studysync®

Teacher's Edition

Grade 6 | Volume 1

studysync.com

ISBN 978-1-94-973923-7

1 2 3 4 5 6 LWI 24 23 22 21 20 19

A

Grade 6

Volume 1 Contents

Authors and Advisors

DR. DOUGLAS FISHER

Dr. Douglas Fisher is Professor of Educational Leadership at San Diego State University and a teacher leader at Health Sciences High & Middle College having been an early intervention teacher and elementary school educator. He is the recipient of a Christa McAuliffe award for excellence in teacher education and is a member of the California Reading Hall of Fame. He is a renowned speaker and author of numerous articles and books and is President of the International Literacy Association (ILA) Board.

DR. TIMOTHY SHANAHAN

Dr. Timothy Shanahan is Distinguished Professor Emeritus at the University of Illinois at Chicago where he is Founding Director of the UIC Center for Literacy. He was Director of Reading for Chicago Public Schools, and, among other awards, received the William S. Gray Citation for Lifetime Achievement and the Albert J. Harris Award for outstanding research on reading disability from the International Literacy Association (ILA). He is the author/editor of more than 200 publications and books, and his research emphasizes the connections between learning to read and learning to write, literacy in the disciplines, and improvement of reading achievement.

DR. MICHELLE H. MARTIN

Dr. Michelle H. Martin is the Beverly Cleary Endowed Professor for Children and Youth Services in the Information School at the University of Washington and from 2011-2016 was the inaugural Augusta Baker Endowed Chair in Childhood Literacy at the University of South Carolina. She published Brown Gold: Milestones of African-American Children's Picture Books, 1845-2002 (Routledge, 2004), and is the founder of Read-a-Rama, a non-profit that uses children's books as the springboard for year-round and summer camp programming.

CATLIN TUCKER

Catlin Tucker is a Google Certified Innovator, bestselling author, international trainer, and frequent Edtech speaker, who teaches in Sonoma County where she was named Teacher of the Year in 2010. Her books Blended Learning in Grades 4-12 and Blended Learning In Action are both bestsellers. She is currently in the doctoral program at Pepperdine University, and writes the Techy Teacher column for ASCD's Educational Leadership.

JEFF ANDERSON

Jeff has inspired writers and teachers with the power and joy of the writing process. His particular area of interest is in making editing and grammar in context a meaning-making experience for students and teachers. He has written five books on writing and teaching writing. More recently, he has taken up writing middle grade novels, including Zack Delacruz: Me and My Big Mouth, which was selected for the Keystone State Reading List in Pennsylvania.

DR. PATRICIA MORALES

Dr. Patricia Morales is founder of ellservices©, consultant, and a professional development provider in English as a Second Language (ESL), Bilingual Education, and Dual Language Education. She is also an independent educational consultant at the Teaching and Learning Division of the Harris County Department of Education in Houston, Texas. She has taught university courses focusing on language acquisition and pedagogy, and continues to prepare thousands of teachers pursuing certifications in bilingual education and English as a Second Language in Texas.

JESSICA ROGERS

Jessica Rogers is a Lecturer at Baylor University and founder of Rogers Education Consulting, which specializes in Balanced Literacy professional development. She has over fifteen years experience in education, including teaching ESL, inclusion, gifted and talented, self-contained classrooms, mentoring teachers, and designing and implementing professional development. Her passion is making abstract educational theory and cutting-edge techniques practical for the classroom teacher.

GERRIT JONES-ROOY

Gerrit Jones-Rooy is Director of Literacy at Collegiate Academies in New Orleans as well as a 9th grade teacher. Previously he worked as a Staff Developer for the Reading and Writing Project, leading work across the country as well as in Saudi Arabia, Colombia, Poland and Thailand. He is the author or co-author of several Teachers College units including "Turning Every Kid into a Reader, Really" and "All About Books: Writing in Non-fiction."

DR. MARCELA FUENTES

Dr. Marcela Fuentes is an Assistant Professor of Creative Writing and Latinx Literature at Texas A&M University. She is a graduate of the Iowa Writers' Workshop, and was the 2016-2017 James C. McCreight Fellow in Fiction at the Wisconsin Institute for Creative Writing. She co-founded The Iowa Youth Writing Project, a nonprofit dedicated to promoting writing programs and events for K-12 students in the Iowa City area.

J. SCOTT BROWNLEE

J. Scott Brownlee is a Career & Talent Development Consultant at UT-Austin's McCombs School of Business, and a core faculty member for Brooklyn Poets, a NYC-based literary nonprofit. The author of four books of poetry, he received the Texas Institute of Letters 2015 Bob Bush Award for Best First Book of Poetry, as well as the 2014 Robert Phillips Prize from Texas Review Press.

DR. LYNNE KNOWLES

Dr. Lynn Knowles spent the majority of her 28-year teaching career at Flower Mound High School in Texas, where she served as English department chair and taught English II pre-AP and Humanities, as well as AP Capstone. She holds a bachelor's degree in Journalism from The University of Texas, a master's in Humanities from the University of Texas at Dallas, and a Ph.D. in Rhetoric from Texas Woman's University.

RICHARD ORLOPP

Richard Orlopp moved to Texas after graduating from Rutgers University with degrees in English and Journalism. He never left. He has taught English for the past 17 years and currently teaches AP Literature and Composition and International Baccalaureate seniors at Coppell High School.

WENDY MASSEY

Wendy Massey has taught high school for 20 years now. She has experience teaching grades 9-12 but primarily has taught English II Pre-AP and PSAT/SAT Prep. She has served several years now as the English department co-chair; in addition, she has served on the curriculum writing team for her district and has been the Academic Decathlon language coach.

MUHAMMAD SHIMAL

Mr. Shimal has been teaching for eleven years now. His teaching experience spans high school to college classes domestically and internationally. He current ly teaches English Language AP/Dual Credit for Juniors and College Prep classes for Seniors. He holds a Bachelor's degree in English Language and Literature, a Masters degree in Linguistics, and is currently finishing his PhD in English at the University of Texas at San Antonio.

VALENTINA GONZALES

Valentina Gonzalez is a Professional Development Specialist for English Language Learners in Texas, coaching teachers in ELL strategies and leading professional development at the state and national level. She has a natural love of language stemming from her experience as an immigrant from Serbia, Yugoslavia. Her years in education include roles as a classroom teacher, ESL Specialty Support Teacher, and ESL Facilitator. She holds a bachelor's degree in Interdisciplinary Studies from The University of Houston, and a master's in Educational Administration from Lamar University.

Testing Our Limits

What do we do when life gets hard?

Integrated Reading and Writing

Genre Focus: FICTION

English Language Learner Resources offer instruction using texts written at four distinct levels that serve as structural and thematic models of authentic texts in the unit.

End-of Unit Assessments gauge students' understanding of key instuctional content and mastery of standards covered in the unit.

Author Biographies

LEWIS CARROLL

Charles Lutwidge Dodgson, better known by his pen name Lewis Carroll (1832–1898), was a British writer of fiction for children. The author's best-known work, *Alice's Adventures in Wonderland* (1865), showcases his playful language and features "Jabberwocky," which is a nonsense poem about a make-believe creature called the Jabberwock. The poem has been so widely read and loved that some of the made-up words in the poem have entered the English dictionary—like the word "chortle."

SANDRA CISNEROS

A dual citizen of Mexico and the United States, Sandra Cisneros (b. 1954) is a writer of poetry, fiction, and essays. Her books have been translated into over twenty languages, and her novel *The House on Mango Street* is required reading in many schools. Cisneros is interested in how writing may serve as activism. In an *Electric Literature* interview, she argued that "the more you reach into the different things that make you who you are, the more you hold up a mirror to what makes you different from others."

CHRISTOPHER PAUL CURTIS

Christopher Paul Curtis (b. 1953) is an American writer of children's books, many of which are set in his hometown of Flint, Michigan. His award-winning book *Bud, Not Buddy* (1999) is based in part on the author's grandfather, who lead the band Herman Curtis and the Dusky Devastators in the 1930s. For Curtis, placing characters against the historical backdrop of the Great Depression is an effective way to highlight the poverty and hunger that millions of people still face every day.

JI-LI JIANG

Ji-Li Jiang (b. 1954) is a Chinese American author from Shanghai, who immigrated to Hawaii shortly after the Cultural Revolution. Her memoir *Red Scarf Girl* (1998) details her teenage years in China, where she found her position as Student Council President at odds with her family's political status. Today, Jiang lives in Seattle and promotes cultural exchange between Western countries and China through nonprofit work, and hopes that literature like her memoir can also nurture understanding and acceptance.

MADELEINE L'ENGLE

Madeleine L'Engle (1918–2007), the only child of a writer and a pianist in New York City, wrote her first story at the age of five. She continued writing as she grew up, and after college pursued a career in theater before publishing her first novel about an aspiring pianist. The author waded through an astounding twenty-six rejections before finding a publisher who championed her well-known novel *A Wrinkle in Time* (1962).

LOIS LOWRY

The author of forty-five children's books, Lois Lowry (b. 1937) is an American author who divides her time between Massachusetts and Maine. Her most famous novel, *The Giver* (1993) has three companion novels and takes place in a fictional future in which technology as we know it has been eliminated. Though Lowry has said she always wanted to be a writer and nothing else, she did not imagine writing books for a young audience until she was asked to do so by her publisher in 1977, with the book *A Summer to Die*.

GARY PAULSEN

Gary Paulsen (b. 1939) is a writer of young adult literature from Minnesota. At the age of seven, on a ship bound for the Philippines, Paulsen witnessed a plane crash and looked on as his mother tended to injured passengers. A plane crash figures prominently in his novel *Hatchet* (1987), which follows a young boy's survival after he is stranded in the wilderness. The author wrote a sequel, *Brian's Winter* (1996), after he received as many as two hundred letters a day from readers who wanted to know more of the story.

RENÉ SALDAÑA JR.

René Saldaña Jr. is an author and teacher who loosely bases many of his fictional works on his experiences growing up in southern Texas near the border of the United States and Mexico. His stories typically follow pre-teen and teenage characters as they address issues of love, danger, loyalty, and family. As an educator, Saldaña has written and stated the need to "simply validate who kids are" through diversity in literature for young readers.

AVI

The name Avi (b. 1937) was given to American writer Edward Irving Wortis by his twin sister at an early age. Though he grew up in a highly literate and creative family of writers, artists, and musicians in Brooklyn, writing has never come easily to Avi, who suffers from dysgraphia. Now an author of over seventy-five books—everything from graphic novels to historical fiction and beyond—Avi enjoys showing error-addled drafts of his work to young writers as encouragement.

UNIT 2

You and Me

How do relationships shape us?

Integrated Reading and Writing

Genre Focus: POETRY

Every lesson in the unit features integrated scaffolding and differentiation for all levels of English Language Learners. Approaching grade-level readers, and Beyond grade-level readers.

478 | Extended Writing Project and Grammar

Grammar instruction is embedded in the Extended Writing Project. Additional grammar lessons are available in the Skills library.

Each Core ELA Unit contains two options for Novel Study with lessons supporting the close reading of the complete text.

Author Biographies

SHARON CREECH

In a suburb of Cleveland, Ohio, Sharon Creech (b. 1945) grew up in a house filled with visiting relatives and friends, along with her parents, sister, and three brothers. Each summer, Creech's parents would pile all five children into the family car to go on a long road trip. On one of these trips, when Creech was twelve years old, they went to Idaho, and that experience became the basis of the story told in the novel *Walk Two Moons* (1994).

COUNTEE CULLEN

In 1918, at the age of fifteen, Countee Cullen (1903-1946) lost the woman who cared for him: his grandmother. His new guardian would be the pastor of Salem Methodist Episcopal Church, which hosted the largest congregation in Harlem. Cullen's poetry is regarded as a significant voice of the Harlem Renaissance, a vibrant period that ushered in an innovative generation of African American writers in New York City. Cullen often expressed that he believed art could transcend race, and hoped his poems would bring together people from all walks of life.

NIKKI GIOVANNI

Nikki Giovanni (b. 1943) is an African American poet who grew up during the Civil Rights Movement and launched her career at the age of twenty-five with her collection of poems, *Black Feeling Black Talk* (1968), published shortly after the assassination of Dr. Martin Luther King Jr. Around the same time, Giovanni was a preeminent author in the Black Arts Movement and was friends with Rosa Parks and Muhammad Ali. She went on to develop a distinguished career as a poet and activist, and is currently a college professor in Virginia.

FRANCISCO JIMÉNEZ

Francisco Jiménez (b. 1943) is a Chicano writer of fiction and memoir who moved from his home in Mexico to California and back several times before he reached adulthood. Along with his family, Jiménez was a migrant field-worker, moving through California to pick crops: Corcoran for cotton, Santa Maria for strawberries, and Fresno for grapes. Despite facing many hardships, including not having a permanent home or consistent education, Jiménez excelled in school and went on to become a college professor and a successful author.

JACKI JING

NCAA Division I athlete Jacki Jing (b. 1986) grew up playing volleyball in Centennial, Colorado. She received a full athletic scholarship to the State University of New York at Binghamton, where she earned degrees in political science and English, and was later inducted into their Athletic Hall of Fame in 2014. Jing went on to become a television journalist, reporting and anchoring for stations in Colorado, New York, Massachusetts, and Louisiana.

DAVID KHERDIAN

"What we learn in childhood is carved in stone. What we learn as adults is carved in ice," writes David Kherdian (b. 1931). The poet, biographer, and editor was born to two survivors of the Armenian Genocide and raised in Wisconsin near Root River. He excelled at sports, especially basketball, football, and softball, and also loved to read and draw. From an early age, he was exposed to and fought against the discrimination he experienced as a child of immigrants.

WALTER DEAN MYERS

Walter Dean Myers (1937–2004) was raised in Harlem by his adopted family. As a child, he was a gifted student and athlete but was teased for having a speech impediment and was known to have a quick temper. He found solace in reading and writing, and would grow up to become an award-winning author of books for young adults and children. His first book, *Where Does the Day Go* (1969), was written for a contest for African American writers, and marked the start of a career-long mission to write literature for and about people of color.

MILDRED TAYLOR

Mildred Taylor (b. 1943) moved with her family from Jackson, Mississippi, to newly-integrated Toledo, Ohio, when she was only three months old. She describes herself as a quiet child in a family of prodigious storytellers. The family visited Mississippi every year, where her great-grandfather had purchased land in the late 1800s that the family still owns. Taylor used those visits to the American South and family lore as the basis for her stories. *Roll of Thunder, Hear My Cry*, the second novel of the saga, won the 1977 Newbery Award.

HOLLY WARLICK

When Holly Warlick (b. 1958) was named head coach of the University of Tennessee's women's basketball team, her predecessor Pat Summitt admitted that Warlick had already been leading the team in her role as assistant coach. The legendary Summitt passed her whistle to Warlick after receiving a diagnosis of Alzheimer's Disease in 2011. Warlick was formerly a player on Summitt's team, and was the first player in Tennessee sports history to have her jersey retired at the end of her playing career.

PAT MORA

Mexican American author Pat Mora (b. 1942) grew up surrounded by books in El Paso, Texas, and fell in love with reading and writing at an early age. Her poetry and stories explore Chicana identity in the region of the border and are written in both English and Spanish. Mora grew up with bilingual parents and says that switching between English and Spanish was the rhythm of her childhood. She went on to replicate a book-loving, bilingual home for her own three children.

Integrated Reading and Writing

Genre Focus: INFORMATIONAL TEXT

Independent Reads provide opportunities to focus on reading comprehension and skills application.

Students self-select a text that corresponds to the unit's theme and essential question and then write a response.

In the Extended Oral Project, students apply the structure and approach of the Extended Writing Project to an oral presentation.

Author Biographies

CARL HIAASEN

Carl Hiaasen (b. 1953) has been a regular columnist for the *Miami Herald* since 1985, reporting and commenting on everything from the Everglades to local politics to Facebook to raccoons. He has also written a number of novels for adults and for younger audiences, all set in Florida. In an interview with *Strand Magazine*, Hiassen stated, "Every writer's obligation is to create enough suspense to keep the readers turning the pages, and it's doubly hard if you're trying to make them laugh along the way."

LANGSTON HUGHES

The final line of the poem "I, Too," by Langston Hughes (1902 – 1967) is chiseled in the stone wall of the National Museum of African American History and Culture in Washington, DC: "I, too, am America." Hughes first wrote these words in 1926 as a young poet at the forefront of the Harlem Renaissance in New York. Through the lasting impact of his poems, Hughes continues to edify and give voice to the African American experience in the United States.

MADELEINE L'ENGLE

American author Madeleine L'Engle (1918–2007) is known primarily for her works of fiction for young adults, including the novels *A Wrinkle in Time* and *A Wind in the Door*. She also wrote poetry and memoir, and served a long career as a librarian in New York. In her acceptance speech for the 1963 Newbery Award, L'Engle commented on how she wrote such resonant, popular work, stating: "Most of what is best in writing isn't done deliberately."

HAMILTON WRIGHT MABIE

After a short time practicing law, Hamilton Wright Mabie (1846–1916) terminated his career as an attorney in 1879 to become an editor at a magazine called *The Outlook*, published weekly in New York City, where he worked alongside Theodore Roosevelt. The first of over thirty books he published in his lifetime was *Norse Stories Retold* (1882), which he later expanded on by writing versions of myths, fairy tales, heroes, and legends for children.

RANDALL MUNROE

From an early age, Randall Munroe (b. 1984) loved reading *Calvin and Hobbes*. Years later, he would himself become a cartoonist after earning a degree in physics and working at NASA. He is most famous for *xkcd*, a stick figure webcomic that draws on technology, math, and science for content. Munroe writes a blog called *What If?* (and has published a book by the same name) which answers questions sent in by fans of his comics, such as: what if a rainstorm dropped all of its water in a single giant drop?

RICK RIORDAN

When Rick Riordan (b. 1964) moved to San Francisco from his native San Antonio around the age of thirty, he began missing Texas so much he was compelled to write a story set in his home state. Not long after, his first book *Big Red Tequila* (1997) was published and his life as an author began. Riordan was a middle school teacher at the time, who transitioned into being a full-time writer when he started writing a popular series about Percy Jackson, a twelve-year-old boy who discovers he is the son of Poseidon.

CATHERINE M. ANDRONIK

Catherine M. Andronik (b. 1958) is a high school librarian and author who shares her Connecticut home with an array of rescue parrots. She primarily writes biographies for a young adult audience, animating such historical figures as England's King Arthur, the mathematician and astronomer Copernicus, the former American president Abraham Lincoln, and the Egyptian pharaoh Hatshepsut. In her spare time, she likes to read, travel, and ride horses.

PAT MORA

Born and raised in El Paso, Texas, as a child of two first-generation Mexican American immigrants, Pat Mora (b. 1942) received her BA from Texas Western College and her MA from the University of Texas at El Paso. She is the author of over forty books, including YA literature, poetry, and children's books. She is a champion of bilingual literacy, and an advocate for "Children's Day, Book Day" which promotes literacy and a love of books. It takes place each year on April 30. She lives in Santa Fe, New Mexico.

Bring Literature to Life

- Instructional choice from thematic units, novel studies, and teacher-created units.

- Interchangeable print and digital use.

- A continuously growing library of over 1,600 classic & contemporary texts.

Student Print Edition

Novel Options

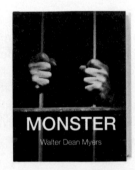

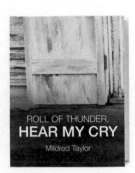

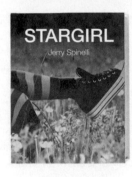

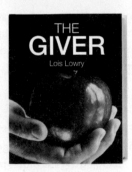

- Extensive writing and research practice.

- Automatically embedded scaffolds so ALL students reach their potential.

- Data-driven assessment to track progress and inform instruction.

Teacher Print Edition

Data Driven Assesment

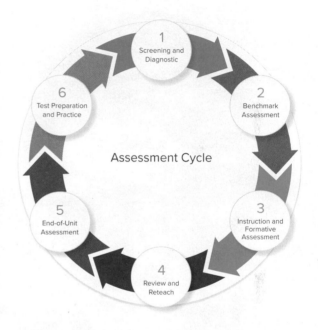

Comprehensive Student and Teacher Digital Experience

Lead to Achievement

StudySync's integrated reading and writing routines hone foundational language, reading comprehension, and analytical reading and writing skills as students respond to multiple genres of increasingly complex texts.

- StudySync's close reading routines ensure progress toward standards mastery.

- Novel Studies provide teachers with key vocabulary, reading quizzes, comparative texts, and other curriculum supports to teach from any of the 12 complete works suggested in each grade.

- Independent and self-selected reading lessons provide students opportunities to practice and apply skills while exercising more choice over their readings and responsesTwo comparative text sets in every unit challenge students to make connections and compare texts within and across genres.

- Extended Writing Projects teach writing with embedded grammar instruction.

Support Every Student

With StudySync, every student has the same opportunity and access regardless of native language, learning level, or physical, social and emotional ability.

Supports for English Language Learners

- Targeted scaffolds for 4 different levels of English Language Learners automatically appear with every digital assignment.

- Two leveled texts per unit introduce English Language Learners to the text types they'll encounter in the core curriculum.

- Additional ELL skills lessons emphasize/ vocabulary development, language acquisition, spelling and grammar, and reading comprehension.

- Extended Oral Projects build language proficiency and offer students opportunities to collaborate and build academic language skills.

Supports for Approaching and Beyond Grade-level Learners

- Intentional scaffolds such as annotation guides, and sentence frames help Approaching-level students interact meaningfully with on grade-level curriculum.

- A digital Library of 1000s of additional skill mini-lessons and texts is searchable by standard and Lexile, allowing teachers to quickly and easily differentiate, remediate, or extend lessons.

- Lesson-specific suggestions such as Beyond the Book and Prepare for Advanced Courses drive Beyond grade-level learners to further engage with texts and extend their learning.

Amplify Student Voices

StudySync helps students think critically and thoughtfully. All StudySync students see themselves in their curriculum. StudySync encourages students to develop their own unique voices while they grow as readers, writers, and future leaders in college and career settings.

- StudySync's curriculum is centered around students. Lesson activities and the digital platform enable teachers to easily facilitate peer review and other on and offline collaborative approaches that transform classrooms into workshops of great reading and writing.

- The Table of Contents for every grade features at least 50% of texts written by female authors and at least 50% of texts written by authors from diverse backgrounds.

- Each grade's Table of Contents includes stories about extraordinary young people. Whether it's Olympic gold medalist Simone Biles or animal rights advocate Thomas Ponce, students will learn how other young people like them are changing the world today.

- Integrated media such as StudySyncTV and SkillsTV models collaborative and academic conversations, providing students the roadmap they need to develop their own voices.

- Unique media like the "School of Thought" podcast series helps teachers meet multimedia and digital literacy standards with high-quality resources that are relevant to the lives of today's students.

- Blast lessons help students understand the most important issues in today's world. Teachers have access to a brand new Blast article - leveled for 3 different Lexiles - every single school day, helping them deliver a fresh, relevant learning experience every year.

Testing Our Limits

What do we do when life gets hard?

UNIT 1

Testing Our Limits

What do we do when life gets hard?

What do we do when life gets hard? How do we respond in a difficult situation? What do we do when our limits are tested? How do we face a challenge? What actions can we take to solve a problem?

These are the questions your students will explore in this Grade 6 unit, which focuses on the genre of fiction.

Life is full of challenges, and some are harder than others. What we choose to do or say in the face of these challenges often varies on the challenge itself. Sometimes we choose to respond to challenges by attempting something that we have never done before, something that might even scare us a little. Often, however, life presents us with difficulties when people least expect it, such as an emergency or a crisis.

Texts within the unit's genre and across other genres present different perspectives on responding to life's unexpected difficulties. Deza Malone in *The Mighty Miss Malone* must deal with the events of the Great Depression when it tears her family apart. In Avi's short story "Scout's Honor" three Boy Scouts from Brooklyn learn a humbling lesson when their limits are tested on a camping trip. After reading about how these and other characters respond when their lives are upended, your students will try their own hands at writing a short story, applying what they have learned about dealing with life's challenges to their own narrative writing projects.

Testing Out Limits

📺 StudySyncTV or SkillsTV Episode

Pacing Guide

Days	Readings	Skill and Standard Instruction	Skill Practice and Spiraling
1-5	**SyncStart: Eleven** 📺 p. 12	• Annotation • Context Clues • Reading Comprehension • Text Dependent Responses • Textual Evidence • Figurative Language • Collaborative Conversations • Short Constructed Responses • Peer Review	• Literary Analysis Writing • Collaborative Conversations
6-7	Essential Question **The Big Idea: What do we do when life gets hard?** p. 46	• Recognizing Genre: Fiction • Academic Vocabulary	• Write: Analyzing Genre
8-10	**The Mighty Miss Malone** p. 50	• Making Connections • Character 📺	• Textual Evidence • Narrative Writing
11-15	PAIRED READINGS **Red Scarf Girl** 📺 p. 70 **Hatchet** 📺 p. 80	• Personal Response • Setting • Compare and Contrast 📺	• Textual Evidence • Comparative Writing • Collaborative Conversations
16-18	**The Magic Marker Mystery** p. 100	• Making and Confirming Predictions • Dramatic Elements and Structure	• Textual Evidence • Character • Literary Analysis Writing

THEMATIC PACING AT A GLANCE – 30 DAYS

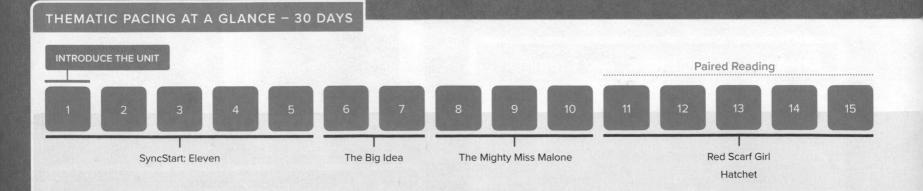

INTRODUCE THE UNIT

1 2 3 4 5   6 7   8 9 10   Paired Reading   11 12 13 14 15

SyncStart: Eleven   The Big Idea   The Mighty Miss Malone   Red Scarf Girl

Hatchet

Days	Readings	Skill and Standard Instruction	Skill Practice and Spiraling
19-20	**Scout's Honor** p. 122	• Story Structure • Plot	• Textual Evidence • Character • Literary Analysis Writing
21-22	**The Good Samaritan** p. 148	• Summarizing	• Textual Evidence • Character • Collaborative Conversations
23-27	**PAIRED READINGS** **Jabberwocky** 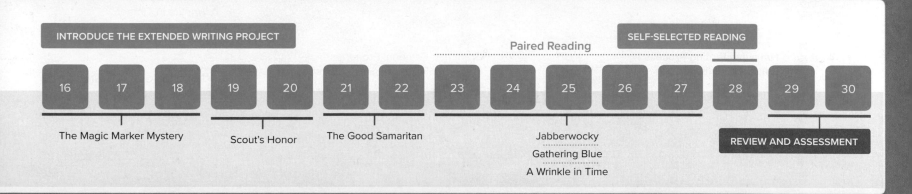 p. 168 **Gathering Blue** p. 178 **A Wrinkle in Time** p. 190	• Context Clues • Analyzing Genre	• Character • Setting • Compare and Contrast • Comparative Writing • Collaborative Conversations
28	**Self-Selected Reading and Response** p. 208	• Independent Reading	• Personal Response Writing

Review and Assessment   See page 292.

Days	Review and Assessment	Skill Practice and Assessment
29	**Skills Review** p. 292	Students will have the opportunity to complete one or more Spotlight Skill lessons in order to improve understanding and further practice skills from the unit that they found most challenging.
30	**End-of-Unit Assessment** p. 293	For more details, please see the End-of-Unit Assessment information for Grade 6 Unit 1 on page 292.

INTRODUCE THE EXTENDED WRITING PROJECT

Paired Reading

SELF-SELECTED READING

| 16 | 17 | 18 | 19 | 20 | 21 | 22 | 23 | 24 | 25 | 26 | 27 | 28 | 29 | 30 |

The Magic Marker Mystery

Scout's Honor

The Good Samaritan

Jabberwocky

Gathering Blue

A Wrinkle in Time

REVIEW AND ASSESSMENT

Extended Writing Project and Grammar

Pacing Guide

In the second half of the unit, students continue exploring texts that address the unit's Essential Question and begin crafting a longer composition to share their own ideas about the Essential Question in the Extended Writing Project. The writing project will take your students through the writing process to produce a narrative essay.

Extended Writing Project Prompt

How can an unexpected event turn into a major challenge?

Imagine the very worst possible day. What event or individual makes that day so terrible? How do your characters respond? Write a story in which the main character faces an unexpected challenge on what was supposed to be a normal day.

Days	Extended Writing Project and Grammar	Skill and Standard Instruction	Connect to Mentor Texts
16	**Narrative Writing Process: Plan** p. 218		
17-18	**Narrative Writing Process: Draft** p. 228	• Organizing Narrative Writing	• Eleven
19-24	**Narrative Writing Process: Revise** p. 246	• Story Beginnings • Descriptive Details • Narrative Techniques • Transitions • Conclusions	• The Mighty Miss Malone • Hatchet • Red Scarf Girl: A Memoir of the Cultural Revolution • Scout's Honor • Gathering Blue • A Wrinkle in Time
25-28	**Narrative Writing Process: Edit and Publish** p. 254	• Grammar: Personal Pronouns • Grammar: Pronouns and Antecedents • Grammar: Consistent Pronoun Use	Additional lessons can be found in the StudySync Skills Library.

Research

The following lessons include opportunities for research:

Blast **Blast Away** Research Links*

Close Read **The Mighty Miss Malone** Beyond the Book

Blast **Moral Quarrel** Research Links*

Independent Read **Red Scarf Girl** Beyond the Book

Close Read **Hatchet** Beyond the Book

Blast **Rewriting History** Research Links*

Independent Read **Gathering Blue** Independent Research (Beyond)

First Read **A Wrinkle in Time** Independent Research (Beyond)

*See the teacher lesson plan online

Self-Selected Reading Prompt

After reading a self-selected text, students will respond to the following argumentative prompt:

A casting director is someone who auditions and hires the right actor for each role for a movie or television show. Choosing the right actor isn't just about finding a pretty face, casting directors must consider an actor's skill set, including relevant portrayals in previous films.

Who can bring a story's character to the big screen?

Imagine that you are the casting director for the film adaptation of the text you just read. Which actor would you cast for the main character's role? Write a response in which you identify an actor that would best portray the main character of your text.

Integrated Scaffolding

ELL and Approaching grade-level students receive scaffolds for every lesson, whether in the Thematic, Novel Study or ELL Resources sections of the unit. Specific scaffolds are intentionally designed to support the needs of English Language Learners and Approaching grade-level students in the ELA classroom. Other scaffolds exist as part of the many standard features in the StudySync digital platform and can be strategically utilized to support students' comprehension and engagement.

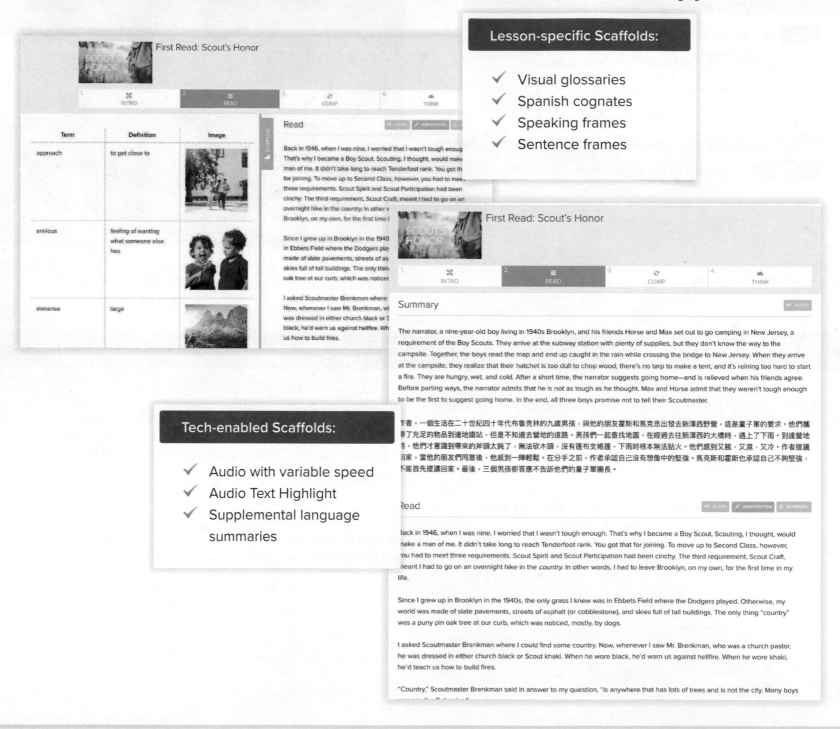

Lesson-specific Scaffolds:

- ✓ Visual glossaries
- ✓ Spanish cognates
- ✓ Speaking frames
- ✓ Sentence frames

Tech-enabled Scaffolds:

- ✓ Audio with variable speed
- ✓ Audio Text Highlight
- ✓ Supplemental language summaries

English Language Learner Resources

Both Thematic and Novel Study units include English Language Learner resources designed to match the thematic focus, text structures, and writing form of the unit. ELL resources include two leveled texts and an extended oral project.

ELL Texts	Differentiated Text Levels	Skill and Standard Instruction
	**BEGINNING** 230L I 255 words **INTERMEDIATE** 360L I 396 words **ADVANCED** 480L I 445 words **ADVANCED HIGH** 600L I 531 words Use this text in place of, or as an extension to *Hatchet*.	• Sight Vocabulary and High-Frequency Words • Seeking Clarification • Analyzing Expressions • Conveying Ideas • Spelling Patterns and Rules
	**BEGINNING** 240L I 310 words **INTERMEDIATE** 300L I 408 words **ADVANCED** 350L I 461 words **ADVANCED HIGH** 500L I 540 words Use this text in place of, or as an extension to *A Wrinkle in Time*.	• Classroom Vocabulary • Taking Notes • Language Structures • Retelling and Summarizing • Subject-Verb Agreement
	In this Extended Oral Project, students will write and perform a dramatic scene. This may be assigned in place of this unit's EWP.	• Acquiring Vocabulary • Sentence Lengths

Focus on English Language Proficiency Levels

ADVANCED HIGH
ADVANCED
INTERMEDIATE
BEGINNING

ELL Resources provide targeted support for four levels of proficiency: Beginning, Intermediate, Advanced, and Advanced High. Instruction and scaffolds, as well as the texts themselves, are differentiated based on these levels.

Additional differentiated scaffolds include visual glossaries, speaking and writing frames, and suggested grouping for peer and teacher support. Lessons also include suggested extension activities to challenge Advanced and Advanced High students as they progress through the year.

Assessment

Assessment in StudySync is built upon a recursive cycle that includes assessment, instruction, and review. Screening, placement, and benchmark assessments help teachers establish baselines and determine scaffold needs. Throughout the course of instruction, teachers regularly assess student progress using formative and summative measures, and use the individualized data from those assessments to guide choices about instruction, review, remediation, and enrichment to bring all students to standards mastery and College and Career Readiness.

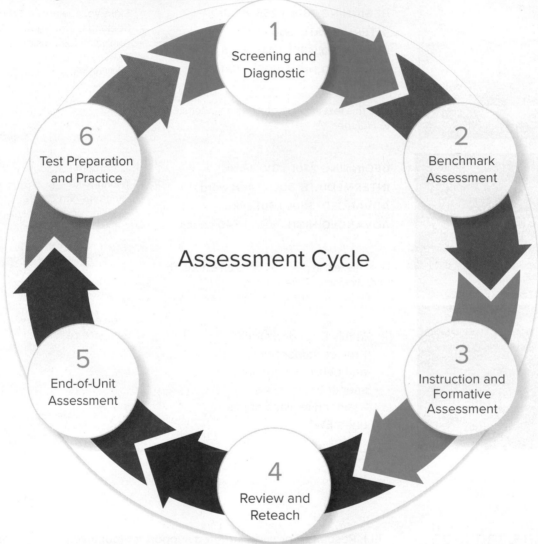

Assessment Cycle

1 Screening and Diagnostic

2 Benchmark Assessment

3 Instruction and Formative Assessment

4 Review and Reteach

5 End-of-Unit Assessment

6 Test Preparation and Practice

What's Next?

Assessment results can be viewed by item, standard, and skill to monitor mastery and make decisions for upcoming instruction.

✓ Reteach skills that students have not yet mastered, using Spotlight Skills or the Test Preparation and Practice book.

✓ Revise your teaching plan to provide more or less explicit instruction into a skill or text, using Beyond the Book activities for enrichment.

✓ Regroup students and levels of scaffolding based on standards progress.

Review

Spotlight Skills Review

A review day before the end-of-unit assessment gives you an opportunity to review difficult concepts with students using Spotlight Skills lessons. Spotlight Skills are targeted lessons that provide you resources to reteach or remediate without assigning additional readings. Every Core ELA Skill lesson has a corresponding Spotlight Skill lesson. Spotlight Skills can be assigned at any point in the year, but the end of each unit provides a natural moment to pause, review data collected throughout the unit, and reteach skills students have not yet mastered.

Progress Monitoring

The Progress Monitoring charts that appear before every text in this unit identify standards and associated Spotlight Skills. On review day, you may want to give preference to reteaching skills that are not revisited in later units. You can see where skills are covered again in the Opportunities to Reteach column.

Opportunities to Learn	Opportunities to Demonstrate Learning	
Context Clues		Unit 1 First Read: The Wise
First Read • Make Predictions about Vocabulary	First Read • Read and Annotate • Think Questions 4, 5	Units 1–6 Various other texts
		Spotlight Skill: Context

StudySync Gradebook

As students submit assignments on StudySync, their mastery of skills and standards is tracked via the gradebook. The gradebook can be sorted and viewed in a variety of ways. Sorting by assignment shows overall student performance, while sorting by standards or by skill lessons displays student progress toward mastery goals.

	First Read	Skill: Text	Close Re...	
MAX SCORE	10	2	12	
STUDENT				
Tate O'Brien	10	2	9	
Olivia Adams	8	1	11	

Skills Library

Spotlight Skills are located in the Skills section of the StudySync Library. You can assign Spotlight Skills to individual students or groups of students. Search tools allow you to search by skill type or name.

End-of-Unit Assessment

Assessed Reading Skills

- ✓ Character
- ✓ Compare and Contrast
- ✓ Context Clues
- ✓ Dramatic Elements and Structure
- ✓ Figurative Language
- ✓ Plot
- ✓ Setting
- ✓ Story Structure
- ✓ Summarizing
- ✓ Textual Evidence

Assessed Revising and Editing Skills

- ✓ Descriptive Details
- ✓ Conclusions
- ✓ Consistent Pronoun Use
- ✓ Narrative Techniques
- ✓ Personal Pronouns
- ✓ Pronouns and Antecedents
- ✓ Story Beginnings
- ✓ Transitions

Introduction

How do I use StudySync? More importantly, how does StudySync design learning today to help my students in the future? SyncStart introduces students and teachers to the instructional routines that figure prominently in StudySync. Built around an existing, grade-level text, each SyncStart Unit instructs and assesses the habits and skills needed to tap student's maximum potential for learning. With SyncStart, teachers have detailed plans for their first two weeks of StudySync instruction. Students and teachers alike reap the benefits of a strong start to a new program--a SyncStart.

What does it take to be a strong reader and writer? Is it enough to just recognize the words on a page, or know how to spell or use punctuation? Are some people born good at it, while others struggle? Attitudes toward learning, particularly learning how to read and write, have changed dramatically over time. What we've now found is that there are a number of specific, individual skills and strategies that can improve the way we access and write about the texts we read.

In this SyncStart unit, students develop these skills in the context of a StudySync reading routine. The unit begins by instructing to foundational best practices for reading—using annotation to record notes and ideas, drawing on context clues to predict the meanings of unknown words, and applying reading comprehension strategies to break down complex texts. From there, students will slowly go through the routine of a First Read, Reading Skills, and a Close Read, pausing intermittently to dive deeply into additional skills and strategies. For example, before participating in their first SyncTV Style Discussion, students will complete a lesson on Collaborative Conversations that explicitly instructs to the behaviors that lead to a successful peer discussion. Similarly, before and after students submit their first Close Read Response, they will analyze and practice the skills of writing Short Constructed Responses and Peer Reviews. Throughout this unit, students are introduced to the skills that will help them grow as readers and writers as they continue to practice throughout the year.

What's different about SyncStart?

In the SyncStart unit, teachers and students become familiar with the lessons, routines, and skills in the StudySync curriculum. StudySync provides this preparation within the curriculum to prepare students for the year ahead in four ways:

1 Routines

The SyncStart unit starts with a Blast and then follows the Integrated Reading and Writing routine of First Read, Skill Lesson, and Close Read. Targeted skill lessons like Short Constructed Response and Peer Review introduce specific skills and give students the instructional tools they'll need to for the year ahead.

2 Habits of Learning

In addition to establishing the routines students will use in StudySync, other skill lessons allow students to develop the skills they will need every day in class like Annotation, Text-Dependent Responses, and Collaborative Conversation. These skills create a foundation of best practices for students so that they can more effectively interact with texts, respond to questions, and collaborate with their peers.

3 PREP

PREP sections in each SyncStart lesson plan explain the purpose behind StudySync's instructional routines. Over the course of the SyncStart lessons, teachers will come to understand and master best practices for the instructional moments in each StudySync lesson.

4 Teaching Lab Videos

These videos show teachers what the routine looks like in action and appear in the Instructional Path alongside the lesson plan for the lesson they illustrate.

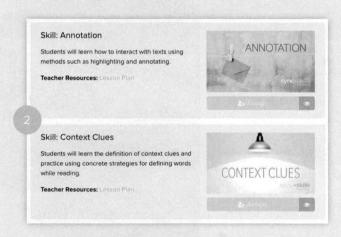

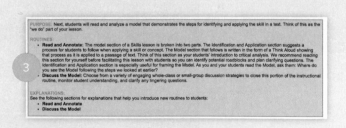

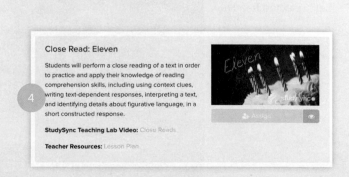

Eleven

FICTION
Sandra Cisneros
1991

Introduction

studysync tv

Sandra Cisneros (b. 1954) is a renowned Chicana writer whose poems, novels, and short stories explore the complicated struggle of finding one's own identity. Cisneros is best known for her novel *The House on Mango Street* and the collection *Woman Hollering Creek and Other Stories*. "Eleven" is from the latter, the story of a girl named Rachel who experiences growing pains on her eleventh birthday. When her teacher insists that an ugly red sweater belongs to Rachel, the eleven-year-old has exceptional thoughts but can't share them. Even so, it's evident that the protagonist of Sandra Cisneros's short story has insight beyond her years.

On her eleventh birthday, Rachel realizes that as she grows up, deep down she retains every age that she's ever been. She describes getting older as the layers of a tree trunk, with each year added to the previous one. However, this morning, Rachel wishes she was even older because she believes that she would know how to stand up for herself when her math teacher, Mrs. Price, insists that an ugly red sweater is hers. As the class watches, Rachel is sick with embarrassment but dons the ugly sweater anyways. Soon thereafter, Rachel breaks down in tears, which leads a classmate to admit that the sweater belongs to her. The story ends with Rachel thinking about the birthday party she will have that evening. She imagines her family will be happy, but she feels that the day is ruined. She wishes she was 102 years old because she thinks being eleven is not what she thought it would be.

 Proficiency-leveled summaries and summaries in multiple languages are available digitally.

 Audio and audio text highlighting are available with this text.

CONNECT TO ESSENTIAL QUESTION

What do we do when life gets hard?

On the day she turns eleven, in Sandra Cisneros's short story "Eleven," Rachel is confronted with an unexpected challenge. Her teacher insists that Rachel is the owner of an old, ugly sweater that has been hanging in the student cloak room for months. But the sweater doesn't belong to Rachel, and to her surprise, she is only able to reply with the most feeble of responses. Finally, she bursts into tears. Rachel's reaction upsets her until she makes the discovery that even though you've just turned eleven, sometimes you can still act as if you were four or five.

Access Complex Text

LEXILE: 1070   WORD COUNT: 1,195

The following areas may be challenging for students, particularly English Language Learners and Ⓐ Approaching grade-level learners.

Organization	Connection of Ideas	Purpose
• Students may not be familiar with first-person stream of consciousness technique.	• Some students may have difficulty linking Cisneros's use of imagery to the plot and theme.	• The author's use of symbolism may be difficult for some students to grasp.
• The use of so many commas in sections connect all of Rachel's thoughts. If sentences were broken up with periods, then they would read more as separate thoughts.	• Point out that when Rachel compares getting older to an onion she is also explaining the reasons behind her behavior in class.	• Point out that the red sweater, because it is so trivial, supports Rachel's idea that sometimes, at eleven, you can still act as if you're four.

 SCAFFOLDS   ENGLISH LANGUAGE LEARNERS   Ⓐ APPROACHING GRADE LEVEL   BEYOND GRADE LEVEL

These icons identify differentiation strategies and scaffolded support for a variety of students. See the digital lesson plan for additional differentiation strategies and scaffolds.

Instructional Path

Blast: Blast Away!

Objectives: Explore background information and research links about a topic, to respond to a question with a 140-character response.

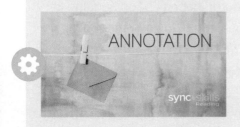

Skill: Annotation

Objectives: Write annotations to ask questions, track information, and respond to the text, as well as understand the purpose of annotations.

Skill: Context Clues

Objectives: Use types of context clues, such as definition, comparisons, and examples, to clarify the meaning of words.

Skill: Reading Comprehension

Objectives: Identify and understand the purpose of various reading comprehension strategies used to develop and deepen comprehension of increasingly complex texts.

First Read: Eleven

Objectives: Use context clues to define new vocabulary, and demonstrate comprehension by responding to questions using textual evidence.

Skill: Text Dependent Responses

Objectives: Write strong text-dependent responses using relevant supporting evidence.

The print teacher's edition includes essential point-of-use instruction and planning tools. Complete lesson plans and program documents appear in your digital teacher account.

Skill: Textual Evidence

Objectives: Cite evidence to support analysis of what the text says explicitly, as well as inferences drawn from the text.

Skill: Figurative Language

Objectives: Identify figurative language and analyze how it is used for descriptive effect in a work of fiction.

Close Read: Eleven

Objectives: Analyze figurative language and cite textual evidence to support their analysis of the narrator's feelings in a short, written response.

Skill: Collaborative Conversations

Objectives: Analyze what elements contribute to successful collaborative conversations.

DIGITAL ONLY

Skill: Short Constructed Responses

Objectives: Break down a literary analysis prompt and answer the prompt in a short, written response.

DIGITAL ONLY

Skill: Peer Review

Objectives: Identify and apply the elements of effective and constructive peer review.

DIGITAL ONLY

Progress Monitoring

Opportunities to Learn	Opportunities to Demonstrate Learning	Opportunities to Reteach
Annotation		
⚙ Skill: Annotation	⚙ Skill: Annotation • Your Turn 🖥 First Read • Read and Annotate • Reading Comprehension Questions 1, 3, 5–8, and 10. • Think Questions 1–3	⚙ Spotlight Skill: Annotation
Context Clues		
⚙ Skill: Context Clues	⚙ Skill: Context Clues • Your Turn 🖥 First Read • Read and Annotate • Think Questions 4 and 5	🖥 Unit 1 First Read: A Wrinkle in Time 🖥 Unit 6 Skill: Letter to His Daughter ⚙ Spotlight Skill: Context Clues
Reading Comprehension		
⚙ Skill: Reading Comprehension	⚙ Skill: Reading Comprehension • Your Turn 🖥 First Read • Read and Annotate	⚙ Spotlight Skill: Reading Comprehension

Progress Monitoring

Opportunities to Learn	Opportunities to Demonstrate Learning	Opportunities to Reteach
Text Dependent Responses		
⚙ Skill: Text-Dependent Responses	⚙ Skill: Text-Dependent Responses • Your Turn ▤ Close Read • Writer's Notebook • Skills Focus • Collaborative Conversation • Write	⚙ Spotlight Skill: Text-Dependent Responses
Textual Evidence		
⚙ Skill: Textual Evidence	⚙ Skill: Textual Evidence • Your Turn ▤ Close Read • Writer's Notebook • Skills Focus • Collaborative Conversation • Write	⚙ Unit 2 Skill: Textual Evidence - Walk Two Moons ⚙ Unit 3 Skill: Textual Evidence - Margaret Bourke-White: Fearless Photographer ⚙ Spotlight Skill: Textual Evidence
Figurative Language		
⚙ Skill: Figurative Language	⚙ Skill: Figurative Language • Your Turn ▤ Close Read • Skills Focus • Collaborative Conversation • Write	⚙ Unit 2 Skill: Figurative Language - Teenagers ⚙ Unit 6 Skill: Figurative Language - Letter to His Daughter ⚙ Spotlight Skill: Figurative Language

Collaborative Conversations

Skill:
Collaborative Conversations

Skill: Collaborative Conversations
- Your Turn

Close Read
- Collaborative Conversation

Spotlight Skill: Collaborative
Conversations

Short Constructed Responses

Skill:
Short Constructed Responses

Skill: Short Constructed Responses
- Your Turn

Close Read
- Write

Spotlight Skill: Short Constructed
Responses

Peer Review

⚙ **Skill: Peer Review**

⚙ **Skill: Peer Review**
- Your Turn

▭ **Close Read**
- Write
- Peer Review

⚙ **Spotlight Skill: Peer Review**

Blast: Blast Away!

How can you be a better learner in the classroom?

TEXT TALK

Where are some places you might already be thinking critically and voicing your opinion about current events?

Paragraph 4: Some places include Facebook, Twitter, and Snapchat.

What are some activities included in a StudySync Blast?

Paragraphs 5 and 6: Weigh in on topical issues, read a short article, research sources, respond to a Driving Question, complete a Number Crunch, QuikPoll, and write a Blast

What's the point of reacting with a short response?

Paragraph 6: The point is to share your opinion with your class, to easily comment on each other's responses, or to learn the opinions of everyone in the class.

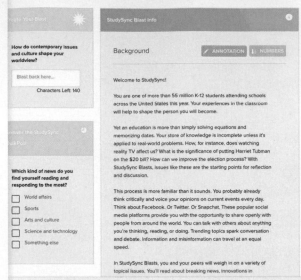

Create Your Own Blast

SCAFFOLDS

Ask students to write a 140-character Blast after they complete the QuikPoll.

Use the scaffolds below to differentiate instruction for your **ELL** English Language Learners.

ELL **BEGINNING** Write a response using the <u>word bank</u> to complete the <u>sentence frame</u>.

INTERMEDIATE Write a response using the <u>sentence frame.</u>

ADVANCED, ADVANCED HIGH Write a response using the <u>sentence starter.</u>

BEGINNING	INTERMEDIATE	ADVANCED, ADVANCED HIGH
Word Bank	Sentence Frame	Sentence Starter
opinions ideas responsible encouraging community listening	I can be a better learner in the classroom by ____ and giving my ____.	• I can be a better learner in the classroom by . . . • When I give my opinion about . . . I should . . . • I contribute to my classroom community by . . .

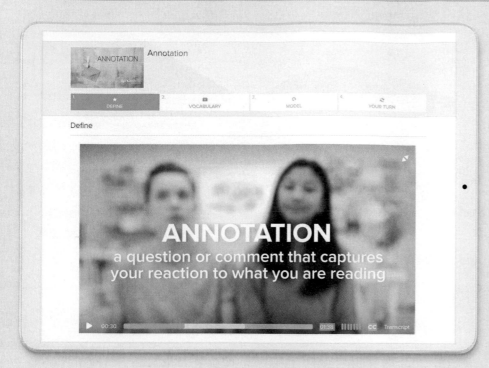

Introduce the Skill

Watch the Concept Definition video and read the following definition with your students.

An **annotation** is a question or comment that you write directly on a text to capture your reaction to what you are reading. When annotating a text, a writer may ask a **question, track** the development of an idea, or **respond** with a personal experience.

Annotations may also include a reader's inferences and evaluations about the text. An **inference** is an idea that a reader forms about a text by combining textual evidence and his or her own reasoning and prior knowledge. An **evaluation** is a judgment about content or the effectiveness of the writer's craft.

To record an annotation, a reader may use the StudySync annotation tool to highlight a selection of text and leave a comment or underline a passage of printed text and write a note in the margin.

Your Turn

Ask students to complete the Your Turn Activity.

Highlighted Text	Annotation	Category
alley	What does *alley* mean? Rachel wants to toss her sweater "in the alley," so it must be a noun. Since Rachel wants to get rid of the sweater, it may be some place where people put their garbage.	Ask Questions
"I don't know why but all of a sudden I'm feeling sick inside, like the part of me that's three wants to come out of my eyes, only I squeeze them shut tight and bite down on my teeth real hard and try to remember today I am eleven, eleven."	Rachel writes that she wants to start crying. But she is in school with her classmates. She's trying hard to remember she's eleven and that she shouldn't cry over the sweater.	Track
"Rachel," Mrs. Price says. She says it like she's getting mad. "You put that sweater on right now and no more nonsense." "But it's not—" "Now!" Mrs. Price says.	This is so weird! What is the problem with Mrs. Price? Why can't Rachel just put the sweater under her desk? No wonder Rachel is upset. No one likes being yelled at.	Respond
"But when the sick feeling goes away and I open my eyes, the red sweater's still sitting there like a big red mountain. I move the red sweater to the corner of my desk with my ruler. I move my pencil and books and eraser as far from it as possible."	Rachel is trying to deal with the sweater problem in the only way she knows how, considering she's in a classroom. She keeps moving it to the corner of her desk so it will be as "out of sight" as possible.	Track

1. What are annotations?
2. What are three purposes of annotations?

ELL **SPEAKING FRAMES**
- Annotations are ____.
- One purpose of annotations is to ____.

Skill: Context Clues

Introduce the Skill

Watch the Concept Definitions video and read the following definition with your students.

When readers come across words they don't know, they often use context to determine the meanings of the unfamiliar words. **Context clues** are hints in the surrounding text that a reader can use to **infer** the meaning of an unfamiliar word. Some common types of context clues include the following:

- **Definition:** an explanation of the word's meaning before or after the word appears, usually set off by a comma

- **Example:** one or more examples in a text that may demonstrate the meaning of a word

- **Comparison:** determining a word's meaning based on how it is like something else in the text

- **Contrast:** determining a word's meaning based on how it is unlike something else in the text

In addition, the genre of a text and what it is about also provide context clues for a word's meaning. Readers can verify their preliminary definitions of words or phrases by using a print or digital resource.

Context Clues

CONTEXT CLUES

Define

CONTEXT CLUE
a hint in the surrounding text that can help a reader infer the meaning of an unfamiliar word

00:35   02:16   CC

TURN AND TALK

1. What are context clues?

2. What are four different types of context clues?

ELL SPEAKING FRAMES

- Context clues are ____.
- One type of context clue is ____.
- It provides a clue to the meaning of a word by ____.

Your Turn

Ask students to complete the Your Turn Activity.

QUESTION 1

A. Incorrect. Taking a sweater, rolling it up, and throwing it away is not by itself behavior that would be called foolish or unacceptable.

B. Incorrect. Thinking about throwing a sweater over a fence, by itself, is not behavior that could be called foolish or unacceptable.

C. Correct. Rachel notes that her sweater is hanging over the edge of her desk "like a waterfall" but she doesn't care. This is a clue that she knows her actions, or behavior, are unacceptable and foolish in a classroom.

D. Incorrect. This describes the reaction Mrs. Price has to Rachel's behavior, but it does not provide a clue to the behavior itself.

QUESTION 2

A. Incorrect. Although the text says the sweater "smells like cottage cheese," it does not suggest that germs have anything to do with causing that smell.

B. Incorrect. Although the text says the sweater is itchy, it does not suggest that germs are causing the itchiness.

C. Incorrect. Although the text says the sweater hurts the narrator, it does not suggest that germs are to blame for her pain.

D. Correct. The phrase "full of germs that aren't even mine" and the narrator's disgust over putting on the sweater suggest that germs are "very small living things that cause sickness."

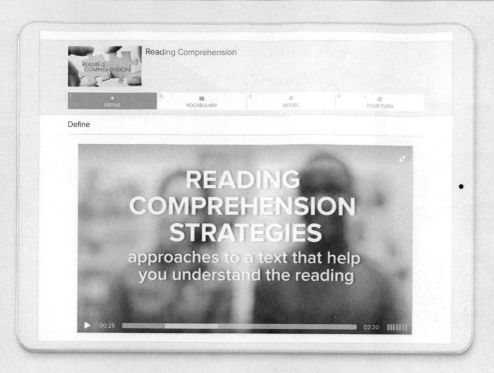

Reading Comprehension

| 1. DEFINE | 2. VOCABULARY | 3. MODEL | 4. YOUR TURN |

Define

READING COMPREHENSION STRATEGIES
approaches to a text that help you understand the reading

00:25 ———————————— 02:20

Skill: Reading Comprehension

Introduce the Skill

Watch the Concept Definition video and read the following definition with your students.

Have you ever felt overwhelmed by the information in a text? There are many **reading comprehension strategies** that can help you. Reading comprehension strategies are conscious, deliberate plans — steps that readers can use to make sense of a text and help them become active readers in control of their own reading comprehension.

Occasionally you will employ a reading comprehension strategy before you begin reading a text, such as **Setting a Purpose for Reading** or **Generating Questions.** To set a purpose for reading means to identify the reason for reading a text. Generating questions means to ask and answer questions before, during, and after reading a text.

Your Turn

Ask students to complete the Your Turn Activity.

Text	Annotation	Strategy
"Eleven" by Sandra Cisneros	I want to find out what the number *eleven* refers to in this story.	setting a purpose for reading
What they don't understand about birthdays and what they never tell you is that when you're eleven, you're also ten, and nine, and eight, and seven, and six, and five, and four, and three, and two, and one. And when you wake up on your eleventh birthday you expect to feel eleven, but you don't.	Who is "they"? Who does the narrator think understands birthdays? Is the narrator talking about herself when she says, "you expect to feel eleven"?	generating questions
Like some days you might say something stupid, and that's the part of you that's still ten. Or maybe some days you might need to sit on your mama's lap because you're scared, and that's the part of you that's five.	I think "that's the part of you that's still ten" means that the narrator feels younger than she is when she behaves a certain way.	making inferences
Because the way you grow old is kind of like an onion or like the rings inside a tree trunk or like my little wooden dolls that fit one inside the other, each year inside the next one. That's how being eleven years old is.	When I picture cutting open an onion, I see the layers that peel back. I think the narrator is saying that you keep your layers with you as you grow older.	visualizing

TURN AND TALK

1. In what ways would you like to improve your reading comprehension?

ELL SPEAKING FRAMES
- I would like to improve ___ when I read.
- I (have/have not) used a reading comprehension strategy before.
- I have used the reading comprehension strategy of ___.

First Read

Sandra Cisneros
Eleven

Introduce the Text

As a class, watch the video preview and have students read the introduction in pairs to make connections to the video preview.

To activate prior knowledge and experiences, ask students:

• How does the information in this video connect to what you already know?

• What kind of story are you going to read? How do you know?

ELL SPEAKING FRAMES

• The ____ in the video makes me think ____.
• The video shows ____. This makes me wonder ____.
• I think the text will ____. I think this because ____.
• I predict that there will be ____. I believe this because ____.

Entry Point

As students prepare to read "Eleven," share the following information with them to provide context.

✓ Sandra Cisneros was born in Chicago in 1954. She has written many books of poetry, short stories, and novels. Her most famous book, *The House on Mango Street*, was published in 1984 but remains required reading in schools across America.

✓ "Eleven" is based on actual events in Cisneros's life, though they actually occured on her ninth birthday.

✓ The story originally appeared in a short story collection titled Woman Hollering Creek, published in 1991.

"You open your eyes and everything's just like yesterday, only it's today. And you don't feel eleven at all."

NOTES

1   What they don't understand about birthdays and what they never tell you is that when you're eleven, you're also ten, and nine, and eight, and seven, and six, and five, and four, and three, and two, and one. And when you wake up on your eleventh birthday you expect to feel eleven, but you don't. You open your eyes and everything's just like yesterday, only it's today. And you don't feel eleven at all. You feel like you're still ten. And you are—underneath the year that makes you eleven.

2   Like some days you might say something stupid, and that's the part of you that's still ten. Or maybe some days you might need to sit on your mama's lap because you're scared, and that's the part of you that's five. And maybe one day when you're all grown up maybe you will need to cry like if you're three, and that's okay. That's what I tell Mama when she's sad and needs to cry. Maybe she's feeling three.

3   Because the way you grow old is kind of like an onion or like the rings inside a tree trunk or like my little wooden dolls that fit one inside the other, each year inside the next one. That's how being eleven years old is.

 Skill: Figurative Language

4   You don't feel eleven. Not right away. It takes a few days, weeks even, sometimes even months before you say Eleven when they ask you. And you don't feel smart eleven, not until you're almost twelve. That's the way it is.

5   Only today I wish I didn't have only eleven years rattling inside me like pennies in a tin Band-Aid box. Today I wish I was one hundred and two instead of eleven because if I was one hundred and two I'd have known what to say when Mrs. Price put the red sweater on my desk. I would've known how to tell her it wasn't mine instead of just sitting there with that look on my face and nothing coming out of my mouth.

The narrator uses similes when she compares aging to everyday things. When I picture onions, tree trunks, and wooden dolls, I notice they all have layers. She must mean that when you get older, you keep getting more layers.

6   "Whose is this?" Mrs. Price says, and she holds the red sweater up in the air for all the class to see. "Whose? It's been sitting in the coatroom for a month."

7   "Not mine," says everybody, "Not me."

Reading & Writing Companion **1**

 ## Analyze Vocabulary Using Context Clues

In paragraph 14, focus on the sentence that uses the word *alley*. Point out these context clues:

1.   The narrator wants to get rid of the sweater.
2.   She considers various methods of disposal - her last thought is to "toss it in the alley."

I look up *alley* in a dictionary, It means "a narrow passageway between or behind buildings."

✓ **CHECK FOR SUCCESS**

Have students work with a partner to determine the meaning of the rest of the bold vocabulary words.

If students are unable to make predictions, revisit the Checklist section of the Grade 6 Context Clues lesson with the class. After revisiting, guide students as they make predictions about the next bold word in the text in paragraph 18.

 ## Figurative Language

How does the figurative language in paragraph 3 help the reader understand Rachel's thoughts about aging?

The similes related to familiar objects help the reader visualize Rachel's idea that people are many ages at the same time.

 ## TEXT TALK

What idea does the narrator have about aging?

See paragraph 1: She thinks people are all the ages they ever have been at once.

Why does the narrator wish she were older after her teacher places the red sweater on her desk?

See paragraphs 5: She thinks if she were older, she would have known what to say to Mrs. Price to make her believe the sweater wasn't hers.

Skills Focus

QUESTION 1: Figurative Language

The narrator uses a simile to make the sweater appear misshapen and ridiculous.

Skills Focus

QUESTION 5: Figurative Language

Exaggeration conveys the narrator's loathing for the shabby, antiquated sweater.

Skills Focus

QUESTION 5: Connect to Essential Question

The narrator can't appeal to Mrs. Price because she's turned into a tongue-tied four-year-old.

Skills Focus

QUESTION 2: Textual Evidence

The text describes the narrator pushing the sweater away from her as if to deny that it's hers.

Skills Focus

QUESTION 2: Textual Evidence

Rachel wants to get rid of the sweater. I infer that she wants it so far from her that nobody will connect it with her.

Text Dependent Responses

What was the first step the writer took to respond to the first Think question?

The writer recalled details from the text and reviewed his annotations to confirm his thinking.

TEXT TALK

Why does the narrator call Sylvia Saldivar "stupid"?

See paragraph 9: She is angry with Sylvia for telling Mrs. Price the sweater belongs to her and thinks Sylvia did it because she doesn't like her.

What happens when Mrs. Price notices Rachel pushing away the sweater, and how does Rachel react?

See paragraphs 14–17: Mrs. Price makes Rachel put on the sweater, and Rachel turns into her four-year-old self and starts to cry.

Eleven

Skill:
Text-Dependent
Responses

Rachel thinks the sweater is old, ugly, and "all stretched out." I don't think she likes it at all.

8   "It has to belong to somebody," Mrs. Price keeps saying, but nobody can remember. It's an ugly sweater with red plastic buttons and a collar and sleeves all stretched out like you could use it for a jump rope. It's maybe a thousand years old and even if it belonged to me I wouldn't say so.

9   Maybe because I'm skinny, maybe because she doesn't like me, that stupid Sylvia Saldivar says, "I think it belongs to Rachel." An ugly sweater like that all **raggedy** and old, but Mrs. Price believes her. Mrs. Price takes the sweater and puts it right on my desk, but when I open my mouth nothing comes out.

10 "That's not, I don't, you're not . . . Not mine." I finally say in a little voice that was maybe me when I was four.

11 "Of course it's yours," Mrs. Price says. "I remember you wearing it once." Because she's older and the teacher, she's right and I'm not.

12 Not mine, not mine, not mine, but Mrs. Price is already turning to page thirty-two, and math problem number four. I don't know why but all of a sudden I'm feeling sick inside, like the part of me that's three wants to come out of my eyes, only I squeeze them shut real hard and bite down on my teeth real hard and try to remember today I am eleven, eleven. Mama is making a cake for me for tonight, and when Papa comes home everybody will sing Happy birthday, happy birthday to you.

13 But when the sick feeling goes away and I open my eyes, the red sweater's still sitting there like a big red mountain. I move the red sweater to the corner of my desk with my ruler. I move my pencil and books and eraser as far from it as possible. I even move my chair a little to the right. Not mine, not mine, not mine.

14 In my head I'm thinking how long till lunchtime, how long till I can take the red sweater and throw it over the schoolyard fence, or leave it hanging on a parking meter, or bunch it up into a little ball and toss it in the **alley.** Except when math period ends Mrs. Price says loud and in front of everybody, "Now, Rachel, that's enough," because she sees I've shoved the red sweater to the tippy-tip corner of my desk and it's hanging all over the edge like a waterfall, but I don't care.

15 "Rachel," Mrs. Price says. She says it like she's getting mad. "You put that sweater on right now and no more **nonsense.**"

16 "But it's not—"

17 "Now!" Mrs. Price says.

18 This is when I wish I wasn't eleven because all the years inside of me—ten, nine, eight, seven, six, five, four, three, two, and one—are pushing at the back of my eyes when I put one arm through one sleeve of the sweater that smells

---

  SELECTION VOCABULARY

raggedy / harapiento/a *adjective* in shabby condition

ELL
- What is being described as "raggedy"?
- What other words are being used to describe the item? Are they positive or negative?

alley / el callejón *noun* a narrow street or area located behind buildings

ELL
- What is happening in the sentence that contains "alley"?

Eleven

like cottage cheese, and then the other arm through the other and stand there with my arms apart like if the sweater hurts me and it does, all itchy and full of **germs** that aren't even mine.

19 That's when everything I've been holding in since this morning, since when Mrs. Price put the sweater on my desk, finally lets go, and all of a sudden I'm crying in front of everybody. I wish I was **invisible** but I'm not. I'm eleven and it's my birthday today and I'm crying like I'm three in front of everybody. I put my head down on the desk and bury my face in my stupid clown-sweater arms. My face all hot and spit coming out of my mouth because I can't stop the little animal noises from coming out of me until there aren't any more tears left in my eyes, and it's just my body shaking like when you have the hiccups, and my whole head hurts like when you drink milk too fast.

20 But the worst part is right before the bell rings for lunch. That stupid Phyllis Lopez, who is even dumber than Sylvia Saldivar, says she remembers the red sweater is hers! I take it off right away and give it to her, only Mrs. Price pretends like everything's okay.

21 Today I'm eleven. There's a cake Mama's making for tonight and when Papa comes home from work we'll eat it. There'll be candles and presents and everybody will sing Happy birthday, happy birthday to you, Rachel, only it's too late.

22 I'm eleven today. I'm eleven, ten, nine, eight, seven, six, five, four, three, two, and one, but I wish I was one hundred and two. I wish I was anything but eleven, because I want today to be far away already, far away like a runaway balloon, like a tiny o in the sky, so tiny-tiny you have to close your eyes to see it.

From WOMAN HOLLERING CREEK. Copyright © 1991 by Sandra Cisneros. Published by Vintage Books, a division of Random House, Inc., New York and originally in hardcover by Random House, Inc. By permission of Susan Bergholz Literary Services, New York, NY and Lamy, NM. All rights reserved

Skill: Textual Evidence

This is the second time Rachel has called one of her classmates stupid.

Rachel shows just how upset with Mrs. Price she really is by lashing out at her classmates. She is 11, but she is acting like a little kid because she doesn't know how else to act.

Reading & Writing Companion 3

Textual Evidence

What textual evidence does the reader cite explicitly from the text? What inference does the reader draw from this textual evidence?

The reader notes that the narrator says people are many different ages at once. The reader infers that the narrator does not always feel her age.

Skills Focus

QUESTION 3: Figurative Language

The narrator uses personification to describe her earlier ages pushing at the back of her eyes, or trying to get out. She says this because she's feeling upset and about to cry, as if she were still a little kid.

Prepare for Advanced Courses

Direct students to reread paragraph 3.

Remind students that a simile is a comparison using like or as.

Ask students: What similes does Cisneros use to describe the way a person ages? Why does she use these three similes specifically? What is the effect of these similes?

Sample answer; answers will vary: The author describes growing up to an onion, a tree, and wooden dolls. She uses these three similes beDcause they are physical examples that a reader can picture in order to understand the narrator's ideas about growing up. These provide characterization for the narrator and allow readers to see how her mind works and how she relates to the world. Putting these similes in the narrator's voice helps the reader see how grown up she can be, even with all those other years inside her.

V SELECTION VOCABULARY

germs / el germen *noun* very small living things that cause sickness COGNATE

- What is happening to the narrator in this paragraph?
- What does the narrator point out about the "germs"?

invisible / invisible *adjective* unable to be seen COGNATE

- What is taking place in this part of the story? How does the narrator feel?
- What does the narrator wish?

nonsense / la tontería *noun* silly behavior

- What is happening in this paragraph? How is Mrs. Price feeling?
- Is "nonsense" a positive or negative word?

Think Questions

Circulate as students answer Think Questions independently. Scaffolds for these questions are shown on the opposite page.

QUESTION 1: Textual Evidence

Rachel strongly dislikes the sweater, stating it is "stretched out" and "maybe a thousand years old." It upsets her so much that she cries in front of her classmates when they think it is hers.

QUESTION 2: Textual Evidence

Rachel says maybe it's because "I'm skinny, maybe because she doesn't like me." For these reasons, Sylvia tells Mrs. Price that she thinks the sweater "belongs to Rachel."

QUESTION 3: Textual Evidence

Rachel states that "Mrs. Price pretends like everything is okay." The reader doesn't know how Mrs. Price feels, but she doesn't apologize to Rachel, maybe because she doesn't realize how humiliated Rachel is, or she's embarrassed about her mistake.

QUESTION 4: Context Clues

The sweater is "all stretched out," and it is "old." These descriptions, plus prior knowledge that a rag is often an old, worn, and possibly torn piece of cloth, hint that *raggedy* means "not in good condition."

QUESTION 5: Context Clues

Mrs. Price tells Rachel that she wants cooperation and "no more nonsense." Since Rachel pushes the sweater away, Mrs. Price thinks Rachel is being dramatic, and she wants Rachel to behave more sensibly. So, *nonsense* means something that is not sensible.

Eleven

First Read

Read "Eleven." After you read, complete the Think Questions below.

☁ THINK QUESTIONS

1. How does Rachel feel about the red sweater that is placed on her desk? Respond with textual evidence from the story as well as ideas that you have inferred from clues in the text.

2. According to Rachel, why does Sylvia say the sweater belongs to Rachel? Support your answer with textual evidence.

3. Write two or three sentences exploring why Mrs. Price responds as she does when Phyllis claims the sweater. Support your answer with textual evidence.

4. Find the word **raggedy** in paragraph 9 of "Eleven." Use context clues in the surrounding sentences, as well as the sentence in which the word appears, to determine the word's meaning. Write your definition here and identify clues that helped you figure out its meaning.

5. Use context clues to determine the meaning of **nonsense** as it is used in paragraph 15 of "Eleven." Write your definition here and identify clues that helped you figure out its meaning. Then check the meaning in a dictionary.

6 📺 Reading & Writing Companion

Think Questions

Use the scaffolds below to differentiate instruction for your ELL English Language Learners and A Approaching grade-level learners.

ELL **BEGINNING** Write a response using the <u>word bank</u> and <u>sentence frames</u>.

INTERMEDIATE Write a response using the <u>sentence frames</u>.

ADVANCED, ADVANCED HIGH Write a response using the <u>Text-Dependent Question Guide</u>.

A **APPROACHING** Write a response using the <u>Text-Dependent Question Guide</u>.

| | INTERMEDIATE | APPROACHING |
BEGINNING		ADVANCED, ADVANCED HIGH
Word Bank	Sentence Frames	Text-Dependent Question Guide
sweater ugly old cry	Mrs. Price gives Rachel the red ____ because the teacher thinks it ____ to her. Rachel thinks the sweater is ____ out and a ____ years old. She dislikes it so much she starts to ____ when she has to wear it.	1. • Why does Mrs. Price give Rachel the red sweater? • How does Rachel feel about it? • How do you know?
belongs thousand silliness	Sylvia says the sweater belongs to ____. Rachel thinks Sylvia must ____ her.	2. • What does Sylvia say about the sweater? • Why does Rachel think Sylvia says this?
Rachel dislike fine damaged	After Mrs. Price gives Phyllis the sweater, the teacher acts like everything is ____. She might respond like this because she doesn't realize how ____ Rachel is or might feel embarrassed about her own ____.	3. • How does Mrs. Price respond after Phyllis claims the sweater? • Why might Mrs. Price respond like this?
upset mistake stretched	The sweater is described as ____ and ____. This gives me a clue that *raggedy* means something that is ____ and not in good condition.	4. • Read: "An ugly sweater like that all **raggedy** and old, but Mrs. Price believes her." • What other word or words are being used to describe the sweater here? • What does that tell me about the meaning of the word "raggedy"?
	Nonsense must mean ____ or *not behaving sensibly*.	5. • Mrs. Price tells Rachel that she wants cooperation and "no more nonsense." • Mrs. Price thinks Rachel is being dramatic, and she wants Rachel to behave more sensibly. • "Nonsense" must mean the reverse or opposite of "sense."

Skill: Text Dependent Responses

Introduce the Skill

Watch the Concept Definition video and read the following definition with your students.

Whether you are reading fiction or poetry, a play or nonfiction, **text-dependent responses** are short, concise answers to questions about a selection that include supporting evidence from the text. In StudySync, every First Read lesson includes a set of Think Questions that require a text-dependent response. To answer a Think Question, you need to use details from the text to make an inference or draw a conclusion, and cite these details to support your response. The strength of your response depends on your ability to use **textual evidence,** or details that a reader can use to support his or her ideas and opinions about a text. Answering such questions allows you to demonstrate your **comprehension,** or understanding of the text before moving on to a deeper analysis in future lessons.

 TURN AND TALK

1. What are some things that you do when writing text-dependent responses?

2. How do you think finding text evidence to support a response might improve your comprehension of the text?

ELL SPEAKING FRAMES

- Text-dependent responses are ____ that include ____.
- The strength of your response depends on your ability to use ____.
- Answering text-dependent responses allows you to demonstrate your ____ of the text before moving on to deeper analysis.

Eleven

Skill: Text-Dependent Responses

Use the Checklist to analyze Text-Dependent Responses in "Eleven." Refer to the sample student annotations about Text-Dependent Responses in the text.

••• CHECKLIST FOR TEXT-DEPENDENT RESPONSES

In order to identify textual evidence to support an analysis of a text, consider the following:

✓ details from the text to make an inference or draw a conclusion. Inferences are logical deductions from information in a text that is not directly, or explicitly, stated by the author

- read carefully and consider why an author gives particular details and information
- think about what you already know and use your own knowledge and experiences to help you figure out what the author does not state directly
- cite textual evidence, or the specific words, phrases, sentences, or paragraphs that led you to make an inference

✓ details that you can use to support your ideas and opinions about a text

✓ explicit evidence of a character's feelings or motivations, or the reasons behind an historical event in a nonfiction text

- explicit evidence is stated directly in the text and must be cited accurately to support a text-dependent answer or analysis

To cite textual evidence to support an analysis, consider the following questions:

✓ What types of textual evidence can I use to support an analysis of a text?

✓ What explicit evidence can I use to support my analysis?

✓ If I infer things in the text that the author does not state directly, what evidence from the text, along with my own experiences and knowledge, can I use to support my analysis?

V SKILL VOCABULARY

text dependent response / la respuesta que depende del texto *noun* short and concise answer to questions about a text that include supporting evidence from the text

textual evidence / la evidencia del texto *noun* details from the text that a reader can use to support his or her ideas and opinions about the text

comprehension / la comprensión *noun* the ability to understand what the text says

Skill:
Text-Dependent Responses

Read the second Think question from the First Read lesson for "Eleven." Then, using the Checklist on the previous page, complete the chart by deciding whether the evidence from the text can be used to form a response.

⟳ YOUR TURN

Evidence Options	
A	"Maybe because I'm skinny. . ."
B	"That's not, I don't, you're not . . . Not mine."
C	"Of course it's yours," Mrs. Price says. "I remember you wearing it once."
D	"Maybe because she doesn't like me . . ."

Would Support a Response	Would Not Support a Response

Please note that excerpts and passages in the StudySync® library and this workbook are intended as touchstones to generate interest in an author's work. The excerpts and passages do not substitute for the reading of entire texts, and StudySync® strongly recommends that students seek out and purchase the whole literary or informational work in order to experience it as the author intended. Links to online resellers are available in our digital library. In addition, complete works may be ordered through an authorized reseller by filling out and returning to StudySync® the order form enclosed in this workbook.

Reading & Writing Companion 5

Your Turn

Ask students to complete the Your Turn Activity.

Would Support a Response	Would Not Support a Response
"Maybe because I'm skinny . . . "	"That's not, I don't, you're not . . . Not mine."
"Maybe because she doesn't like me . . . "	"Of course it's yours," Mrs. Price says. "I remember you wearing it once."

Reading Comprehension OPTIONAL

Have students complete the digital reading comprehension questions ✓ when they finish reading.

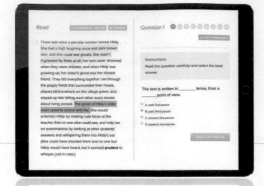

ANSWER KEY

QUESTION 1: B	**QUESTION 5:** D	**QUESTION 9:**
QUESTION 2: C	**QUESTION 6:** C	*See first chart.*
QUESTION 3: D	**QUESTION 7:** A	**QUESTION 10:**
QUESTION 4: C	**QUESTION 8:** B	*See second chart.*

Description	Character
Frustrated that no one will claim the sweater	Mrs. Price
Embarrassed in front of the class	Rachel
Doesn't like Rachel for some reason	Sylvia Saldivar
The person the sweater actually belongs to	Phyllis Lopez

First	Second	Third	Fourth	Fifth	Sixth
Rachel explains in detail how it feels to be eleven years old.	Mrs. Price asks the class to tell her who owns a particular red sweater.	Mrs. Price tells Rachel to put the sweater on.	Rachel cries in front of the class when she feels overwhelmed.	A student claims the red sweater is hers before the end of class.	Rachel wishes her birthday day were over.

Connect and Extend OPTIONAL

CONNECT TO EXTENDED WRITING PROJECT

Students can use "Eleven" as a mentor text for their Extended Writing Project. They may adopt some of Sandra Cisneros's descriptive language as they craft their own suspenseful narrative.

BEYOND THE BOOK

Game: How would you respond?

Put students in groups of 6. Give each group a stack of 12 index cards. Instruct students to:

1. Write a real-life scenario on one index card then write an age between three and their current age on a second card.

2. Mix the scenario cards in one stack and mix the age cards in a second stack.

3. Draw a real-life scenario card and an age card from each stack then act out how you think a child would respond to that situation at that age.

Select the "best performance" and have students selected by each group perform for the class.

To reflect, ask students:

• When do people become more logical and less emotional?

• What behavior is common for younger children? What does this reveal?

Skill:
Textual Evidence

Use the Checklist to analyze Textual Evidence in "Eleven." Refer to the sample student annotations about Textual Evidence in the text.

••• CHECKLIST FOR TEXTUAL EVIDENCE

In order to support an analysis by citing textual evidence that is explicitly, or clearly, stated in the text, do the following:

- ✓ read the text closely and critically
- ✓ identify what the text says explicitly
- ✓ find the most relevant textual evidence that supports your analysis
- ✓ consider why an author explicitly states specific details and information
- ✓ cite the specific words, phrases, sentences, or paragraphs from the text that support your analysis

In order to interpret implicit meanings in a text by making inferences, do the following:

- ✓ combine information directly stated in the text with your own knowledge, experiences, and observations
- ✓ cite the specific words, phrases, sentences, or paragraphs from the text that led to and support this inference.

In order to cite textual evidence to support an analysis of what the text says explicitly as well as inferences drawn from the text, consider the following questions:

- ✓ Have I read the text closely and critically?
- ✓ What inferences am I making about the text? What textual evidence am I using to support these inferences?
- ✓ Am I quoting the evidence from the text correctly?
- ✓ Does my textual evidence logically relate to my analysis?

Reading & Writing Companion   **7**

V SKILL VOCABULARY

cite / citar *verb* to quote as evidence to support a response

textual evidence / la evidencia del texto *noun* details from the text that a reader can use to support his or her ideas and opinions about the text

explicit / explícito/a *adjective* precisely and clearly expressed COGNATE

implicit / implícito/a *adjective* implied but not stated directly COGNATE

Skill: Textual Evidence

Introduce the Skill

Watch the Concept Definition video and read the following definition with your students.

Any time you're discussing a text, you need to cite, or point out, textual evidence, the details that readers use to support their ideas and opinions. Readers may cite evidence that is directly stated, or explicit, in the text. Other times, textual evidence may be implicit, which means it is suggested but not directly stated. One way to interpret implicit meanings is to make inferences, using clues from the text and your own experiences to make logical decisions about characters and events that are not stated directly.

Readers must also refer to textual evidence when they analyze and examine the different parts of a text. Analyzing specific parts of the text, such as the actions of a character or the cause-and-effect relationships between events in nonfiction, helps a reader interpret and explain the meaning, theme, or central idea of the text as a whole. When you cite textual evidence, someone else can look back at a particular part of a text you read and understand your analysis.

TURN AND TALK

1. What are the two types of textual evidence you might cite while trying to interpret a text and how are they different?

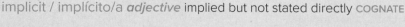

ELL SPEAKING FRAMES

- The purpose of citing textual evidence is ___.
- One type of textual evidence is ___.
- Readers can find textual evidence that is explicitly stated by ___.
- Readers can draw inferences from the text by ___.

⚙ Your Turn

Ask students to complete the Your Turn Activity.

Text	Evidence found explicitly in the text	Inference drawn from the text
Today I wish I was one hundred and two instead of eleven because if I was one hundred and two I'd have known what to say when Mrs. Price put the red sweater on my desk.	The narrator wishes she were 102 years old.	The narrator wishes she were older so she would know how to deal with difficult situations.
It's maybe a thousand years old and even if it belonged to me I wouldn't say so.	The narrator thinks the sweater is old, and she dislikes it.	The narrator dislikes the old sweater and wants to distance herself from it.
"Of course it's yours," Mrs. Price says. "I remember you wearing it once." Because she's older and the teacher, she's right and I'm not.	Because Mrs. Price is older and the teacher, her opinion about the sweater is correct.	Rachel is saying that Mrs. Price makes her feel powerless.

Skill:
Textual Evidence

sync•skills

Read the following excerpts from the story. Then, match the evidence found explicitly in the text and the inference drawn from the text for each excerpt. The first one is done for you.

🔄 YOUR TURN

Evidence Options	
A	The narrator dislikes the old sweater and wants to distance herself from it.
B	Because Mrs. Price is older and the teacher, her opinion about the sweater is correct.
C	Rachel is saying that Mrs. Price makes her feel powerless.
D	The narrator thinks the sweater is old, and she dislikes it.

Text	Evidence found explicitly in the text	Inference drawn from the text
Today I wish I was one hundred and two instead of eleven because if I was one hundred and two I'd have known what to say when Mrs. Price put the red sweater on my desk.	The narrator wishes she were 102 years old.	The narrator wishes she were older so she would know how to deal with difficult situations.
It's maybe a thousand years old and even if it belonged to me I wouldn't say so.		
"Of course it's yours," Mrs. Price says. "I remember you wearing it once." Because she's older and the teacher, she's right and I'm not.		

Ⅴ SKILL VOCABULARY

make inferences / hacer inferencias *verb* to use your understanding of a text and your own experiences, to draw conclusions

analyze / analizar *verb* to consider in detail and discover essential features or meaning COGNATE

interpret / interpretar *verb* to explain the meaning of (information, words, or actions) COGNATE

Eleven

Skill: Figurative Language

Use the Checklist to analyze Figurative Language in "Eleven." Refer to the sample student annotations about Figurative Language in the text.

••• CHECKLIST FOR FIGURATIVE LANGUAGE

To determine the meaning of figures of speech in a text, note the following:

- ✓ words that mean one thing literally and suggest something else
- ✓ similes, such as "strong as an ox"
- ✓ metaphors, such as "her eyes were stars"
- ✓ personification, such as "the daisies danced in the wind"

In order to interpret the meaning of a figure of speech in context, ask the following questions:

- ✓ Does any of the descriptive language in the text compare two seemingly unlike things?
- ✓ Do any descriptions include "like" or "as" that indicate a simile?
- ✓ Is there a direct comparison that suggests a metaphor?
- ✓ Is a human quality is being used to describe this animal, object, force of nature or idea that suggests personification?
- ✓ How does the use of this figure of speech change your understanding of the thing or person being described?

In order to analyze the impact of figurative language on the meaning of a text, use the following questions as a guide:

- ✓ Where does figurative language appear in the text? What does it mean?
- ✓ Why does the author use figurative language rather than literal language?

Reading & Writing Companion **9**

Skill: Figurative Language

Introduce the Skill

Watch the Concept Definition video and read the following definition with your students.

Figurative language is language used for descriptive effect, often to illustrate or imply ideas indirectly. Figures of Speech include simile, metaphor, and personification. A **simile** uses words *like* or *as* to compare two seemingly unlike things. A **metaphor** directly compares two seemingly unlike things without using like or as. **Personification** is a **figure of speech** in which an animal, object, force of nature, or an idea is ascribe human qualities.

When reading prose, and especially poetry, readers use **context**—including when and where a text was written, —to analyze the impact of word choice and to help interpret the meaning of figurative words and phrases.

⚙ TURN AND TALK

1. How did the figurative language help you better understand the text?

> **ELL** SPEAKING FRAMES
> - One example of figurative language from my favorite story or song is ____. ____ was compared to ____. This made me feel ____.
> - One feeling I had was ____. It felt like ____. I compared it to ____.

V SKILL VOCABULARY

figurative language / el lenguaje figurativo *noun* expressions used for descriptive or rhetorical effect that are not literally true but that express some truth beyond the literal level) COGNATE

simile / el símil *noun* a figure of speech that uses the words like or as to compare two seemingly unlike things COGNATE

metaphor / la metáfora *noun* a figure of speech that compares two seemingly unlike things but implies a comparison instead of stating it directly with the words like or as COGNATE

personification / la personificación *noun* a figure of speech in which an animal, object, force of nature, or an idea is given human form or qualities COGNATE

figure of speech / la figura literaria *noun* a word or phrase not meant to be taken literally, but rather used for effect

context / el contexto *noun* the set of facts or circumstances that surround a situation or event COGNATE

Your Turn

Ask students to complete the Your Turn Activity.

QUESTION 1

A. Incorrect. The figurative language in the paragraph is similes, not metaphors.

B. **Correct.** The similes in the paragraph—"smells like cottage cheese" and "like if the sweater hurts me"—tell readers that Rachel finds the sweater smelly and uncomfortable.

C. Incorrect. The figurative language in the paragraph makes Rachel's discomfort clear but does not suggest she is overreacting. The paragraph also contains similes, not metaphors.

D. Incorrect. The figurative language in the paragraph makes Rachel's discomfort clear but does not suggest she is overreacting.

QUESTION 2

A. Incorrect. This metaphor helps us picture Rachel's behavior but does not go so far as to suggest she is behaving like an animal.

B. Incorrect. The text does not suggest that Rachel finds any humor in her experience with the sweater.

C. **Correct.** These similes help readers visualize her experience by comparing her reaction to unpleasant emotions most readers have experienced and can easily picture.

D. Incorrect. Rachel is still very upset at this point in the story, and nothing in the story suggests she is about to calm down.

Eleven

Skill: Figurative Language

Reread paragraphs 18 and 19 of "Eleven." Then, using the Checklist on the previous page, answer the multiple-choice questions below.

⟳ YOUR TURN

1. How does the figurative language in paragraph 18 help readers understand Rachel's reaction to the sweater?

    ○ A. The metaphors in the paragraph help readers understand how uncomfortable Rachel feels in the sweater.

    ○ B. The similes in the paragraph help readers understand how uncomfortable Rachel feels in the sweater.

    ○ C. The metaphors in the paragraph make it clear to readers that Rachel is overreacting about the sweater.

    ○ D. The similes in the paragraph make it clear to readers that Rachel is overreacting about the sweater.

2. How does the figurative language in paragraph 19 help readers visualize Rachel's behavior?

    ○ A. The mention of "little animal noises" tells readers that Rachel is acting more like an animal than a human.

    ○ B. The metaphor of "clown-sweater arms" shows that Rachel is able to see the humorous side in her experience.

    ○ C. The similes about her body shaking "like when you have the hiccups" and her head hurting "like when you drink milk too fast" connect to unpleasant experiences most readers have had.

    ○ D. The statement that "there aren't any more tears left in [her] eyes" suggests that Rachel is starting to calm down.

Close Read

Close Read

Reread "Eleven." As you reread, complete the Skills Focus questions below. Then use your answers and annotations from the questions to help you complete the Write activity.

◎ SKILLS FOCUS

1. Identify examples of figurative language and explain the purpose they achieve in the story.

2. Explain what you can infer about the narrator's feelings about the sweater based on her descriptions, actions, and reactions.

3. The narrator uses figurative language, including similes and metaphors, to describe aging. Identify these in the text. Explain what type of figurative language each one is an example of and what each piece of figurative language means.

4. Explain what the author implies about what the narrator really wants when she says, "today I wish I was one hundred and two."

5. Getting older can be tough. Identify and explain the textual evidence in the story that supports this statement.

✏ WRITE

LITERARY ANALYSIS: How does the author's use of figurative language help readers understand the feelings that the narrator is expressing? Write a response of at least 200 words. Support your writing with evidence from the text.

Reading & Writing Companion   **11**

Close Read

Skills Focus

QUESTION 1: Figurative Language

See paragraph 8.

QUESTION 2: Textual Evidence

See paragraphs 13 and 14.

QUESTION 3: Figurative Language

See paragraph 3.

QUESTION 3: Figurative Language

See paragraph 18.

QUESTION 4: Textual Evidence

Paragraph 4: The explicit meaning of this statement is that the narrator wishes she were 102 years old. The implicit meaning is that she wishes she had the knowledge and experience of someone older to be able to convince Mrs. Price the sweater wasn't hers. See paragraph 5.

QUESTION 5: Connect to Essential Question

See paragraph 10.

✓ CHECK FOR SUCCESS

If students struggle to respond to Skills Focus Question #1, ask students the following questions:

- What does the narrator say about the sweater in paragraph 8?

- What types of figurative language do you find in that paragraph?

- Why does the narrator describe the sweater this way? What does this tell readers about how the narrator views the sweater?

Writer's Notebook

Connect to Essential Question: Give students time to reflect on how "Eleven" connects to the unit's essential question "What do we do when life gets hard?" by freewriting in their Writer's Notebooks.

ELL **Beginning & Intermediate**

Read aloud the unit's essential question: "What do we do when life gets hard?". Encourage students to draw their connections or allow students to write in their native language. Circulate around the room, prompting students for their thoughts as they respond orally or through pantomime.

Advanced & Advanced High

Allow students to share their reflections orally in pairs or small groups before freewriting.

Skill: Collaborative Conversations

Introduce the Skill

Watch the Concept Definitions video and read the following definition with your students.

A **collaborative conversation** is a discussion among individuals in which the participants engage in collaboration. **Collaboration** is the process of working together to achieve a shared goal.

Collaborative conversation involves offering insights and ideas, listening carefully to the ideas of others, and responding thoughtfully to each other. Participants in a collaborative conversation choose language that is respectful and encouraging and are careful not to dismiss or ignore others' opinions. Participants must **reflect** on the ideas of others and **adjust** their own responses when **valid evidence** indicates an adjustment is warranted. When defending or challenging an author's **claim**, a speaker must use relevant **text evidence**. The outcome of the collaboration is, ideally, the fulfillment of a stated plan or goal.

Learning to listen to and respond appropriately and thoughtfully to the ideas of others and working to express your own relevant ideas and opinions are essential life skills.

Your Turn

Your Turn 1

Helps the Collaborative Conversation	Distracts from the Collaborative Conversation
"Whoa, whoa! Can someone read the prompt first?"	"She should think of it as an unexpected present."
"'Oh yeah! She explains it at the beginning of the story."	"An ugly sweater that smells like cottage cheese?"

Your Turn 2

Helps the Collaborative Conversation	Distracts from the Collaborative Conversation
"I'm going to write down that idea to use in my response."	"That's really great."
"What paragraph did you find that evidence in?"	"I hope I don't forget this idea later on."

TURN AND TALK

1. What are some ways you can make sure a collaborative conversation stays on track and doesn't move off topic?

2. If you disagree with someone during a collaborative conversation, what are some respectful ways to voice your differing opinion?

> **ELL SPEAKING FRAMES**
> - Collaboration is the process of working together to ____.
> - A collaborative conversation is a discussion between ____. It involves ____.
> - During collaborative conversations, it's important to choose language that is ____ and be careful not to dismiss or ignore ____.

StudySyncTV   Project the StudySyncTV episode  and pause at the following times to prompt discussion:

0:16–0:39   What do the students disagree about at the start of the discussion?

1:16   Nik says Rachel "acts like a four-year-old when it comes to that red sweater." Why does he say that, and how does this statement connect to the narrator's ideas about aging?

2:57   What do Nik and Donovan point out about how Rachel sounds when she is describing her ideas about aging? What does this reveal about Rachel's character?

3:37   Delaney points out that readers "get the feeling of what it's like" at Rachel's home. What textual evidence does the group share to support this conclusion?

 ## Collaborative Conversation

Break students into collaborative conversation groups to discuss the writing prompt. Ask students to use the StudySyncTV episode as a model for their discussion. Remind them to reference their Skills Focus annotations in their discussion.

How does the author's use of figurative language help readers understand the feelings that the narrator is expressing?

Use the scaffolds below to differentiate instruction for your **ELL** English Language Learners and **A** Approaching grade-level learners.

ELL   BEGINNING, INTERMEDIATE   Use the <u>discussion guide</u> and <u>speaking frames</u> to facilitate the discussion with support from the teacher.

ADVANCED, ADVANCED HIGH   Use the <u>discussion guide</u> and <u>speaking frames</u> to facilitate the discussion in mixed-level groups.

A   APPROACHING   Use the <u>discussion guide</u> to facilitate the discussion in mixed-level groups.

APPROACHING
ADVANCED, ADVANCED HIGH
BEGINNING, INTERMEDIATE

Discussion Guide	Speaking Frames
1. What examples of figurative language are used in the text?	• In paragraph 3, the author uses similes to ____. • In paragraph 8, the author uses exaggeration to ____.
2. What does the narrator say about the sweater?	• The narrator describes the sweater as ____. • The narrator's reaction to putting on the sweater is ____.
3. What feelings does the narrator express through the descriptions of the sweater?	• The narrator's descriptions of the sweater suggest that she feels ____ about the sweater. • The narrator reacts that way to putting on the sweater because ____.

Review Prompt and Rubric

Before students begin writing, review the writing prompt and rubric with the class.

LITERARY ANALYSIS: How does the author's use of figurative language help readers understand the feelings that the narrator is expressing? Write a response of at least 200 words. Support your writing with evidence from the text.

 PROMPT GUIDE

- What is figurative language?
- What does the narrator say about the sweater?
- What feelings does the narrator express through the descriptions of the sweater?

- How does the author's use of figurative language help readers understand the narrator's explicit and implicit feelings?

Score	Figurative Language	Textual Evidence	Language and Conventions
4	The writer clearly analyzes and explains the author's use of figurative language. The writer provides exemplary analysis, using relevant evidence from the text.	The writer clearly analyzes and explains the feelings that the narrator is expressing. The writer provides exemplary analysis, using relevant evidence from the text.	The writer demonstrates a consistent command of grammar, punctuation, and usage conventions. Although minor errors may be evident, they do not detract from the fluency or the clarity of the essay.
3	The writer analyzes and explains the author's use of figurative language. The writer provides sufficient analysis, using relevant evidence from the text most of the time.	The writer analyzes and explains the feelings that the narrator is expressing. The writer provides sufficient analysis, using relevant evidence from the text most of the time.	The writer demonstrates an adequate command of grammar, punctuation, and usage conventions. Although some errors may be evident, they create few (if any) disruptions in the fluency of the writing or the clarity of the essay.
2	The writer begins to analyze or explain the author's use of figurative language, but the analysis is incomplete. The writer uses relevant evidence from the text only some of the time.	The writer begins to analyze or explain the feelings that the narrator is expressing, but the analysis is incomplete. The writer uses relevant evidence from the text only some of the time.	The writer demonstrates a partial command of grammar, punctuation, and usage conventions. Some distracting errors may be evident, at times creating minor disruptions in the fluency or clarity of the writing.
1	The writer attempts to analyze or explain the author's use of figurative language, but the analysis is not successful. The writer uses little or no relevant evidence from the text.	The writer attempts to analyze or explain the feelings that the narrator is expressing, but the analysis is not successful. The writer uses little or no relevant evidence from the text.	The writer demonstrates little or no command of grammar, punctuation, and usage conventions. Serious and persistent errors create disruptions in the fluency of the writing and sometimes interfere with meaning.
0	The writer does not provide a relevant response to the prompt or does not provide a response at all.	The writer does not provide a relevant response to the prompt or does not provide a response at all.	Serious and persistent errors overwhelm the writing and interfere with the meaning of the response as a whole, making the writer's meaning impossible to understand.

Short Constructed Responses

1. ★ DEFINE   2. 📷 VOCABULARY   3. ⏱ MODEL   4. ⟳ YOUR TURN

Define

SHORT CONSTRUCTED RESPONSE
a brief, organized written composition answering a prompt

00:35 ━━━━━━━━━━━━━━ 02:16 ▐▐▌▌ CC

Skill: Short Constructed Responses

Introduce the Skill

Watch the Concept Definitions video and read the following definition with your students.

A **short constructed response** is a brief, organized written composition that answers a **prompt**. A prompt asks you to define, explain, analyze, interpret, or respond to a topic, idea, or issue. The prompt may include statements and questions to guide or inspire a reader's response.

Types of responses vary for different texts and lessons. For instance, you may analyze an extended metaphor in a poem, argue your point of view after reading an article, or even imagine yourself as a character in a short story.

To write your response, you first paraphrase the prompt to guide your thinking. To **paraphrase** means to restate the directions of the prompt in your own words. Next, you plan your analysis and write your response using text evidence collected in annotations. **Text evidence** refers to the details from the text that you can use to support your ideas.

Writing short constructed responses helps you to develop a routine to support your thinking with evidence, as well as giving you practice using newly acquired content and academic vocabulary.

Your Turn

Ask students to complete the Your Turn Activity.

QUESTION 1

A. **Correct.** The sentence paraphrases the prompt correctly.

B. Incorrect. This sentence does not clearly paraphrase the prompt because it mentions the author's feelings toward the narrator, not the narrator's feelings in general.

C. Incorrect. This sentence mentions only metaphors, not similes or other types of figurative language.

D. Incorrect. This sentence leaves out inferences that the reader makes about Rachel's feelings and ideas.

QUESTION 2

A. Incorrect. The phrase "just like yesterday" contains the word "like," but it is not a simile.

B. **Correct.** The narrator uses a simile to compare the red sweater hanging over the edge of her desk to a waterfall.

C. Incorrect. This describes a response you might have when you're scared, but it is not an example of figurative language.

D. Incorrect. This describes what the sweater smells like, but it is a description, not an example of figurative language such as a simile or metaphor.

TURN AND TALK

1. What was the last prompt you had to respond to in a class?

2. What did you do to plan your analysis, and what evidence did you include to support your ideas?

ELL SPEAKING FRAMES

- A short constructed response is a written composition that answers a ____. A prompt is a ____.
- To write a response, it's a good idea to first ____ your prompt, or restate it in your own words.
- As you plan and write your analysis, include ____ to support your ideas.

Skill: Peer Review

Introduce the Skill

Watch the Concept Definition video  and read the following definition with your students.

Peer review is the act of one student reading over, commenting on, and **critiquing** another student's written work. This collaborative process allows for input from a variety of perspectives, providing a writer with more complete feedback on his or her writing. What one reviewer notices, another might miss.

Peer reviewers should strive to give **constructive** feedback that will help the writer improve his or her work. To provide constructive feedback, include **specific comments** that identify strengths or areas for improvement, and offer clear suggestions on how to improve the writing. Peer reviewers should always maintain a **respectful tone.** That means expressing their thoughts and opinions in a way that shows consideration for the writer's feelings, keeping in mind that it can be difficult for a writer to receive criticism.

TURN AND TALK

1. What are the most important things to keep in mind when writing a peer review?

2. What are some ways you can phrase negative feedback so that it is respectful and not discouraging to the writer?

ELL SPEAKING FRAMES

- A peer review is ____. It is helpful because it gives a writer input from ____.
- Peer reviewers should provide feedback that is ____ and ____.
- A specific comment identifies a strength or an area for improvement and offers a suggestion for ____.
- Peer reviewers should maintain a ____ tone in order to show consideration for the writer's feelings.

Your Turn

Ask students to complete the Your Turn Activity.

Description	Peer Reviews
Specific	The textual evidence in your second paragraph is very strong.
Vague	I like how you used textual evidence.
Positive	You did a really great job of selecting details from the story!
Negative	I don't like the quotes that you chose.
Constructive	You may want to add an explanation after your first paragraph, the evidence is good but I'm not sure how it supports your claim.

Write

Ask students to complete the writing assignment using textual evidence to support their answers.

Use the scaffolds below to differentiate instruction for your **ELL** English Language Learners and **A** Approaching grade-level learners.

ELL **BEGINNING** With the help of the <u>word bank</u>, write a response using <u>paragraph frame 1</u>.

INTERMEDIATE With the help of the <u>word bank</u>, write a response using <u>paragraph frames 1 and 2</u>.

ADVANCED, ADVANCED HIGH Write a response of differentiated length using the <u>sentence starters</u>.

A **APPROACHING** Write a response of differentiated length using the <u>sentence starters</u>.

BEGINNING	ADVANCED, ADVANCED HIGH
INTERMEDIATE	APPROACHING

Word Bank	Paragraph Frame 1	Paragraph Frame 2	Sentence Starters
onion figurative language aging similes ages	The author uses ___ such as ___ and metaphors to help readers understand the narrator's feelings. For example, she describes ___ as being like an ___ or the rings of a tree trunk because people are many different ___ at once.	When you need to ___, the narrator says, that's the part of you that's still ___. When the narrator tries to speak up and tell ___ the sweater isn't ___, she speaks quietly and isn't convincing. That's the part of her that's still ___. Even though the narrator has just turned ___, she doesn't feel older yet because of her ___ over the sweater.	• The author uses figurative language such as . . . • The narrator expresses her feelings about aging by . . . • The use of figurative language helps the reader understand . . .

Peer Review

Students should submit substantive feedback to two peers using the review instructions below.

- How well does this response answer the prompt?
- How well does the writer support ideas with details and examples from the text?
- Which sentence in the writer's response made you think differently about the text?
- What did the writer do well in this response? What does the writer need to work on? Remember that your comments are most useful when they are kind and constructive.

Rate

Respond to the following with a point rating that reflects your opinion.

	1 2 3 4
Ideas	▪▪▪☐
Evidence	▪▪▪▪
Language and Conventions	▪▪☐☐

Submit

ELL **A** **SENTENCE FRAMES**

- You were able to (completely / partly / almost) ___ answer the prompt because . . .
- You could answer the prompt more completely by . . .
- You supported the idea of . . . with the detail of . . .

- One idea that needs more support is . . .
- I thought differently about the texts after reading . . .
- The part of your response that needs the most improvement is . . .
- My favorite part of your response is . . .

Unit Preview

Introduce the Unit

As a class, watch the unit preview ▶ and discuss the questions below.

- What two words would you use to describe this video?

- What key words or images from the video do you think will be most important to this unit?

Instructional Path

Big Idea Blast

Objectives: After exploring background information and research links about a topic, students will respond to a question with a 140-character response.

Skill: Recognize Genre

Objectives: After learning about the genre of fiction, students will be able to identify and describe characteristics of fantasy, mystery, and realistic and historical fiction.

Skill: Academic Vocabulary

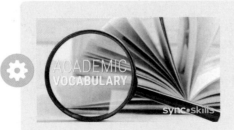

Objectives: After learning the meanings of ten academic vocabulary words, students will be able to recognize and use them in a variety of contexts.

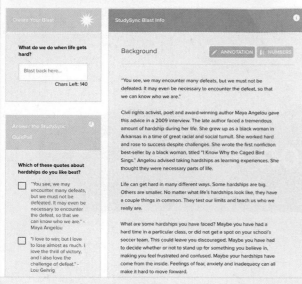

 ## Blast: Testing Our Limits

What do we do when life gets hard?

✺ TEXT TALK

What do most hardships have in common?

They test our limits and help us know who we really are inside.

What kind of hardships did Paul Allen and Bill Gates face? How did it help them to eventually achieve success?

Their first invention, a machine that would count traffic, was a failure. Rather than give up, it gave them the motivation to build Microsoft, which became a runaway success.

What kinds of hardships do you think are more difficult to face, those that come from inside, such as feelings of anxiety, or those that test a person's motivation? Explain.

Answers will vary.

✺ Create Your Own Blast

SCAFFOLDS

Ask students to write a 140-character Blast after they complete the QuikPoll.

Use the scaffolds below to differentiate instruction for your **ELL** English Language Learners.

ELL BEGINNING Write a response using the underline{word bank} to complete the sentence frame.

INTERMEDIATE Write a response using the underline{sentence frame}.

ADVANCED, ADVANCED HIGH Write a response using the underline{sentence starter}.

BEGINNING	INTERMEDIATE	ADVANCED, ADVANCED HIGH
Word Bank	**Sentence Frame**	**Sentence Starter**
hard limits scary selves difficult lives	Facing hardship is often ____, but it can teach us things about our ____.	• Facing a challenge can teach us things about . . .

Skill: Recognize Genre

Introduce the Genre: Fiction

Watch the Concept Definition video  and read the following definition with your students.

Fiction is writing about invented people, places, and events. It includes both long and short written works. **Novels** are long works of fiction. **Short stories,** myths, and folktales are examples of short works of fiction. Short fiction focuses on a small number of events or on just one event. You can usually read a short work of fiction in a single sitting. Short works contain the same elements as do longer works of fiction. These elements include character, plot, setting, point of view, and theme.

In addition, there are many different **literary genres,** or specific categories, of fiction writing. Examples of literary genres include realistic fiction, adventure stories, historical fiction, mysteries, humor, myths, fantasy, and science fiction. Each literary genre has certain characteristics that define the content of the writing.

 TURN AND TALK

1. How do you know when you are reading fiction as opposed to other kinds of writing?

2. What features of fiction do you notice first?

ELL SPEAKING FRAMES
- I know I am reading fiction when ____.
- The first features I notice in fiction are ____.

 Your Turn

Ask students to complete the Your Turn activity.

Description	Literary Genre
A teenage girl embarks on a journey across the Great Desert to find the magic stone that will unlock her ability to see the future.	fantasy
A short story about a farm boy takes place on the night of Paul Revere's famous Midnight Ride in 1775.	historical fiction
Two sisters move to a new city in a new country and are faced not just with learning a new language, but also making new friends.	realistic fiction
On a dark and stormy night, someone kidnaps the Smiths' beloved poodle. The search takes the family to a surprising location.	mystery

Skill: Academic Vocabulary

Introduce the Terms

analyze / analizar *verb* to consider in detail and discover essential features or meaning COGNATE

approach / la estrategia *noun* ideas or actions intended to deal with a problem or situation

assume / asumir *verb* to accept to be true without proof COGNATE

conclude / concluir *verb* to decide by reasoning COGNATE

context / el contexto *noun* the set of facts or circumstances that surround a situation or event COGNATE

derive / obtener *verb* to reason by deduction; to receive from a source

indicate / indicar *verb* to state or express briefly COGNATE

interpret / interpretar *verb* to explain the meaning of (information, words, or actions) COGNATE

obtain / obtener *verb* to come into possession of COGNATE

seek / buscar *verb* to try to locate or discover

Your Turn

Ask students to complete the Your Turn activities.

Your Turn 1

See digital teacher's edition for sample answers.

Your Turn 2

QUESTION 1: B   **QUESTION 2:** D   **QUESTION 3:** A   **QUESTION 4:** C   **QUESTION 5:** C

Your Turn 3

See digital teacher's edition for sample answers.

Practice Using Vocabulary

Divide the vocabulary words into two lists. Pair students and give each student one half of the list. Challenge students to have a casual conversation with each other that uses every word on their list. Students should aim to insert their vocabulary words in a way that sounds natural. You may wish to turn this activity into a game, allowing partners to award each other points if they effectively use each word on their list.

The Mighty Miss Malone

FICTION
Christopher Paul Curtis
2012

Introduction

The Mighty Miss Malone is author Christopher Paul Curtis's follow-up to 2000's Newbery Award-winning Bud, Not Buddy, both stories of young African Americans set in Great Depression-era Flint, Michigan. This time, twelve-year-old Deza Malone—new in Flint from Gary, Indiana, where she was at the top of her class—is the narrator. When her father doesn't return from a trip to find work, Deza, her brother Jimmie, and her mother go looking for him, journeying across the land by hopping aboard a boxcar. For a time, the Malones make their home outside of Flint, Michigan, in a "Hooverville," a ragtag encampment of hoboes and wayfarers. When Deza begins again at a new school, her teachers, unlike her beloved former teacher Mrs. Needham, treat her unfairly because of her race. As this excerpt begins, Deza has been busying herself helping Stew, the woman in charge.

During the Great Depression, twelve-year-old Deza Malone must adjust to life in Flint, Michigan after her family leaves Gary, Indiana in search of her father, who left home earlier to find work. Her family makes a temporary home in an encampment run by a woman named Stew. At the beginning of this excerpt, Deza reflects on the racism that she encounters at her new school. Her math teacher is astounded when Deza, an African American girl, solves all the problems correctly; and in English class, Mr. Smith gives Deza a C+ on an essay even though she did a "very good job." In the camp, Deza becomes a mentor to the new children, some of whom don't have parents. One evening while washing dishes with an orphan boy, Deza is surprised when he kisses her. Rather than hit him like she wants to, Deza pities and comforts him. She reminds herself that he is all alone and reflects on how lucky she is to still have her family.

 Proficiency-leveled summaries and summaries in multiple languages are available digitally.

🔊 Audio and audio text highlighting are available with this text.

CONNECT TO ESSENTIAL QUESTION

What do we do when life gets hard?

In Christopher Paul Curtis's *The Mighty Miss Malone*, twelve-year-old Deza Malone is a bright student with a promising future. But when the Great Depression hits Gary, Indiana, her family is confronted with many new challenges. Deza's father leaves town to find work, and when he doesn't return, Deza, her mother, and her brother go looking for him. They journey across the state by boxcar until they wind up in a "Hooverville" outside of Flint, Michigan.

Access Complex Text

LEXILE: 750   WORD COUNT: 1,382

The following areas may be challenging for students, particularly **ELL** English Language Learners and **A** Approaching grade-level learners.

Prior Knowledge	Sentence Structure	Organization
• Some students may not be familiar with the term "Hooverville." • Hoovervilles were towns of crudely built houses built by unemployed people in the Depression. They were named after Herbert Hoover, the president in the early years of the Depression.	• The selection contains examples of dialect and unusual sentence structure. • Point out that phrases such as 'I'MNOTAFRAIDOFGIRLS!'" enable the reader to *hear* as well as read the dialogue, and serve as clues to character.	• Students may be confused by the jump in the narrative that takes place between paragraphs three and four. • Explain that Miss Stew helps run the camp where Deza's family is staying, and Miss Needham was one of Deza's teachers in Gary.

 **SCAFFOLDS** 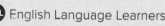 **ENGLISH LANGUAGE LEARNERS** **A** **APPROACHING GRADE LEVEL** **B** **BEYOND GRADE LEVEL**

These icons identify differentiation strategies and scaffolded support for a variety of students. See the digital lesson plan for additional differentiation strategies and scaffolds.

Instructional Path

The print teacher's edition includes essential point-of-use instruction and planning tools. Complete lesson plans and program documents appear in your digital teacher account.

Skill: Making Connections

Objectives: After reading and discussing a model of close reading, students will be able to make connections in order to improve reading comprehension.

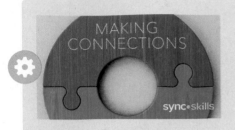

First Read: *The Mighty Miss Malone*

Objectives: After an initial reading and discussion of the story, students will be able to identify and describe character traits, key events, as well as articulate the conflict that is integral to the story's plot.

Skill: Character

Objectives: After reading and discussing a model of close reading, students will be able to analyze how the characters' reactions and changes contribute to the plot.

Close Read: *The Mighty Miss Malone*

Objectives: After engaging in a close reading and discussion of the text, students will be able to analyze character and show how characters respond to change in a short, written response.

Blast: Moral Quarrel

Objectives: After exploring background information and research links about a topic, students will respond to a question with a 140-character response.

Progress Monitoring

Opportunities to Learn	Opportunities to Demonstrate Learning	Opportunities to Reteach

Making Connections

⚙ Skill: Making Connections	💬 First Read • Read and Annotate	⚙ Spotlight Skill: Making Connections

Character

⚙ Skill: Character	⚙ Skill: Character • Your Turn 📄 Close Read • Skills Focus • Collaborative Conversations • Write	⚙ Unit 3 Skill: Character - Heroes Every Child Should Know: Perseus ⚙ Unit 5 Skill: Character - Amigo Brother ⚙ Spotlight Skill: Character

First Read

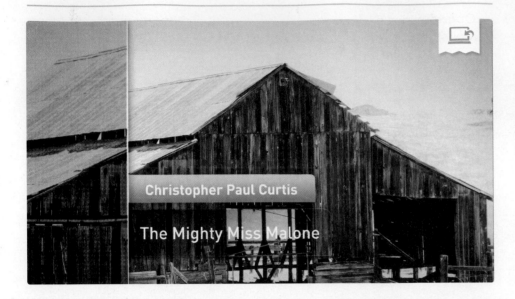

Christopher Paul Curtis

The Mighty Miss Malone

Introduce the Text

As a class, watch the video preview  and have students read the introduction in pairs to make connections to the video preview.

To activate prior knowledge and experiences, ask students:

- What part of the video stood out to you the most?

- What kind of story are you about to read? How can you tell?

ELL SPEAKING FRAMES

- The ____ in the video makes me think ____.
- The video shows ____. This makes me wonder ____.
- I think the text will ____. I think this because ____.
- I predict that there will be ____. I believe this because ____.

Entry Point

As students prepare to read *The Mighty Miss Malone*, share the following information with them to provide context.

✓ *The Mighty Miss Malone* is set during the Great Depression, which lasted from the stock market crash of 1929 until 1939. This was a time of great economic despair and poverty in America. Families were separated, often due to the quest to find work. In the story, Deza, her mother, and her brother set out to find her father who had to travel to find work, like many of the 15 million unemployed Americans during the Great Depression.

✓ Deza Malone was a character in the book *Bud, Not Buddy* written by Christopher Paul Curtis and published in 2000, twelve years before *The Mighty Miss Malone*. Both stories have a similar setting and theme. Bud is a boy living during the Great Depression who is also on a quest to find his father. He meets Deza in a Hooverville in Flint, Michigan. Hoovervilles are shanty homes that were built to provide shelters for the poor and homeless during the Great Depression and were named after President Hoover, who was blamed for the economic problems of the country.

✓ Although the Great Depression was hard on all Americans, African Americans were affected the most. Violence against black people was common. By the year 1932, it was estimated that nearly 50% of African Americans were unemployed.

"You must be a genius to get a C plus!"

from Chapter Twenty-Two: Learning How to Settle in Flint

1 I'd been having such a good time being Little Stew and trying to fill in all the missing words from the *Reader's Digest* that time had completely run off and forgot all about me!

2 "But, Mother, Miss Stew needs me to—"

3 "You aren't suggesting you stay here and help Stew instead of going to school, are you?" When she said it like that, it did seem silly.

. . .

4 On the outside, schools in Flint seemed a lot like schools in Gary, but they weren't. Instead of having one teacher all day, in Flint we went from classroom to classroom and teacher to teacher for each subject. The teachers were different too. First, all of them were white, and second, they weren't anywhere as nice as the teachers in Gary. But one of Mrs. Needham's lessons stuck: I was learning how to toughen up.

5 I got my usual As on the tests in mathematics, geography, civics and history.

6 After my first mathematics test, when class was dismissed, Mrs. Scott called me to her desk.

7 "Deza, have you always done so well in math? You're the only student who got a perfect score."

8 I sounded very **humble,** but the truth's the truth. "Yes, ma'am. Mathematics is one of my favorite subjects."

9 It was great to be back in school!

10 "Could I ask you a favor?"

11 Maybe she wanted me to help some of my classmates. Even though they were white, some of them were the spittin' image of Dolly Peaches and Benny Cobb.

NOTES

Reading & Writing Companion   **13**

SELECTION VOCABULARY

humble / humilde *adjective* modest; without pride or arrogance

Analyze Vocabulary Using Context Clues

In paragraph 8, focus on the sentence that uses the word *humble*. Point out these context clues:

1. First I notice the word *but*, which often indicates a contrast or contradiction. Deza's voice may sound humble, but she thinks and feels something different.

2. When I read the sentences again, I notice that Deza is talking to her teacher, so she would want to sound respectful.

3. I also notice that Deza says, "the truth's the truth." She doesn't want to sound like she's bragging about her skills, but she's proud of them. And she's honest. *Humble* must mean the opposite of boastful: "without pride."

✓ CHECK FOR SUCCESS

Have students work with a partner to determine the meaning of the rest of the bold vocabulary words.

If students are unable to make predictions, revisit the Checklist section of the Grade 6 Context Clues lesson with the class. After revisiting, guide students as they make predictions about the next bold word in the text in paragraph 19.

TEXT TALK

Why does Mrs. Scott call Deza to her desk after Deza gets a perfect score on her math test?

See paragraphs 7, 10, 12, 13: Mrs. Scott wants to find out if Deza cheated on her test, so she gives her some problems to solve right in front of her.

Skills Focus

QUESTION 1: Character

Deza thinks Mrs. Scott wants to see if she is ready for harder work. But the word "maybe" suggests she has doubts. When Mrs. Scott simply dismisses her, Deza is surprised. She still isn't sure why Mrs. Scott asked her to solve the problems.

Skills Focus

QUESTION 1: Character

Deza is irritated that Flint teachers don't share grades like the teachers in Gary. This is evidence that Deza likes people to acknowledge that she is smart.

Skills Focus

QUESTION 4: Connect to Essential Question

Even though Deza is upset, she thinks of Jimmie's little joke rather than crying.

Character

How does the reader use the character's reaction to analyze how she feels about an event in the plot?

The reader notes that Deza smiles when she tries Jimmie's little joke. She realizes that of course her grade hasn't changed.

TEXT TALK

How are African American children such as Deza treated at the school in Flint?

See paragraphs 13–25: There are low expectations for the students, who automatically receive poor grades and are suspected of cheating when they do well.

The Mighty Miss Malone

NOTES

12 She slid a paper toward me. It had five unsolved story problems on it.

13 "Could you sit right there, right now, and solve these for me?"

14 Maybe Mrs. Scott was seeing if I was ready for harder work. I finished in no time.

15 She looked them over. "Hmm, perfect again, but next time you *must* make sure to show all your work. You're dismissed."

16 I was surprised that was all she said.

17 In English class I *really* showed how much I'd toughened up.

18 Flint teachers don't have the imaginations that Gary teachers do, so instead of giving grades back so everyone knows what you got, they walk around the class and hand your test or paper back to you. Upside down.

19 Mr. Smith was passing out our first essay. I'd followed all of Mrs. Needham's advice. I'd written it at the Flint Public Library and was very careful not to use the dictionary or the thesaurus too much. And I didn't **digress** at all.

20 I made sure my posture was good, crossed my ankles and folded my hands on the desk when he got close to me.

21 He handed me my paper and smiled. "Very good job."

22 My heart flew! "Thank you, sir."

23 I turned my paper over.

24 He'd written, "Good for you!" and put a giant C+ with three exclamation points.

25 I turned the paper back over. Maybe I saw it wrong.

26 I looked again but it was the same.

27 One sign that I had toughened up was that instead of crying I thought of a little joke that Jimmie said he did whenever he didn't like his grade.

28 "I turn the paper over, then, the same way people bang on a machine it if ain't acting right, I smack my hand on the paper. Maybe if I bang it hard enough my grade will jump up a mark!"

29 It was nonsense, but I slapped my hand on Mr. Smith's essay.

30 I turned the paper back over and smiled.

Skill: Character

Deza's reaction to her grade is to follow her brother's advice. When Deza turns the paper over, I notice she doesn't start crying or display irritation. She smiles. This reaction shows me that Deza knows her essay is good. She's changed - before she would have cried, but now she's strong.

🅥 SELECTION VOCABULARY

digress / divagar *verb* to get sidetracked in conversation or writing; to deviate from the main subject of interest

ELL
- What advice from Mrs. Needham does Deza follow when she writes her essay?
- Why is it good not to digress from a topic when writing an essay?

NOTES

31 I'd have to tell Jimmie that it still wasn't working.

32 Mrs. Needham would've been proud. Instead of bawling, I looked at Mr. Smith's back and said to myself, "OK, buster, I'm going to make sure my next essay is the best thing I've ever written. You won't have any choice but to give me my A plus."

33 When me and Loretta were walking back to camp I asked, "What grade did you get on your essay?"

34 "I don't know, the same old D. What'd you get?"

35 "C plus."

36 She stopped walking. "Uh-oh, no, you didn't!"

37 I showed her my grade.

38 "Ooh, girl, you must be *real* smart."

39 "For getting a C plus?"

40 "All these teachers up here at Whittier's prejudice. Katherine Williams was the smartest colored girl in the school and all she use to get was a C. You must be a genius to get a C plus!"

41 She laughed. "I'm gonna see if I can sit next to you when we take our next exam!"

. . .

42 Early every morning, Mother and I would leave the camp and walk for half an hour to downtown Flint. Jimmie would go his own way.

43 After school I'd go to the library and read until Mother picked me up. We didn't have a official address so I couldn't check out any books, but I still got to read.

44 It wasn't long before we stopped looking fresh and had **seniority** in camp. Stew said I had a **bubbly** personality so she had me help the new children get used to living here. Some of them didn't have any idea what to do, mostly the boys.

45 I pretended they were my students and was very patient.

46 Two little boys from Flint came in one day all by themselves. One of them reminded me of myself. He seemed scareder than his friend so I took him under my wing.

47 He was very nervous and shy, but you could see how sweet he was too.

Copyright © BookheadEd Learning, LLC

Reading & Writing Companion **15**

Skill: Character

Instead of complaining about her grade, Deza feels inspired to prove her teacher wrong. Instead of feeling sorry for herself, Deza is determined to impress her teacher and get a better grade.

Skills Focus

QUESTION 4: Connect to Essential Question

After trying Jimmie's little joke, Deza thinks how she will force Mr. Smith to give her the A+ she deserves by writing the best essay she has ever written.

Skills Focus

QUESTION 3: Character

Deza must be getting used to the camp. If her personality is bubbly, she is happier. She's also taking on more responsibility.

Skills Focus

QUESTION 2: Character

Deza shows compassion when she takes the little boys under her wing. It shows that she is concerned about others.

Character

How does the reader analyze Deza's reaction to her grade?

The reader understands that Deza is fully aware of her academic abilities. She does not need the teacher's approval to know that her writing is good.

TEXT TALK

Why does Deza's family live in a camp?

See paragraph 43: They are homeless.

V SELECTION VOCABULARY

seniority / la antigüedad *noun* to have a higher rank based on experience or age

ELL
- Since Deza's family no longer looks "fresh," are they new to the camp or have they been there awhile?
- How does the length of their stay give them seniority?

bubbly / alegre *adjective* cheerful; bright; animated

ELL
- Is Deza a person who talks a lot, or is she shy?
- Why might Stew want someone with a bubbly personality to greet new children?

Skills Focus

QUESTION 2: Character

Deza puts the boys to work so that they understand they have responsibilities. This is like her own approach to her school work. Deza is willing to work hard to get the English grade she thinks she deserves.

Skills Focus

QUESTION 4: Connect to Essential Question

Deza lets the reader know that she is angry with the little boy. At first she wants to slug him. When Deza sees how sad he is she feels sorry for him instead.

NOTES

48   His first evening in the camp, I didn't want him and his friend to think they were going to get a free ride so I had them help me with the dishes. I took the little boy and showed him the creek where we clean the camp's pots and dishes. We sat on a big rock and I washed and had him dry.

49   He said, "Are you leaving on the train tomorrow?"

50   "Uh-uh." I'd been lying so much about how we weren't alone that without thinking, I said, "My father's going out on it, he might leave for a day or two for work.'

51   "Where do you go to school?"

52   "Well, Mother says I might have to keep going here in Flint at Whittier."

53   The sad-eyed little boy said, "I'm hopping the freight to go west, me and Bugs are gonna pick fruit."

54   "I wish you two well."

55   I'd hand him the dish after I'd washed it and when my hand touched his he'd start blinking a lot and would get twitchity and **fumble** the cloth when he tried to dry the dish.

56   After a while I started touching his hand just to make him squirm. And squirm he did!

57   He counted softly, "One, two, three . . . ," then blurted out, "I'MNOTAFRAIDOFGIRLS!"

58   I laughed. "You aren't?"

59   "Uh-uh. I even kissed some in the home."

60   "Really?"

61   "Yup, I got three kisses."

62   He held up four fingers.

63   I looked up at the moon. It was huge and yellow and yolky. "Isn't the moon lovely?"

64   I looked back. The little boy had closed his eyes, puckered his lips and leaned in toward me!

65   I started to slug him, just a arm punch. But looking at how sad he was made my heart melt.

66   He was all alone except for a person named Bugs.

TEXT TALK

How does Deza make the little boy from Flint, Michigan feel at home?

See paragraphs 48–78: She gives him chores, kisses his forehead, holds his hand, and sings to him.

SELECTION VOCABULARY

fumble / dejar caer *verb* to move one's hands or handle something in a clumsy, erratic way

ELL
- What does it mean to twitch?
- If a person twitches, is he or she more likely to hold on to something or to fumble it?

67 What else could I do?

68 I kissed his forehead three times and said, "Kisses . . . kisses . . . kisses make you stronger."

69 He blinked six or seven times and when his eyes came open he looked lost and befumbled.

70 I put his hand in mine.

71 The harmonica man started playing "Shenandoah."

72 "Do you know that song?"

73 His head was wobbling back and forth and I wasn't sure if he was saying no or getting ready to swoon.

74 I said, "It's about a Indian princess who hasn't seen her husband for seven years."

75 I sang a little.

76 He said, "You sing beautiful."

77 Wow! He *was* befumbled!

78 "You should hear my brother, now that's a real singer."

79 I helped him up and we carried the dishes back to the camp.

80 As bad as things were for me, they were much worse for him. I still had my family, and like Mother always says, without a family you're nothing but dust on the wind.

81 I hoped he'd find kindness somewhere, but even with my exploding imagination, I couldn't figure out where that would be.

Excerpted from *The Mighty Miss Malone* by Christopher Paul Curtis, published by Wendy Lamb Books.

NOTES

Reading & Writing Companion **17**

Skills Focus

QUESTION 3: Character

Over time, Deza has come to realize that she is luckier than some people because she has a family.

TEXT TALK

Why does Deza think that she is better off than this little boy?

See paragraph 80: Deza still has her family.

What other connections are you able to make with this text?

Answers will vary.

B BEYOND TEXT TALK

How is Deza Malone coping with injustice?

Think Questions

Circulate as students answer Think Questions independently. Scaffolds for these questions are shown on the opposite page.

QUESTION 1: Textual Evidence

When Deza went to school in Gary, she had one teacher, Mrs. Needham, all day. In Flint, Deza and the other students "went from classroom to classroom and teacher to teacher for each subject." All of the teachers in Flint are white, and Deza doesn't think they are "anywhere as nice as the teachers in Gary."

QUESTION 2: Textual Evidence

Loretta is so surprised at the grade Deza received that she stops walking. She tells Deza that she must be real smart, because all the teachers at Whittier's are prejudiced.

QUESTION 3: Textual Evidence

Deza is kind and sensitive. She thinks that the boy "seemed scareder than his friend so I took him under my wing." Later, she kisses him on the forehead three times, telling him that "kisses make you stronger."

QUESTION 4: Context Clues

I think *seniority* must mean "higher rank or experience." The word is used to describe Deza's family's status in the camp after they have been there for a while. Deza says the family "stopped looking fresh" and had "seniority in the camp." So they are no longer new and have experience with the way things are done.

QUESTION 5: Context Clues

I think *fumble* must mean "to be clumsy with one's hands." The word is used to describe the boy as he tries to dry the dish with a cloth. He is "twitchity," or shaky, so he's clumsy and almost drops the cloth.

First Read

Read *The Mighty Miss Malone*. After you read, complete the Think Questions below.

THINK QUESTIONS

1. What are the differences between Deza's old school in Gary, Indiana, and her new school in Flint, Michigan? Cite textual evidence to support your answer.

2. Write two or three sentences describing how Loretta reacts when she finds out what grade Deza received on her essay. Support your answer with evidence from the text.

3. What does Deza's attitude toward the little boy she meets in the camp reveal about her character? Cite textual evidence from the selection to support your answer.

4. Find the word **seniority** in paragraph 44 of "The Mighty Miss Malone." Use context clues in the surrounding sentences, as well as the sentence in which the word appears, to determine the word's meaning. Write your definition here and identify clues that helped you figure out the meaning.

5. Use context clues to determine the meaning of **fumble** as it is used in paragraph 55 of "The Mighty Miss Malone." Write your definition here and identify clues that helped you figure out the meaning. Then check the meaning in the dictionary.

Think Questions

Use the scaffolds below to differentiate instruction for your **ELL** English Language Learners and **A** Approaching grade-level learners.

ELL **BEGINNING** Write a response using the <u>word bank</u> and <u>sentence frames</u>.

INTERMEDIATE Write a response using the <u>sentence frames</u>.

ADVANCED, ADVANCED HIGH Write a response using the <u>Text-Dependent Question Guide</u>.

A **APPROACHING** Write a response using the <u>Text-Dependent Question Guide</u>.

BEGINNING	INTERMEDIATE	APPROACHING / ADVANCED, ADVANCED HIGH
Word Bank	Sentence Frames	Text-Dependent Question Guide
higher rank experience drops teacher well while white walking clumsy prejudice nice smart stronger scared	When Deza went to school in Gary, she had one ____. All of the teachers at Deza's new school are ____. Deza does not think the teachers at her new school are as ____ as the teachers in Gary.	1. • How many teachers did Deza have at her school in Gary? • Are the teachers in Flint white or black? • Does Deza think the teachers in Flint are nice?
	When Loretta hears that Deza got a C+ on her essay she stops ____. Loretta tells Deza that the teachers at Whittier are ____. She tells Deza she wants to sit next to her during the next exam because Deza is real ____.	2. • What does Loretta stop doing when she hears Deza's grade? • What does Loretta tell Deza about the teachers at Whittier? • Why does Loretta tell Deza she wants to sit next to her when they take their next exam?
	Deza decides to take care of the little boy because he seems more ____ than his friend. Deza kisses the boy on the forehead and tells him kisses make you ____. Deza wishes the boy and his friend ____.	3. • Why does Deza take care of the little boy? • Why does Deza kiss the boy on the forehead? • What does Deza wish for the little boy?
	Deza's family's has been at the camp for a ____. This gives me a clue that *seniority* means having ____ or a ____.	4. • Read: "It wasn't long before we stopped looking fresh and had **seniority** in camp." • What does it mean to be fresh to camp? • What is the opposite of being fresh to camp?
	Because the little boy twitches, he almost ____ the cloth. This gives me a clue that *fumble* means to be ____.	5. • Read: "I'd hand him the dish after I'd washed it and when my hand touched his he'd start blinking a lot and would get twitchity and **fumble** the cloth when he tried to dry the dish." • What does it mean to twitch? • Are you more or less likely to drop something when you twitch?

Reading Comprehension OPTIONAL

Have students complete the digital reading comprehension questions ✅ when they finish reading.

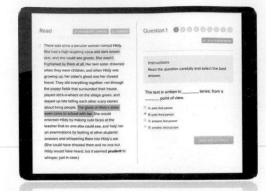

ANSWER KEY

QUESTION 1: A	QUESTION 5: C	QUESTION 9:
QUESTION 2: A	QUESTION 6: A	*See first chart.*
QUESTION 3: D	QUESTION 7: D	QUESTION 10:
QUESTION 4: B	QUESTION 8: B	*See second chart.*

Synonym	Word
modest	humble
deviate	digress
rank	seniority
cheerful	bubbly
mishandle	fumble

First	Second	Third	Fourth
Deza shows the nervous boy that there are responsibilities at the camp.	The nervous boy reveals that he is planning to hop train cars once he leaves the camp.	The nervous boy gets extra nervous about having a crush on Deza.	Deza takes pity on the nervous boy and makes sure not to completely reject his flirtation.

Connect and Extend OPTIONAL

CONNECT TO EXTENDED WRITING PROJECT

Students can use *The Mighty Miss Malone* as a mentor text for their Extended Writing Project. They may note how Curtis uses an historical event—in this case the Great Depression—to create unexpected challenges for his characters.

BEYOND THE BOOK

Research Project: School Then and Now

To help students learn more about life in Depression-era Flint, organize students in groups. Ask each group to research one of the following topics related to the Great Depression:

- Hoovervilles
- Unemployment
- Schools
- Migrant workers

Have groups design visual aids and present their findings informally to the class.

To reflect, ask students:

- How did this research help you better understand Deza's daily life?
- What was life like in Hoovervilles and how might that have impacted Deza's ability to do well in school?

Skill:
Character

Use the Checklist to analyze Character in *The Mighty Miss Malone*. Refer to the sample student annotations about Character in the text.

••• CHECKLIST FOR CHARACTER

In order to determine how the characters respond or change as the plot moves toward a resolution, note the following:

- ✓ the characters in the story, including the protagonist and antagonist
- ✓ key events or series of episodes in the plot, especially events that cause characters to react, respond, or change in some way
- ✓ characters' responses as the plot reaches a climax, and moves toward a resolution of the problem facing the protagonist
- ✓ the resolution of the conflict in the plot and the ways that it affects each character

To describe how a particular story's or drama's plot unfolds in a series of episodes as well as how the characters respond or change as the plot moves toward a resolution, consider the following questions:

- ✓ How do the characters' responses change or develop from the beginning to the end of the story?
- ✓ Do the characters in the story change? Which event or events in the story cause a character to change?
- ✓ Is there an event in the story that provokes, or causes, a character to make a decision?
- ✓ Do the characters' problems reach a resolution? How?
- ✓ How does the resolution affect the characters?

Reading & Writing Companion 19

Skill: Character

Introduce the Skill

Watch the Concept Definition video and read the following definition with your students.

A **character** is a person, animal, or other being portrayed in a story. Every kind of fiction and drama needs characters. Characters' thoughts, feelings, actions, and reactions drive the **plot**, or the events that take place in the story. The **resolution** is the outcome of the story's conflict. Writers use several techniques to develop characters and reveal aspects of their personality including **dialogue,** or conversation, description, and plot events. Character **traits** are the defining qualities of or behavior, good or bad, that make each character unique.

The main character—the one the story revolves around and who usually has a problem to solve—is called the **protagonist.** The character who opposes the protagonist is called the **antagonist.** Minor characters provide support for the protagonist or antagonist.

⚙ TURN AND TALK

1. In a book, would you rather read about a character's actions or about the character's thoughts and feelings? Why?

> **ELL SPEAKING FRAMES**
> - One of my favorite characters is ____. I like this character because ____.
> - A character that changes is ____. This character changes because ____.
> - A character that does not change is ____. This character does not change even though ____.

SKILL VOCABULARY

character / el personaje *noun* an individual in a literary work whose thoughts, feelings, actions, and reactions move the action of the plot forward

plot / la trama *noun* the sequence of events that form a story

resolution / la resolución *noun* the final outcome of the story's conflict COGNATE

dialogue / el diálogo *noun* the conversation between characters COGNATE

trait / el rasgo *noun* an aspect of a character's behavior and attitude that make up that character's personality

protagonist / el/la protagonista *noun* the main character—the one the story revolves around and who usually has a problem to solve COGNATE

antagonist / el/la antagonista *noun* the character whose goals work against the protagonist COGNATE

Your Turn

Ask students to complete the Your Turn Activity.

QUESTION 1

A. Incorrect. Mrs. Scott never mentions extra credit.

B. **Correct.** This is why Mrs. Scott wants Deza to solve the five story problems "right here, right now." That way she can watch Deza as she works.

C. Incorrect. Mrs. Scott already told Deza she got a "perfect score," so she must have finished the test.

D. Incorrect. Mrs. Scott never mentions becoming a tutor with Deza.

QUESTION 2

Part A

A. Incorrect. Although the text says that Deza thinks Mrs. Scott might want her to help other students, she is not "anxious" to do so.

B. Incorrect. Deza has a number of internal responses to Mrs. Scott's request, but the fact that Mrs. Scott thinks she might have cheated is not one of them.

C. **Correct.** The number of reactions, or thoughts, that Deza has about Mrs. Scott's request show that she has no idea her teacher suspects her of cheating. She thinks, for example, that Mrs. Scott might want to find out if Deza is ready for harder work.

D. Incorrect. At this point in the story Deza has no idea that the teachers are prejudiced against African American students.

Part B

A. Incorrect.

B. Incorrect.

C. Incorrect.

D. **Correct.** After Deza answers the five story problems correctly, Mr.s Scott still wants Deza to show her work in the future so her teacher can be sure Deza isn't making any lucky guesses. But Deza is surprised by what Mrs. Scott says so she still has no idea why Mrs. Scott has asked to see her.

The Mighty Miss Malone

 Skill: Character

Reread paragraphs 6–16 from the text. Then, using the Checklist on the previous page, answer the multiple-choice questions below.

🔁 **YOUR TURN**

1. Based on Mrs. Scott's actions in paragraphs 12 and 13, the reader can conclude that —

   ○ A. Mrs. Scott wanted Deza to solve more math problems for extra credit.
   ○ B. Mrs. Scott suspects that Deza may have cheated on her math test.
   ○ C. Deza did not finish the test.
   ○ D. Mrs. Scott wanted to see if Deza was good enough to be a tutor.

2. This question has two parts. First, answer Part A. Then, answer Part B.

   Part A: Deza's reaction to Mrs. Scott's request reveals that Deza —

   ○ A. is anxious to help other students succeed in math.
   ○ B. is aware that Mrs. Scott thinks she might have cheated on her test.
   ○ C. is not aware that Mrs. Scott thinks she might have cheated on her test.
   ○ D. is aware that Mrs. Scott is prejudiced against African American students.

   Part B: Which paragraph best shows evidence for the answer to Part A?

   ○ A. 8
   ○ B. 9
   ○ C. 15
   ○ D. 16

SkillsTV

 Project the SkillsTV episode ▶ and pause at the following times to prompt discussion:

1:40 How do the students make an inference about Deza's character?

2:32 How do the students use what Deza doesn't say as well as what she does say, to figure out they type of person she is?

3:13 How do the students know that Deza's response is internal?

Close Read

Reread *The Mighty Miss Malone*. As you reread, complete the Skills Focus questions below. Then use your answers and annotations from the questions to help you complete the Write activity.

◎ SKILLS FOCUS

1. Recall Deza's initial thoughts about what her Flint teachers say and do. Explain what these thoughts reveal about Deza's character.

2. Focus on Deza's words and actions as she interacts with the little boys who come to the camp. Identify what these indicate about her character.

3. Analyze how Deza's responses to change develop the plot by identifying evidence that shows how her relationship with the camp and Flint changes over time.

4. When life gets hard for Deza, what does she do? Identify evidence of her reactions to challenges and explain whether there are any differences between her thoughts and actions.

✎ WRITE

NARRATIVE: Describe how Deza's responses to the C+ she received on her essay show how her character has changed. Then imagine how she will approach the next assignment she receives from Mr. Smith. Use the information you learned about both characters to write a short scene that describes this event.

Close Read

Skills Focus

QUESTION 1: Character

See paragraphs 13–16 and 18.

QUESTION 2: Character

Paragraph 4: Deza seems to prefer Gary teachers over Flint teachers. She misses her teachers in Gary. See paragraphs 46 and 48.

QUESTION 3: Character

See paragraphs 44 and 80.

QUESTION 4: Connect to Essential Question

See paragraphs 25–27, 32, and 64–65.

✓ CHECK FOR SUCCESS

If students struggle to respond to Skills Focus Question 1, ask students the following questions:

- In paragraph 18, why does Deza think Flint teachers lack imagination?

- What does this evidence tell you about Deza?

📖 Writer's Notebook

Connect to Essential Question: Give students time to reflect on how "*The Mighty Miss Malone*" connects to the unit's essential question "What do we do when life gets hard?" by freewriting in their Writer's Notebooks.

 Beginning & Intermediate

Read aloud the unit's essential question: "What do we do when life gets hard?" Encourage students to draw their connections or allow students to write in their native language. Circulate around the room, prompting students for their thoughts as they respond orally or through pantomime.

Advanced & Advanced High

Allow students to share their connections orally in pairs or small groups before freewriting.

Collaborative Conversation

Break students into collaborative conversation groups to discuss the Close Read prompt. Ask students to use the StudySyncTV episode as a model for their discussion. Remind them to reference their Skills Focus annotations in their discussion.

Describe how Deza's responses to the C+ she received on her essay show how her character has changed. Then imagine how she will approach the next assignment she receives from Mr. Smith. Use the information you have learned about both characters to write a short scene that describes this event.

Use the scaffolds below to differentiate instruction for your **ELL** English Language Learners and **A** Approaching grade-level learners.

ELL **BEGINNING, INTERMEDIATE** Use the <u>discussion guide</u> and <u>speaking frames</u> to facilitate the discussion with support from the teacher.

ADVANCED, ADVANCED HIGH Use the <u>discussion guide</u> and <u>speaking frames</u> to facilitate the discussion in mixed-level groups.

A **APPROACHING** Use the <u>discussion guide</u> to facilitate the discussion in mixed-level groups.

APPROACHING
ADVANCED, ADVANCED HIGH
BEGINNING, INTERMEDIATE

Discussion Guide	Speaking Frames
1. What are Deza's reactions as Mr. Smith approaches her?	• As Mr. Smith approaches, Deza ____. • This is important because ____.
2. What are Deza's thoughts when Mr. Smith comments on her essay?	• Deza responds to his comments by ____. • This is important because ____.
3. How do Deza's responses help you imagine how she will approach her next assignment?	• The responses help by ____. • On the next assignment, I think she will ____.

Review Prompt and Rubric

Before students begin writing, review the writing prompt and rubric with the class.

NARRATIVE: Describe how Deza's responses to the C+ she received on her essay show how her character has changed. Then imagine how she will approach the next assignment she receives from Mr. Smith. Use the information you learned about both characters to write a short scene that describes this event.

ELL **PROMPT GUIDE**

A
- What are Deza's thoughts about her grade?
- What are Deza's reactions to her grade?
- What is meant by approach?

- How do Deza's responses help you imagine how she will approach her next assignment?

Score	Character	Language and Conventions
4	The writer clearly explains how Deza's character has changed through her response to her C+. The writer skillfully imagines and describes Deza's approach to her next assignment. Descriptive details and clear transitions contribute to the strength and unity of the narrative.	The writer demonstrates a consistent command of grammar, punctuation, and usage conventions. Although minor errors may be evident, they do not detract from the fluency or the clarity of the essay.
3	The writer explains how Deza's character has changed through her response to her C+. The writer is able to clearly imagine and describe Deza's approach to her next assignment. Most details and transitions contribute to the strength and unity of the narrative, despite minor lapses in focus.	The writer demonstrates an adequate command of grammar, punctuation, and usage conventions. Although some errors may be evident, they create few (if any) disruptions in the fluency of the writing or the clarity of the essay.
2	The writer incompletely explains how Deza's character has changed through her response to her C+ . The writer is able to imagine and describe Deza's approach to her next assignment. Some details do not contribute to the narrative, which limits the unity and coherence of the narrative.	The writer demonstrates a partial command of grammar, punctuation, and usage conventions. Some distracting errors may be evident, at times creating minor disruptions in the fluency or clarity of the writing.
1	The writer does not explain how Deza's character has changed through her response to her C+. The narrative is presented illogically. The writer is not able to imagine and describe Deza's approach to her next assignment. Many of the details and transitions do not contribute to the narrative.	The writer demonstrates little or no command of grammar, punctuation, and usage conventions. Serious and persistent errors create disruptions in the fluency of the writing and sometimes interfere with meaning.
0	The writer does not provide a relevant response to the prompt or does not provide a response at all.	Serious and persistent errors overwhelm the writing and interfere with the meaning of the response as a whole, making the writer's meaning impossible to understand.

Write

Ask students to complete the writing assignment using textual evidence to support their answers.

Use the scaffolds below to differentiate instruction for your **ELL** English Language Learners and **A** Approaching grade-level learners.

ELL **BEGINNING** With the help of the <u>word bank</u>, write a response using <u>paragraph frame 1</u>.

INTERMEDIATE With the help of the <u>word bank</u>, write a response using <u>paragraph frames 1 and 2</u>.

ADVANCED, ADVANCED HIGH Write a response of differentiated length using the <u>sentence starters</u>.

A **APPROACHING** Write a response of differentiated length using the <u>sentence starters</u>.

| BEGINNING | | ADVANCED, ADVANCED HIGH |
| INTERMEDIATE | | APPROACHING |

Word Bank	Paragraph Frame 1	Paragraph Frame 2	Sentence Starters
approach capable assigned humble attitude	Mr. Smith has ____ a new essay. I'm going to ____ this assignment with a positive ____. I know I'm ____ of getting an A+. I'll be ____ when Mr. Smith admits how smart I am.	Mrs. Needham taught me to ____. She also gave me good advice about ____. I'll prove to Mr. Smith that I deserve ____. I don't want to have to ____!	• Mr. Smith has assigned . . . • I'm going to . . . • I know that I'm capable of . . . • I'll be very happy when . . . • I don't want to have to . . .

Peer Review

Students should submit substantive feedback to two peers using the review instructions below.

- How well does this response answer the prompt?
- How well does the writer apply analysis of the characters' responses when writing about Deza's approach to the next assignment?
- Which sentence in the writer's short scene made you think differently about the plot development?
- What did the writer do well in this response? What does the writer need to work on?

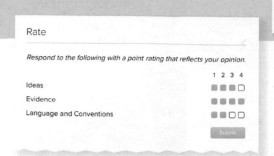

Rate

Respond to the following with a point rating that reflects your opinion.

	1 2 3 4
Ideas	■ ■ ■ □
Evidence	■ ■ ■ ■
Language and Conventions	■ ■ □ □

Submit

 SENTENCE FRAMES

- You were able to (completely / partly / almost) ____ address the prompt because . . .
- You could address the prompt more completely by . . .
- You were able to (completely / partly / almost) . . . apply your analysis of the characters' responses.

- You could apply your analysis more completely by . . .
- I thought differently about the plot development after reading . . .
- My favorite part of your story is . . .

Red Scarf Girl: A Memoir of the Cultural Revolution

INFORMATIONAL TEXT
Ji-Li Jiang
1997

Introduction

studysync

Red Scarf Girl: A Memoir of the Cultural Revolution is an autobiography about the teenage life of Ji-Li Jiang, who lived with her family in Shanghai during the 1960s when Communist Party leader Mao Zedong effectively declared war against capitalist and anti-establishment forces throughout China. As Zedong launched a series of purges aimed at purifying the Communist party, Ji Li and her family were dedicated Communists; she was initially embarrassed by her family's "landlord" background when the Cultural Revolution began in 1966. However, her feelings began to change when the government started attacking her family. In this excerpt, she has been pulled out of class and is being interrogated by people from her father's theater.

Red Scarf Girl depicts Ji-Li Jiang's experiences as a teen during the 1960s in Shanghai when Communist party leader Mao Zedong declared war against capitalist and establishment forces throughout China. In this excerpt, Ji-Li is pulled out of class to be interrogated by party members from her father's theater. A man Ji-Li refers to as Thin-Face asks her to denounce her father. As the other adults in the room encourage her to testify, Ji-Li imagines the sadness this would cause her father. They pressure her to prove that she is loyal to Chairman Mao, and not her father. Ji-Li insists that her father never said anything against the Chairman. Thin-Face tells her that she has two options: to follow Chairman Mao and break ties with her father, or stand by her father and become an enemy of the people. In the end, Ji-Li finds herself in an alleyway, feeling trapped and alone.

 Proficiency-leveled summaries and summaries in multiple languages are available digitally.

 Audio and audio text highlighting are available with this text.

COMPARING WITHIN AND ACROSS GENRES

 In her memoir, *Red Scarf Girl*, Ji-Li Jiang recounts how hard it is to grow up dedicated to the Communist Party. Much like the main character in Hatchet, which follows this text, Ji-Li Jiang must make important decisions while under pressure.

In Gary Paulsen's Hatchet 13-year-old Brian Robeson discovers just how hard life can be when he is stranded in the Canadian wilderness after his pilot has a heart attack and their plane crashes into a lake.

Access Complex Text

LEXILE: 740 · WORD COUNT: 871

The following areas may be challenging for students, particularly English Language Learners and Approaching grade-level learners.

Organization	Specific Vocabulary	Prior Knowledge
• *Red Scarf Girl* includes dialogue as well as first-person narration. • Students need to draw details from both to understand the relationships between individuals, events, and ideas.	• Many words, such as *comrades,* or *study session,* had special connotations during the Chinese Cultural Revolution. Students will need to consider these connotations while reading. • The memoir does not always provide exact details about the study session. Students will need to consider the shades of meaning of various words to understand what is happening and how Ji-Li Jiang feels.	• The focus on Chinese culture during a specific period in history may present special challenges for students. • Many students may lack prior knowledge of the Chinese Communist Party and events surrounding the Cultural Revolution.

 SCAFFOLDS   **ENGLISH LANGUAGE LEARNERS**   **A APPROACHING GRADE LEVEL**   **BEYOND GRADE LEVEL**

These icons identify differentiation strategies and scaffolded support for a variety of students. See the digital lesson plan for additional differentiation strategies and scaffolds.

Instructional Path

The print teacher's edition includes essential point-of-use instruction and planning tools. Complete lesson plans and program documents appear in your digital teacher account.

Skill: Personal Response

Objectives: After rereading and discussing a model of close reading, students will be able to write a personal response comparing and contrasting their life experiences with those of the main character in the text.

Independent Read: Red Scarf Girl: A Memoir of the Cultural Revolution

Objectives: After reading the text, students will demonstrate their understanding of how plot is developed through characterization and setting in a short, written response.

Independent Read

Ji-li Jiang

Red Scarf Girl

Introduce the Text

As a class, watch the video preview ▶ and have students read the introduction in pairs to make connections to the video preview.

- How do the images contrast with the narration? Why do you think that is? How does it make you feel?

- What do you think *purges* means?

ELL **SPEAKING FRAMES**

- The ___ in the video makes me think ___.
- The video shows ___. This makes me wonder ___.
- I think the text will ___. I think this because ___.
- I predict that there will be ___. I believe this because ___.

Entry Point

As students prepare to read, share the following information with them to provide context.

✓ China's Cultural Revolution was initiated in August, 1966 under the leadership of Mao Zedong, with the intention of eradicating capitalism as a threat to the Communist state.

✓ Mao Zedong wanted to purge China of "The Four Olds," old culture, old customs, old habits, and old beliefs.

✓ The Communist Party put pressure on China's youth to report anyone critical of Mao, and young informers rushed forward to name teachers, neighbors, and even their own parents.

Red Scarf Girl: A Memoir of the Cultural Revolution

"I saw Dad looking at me hopelessly, tears on his face."

1 "Sit down, sit down. Don't be afraid." Chairman Jin pointed to the empty chair. "These comrades from your father's work unit are just here to have a study session with you. It's nothing to worry about."

2 I sat down dumbly.

3 I had thought about their coming to my home but never imagined this. They were going to **expose** my family in front of my teachers and classmates. I would have no pride left. I would never be an educable child again.

4 Thin-Face sat opposite me, with a woman I had never seen before. Teacher Zhang was there too, his eyes encouraging me.

5 Thin-Face came straight to the point. "Your father's problems are very serious." His cold eyes nailed me to my seat. "You may have read the article in the *Workers' Revolt* that exposed your family's filthy past." I slumped down in my chair without taking my eyes off his face. "In addition to coming from a landlord family, your father committed some serious mistakes during the Antirightist[1] Movement several years ago, but he still obstinately refuses to confess." His cold manner became a little more animated. "Of course we won't tolerate this. We have decided to make an example of him. We are going to have a struggle meeting of the entire theater system to criticize him and force him to confess." He suddenly pounded the table with his fist. The cups on the table rattled.

6 I tore my eyes away from him and stared at a cup instead.

7 "As I told you before, you are your own person. If you want to make a clean break with your black family, then you can be an educable child and we will welcome you to our **revolutionary** ranks." He gave Chairman Jin a look, and Chairman Jin chimed in, "That's right, we welcome you."

8 "Jiang Ji-li has always done well at school. In addition to doing very well in her studies, she participates in educational reform," Teacher Zhang added.

---

1. **Antirightist Movement** a campaign, from roughly 1957 to 1959, to purge people in the Communist Party with alleged capitalist or anti-establishment sympathies

Reading & Writing Companion **23**

SELECTION VOCABULARY

expose / exponer *verb* to show or make visible or apparent COGNATE

revolutionary / revolucionario/a *adjective* involved in a political revolution or change COGNATE

 ELL
- Who is speaking in this paragraph?
- What does he want Jiang to do?

 ## Analyze Vocabulary Using Context Clues

As students read the text, ask them to make predictions about each bold vocabulary word based on the context clues in the sentence. Have students use the annotation tool to make their predictions.

 CHECK FOR SUCCESS

If students are unable to determine the meaning of one or more bolded vocabulary words, project the Checklist section of the Grade 6 Context Clues lesson with the class. After revisiting, guide students as they make predictions about the bold word in paragraph 3 using the following routine:

- Is the word a noun, a verb, an adjective, or an adverb?
- Who is going to expose Jiang's family?
- Why will she have no pride left?

TURN AND TALK

Have students discuss their original vocabulary predictions with a neighbor. Come to a consensus as a class before confirming their definitions.

 ### TEXT TALK

What does the committee want Jiang Ji-li to do, and for what reward?

See paragraphs 7–9: They want her to testify against her father; if she does, they will honor her as 'truly Chairman Mao's child'.

Author's Word Choice

Look at the way that the author describes how people look at each other in paragraphs 5, 6, and 13.

Ask students to examine the author's use of the various phrases that describe the manner in which the characters look at one another. How does the author's word choice help readers understand the tone of the conversation in that section? How do those details add to your understanding of the characters? What does it tell you about the narrator's emotions?

Red Scarf Girl: A Memoir of the Cultural Revolution

NOTES

9 "That's very good. We knew that you had more sense than to follow your father," Thin-Face said with a brief, frozen smile. "Now you can show your revolutionary determination." He paused. "We want you to **testify** against your father at the struggle meeting."

10 I closed my eyes. I saw Dad standing on a stage, his head bowed, his name written in large black letters, and then crossed out in red ink, on a sign hanging from his neck. I saw myself standing in the middle of the stage, facing thousands of people, condemning Dad for his crimes, raising my fist to lead the chant, "Down with Jiang Xi-reng." I saw Dad looking at me hopelessly, tears on his face.

11 "I...I..." I looked at Teacher Zhang for help. He looked away.

12 The Woman from the theater spoke. "It's really not such a hard thing to do. The key is your class stance. The daughter of our former Party Secretary resolved to make a clean break with her mother. When she went onstage to condemn her mother, she actually slapped her face. Of course, we don't mean that you have to slap your father's face. The point is that as long as you have the correct class stance, it will be easy to testify." Her voice grated on my ears.

13 "There is something you can do to prove you are truly Chairman Mao's child." Thin-Face spoke again. "I am sure you can tell us some things your father said and did that show his landlord and rightist mentality." I stared at the table, but I could feel his eyes boring into me. "What can you tell us?"

14 "But I don't know anything," I whispered." I don't know—"

15 "I am sure you can remember something if you think about it," Thin-Face said. "A man like him could not hide his true beliefs from a child as smart as you. He must have made comments **critical** of Chairman Mao and the Cultural Revolution. I am sure you are loyal to Chairman Mao and the Communist[2] Party. Tell us!"

16 "But my father never said anything against Chairman Mao," I protested weakly. "I would tell you if he did." My voice grew stronger with conviction. "He never said anything against the Party."

_____
2. **Communist Party** the ruling party of the People's Republic of China, established in 1949 and led by Chairman Mao Zedong

 24 Reading & Writing Companion

Copyright © BookheadEd Learning, LLC

 TEXT TALK

What does Jiang Ji-li imagine will happen at the struggle meeting?

See paragraph 10: She imagines her father onstage wearing a humiliating sign and crying as she leads a chant against him.

What does Thin-Face want Jiang Ji-li to tell him to prove her loyalty?

See paragraphs 13–15: He wants her to tell him something he can use as proof that her father is a capitalist and a critic of Mao:

 SELECTION VOCABULARY

testify / testificar *verb* to speak in a formal setting such as a court COGNATE

ELL • What do you know about the struggle meeting?
     • What will Jiang have to do at the meeting?

critical / crítico/a *adjective* expressing disapproval COGNATE

ELL • What does Thin-Face say Jiang's father can't do?
     • Who does Thin-Face say Jiang's father made comments about?

Red Scarf Girl: A Memoir of the Cultural Revolution

17 "Now, you have to choose between two roads." Thin-Face looked straight into my eyes. "You can break with your family and follow Chairman Mao, or you can follow your father and become an enemy of the people." His voice grew more **severe.** "In that case we would have many more study sessions, with your brother and sister too, and the Red Guard Committee[3] and the school leaders. Think about it. We will come back to talk to you again."

18 Thin-Face and the woman left, saying they would be back to get my statement. Without knowing how I got there, I found myself in a narrow passageway between the school building and the school-yard wall. The gray concrete walls closed around me and a slow drizzle dampened my cheeks. I could not go back to the classroom, and I could not go home. I felt like a small animal that had fallen into a trap, alone and helpless, and sure that the hunter was coming.

Excerpted from *Red Scarf Girl* by Ji-li Jiang, published by HarperCollins Publishers

 WRITE

PERSONAL RESPONSE: Jiang is facing a challenging decision—between defending her father and protecting herself. Think about a time you had to make a difficult decision. Explain the decision you had to make, why you had to make it, and who, if anyone, helped you. Does your experience help you empathize with Jiang? Use evidence from the text to support your response.

3. **Red Guard Committee** a student paramilitary organization that organized on behalf of Chairman Mao and the Communist Party, using violence as a means of coercion

Reading & Writing Companion **25**

SELECTION VOCABULARY

severe / severo/a *adjective* harsh or unpleasant COGNATE

ELL
• What is Thin-Face doing in this paragraph?
• What does he say the Red Guard will do?

 TEXT TALK

How does Jiang Ji-li feel at the end of the excerpt?

See paragraph 18: She is afraid, saying she feels like a trapped animal waiting for the hunter.

B Ask each Beyond grade level student to write one additional discussion question. Then, have one or two students facilitate a discussion, using their questions to guide the conversation.

Reading Comprehension OPTIONAL

Have students complete the digital reading comprehension questions ✓ when they finish reading.

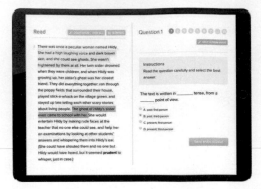

ANSWER KEY

QUESTION 1: A	**QUESTION 5:** B	**QUESTION 9:**
QUESTION 2: B	**QUESTION 6:** D	*See first chart.*
QUESTION 3: B	**QUESTION 7:** C	**QUESTION 10:**
QUESTION 4: C	**QUESTION 8:** B	*See second chart.*

Dialogue	Characte
"Jiang Ji-li has always done well at school."	Teacher Zhang
"When she went onstage to condemn her mother, she actually slapped her face".	The Woman from the theater
"That's right, we welcome you."	Chairman Jin
"There is something you can do to prove you are truly Chairman Mao's child."	Thin-Face

Definition	Word
Process of correcting what is wrong	reform
Able to be taught	educable
Stating that something is completely wrong	condemning
Strong belief	conviction
To speak on record in court	testify

Connect and Extend OPTIONAL

CONNECT TO EXTENDED WRITING PROJECT

Students can draw inspiration from *Red Scarf Girl* as they consider a narrative for their Extended Writing Project. The memoir is set in the recent past, and features challenges connected to a specific time and place.

BEYOND THE BOOK

Mock Trial: Defending a Loved One

Break into groups of 6-8 students. Ask groups to:

1. Select a person they care about to put on trial for a crime that this person did not commit.

2. Identify the people involved in the case—plaintiff, defendant, witnesses, judge, jury, and lawyers.

3. Assign each group member a role.

4. Send the plaintiff and defendant out of the room to record "the facts" of the case. Then they should give the facts to the witnesses and lawyers to review.

5. While the plaintiff and defendant record the facts, the rest of the group should research the law relating to this crime. What is the punishment for this crime? What types of evidence are typically introduced in court for this crime?

6. Have each group perform a brief mock trial for the class.

To reflect, ask students:

- Were any of the facts of the case unclear?

- Did the outcome of the trial surprise you? Was justice served?

StudySyncTV Project the StudySyncTV episode ▶ and pause at the following times to prompt discussion:

1:17 What is the students' first step in understanding how Ji-Li's feelings change? What feelings do they identify during this step?

2:52 What first conflict do the students identify? Why is this conflict so significant for Ji-Li?

4:35 Sohini says she's glad Ji-Li didn't change "just out of family loyalty," because the debate gets more interesting when "values and ethics" are added. Do you agree with Sohini? Why or why not?

Collaborative Conversation

Break students into collaborative conversation groups to discuss the writing prompt. Ask students to use the StudySyncTV episode as a model for their discussion. Remind them to reference their Skills Focus annotations in their discussion.

Jiang is facing a challenging decision—between defending her father and protecting herself. Think about a time when you had to make a difficult decision. Explain the decision you had to make, why you had to make it, and who, if anyone, helped you. Does your experience help you empathize with Jiang? Use evidence from the text to support your response.

Use the scaffolds below to differentiate instruction for your **ELL** English Language Learners and **A** Approaching grade-level learners.

ELL **BEGINNING, INTERMEDIATE** Use the discussion guide and speaking frames to facilitate the discussion with support from the teacher.

ADVANCED, ADVANCED HIGH Use the discussion guide and speaking frames to facilitate the discussion in mixed-level groups.

A **APPROACHING** Use the discussion guide to facilitate the discussion in mixed-level groups.

APPROACHING
ADVANCED, ADVANCED HIGH
BEGINNING, INTERMEDIATE

Discussion Guide	Speaking Frames
1. Do you think that Jiang's decision was hard to make? Why or why not?	• I think Jiang's decision was ____ to make. • I think Jiang's decision was ____ because ____.
2. What connections can you make between Jiang's decision and the time you made a hard decision?	• Jiang's decision reminds me of ____. • Jiang's decision connects to ____.
3. How has Jiang's experience changed the way you think about what it means to make a decision?	• Jiang's experience has made me realize that ____. • I used to think ____. Now I think ____.

Review Prompt and Rubric

Before students begin writing, review the writing prompt and rubric with the class.

PERSONAL RESPONSE: Jiang is facing a challenging decision—between defending her father and protecting herself. Think about a time when you had to make a difficult decision. Explain the decision you had to make, why you had to make it, and who, if anyone, helped you. Does your experience help you empathize with Jiang? Use evidence from the text to support your response.

 PROMPT GUIDE

- Do you think that Jiang's decision was hard to make? Why or why not?
- What connections can you make between Jiang's decision and the time you made a hard decision?

- How has Jiang's experience changed the way you think about what it means to make a decision?

Score	Personal Response	Language and Conventions
4	The writer clearly explains his or her personal connection to the text, using relevant evidence from the text.	The writer demonstrates a consistent command of grammar, punctuation, and usage conventions. Although minor errors may be evident, they do not detract from the fluency or the clarity of the essay.
3	The writer sufficiently explains his or her personal connection to the text, using relevant evidence from the text most of the time.	The writer demonstrates an adequate command of grammar, punctuation, and usage conventions. Although some errors may be evident, they create few (if any) disruptions in the fluency of the writing or the clarity of the essay.
2	The writer begins to explain his or her personal connection to the text, but the explanation is incomplete. The writer uses relevant evidence from the text only some of the time.	The writer demonstrates a partial command of grammar, punctuation, and usage conventions. Some distracting errors may be evident, at times creating minor disruptions in the fluency or clarity of the writing.
1	The writer attempts to explain his or her personal connection to the text, but the explanation is not successful. The writer uses little or no relevant evidence from the text.	The writer demonstrates little or no command of grammar, punctuation, and usage conventions. Serious and persistent errors create disruptions in the fluency of the writing and sometimes interfere with meaning.
0	The writer does not provide a relevant response to the prompt or does not provide a response at all.	Serious and persistent errors overwhelm the writing and interfere with the meaning of the response as a whole, making the writer's meaning impossible to understand.

Write

SCAFFOLDS

Ask students to complete the writing assignment using textual evidence to support their answers.

Use the scaffolds below to differentiate instruction for your **ELL** English Language Learners and **A** Approaching grade-level learners.

ELL **BEGINNING** With the help of the <u>word bank</u>, write a response using <u>paragraph frame 1</u>.

INTERMEDIATE With the help of the <u>word bank</u>, write a response using <u>paragraph frames 1 and 2</u>.

ADVANCED, ADVANCED HIGH Write a response of differentiated length using the <u>sentence starters</u>.

A **APPROACHING** Write a response of differentiated length using the <u>sentence starters</u>.

BEGINNING / INTERMEDIATE		ADVANCED, ADVANCED HIGH / APPROACHING

Word Bank		Paragraph Frame 1	Paragraph Frame 2	Sentence Starters
choice decision against important	hard loyalty changed hurt	Jiang is told to speak out ____ her father. Jiang is forced to choose between her family and her ____ to the government. I think this decision is ____ to make. Jiang's situation reminds me of a ____ I once had to make. I was forced to make a ____. It was difficult because I didn't want to ____ a friend. Jiang's experience has ____ the way I think about making a decision.	Jiang's experience makes me feel more ____ toward people who have to make hard decisions. For example, when I read ____, I felt ____. This text reminds me that ____ .	• I think that Jiang's decision was difficult because . . . • The text reminds me of . . . • I was able to connect to . . . • This text made me realize . . . , • I thought . . . when I read the text. . . . • I used to think . . . , but now I think . . .

Peer Review

Students should submit substantive feedback to two peers using the review instructions below.

- How well does this response answer the prompt?
- How effectively does the writer relate a personal decision to Jiang's experience?
- Which of the writer's comments inspired you to think differently about the text?
- What did the writer do well in this response? What does the writer need to work on?

Rate

Respond to the following with a point rating that reflects your opinion.

	1	2	3	4
Ideas	■	■	■	□
Evidence	■	■	■	■
Language and Conventions	■	■	□	□

Submit

ELL **A** **SENTENCE FRAMES**

- You were able to (completely / partly / almost) ____ answer the prompt.
- You could answer the prompt more completely by . . .

- I thought differently about the text after reading . . .
- My favorite part of your response is . . .

Hatchet

FICTION
Gary Paulsen
1987

Introduction

studysync

atchet is the first in a series of five novels by Gary Paulsen (b. 1939), who won a Newbery Honor in 1988 for this gripping tale of survival. The hero of *Hatchet* and its follow-ups is young Brian Robeson, who must rely on his wits and instincts alone to stay alive in the Canadian wilderness. Preceding this excerpt from Chapter 5, thirteen-year-old Brian is left stranded on his own after his pilot has a heart attack and their plane crashes in a lake. The excerpt describes the day after the crash.

Thirteen-year-old Brian Robeson is stranded in the Canadian wilderness after his pilot has a heart attack and their plane crashes in a lake. This excerpt describes the day after the crash when his clothes are drying, and he's trying to convince himself that a search party will come soon. Brian daydreams of eating a hamburger. With no food and no way to start a fire, he recognizes that he has nothing. However, he remembers an old English teacher, Perpich, who always talked about being positive and motivated, so Brian takes stock of everything he has with him such as shoes, clothes, a hatchet, and a watch. When he's finished, Brian realizes that he forgot one more thing in his possession: himself. He recalls Perpich's words: "You are your most valuable asset." The excerpt closes with Brian wishing that Perpich could be there with him and thinking about how he would trade everything he has for a hamburger.

 Proficiency-leveled summaries and summaries in multiple languages are available digitally.

 Audio and audio text highlighting are available with the text.

COMPARING WITHIN AND ACROSS GENRES

After engaging in a close reading and discussion of *Hatchet*, students will be able to compare and contrast how the setting in *Hatchet* and *Red Scarf Girl* provides context to the main conflict in a short, written response.

Access Complex Text

LEXILE: 730   WORD COUNT: 943

The following areas may be challenging for students, particularly English Language Learners and Approaching grade-level learners.

Organization	Genre	Specific Vocabulary
• Longer paragraphs in the selection are frequently followed by one-sentence or one-word paragraphs, which function to slow the pace of the text and allow readers to follow Brian's muddled post-crash thinking. • These one-word paragraphs also serve to emphasize the seriousness of Brian's situation, as when *Nothing* is repeated in paragraphs 9 and 12 and is the only word in the paragraph.	• The limited-third person narrator focuses on Brian and his situation and relays Brian's thoughts, words, and actions. • This narrative choice allows readers to sympathize with Brian as they are also left to wonder whether a rescue mission is in progress.	• The selection contains examples of domain-specific vocabulary. • Aviation terms, such as *flight plan*, *amphibious planes*, and *bushplanes*, may need to be defined.

SCAFFOLDS   **ENGLISH LANGUAGE LEARNERS**   **APPROACHING GRADE LEVEL**   **BEYOND GRADE LEVEL**

These icons identify differentiation strategies and scaffolded support for a variety of students. See the digital lesson plan for additional differentiation strategies and scaffolds.

Instructional Path

The print teacher's edition includes essential point-of-use instruction and planning tools. Complete lesson plans and program documents appear in your digital teacher account.

First Read: Hatchet

Objectives: After an initial reading and discussion of the text, students will be able to identify and describe character traits and setting details, as well as articulate the conflict that is integral to the story's plot.

Skill: Setting

Objectives: After rereading and discussing a model of close reading, students will be able to describe how a particular story or drama's plot unfolds in a series of episodes as well as how the characters respond or change as the plot moves toward a resolution.

Skill: Compare and Contrast

Objectives: After rereading and discussing a model of close reading, students will be able to compare and contrast texts in different forms or genres in terms of their approaches to similar themes.

Close Read: Hatchet

Objectives: After engaging in a close reading and discussion of the text, students will be able compare and contrast how the setting in *Hatchet* and *Red Scarf Girl* provides context to the main conflict in a short, written response.

Progress Monitoring

Opportunities to Learn	Opportunities to Demonstrate Learning	Opportunities to Reteach

Setting

Opportunities to Learn	Opportunities to Demonstrate Learning	Opportunities to Reteach
⚙ Skill: Setting	⚙ Skill: Setting • Your Turn ▣ Close Read • Skills Focus • Collaborative Conversation • Write	⚙ Unit 5 Skill: Setting - The All-American Slurp ⚙ Units 6 Skill: Setting - Touching Spirit Bear ⚙ Spotlight Skill: Setting

Compare and Contrast

Opportunities to Learn	Opportunities to Demonstrate Learning	Opportunities to Reteach
⚙ Skill: Compare and Contrast	⚙ Skill: Compare and Contrast • Your Turn ▣ Close Read • Skills Focus • Collaborative Conversation • Write	⚙ Unit 2 Skill: Compare and Contrast - A Poem for My Librarian, Mrs. Long ⚙ Unit 4 Skill: Compare and Contrast - Freedom's Daughters: The Unsung Heroines of the Civil Rights Movement from 1830 to 1970 ⚙ Spotlight Skill: Compare and Contrast

First Read

Gary Paulsen

Hatchet

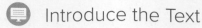 Introduce the Text

As a class, watch the video preview ▶ and have students read the introduction in pairs to make connections to the video preview.

To activate prior knowledge and experiences, ask students:

- What image from the video was your favorite? Why?
- How do you think this story will relate to Hatchet?

ELL SPEAKING FRAMES

- The ____ in the video makes me think ____.
- The video shows ____. This makes me wonder ____.
- I think the text will ____. I think this because ____.
- I predict that there will be ____. I believe this because ____.

Entry Point

As students prepare to read *Hatchet*, share the following information with them to provide context.

✓ Growing up, Gary Paulsen was never an exemplary student. He struggled with school and didn't always enjoy reading. After a local librarian gave him a library card, Paulsen explained, ". . . the most astonishing thing happened. This silly little card with my name on it gave me an identity I had not had. I felt I had become somebody." This experience sparked his interest in reading and eventually writing.

✓ From a young age, Paulsen was intrigued by adventure. After running away from home at 14, he worked many odd jobs including traveling with a carnival. He ultimately settled on writing as a career.

✓ Living in the woods of Minnesota, Paulsen drew inspiration for many of his books from the great outdoors and one's harmony with nature.

"Nothing.
It kept coming back to that.
He had nothing."

from Chapter 5

1 They would look for him, look for the plane. His father and mother would be frantic. They would tear the world apart to find him. Brian had seen searches on the news, seen movies about lost planes. When a plane went down they mounted **extensive** searches and almost always they found the plane within a day or two. Pilots all filed flight plans—a detailed plan for where and when they were going to fly, with all the courses explained. They would come, they would look for him. The searchers would get government planes and cover both sides of the flight plan filed by the pilot and search until they found him.

2 Maybe even today. They might come today. This was the second day after the crash. No. Brian frowned. Was it the first day or the second day? They had gone down in the afternoon and he had spent the whole night out cold. So this was the first real day. But they could still come today. They would have started the search immediately when Brian's plane did not arrive.

3 Yeah, they would probably come today.

4 Probably come in here with **amphibious** planes, small bushplanes with floats that could land right here on the lake and pick him up and take him home.

5 Which home? The father home or the mother home? He stopped the thinking. It didn't matter. Either on to his dad or back to his mother. Either way he would probably be home by late night or early morning, home where he could sit down and eat a large, cheesy, juicy burger with tomatoes and double fries with ketchup and a thick chocolate shake.

6 And there came hunger.

7 Brian rubbed his stomach. The hunger had been there but something else—fear, pain—had held it down. Now, with the thought of the burger, the emptiness roared at him. He could not believe the hunger, had never felt it this way. The lake water had filled his stomach but left it hungry, and now it demanded food, screamed for food.

8 And there was, he thought, absolutely nothing to eat.

Skill:
Setting

It's obvious that Brian is anxious to be rescued. He's alone and afraid in the wilderness. He's trying to calm himself down by guessing when his rescuers will come, but he has no idea if they ever will.

Reading & Writing Companion **27**

Analyze Vocabulary Using Context Clues

In paragraph 1, focus on the sentence that uses the word *extensive*. Point out these context clues:

1. The word *extensive* makes me think of the word *extend*. I think of making something longer or going out farther.

2. I notice that *extensive* describes *searches*, which are about looking for something.

3. I think an *extensive* search would cover a large area. This makes sense in the sentence because the search would be for a lost plane that might not be found for two days.

Setting

How did the reader use details in the text to determine the setting and conflict?

The reader used the narrator's remarks about planes and flight plans to identify the setting and noted how the setting contributes to the conflict: Brian's plane has crashed and he's lost in the wilderness.

SELECTION VOCABULARY

extensive / extenso/a *adjective* covering or extending over a large area; great in extent

amphibious / anfibio/a *adjective* able to live or operate on both land and water COGNATE

 • What does an amphibious plane have?
• How would this kind of plane help Brian?

TEXT TALK

What does Brian believe will happen right away?

See paragraphs 1-4: Brian believes that people will search for him right away and rescue him within two days.

What is the first thing Brian thinks about doing when he gets home?

See paragraph 5: Brian plans to eat a big, juicy hamburger and fries and drink a chocolate shake.

Skills Focus

QUESTION 1: Setting

Meadows, marshland and a beaver suggest to Brian that he is close to a lake.

Skills Focus

QUESTION 2: Setting

Brian is hungry, but he can see nothing among the local wildlife appeals to him as food.

Skills Focus

QUESTION 3: Setting

Brian is so sure he has nothing that he hasn't bothered to check. Bothering to check can, however, yield unexpected benefits.

Skills Focus

QUESTION 4: Compare and Contrast

The fact that the confrontation was at school creates a mood of helplessness and isolation for Jiang. This is similar to the mood of helplessness that being stranded in the wilderness creates for Brian.

Skills Focus

QUESTION 5: Connect to Essential Question

After feeling helpless because he thinks that he has nothing. Brian reaches a turning point. He decides to get motivated and look at everything he has that might help him.

TEXT TALK

What does Brian remember his English teacher saying?

See paragraph 15: Brian remembers that his English teacher was always talking about "staying positive" and "staying on top of things."

What does Brian see that he has with him?

See paragraphs 16-18 and 19-20: The only things Brian has are some coins, a $20 bill, a fingernail clipper, a hatchet, and his clothes.

Hatchet

NOTES

9 Nothing.

10 What did they do in the movies when they got stranded like this? Oh, yes, the hero usually found some kind of plant that he knew was good to eat and that took care of it. Just ate the plant until he was full or used some kind of cute trap to catch an animal and cook it over a slick little fire and pretty soon he had a full eight-course meal.

11 The trouble, Brian thought, looking around, was that all he could see was grass and brush. There was nothing **obvious** to eat and aside from about a million birds and the beaver he hadn't seen animals to trap and cook, and even if he got one somehow he didn't have any matches so he couldn't have a fire. . .

12 Nothing.

13 It kept coming back to that. He had nothing.

14 Well, almost nothing. As a matter of fact, he thought, I don't know what I've got or haven't got. Maybe I should try and figure out just how I stand. It will give me something to do—keep me from thinking of food. Until they come to find me.

15 Brian had once had an English teacher, a guy named Perpich, who was always talking about being positive, thinking positive, staying on top of things. That's how Perpich had put it—stay positive and stay on top of things. Brian thought of him now—wondered how to stay positive and stay on top of this. All Perpich would say is that I have to get **motivated.** He was always telling kids to get motivated.

16 Brian changed position so he was sitting on his knees. He reached into his pockets and took out everything he had and laid it on the grass in front of him.

17 It was pitiful enough. A quarter, three dimes, a nickel, and two pennies. A fingernail clipper. A billfold with a twenty dollar bill—"In case you get stranded at the airport in some small town and have to buy food," his mother had said—and some odd pieces of paper.

18 And on his belt, somehow still there, the hatchet his mother had given him. He had forgotten it and now reached around and took it out and put it in the grass. There was a touch of rust already forming on the cutting edge of the blade and he rubbed it off with his thumb.

19 That was it.

20 He frowned. No, wait—if he was going to play the game, might as well play it right. Perpich would tell him to quit messing around. Get motivated. Look at *all* of it, Robeson.

28 Reading & Writing Companion

V SELECTION VOCABULARY

obvious / obvio/a *adjective* easily perceived by the senses or grasped by the mind COGNATE

ELL • What does Brian see and not see?
     • What is obvious to Brian about satisfying his hunger?

21 He had on a pair of good tennis shoes, now almost dry. And socks. And jeans and underwear and a thin leather belt and a T-shirt with a windbreaker so torn it hung on him in tatters.

22 And a watch. He had a digital watch still on his wrist but it was broken from the crash—the little screen blank—and he took it off and almost threw it away but stopped the hand motion and lay the watch on the grass with the rest of it.

23 There. That was it.

24 No, wait. One other thing. Those were all the things he had, but he also had himself. Perpich used to drum that into them—"You are your most valuable **asset.** Don't forget that. *You* are the best thing you have."

25 Brian looked around again. I wish you were here, Perpich. I'm hungry and I'd trade everything I have for a hamburger.

Excerpted from *Hatchet* by Gary Paulsen, published by Simon & Schuster.

Skills Focus

QUESTION 5: Connect to Essential Question

Brian realizes that he is his own most valuable asset. Now he is in a better position to tackle the challenges he faces.

Analyze for Enrichment

Look at paragraph 20:

He frowned. No, wait—if he was going to play the game, might as well play it right . . .

Ask students: What "game" is Brian playing? How does this word choice affect your interpretation of the scene? Why does Brian refer to his situation and activity in this section as a game?

TEXT TALK

What are Brian's core values, given that he has been snatched from everything familiar?

Answers will vary.

Reading & Writing Companion   **29**

SELECTION VOCABULARY

motivated / motivar *verb* to have a strong reason to do something; inspired; enthusiastic COGNATE

ELL
• What is Brian motivated to do?
• What does Brian remember his teacher saying to help him get motivated?

asset / el recurso *noun* something valuable to have or own

ELL
• What is Brian's most valuable asset?
• What nearby word in paragraph 24 describes asset? Is it positive or negative?

Think Questions

Circulate as students answer Think Questions independently. Scaffolds for these questions are shown on the opposite page.

QUESTION 1: Textual Evidence

The small plane that Brian was traveling in has crashed. He is in the wilderness alone. In the text, Brian says he has "nothing." He has no food or matches to start a fire.

QUESTION 2: Textual Evidence

When Brian thinks about being home, he is insure whether he means the father home or the mother home. This must mean that his parents are separated or divorced.

QUESTION 3: Textual Evidence

Brian's stomach is personified when he realizes how hungry he is as he thinks about eating a hamburger. The text says that "the emptiness roared at him" and "now it demanded food, screamed for food."

QUESTION 4: Context Clues

I think *obvious* must mean "clear" or "noticeable." The word is used to describe Brian's options for eating. In the previous sentence, the narrator tells us that "all he could see was grass and brush." Brian is looking for food, and he says there is "nothing obvious to eat," so that must mean there is nothing that is clearly edible, just "grass and brush."

QUESTION 5: Context Clues

I think *asset* means "something of value or worth," like a resource. After deciding that Brian had nothing, he recalls when Peprich said, "*You* are the best thing you have." So, even if he doesn't have tools, he has himself. In this case, Brian is the asset. He is the most valuable resource that he has.

Hatchet

First Read

Read *Hatchet*. After you read, complete the Think Questions below.

  THINK QUESTIONS

1. What happens to Brian? What problem does he have? Cite textual evidence from the selection to support your answer.

2. What is Brian's family situation? What makes you think so? State details from the text or ideas you have inferred from clues in the text.

3. Figurative language is language used for descriptive effect, often to illustrate or imply ideas indirectly. A type of figurative language is **personification**, in which an animal, object, force of nature, or an idea is given human form or qualities. Can you identify an example of personification from *Hatchet* that illustrates one of the problems Brian is facing? Cite textual evidence from the selection to support your answer.

4. Find the word **obvious** as used in paragraph 11 in *Hatchet*. Use context clues in the surrounding sentences, as well as the sentence in which the word appears, to determine the word's meaning. Write your definition here and identify clues that helped you figure out its meaning.

5. Use context clues to determine the meaning of **asset** as it is used in paragraph 24 of the excerpt. Write your definition here and identify clues that helped you figure out its meaning. Then check the meaning in a dictionary.

Please note that excerpts and passages in the StudySync® library and this workbook are intended as touchstones to generate interest in an author's work. The excerpts and passages do not substitute for the reading of entire texts, and StudySync® strongly recommends that students seek out and purchase the whole literary or informational work in order to experience it as the author intended. Links to online resellers are available in our digital library. In addition, complete works may be ordered through an authorized reseller by filling out and returning to StudySync® the order form enclosed in this workbook.

Think Questions

Use the scaffolds below to differentiate instruction for your **ELL** English Language Learners and **A** Approaching grade-level learners.

ELL **BEGINNING** Write a response using the <u>word bank</u> and <u>sentence frames.</u>

INTERMEDIATE Write a response using the <u>sentence frames.</u>

ADVANCED, ADVANCED HIGH Write a response using the <u>Text-Dependent Question Guide.</u>

A **APPROACHING** Write a response using the <u>Text-Dependent Question Guide.</u>

BEGINNING	INTERMEDIATE	APPROACHING / ADVANCED, ADVANCED HIGH
Word Bank	Sentence Frames	Text-Dependent Question Guide
rescued food demands roars father home resource divorced best hungry crashed mother home noticed search	The plane that Brian was in has ____. Brian needs to be ____. I know this because Brian thinks about how people will ____ for him.	1. • What happened to the plane that Brian was in? • What does Brian need? • How do I know what Brian needs?
	Brian asks himself if he will go to the ____ or the ____. This means that his parents are probably ____.	2. • What does Brian ask himself after he thinks about a plane picking him up? • How does Brian answer his question? • What does his answer tell you about Brian's family?
	Brian realizes that he is ____ after he thinks about eating at home. The emptiness in Brian's stomach ____. Brian's stomach is like a person because it ____ food.	3. • What does Brian realize after he thinks about eating at home? • How is the emptiness in Brian's stomach described? • What does Brian realize when he thinks about how people in movies survive his kind of situation?
	Obvious describes the ____ that Brian can't see. This gives me a clue that *obvious* means something that can be easily ____.	4. • Read: "There was nothing **obvious** to eat and aside from about a million birds and the beaver he hadn't seen animals to trap and cook, and even if he got one somehow he didn't have any matches so he couldn't have a fire." • What is *obvious* referring to in this sentence? • What does that tell me about the meaning of the word *obvious*?
	Brian remembers that his teacher used to say that you are the ____ thing you have. This tells me that *asset* means ____.	5. • Read: "You are your most valuable **asset**. Don't forget that. You are the best thing you have." • What advice did Brian's teacher, Mr. Perpich, give? • What does this tell you about what *asset* means?

Reading Comprehension OPTIONAL

Have students complete the digital reading comprehension questions ✓ when they finish reading.

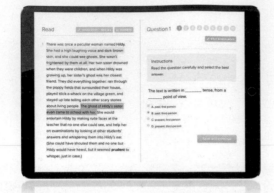

ANSWER KEY

QUESTION 1: B	QUESTION 5: B	QUESTION 9: B
QUESTION 2: C	QUESTION 6: C	QUESTION 10:
QUESTION 3: D	QUESTION 7: A	*See chart below.*
QUESTION 4: C	QUESTION 8: A	

First	Second	Third	Fourth
Brian reassures himself that he will be rescued soon.	Brian momentarily thinks about his complex situation with his parents.	Brian realizes he is extremely hungry.	Brian takes stock of all of his supplies and materials.

Connect and Extend OPTIONAL

CONNECT TO EXTENDED WRITING PROJECT

Students can use Gary Paulsen's *Hatchet* as a mentor text for their Extended Writing Project. Paulsen's narrative is a classic tale of a fictional character meeting an unexpected, life-or-death challenge.

BEYOND THE BOOK

Debate: Selecting Your Survival Tool

In *Hatchet,* Brian survives, in large part, because of his hatchet. Ask students to:

- Imagine they have been stranded in the Alaskan wilderness in April.

- Research conditions in Alaska during this time of year. Students might consider questions such as:

    a. What types of trees and plants might you encounter?

    b. What is the typical temperature?

    c. What food sources are available?

    d. What predators or dangerous animals are common?

- Select one survival tool they would take if they were going to be stranded for an indefinite amount of time.

- Provide three clear reasons for this choice.

- Draw a picture of their chosen tool and write a brief explanation of why they selected it.

Finally, invite students to debate why their survival tool is the best choice.

Skill: Setting

Skill:
Setting

Use the Checklist to analyze Setting in *Hatchet*. Refer to the sample student annotations about Setting in the text.

••• CHECKLIST FOR SETTING

In order to identify how a particular story's or drama's plot unfolds in a series of episodes, note the following:

- ✓ key elements in the plot
- ✓ the setting(s) in the story
- ✓ how the plot unfolds in a series of episodes
- ✓ how the setting shapes the plot

To describe how a particular story's or drama's plot unfolds in a series of episodes, consider the following questions:

- ✓ When and where does this story take place?
- ✓ How does the plot unfold in a series of episodes?
- ✓ How does the setting affect the plot? How does it affect the characters and their responses to events? How does the setting help move the plot to a resolution?

Introduce the Skill

Watch the Concept Definition video and read the following definition with your students.

The **setting** of a story is the time and place in which the events of the **plot** unfold. A narrative can be set at a particular point in the past or future, and the setting may be familiar or unfamiliar to readers. Either way, it is one of the most important elements in a story.

Authors frequently use setting to create **mood,** sometimes using only a single sentence to describe, for example, a raging blizzard. Settings can draw the reader into a work of literature while also making it easier to understand the development of the **characters** and the events in the plot. The behavior of fictional characters is often influenced by their environment. Sometimes the setting of a story *is* the problem a character confronts. The character, such as Dorothy in *The Wizard of Oz,* may want to leave a certain place or go somewhere else.

TURN AND TALK

1. Think of a book, movie, or TV show you have enjoyed in which the setting was important to the plot. How did the setting influence the plot?

2. How did the setting influence the conflict of the story and the characters involved?

V SKILL VOCABULARY

setting / el escenario *noun* the time and place of the story

plot / la trama *noun* the sequence of events that form a story

mood / el tono *noun* the emotional quality or atmosphere of a story or poem

character / el personaje *noun* an individual in a literary work whose thoughts, feelings, actions, and reactions move the action of the plot forward

ELL SPEAKING FRAMES

- The setting affected the plot by ____.
- One action affected by the setting was ____.
- One belief affected by the setting was ____.
- One value affected by the setting was ____.

Your Turn

Ask students to complete the Your Turn Activity.

QUESTION 1

A. Incorrect. The presence of beavers indicates nearby water.

B. Incorrect. There is no mention of forests in the paragraph.

C. Incorrect. Brian does not see anything obvious to eat.

D. **Correct.** All Brian sees is grass and brushland.

QUESTION 2

A. **Correct.** Brian shifts from thinking he has nothing to being unsure of what he has.

B. Incorrect. Brian wonders how he can stay positive in the situation.

C. Incorrect. Brian knows he should get motivated but not how to do it.

D. Incorrect. Brian keeps repeating that he has nothing, not even matches.

QUESTION 3

A. Incorrect.

B. **Correct.** Brian's thoughts indicate that he does not see anything obvious in the setting that will help him survive.

C. Incorrect.

D. Incorrect

Hatchet

SETTING   Skill:
Setting

sync

Reread paragraphs 10–15 from the text. Then, using the Checklist on the previous page, answer the multiple-choice questions below.

↻ YOUR TURN

1. Based on the description in paragraph 11, the reader can conclude that —

   ○ A. the story is set in a place far from water.
   ○ B. the story is set in a place that is heavily forested.
   ○ C. the story is set in a place with an obvious food source.
   ○ D. the story is set in a place covered with grass and brushland.

2. The description of Brian's thoughts in paragraphs 11–15 indicates that he feels —

   ○ A. unsure.
   ○ B. positive.
   ○ C. motivated.
   ○ D. resourceful.

3. Which paragraph best shows how the setting contributes to the conflict in the plot?

   ○ A. 10
   ○ B. 11
   ○ C. 14
   ○ D. 15

Ⓥ SKILL VOCABULARY

comparative response / la respuesta comparativa *noun* an oral or written response in which a reader explains the similarities and differences between two or more things

textual evidence / la evidencia del texto *noun* details from the text that a reader can use to support his or her ideas and opinions about the text

quote / citar *verb* to use an author's exact words and place them within quotation marks

paraphrase / parafrasear *verb* to restate the author's words in your own words COGNATE

Skill:
Compare and Contrast

Use the Checklist to analyze Compare and Contrast in *Hatchet*.

••• CHECKLIST FOR COMPARE AND CONTRAST

In order to determine how to compare and contrast texts in different forms or genres, use the following steps:

✓ first, choose texts with similar subjects or topics

✓ next, identify the qualities or characteristics of each genre

✓ after, identify the theme in each work

✓ finally, analyze ways in which the texts are similar and different in the way they approach similar themes and topics

 • think about what the characters do and say

 • think about what happens as a result of the characters' words and actions

To compare and contrast texts in different forms or genres in terms of their approaches to similar themes and topics, consider the following questions:

✓ How does each text approach the theme and topic? How does the form or genre of the text affect this approach?

✓ What are the similarities and differences in the subjects or topics of the texts I have chosen?

 Skill: Compare and Contrast

Introduce the Skill

Watch the Concept Definition video ▶ and read the following definition with your students.

To **compare** two or more texts means to explain how they are similar. To **contrast** texts means to explain how they are different. A reader may compare and contrast texts within and across genres. **Genre** refers to a specific category of literary text, such as science fiction, satire, historical drama, epic poetry, and the essay. Genre may also refer to a specific category of creative expression in other **media,** such as film, fine art, and music—examples include the Western, Impressionism, and jazz.

Readers may write or deliver **comparative responses** in which they use evidence to analyze the similarities and differences between two or more texts or other media. **Textual evidence** refers to details from the texts that support ideas and opinions about similarities and differences between them. Evidence may be **quoted** directly by including the author's exact words and placing them within quotation marks. Readers may also **paraphrase,** or restate the evidence in their own words.

 TURN AND TALK

1. What kinds of things do you compare in your daily life? How are the comparisons helpful?

2. Think of two of your favorite stories, poems, or songs. How are they similar? How are they different? What could you learn by comparing them?

ELL **SPEAKING FRAMES**

 • I compare ____. This helps me ____.
 • One way they are similar is ____. This teaches me ____.
 • One way they are different is ____. This teaches me ____.

V **SKILL VOCABULARY**

compare / comparar *verb* to explain how two or more things are similar COGNATE

contrast / contrastar *verb* to explain how two or more things are different COGNATE

genre / el género *noun* the different categories or types of literature, in which the main categories are fiction, nonfiction, poetry, and drama

media / los medios *noun* the plural form of the word medium; a means of sending a communication to an intended audience

Your Turn

Ask students to complete the Your Turn Activity.

Hatchet	Both	Red Scarf Girl
The main character is alone in a strange, challenging setting.\n\nThe genre is fiction.	Both characters have to rely on their own intelligence and good sense in order to solve a problem. No one can really help them.\n\nTheme, or message, of survival.	The main character is trapped into making a difficult decision.\n\nThe genre is nonfiction.

Hatchet

Skill:
Compare and Contrast

Reread paragraphs 8–13 from *Hatchet* and paragraphs 17 and 18 from *Red Scarf Girl*. Then, using the Checklist on the previous page, complete the chart below to compare and contrast the passages.

↻ YOUR TURN

	Inference Options
A	Both characters have to rely on their own intelligence and good sense in order to solve a problem. No one can really help them. Theme, or message, of survival.
B	The main character is trapped into making a difficult decision. The genre is nonfiction.
C	The main character is alone in a strange, challenging setting. The genre is fiction.

Hatchet	Both	Red Scarf Girl

SkillsTV

Project the SkillsTV episode ▶ and pause at the following times to prompt discussion:

2:54 What gives students a clue that these two stories "might be similar"?

3:37 How do the students use the opening of each story to determine similarities and differences?

4:00 How does realizing what the characters from each story want help the students to compare and contrast?

Close Read

Reread *Hatchet*. As you reread, complete the Skills Focus questions below. Then use your answers and annotations from the questions to help you complete the Write activity.

◎ SKILLS FOCUS

1. Identify details that Brian shares about his surroundings and explain how the evidence helps you determine the setting.

2. Identify evidence of how Brian evaluates his surroundings and explain why the details are so important to him.

3. Identify details about the setting that contribute to the conflict in *Hatchet*, and explain how these details directly affect the plot.

4. In *Red Scarf Girl*, Ji-Li Jiang is pulled out of class by Communist Party officials and questioned about her family's loyalty to the Cultural Revolution. Identify details in *Red Scarf Girl* that tell you about the setting, and explain how the details help you compare this setting to the setting in *Hatchet*.

5. Identify details that demonstrate how Brian deals with the challenges he faces.

✏ WRITE

COMPARATIVE: *Red Scarf Girl* and *Hatchet* feature young people trapped in challenging situations. In both texts, the setting provides the context for the main conflict or problem. Compare and contrast the role that the setting plays in influencing the characters and events of the two texts.

Reading & Writing Companion **35**

Close Read

Skills Focus

QUESTION 1: Setting

See paragraph 11.

QUESTION 2: Setting

See paragraph 11.

QUESTION 3: Setting

See paragraphs 12–14.

QUESTION 4: Compare and Contrast

Paragraph 3: Jiang is terrified because the theater group confronts her at school, so everyone at school will know, and she will be an outcast. Like Brian, she is in a setting that can do her harm. It is different because she knows where she is and only her way of life, not her life itself, is in danger.

QUESTION 4: Compare and Contrast

See paragraph 18.

QUESTION 5: Connect to Essential Question

See paragraphs 20 and 24.

▣ Writer's Notebook

Connect to Essential Question: Give students time to reflect on how "Hatchet" and "Red Scarf Girl" connect to the unit's essential question "What do we do when life gets hard?" by freewriting in their Writer's Notebooks.

ⓔ Beginning & Intermediate

Read aloud the unit's essential question: "What do we do when life gets hard?" Encourage students to draw their connections or allow students to write in their native language. Circulate, prompting students for their thoughts as they respond orally or through pantomime.

Advanced & Advanced High

Allow students to share their connections orally in pairs or small groups before freewriting.

StudySyncTV   Project the StudySyncTV episode and pause at the following times to prompt discussion:

2:16   What points do Chloe and Alex make about Brian's point of view? How does the group use textual evidence to determine how Brian's point of view changes?

3:07   Why does Josh find the words *might* and *probably* significant? What conclusion does this textual evidence help the classmates draw?

4:17   What does Connor suggest is the turning point in Brian's thinking? How does the group use textual evidence to explore Connor's idea of a turning point?

Collaborative Conversation

Break students into collaborative conversation groups to discuss the Close Read prompt. Ask students to use the StudySyncTV episode as a model for their discussion. Remind them to reference their Skills Focus annotations in their discussion.

Red Scarf Girl and *Hatchet* feature young people trapped in challenging situations. In both texts, the setting provides the **context** to the main conflict or problem. Compare and contrast the role that the setting plays in influencing the characters and events of the two texts.

Use the scaffolds below to differentiate instruction for your **ELL** English Language Learners and **A** Approaching grade-level learners.

ELL BEGINNING, INTERMEDIATE Use the <u>discussion guide</u> and <u>speaking frames</u> to facilitate the discussion with support from the teacher.

ADVANCED, ADVANCED HIGH Use the <u>discussion guide</u> and <u>speaking frames</u> to facilitate the discussion in mixed-level groups.

A APPROACHING Use the <u>discussion guide</u> to facilitate the discussion in mixed-level groups.

APPROACHING
ADVANCED, ADVANCED HIGH
BEGINNING, INTERMEDIATE

Discussion Guide	Speaking Frames
1. What is the setting in each story?	• The setting is ____. • The setting is challenging because ____.
2. How does the setting influence the main character in each story?	• (Jiang/Brian) responds to the setting by ____. • (Jiang/Brian) does this because because ____.
3. How does the setting influence events in each story?	• The setting influences events by ____. • The setting does this because ____.

Review Prompt and Rubric

Before students begin writing, review the writing prompt and rubric with the class.

COMPARATIVE: Red Scarf Girl and Hatchet feature young people trapped in challenging situations. In both texts, the setting provides the context to the main conflict or problem. Compare and contrast the role that the setting plays in influencing the characters and events of the two texts.

ELL PROMPT GUIDE

A
- What is the setting of each story?
- What conflict does each setting produce?
- How does each setting influence the characters?

- How does each setting influence events?
- How are the stories similar?
- How are they different?

Score	Setting	Comparative	Language and Conventions
4	The writer clearly analyzes and explains how the setting influences characters and events in each text. The writer provides exemplary analysis, using relevant evidence from the text.	The writer clearly compares and contrasts the texts. The writer provides exemplary analysis, using relevant evidence from the text.	The writer demonstrates a consistent command of grammar, punctuation, and usage conventions. Although minor errors may be evident, they do not detract from the fluency or the clarity of the essay.
3	The writer analyzes and explains how the setting influences characters and events in each text. The writer provides sufficient analysis, using relevant evidence from the text most of the time.	The writer compares and contrasts the texts. The writer provides sufficient analysis, using relevant evidence from the text most of the time.	The writer demonstrates an adequate command of grammar, punctuation, and usage conventions. Although some errors may be evident, they create few (if any) disruptions in the fluency of the writing or the clarity of the essay.
2	The writer begins to analyze or explain how the setting influences characters and events in each text, but the analysis is incomplete. The writer uses relevant evidence from the text only some of the time.	The writer begins to compare and contrast the texts, but the comparison is incomplete. The writer uses relevant evidence from the text only some of the time.	The writer demonstrates a partial command of grammar, punctuation, and usage conventions. Some distracting errors may be evident, at times creating minor disruptions in the fluency or clarity of the writing.
1	The writer attempts to analyze or explain how the setting influences characters and events in each text, but the analysis is not successful. The writer uses little or no relevant evidence from the text.	The writer attempts to compare and contrast the texts, but the comparison is not successful. The writer uses little or no relevant evidence from the text.	The writer demonstrates little or no command of grammar, punctuation, and usage conventions. Serious and persistent errors create disruptions in the fluency of the writing and sometimes interfere with meaning.
0	The writer does not provide a relevant response to the prompt or does not provide a response at all.	The writer does not provide a relevant response to the prompt or does not provide a response at all.	Serious and persistent errors overwhelm the writing and interfere with the meaning of the response as a whole, making the writer's meaning impossible to understand.

Write

Ask students to complete the writing assignment using textual evidence to support their answers.

Use the scaffolds below to differentiate instruction for your **ELL** English Language Learners and **A** Approaching grade-level learners.

ELL **BEGINNING** With the help of the <u>word bank</u>, write a response using <u>paragraph frame 1</u>.

INTERMEDIATE With the help of the <u>word bank</u>, write a response using <u>paragraph frames 1 and 2</u>.

ADVANCED, ADVANCED HIGH Write a response of differentiated length using the <u>sentence starters</u>.

A **APPROACHING** Write a response of differentiated length using the <u>sentence starters</u>.

| BEGINNING | | ADVANCED, ADVANCED HIGH | |
| INTERMEDIATE | | APPROACHING | |

Word Bank	Paragraph Frame 1	Paragraph Frame 2	Sentence Starters
wilderness survive classroom food testify	Jiang has been pulled from her ____. People from her father's theater group want her to ____ against her father. Brian has crashed in the Canadian ____. Brian lacks ____ and resources to ____.	Brian and Jiang both face ____ settings. Jiang feels ____. She cannot go ____ or back to her ____. Brian cannot go home unless he is ____. Jiang is worried that she will ____ the life she knows. Brian is worried that he will lose his ____.	• Jiang and Brian both face settings that are . . . • For Jiang, the setting is a problem because . . . • Within this context, Jiang worries that . . . • This causes her to . . . • For Brian, the setting is a problem because . . . • Within this context, Brian worries that . . . • This causes him to . . . • What is at stake differs for Jiang and Brian because . . .

Peer Review

Students should submit substantive feedback to two peers using the review instructions below.

- How well does this response answer the prompt?
- How well does the writer support ideas with details and examples from each text?
- Which sentence in the writer's response made you think differently about each text?
- What did the writer do well in this response? What does the writer need to work on?

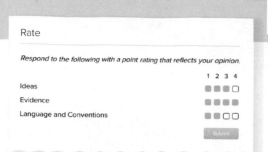

Rate

Respond to the following with a point rating that reflects your opinion.

	1	2	3	4
Ideas	■	■	■	□
Evidence	■	■	■	■
Language and Conventions	■	■	□	□

Submit

ELL **SENTENCE FRAMES**

A
- You were able to (completely / partly / almost) ___ answer the prompt because . . .
- You could answer the prompt more completely by . . .
- You supported the idea of . . . with the detail of . . .

- One idea that needs more support is . . .
- I thought differently about the texts after reading . . .
- My favorite part of your response is . . .

The Magic Marker Mystery

DRAMA
René Saldaña, Jr.
2013

Introduction

Author René Saldaña, Jr. draws from both his Texas upbringing and his past as a middle-school teacher to create characters like the young sleuth Mickey Rangel. In this short play, Mickey is employed by his principal in order to find out who is behind some graffiti that has recently turned up at the school. Mickey is forced to use his detective skills, as well as a recent English class lesson on homophones, to figure out which of his classmates has been defacing school property.

Middle-schooler Mickey Rangel is enlisted by his principal to find out who is responsible for the recent appearance of graffiti on the school's walls. While certain clues point to a bully named Bucho, Principal Abrego thinks otherwise. Mickey finds his first clue when he notices a spelling error in the graffiti. During lunch, Mickey's friends are convinced Bucho is to blame, but Mickey reminds them that the existing evidence is only circumstantial. He must find solid proof to determine who is guilty. Later, Bucho pleads with Mickey to uncover the truth. Bucho proves his innocence by correctly spelling the misspelled word in the graffiti. Out in the schoolyard, Mickey gives Joe a spelling test based on a homophone lesson from English class and discovers that he is the culprit. Principal Abrego takes Joe away to her office, and Bucho thanks Mickey for his detective work.

 Proficiency-leveled summaries and summaries in multiple languages are available digitally.

 Audio and audio text highlighting are available with this text.

CONNECT TO ESSENTIAL QUESTION

What do we do when life gets hard?

As a budding private investigator, Mickey Rangel is asked to solve a difficult case at the middle school he attends, and to find out who is marking up the school grounds with graffiti in René Saldaña Jr.'s "The Magic Marker Mystery."

Access Complex Text

LEXILE: N/A   WORD COUNT: 2,692

The following areas may be challenging for students, particularly **ELL** English Language Learners and **A** Approaching grade-level learners.

Purpose	Genre	Specific Vocabulary
• The author's intentions for writing the play may be ambiguous to some students.	• Some students may have limited experience reading plays.	• The selection contains idioms that may be unfamiliar.
• Point out how the play might have had a different ending if both Joe and Bucho had paid attention in class.	• Point out that in this play, "Lights Out" indicates the end of an act. It refers to the lights going out on stage before the next act begins.	• Explain that "a leopard doesn't change its spots" is an idiom that means a person doesn't change his or her behavior.

SCAFFOLDS   **ELL** ENGLISH LANGUAGE LEARNERS   **A** APPROACHING GRADE LEVEL   **B** BEYOND GRADE LEVEL

These icons identify differentiation strategies and scaffolded support for a variety of students. See the digital lesson plan for additional differentiation strategies and scaffolds.

Instructional Path

The print teacher's edition includes essential point-of-use instruction and planning tools. Complete lesson plans and program documents appear in your digital teacher account.

Skill: Making and Confirming Predictions

Objectives: After reading and discussing a model, students will be able to make and confirm predictions to ensure understanding and gain information.

DIGITAL ONLY

First Read: The Magic Marker Mystery

Objectives: After an initial reading and discussion of the drama, students will be able to identify and describe character traits, setting details, and key events, as well as articulate the conflict that is integral to the story's plot.

Skill: Dramatic Elements and Structure

Objectives: After rereading and discussing a model of close reading, students will be able to analyze dramatic elements, including character, setting, plot, theme, dialogue, and stage directions.

Close Read: The Magic Marker Mystery

Objectives: After engaging in a close reading and discussion of the text, students will be able to explain how dramatic elements and the structure of a drama affect the plot in a short, written response.

Progress Monitoring

Opportunities to Learn	Opportunities to Demonstrate Learning	Opportunities to Reteach
Making and Confirming Predictions		
⚙ Skill: Making and Confirming Predictions	🖥 First Read • Read and Annotate	⚙ Spotlight Skill: Making and Confirming Predictions
Dramatic Elements and Structure		
⚙ Skill: Dramatic Elements and Structure	⚙ Skill: Dramatic Elements and Structure • Your Turn 📄 Close Read • Skills Focus • Collaborative Conversation • Write	⚙ Unit 5 Skill: Dramatic Elements and Structure - The Miracle Worker ⚙ Spotlight Skill: Dramatic Elements and Structure

First Read

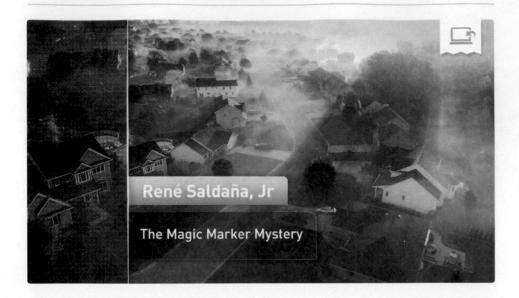

René Saldaña, Jr

The Magic Marker Mystery

Introduce the Text

As a class, watch the video preview and have students read the introduction in pairs to make connections to the video preview.

To activate prior knowledge and experiences, ask students:

- What key words or images from the video do you think will be most important to the drama you are about to read?

- What is one prediction you can make about this drama?

ELL SPEAKING FRAMES

- The ____ in the video makes me think ____.
- The video shows ____. This makes me wonder ____.
- I think the text will ____. I think this because ____.
- I predict that there will be ____. I believe this because ____.

Entry Point

As students prepare to read "The Magic Marker Mystery," share the following information with them to provide context.

✓ From a young age author René Saldaña, Jr. remembers being captivated by the genre of mystery and writes a series about Mickey Rangel, kid detective.

✓ Told in the form of a play, this mystery contains the key elements of suspense, overt clues, and a conclusion that helps the reader better understand the human condition.

✓ In the fashion of a typical mystery, the once tranquil setting of a school is disrupted by a crime. The hero, Mickey, must identify the villain to restore order in the community.

"I've got to do the job right, even if it means going against my gut instinct. . ."

Characters

Mickey Rangel
Principal Abrego
Bucho
Joe
Belinda
Johnny

Setting

A middle school in a Midwestern suburb

1 **ACT ONE:** PRINCIPAL ABREGO's office. The principal is sitting at a large wooden desk. Sunlight streams in from two large windows to her right.

2 PRINCIPAL ABREGO (*buzzes phone*): Angie, can you please send Mickey in now?

3 (*door opens, MICKEY RANGEL reluctantly walks in*)

4 PRINCIPAL ABREGO (*shuffling papers, and without looking at MICKEY*): Won't you have a seat, Mr. Rangel? I'll be just a moment. (*continues shuffling papers for a couple more seconds, then sets them in order and places them on the desk*) So, (*looks up at MICKEY finally*) you must be wondering why I've called you to my office?

5 MICKEY (*leg shaking, swallows hard*): Sort of. I've been going over in my head what I could have possibly done to **merit** being summoned to the principal's office, and though there is that spitball **incident** from this morning on the bus, it was only this morning and mostly between my brother Ricky and me, so word couldn't have gotten to you this quickly, and even if it had, my actions weren't so bad that. . .(*MICKEY notices PRINCIPAL ABREGO has reached for a pen to begin taking notes, and that she also has the traces of a smile on her face.*) I mean, yes, ma'am, I am wondering why you would call me here.

 NOTES

Skill: Dramatic Elements and Structure

I know that this is a drama about a student, and this scene shows me that the play takes place at school because he's talking to the principal.

Mickey seems nervous in this setting, but the principal is smiling. I wonder if Mickey is in trouble or not, and what will happen next...

Reading & Writing Companion **37**

 SELECTION VOCABULARY

merit / merecer *verb* to deserve or be worthy of

incident / el incidente *noun* an event or happening COGNATE

 ELL
- What happened on the bus?
- What is Mickey feeling worried?

Analyze Vocabulary Using Context Clues

In paragraph 5, focus on the sentence that uses the word *merit*. Point out these context clues:

1. First, I notice that Mickey doesn't know what he could have done to be called to the principal's office.

2. He assumes he's in trouble and tries to think of something he did wrong. He remembers a spitball fight he had on the bus that morning.

3. Mickey is trying to figure out what he did to be worthy of this visit to the principal's office, so *merit* must mean "deserve or be worthy of." When I check the meaning in a dictionary, I see that I'm correct.

✓ CHECK FOR SUCCESS

If students are unable to make predictions, revisit the Checklist section of the Grade 6 Context Clues lesson with the class. After revisiting, guide students as they make predictions about the next bold word in the text in paragraph 5.

Dramatic Elements and Structure

How do the stage directions help readers learn more about the setting?

The stage directions let readers know that Mickey has been called to Principal Abrego's office. The reader is then able to infer that the setting of this drama is a school.

Skills Focus

QUESTION 1: Dramatic Elements and Structure

Graffiti is the cause of the main conflict in the story, and Mickey's quest to find the person responsible drives the rest of the plot.

Skills Focus

QUESTION 4: Connect to Essential Question

The main challenge of the drama is finding the perpetrator of the graffiti. Principal Abrego has decided to use Mickey's detective skills to solve the mystery.

Dramatic Elements and Structure

What does the reader learn by analyzing the dialogue?

He confirms that Mickey is not in trouble and learns that he is actually a detective. He predicts that Mickey will help solve who is responsible for the graffiti.

The Magic Marker Mystery

NOTES

6 PRINCIPAL ABREGO: Well. . .never mind about the, uh, spitball episode, at least for now. (*raises an eyebrow, then smiles*) As to why I've asked you to my office this morning, Mr Rangel—may I call you Mickey?

7 MICKEY: Certainly, ma'am.

8 PRINCIPAL ABREGO: I'm sure you've seen the graffiti marring our walls lately. The substance of the messages, mostly aimed at me, is fairly harmless. I'm a principal, so I've had to grow a thick skin over the years. What is bothersome beyond belief, though, is that someone thinks so very little of our school that they would show such disrespect. (*shakes her head*)

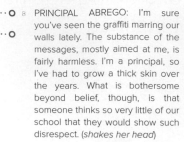
Graffiti

9 MICKEY: Mrs. Abrego, you don't think that I. . .?

10 PRINCIPAL ABREGO: Oh, goodness, no, Mickey. I'm sorry I haven't made myself clear. No, I don't think for a second you have anything to do with this.

11 MICKEY (*sighs in relief*): So then why am I here, if you don't mind me asking?

12 PRINCIPAL ABREGO: Am I right in saying you're sort of a detective, young though you are?

13 MICKEY: Actually, Mrs. Abrego, I'm the real deal. I took the required online courses to earn my degree. I've got a framed diploma at home to prove it. (*pulls wallet from back pocket, rifles through it as though in search of something*) I also carry my official P.I. ID card. P.I.—that stands for private investigator. You want to see it? (*finds it and offers it to PRINCIPAL ABREGO*)

14 PRINCIPAL ABREGO (*takes it from MICKEY and studies it briefly, then returns it*): That's very impressive, Mickey.

15 MICKEY: Thank you, ma'am. But I still don't understand why I'm here.

16 PRINCIPAL ABREGO: Mickey, I'll be frank with you: I'm in a bit of a sticky situation. (*pushes aside a few papers on her desk, stands, and walks to the window overlooking the playground*) Take a look out the window with me and tell me what you see.

17 MICKEY: Yes, ma'am. (*rises, makes his way around the desk, and walks over to the window*)

18 PRINCIPAL ABREGO: Can you read it from here?

Skill: Dramatic Elements and Structure

Principal Abrego didn't call Mickey to her office because he's in trouble. She's asking for his help! She must want him to use his detective skills to find the person responsible for the graffiti.

38 Reading & Writing Companion

NOTES

19 MICKEY (*reads aloud*): "Our Principle's no pal of nobodies!" Interesting spelling and punctuation choices this Magic Marker Mischief Maker has made.

20 PRINCIPAL ABREGO: You noticed? Good. Yes, it should read "principal," ending in "PAL," not "PLE." Major difference.

21 MICKEY: Yes, and "nobody" is spelled as though it were plural, ending in "-dies," though it should not be a plural. And is that a small letter "B" at the bottom right corner, like a signature?

22 PRINCIPAL ABREGO: You caught that too? Most impressive Mickey.

23 MICKEY (*smiles*): Thanks, ma'am.

24 PRINCIPAL ABREGO: I also got this anonymous email this morning right as I turned on my computer. The author claims to be an eye-witness to the wrongdoing. What do you make of it? (*hands MICKEY the sheet of paper*)

25 MICKEY (*reads the email*): Hmmmm. Incriminating, to say the least. So the letter "B" on the wall would make sense. Based on these two clues, all fingers point to Bucho being our mischief maker.

26 PRINCIPAL ABREGO: Yes, that's what I thought. But here's the thing, Mickey. I confronted him with this evidence, and he denies having anything to do with marking up our walls. Believe it or not, tough though he comes across, he was nearly in tears.

27 MICKEY: Ma'am, I'm not so sure you should be telling me this. Isn't there some kind of student-principal privilege?

28 PRINCIPAL ABREGO: Normally, yes, but he gave me permission to discuss this whole matter with you, every bit of it.

29 MICKEY: Wait—what? You mean he told you it was okay to talk to me about this? Why would he do that?

30 PRINCIPAL ABREGO: Mickey, Bucho was so **adamant** that he wasn't the **culprit** that he recommended I bring you in on the case. He's the one who told me you were a detective.

31 MICKEY: He said that?

32 PRINCIPAL ABREGO: Are you surprised?

33 MICKEY: Yes, ma'am. You might not know this about us, but he and I are not the best of friends. To be honest, Mrs. Abrego, he's a bit of a bully.

34 PRINCIPAL ABREGO: That he is. But he and I have been trying to work on that part of his life. In the last few months he's made some great strides, and so

Reading & Writing Companion **39**

Skills Focus

QUESTION 1: Dramatic Elements and Structure

Here we learn about another main character, the bully Bucho. This dialogue is an early hint that Bucho may be innocent, considering that he asks for Mickey's help.

Skills Focus

QUESTION 4: Connect to Essential Question

Bucho's reaction to the challenge is to urge Principal Abrego to use Mickey's detective skills to solve the mystery and clear Bucho's name despite his past behavior.

TEXT TALK

What is the relationship between Bucho and Mickey?

See paragraphs 30 through 33: They are not friends and Mickey may have been a victim of Bucho's bullying in the past, but Bucho asks the principal in good faith for Mickey's help to find the real graffiti artist.

V SELECTION VOCABULARY

adamant / firme *adjective* determined

- What does Bucho say about being the graffiti writer?
- Are Bucho's words strong or weak?

culprit / culpable *noun* person who has done a crime

- Who wrote graffiti on the school wall?
- Whom will Mickey investigate?

Skills Focus

QUESTION 4: Connect to Essential Question

Mickey's reaction to the challenge is to step up and help out. He tells the principal that he can be counted on.

Skills Focus

QUESTION 2: Character

Belinda still thinks of Bucho as a bully, even though she acknowledges that his behavior has improved recently.

Skills Focus

QUESTION 2: Character

Johnny admits that Bucho may be improving, but would still prefer it if it turned out Bucho was guilty of the graffiti and were punished for it.

The Magic Marker Mystery

 NOTES

when I got this email and put it together with the so-called signature, it was easy to jump to conclusions. And this is where you come in, Mickey. I was filled with indecision about what I should do about this, but now I think I've found an answer. I need you to find out who is to blame for the graffiti. Can you help me?

35 MICKEY: You can count on me. Mickey Rangel is on the case.

36 PRINCIPAL ABREGO: Good. Whatever you need, please don't hesitate to ask. In fact, think of me as your benefactor.

37 **ACT TWO, SCENE 1:** First lunch period. MICKEY is eating at a table in the school cafeteria; with him are his friends BELINDA and JOHNNY. JOE, another student, is sitting alone at a nearby table, eavesdropping on MICKEY and friends.

38 BELINDA: You know, Mickey, I'm not the only one who thinks this school would be a better place without that bully, Bucho. I can't even count the multitude of times he's knocked my book bag off my shoulder, as if that were some kind of big joke. (*BELINDA looks reflective for a moment.*) Come to think of it, though, he's walked past me a couple of times the past few weeks and nothing's happened.

39 JOHNNY: Well, all I can say is, I thought it was just a myth about the school bully taking your lunch, but it's true. He hasn't done it for a while, but I still bring rice cakes and celery sticks for lunch because it's the only stuff he won't try and steal from me.

40 MICKEY: Yeah, but what kind of a detective would I be if I'm **presuming** a kid is guilty instead of presuming he's innocent? Not a very good one. And Principal Abrego has been having talks with him, and she claims he's really trying hard to be less of a bully lately.

41 JOHNNY: You might be right about that, but I'd be able to bring a sandwich for lunch again if you did assume he's guilty and found the proof of it. I mean, it's Bucho we're talking about here.

42 *JOE looks over his shoulder at MICKEY and friends, smiles to himself and rubs his hands as if he's won a game of chess; he coughs into his fist: "Bucho's a loser!")*

43 MICKEY: (*turns to JOE*) I'm sorry; did you say something, Joe?

44 JOE: Who, me? Nope. You must be hearing things.

45 MICKEY: Maybe, Joe. But I thought I heard you say, "Bucho's a loser."

46 JOE: I said no such thing. Like I told you, Mickey, you must be hearing things. Get your ears checked.

---

40 Reading & Writing Companion

V SELECTION VOCABULARY

presume / asumir *verb* verb to think something is true without facts

 ELL
• What is Mickey trying to decide?
• What does Mickey point out about Bucho?

47 MICKEY: You're probably right. (*turns back to his friends, thinks for a split second, then turns back to JOE*) Say, Joe, why are you eating all alone? Don't you normally eat lunch with Bucho? He is your best friend, isn't he?

48 JOE: Yeah, well. . . (*JOE scans the room as if looking for somebody.*) Maybe he is and maybe he isn't. Anyway, I'll bet he's probably out marking up a wall somewhere. And I think your pals here are right: Bucho's your man. What is it they say about leopards and their dots?

49 MICKEY: Spots, Joe, you mean "spots."

50 JOE: Yeah, whatever. But like I'm saying, he's so dumb he's even signing his tags with a "B" right? (*JOE stands up and takes his tray off the table.*)

51 MICKEY: Funny way to talk about your best friend. (*JOE gives MICKEY a hard look and then departs without saying anything.*)

52 MICKEY (*turns back to his friends, thinks for a couple short beats*): Anyhow, I'd like to see Bucho gone, too, but I made a promise, Johnny. It's not so simple for me. I've got to do the job right, even if it means going against my gut instinct.

53 BELINDA: So what are you saying, Mickey? You think he's innocent? If you ask a hundred kids who they think is leaving those messages around the school, a hundred of them will say it's got to be Bucho. Who else would it be? He's probably not bullying people as much now because he has a new endeavor—writing graffiti.

54 MICKEY: But a survey isn't evidence.

55 JOHNNY: But you do have evidence, don't you? You said the principal showed you the email in which someone claimed to have seen Bucho in action, writing on the wall.

56 MICKEY: That's circumstantial. Not in the least incriminating without anything else of substance.

57 BELINDA: So, what about the letter "B" the culprit has left behind as a kind of signature—is Joe lying about that?

58 MICKEY: Also circumstantial. I mean, if a "B" is all we've got, who's to say it doesn't stand for "Belinda"? (*BELINDA looks as though she's been accused.*) Don't get me wrong—I'm not saying it's you, I'm saying a "B" is not enough to prove a guy's guilt.

59 BELINDA: Are you saying you're not willing to stand with me—(*looks at JOHNNY*) with us—and instead you're going to side with Bucho?

Reading & Writing Companion 41

Skills Focus

QUESTION 2: Character

Joe used to be Bucho's best friend, but isn't sitting with him at lunch and even suggests that Bucho is guilty. He clearly doesn't like his friend anymore.

Skills Focus

QUESTION 4 Connect to Essential Question

Joe's reaction to the challenge is to throw suspicions off himself and onto Bucho.

TEXT TALK

What is the relationship between Bucho and Joe?

See paragraphs 47 and 48: Bucho and Joe used to be best friends, but they've had a falling out that Joe seems angry over.

The Magic Marker Mystery

60   MICKEY: That's not it at all. What I'm saying is that I've got to do this the right way. I would think you'd understand that my work and doing it right are important to me.

61   BELINDA: No, Mickey. There's nothing "right" about Bucho's ugly behavior all these years. Do you really think a few weeks of acting nice can erase years of mean behavior? Whatever! It's up to you to do the right thing. (*BELINDA stands suddenly and walks away.*)

62   MICKEY: Belinda just doesn't get it, Johnny. I'm a detective; I took an oath to dig and dig until I find the truth, even if I don't like the outcome. I'm not saying it's not Bucho, it's just that I need extensive evidence to prove that it is him. (*he pauses, then looks at JOHNNY*) Besides, putting the blame on Bucho without evidence is just another form of bullying, isn't it? Only this time, we'd be the bullies. (*JOHNNY looks thoughtful and walks away.*)

63   **ACT TWO, SCENE 2:** Second lunch period. MICKEY is sitting alone, deep in thought, unaware that the bell has rung. Suddenly, BUCHO looms in front of MICKEY.

64   BUCHO: Hey, Mickey. . .I imagine Mrs. A told you the story. Somebody's trying to frame me for all this graffiti, and I bet you won't believe me, but it wasn't me. And you're the only one I trust to uncover the truth.

65   MICKEY: I told Mrs. A I would, so I'm going to help any way I can.

66   BUCHO: Ok, bro. Say, you going to eat that? (*Before MICKEY can answer, BUCHO reaches for MICKEY's brownie and swallows it in one bite; then he walks away from the table with his own tray in hand.*)

67   MICKEY: Hey, Bucho. (*BUCHO turns*) How do you spell "principal"? As in Mrs. Abrego, the school's big cheese?

68   BUCHO: First, are you kidding? What other kind of principal is there? Second, are you making fun of me? Because if you are. . .(*BUCHO shakes a fist at MICKEY, but then he thinks better of it and puts his hand down.*)

69   MICKEY: So spell it.

70   BUCHO (*scowling, exaggerating his pronunciation*): P-R-I-N-C-I-P-A-L. As in, Mrs. Abrego is our PAL. Satisfied?

71   MICKEY: Yup. (*BUCHO walks away, this time for good.*)

72   **ACT THREE:** Outside, the school playground, where PRINCIPAL ABREGO, BUCHO, and OTHERS have gathered in front of the site of the latest graffiti. BELINDA stands against a wall nearby. MICKEY enters from stage right.

42   Reading & Writing Companion

Skills Focus

QUESTION 3: Dramatic Elements and Structure

Bucho is still in the habit of trying to be intimidating to his classmates, but is starting to catch himself and correct his behavior.

TEXT TALK

How does Mickey prove that Bucho wasn't responsible for the graffiti?

See paragraph 70: Bucho correctly spells "principal."

73　PRINCIPAL ABREGO: There you are, Mickey. As you can see, I've asked Bucho to join us, as you requested. Can we get started now? (*Beyond PRINCIPAL ABREGO and BUCHO are a multitude of kids playing different games. Among them are JOE, who is noticeably nervous and keeping a careful eye on the developments from a safe distance, and BELINDA, who is standing against a wall nearby.*)

74　MICKEY: Sure thing. First of all, you were right. In the case of The Magic Marker Mischief Maker, someone other than Bucho is responsible for this graffiti. My first clue was the curious spelling. Only two weeks ago in English we were studying homophones. One set of words we were asked to learn included the "principal/principle" set.

75　BUCHO: Yeah, that's right. Miss Garza gave us a trick to remember how to spell it: "Mrs. Abrego, the principal, is our pal." (*BUCHO looks at MICKEY.*) Like I told you at lunch.

76　MICKEY: Exactly, but at lunch you also said, "What other kind of "principal" is there?" when in fact there are two. You had no clue about the other spelling; P-R-I-N-C-I-P-L-E, which means "a high standard that guides one's actions and reactions." You must've been looking at the insides of your eyelids when Miss Garza was going over that one.

77　BUCHO: Watch yourself.

78　PRINCIPAL ABREGO: No, watch yourself, Bernard. Mickey's trying to help, so help yourself by minding your temper.

79　BUCHO: Yes, ma'am.

80　MICKEY: *Bernard?* Really?

81　(*BUCHO scowls and tentatively takes a step in MICKEY's direction, but then he steps back.*)

82　MICKEY: Allow me to go on. If you don't know how to spell both words, much less that there are two variations, then you couldn't have written this graffiti. (*waves a hand at the wall*) This tells me that our culprit is also studying vocabulary in Miss Garza's class, though it's obvious he's not learning.

83　BUCHO: Well, spit it out: if it wasn't me, then who?

84　MICKEY: Hey, Joe, can you come here?

85　JOE (*walks over*): What's up, man? (*He refuses to acknowledge BUCHO.*)

86　MICKEY: Can you spell the word "principal" for us, as in Mrs. Abrego, our school's principal? You know, like we were supposed to have learned in Miss Garza's class.

Skills Focus

QUESTION 3: Dramatic Elements and Structure

Bucho can't help but respond to Mickey with a threat. However, he changes his tone when he is corrected by Principal Abrego. He even calls her ma'am!

Skills Focus

QUESTION 3: Dramatic Elements and Structure

Bucho is embarrassed by his full name but catches himself before lashing out.

TEXT TALK

How does Mickey identify Joe as the guilty person?

See paragraphs 84-91: Mickey notices Joe's anger toward Bucho; Joe spells *principal* incorrectly.

Prepare for Advanced Courses

Use the activity below to differentiate instruction for your Beyond grade - level learners.

One of the most sacred principles in the American criminal justice system is the idea of innocent until proven guilty. How important is remaining objective when solving a mystery? What other stories and events have followed this principle?

TEXT TALK

What other predictions can you make and confirm or correct?

Answers will vary.

Do you think Mickey let people's assumptions of Bucho affect his investigation for the truth? Why or why not?

Answers will vary.

B   BEYOND TEXT TALK

Ask each Beyond grade level student to write one additional discussion question. Then, have one or two students facilitate a discussion, using their questions to guide the conversation.

The Magic Marker Mystery

NOTES

87   JOE: Are you kidding me?

88   PRINCIPAL ABREGO: Mickey?

89   MICKEY: Ma'am? (*motions as though for support from MRS. ABREGO*)

90   PRINCIPAL ABREGO: Okay, then. Go on, Joe, do as he says.

91   JOE (*puffs his chest out proudly*): P-R-I-N-C-I-P-L-E, "principle," as in "The last thing I want is to be sent to the principle's office." Satisfied?

92   MICKEY: Quite.

93   PRINCIPAL ABREGO: Quite indeed. (*speaking to JOE*) Young man, though it's the last thing you want to do, you will follow me to my office. (*The two leave, though MRS. ABREGO does put an arm around JOE's shoulders indicating she will want to "work with" him in the same way she's been working with BUCHO.*)

94   BUCHO: Mickey, you did it! You proved my innocence!

95   MICKEY: I also proved you need to pay more attention in class.

96   BUCHO (*looks to make sure MRS. ABREGO is out of sight before taking a menacing step toward MICKEY*): Why, I oughta…

Used with permission of McGraw-Hill Education

Reading Comprehension OPTIONAL

Have students complete the digital reading comprehension questions ✔ when they finish reading.

ANSWER KEY

QUESTION 1: D	**QUESTION 5:** B	**QUESTION 9:**
QUESTION 2: C	**QUESTION 6:** D	*See first chart.*
QUESTION 3: B	**QUESTION 7:** A	**QUESTION 10:**
QUESTION 4: B	**QUESTION 8:** A	*See second chart.*

Synonym	Word
deserve	merit
happening	incident
certain	adamant
criminal	culprit
supposing	presuming
rule	principle

Dialogue	Character
"But like I'm saying, he's so dumb he's even signing his tags with a 'B' right?"	Joe
"Ok, bro. Say, you going to eat that?"	Bucho
"No, watch yourself, Bernard."	Principal Abrego
"I've got a framed diploma at home to prove it."	Mickey

Connect and Extend OPTIONAL

CONNECT TO EXTENDED WRITING PROJECT

Students may find inspiration in René Saldaña Jr.'s mystery play, both in its format and in the way the twists and turns of a mystery can lead characters to face unexpected challenges.

BEYOND THE BOOK

Writing: It Takes Two to Solve a Mystery

Pair students for this collaborative writing exercise. The pairs will need to decide:

- Where does your mystery take place?
- Who do you want to be in this mystery?

Once they decide on their mystery's setting, students will take turns passing one paper between them. Each time they get the paper, they can write 1-3 lines of dialogue for their character. It's important that they not talk during this activity, but instead allow the mysterious scene to unfold naturally as they add dialogue.

To reflect, ask students

- How did you initiate the mysterious situation in your scene?
- How did your dialogue build tension and create mystery?

Dialogue	Character
"He hasn't done it for awhile, but I still bring rice cakes and celery sticks for lunch because it's the only stuff he won't try and steal from me."	Johnny

Think Questions

Circulate as students answer Think Questions independently. Scaffolds for these questions are shown on the opposite page.

QUESTION 1: Textual Evidence

In the past Bucho has acted like a bully, but Principal Abrego explains that Bucho has tried to make positive changes in his life. However, his classmates do not see this side of him. Belinda states, "If you ask a hundred kids who they think is leaving those messages around the school, a hundred of them will say it's got to be Bucho." Bucho's years of bad behavior make it easy for his classmates to jump to the conclusion that he's responsible for the graffiti.

QUESTION 2: Textual Evidence

Although Bucho feels upset at first, he is active in trying to clear his name. He explains, "Somebody's trying to frame me for all this graffiti. . ." When Principal Abrego first confronts Bucho, he is so frustrated that he almost cries. Then he asks her to enlist the help of private detective Mickey Rangel.

QUESTION 3: Textual Evidence

Belinda's behavior suggests she's interested to find out who wrote the graffiti, but she's still upset with Mickey for not believing that it was Bucho. At lunch, Mickey and Belinda argue about Bucho's guilt. She says, "Whatever!" and then "stands suddenly and walks away." She's mad, but also curious.

QUESTION 4: Context Clues

I think *culprit* must mean "guilty person." The word is used to describe Bucho, who has been suspected of writing the graffiti. Also, Mickey has been brought in to solve the case, and detectives often search for a person guilty of a crime.

QUESTION 5: Context Clues

I think *presuming* must mean "deciding ahead of time." Mickey argues that he wouldn't be a good detective if he presumed that Bucho was guilty even though his friends think so. He is keeping an open mind about Bucho's innocence, and isn't deciding ahead of time that Bucho is guilty.

First Read

Read *The Magic Marker Mystery*. After you read, complete the Think Questions below.

☁ THINK QUESTIONS

1. How does Bucho's past behavior make him an easy target for the real graffiti artist? Cite textual evidence from the selection to support your answer.

2. Write two to three sentences describing how Bucho reacts to being the target of bullying. Cite textual evidence from the selection to support your answer.

3. The stage directions for Act Three say that Belinda stands "against a wall nearby." How would you explain Belinda's behavior during this scene? Cite textual evidence from the selection to support your answer.

4. Find the word **culprit** in paragraph 30 of *The Magic Marker Mystery*. Use context clues in the surrounding sentences, as well as the sentence in which the word appears, to determine the word's meaning. Write your definition here and identify clues that helped you figure out its meaning.

5. Use context clues to determine the meaning of **presuming** as it is used in paragraph 40 of *The Magic Marker Mystery*. Write your definition here and identify clues that helped you figure out its meaning. Then check the meaning in a dictionary.

Reading & Writing Companion **45**

Copyright © BookheadEd Learning, LLC

Think Questions

Use the scaffolds below to differentiate instruction for your **ELL** English Language Learners and **A** Approaching grade-level learners.

ELL **BEGINNING** Write a response using the <u>word bank</u> and <u>sentence frames</u>.

INTERMEDIATE Write a response using the <u>sentence frames</u>.

ADVANCED, ADVANCED HIGH Write a response using the <u>Text-Dependent Question Guide</u>.

A **APPROACHING** Write a response using the <u>Text-Dependent Question Guide</u>.

| | INTERMEDIATE | APPROACHING |
| BEGINNING | | ADVANCED, ADVANCED HIGH |

Word Bank	Sentence Frames	Text-Dependent Question Guide
ahead of time person bully	Bucho used to be a ____. His classmates do not ____ him. They think he is ____.	1. • How did Bucho act in the past? • How do his classmates feel about him?
cries decide mean	When Principal Brego asks Bucho about the graffiti, he ____. Bucho asks Principal Abrego to get ____.	2. • What does Bucho do when Principal Abrego asks him about the graffiti? • What does Bucho ask for? • How does Bucho act toward Mickey?
Bucho Mickey know	Belinda thinks that ____ is guilty. When Mickey disagrees, Belinda gets ____. Belinda still goes to the meeting because she wants to ____ who did the graffiti.	3. • What does Belinda think about Bucho? • How does Belinda act when Mickey disagrees? • Why would Belinda still go to the meeting?
wrote guilty mad	Bucho is accused of writing the ____ on the school wall. Mickey is trying to find the person who is ____. This gives me a clue that *culprit* means a ____ who is suspected of a crime.	4. • Read: "Mickey, Bucho was so adamant that he wasn't the **culprit** that he recommended I bring you in on the case." • What is Bucho being accused of? • What is Mickey trying to do?
graffiti like	Mickey is trying to decide who ____ the graffiti. Mickey is careful not to ____ too soon. This gives me a clue that *presuming* means deciding something ____.	5. • Read: "Yeah, but what kind of a detective would I be if I'm **presuming** a kid is guilty instead of presuming he's innocent?" • What is Mickey trying to decide? • What is Mickey careful to not do?

Skill: Dramatic Elements and Structure

Introduce the Skill

Watch the Concept Definition video and read the following definition with your students.

A drama, or play, is a story performed by actors before an audience. The script of a dramatic work contains certain **dramatic elements,** such as character, setting, plot, theme, dialogue, and stage directions. The **setting** of a play is the time and place in which the events of the story unfold. The events that unfold throughout a drama are called **plot. Dialogue** refers to the conversation between characters in a script. **Stage directions** are the instructions written by the playwright to describe the appearance and actions of the characters as well as the sets, props, costumes, sound effects, and lighting.

Dramas are structured in acts and scenes. An **act** is a major unit of a dramatic work. A play may be divided into several acts. Acts may be further divided into **scenes.** A new act or scene may indicate a change in location or the passage of time.

 TURN AND TALK

1. What are some dramas you have seen?

2. Do you find it easier or more challenging to follow along with a drama than read a narrative

3. What are some ways that information is presented differently and a drama and a traditional story?

ELL SPEAKING FRAMES

- One drama that I have seen is ____.
- I think it is (easier/harder) ____ to follow along with a drama.
- One way that information is presented differently is ____.

The Magic Marker Mystery

DRAMATIC ELEMENTS AND STRUCTURES
sync·Skills

Skill: Dramatic Elements and Structure

Use the Checklist to analyze Dramatic Elements and Structure in *The Magic Marker Mystery*. Refer to the sample student annotations about Dramatic Elements and Structure in the text.

••• CHECKLIST FOR DRAMATIC ELEMENTS AND STRUCTURE

In order to identify the dramatic elements and structure of a play, note the following:

✓ the order of acts and scenes in the play

✓ what happens in each act and scene

✓ how the acts and scenes work together to develop the plot

✓ the setting of the play and how it changes by act and scene

✓ the information in stage directions, including lighting, sound, and set, as well as details about characters, including exits and entrances

To analyze how a particular scene fits into the overall structure of a text and contributes to the development of the theme, setting, or plot, consider the following questions:

✓ When does this particular scene appear?

✓ How does this scene fit into the overall structure of the text?

✓ How do setting, characters, and other elements in the scene contribute to the development of the plot?

✓ What does the scene contribute to the theme or message of the drama?

v SKILL VOCABULARY

dramatic elements / los elementos del género dramático *noun* essential components of a drama, such as plot, characters, theme, and costumes

setting / el escenario *noun* the time and place of the story

plot / la trama *noun* the sequence of events that form a story

dialogue / el diálogo *noun* the conversation between characters   COGNATE

Skill: Dramatic Elements and Structure

sync•skills

Reread paragraphs 75–92 from Act Three of *The Magic Marker Mystery*. Then, using the Checklist on the previous page, answer the multiple-choice questions below.

↻ YOUR TURN

1. Why is mentioning the conversation in the lunchroom (paragraphs 75–76) important to the plot?

   ○ A. Mickey understands that Bucho never pays attention in class.
   ○ B. Mickey is able to grasp that Bucho is not the guilty party.
   ○ C. Bucho realizes that Mickey is attempting to make fun of him.
   ○ D. Bucho admires Mickey's thorough detective skills.

2. What does the dialogue exchanged between Mickey and Principal Abrego in paragraphs 88–90 reveal about the plot?

   ○ A. Principal Abrego is upset with Mickey for overstepping his authority in the situation.
   ○ B. Principal Abrego shows amazement at Mickey's detective skills.
   ○ C. Mickey checks in with Principal Abrego when he needs help solving the case.
   ○ D. Mickey is disappointed that Principal Abrego doesn't trust him to solve the case.

3. In the drama, Mickey asks Joe to spell the word "principal." What does the dialogue exchanged between Mickey and Joe in paragraphs 84–92 reveal about the plot?

   ○ A. Joe admires Miss Garza's clever vocabulary tricks.
   ○ B. Joe makes fun of Mickey for being called to the principal's office.
   ○ C. Joe is a top vocabulary student in Miss Garza's class.
   ○ D. Joe is the culprit because this spelling matches the graffiti.

⊻ SKILL VOCABULARY

stage direction / la dirección en el escenario *noun* an instruction written by the playwright that may describe the set, a sound effect, the lighting, or the appearance or actions of a character

act / el acto *noun* a major unit of a drama COGNATE

scene / la escena *noun* a subdivision of an act in a drama COGNATE

dramatic conventions / las convenciones dramáticas *noun* rules or techniques, accepted by the audience, that an actor or playwright uses to achieve a certain dramatic effect and style COGNATE

The Magic Marker Mystery

⚙ Your Turn

Ask students to complete the Your Turn Activity.

QUESTION 1

A. **Incorrect.** Bucho pays enough attention in class to understand how to spell "principal."

B. **Correct.** Bucho only knows how to spell "principal" one way, thus he could not have spelled "principle" in graffiti.

C. **Incorrect.** Mickey is not attempting to make fun of Bucho; he is trying to prove his innocence.

D. **Incorrect.** These paragraphs reveal that Bucho is initially irritated. It is not until later that he compliments Mickey on his detective skills.

QUESTION 2

A. **Incorrect.** Principal Abrego gives in and allows Mickey to question Joe.

B. **Incorrect.** Principal Abrego initially questions Mickey's desire to interrogate Joe.

C. **Correct.** Mickey proceeds with the case as he desires with support from Principal Abrego.

D. **Incorrect.** Mickey uses his communication skills to assert his expertise in the situation.

QUESTION 3

A. **Incorrect.** Joe has not learned Miss Garza's lesson about homophones.

B. **Incorrect.** There is no evidence of Joe knowing that Mickey was called to the principal's office.

C. **Incorrect.** Joe spells the word incorrectly; he is not a top vocabulary student.

D. **Correct.** Joe reveals a pattern by spelling *principal* incorrectly two times.

Close Read

Skills Focus

QUESTION 1: Dramatic Elements and Structure

Paragraphs 2–4: The opening lines introduce two of the main characters: Principal Abrego and Mickey Rangel. We also learn that Principal Abrego needs something from Mickey.

QUESTION 1: Dramatic Elements and Structure

See paragraphs 8 and 30–33.

QUESTION 2: Character

See paragraphs 38, 41, and 48.

QUESTION 3: Dramatic Elements and Structure

See paragraphs 68, 76–79, and 80–81.

QUESTION 4: Connect to Essential Question

See paragraphs 8–12, 30, 35–36, and 48.

CHECK FOR SUCCESS

If students struggle to respond to Skills Focus Question #1, ask students the following questions:

- According to Principal Abrego in paragraph 30, who is asking for Mickey's help?
- What is Mickey being asked to do?
- Why is Mickey surprised in paragraph 33?

The Magic Marker Mystery

THE MAGIC MARKER MYSTERY

Close Read

Reread *The Magic Marker Mystery*. As you reread, complete the Skills Focus questions below. Then use your answers and annotations from the questions to help you complete the Write activity.

 SKILLS FOCUS

1. Identify a scene or line of dialogue in Act 1 that helps to develop or move the plot forward.

2. Identify how the other characters feel about Bucho in Act Two, Scene 1.

3. Identify lines of dialogue or stage directions that show Bucho's attempt to change from being a bully.

4. Think about the challenges the characters face in *The Magic Marker Mystery*. Identify the challenges and what the characters choose to do about it.

 WRITE

LITERARY ANALYSIS: Think about how the playwright uses specific scenes to develop the plot. How would Act Three of *The Magic Marker Mystery* would be different if it were told from Joe's perspective? In your response, indicate how this would affect the structure of the play as a whole. Write a response of at least 200 words. Support your writing with specific evidence from the text.

Please note that excerpts and passages in the StudySync® library and this workbook are intended as touchstones to generate interest in an author's work. The excerpts and passages do not substitute for the reading of entire texts, and StudySync® strongly recommends that students seek out and purchase the whole literary or informational work in order to experience it as the author intended. Links to online resellers are available in our digital library. In addition, complete works may be ordered through an authorized reseller by filling out and returning to StudySync® the order form enclosed in this workbook.

 ## Writer's Notebook

Connect to Essential Question: Give students time to reflect on how "The Magic Marker Mystery" connects to the unit's essential question "What do we do when life gets hard?" by freewriting in their Writer's Notebooks.

 ELL **Beginning & Intermediate**

Read aloud the unit's essential question: "What do we do when life gets hard?" Encourage students to draw their connections or allow students to write in their native language. Circulate around the room, prompting students for their thoughts as they respond orally or through pantomime.

Advanced & Advanced High

Allow students to share their connections orally in pairs or small groups before freewriting.

Collaborative Conversation

Break students into collaborative conversation groups. Using StudySyncTV as a model, have students begin by reading the Close Read prompt. They should then use their Skills focus annotations, their own ideas and reactions to the text, and any other notes and annotations they have to collaboratively explore the text.

- How does the playwright use dialogue to **indicate** how the character's role in the drama advances the plot?

- What is the importance of the setting, and how does the setting contribute to the plot?

Use the scaffolds below to differentiate instruction for your **ELL** English Language Learners and **A** Approaching grade-level learners.

ELL **BEGINNING, INTERMEDIATE** Use the <u>discussion guide</u> and <u>speaking frames</u> to facilitate the discussion with support from the teacher.

ADVANCED, ADVANCED HIGH Use the <u>discussion guide</u> and <u>speaking frames</u> to facilitate the discussion in mixed-level groups.

A **APPROACHING** Use the <u>discussion guide</u> to facilitate the discussion in mixed-level groups.

APPROACHING
ADVANCED, ADVANCED HIGH
BEGINNING, INTERMEDIATE

Discussion Guide	Speaking Frames
1. How does the playwright use dialogue to **indicate** how the character's role in the drama advances the plot?	• The dialogue shows me that ____'s (Principal Abrego/Mickey/Bucho/Joe) role is ____. • This character is important to the story because ____.
2. What is the importance of the setting?	• The setting is important because ____. • The setting helps me understand ____.
3. How does the setting contribute to the plot?	• The setting helps to move the plot in paragraph ____. • The information helps me because ____.

Review Prompt and Rubric

Before students begin writing, review the writing prompt and rubric with the class.

LITERARY ANALYSIS: Think about how the playwright uses specific scenes to develop the plot. How would Act Three of "The Magic Marker Mystery" be different if it were told from Joe's perspective? In your response, **indicate** how this would affect the structure of the play as a whole. Write a response of at least 200 words. Support your writing with specific evidence from the text.

  PROMPT GUIDE

- What does the dialogue tell you about a character?
- How does the playwright use dialogue to **indicate** the character's role?
- How does the dialogue help move the story or plot forward?

- What is the setting?
- Why is the setting important to the story?

Score	Dramatic Elements and Structure	Language and Conventions
4	The writer clearly explains how Act Three would differ if it were told from Joe's perspective and how this would affect the overall structure of the play. The writer provides exemplary analysis, using relevant evidence from the text.	The writer demonstrates a consistent command of grammar, punctuation, and usage conventions. Although minor errors may be evident, they do not detract from the fluency or the clarity of the essay.
3	The writer explains how Act Three would differ if it were told from Joe's perspective and how this would affect the overall structure of the play. The writer provides analysis, using evidence from the text.	The writer demonstrates an adequate command of grammar, punctuation, and usage conventions. Although some errors may be evident, they create few (if any) disruptions in the fluency of the writing or the clarity of the essay.
2	The writer begins to explain how Act Three would differ if it were told from Joe's perspective and how this would affect the overall structure of the play, but the analysis is incomplete. The writer uses relevant evidence from the text only some of the time.	The writer demonstrates a partial command of grammar, punctuation, and usage conventions. Some distracting errors may be evident, at times creating minor disruptions in the fluency or clarity of the writing.
1	The writer attempts to explain how Act Three would differ if it were told from Joe's perspective and how this would affect the overall structure of the play, but the analysis is not successful. The writer uses little or no relevant evidence from the text.	The writer demonstrates little or no command of grammar, punctuation, and usage conventions. Serious and persistent errors create disruptions in the fluency of the writing and sometimes interfere with meaning.
0	The writer does not provide a relevant response to the prompt or does not provide a response at all.	Serious and persistent errors overwhelm the writing and interfere with the meaning of the response as a whole, making the writer's meaning impossible to understand.

Write

Ask students to complete the writing assignment using textual evidence to support their answers.

Use the scaffolds below to differentiate instruction for your **ELL** English Language Learners and **A** Approaching grade-level learners.

ELL **BEGINNING** With the help of the word bank, write a response using paragraph frame 1.

INTERMEDIATE With the help of the word bank, write a response using paragraph frames 1 and 2.

ADVANCED, ADVANCED HIGH Write a response of differentiated length using the sentence starters.

A **APPROACHING** Write a response of differentiated length using the sentence starters.

	BEGINNING INTERMEDIATE		ADVANCED, ADVANCED HIGH APPROACHING
Word Bank	**Paragraph Frame 1**	**Paragraph Frame 2**	**Sentence Starters**
spelling culprit punctuation character guilty	The playwright René Saldaña, Jr. uses Act Three to identify the ____ of the magic marker mystery. Through this scene, the reader discovers that Joe is ____ because of the ____ and ____ errors. If Joe were the narrator, the reader would know more about his ____.	The structure of the play itself would be different as the reader could learn more about Joe's ____ through his inner ____. A difference in stage directions could also change how the reader ____ Joe's character. Overall, a difference in perspective may ____ how the audience feels about Joe and the overall tone of the ____.	• The playwright uses scenes to . . . • If the narrator of this scene changed . . . • An example of this is when the character____ . . . • This shows that the structure . . . • Another example is . . . • This also shows that the structure . . . • It shows this because . . .

Peer Review

Students should submit substantive feedback to two peers using the review instructions below.

- How well does this response answer the prompt?
- How well does the writer support his ideas with specific scenes and dialogue from the drama?
- Did the writer give examples of how the story would be different from Joe's perspective? Did the writer explain how this would affect the play's structure?
- What did the writer do well in this response? What does the writer need to work on?

Rate

Respond to the following with a point rating that reflects your opinion.

	1 2 3 4
Ideas	■ ■ ■ ☐
Evidence	■ ■ ■ ■
Language and Conventions	■ ■ ☐ ☐

Submit

ELL **SENTENCE FRAMES**

A
- You were able to (completely / partly / almost) ____ answer the prompt because . . .
- You could answer the prompt more completely by . . .
- You supported the idea of . . . with the detail of . . .

- One idea that needs more support is . . .
- I thought differently about the text after reading . . .
- My favorite part of your response is . . .

Scout's Honor

FICTION
Avi
1996

Introduction

Avi is the pen name of Edward Irving Wortis (b. 1937), the Newbery Award-winning author of more than seventy-five books for children and young adults. Avi was born and raised in New York City, and his childhood and adolescence were an inspiration for many of his stories and books. "Scout's Honor," presented here, is the humorous story of a nine-year-old boy and his Boy Scout friends who set out to the New Jersey "wilderness" to prove their toughness. Avi's body of work spans many genres, from historical fiction to graphic novels. Yet his stories and books are united by their relatable and evocative depictions of young people in challenging circumstances, struggling to learn and to grow.

The narrator, a nine-year-old boy living in 1940s Brooklyn, and his friends Horse and Max set out to go camping in New Jersey, a requirement of the Boy Scouts. They arrive at the subway station with plenty of supplies, but they don't know the way to the campsite. Together, the boys read the map and end up caught in the rain while crossing the bridge to New Jersey. When they arrive at the campsite, they realize that their hatchet is too dull to chop wood, there's no tarp to make a tent, and it's raining too hard to start a fire. They are hungry, wet, and cold. After a short time, the narrator suggests going home—and he's mightily relieved when his friends agree. Before parting ways, the narrator admits that he is not as tough as he thought. Max and Horse admit that they weren't tough enough to be the first to suggest going home. In the end, all three boys promise not to tell their Scoutmaster.

 Proficiency-leveled summaries and summaries in multiple languages are available digitally.

 Audio and audio text highlighting are available with this text.

CONNECT TO ESSENTIAL QUESTION

What do we do when life gets hard?

In "Scout's Honor," by Avi, three friends from Brooklyn, all Boy Scouts, go camping by themselves in the Palisades of New Jersey in order to earn merit badges and prove they are "tough." But their trip turns out to be much more of a challenge than they expected.

Access Complex Text

LEXILE: 660   WORD COUNT: 3,133

The following areas may be challenging for students, particularly English Language Learners and Ⓐ Approaching grade-level learners.

Prior Knowledge	Specific Vocabulary	Sentence Structure
• Some students may be unfamiliar with the location of Brooklyn and the Palisades in New Jersey. • Point out that Brooklyn is a borough of New York City. The Palisades Interstate Park contains 2,500 acres and is located about an hour from Brooklyn on a subway train.	• The selection contains some words that are specific to the time period of the late 1940s. • Words and terms such as *Buster Brown shoes, F-36 fighter plane,* and *Hell-cat dive-bomber* may need to be explained or defined.	• Following the dialogue in the story may be difficult for some readers. • Point out that the speaker is not always identified, and students should note that the dialogue is separated into paragraphs for each new speaker.

 SCAFFOLDS   **ENGLISH LANGUAGE LEARNERS**   Ⓐ **APPROACHING GRADE LEVEL**   **BEYOND GRADE LEVEL**

These icons identify differentiation strategies and scaffolded support for a variety of students. See the digital lesson plan for additional differentiation strategies and scaffolds.

Instructional Path

The print teacher's edition includes essential point-of-use instruction and planning tools. Complete lesson plans and program documents appear in your digital teacher account.

First Read: Scout's Honor

Objectives: After an initial reading and discussion of "Scout's Honor," students will be able to identify and describe character traits and setting details as well as articulate the conflict that is integral to the story's plot.

Skill: Story Structure

Objectives: After rereading and discussing a model of close reading, students will be able to analyze how a particular sentence/chapter fits into the overall structure of a text and contributes to the development of theme, setting, or plot.

Skill: Plot

Objectives: After rereading and discussing a model of close reading, students will be able to describe how a particular story's plot unfolds in a series of episodes as well as how the characters respond or change as the plot moves toward a resolution.

Close Read: Scout's Honor

Objectives: After engaging in a close reading and discussion of "Scout's Honor," students will be able to analyze how the plot of the story is developed through the characters' dialogue, actions, and motivations in a short, written response.

Progress Monitoring

Opportunities to Learn	Opportunities to Demonstrate Learning	Opportunities to Reteach
Story Structure		
⚙ Skill: Story Structure	⚙ Skill: Story Structure • Your Turn ▣ Close Read • Skills Focus • Collaborative Conversation • Write	⚙ Unit 2 Skill: Story Structure - Roll of Thunder, Hear My Cry ⚙ Unit 3 Skill: Story Structure - The Lightning Thief ⚙ Spotlight Skill: Story Structure
Plot		
⚙ Skill: Plot	⚙ Skill: Plot • Your Turn ▣ Close Read • Skills Focus • Collaborative Conversation • Write	⚙ Unit 5 Skill: Plot - Damon and Pythias ⚙ Spotlight Skill: Plot

First Read

Avi

Scout's Honor

Entry Point

 ## Introduce the Text

As a class, watch the video preview ▶ and have students read the introduction in pairs to make connections to the video preview.

To activate prior knowledge and experiences, ask students:

- What information in this video was new to you?

- How does this information connect to something you already know?

ELL SPEAKING FRAMES

- The ____ in the video makes me think ____.
- The video shows ____. This makes me wonder ____.
- I think the text will ____. I think this because ____.
- I predict that there will be ____. I believe this because ____.

As students prepare to read "Scout's Honor," share the following information with them to provide context.

✓ The Boy Scouts of America is a large organization comprised of boys and volunteers. The goal of the BSA is to mentor youth in the areas of character, education, career, and outdoor skills.

✓ Scouts earn proficiency badges as they advance through the ranks. A scout must successfully demonstrate knowledge of the requirements for the badge as listed in the Boy Scout Handbook.

✓ "Scout's honor" is a phrase used by scouts to affirm their fidelity to the Scout Oath "On my honor I will do my best to do my duty to God and my country and to obey the Scout Law; to help other people at all times; to keep myself physically strong, mentally awake, and morally straight." This is the pledge each scout takes and lives by.

"The way they agreed made me nervous. Now I really was going to have to be tough."

 NOTES

 Skill: Story Structure

These sentences tell me that this story will be about an overnight camping adventure. It will be a new experience for the narrator since he will be leaving Brooklyn for the first time, without adult supervision.

This sentence in paragraph 2 tells me that the setting plays an important role in the story. It will probably have an effect on what happens to the boys because the narrator isn't used to the country.

1 Back in 1946, when I was nine, I worried that I wasn't tough enough. That's why I became a Boy Scout. Scouting, I thought, would make a man of me. It didn't take long to reach Tenderfoot rank. You got that for joining. To move up to Second Class, however, you had to meet three requirements. Scout Spirit and Scout Participation had been cinchy. The third requirement, Scout Craft, meant I had to go on an overnight hike in the *country*. In other words, I had to leave Brooklyn, on my own, for the first time in my life.

2 Since I grew up in Brooklyn in the 1940s, the only grass I knew was in Ebbets Field where the Dodgers played. Otherwise, my world was made of slate pavements, streets of asphalt (or cobblestone), and skies full of tall buildings. The only thing "country" was a puny pin oak tree at our curb, which was noticed, mostly, by dogs.

3 I asked Scoutmaster Brenkman where I could find some country. Now, whenever I saw Mr. Brenkman, who was a church pastor, he was dressed in either church black or Scout khaki. When he wore black, he'd warn us against hellfire. When he wore khaki, he'd teach us how to build fires.

4 "Country," Scoutmaster Brenkman said in answer to my question, "is anywhere that has lots of trees and is not the city. Many boys camp in the Palisades."

5 "Where's that?"

6 "Just north of the city. It's a park in Jersey."

7 "Isn't that a zillion miles from here?"

8 "Take the subway to the George Washington Bridge, then hike across."

9 I thought for a moment, then asked, "How do I prove I went?"

10 Mr. Brenkman looked deeply shocked. "You wouldn't *lie*, would you? What about Scout's honor?"

11 "Yes, sir," I replied meekly.

Copyright © BookheadEd Learning, LLC

 ## Analyze Vocabulary Using Context Clues

In paragraph 29, focus on the sentence that uses the word *courteous*. Point out these context clues:

1. First, I notice that all the words associated with Scout law are positive.

2. When I read the sentence again, it appears that all of these words refer to natural human traits. Some people are cheerful, while others are friendly or thrifty. Some can be all three and more. So these words refer to characteristics that all scouts should display.

3. Finally, I notice the word that comes before *courteous* is *friendly*, which means "kind and pleasant." The word *kind* in fact, follows courteous. So *courteous* may have something to do with showing kindness, too, because the words are grouped together in the list. A person who is friendly by showing good manners is courteous.

 ## Story Structure

What is the setting of the story?

The reader infers that the setting is new to the narrator, and notes that this is important to the plot.

 ## TEXT TALK

Why does the narrator join the Boy Scouts?

See paragraph 1: He fears he isn't tough enough, and he thinks the Boy Scouts will make a man of him.

Skills Focus

QUESTION 1: Character

The narrator admits that he and his friends are rivals. That makes his fear that he isn't tough enough more challenging.

Skills Focus

QUESTION 2: Story Structure

The narrator at the beginning of the story tells the reader about the type of relationship that he and his friends have. The narrator states that his motivation for camping is "wanting to be tougher." Going camping will provide the setting for the main theme of the story: how far will you go before admitting "weakness"?

Skills Focus

QUESTION 1: Character

The narrator is so determined to accept the challenge of proving his toughness by camping that he is willing to lie to his parents and break a Scout law.

Plot

How does the reader use the inciting incident to understand the main character's problem?

He notices that the plot will involve friends who are trying to prove they're tough. He notes this as the inciting incident because it seems to set up the rest of the story.

TEXT TALK

How does the narrator think he compares with his two best friends?

See paragraph 15: He thinks he is not as tough

---

12 My two best friends were Philip Hossfender, whom we nicknamed Horse, and Richard Macht, called Max because we were not great spellers. They were also Scouts, Tenderfoots like me.

13 Horse was a skinny little kid about half my size whose way of arguing was to ball up his fist and say, "Are you saying. . .?" in a threatening tone.

14 Max was on the pudgy side, but he could talk his way out of a locked room. More importantly, he always seemed to have pocket money, which gave his talk real power.

15 I wasn't sure why, but being best friends meant we were rivals too. One of the reasons for my wanting to be tougher was a feeling that Horse was a lot tougher than I was, and that Max was a little tougher.

16 "I'm going camping in the Palisades next weekend," I casually informed them.

17 "How come?" Max challenged.

18 "Scout Craft," I replied.

19 "Oh, *that*," Horse said with a shrug.

20 "Look," I said, "I don't know about you, but I don't intend to be a Tenderfoot all my life. Anyway, doing stuff in the city is for sissies. Scouting is real camping. Besides, I like roughing it."

21 "You saying I don't?" Horse snapped.

22 "I'm not saying nothing," I said.

23 They considered my idea. Finally, Horse said, "Yeah, well, I was going to do that, but I didn't think you guys were ready for it."

24 "I've been ready for *years*," Max protested.

25 "Then we're going, right?" I said.

26 They looked around at me. "If you can do it, I can do it," Max said.

27 "Yeah," Horse said thoughtfully.

28 The way they agreed made me nervous. Now I really was going to have to be tough.

29 We informed our folks that we were going camping overnight (which was true) and that the Scoutmaster was going with us—which was a lie. We did remember what Mr. Brenkman said about honesty, but we were baseball fans too, and since we were prepared to follow Scout law—being loyal, helpful, friendly, **courteous,** kind, obedient, cheerful, thrifty, brave, clean *and* reverent—we figured a 900 batting average was not bad.

Skill: Plot

These early paragraphs tell me that the plot will involve friends who are trying to prove they're tough. I think it is the inciting incident because it seems to set up the rest of the story.

Reading & Writing Companion 51

SELECTION VOCABULARY

courteous / cortés *adjective* polite or respectful

NOTES

30   So Saturday morning we met at the High Street subway station. I got there first. Stuffed in my dad's army surplus knapsack was a blanket, a pillow, and a paper bag with three white-bread peanut-butter-and-jelly sandwiches—that is, lunch, supper, and Sunday breakfast. My pockets were full of stick matches. I had an old flashlight, and since I lived by the Scout motto—Be Prepared—I had brought along an umbrella. Finally, being a serious reader, I had the latest Marvel Family comics.

31   Horse arrived next, his arms barely managing to hold on to a mattress that seemed twice his size. As for food, he had four cans of beans jammed into his pockets.

32   Max came last. He was lugging a new knapsack that contained a cast-iron frying pan, a packet of hot dogs, and a box of saltine crackers—plus two bottles. One bottle was mustard, the other, celery soda. He also had a bag of Tootsie Rolls and a shiny hatchet. "To build a lean-to," he explained.

33   Max's prize **possession,** however, was an official Scout compass. "It's really swell," he told us. "You can't ever get lost with it. Got it at the Scout store."

34   "I hate that place," Horse informed us. "It's all new. Nothing real."

35   "This compass is real," Max retorted. "Points north all the time. You can get cheaper ones, but they point all different directions."

36   "What's so great about the north?" Horse said.

37   "That's always the way to go," Max insisted.

38   "Says who?" I demanded.

39   "Mr. Brenkman, dummy," Horse cried. "Anyway, there's always an arrow on maps pointing the way north."

40   "Cowboys live out west," I reminded them. They didn't care.

41   On the subway platform, we realized we did not know which station we were heading for. To find out, we studied the system map, which looked like a noodle factory hit by a bomb. The place we wanted to go (north) was at the top of the map, so I had to hoist Horse onto my shoulders for a closer look. Since he refused to let go of his mattress—or the tin cans in his pockets—it wasn't easy. I asked him—in a kindly fashion—to put the mattress down.

42   No sooner did he find the station—168th Street—than our train arrived. We rushed on, only to have Horse scream, "My mattress!" He had left it on the platform. Just before the doors shut, he and I leaped off. Max, however, remained on the train. Helplessly, we watched as his horror-stricken face slid away from us. "Wait at the next station!" I bellowed. "Don't move!"

---

52   Reading & Writing Companion

Skills Focus

QUESTION 3: Plot

Horse jumps off the train, even though the doors are about to close. The narrator follows, either to help his friend or not be separated from him. Max is slow to react and is carried away. This adds tension to the rising action.

 SELECTION VOCABULARY

possession / la posesión *noun* something belonging to someone COGNATE

ELL • Where does Max get the compass?
     • Does he own or borrow the compass?

TEXT TALK

Are the boys prepared for their camping trip in New Jersey?

See paragraphs 30–32: No; they haven't packed the right food, equipment, or sleeping gear; they aren't prepared for the weather

43 The next train took forever to come. Then it took even longer to get to the next stop. There was Max. All around him—like fake snow in a glass ball—were crumbs. He'd been so nervous he had eaten all his crackers.

44 "Didn't that make you thirsty?"

45 "I drank my soda."

46 I noticed streaks down his cheeks. Horse noticed them too. "You been crying?" he asked.

47 "Naw," Max said. "There was this water dripping from the tunnel roof. But, you said don't move, right? Well, I was just being obedient."

48 By the time we got on the next train—with all our possessions—we had been traveling for an hour. But we had managed to go only one stop.

49 During the ride, I got hungry. I pulled out one of my sandwiches. With the jelly soaked through the bread, it looked like a limp scab.

50 Horse, **envious,** complained *he* was getting hungry.

51 "Eat some of your canned beans," I suggested.

52 He got out one can without ripping his pocket too badly. Then his face took on a mournful look.

53 "What's the matter?" I asked.

54 "Forgot to bring a can opener."

55 Max said, "In the old days, people opened cans with their teeth."

56 "You saying my teeth aren't strong?"

57 "I'm just talking about history!"

58 "You saying I don't know history?"

59 Always kind, I plopped half my sandwich into Horse's hand. He squashed it into his mouth and was quiet for the next fifteen minutes. It proved something I'd always believed: The best way to stop arguments is to get people to eat peanut butter sandwiches. They can't talk.

60 Then we became so **absorbed** in our Marvel Family comics we missed our station. We got to it only by coming back the other way. When we reached street level, the sky was dark.

61 "I knew it," Max announced. "It's going to rain."

NOTES

Skill:
Plot

I see that the boys' adventure is going from bad to worse. Max began by being brave, but now I see that he has been crying. This is the conflict at work, and it suggests to me that there will be more challenges ahead before the resolution comes.

Skills Focus

QUESTION 5: Connect to Essential Question

Once they start out, the narrator is helpful when Horse faces the challenge of having nothing to eat because he didn't bring a can opener.

Plot

What does the reader notice in the conflict?

The reader notices that the boys' adventure is not going well. The boys are no longer brave. The reader notes that this is the conflict in action, and there will be more challenges before the resolution.

Reading & Writing Companion 53

 SELECTION VOCABULARY

envious / envidioso/a *adjective* showing desire for what someone else has COGNATE

ELL
• What is the narrator eating?
• How does Horse feel?

absorb / absorber *verb* to mentally take in information; to comprehend COGNATE

ELL
• What are the boys doing?
• Why do the boys miss their station?

Scout's Honor

62 "Don't worry," Horse said. "New Jersey is a whole other state. It probably won't be raining there."

63 "I brought an umbrella," I said smugly, though I wanted it to sound helpful.

64 As we marched down 168th Street, heading for the George Washington Bridge, we looked like European war refugees. Every few paces, Horse cried, "Hold it!" and adjusted his arms around his mattress. Each time we paused, Max pulled out his compass, peered at it, then announced, "Heading north!"

65 I said, "The bridge goes from east to west."

66 "Maybe the bridge does," Max insisted with a show of his compass, "but guaranteed, *we* are going north."

67 About then, the heel of my left foot, encased in a heavy rubber boot over an earth-crushing Buster Brown shoe, started to get sore. Things weren't going as I had hoped. Cheerfully, I tried to ignore the pain.

68 The closer we drew to the bridge, the more **immense** it seemed. And the clouds had become so thick, you couldn't see the top of the far side.

69 Max eyed the bridge with deep suspicion. "I'm not so sure we should go," he said.

70 "Why?"

71 "Maybe it doesn't have another side."

72 We looked at him.

Skill: Story Structure

I think the boys are trying to prove that they're tough. I think this event is important to the theme since the narrator wants to prove he's brave in front of his friends. I wonder if this attitude will continue throughout the whole story.

73 "No, seriously," Max explained, "they could have taken the Jersey side away, you know, for repairs."

74 "Cars are going across," I pointed out.

75 "They could be dropping off," he suggested.

76 "You would hear them splash," Horse argued.

77 "I'm going," I said. Trying to look brave, I started off on my own. My bravery didn't last for long. The walkway was narrow. When I looked down, I saw only fog. I could feel the bridge tremble and sway. It wasn't long before I was convinced the bridge was about to collapse. Then a ray of hope struck me: Maybe the other guys had chickened out. If they had, I could quit because of *them.* I glanced back. My heart sank. They were coming.

78 After they caught up, Horse looked me in the eye and said, "If this bridge falls, I'm going to kill you."

SELECTION VOCABULARY

immense / inmenso/a *adjective* very great or large   COGNATE

ELL
• Is the bridge big or small?
• Does the idea of crossing the bridge make the boys feel scared or safe?

Skills Focus

QUESTION 1: Character

The narrator shows determination. He is willing to carry on, even when he is in pain.

Skills Focus

QUESTION 3: Plot

The narrator's external and internal reactions don't match. He acts brave, but internally he is getting more and more frightened and hopes the others won't follow him. When they do, the tension rises and the narrator is forced to keep going.

Story Structure

How does this contribute to the developing theme?

The reader notes character traits by analyzing dialogue and infers that this will be a pattern of events.

TEXT TALK

What happens when the boys get to the bridge?

See paragraphs 68–72: The clouds are so thick that the boys can't see the other side; they are afraid to cross.

Skills Focus

QUESTION 3: Plot

Things are going from bad to worse. Horse trips and his mattress gets soaking wet. Still, he doesn't say anything about giving up.

Analyze for Enrichment

Look at the simile in paragraph 97:

"Unfortunately, he landed like a Hell-cat dive-bomber as his mattress unspooled before him and then slammed into a big puddle."

Remind students that a simile is a figure of speech that makes a comparison, showing similarities between two different things using *like* or *as*. Ask students: What two different things are being compared here? How does the use of a simile here impact the reader? What is the significance of the simile?

79 A quarter of a mile farther across, I gazed around. We were completely fogged in.

80 "I think we're lost," I announced.

81 "What do we do?" Horse whispered. His voice was jagged with panic. That made me feel better.

82 "Don't worry," Max said. "I've got my compass." He pulled it out. "North is that way," he said, pointing in the direction we had been going.

83 Horse said, "You sure?"

84 "A Scout compass never lies," Max insisted.

85 "*We* lied," I reminded him.

86 "Yeah, but this is an *official* Scout compass," Max returned loyally.

87 "Come on," Max said and marched forward. Horse and I followed. In moments, we crossed a metal bar on the walkway. On one side, a sign proclaimed: NEW YORK; on the other, it said: NEW JERSEY.

88 "Holy smoke," Horse said with reverence as he straddled the bar. "Talk about being tough. We're in two states at the same time."

89 It began to rain. Max said, "Maybe it'll keep us clean."

90 "You saying I'm not clean?" Horse shot back.

91 Ever friendly, I put up my umbrella.

92 We went on—Max on one side, Horse on the other, me in the middle—trying to avoid the growing puddles. After a while, Max said, "Would you move the umbrella? Rain is coming down my neck."

93 "We're supposed to be roughing it," I said.

94 "Being in the middle isn't roughing it," Horse reminded me.

95 I folded the umbrella up so we could all get soaked equally.

96 "Hey!" I cried. "Look!" Staring up ahead, I could make out tollbooths and the dim outlines of buildings.

97 "Last one off the bridge is a rotten egg!" Horse shouted and began to run. The next second, he tripped and took off like an F-36 fighter plane. Unfortunately, he landed like a Hell-cat dive-bomber as his mattress unspooled before him and then slammed into a big puddle.

NOTES

98 Max and I ran to help. Horse was damp. His mattress was soaked. When he tried to roll it up, water cascaded like Niagara Falls.

99 "Better leave it," Max said.

100 "It's what I sleep on at home," Horse said as he slung the soaking, dripping mass over his shoulder.

101 When we got off the bridge, we were in a small plaza. To the left was the roadway, full of roaring cars. In front of us, aside from the highway, there was nothing but buildings. Only to the right were there trees.

102 "North is that way," Max said, pointing toward the trees. We set off.

103 "How come you're limping?" Horse asked me. My foot *was* killing me. All I said, though, was, "How come you keep rubbing your arm?"

104 "I'm keeping the blood moving."

105 We **approached** a grove of trees. "Wow," Horse exclaimed. "Country." But as we drew closer, what we found were discarded cans, bottles, and newspapers—plus an old mattress spring.

106 "Hey," Max cried, sounding relieved, "this is just like Brooklyn."

107 I said, "Let's find a decent place, make camp, and eat."

108 It was hard to find a campsite that didn't have junk. The growing dark didn't help. We had to settle for the place that had the least amount of garbage.

109 Max said, "If we build a lean-to, it'll keep us out of the rain." He and Horse went a short distance with the hatchet.

110 Seeing a tree they wanted, Max whacked at it. The hatchet bounced right out of his hand. There was not even a dent in the tree. Horse retrieved the hatchet and checked the blade. "Dull," he said.

111 "Think I'm going to carry something sharp and cut myself?" Max protested. They contented themselves with picking up branches.

112 I went in search of firewood, but everything was wet. When I finally gathered some twigs and tried to light them, the only thing that burned was my fingers.

113 Meanwhile, Horse and Max used their branches to build a lean-to directly over me. After many collapses—which didn't help my work—they finally got the branches to stand in a shaky sort of way.

114 "Uh-oh," Horse said. "We forgot to bring something for a cover."

115 Max eyed me. "Didn't you say you brought a blanket?"

 SELECTION VOCABULARY

approach / acercarse *verb* to come near

 ELL
- What are the boys doing?
- How does what they see change?

 Skills Focus

QUESTION 5: Connect to Essential Question

When it comes to the issue of toughness, the narrator continues to pretend he is tough, even when suffering the pain of a sore foot.

 TEXT TALK

What difficulties do Max, Horse and the narrator have when they try to build a lean-to and start a fire?

See paragraphs 109–112: Max's hatchet bounces right out of his hand when he tries to cut down a tree, and all of the branches are wet from the rain.

Skills Focus

QUESTION 4: Plot

The narrator is very close to giving up in the midst of the conflict. He seems determined, though, if his friends still appear to be tough.

116 "No way!" I cried.

117 "All in favor of using the blanket!"

118 Horse and Max both cried, "Aye."

119 Only after I built up a mound of partially burned match sticks and lit *them*, did I get the fire going. It proved that where there's smoke there doesn't have to be much fire. The guys meanwhile draped my blanket over their branch construction. It collapsed twice.

120 About an hour after our arrival, the three of us were gathered inside the tiny space. There was a small fire, but more light came from my flickering flashlight.

121 "No more rain," Horse said with pride.

122 "Just smoke," I said, rubbing my stinging eyes.

123 "We need a vent hole," Horse pointed out.

124 "I could cut it with the hatchet," Max said.

125 "It's my mother's favorite blanket."

126 "And you took it?" Max said.

127 I nodded.

128 "You *are* tough," Horse said.

129 Besides having too much smoke in our eyes and being wet, tired, and in pain, we were starving. I almost said something about giving up, but as far as I could see, the other guys were still tough.

130 Max put his frying pan atop my smoldering smoke. After dumping in the entire contents of his mustard bottle, he threw in the franks. Meanwhile, I bolted down to my last sandwich.

131 "What am I going to eat?" Horse suddenly said.

132 "Your beans," I reminded him.

133 Max offered up his hatchet. "Here. Just chop off the top end of the can."

134 "Oh, right," Horse said. He selected a can, set it in front of him, levered himself onto his knees, then swung down—hard. There was an explosion. For a stunned moment, we just sat there, hands, face, and clothing dripping with beans.

Copyright © BookheadEd Learning, LLC

Reading & Writing Companion

57

NOTES

135   Suddenly Max shouted, "Food fight! Food fight!" and began to paw the stuff off and fling it around.

136   Having a food fight in a cafeteria is one thing. Having one in the middle of a soaking wet lean-to with cold beans during a dark, wet New Jersey night is another. In seconds, the lean-to was down, the fire kicked over, and Max's frankfurters dumped on the ground.

137   "The food!" Max screamed, and began to snatch up the franks. Coated with mustard, dirt, grass, and leaves, they looked positively prehistoric. Still, we wiped the franks clean on our pants then ate them—the franks, that is. Afterward, we picked beans off each other's clothes—the way monkeys help friends get rid of lice.

138   For dessert, Max shared some Tootsie Rolls. After Horse swallowed his sixteenth piece, he announced, "I don't feel so good."

139   The thought of his getting sick was too much. "Let's go home," I said, ashamed to look at the others. To my surprise—and relief—nobody objected.

140   Wet and cold, our way lit by my fast-fading flashlight, we gathered our belongings—most of them, anyway. As we made our way back over the bridge, gusts of wind-blown rain pummeled us until I felt like a used-up punching bag. By the time we got to the subway station, my legs were melting fast. The other guys looked bad too. Other riders moved away from us. One of them murmured, "Juvenile delinquents." To cheer us up, I got out my comic books, but they had congealed into a lump of red, white, and blue pulp.

141   With the subways running slow, it took hours to get home. When we emerged from the High Street Station, it was close to midnight.

142   Before we split up to go to our own homes, we just stood there on a street corner, embarrassed, trying to figure out how to end the day gracefully. I was the one who said, "Okay, I admit it. I'm not as tough as you guys. I gave up first."

143   Max shook his head. "Naw. I wanted to quit, but I wasn't tough enough to do it." He looked to Horse.

144   Horse made a fist. "You saying I'm the one who's tough?" he demanded. "I hate roughing it!"

145   "Me too," I said quickly.

146   "Same for me," Max said.

147   Horse said, "Only thing is, we just have to promise not to tell Mr. Brenkman."

Skills Focus

QUESTION 4: Plot

After the food fight and the collapse of the lean-to, the thought of Horse getting sick is too much for the narrator. This is the turning point in the story. He quits trying to prove to the others how tough he is. I notice that he is ashamed to look at his friends, however, when he suggests they go home.

Skills Focus

QUESTION 4: Plot

In the resolution, the narrator risks opening up about his feelings and discovers that his friends never thought that he wasn't as tough as they are. I think when Max says he wanted to quit but he wasn't tough enough to do it, he's showing that it takes a really tough character to accept and admit defeat.

TEXT TALK

Why do the boys give up on their camping trip and go home?

See paragraphs 139 and 142–146: They are willing to admit that they aren't tough enough to last overnight.

Skills Focus

QUESTION 5: Connect to Essential Question

After opening up about not being as tough as they might seem, the boys grow closer. Sometimes dealing with obstacles helps when you have good friends!

TEXT TALK

What other connections are you able to make with the story?

Answers will vary.

Why didn't the boys give up on the camping trip sooner?

Answers will vary.

B   BEYOND TEXT TALK

Ask each Beyond grade-level student to write one additional discussion question. Then, have one or two students facilitate a discussion, using their questions to guide the conversation.

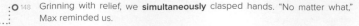

148 Grinning with relief, we **simultaneously** clasped hands. "No matter what," Max reminded us.

149 To which I added, "Scout's Honor."

Reading & Writing Companion   **59**

V   SELECTION VOCABULARY

simultaneously / simultaneamente *adverb* at the same time   COGNATE

ELL
- What are the boys doing?
- Do they agree or disagree?

Reading Comprehension OPTIONAL

Have students complete the digital reading comprehension questions ✔ when they finish reading.

ANSWER KEY

QUESTION 1: A	**QUESTION 5:** B	**QUESTION 9:**
QUESTION 2: C	**QUESTION 6:** C	*See first chart.*
QUESTION 3: B	**QUESTION 7:** D	**QUESTION 10:**
QUESTION 4: A	**QUESTION 8:** B	*See second chart.*

First	Second	Third	Fourth
Horse leaves his mattress on the subway platform unattended.	The boys cross the George Washington Bridge into New Jersey.	Max and Horse assemble a "lean-to" and finally get it to stand successfully.	The narrator discovers that his comic books have been ruined by water damage.

Dialogue	Speaker
"Yeah, but this is an *official* Scout compass."	Max
"You saying I'm the one who's tough?"	Horse
"Okay, I admit it. I'm not as tough as you guys. I gave up first."	Narrator
"You wouldn't *lie*, would you? What about Scout's honor?"	Mr. Brenkman

Connect and Extend OPTIONAL

CONNECT TO EXTENDED WRITING PROJECT

Students may find inspiration in Avi's memoir about a scouting trip gone awry, and see how proper preparation can sometimes prevent a disaster.

BEYOND THE BOOK

Photography: What's in Your Bag?

In "Scout's Honor," each boy packs different items in preparation for the trip. These items reveal important information about each of them. Ask students to:

- Photograph three items of their own that reveal something unique about them.

- In small groups, have students take turns showing their photographs and explaining the significance of their items.

To reflect, ask students:

- What was the most interesting thing you learned about your peers from the items they shared?

- Why do some objects have a deeper meaning than others?

Think Questions

Circulate as students answer Think Questions independently. Scaffolds for these questions are shown on the opposite page.

QUESTION 1: Textual Evidence

The narrator grew up in Brooklyn in the 1940s. Before joining the Boy Scouts, he had never left Brooklyn, so he thinks "anywhere that has lots of trees and is not the city" is country.

QUESTION 2: Textual Evidence

The narrator and Horse jump out of the subway car to get Horse's mattress, but Max is left stuck on the train. It takes the boys a long time to join up again with Max and they find him with "streaks down his cheeks." Max won't admit he was crying, and this shows that even though the boys are friends, they don't want to show any weakness.

QUESTION 3: Textual Evidence

Max and Horse do not object. This surprises the narrator, who thought that he was the only one not tough enough to last through the trip. When they arrive back in Brooklyn, Max admits that he "wanted to quit, but I wasn't tough enough to do it."

QUESTION 4: Context Clues

I think *absorbed* means "focused on." In the story, the boys are reading their comics and miss their subway stop. This shows that they were so focused on the comics that they didn't notice what was going on around them.

QUESTION 5: Context Clues

I think *simultaneously* must mean "at the same time." The word describes the boys clasping hands when they agree that they won't tell Mr. Brenkman about their failed camping trip. Because the boys agree, they act in unity.

Scout's Honor

First Read

Read "Scout's Honor." After you read, complete the Think Questions below.

  THINK QUESTIONS

1. Where did the narrator grow up? How does that influence his idea of the "country"? Cite textual evidence from the selection to support your answer.

2. What happens to Max on the subway? What does the event reveal about their friendship?

3. How do Max and Horse react when the narrator suggests they head back home? Why does this surprise the narrator? Cite textual evidence from the selection to support your answer.

4. Find the word **absorbed** in paragraph 60 of "Scout's Honor." Use context clues in the surrounding sentences, as well as the sentence in which it appears, to determine the word's meaning. Write your definition here and identify clues that helped you figure out its meaning.

5. Use context clues to determine the meaning of **simultaneously** as it is used in paragraph 148 of "Scout's Honor." Write your definition here and identify clues that helped you figure out its meaning. Then check the meaning in a dictionary.

Think Questions

Use the scaffolds below to differentiate instruction for your **ELL** English Language Learners and **A** Approaching grade-level learners.

ELL **BEGINNING** Write a response using the <u>word bank</u> and <u>sentence frames</u>.

INTERMEDIATE Write a response using the <u>sentence frames</u>.

ADVANCED, ADVANCED HIGH Write a response using the <u>Text-Dependent Question Guide</u>.

A **APPROACHING** Write a response using the <u>Text-Dependent Question Guide</u>.

| | INTERMEDIATE | APPROACHING |
| BEGINNING | | ADVANCED, ADVANCED HIGH |

Word Bank	Sentence Frames	Text-Dependent Question Guide
tough Brooklyn focus	The narrator grew up in ____. In the 1940s, Brooklyn did not have a lot of ____. It was very different from the ____.	1. • Where is the narrator from? • When did the narrator grow up there? • What was it like?
think comics country	Max is ____ from his friends. He is scared, and looks like he's been ____. He lies because he is ____. He cares about what his friends ____.	2. • Why does Max end up alone? • What does he look like? • Why does he lie?
separated hold crying	The narrator is worried about being ____. However, Max and Horse also want to go ____. They promise not to ____ anyone that they didn't spend the night.	3. • What was the narrator worried about? • How did Max and Horse feel? • What did the boys agree on?
same time tell trees	The boys are looking at their ____. They miss their train ____. This gives me a clue *absorbed* means to "____ on."	4. • Read: "Then we became so **absorbed** in our Marvel Family comics we missed our station." • What are the boys looking at? • What do the boys miss?
home happened embarrassed stop	The boys ____ hands with each other and feel the same way about what ____. This gives me a clue that *simultaneously* means "at the ____."	5. • Read: "Grinning with relief, we **simultaneously** clasped hands." • What are the boys doing? • How are they feeling?

Skill: Story Structure

Introduce the Skill

Watch the Concept Definition video and read the following definition with your students.

Story structure is the framework writers use to develop the events of the **plot**. Any plot has a central problem or conflict which the story introduces, builds to a climax, and finally solves. The story may be character-driven, exploring one person's emotions, or it could be driven by suspense, with a complicated sequence of events that takes many twists and turns. The events may or may not be presented in chronological order. For example, an author who wishes to build tension may begin with a dramatic **flashback** before introducing the present situation in a story. A character-driven novel might describe events from the point of view of one character, and how the events change him or her. Whatever story structure an author chooses to use, **analyzing** how the events of a chapter or scene fit into the overall structure can help readers identify how it also contributes to the development of the **theme** and **setting**.

 TURN AND TALK

1. What is the plot of your favorite book or movie?

2. How does the plot unfold?

3. What can you learn from the way a book or movie is structured?

ELL **SPEAKING FRAMES**
- The plot of [book/movie title] was ___.
- The [author/director] uses ___ to unfold the events in the plot.
- I can learn about ___ from the structure of a story.

Skill:
Story Structure

Use the Checklist to analyze Story Structure in "Scout's Honor." Refer to the sample student annotations about Story Structure in the text.

••• CHECKLIST FOR STORY STRUCTURE

In order to identify how a particular sentence, chapter, or scene fits into the overall structure of a text, note the following:

✓ the author's use of description, dialogue, and narration and how each develops the events of the plot

✓ the pattern the author uses to organize the events within a story or chapter
  - chronological, or in time order
  - events out of time order

✓ any literary devices the author uses, such as flashback, a part of a story that shows something that happened in the past

✓ any particular sentence, chapter, or scene that contributes to the development of the setting, the plot, and the theme

✓ how a particular sentence, chapter, or scene fits into the overall structure

To analyze how a particular sentence, chapter, or scene fits into the overall structure of a text and contributes to the development of the theme, setting, or plot, consider the following questions:

✓ What are the key events in the story and when did they take place?

✓ What impact does the order of events that take place in the story have on the theme, setting, or plot?

✓ What literary devices does the author use? How do they affect the development of the plot?

✓ How does a particular sentence, chapter, or scene fit into the overall structure? How does it contribute to the development of the theme, setting, or plot?

V   SKILL VOCABULARY

story structure / la estructura de la historia *noun* the outline a writer uses to organize and tell a story

plot / la trama *noun* the sequence of events that form a story

flashback / la escena retrospectiva *noun* a scene in a story, play, movie, or TV show that is set in a time earlier than the events in the main story

Scout's Honor

Skill:
Story Structure

Reread paragraphs 80–98 of "Scout's Honor." Then, using the Checklist on the previous page, answer the multiple-choice questions below.

YOUR TURN

1. Reread paragraph 81. Based on this paragraph, what can the reader conclude about the narrator?

   ○ A. The narrator is irritated with Horse because he does not know how to proceed bravely in this situation.

   ○ B. Although he attempts to be brave, the narrator is still feeling anxious about the journey to the country.

   ○ C. The narrator understands that Horse is unable to stay calm and tries to comfort him in his time of need.

   ○ D. Horse's anxiety creates a sense of tension between the boys, thus the narrator is unsettled.

2. Which of the following best describes the theme based on the passage provided?

   ○ A. Desperate times call for desperate measures.

   ○ B. In dark times, friends can offer the best support.

   ○ C. Blindly following others can cause trouble.

   ○ D. In life, we sometimes take on more than we can handle.

3. How does this passage contribute to the rest of the story's plot?

   ○ A. The events in the passage highlight the turning point of the plot because the boys are afraid.

   ○ B. The dialogue in the passage conveys a sense of urgency because the boys are not sure they will survive.

   ○ C. The passage emphasizes key, humbling events in the story that support the overall theme.

   ○ D. The narration in the passage highlights a dark tone that is maintained throughout the plot.

Please note that excerpts and passages in the StudySync® library and this workbook are intended as touchstones to generate interest in an author's work. The excerpts and passages do not substitute for the reading of entire texts, and StudySync® strongly recommends that students seek out and purchase the whole literary or informational work in order to experience it as the author intended. Links to online resellers are available in our digital library. In addition, complete works may be ordered through an authorized reseller by filling out and returning to StudySync® the order form enclosed in this workbook.

62   Reading & Writing
Companion

V SKILL VOCABULARY

analyze / analizar *verb* to consider in detail and discover essential features or meaning   COGNATE

theme / el tema *noun* the central idea or message of a work of literature, often expressed as a general statement about life

setting / el escenario *noun* the time and place of the story

---

 ## Your Turn

Ask students to complete the Your Turn Activity.

QUESTION 1

A. Incorrect. The narrator is not irritated with Horse; he is nervous about the situation at hand.

B. **Correct.** The narrator feels better when he understands that Horse feels the same way about the journey as he does. They are both anxious.

C. Incorrect. The narrator does not attempt to comfort Horse when he sees that he is panicked.

D. Incorrect. The narrator feels unsettled about the journey, not because Horse is nervous.

QUESTION 2

A. Incorrect. While the boys are feeling anxious, they do not resort to desperate actions in their time of need.

B. Incorrect. Although this is a dark time for the boys, they do not offer one another direct support.

C. Incorrect. The boys are in this together as an assignment from the Boy Scouts. They are not blindly following anyone.

D. **Correct.** The boys attempt to remain brave despite the fact that they really do not know what they are doing.

QUESTION 3

A. Incorrect. This scene is part of the conflict, not the turning point. The boys are not afraid; they are just becoming skeptical of their decision to camp.

B. Incorrect. The boys are having a rough time, but there is no evidence to support the idea that they will not survive.

C. **Correct.** This passage highlights one of the moments when the boys come to understand that they are not as tough as they think.

D. Incorrect. Although the boys are struggling, there are hints of humor sprinkled throughout the passage. A dark tone is not maintained.

Skill: Plot

Introduce the Skill

Watch the Concept Definition video and read the following definition with your students.

The events that take place in a story or **narrative** are called the **plot**. These events give the story a beginning, a middle, and an end, and they are influenced by literary elements such as character and setting. Events in a story begin with the **inciting incident**, or the moment in which the **conflict**, or main problem, is introduced. As characters attempt to solve the problem, it may become more complicated, and the characters may undergo changes as they respond to rising tension. For example, the main character may learn the value of patience as he or she works toward finding a solution, or may begin to understand or sympathize with another character's difficulties. The **turning point** in a plot occurs when a key event or decision leads to a **resolution**, or a way to solve the problem.

TURN AND TALK

1. What are some memorable plot elements from your favorite books, TV shows, or movies?

2. What conflict or problem do the characters have? What event in the inciting incident reveals the conflict and creates tension?

ELL SPEAKING FRAMES

- The plot element I remember best is ____. I liked this part of the story because ____.
- The characters' conflict was ____. The event that introduced the conflict was ____.
- The resolution of the conflict came when ____.

Scout's Honor

PLOT

Skill: Plot

sync•skills

Use the Checklist to analyze Plot in "Scout's Honor." Refer to the sample student annotations about Plot in the text.

••• CHECKLIST FOR PLOT

In order to determine the plot and how a particular story's or drama's plot unfolds, note the following:

✓ specific plot events as they occur in the story

✓ series of episodes in the plot

✓ ways characters respond or change as the plot moves toward a resolution

✓ dialogue between or among characters that reveals their growth or change

To describe how a particular story's or drama's plot unfolds in a series of episodes as well as how the characters respond or change as the plot moves toward a resolution, consider the following questions:

✓ What is the plot? What are the key events in the plot?

✓ How does the series of episodes in the story help unfold the plot?

✓ How do the characters respond or change as the plot moves through the conflict and toward a resolution?

Reading & Writing Companion **63**

V SKILL VOCABULARY

narrative / la narración *noun* a story, real or imagined, consisting of connected events

plot / la trama *noun* the sequence of events that form a story

inciting incident / el incidente generador *noun* the first event in which the conflict becomes apparent

PLOT

Skill:
Plot

Reread paragraphs 129–139 from the text. Then, using the Checklist on the previous page, answer the multiple-choice questions below.

↻ YOUR TURN

1. Based on the narrator's thoughts in paragraph 129, the reader can conclude that —

   ○ A. the narrator's friends are close to giving up.
   ○ B. the narrator still doesn't think he's tough enough.
   ○ C. the boys are out of food.
   ○ D. the narrator is going to tell his friends that he gives up and wants to go home.

2. The turning point of the story is when —

   ○ A. Max shouts "food fight!"
   ○ B. the lean-to is knocked down.
   ○ C. the can of beans explodes all over them.
   ○ D. the boys eat the dirty franks.

3. Which paragraph includes the resolution of the story's conflict?

   ○ A. 138
   ○ B. 136
   ○ C. 139
   ○ D. 135

SKILL VOCABULARY

conflict / el conflicto *noun* the main problem or struggle that characters face in a story   COGNATE

turning point / el clímax *noun* a moment when the series of events in a plot suddenly changes

resolution / la resolución *noun* the final outcome of the story's conflict   COGNATE

⚙ Your Turn

Ask students to complete the Your Turn Activity.

QUESTION 1

A. Incorrect. There is no evidence at this point in the story that the narrator's friends are close to giving up.

B. Correct. The narrator thinks that his friends Horse and Max are "still tough," and because he wants to go home, that means they are tougher than he is.

C. Incorrect. The boys are "starving," but they still have food that they haven't eaten yet.

D. Incorrect. The narrator thinks that his friends are "still tough," and so he is afraid to tell them he wants to give up.

QUESTION 2

A. Incorrect. The food fight comes after the turning point.

B. Incorrect. The lean-to falling down is just one event that happens after the beans explode.

C. Correct. The explosion is the big event, or "stunned moment," that leads the boys to make a decision to give up and go home.

D. Incorrect. Eating the dirty franks is just another event after the food fight.

QUESTION 3

A. Incorrect.

B. Incorrect.

C. Correct. The boys finally agree to give up and go home as the best way to resolve all the problems with the camping trip.

D. Incorrect.

Close Read

Skills Focus

QUESTION 1: Character

See paragraphs 15, 29, and 67.

QUESTION 2: Story Structure

See paragraphs 15–24.

QUESTION 3: Plot

See paragraphs 42, 77, and 97–100.

QUESTION 4: Plot

See paragraphs 129, 138–139, and 142–144.

QUESTION 5: Connect to Essential Question

See paragraphs 59, 103, and 148–149.

✔ CHECK FOR SUCCESS

If students struggle to respond to Skills Focus Question 1, ask students the following questions:

- What does the narrator tell you about his relationship with his friends in paragraph 15?

- How would you describe the narrator's character in paragraphs 16-20?

- What personality trait does the narrator display in paragraph 67?

Close Read

Reread "Scout's Honor." As you reread, complete the Skills Focus questions below. Then use your answers and annotations from the questions to help you complete the Write activity.

◎ SKILLS FOCUS

1. Think about how the narrator reacts to the challenges the characters face. Identify what these reactions tell you about his personality.

2. Think about the beginning of the "Scout's Honor" when the narrator tells his friends he's going camping. Using textual evidence, identify how this scene is important to the rest of the story.

3. How boys can prove they are tough: this is the central conflict of Avi's story. Identify how each character reacts to key events in the plot as the boys try to resolve the conflict through their camping trip.

4. Use key events, including the inciting incident and moments of conflict, to determine how the resolution of the conflict contributes to the meaning of the story.

5. Identify how the development of the characters and plot in "Scout's Honor" connects to the Essential Question: "What do we do when life gets hard?"

✏ WRITE

LITERARY ANALYSIS: There are many challenges in "Scout's Honor" that the boys face. How do the characters' responses to these challenges help develop the plot and help readers interpret the events in the plot—such as the inciting incident, conflict, turning point and resolution—as they take place? Write a response of 200 words. Support your writing with evidence from the text.

Reading & Writing Companion   **65**

Writer's Notebook

Connect to Essential Question: Give students time to reflect on how "Scout's Honor" connects to the unit's essential question "What do we do when life gets hard?" by freewriting in their Writer's Notebooks.

ELL **Beginning & Intermediate**

Read aloud the unit's essential question: "What do we do when life gets hard?" Encourage students to draw their connections or allow students to write in their native language. Circulate around the room, prompting students for their thoughts as they respond orally or through pantomime.

Advanced & Advanced High

Allow students to share their reflections orally in pairs or small groups before freewriting.

Collaborative Conversation

SCAFFOLDS

Break students up into collaborative conversation groups to discuss the Close Read prompt. Ask students to use the StudySyncTV episode as a model for their discussion. Remind them to reference their Skills Focus annotations in their discussion.

There are many challenges in "Scout's Honor" that the boys face. How do the characters' responses to these challenges help develop the plot and help readers interpret (AV) the events in the plot--such as the inciting incident, conflict, turning point and resolution--as they take place? Write a response of 200 words. Support your writing with evidence from the text.

Use the scaffolds below to differentiate instruction for your **ELL** English Language Learners and **A** Approaching grade-level learners.

ELL **BEGINNING, INTERMEDIATE** Use the discussion guide and speaking frames to facilitate the discussion with support from the teacher.

ADVANCED, ADVANCED HIGH Use the discussion guide and speaking frames to facilitate the discussion in mixed-level groups.

A **APPROACHING** Use the discussion guide to facilitate the discussion in mixed-level groups.

APPROACHING

ADVANCED, ADVANCED HIGH

BEGINNING, INTERMEDIATE

Discussion Guide	Speaking Frames
1. How do the characters respond to challenges in the plot?	• The characters respond to challenges by ____. • Their responses tell me that ____.
2. What are some events the boys experience while camping, and why are they important to the plot?	• While camping, the boys ____. • This is important because ____.

Review Prompt and Rubric

Before students begin writing, review the writing prompt and rubric with the class.

LITERARY ANALYSIS: The boys face many challenges in 'Scout's Honor". How do their responses to these challenges help develop the plot and help readers interpret (AV) the events in the plot? Write a response of 200 words. Support your writing with evidence from the text.

ELL PROMPT GUIDE

A
- In which part of the story does the narrator respond to a challenge?
- What other characters react to challenges in the story?
- How do characters' responses help you interpret the plot?

Score	Story Structure	Plot	Language and Conventions
4	The writer clearly analyzes and explains how the characters' responses to challenges help develop the plot.The writer provides exemplary analysis, using relevant evidence from the text.	The writer clearly analyzes and explains how the characters' responses to challenges help readers **interpret** the events in the plot as they unfold. The writer provides exemplary analysis, using relevant evidence from the text.	The writer demonstrates a consistent command of grammar, punctuation, and usage conventions. Although minor errors may be evident, they do not detract from the fluency or the clarity of the essay.
3	The writer analyzes and explains how the characters' responses to challenges help develop the plot. The writer provides sufficient analysis, using relevant evidence from the text most of the time.	The writer analyzes and explains how the characters' responses to challenges help readers **interpret** the events in the plot as they unfold. The writer provides sufficient analysis, using relevant evidence from the text most of the time.	The writer demonstrates an adequate command of grammar, punctuation, and usage conventions. Although some errors may be evident, they create few (if any) disruptions in the fluency of the writing or the clarity of the essay.
2	The writer begins to analyze or explain how the characters' responses to challenges help develop the plot, but the analysis is incomplete. The writer uses relevant evidence from the text only some of the time.	The writer begins to analyze or explain how the characters' responses to challenges help readers **interpret** the events in the plot as they unfold, but the analysis is incomplete. The writer uses relevant evidence from the text only some of the time.	The writer demonstrates a partial command of grammar, punctuation, and usage conventions. Some distracting errors may be evident, at times creating minor disruptions in the fluency or clarity of the writing.
1	The writer attempts to analyze or explain how the characters' responses to challenges help develop the plot, but the analysis is not successful. The writer uses little or no relevant evidence from the text.	The writer attempts to analyze or explain how the characters' responses to challenges help readers **interpret** the events in the plot as they unfold, but the analysis is not successful. The writer uses little or no relevant evidence from the text.	The writer demonstrates little or no command of grammar, punctuation, and usage conventions. Serious and persistent errors create disruptions in the fluency of the writing and sometimes interfere with meaning.
0	The writer does not provide a relevant response to the prompt or does not provide a response at all.	The writer does not provide a relevant response to the prompt or does not provide a response at all.	Serious and persistent errors overwhelm the writing and interfere with the meaning of the response as a whole, making the writer's meaning impossible to understand.

Write

Ask students to complete the writing assignment using textual evidence to support their answers.

Use the scaffolds below to differentiate instruction for your **ELL** English Language Learners and **A** Approaching grade-level learners.

ELL **BEGINNING** With the help of the <u>word bank</u>, write a response using <u>paragraph frame 1</u>.

INTERMEDIATE With the help of the <u>word bank</u>, write a response using <u>paragraph frames 1 and 2</u>.

ADVANCED, ADVANCED HIGH Write a response of differentiated length using the <u>sentence starters</u>.

A **APPROACHING** Write a response of differentiated length using the <u>sentence starters</u>.

| BEGINNING | | ADVANCED, ADVANCED HIGH | |
| INTERMEDIATE | | APPROACHING | |
Word Bank	**Paragraph Frame 1**	**Paragraph Frame 2**	**Sentence Starters**
challenge plot conflict around tough	The narrator faces a ____ when he crosses the bridge. He wants to turn ____, but he doesn't. This helps me understand that the narrator wants to be ____, which is the ____ of the story. When his friends start to cross, I know that the ____ will continue.	Later in the story, the boys have lots of ____ while camping. The boys don't decide to go home until ____. This helps me understand that the resolution is ____.	• The conflict of the story is . . . • In paragraph ____, the narrator responds to a challenge by . . . • In paragraph ____, the character ____ responds to a challenge by____ . . . • To resolve the conflict, the characters . . . • I understand this plot development because . . .

Peer Review

Students should submit substantive feedback to two peers using the review instructions below.

- How well does this response answer the prompt?
- How well does the writer support his or her ideas with details and examples from the text?
- Which sentence in the writer's response made you think differently about the text?
- What did the writer do well in this response? What does the writer need to work on?

Rate

Respond to the following with a point rating that reflects your opinion.

	1 2 3 4
Ideas	■ ■ ■ □
Evidence	■ ■ ■ ■
Language and Conventions	■ ■ □ □

Submit

ELL **A** **SENTENCE FRAMES**

- You were able to (completely / partly / almost) ____ answer the prompt because ____.
- You could answer the prompt more completely by ____.
- You supported the idea of . . . with the detail of ____.

- One idea that needs more support is ____.
- I thought differently about the text after reading ____.
- My favorite part of your response is ____.

The Good Samaritan

FICTION
René Saldaña, Jr.
2007

Introduction

René Saldaña, Jr.'s 2003 collection of short stories, *Finding Our Way*, features adolescents and young adults searching for answers wherever they are to be found. Encompassing universal experiences and rites of passage, Saldaña, Jr.'s stories take place in Hispanic neighborhoods ranging from Georgia to the south of Texas, where the author was born and raised. The collection's opening story, "The Good Samaritan," is told through the eyes of teenage Rey. As Rey's relationship with a neighborhood family turns sour, he soon finds himself faced with an age-old moral dilemma.

The story opens with Rey standing outside his friend Orlando's house, where he had been invited to swim in the pool. Orlando's mom tells Rey that Orlando is not home. Orlando's father, Mr. Sánchez, also breaks promises. For instance, Mr. Sánchez asked Rey to help build a basketball court and do yard work in exchange for some pool time, but didn't follow through. Later in the day, Rey is on his way to pick up his younger brother from summer school when he sees Mr. Sánchez stranded on the side of the road with a flat tire. Rey decides not to help him because he thinks that Mr. Sánchez doesn't deserve his assistance. However, when he imagines his own father in Mr. Sánchez's position, Rey reconsiders and turns the car around. To thank Rey, Mr. Sánchez invites him over for a barbecue. Rey declines, choosing to play basketball with his friends instead.

 Proficiency-leveled summaries and summaries in multiple languages are available digitally.

 Audio and audio text highlighting are available with this text.

CONNECT TO ESSENTIAL QUESTION

What do we do when life gets hard?

From René Saldaña, Jr.'s 2003 collection of short stories, "The Good Samaritan" is told through the eyes of a teenage boy named Rey. When his relationship with a neighborhood family turns sour, Rey soon finds himself faced with an age-old moral dilemma.

Access Complex Text

LEXILE: 720   WORD COUNT: 2,553

The following areas may be challenging for students, particularly **ELL** English Language Learners and **A** Approaching grade-level learners.

Purpose	Sentence Vocabulary	Prior Knowledge
• The author's purpose for writing the selection may be rather ambiguous to some students. • Point out Mr. Sánchez's reaction when Hernando calls him *vato* (dude). Then have students reread the last line of the story to determine how the narrator responds to Mr. Sánchez's invitation and what that implies.	• The selection contains some words in Spanish. • Words and phrases such as *mejor con regresen mañana* (better come back tomorrow), *pues* (well), and *barrio* (neighborhood) may need to be defined.	• Some of the Spanish words in the text have connotations that may be unfamiliar to students. • Point out that a *barrio* is a neighborhood where people usually know one another. This explains why Mr. Sánchez would walk around the neighborhood visiting.

 SCAFFOLDS **ELL** ENGLISH LANGUAGE LEARNERS   **A** APPROACHING GRADE LEVEL   **B** BEYOND GRADE LEVEL

These icons identify differentiation strategies and scaffolded support for a variety of students. See the digital lesson plan for additional differentiation strategies and scaffolds.

Instructional Path

The print teacher's edition includes essential point-of-use instruction and planning tools. Complete lesson plans and program documents appear in your digital teacher account.

First Read: The Good Samaritan

Objectives: After an initial reading and discussion of the text, students will be able to identify and describe character traits and setting details as well as articulate the conflict that is integral to the story's plot.

Skill: Summarizing

Objectives: After rereading and discussing a model of close reading, students will be able to provide a summary of the text free of personal opinions or judgments.

Close Read: The Good Samaritan

Objectives: After engaging in a close reading and discussion of the text, students will be able to summarize the story's plot through the characters' dialogue, actions, and motivations in a response for a debate.

Blast: Rewriting History

Objectives: After exploring background information and research links about a topic, students will respond to a question with a 140-character answer.

DIGITAL ONLY

Progress Monitoring

Opportunities to Learn	Opportunities to Demonstrate Learning	Opportunities to Reteach
Summarizing		
⚙ Skill: Summarizing	⚙ Skill: Summarizing • Your Turn ▣ Close Read • Skills Focus • Collaborative Conversation • Write	⚙ Unit 2 Skill: Summarizing - We're On The Same Team ⚙ Unit 6 Skill: Summarizing - Bronx Masquerade ⚙ Spotlight Skill: Summarizing

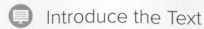 # First Read

René Saldaña, Jr.

The Good Samaritan

Entry Point

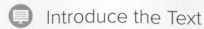 ## Introduce the Text

As a class, watch the video preview ▶ and have students read the introduction in pairs to make connections to the video preview.

To activate prior knowledge and experiences, ask students:

- What part of the video stood out to you the most?
- What is one prediction you can make about the story you're going to read?

ELL SPEAKING FRAMES

- The ____ in the video makes me think ____.
- The video shows ____. This makes me wonder ____.
- I think the text will ____. I think this because ____.
- I predict that there will be ____. I believe this because ____.

As students prepare to read "The Good Samaritan," share the following information with them to provide context.

✓ René Saldaña, Jr.'s experiences during his days teaching middle and high school in Texas have deeply influenced his writing. While grappling with how to best teach authentic writing, he drew inspiration from his Abuelo Federico (Uncle Federico) and began telling short stories as a way to deliver a stimulating form of writing instruction.

✓ As he is a young adult novelist, many of the stories René Saldaña, Jr. writes are about the spirit and strength of teens.

"Let him do his own dirty work for once. He could stay out there and melt in this heat for all I cared."

1 I know he's in there, I thought. I saw the curtains of his bedroom move, only a little, yes, but they moved.

2 Yesterday Orlie told me, "Come over tomorrow afternoon. We'll hang out by the pool."

3 I rang the doorbell again. Then I knocked.

4 The door creaked open. The afternoon light crept into the dark living room inch by slow inch. Mrs. Sánchez, Orlie's mom, stuck her head through the narrow opening, her body hidden behind the door. "Hi, Rey, how can I help you?"

5 "Ah, Mrs. Sánchez, is Orlando here?" I tried looking past her but only saw a few pictures hanging on the wall. One of the Sánchez family all dressed up fancy and smiling, standing in front of a gray marble background.

6 "No, he's not. He went with his father to Mission."

7 "Oh, because Orlando said he would be here, and told me to come over."

8 "They won't be back until later tonight," she said. "You can come by tomorrow and see if he's here. You know how it is in the summer. He and his dad are always doing work here and there. Come back tomorrow, but call first."

9 "It's just that he said I could come by and swim in your pool. Dijo, 'Tomorrow, come over. I'll be here. We'll go swimming.'"

10 "I'm sorry he told you that, but without him or my husband here, you won't be able to use the pool," me dijo Mrs. Sánchez.

11 "Okay," I said.

12 "Maybe tomorrow?"

13 "Yeah, maybe."

14 But there was no maybe about it. I wouldn't be coming back. Because I knew that Orlando was in the house, he just didn't want to hang out. Bien codo con

Analyze Vocabulary Using Context Clues

In paragraph 17, focus on the sentence that uses the word *supervision*. Point out these context clues:

1. First I notice the word *vision,* which can mean "the act of seeing," inside the word *supervision.* I also notice the word *super,* which as a prefix can mean "over."

2. When I read the sentence again, I notice that Mr. Sánchez is heading out right after lunch and doesn't feel safe leaving the boys alone. If he isn't there, he can't keep an eye on the boys and check their behavior.

CHECK FOR SUCCESS

If students are unable to make predictions, revisit the Checklist section of the Grade 6 Context Clues lesson with the class. After revisiting, guide students as they make predictions about the next bold word in the text in paragraph 19.

TEXT TALK

How does Rey know that Orlie is home even though his mom says he went to Mission?

See paragraph 1: Rey sees the curtain move.

How does Mr. Sánchez break his promise about swimming in exchange for yard work?

See paragraphs 14–18: Mr. Sánchez keeps finding reasons and making excuses why the boys cannot use the pool.

Skills Focus

QUESTION 1: Summarizing

Mr. Sánchez promises the boys they can swim in the pool if they help him with yard work, but he keeps putting them off with excuses. Rey and his friends realize that Mr. Sánchez has suckered them.

Skills Focus

QUESTION 3: Connect to Essential Question

Rey can't forget the times that Mr. Sánchez has hustled the boys by making promises, but not delivering.

Skills Focus

QUESTION 1: Summarizing

Here is further proof that Mr. Sánchez takes advantage of the boys. He doesn't exactly lie this time—he does provide a bottle of Coke and a bag of chips. He makes an excuse when he says that he didn't know there would be so many boys.

Summarizing

Which characters are involved in this event, and what happens?

The reader highlighted sections that describe how Rey and his friends think that Mr. Sánchez takes advantage of their help.

TEXT TALK

What happens when Mr. Sánchez promises the boys they can use the basketball court in exchange for helping build it?

See paragraphs 22–33: Although Mr. Sánchez tells them they can use the court anytime, he chases them away the first time they use it when he isn't home.

The Good Samaritan

 NOTES

su pool. Plain stingy. And tricky. This guy invited me and a few others over all summer to help his dad with some yard work because Mr. Sánchez told us, "If you help clean up the yard, you boys can use the pool any time you want so long as one of us is here." And we cleaned up his yard. On that hot day the water that smelled of chlorine looked delicious to me. And after a hard day's work cleaning his yard, I so looked forward to taking a dip. I'd even worn my trunks under my work clothes. Then Mr. Sánchez said, "Come by tomorrow. I don't want you fellas to track all this dirt into the pool."

15 "We can go home and shower and be back," said Hernando.

16 "No, mejor que regresen mañana. I'll be here tomorrow and we can swim. After lunch, okay. For sure we'll do it tomorrow," said Mr. Sánchez.

17 The following day he was there, but he was headed out right after lunch and he didn't feel safe leaving us behind without **supervision**. "If one of you drowns, your parents will be angry at me and…" He didn't say it, but he didn't need to. One of our parents could sue him. And he needed that like I needed another F in my Geometry I class!

18 Or, we figured out later, he could have just said, "I used you saps to do my dirty work. And I lied about the pool, suckers!"

19 I don't know why we hadn't learned our lesson. Twice before he had **hustled** us this way of our time and effort. Always dangling the carrot in front of our eyes, then snatching it away last second.

20 One of those times he promised us soft drinks and snacks if we helped clean up a yard across the street from his house. It wasn't his yard to worry about, but I guess he just didn't like to see the weeds growing as tall as dogs. What if he had company? What would they think? And he was angling for a position on the school board. How could a politico live in such filth!

21 Well, we did get a soft drink and chips, only it was one two-liter bottle of Coke and one bag of chips for close to ten of us. We had no cups, and the older, stronger boys got dibs on most of the eats. "I didn't know there'd be so many of you," he said. "Well, share. And thanks. You all are good, strong boys."

22 The next time was real hard **labor**. He said, "Help me dig these holes here, then we can put up some basketball rims. Once the cement dries on the court itself, you all can come over and play anytime since it's kind of your court too. That is, if you help me dig the holes."

23 And we did. We dug and dug and dug for close to six hours straight until we got done, passing on the shovel from one of us to the next. But we got it done. We had our court. Mr. Sánchez kept his word. He reminded us we could come over to play anytime, and we took special care not to dunk and grab hold of the rim. Even the shortest kid could practically dunk it because

---

 SELECTION VOCABULARY

supervision / *noun* the act of watching over or directing COGNATE

ELL
- Who is being "supervised"? Who is doing the act of "supervising"?
- What is Mr. Sánchez doing right after lunch? What does he not feel safe doing?

hustle / *estafar* **verb** to get what one wants by force or persuasion

ELL
- What are the boys being "hustled" out of?
- What does Rey accuse Mr. Sánchez of doing?

NOTES

the baskets were so low. But we'd seen the rims all bent down at the different yards at school. And we didn't want that for our court.

24 One day, we wanted to play a little three on three. After knocking on the different doors several times and getting no answer, we figured the Sánchez family had gone out. We decided that it'd be okay to play. We weren't going to do anything wrong. The court was far enough from the house that we couldn't possibly break a window. And Mr. Sánchez had said we could come over any time we wanted. It was our court, after all. Those were his words exactly.

25 A little later in the afternoon, Mr. Sánchez drove up in his truck, honking and honking at us. "Here they come. Maybe Orlando and Marty can play with us," someone said.

26 Pues, it was not to be. The truck had just come to a standstill when Mr. Sánchez shot out of the driver's side. He ran up to us, waving his hands in the air like a crazy man, first saying, then screaming, "What are you guys doing here? You all can't be here when I'm not here."

27 "But you told us we could come over anytime. And we knocked and knocked, and we were being very careful.'

28 "It doesn't matter. You all shouldn't be here when I'm not home. What if you had broken something?" he said.

29 "But we didn't," I said.

30 "But if you had, then who would have been responsible for paying to replace it? I'm sure every one of you would have denied breaking anything."

31 "Este vato!" said Hernando.

32 "Vato? Is that what you called me? I'm no street punk, no hoodlum. I'll have you know, I've worked my whole life, and I won't be called a vato. It's Mr. Sánchez. Got that? And you boys know what—from now on, you are not allowed to come here whether I'm home or not! You all messed it up for yourselves. You've shown me so much disrespect today you don't deserve to play on my court. It was a **privilege** and not a right, and you messed it up. Now leave!"

33 Hernando, who was fuming, said, "Orale, guys, let's go." He took the ball from one of the smaller boys and began to run toward the nearest basket. He slowed down the closer he came to the basket and leapt in the air. I'd never seen him jump with such grace. He floated from the foul line, his long hair like wings, all the way to the basket. He grabbed the ball in both his hands and let go of it at the last moment. Instead of dunking the ball, he let it shoot up to the sky; then he wrapped his fingers around the rim and pulled down as hard as

Skill:
Summarizing

Mr. Sánchez angrily kicks the boys off of his volleyball court. He feels disrespected. Mr. Sánchez says the boys were wrong to let themselves onto his property when he wasn't home.

Reading & Writing Companion **69**

Summarizing

What does the reader note about the event?

The reader gives an objective account of Mr. Sánchez kicking the boys off the court.

SELECTION VOCABULARY

labor / el trabajo *noun* work

ELL
- What does Mr. Sánchez want the boys to do?
- What do the boys do for six hours?

privilege / el privilegio *noun* a special opportunity or benefit COGNATE

ELL
- What are the boys no longer allowed to do?
- What does Mr. Sánchez say "privilege" is not?

The Good Samaritan

he could, hanging on for a few seconds. Then the rest of us walked after him, dejected. He hadn't bent the rim even a millimeter. Eventually Orlie talked us into going back when his dad wasn't home. His baby brother, Marty, was small and slow, and Orlie wanted some competition on the court.

34   Today was it for me, though. I made up my mind never to go back to the Sánchezes'. I walked to the little store for a Fanta Orange. That and a grape Popsicle would cool me down. I sat on the bench outside, finished off the drink, returned the bottle for my nickel refund, and headed for home.

35   As soon as I walked through our front door, my mother said, "Mi'jo, you need to go pick up your brother at summer school. He missed the bus."

36   "Again? He probably missed it on purpose, Ama. He's always walking over to Leo's Grocery to talk to his little girlfriends, then he calls when he needs a ride." I turned toward the bedroom.

37   "Come back here," she said. So I turned and took a seat at the table. "Have you forgotten the times we had to go pick you up? Your brother always went with us, no matter what time it was."

38   "Yeah, but I was doing school stuff. Football, band. He's in summer school just piddling his time away!"

39   She looked at me as she brushed sweat away from her face with the back of her hand and said, "Just go pick him up, and hurry home. On the way back, stop at Circle Seven and buy some tortillas. There's money on the table."

40   I shook my head in disgust. Here I was, already a senior, having to be my baby brother's chauffeur.

41   I'd driven halfway to Leo's Grocery when I saw Mr. Sánchez's truck up ahead by the side of the road. I could just make him out sitting under the shade of his truck. Every time he heard a car coming his way, he'd raise his head slightly, try to catch the driver's attention by staring at him, then he'd hang his head again when the car didn't stop.

42   I slowed down as I **approached.** Could he tell it was me driving? When he looked up at my car, I could swear he almost smiled, thinking he had been saved. He had been leaning his head between his bent knees, and I could tell he was tired; his white shirt stuck to him because of all the sweat. His sock on one leg was bunched up at his ankle like a carnation. He had the whitest legs I'd ever seen on a Mexican. Whiter than even my dad's. I kept on looking straight; that is, I made like I was looking ahead, not a care in the world, but out of the corner of my eye I saw that he had a flat tire, that he had gotten two of the lug nuts off but hadn't gotten to the others, that the crowbar lay half on his other foot and half on the ground beside him, that his hair was matted by sweat to his forehead.

70   Reading & Writing Companion

 TEXT TALK

What does Rey first do when he sees Mr. Sánchez by the side of the road?

See paragraphs 42–44: Rey drives by, pretending not to see Mr. Sánchez.

 SELECTION VOCABULARY

approach / acercarse *verb* to come near

ELL
- What does Rey see ahead?
- Who is Rey "approaching"?

NOTES

43 I knew that look. I'd probably looked just like that digging those holes for our basketball court, cleaning up his yard and the one across the street from his house. I wondered if he could use a cold two-liter Coke right about now! If he was dreaming of taking a dip in his pool!

44 I drove on. No way was I going to help him out again! Let him do his own dirty work for once. He could stay out there and melt in this heat for all I cared. And besides, someone else will stop, I thought. Someone who doesn't know him like I do.

45 And I knew that when Mr. Sánchez got home, he'd stop at my house on his walk around the barrio. My dad would be watering the plants, his evening ritual to relax from a hard day at work, and Mr. Sánchez would mention in passing that I had probably not seen him by the side of the road so I hadn't stopped to help him out; "Kids today" he would say to my dad, "not a care in the world, their heads up in the clouds somewhere." My dad would call me out and ask me to tell him and Mr. Sánchez why I hadn't helped out a neighbor when he needed it most. I'd say, to both of them, "That was you? I thought you and Orlie were in Mission taking care of some business, so it never **occurred** to me to stop to help a neighbor. Geez, I'm so sorry." Or I could say, "You know, I was in such a hurry to pick up my brother in La Joya that I didn't even notice you by the side of the road."

46 I'd be off the hook. Anyways, why should I be the one to extend a helping hand when he's done every one of us in the barrio wrong in one way or another! He deserves to sweat a little. A taste of his own bad medicine. Maybe he'll learn a lesson.

47 But I remembered the look in his eyes as I drove past him. That same tired look my father had when he'd get home from work and he didn't have the strength to take off his boots. My father always looked like he'd been working for centuries without any rest. He'd sit there in front of the television on his favorite green vinyl sofa chair and stare at whatever was on TV. He'd sit there for an hour before he could move, before he could eat his supper and take his shower, that same look on his face Mr. Sánchez had just now.

48 What if this were my dad stranded on the side of the road? I'd want someone to stop for him.

49 "My one good deed for today," I told myself. "And I'm doing it for my dad really, not for Mr. Sánchez."

50 I made a U-turn, drove back to where he was still sitting, turned around again, and pulled up behind him.

51 "I thought that was you, Rey," he said. He wiped at his forehead with his shirtsleeve. "And when you drove past, I thought you hadn't seen me. Thank

Reading & Writing Companion   71

Skills Focus

QUESTION 3: Connect to Essential Question

It's a challenge to help someone you don't like or think of as deserving your help. Past experiences make Rey want to teach Mr. Sánchez a lesson by letting him solve his own problem. And Rey could probably get away with not helping without getting in trouble. In the end, though, Rey can't leave Mr. Sánchez stranded because he wouldn't want his father stranded in the same situation.

Skills Focus

QUESTION 2: Character

Rey doesn't trust or like Mr. Sánchez. But he does love and care about his dad. When he sees that look on Mr. Sánchez's face, Rey thinks of his dad. Since he would want someone to help his dad in the same situation, he decides to help Mr. Sánchez. But he does it for his dad, not for Mr. Sánchez. This makes me think that Rey has a big heart. He is generous.

TEXT TALK

Why does Rey change his mind?

See paragraphs 47–48: Rey remembers the look on Mr. Sánchez's face and it reminds him of his father. This makes him realize that he would want someone to help his father.

SELECTION VOCABULARY

occur / ocurrir *verb* to come to mind   COGNATE

• What does Rey plan to tell his dad?
• What never "occurred" to Rey?

Prepare for Advanced Courses

Direct students to reread paragraphs 19–31.

Use the activity below to differentiate instruction for your **B** Beyond grade-level learners.

Ask students: How would you describe Rey's tone in this section of the story? How does his tone affect the reader's opinion of Mr. Sánchez?

Sample answer; answers will vary: Rey's tone in this section is annoyed. Mr. Sánchez has taken advantage of Rey and his friends multiple times, "Always dangling the carrot in front of [their] eyes, then snatching it away last second." Rey is fed up with helping him out, only for Mr. Sánchez to ignore his end of the bargain. Hearing Rey describe Mr. Sánchez this way makes the reader feel similarly toward Mr. Sánchez, sympathizing with Rey.

TEXT TALK

What does Rey finally do?

See paragraphs 50–56: Rey changes the tire for Mr. Sánchez but declines his invitation to the barbecue.

What are the positive relationship skills that Rey displays in the story?

Answers may vary.

> **B** Ask each Beyond grade level student to write one additional discussion question. Then, have one or two students facilitate a discussion, using their questions to guide the conversation.

The Good Samaritan

NOTES

goodness you stopped. I've been here for close to forty-five minutes and nobody's stopped to help. Thank goodness you did. I just can't get the tire off."

52   Thank my father, I thought. If it weren't for my father, you'd still be out here.

53   I had that tire changed in no time. All the while Mr. Sánchez stood behind me and a bit to my left saying, "Yes, thank God you came by. Boy, it's hot out here. You're a good boy, Rey. You'll make a good man. How about some help there?"

54   "No, I've got it," I answered. "I'm almost done."

55   "Oyes, Rey, what if you come over tomorrow night to my house? I'm having a little barbecue for some important people here in town. You should come over. We're even going to do some swimming. What do you say?"

56   I tightened the last of the nuts, replaced the jack, the flat tire, and the crowbar in the bed of his truck, looked at him, and said, "Thanks. But I'll be playing football with the vatos."

Reading Comprehension OPTIONAL

Have students complete the digital reading comprehension questions ✅ when they finish reading.

ANSWER KEY

QUESTION 1: A	QUESTION 5: B	QUESTION 9:
QUESTION 2: A	QUESTION 6: C	*See first chart.*
QUESTION 3: D	QUESTION 7: B	QUESTION 10:
QUESTION 4: D	QUESTION 8: A	*See second chart.*

First	Second	Third	Fourth
Mr. Sánchez uses the boys to help him clean up a yard nearby, but feeds them very little.	Mr. Sánchez offers the boys use of his basketball court if they help him dig holes for cement.	Mr. Sánchez becomes angry when he comes home to find the boys playing basketball.	Rey goes over to swim at the Sánchez house, but Mrs. Sánchez doesn't let him in.

Dialogue	Speaker
"Thanks. But I'll be playing football with the vatos."	Rey
"Come by tomorrow. I don't want you fellas to track all this dirt into the pool."	Mr. Sánchez
"Hi, Rey, how can I help you?"	Mrs. Sánchez
"Este vato!"	Hernando
"Have you forgotten the times we had to go pick you up?"	Rey's mother

Connect and Extend OPTIONAL

CONNECT TO EXTENDED WRITING PROJECT

Students can use "The Good Samaritan" as a mentor text for their Extended Writing Project. They may adapt one of the themes René Saldaña, Jr. explores: that an unexpected challenge might sometimes come from within us.

BEYOND THE BOOK

Performance: Betrayal and Forgiveness

In "The Good Samaritan," Rey feels betrayed by Mr. Sánchez. Pair students. Ask them to:

- Reflect on a time when they experienced a betrayal.
- Design two short skits to act out these moments. Their performance should answer the following:
  > What happened? Who betrayed you?
  > How did the betrayal make you feel?
  > How did you respond to the betrayal?
  > Did you forgive the person who betrayed you?

To reflect, ask students:

- How were these betrayals similar or different?
- Why is it hard for a child to forgive an adult who has betrayed them?

Think Questions

Circulate as students answer Think Questions independently. Scaffolds for these questions are shown on the opposite page.

QUESTION 1: Textual Evidence

When Rey comes to Orlie's house, Orlie doesn't answer the door, even though he invited his friend to "hang out by the pool." Orlie's mother says that her son "went with his father to Mission," but Rey knows he is home.

QUESTION 2: Textual Evidence

Mr. Sánchez promised the neighborhood boys that they could use the Sánchez pool if they helped him with yard work. Earlier, he promised to provide snacks in exchange for cleaning up a neighborhood yard and to let them use his basketball court in exchange for digging the holes for the basketball rims. The boys did the work, but Mr. Sánchez was stingy with the snacks and did not keep his other two promises.

QUESTION 3: Textual Evidence

Rey faces the decision of whether to stop and help Mr. Sánchez change a flat tire. At first he keeps driving, thinking Sánchez should "do his own dirty work for once." But then Rey thinks of his dad and decides to turn around even though Mr. Sánchez has treated him poorly.

QUESTION 4: Context Clues

I think *labor* must mean "work." The word is used in reference to Rey and the boys helping Mr. Sánchez dig holes for the basketball rims. Rey says that they "dug and dug and dug for close to six hours straight," which sounds like really hard work.

QUESTION 5: Context Clues

I think *approach* must mean "to come near." The word is used to describe Rey's car coming up to where Mr. Sánchez is by the side of the road before with "he decides to drive right on" [as "right on past"] past.

First Read

Read "The Good Samaritan." After you read, complete the Think Questions below.

☁ THINK QUESTIONS

1. Why is Rey upset with Orlie at the beginning of the story? Cite textual evidence from the selection to support your answer.

2. Why does Rey hold a grudge against Mr. Sánchez? Cite textual evidence from the selection to support your answer.

3. What is the main problem Rey faces at the end of the story? What actions does he take? Cite textual evidence from the selection to support your answer.

4. Find the word **labor** in paragraph 22 of "The Good Samaritan." Use context clues in the surrounding sentences, as well as the sentence in which the word appears, to determine the word's meaning. Write your definition here and identify clues that helped you figure out its meaning.

5. Use context clues to determine the meaning of **approached** as it is used in paragraph 42 of "The Good Samaritan." Write your definition here and identify clues that helped you figure out its meaning. Then check the meaning in a dictionary.

Reading & Writing Companion   73

Think Questions

SCAFFOLDS

Use the scaffolds below to differentiate instruction for your **ELL** English Language Learners and **A** Approaching grade-level learners.

ELL **BEGINNING** Write a response using the <u>word bank</u> and <u>sentence frames</u>.

INTERMEDIATE Write a response using the <u>sentence frames</u>.

ADVANCED, ADVANCED HIGH Write a response using the <u>Text-Dependent Question Guide</u>.

A **APPROACHING** Write a response using the <u>Text-Dependent Question Guide</u>.

	INTERMEDIATE	APPROACHING
BEGINNING		ADVANCED, ADVANCED HIGH

Word Bank	Sentence Frames	Text-Dependent Question Guide
bad basketball court broke	Rey is upset because Orlie will not answer the ____. Rey thinks Orlie does not want to share the ____ and ____. I know this because Rey says Orlie is ____.	1. • Why is Rey upset with Orlie? • What does Rey think Orlie doesn't want to share? • What does Rey conclude about Orlie?
changing the tire digging door	Mr. Sánchez ____ the boys into ____. Mr. Sánchez ____ that the boys could use the pool and ____. Mr. Sánchez ____ his promise.	2. • How does Rey feel about Mr. Sánchez? • Why does Rey feel this way? • What did Mr. Sánchez do or not do?
flat tire hang out pool	Ray sees that Mr. Sánchez has a ____. Rey does not ____. Ray feels ____ so he makes a ____. Rey helps Mr. Sánchez by ____.	3. • What must Rey decide at the end of the story? • What does he do first? • What does he finally do?
promised stingy stop come near toward	The boys are ____. This gives me a clue that *labor* means "____."	4. • In paragraph 22 read: "The next time was real hard **labor.** He said, 'Help me dig these holes here, then we can put up some basketball rims.'" In paragraph 23 read: "We dug and dug and dug for close to six hours straight until we got done, passing on the shovel from one of us to the next." • What are the boys doing in these paragraphs? • What does that tell me about the meaning of the word *labor*?
tricked U-turn work working	Rey's car is moving ____ Mr. Sánchez. This gives me a clue that *approach* means "____."	5. • Read: "I slowed down as I **approached.** Could he tell it was me driving? When he looked up at my car, I could swear he almost smiled, thinking he had been saved." • What is Rey's car doing? • Where is Mr. Sánchez? • What does that tell me about the meaning of the word *approach*?

Skill: Summarizing

Introduce the Skill

Watch the Concept Definitions video and read the following definition with your students.

When you **summarize** a text, you briefly state the main points and most important details in your own words. Summarizing can help you organize, explain, and remember concepts in an informational text or the events that take place in a story.

To summarize, you must decide what is most important as you read. Ask the basic questions: *who, what, when, where, why,* and *how.* Using your own words, write your answers to these questions from an **objective** point of view, without inserting your own feelings and opinions.

Summarizing is sometimes confused with paraphrasing. When you **paraphrase,** you do not condense a text to its most important details. Instead, you restate the entire text in your own words. A summary is much shorter than the original text, while a paraphrase may be the same length as the original text.

 TURN AND TALK

1. What are the most important events in the plot of your favorite book or movie?

2. Based on these events, how would you summarize your favorite book or movie?

ELL SPEAKING FRAMES
- One major event in [book/movie title] is ____.
- Another major event is ____.
- I think the final major event is ____.
- A summary of [book/movie title] is ____.

The Good Samaritan

Skill: Summarizing

Use the Checklist to analyze Summarizing in "The Good Samaritan." Refer to the sample student annotations about Summarizing in the text.

••• CHECKLIST FOR SUMMARIZING

In order to determine how to write an objective summary of a text, note the following:

✓ in literature, note the setting, characters, and events in the plot, taking into account the main problem the characters face and how it is solved

✓ answers to the basic questions *who, what, where, when, why,* and *how*

✓ stay objective, and do not add your own personal thoughts, judgments, or opinions to the summary

To provide an objective summary of a text not influenced by personal opinions or judgments, consider the following questions:

✓ What are the answers to basic *who, what, where, when, why,* and *how* questions in literature?

✓ Are all of the details I have included in my summary of a work of literature related to the theme?

✓ Is my summary objective, or have I added my own thoughts, judgments, or personal opinions?

Please note that excerpts and passages in the StudySync® library and this workbook are intended as touchstones to generate interest in an author's work. The excerpts and passages do not substitute for the reading of entire texts, and StudySync® strongly recommends that students seek out and purchase the whole literary or informational work in order to experience it as the author intended. Links to online resellers are available in our digital library. In addition, complete works may be ordered through an authorized reseller by filling out and returning to StudySync® the order form enclosed in this workbook.

V SKILL VOCABULARY

summarize / resumir *verb* to restate briefly the most important points in a text

objective / objetivo/a *adjective* undistorted by emotion or personal bias COGNATE

paraphrase / parafrasear *verb* to restate the author's words in your own words COGNATE

The Good Samaritan

Skill: Summarizing

Reread paragraphs 42–44 of "The Good Samaritan." Then, using the Checklist on the previous page, answer the multiple-choice questions below.

⟳ YOUR TURN

1. Which of the following best describes Rey's relationship with Mr. Sánchez in this selection?

   ○ A. Mr. Sánchez is like a father figure to Rey.
   ○ B. Rey thinks that Mr. Sánchez treats him unfairly.
   ○ C. Mr. Sánchez relies on Rey to do things that he cannot.
   ○ D. Rey pities Mr. Sánchez as he wishes he could help.

2. Which of the following answer choices provides the best summary of this selection?

   ○ A. Rey recalls times when Mr. Sánchez has used him and does not want to help him fix the flat tire.
   ○ B. Mr. Sánchez gets a flat tire and wishes he hadn't taken advantage of Rey in the past.
   ○ C. Rey sees Mr. Sánchez struggling to fix a flat tire and decides to help him out.
   ○ D. Mr. Sánchez observes Rey passing him up in his time of need.

Your Turn

Ask students to complete the Your Turn Activity.

QUESTION 1

A. **Incorrect.** Rey never thinks of Mr. Sánchez as a father; he does not look up to him.

B. **Correct.** Rey is annoyed that Mr. Sánchez constantly takes advantage of him and the work he does for him.

C. **Incorrect.** Mr. Sánchez can do the same jobs as Rey, but he prefers to ask Rey to do it.

D. **Incorrect.** Rey does not pity Mr. Sánchez in this excerpt; he ignores Mr. Sánchez and keeps driving.

QUESTION 2

A. **Correct.** Rey thinks about times when Mr. Sánchez has taken advantage of him, thus causing him to feel angry and not want to help him fix his flat tire.

B. **Incorrect.** Mr. Sánchez does have a flat tire, but there is no evidence to suggest that he wishes he hadn't mistreated Rey in the past.

C. **Incorrect.** Rey does not decide to help Mr. Sánchez out in this passage. This passage ends with Rey stating that he does not want to help.

D. **Incorrect.** The reader does not know if Mr. Sánchez sees Rey drive by, and there is no evidence to support this statement.

Close Read

Skills Focus

QUESTION 1: Summarizing

See paragraphs 16–18 and 20–21.

QUESTION 2: Character

See paragraphs 47–49: Rey can't forget about all the times that Mr. Sánchez hustled the boys. He's suspicious of the invitation. This makes Rey turn it down. He would rather hang out with his friends. I think this means that Rey is also skeptical.

QUESTION 3: Connect to Essential Question

See paragraphs 19 and 46–48.

CHECK FOR SUCCESS

If students struggle to respond to Skills Focus Question #1, ask students the following questions:

- What does Mr. Sánchez promise in paragraph 16?
- What does Mr. Sánchez do in paragraph 17?
- What do Rey and the boys conclude in paragraph 18?

Close Read

Reread "The Good Samaritan." As you reread, complete the Skills Focus questions below. Then use your answers and annotations from the questions to help you complete the Write activity.

 SKILLS FOCUS

1. Summarize the lessons Rey learns as he deals with the Sánchez family without giving your personal opinion.

2. Think about how Rey makes decisions in "The Good Samaritan." Use evidence of Rey's decision-making to explain his character.

3. Use textual evidence to explain why making the decision to help Mr. Sánchez was hard for Rey.

 WRITE

DEBATE: Rey lives up to the story's title, "The Good Samaritan," when he stops to help Mr. Sánchez. However, do you think Rey made the right decision in stopping to help? Summarize Rey's experiences dealing with the Sánchez family and use them to prepare an argument for a debate. Use evidence from the text to support your position.

Writer's Notebook

Connect to Essential Question: Give students time to reflect on how "The Good Samaritan" connects to the unit's essential question "What do we do when life gets hard?" by freewriting in their Writer's Notebooks.

ELL **Beginning & Intermediate**

Read aloud the unit's essential question: "What do we do when life gets hard?" Encourage students to draw their reflections and allow students to write in their native language. Circulate around the room, prompting students for their thoughts as they respond orally or through pantomime.

Advanced & Advanced High

Allow students to share their reflections orally in pairs or small groups before freewriting.

Collaborative Conversation

Break students into collaborative conversation groups to discuss the Close Read prompt. Ask students to use the StudySyncTV episode as a model for their discussion. Remind them to reference their Skills Focus annotations in their discussion.

Rey lives up to the story's title, "The Good Samaritan," when he stops to help Mr. Sánchez. But do you think Rey made the right decision in stopping to help? Summarize Rey's experiences dealing with the Sánchez family and use your summary to prepare an argument for a debate. Use evidence from the text to support your position.

Use the scaffolds below to differentiate instruction for your **ELL** English Language Learners and **A** Approaching grade-level learners.

ELL **BEGINNING, INTERMEDIATE** Use the discussion guide and speaking frames to facilitate the discussion with support from the teacher.

ADVANCED, ADVANCED HIGH Use the discussion guide and speaking frames to facilitate the discussion in mixed-level groups.

A **APPROACHING** Use the discussion guide to facilitate the discussion in mixed-level groups.

APPROACHING

ADVANCED, ADVANCED HIGH

BEGINNING, INTERMEDIATE

Discussion Guide	Speaking Frames
1. What relationship do Rey and his friends have with Mr. Sánchez when the story starts?	• Rey and his friends ____ for Mr. Sánchez. • The boys feel that Mr. Sánchez is ____.
2. Did Rey make the right decision by turning around to help Mr. Sánchez?	• I think Rey made the ____ decision. • I think this because ____.

Review Prompt and Rubric

Before students begin writing, review the writing prompt and rubric with the class.

REFLECTION: As you write, be sure to

- describe your best contribution to the discussion;
- identify a specific goal for improving your contributions to future discussions.

ELL PROMPT GUIDE

A
- What did Rey do when he first saw Mr. Sánchez on the side of the road?
- Why did Rey decide to turn around?
- Do you think Rey made the right decision by turning around?

Score	Reflection	Language and Conventions
4	The writer clearly reflects on how well he or she adjusted prepared responses as new evidence was presented, and evaluates his or her own participation with complete objectivity. The writer consistently refers to specific examples from the discussion.	The writer demonstrates a consistent command of grammar, punctuation, and usage conventions. Although minor errors may be evident, they do not detract from the fluency or the clarity of the essay.
3	The writer reflects on how well he or she adjusted prepared responses as new evidence was presented, and evaluates his or her own participation objectively most of the time. The writer often refers to specific examples from the discussion.	The writer demonstrates an adequate command of grammar, punctuation, and usage conventions. Although some errors may be evident, they create few (if any) disruptions in the fluency of the writing or the clarity of the essay.
2	The writer begins to reflect on how well he or she adjusted prepared responses as new evidence was presented, and makes some effort to be objective in evaluating his or her own participation. The writer refers to specific examples from the discussion some of the time.	The writer demonstrates a partial command of grammar, punctuation, and usage conventions. Some distracting errors may be evident, at times creating minor disruptions in the fluency or clarity of the writing.
1	The writer has difficulty reflecting on how well he or she adjusted prepared responses as new evidence was presented, and attempts with limited success to make an objective evaluation of his or her own participation. The writer refers to few, if any examples from the discussion.	The writer demonstrates little or no command of grammar, punctuation, and usage conventions. Serious and persistent errors create disruptions in the fluency of the writing and sometimes interfere with meaning.
0	The writer does not provide a relevant response to the prompt or does not provide a response at all.	Serious and persistent errors overwhelm the writing and interfere with the meaning of the response as a whole, making the writer's meaning impossible to understand.

Write

Ask students to complete the writing assignment using textual evidence to support their answers.

Use the scaffolds below to differentiate instruction for your **ELL** English Language Learners and **A** Approaching grade-level learners.

ELL **BEGINNING** With the help of the word bank, write a response using paragraph frame 1.

INTERMEDIATE With the help of the word bank, write a response using paragraph frames 1 and 2.

ADVANCED, ADVANCED HIGH Write a response of differentiated length using the sentence starters.

A **APPROACHING** Write a response of differentiated length using the sentence starters.

| BEGINNING | | | ADVANCED, ADVANCED HIGH |
| INTERMEDIATE | | | APPROACHING |

Word Bank	Paragraph Frame 1	Paragraph Frame 2	Sentence Starters
should not trustworthy counted on cannot right	I conclude that Rey made the ____ decision. Rey ____ count on Mr. Sánchez. This does not mean that Rey ____ help. Rey proves that he can be ____. If Rey drove on, the story's message could not be about the importance of being ____.	Rey turns around because of ____. He would want someone to ____. Rey is willing to help even though he does not ____. If Rey drove on, the story's message would change because ____.	• I think Rey made the ____ decision. • Evidence of this is . . . • Rey thinks Mr. Sánchez is . . . • I know this because . . . • Rey is . . . • If Rey did . . .

Peer Review

Students should submit substantive feedback to two peers using the instructions below.

- How well does the writer explain his or her position on Rey's decision?
- How well does the writer summarize Rey's experiences dealing with the Sánchez family?
- Which of the writer's comments or questions do you think helped drive the debate?
- How well did the writer address how the participants adjusted their prepared responses during the debate?
- What does the writer do well in this reflection? What does the writer need to work on?

Rate

Respond to the following with a point rating that reflects your opinion.

	1 2 3 4
Ideas	■ ■ ■ ☐
Evidence	■ ■ ■ ■
Language and Conventions	■ ■ ☐ ☐

Submit

ELL **A** **SENTENCE FRAMES**

- You were able to (completely / partly / almost) ____ answer the prompt because . . .
- You could answer the prompt more completely by . . .

- You supported the idea of . . . with the detail of . . .
- One idea that needs more support is . . .
- My favorite part of your response is . . .

Jabberwocky

POETRY
Lewis Carroll
1872

Introduction

studysync

This whimsical poem about a heroic quest was first published in its entirety in author Lewis Carroll's *Through the Looking Glass*. Carroll (1832–1898) is best known for his fanciful stories and his contributions to the genre of literary nonsense. His most famous work, *Alice's Adventures in Wonderland*, has been adapted for film and television, and continues to be well-beloved today. Alice finds this particular poem in a book after she steps through a mirror into an odd new world. The poem's fantastical characters, invented language, and formal structure have made it a classic in its own right.

This classic poem opens with a playful, nonsensical stanza, setting the scene for a story about a boy and his father. The father warns his son to watch out for a monstrous creature that lurks in the woods: the Jabberwock. Eager to do battle with such an adversary, the boy takes his sword into the forest and waits for the Jabberwock to appear. Eventually, the boy hears it coming through the brush. When the Jabberwock arrives, its eyes are aflame, but the boy succeeds in killing it. He runs back to his father to present him with the creature's head and is met with celebration and praise for his courage.

 Proficiency-leveled summaries and summaries in multiple languages are available digitally.

 Audio and audio text highlighting are available with this text.

COMPARING WITHIN AND ACROSS GENRES

 The first of three selections, Lewis Carroll's whimsical poem "Jabberwocky" combines fantastical characters, invented language and formal structure to tell a heroic tale. Read alongside *Gathering Blue* and *A Wrinkle in Time,* students will consider how the language, setting, and events make the reader feel uncertain, and what steps the reader can take to better understand these selections.

Access Complex Text

LEXILE: N/A   WORD COUNT: 166

The following areas may be challenging for students, particularly English Language Learners and Approaching grade-level learners.

Genre	Purpose	Connection of Ideas
• Although it contains many made up words, the poem is a ballad written in four-line stanzas. • Each stanza has four stressed syllables in the first three lines and three stressed syllables in the fourth line. Each stanza has a regular ABAB rhyme scheme.	• Words are chosen and made up because of the impression they create. • Carroll often invented words by blending the sounds and meanings of two or more other words--"slithy" is a blend of "lithe" and "slimy." Words like these are known as "portmanteau words."	• The poem has a slim narrative. A hero leaves home to test his bravery. He comes home triumphant. This plot has been treated over and over, from *Beowulf* to *The Lord of the Rings*. • Point out that the strict form of the poem stands in sharp contrast to and accentuates the fact that it is pure nonsense.

 SCAFFOLDS   ENGLISH LANGUAGE LEARNERS   APPROACHING GRADE LEVEL   Ⓑ BEYOND GRADE LEVEL

These icons identify differentiation strategies and scaffolded support for a variety of students. See the digital lesson plan for additional differentiation strategies and scaffolds.

Instructional Path

The print teacher's edition includes essential point-of-use instruction and planning tools. Complete lesson plans and program documents appear in your digital teacher account.

Independent Read: Jabberwocky

Objectives: After reading the text, students will demonstrate their ability to determine the meaning and purpose of nonsense words by creating a short, written poem.

Independent Read

Lewis Carroll

Jabberwocky

Introduce the Text

As a class, watch the video preview ▶ and have students read the introduction in pairs to make connections to the video preview.

- What key words or images from the video do you think will be most important to the poem you are about to read?

- How do the images, words, and music in the video connect to the information in the introduction?

- What do you think *whimsical* means?

ELL SPEAKING FRAMES

- The ____ in the video makes me think ____..
- The video shows ____. This makes me wonder ____.
- I think the text will ____. I think this because ____.
- I predict that there will be ____. I believe this because ____.

Entry Point

As students prepare to read "Jabberwocky," share the following information with them to provide context.

✓ Lewis Carroll, the pen name of British author Charles Lutwidge Dodgson (1832–1898), is best known for his novels *Alice's Adventures in Wonderland* and *Through the Looking-Glass.* These books were inspired by the stories that he told the children of friends and colleagues at the University of Oxford, and Alice is closely modeled on Alice Liddell, whose father was Dean of Christ Church--the college where Dodgson taught mathematics.

✓ "Jabberwocky" appears in *Through the Looking-Glass.* In the story, Alice finds the poem in a book printed backwards.

✓ Though Carroll did not invent nonsense verse, "Jabberwocky" has become the most famous example of it. Many words from the poem which Carroll invented have become part of the English lexicon.

"'Beware the Jabberwock, my son! The jaws that bite, the claws that catch!'"

 NOTES

from Chapter 1: "Looking-Glass House"

1 'Twas brillig, and the slithy toves
2 Did gyre and gimble in the wabe;
3 All mimsy were the borogoves,
4 And the mome raths outgrabe.

5 'Beware the Jabberwock, my son!
6 The jaws that bite, the claws that catch!
7 Beware the Jubjub bird, and **shun**
8 The frumious Bandersnatch!'

9 He took his vorpal sword in hand:
10 Long time the manxome **foe** he **sought**—
11 So rested he by the Tumtum tree
12 And stood awhile in thought.

13 And, as in uffish thought he stood,
14 The Jabberwock, with eyes of flame,
15 Came whiffling through the tulgey wood,
16 And burbled as it came!

17 One, two! One, two! And through and through
18 The vorpal blade went snicker-snack!
19 He left it dead, and with its head
20 He went **galumphing** back.

21 'And hast thou slain the Jabberwock?
22 Come to my arms, my beamish boy!
23 O frabjous day! Callooh! Callay!'
24 He **chortled** in his joy.

25 'Twas brillig, and the slithy toves
26 Did gyre and gimble in the wabe;
27 All mimsy were the borogoves,
28 And the mome raths outgrabe.

The Jabberwock

Copyright © BookheadEd Learning, LLC

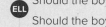 **V SELECTION VOCABULARY**

shun / evitar *verb* to avoid purposefully

ELL Should the boy go near or stay away from the Jubjub bird?
Should the boy go near or stay away from the Bandersnatch?

foe / el enemigo *noun* enemy or opponent

ELL Why might the boy take a sword in hand?
Would the boy fight a friend or enemy with a sword?

 ## Analyze Vocabulary Using Context Clues

As students read the text, ask them to make predictions about each bold vocabulary word based on the context clues in the sentence. Have students use the annotation tool to make their predictions.

 ✓ CHECK FOR SUCCESS

If students are unable to determine the meaning of one or more bolded vocabulary words, project the Checklist from the Grade 6 Context Clues lesson with the class. After revisiting, guide students as they make predictions about the bold word in line 7.

⚙ TURN AND TALK

Have students discuss their original vocabulary predictions with a neighbor. Come to a consensus as a class before confirming their definitions.

 TEXT TALK

What do you think you're being told about the setting of the poem in stanza 1?

See stanza 1: Either the time of day or the weather is "brillig." Animals or plants called "toves," "borogoves," and "raths" are moving about or looking a certain way

In stanza 2, who is speaking and what is the message?

See stanza 2: A cautious father is warning his son to avoid the Jabberwock, the Jubjub bird, and the Bandersnatch

✏ WRITE

POEM: The poem "Jabberwocky" uses nonsense language to describe a heroic battle. Choose three nonsensical words from the first stanza of "Jabberwocky" and create a definition for each based on context, sound, and the image you picture in your head. Then write a poem about a time you overcame an obstacle incorporating each of the three words.

🔊 TEXT TALK

Who is performing the action in stanza 3, and what is he doing ?

See stanza 3: the son is hunting the Jabberwock, "vorpal sword in hand".

Who wins the battle?

See stanza 5: The son wins, killing the Jabberwock with his "vorpal blade" and riding off with its head.

How does the father react to the outcome of the battle?

See stanza 6: He hugs his son, makes exclamations, and chortles (laughs) in his joy.

> **B** Ask each Beyond grade level student to write one additional discussion question. Then, have one or two students facilitate a discussion, using their questions to guide the conversation.

Copyright © BookheadEd Learning, LLC

Ⓥ SELECTION VOCABULARY

sought / buscar *verb* to try to locate or discover

> **ELL** Is the boy looking for or running away from his foe?
> Why does the boy want to find his foe?

galumphing / corretear *verb* to move in a loud and clumsy way

> **ELL** Does the boy win or lose the fight?
> Afterward, does he move around quietly or loudly?

chortled / translation *verb* to laugh or chuckle

> **ELL** What do the exclamation marks show about how the father feels about his son's win?
> What joyous sounds might the father make?

Reading Comprehension OPTIONAL

Have students complete the digital reading comprehension questions ✔ when they finish reading.

ANSWER KEY

QUESTION 1: C	**QUESTION 3:** B	**QUESTION 5:** B
QUESTION 2: B	**QUESTION 4:** A	*See chart below.*

First	Second	Third	Fourth
The slithy toves gyre and gimble.	The hero is warned about the Jabberwock, the Jubjub, and the frumious Bandersnatch.	The hero decapitates the Jabberwok.	The hero proudly returns to his father.

Connect and Extend OPTIONAL

CONNECT TO EXTENDED WRITING PROJECT

As they craft their own narratives for the Extended Writing Project, students may find inspiration in Lewis Carroll's unorthodox use of language as a way to depict a main character who faces an unexpected challenge.

BEYOND THE BOOK

Writing: An Epic Battle

Ask students to let their imaginations run wild and invent a monstrous creature.

- What's its name?
- What does it look like?
- Where does it live?
- What are some of its personality traits?

Once students have written a description and drawn a picture of their monster, ask them to write an epic poem in which a hero fights this creature. Their epic poems should use the same rhyme scheme as "Jabberwocky" (ABAB, CDCD, EFEF).

StudySyncTV   Project the StudySyncTV episode  and pause at the following times to prompt discussion:

1:43   What setting did Isaiah and Daniela imagine "wabe" described? Why do you think they both had the same image in mind?

3:03   Isaiah calls the structure of the poem a "ballad stanza." How does this structure make the students feel? What contrast does Ethan point out?

4:29   How do Daniela and Erica feel about the made-up language in the poem? Do you agree?

 ## Collaborative Conversation

 **SCAFFOLDS**

Break students into collaborative conversation groups to discuss the writing prompt. Ask students to use the StudySyncTV episode as a model for their discussion. Remind them to reference their Skills Focus annotations in their discussion.

The poem "Jabberwocky" uses nonsensical language to describe a heroic battle. Do you think that the made-up words effectively communicate what happens in the fight? Why or why not? Use evidence from the text to support your response.

Use the scaffolds below to differentiate instruction for your **ELL** English Language Learners and **A** Approaching grade-level learners.

ELL **BEGINNING, INTERMEDIATE** Use the discussion guide and speaking frames to facilitate the discussion with support from the teacher.

ADVANCED, ADVANCED HIGH Use the discussion guide and speaking frames to facilitate the discussion in mixed-level groups.

A **APPROACHING** Use the discussion guide to facilitate the discussion in mixed-level groups.

APPROACHING
ADVANCED, ADVANCED HIGH
BEGINNING, INTERMEDIATE

Discussion Guide	Speaking Frames
1. How do the made-up words make you feel?	• The made-up words make me feel ____. • They make me feel that way because ____.
2. Are the made-up words appropriate for a fight scene?	• The made-up words ____ (are/are not) appropriate. • I think this way because ____.
3. What textual evidence supports your opinion?	• The text says ____, which shows ____. • The text says ____, which does not show ____.

Review Prompt and Rubric

Before students begin writing, review the writing prompt and rubric with the class.

LITERARY - POETRY: The poem "Jabberwocky" uses nonsense language to describe a heroic battle. Choose three nonsensical words from the first stanza of "Jabberwocky" and create a definition for each based on context, sound, and the image you picture in your head. Then write a poem about a time you overcame an obstacle incorporating each of the three words.

 PROMPT GUIDE

A
- How would you define two made-up words from the poem?
- What is an obstacle that you have had to overcome in your life?

- Use the two made-up words to write a poem about the obstacle.

Score	Poem	Language and Conventions
4	The writer clearly writes a poem about an obstacle, using nonsense words from the text.	The writer demonstrates a consistent command of grammar, punctuation, and usage conventions. Although minor errors may be evident, they do not detract from the fluency or the clarity of the poem.
3	The writer sufficiently writes a poem about an obstacle, using three nonsense words, nonsensical words from the text most of the time.	The writer demonstrates an adequate command of grammar, punctuation, and usage conventions. Although some errors may be evident, they create few (if any) disruptions in the fluency of the writing or the clarity of the poem.
2	The writer begins to write a poem about an obstacle, using nonsense words, but the poem is incomplete. The writer uses inspiration or relevant evidence from the text only some of the time.	The writer demonstrates a partial command of grammar, punctuation, and usage conventions. Some distracting errors may be evident, at times creating minor disruptions in the fluency or clarity of the writing.
1	The writer attempts to write a poem about an obstacle, using nonsense words, but the attempt is not successful. The writer doesn't discuss an obstacle and uses little or no nonsensical words from the text.	The writer demonstrates little or no command of grammar, punctuation, and usage conventions. Serious and persistent errors create disruptions in the fluency of the writing and sometimes interfere with meaning.
0	The writer does not provide a relevant response to the prompt or does not provide a response at all.	Serious and persistent errors overwhelm the writing and interfere with the meaning of the response as a whole, making the writer's meaning impossible to understand.

Write

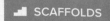

Ask students to complete the writing assignment using textual evidence to support their answers.

Use the scaffolds below to differentiate instruction for your **ELL** English Language Learners and **A** Approaching grade-level learners.

ELL **BEGINNING** With the help of the word bank, write a response using paragraph frame 1.

INTERMEDIATE With the help of the word bank, write a response using paragraph frames 1 and 2.

ADVANCED, ADVANCED HIGH Write a response of differentiated length using the sentence starters.

A **APPROACHING** Write a response of differentiated length using the sentence starters.

| BEGINNING | | ADVANCED, ADVANCED HIGH |
| INTERMEDIATE | | APPROACHING |

Word Bank	Paragraph Frame 1	Paragraph Frame 2	Sentence Starters
scary	The word "frumious" means ____. The word "uffish" means ____. One time I had to ____. The obstacle was ____. I felt ____. I succeeded by ____.	The word "frumious" means ____. In the poem, "frumious" describes ____. The word "uffish" means ____. In the poem, "uffish" describes ____. One time I had to ____. The obstacle was ____. It was ____. I felt ____. I succeeded by ____. I learned that ____. After, I felt ____.	• The made-up word means . . . • When I read the word in the text, I picture . . . • An obstacle I experienced . . . • I felt . . . • I overcame the obstacle by . . . • After, I felt . . . • I learned that . . .
trouble			
choose			
deep			
hard			
afraid			
excited			
happy			
thoughtful			
brave			

Peer Review

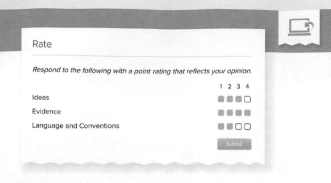

Rate

Respond to the following with a point rating that reflects your opinion.

	1 2 3 4
Ideas	▪▪▪☐
Evidence	▪▪▪▪
Language and Conventions	▪▪☐☐

Submit

Students should submit substantive feedback to two peers using the review instructions below.

- How well does this response answer the prompt?
- Does the writer define three nonsensical words using context, sound, and the image you picture in your head?
- Does the writer incorporate the words into an original poem?
- Does the writer write about a personal obstacle in the poem?
- Which of the writer's lines inspired you to think differently about a nonsensical word from "Jabberwocky"?
- What did the writer do well in this poem? What does the writer need to work on?

 SENTENCE FRAMES

A
- You were able to (completely / partly / almost) ____ answer the prompt.
- You could answer the prompt more completely by . . .

- I thought differently about the text after reading . . .
- My favorite part of your response is . . .

Gathering Blue

FICTION
Lois Lowry
2000

Introduction

Lois Lowry (b. 1937) has written more than thirty novels for children and young adults in her long career. The novel excerpted here, *Gathering Blue*, takes place in the same universe as several other novels of Lowry's, including 1993's Newbery-winning *The Giver*. Prior to this excerpt from Chapter 5, a crippled young girl, Kira, has been left an orphan after her mother's death. In a place where the weak or disabled are typically left in the fields to die, Kira fears she will be forced to leave—but her talent for embroidery may earn her a role in society. She awaits judgment from Jamison and the Council of Guardians, whose members will settle a dispute between her and Vandara, an enemy of hers who seeks her expulsion from the village.

In a dystopian society where individuals with physical disabilities are left to die, a young orphan named Now Kira hopes the skills her mother passed down to her will grant her a future. So far the slight deformity in her lower leg has gone unnoticed. Now Kira awaits judgment from the Council of Guardians to settle her dispute with Vandara, who wants to expel Kira from their village. To secure Kira's place in society, her advocate, Jamison, introduces the Singer's robe—a magnificent ceremonial artifact—into evidence. Kira's mother was the only one who had the expertise to create its embroidery. Kira explains that her mother taught her these same skills. Upon hearing this, the Council decides in Kira's favor and assigns her the task of completing the Singer's robe that her mother started. After the judgment, Kira steps into the street and is surprised to see that the central plaza remains the same. She muses that no one's life has changed—except her own.

  Proficiency-leveled summaries and summaries in multiple languages are available digitally.

 Audio and audio text highlighting are available with this text.

COMPARING WITHIN AND ACROSS GENRES

 In Lowry's futuristic novel, *Gathering Blue,* a young girl named Kira fears she will be banished because of her disability—but her talent for embroidery may earn her a role in society. As Kira's limits are tested in this excerpt of *Gathering Blue,* students will consider how to use context clues to understand the settings in "Jabberwocky" and *A Wrinkle in Time.*

Access Complex Text

LEXILE: 670   WORD COUNT: 1,014

The following areas may be challenging for students, particularly English Language Learners and Ⓐ Approaching grade-level learners.

Prior Knowledge	Connection of Ideas	Sentence Structure
• Students may not know that the selection is a companion piece to a novel entitled *The Giver.* • The societies in both stories are controlled by ruthless authorities. At the center of each is a young person who is given the responsibility of preserving the culture.	• Some students may have difficulty synthesizing information throughout the text. • Point out that the character Annabel is now called Annabella. The increasing number of syllables in a person's name indicates rising social status.	• Some students may have difficulty following the dialogue in the selection. They must determine when Jamison is speaking from the surrounding dialogue. • In lines 14 and 20, the author italicizes the first sentence in each paragraph. These are meant to convey Kira's thoughts and not dialogue.

  SCAFFOLDS   **ENGLISH LANGUAGE LEARNERS**   Ⓐ **APPROACHING GRADE LEVEL**   Ⓑ **BEYOND GRADE LEVEL**

These icons identify differentiation strategies and scaffolded support for a variety of students. See the digital lesson plan for additional differentiation strategies and scaffolds.

Instructional Path

The print teacher's edition includes essential point-of-use instruction and planning tools. Complete lesson plans and program documents appear in your digital teacher account.

Independent Read: Gathering Blue

Objectives: After reading "Gathering Blue," students will demonstrate their grasp of how context clues enable our understanding of characters and plot in a short, written response.

Independent Read

Introduce the Text

As a class, watch the video preview ▶ and have students read the introduction in pairs to make connections to the video preview.

- How do the images, words, and music in this video make you feel?
- How does this information connect to a challenge you have faced?
- What do you think the word fate means?

> **ELL SPEAKING FRAMES**
> - The ____ in the video makes me think ____.
> - The video shows ____. This makes me wonder ____.
> - I think the text will ____. I think this because ____.
> - I predict that there will be____. I believe this because ____.

Entry Point

As students prepare to read *Gathering Blue*, share the following information with them to provide context.

✓ Lois Lowry's *Gathering Blue* is in a genre of its own; it's a cross between fantasy and realistic fiction, and it's set in a future dystopia where the people live in poverty and the sick are uncared for.

✓ The reader might find it difficult to compare Kira's society to his or her own, so comparing the setting of *Gathering Blue* to other genre selections, such as *Jabberwocky* and "A Wrinkle in Time", might provide helpful context.

✓ Lois Lowry wrote four books with a dystopian theme; these books are *The Giver, Gathering Blue,* Messenger, and Son. These novels are part of a series known as "The Giver Quartet." *The Giver* is arguably Lowry's most famous book. It was the 1994 Newbery Medal winner and was made into a movie with Meryl Streep in 2014.

"The proceedings are complete. We have reached our decision."

from Chapter 5

NOTES

1 Kira noticed for the first time that a large box had been placed on the floor behind the seats of the Council of Guardians.

2 It had not been there before the lunchtime break.

3 As she and Vandara watched, one of the guards, responding to a nod from the chief guardian, lifted the box to the table and raised its lid. Her defender, Jamison, removed and unfolded something that she recognized immediately.

4 "The Singer's robe!" Kira spoke aloud in delight.

5 "This has no **relevance,**" Vandara muttered. But she too was leaning forward to see.

6 The magnificent robe was laid out on the table in display. Ordinarily it was seen only once a year, at the time when the village gathered to hear the Ruin Song, the lengthy history of their people. Most citizens, crowded into the auditorium for the occasion, saw the Singer's robe only from a distance; they shoved and pushed, trying to nudge closer for a look.

7 But Kira knew the robe well from watching her mother's meticulous work on it each year. A guardian had always stood nearby, attentive. Warned not to touch, Kira had watched, marveling at her mother's skill, at her ability to choose just the right shade.

8 There, on the left shoulder! Kira remembered that spot, where just last year some threads had pulled and torn and her mother had carefully coaxed the broken threads free. Then she had selected pale pinks, slightly darker roses, and other colors darkening to crimson, each hue only a hint deeper than the one before; and she had stitched them into place, blending them flawlessly into the edges of the **elaborate** design.

9 Jamison watched Kira as she remembered. Then he said, "Your mother had been teaching you the art."

10 Kira nodded. "Since I was small," she acknowledged aloud.

Reading & Writing Companion 81

SELECTION VOCABULARY

relevance / la relevancia *noun* a relationship to a subject or topic in an appropriate way COGNATE

elaborate / elaborado/a *adjective* having many parts; complicated in design

ELL
- Does embroidery take a lot of attention or a little?
- Is the Singer's robe very detailed or not very detailed?

Analyze Vocabulary Using Context Clues

As students read the text, ask them to make predictions about each bold vocabulary word based on the context clues in the sentence. Have students use the annotation tool to make their predictions.

CHECK FOR SUCCESS

If students are unable to determine the meaning of one or more bolded vocabulary words, project the Checklist from the Grade 6 Context Clues lesson with the class. After revisiting, guide students as they make predictions about the bold word in paragraph 5.

TURN AND TALK

Have students discuss their original vocabulary predictions with a partner. Come to a consensus as a class before confirming their definitions.

TEXT TALK

What is taking place at the beginning of the excerpt?

See paragraphs 1–3: The Council of Guardians is hearing a civil case, and the main character, Kira, notices that a box has been brought in.

What is Kira's connection to the Singer's robe that arrives in the box?

See paragraphs 6–8: All the village sees the robe once a year, when they hear their history sung. Kira's mother used to repair and continue to decorate the robe each year as Kira watched.

Gathering Blue

11 "Your mother was a skilled worker. Her dyes were **steadfast.** They have not faded."

12 "She was careful," Kira said, "and thorough."

13 "We are told that your skill is greater than hers."

14 *So they knew.* "I still have much to learn," Kira said.

15 "And she taught you the coloring, as well as the stitches?"

16 Kira nodded because she knew he expected her to. But it was not exactly true. Her mother had planned to teach her the art of the dyes, but the time had not yet come before the illness struck. She tried to be honest in her answer. "She was beginning to teach me," Kira said. "She told me that she had been taught by a woman named Annabel."

17 "Annabella now," Jamison said.

18 Kira was startled. "She is still alive? And four syllables?"

19 "She is very old. Her sight is somewhat **diminished.** But she can still be used as a **resource.**"

20 *Resource for what?* But Kira stayed silent. The scrap in her pocket was warm against her hand.

21 Suddenly Vandara stood. "I request that these proceedings continue," she said abruptly and harshly. "This is a delaying tactic on the part of the defender."

22 The chief guardian rose. Around him, the other guardians, who had been murmuring among themselves, fell silent.

23 His voice, directed at Vandara, was not unkind. "You may go," he said. "The proceedings are complete. We have reached our decision."

24 Vandara stood silent, unmoving. She glared at him defiantly. The chief guardian nodded, and two guards moved forward to escort her from the room.

25 "I have a right to know your decision!" Vandara shouted, her face twisted with rage. She wrested her arms free of the guards' grasp and faced the Council of Guardians.

26 "Actually," the chief guardian said in a calm voice, "you have no rights at all. But I am going to tell you the decision so that there will be no misunderstanding.

27 "The orphan girl Kira will stay. She will have a new role."

TEXT TALK

What do the guardians decide regarding Kira?

See paragraphs 26–27: They will let her stay, and she will take over her mother's work maintaining the robe.

 SELECTION VOCABULARY

steadfast / firme *adjective* unchanging over time

• What does "steadfast" dye not do?
• Is this a good or bad quality?

diminished / disminuir *verb* made or became less COGNATE

ELL
• How would you expect the sight of a very old person to be?
• Does "somewhat" mean the same as "completely"?

resource / el recurso *noun* a place, person, or thing that provides something useful COGNATE

• How might Annabella be "used"?
• Will Annabella's age and eyesight keep her from being a resource?

28 He gestured toward the Singer's robe, still spread out on the table. "Kira," he said, looking at her, "you will continue your mother's work. You will go beyond her work, actually, since your skill is far greater than hers was. First, you will repair the robe, as your mother always did. Next, you will restore it. Then your true work will begin. You will *complete* the robe." He gestured toward the large undecorated expanse of fabric across the shoulders. He raised one eyebrow, looking at her as if he were asking a question.

29 Nervously Kira nodded in reply and bowed slightly.

30 "As for you?" The chief guardian looked again at Vandara, who stood sullenly between the guards. He spoke politely to her. "You have not lost. You demanded the girl's land, and you may have it, you and the other women. Build your pen. It would be wise to pen your tykes; they are troublesome and should be better contained.

31 "Go now," he commanded.

32 Vandara turned. Her face was a mask of fury. She shrugged away the hands of the guards, leaned forward, and whispered harshly to Kira, "You will fail. Then they will kill you."

33 She smiled coldly at Jamison. "So, that's it, then," she said. "The girl is yours." She stalked down the aisle and went through the broad door.

34 The chief guardian and the other Council members ignored the outburst, as if it were merely an annoying insect that had finally been swatted away. Someone was refolding the Singer's robe.

35 "Kira," Jamison said, "go and gather what you need. Whatever you want to bring with you. Be back here when the bell rings four times. And we will take you to your quarters, to the place where you will live from now on."

36 Puzzled, Kira waited a moment. But there were no other instructions. The guardians were straightening their papers and collecting their books and belongings. They seemed to have forgotten she was there. Finally she stood, straightened herself against her walking stick, and limped from the room.

37 Emerging from the Council Edifice into bright sunlight and the usual chaos of the village central plaza, she realized that it was still midafternoon, still an ordinary day in the existence of the people, and that no one's life had changed except her own.

Excerpted from *Gathering Blue* by Lois Lowry, published by Ember.

TEXT TALK

How does Vandara feel about the decision?

See paragraphs 31–32: She is angry; her face is "a mask of fury" and she apparently hopes that Kira will fail and they will kill her.

How does Kira react to the decision?

See paragraphs 36–37: She is puzzled and then realizes that her life will change completely.

From Kira's perspective, what might be difficult in taking over her mother's work of maintaining the robe? Why?

Answers may vary.

Gathering Blue

✎ WRITE

PERSONAL RESPONSE: Think back to a challenge that you've faced in your life. How did you feel facing it? How were you able to respond? With that memory in mind, what advice would you give Kira from *Gathering Blue* to help her with the challenge she faces now?

Reading Comprehension OPTIONAL

Have students complete the digital reading comprehension questions ✅ when they finish reading.

ANSWER KEY

QUESTION 1: D	**QUESTION 5:** A	**QUESTION 9:** C
QUESTION 2: A	**QUESTION 6:** D	**QUESTION 10:**
QUESTION 3: B	**QUESTION 7:** C	*See chart below.*
QUESTION 4: A	**QUESTION 8:** D	

First	Second	Third	Fourth
Jamison takes the Singer's Robe out of the box	Kira remembers watching her mother work on the Robe	The Council gives Vandara Kira's land	Kira steps into the street realizing her life has changed

Connect and Extend OPTIONAL

CONNECT TO EXTENDED WRITING PROJECT

Students may find inspiration in Lois Lowry's use of an unusual setting and a surprise ending as they discover that someone's worst possible day can turn out to be another character's best possible day.

BEYOND THE BOOK

Art: The Singer's Robe

In preparation for creating their own singer's robe, invite students to think about the following questions:

- What stories have you heard about your family growing up?

- Are there objects in your home that have a deeper meaning or symbolize something important for your family?

- Do you have family members living in different parts of the country or the world? Have you traveled to visit them?

- What traditions, however small, make your family unique?

Once students have had a chance to consider these questions, ask them to create a "Singer's Robe" to reflect their personal history, culture, and family using a mix of colors, images, and symbols.

Collaborative Conversation

Break students into collaborative conversation groups to discuss the writing prompt. Ask students to use the StudySyncTV episode as a model for their discussion. Remind them to reference their Skills Focus annotations in their discussion.

Think back to a challenge that you've faced in your life. How did you feel facing it? How were you able to respond? With that memory in mind, what advice would you give Kira from Gathering Blue to help her with the challenge she faces now?

Use the scaffolds below to differentiate instruction for your **ELL** English Language Learners and **A** Approaching grade-level learners.

ELL **BEGINNING, INTERMEDIATE** Use the discussion guide and speaking frames to facilitate the discussion with support from the teacher.

ADVANCED, ADVANCED HIGH Use the discussion guide and speaking frames to facilitate the discussion in mixed-level groups.

A **APPROACHING** Use the discussion guide to facilitate the discussion in mixed-level groups.

APPROACHING
ADVANCED, ADVANCED HIGH
BEGINNING, INTERMEDIATE

Discussion Guide	Speaking Frames
1. Did you ever feel uncertain about something in the future?	• I ___ (did/did not) feel uncertain about something in the future. • I once felt uncertain when ___.
2. How did this feeling challenge you and how did you respond to it?	• It was a challenge because ___. • I responded to this challenge by ___.
3. Based on your experience, what advice would you give Kira?	• I would tell Kira to ___. • This is good advice for her because ___.

Review Prompt and Rubric

Before students begin writing, review the writing prompt and rubric with the class.

PERSONAL RESPONSE: Think back to a challenge that you've faced in your life. How did you feel facing it? How were you able to respond? With that memory in mind, what advice would you give Kira from Gathering Blue to help her with the challenge she faces now?

ELL **PROMPT GUIDE**

 A
- Did you ever feel uncertain about something in the future?
- How did this feeling challenge you?

- How did you respond to this challenge?
- Based on your experience, what advice would you give Kira?

Score	Personal Response	Language and Conventions
4	The writer clearly explains his or her personal connection to the text, using relevant evidence from the text.	The writer demonstrates a consistent command of grammar, punctuation, and usage conventions. Although minor errors may be evident, they do not detract from the fluency or the clarity of the essay.
3	The writer sufficiently explains his or her personal connection to the text, using relevant evidence from the text most of the time.	The writer demonstrates an adequate command of grammar, punctuation, and usage conventions. Although some errors may be evident, they create few (if any) disruptions in the fluency of the writing or the clarity of the essay.
2	The writer begins to explain his or her personal connection to the text, but the explanation is incomplete. The writer uses relevant evidence from the text only some of the time.	The writer demonstrates a partial command of grammar, punctuation, and usage conventions. Some distracting errors may be evident, at times creating minor disruptions in the fluency or clarity of the writing.
1	The writer attempts to explain his or her personal connection to the text, but the explanation is not successful. The writer uses little or no relevant evidence from the text.	The writer demonstrates little or no command of grammar, punctuation, and usage conventions. Serious and persistent errors create disruptions in the fluency of the writing and sometimes interfere with meaning.
0	The writer does not provide a relevant response to the prompt or does not provide a response at all.	Serious and persistent errors overwhelm the writing and interfere with the meaning of the response as a whole, making the writer's meaning impossible to understand.

Write

Ask students to complete the writing assignment using textual evidence to support their answers.

Use the scaffolds below to differentiate instruction for your **ELL** English Language Learners and **A** Approaching grade-level learners.

ELL **BEGINNING** With the help of the <u>word bank</u>, write a response using <u>paragraph frame 1</u>.

INTERMEDIATE With the help of the <u>word bank</u>, write a response using <u>paragraph frames 1 and 2</u>.

ADVANCED, ADVANCED HIGH Write a response of differentiated length using the <u>sentence starters</u>.

A **APPROACHING** Write a response of differentiated length using the <u>sentence starters</u>.

BEGINNING	ADVANCED, ADVANCED HIGH
INTERMEDIATE	APPROACHING

Word Bank	Paragraph Frame 1	Paragraph Frame 2	Sentence Starters
decision problems uncertain thinking learned difficulty working act	I felt uncertain about the future when I ____ we might have to move. This feeling challenged me because I have always had ____ making new friends. I responded to this challenge by ____ I would join some clubs at my new school. Based on my experience, I would advise Kira to ____.	This experience taught me ____. Kira can learn from my experience by ____.	• I faced a challenge in my life when . . . • This challenge made me feel . . . • I felt this way because . . . • I responded to the challenge by . . . • I think Kira should . . . • This will help Kira because . . .

Peer Review

Students should submit substantive feedback to two peers using the review instructions below.

- How well does this response answer the prompt?
- How well does the writer connect a personal experience to Kira's situation?
- Does the writer connect his or her response to a challenge directly to Kira's situation?
- Does the advice make sense in terms of the writer's situation and Kira's?
- Which of the writer's comments inspired you to think differently about the text?
- What did the writer do well in this response? What does the writer need to work on?

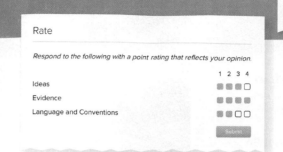

Rate

Respond to the following with a point rating that reflects your opinion.

	1 2 3 4
Ideas	■■■□
Evidence	■■■■
Language and Conventions	■■□□

Submit

 SENTENCE FRAMES

- You were able to (completely / partly / almost) ___ answer the prompt.
- You could answer the prompt more completely by . . .

- I thought differently about the text after reading . . .
- My favorite part of your response is . . .

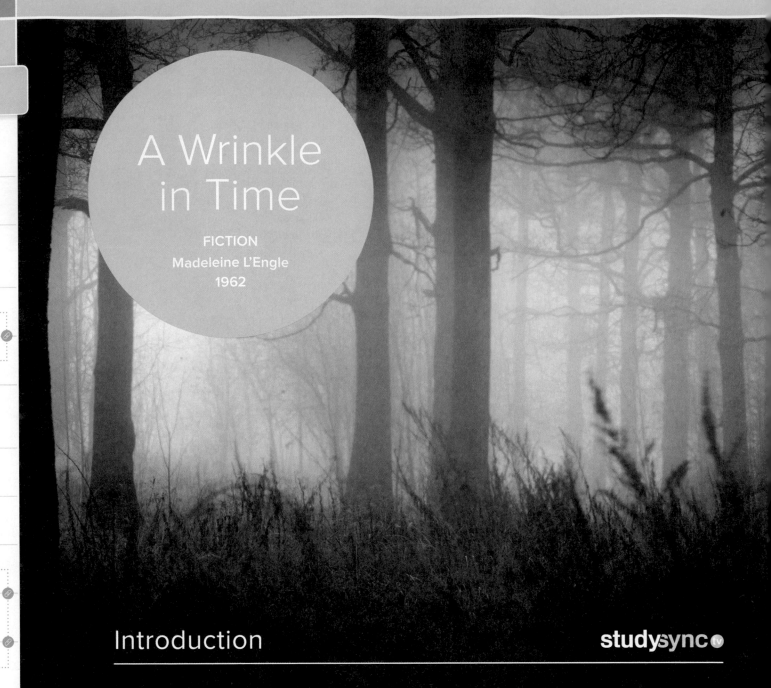

A Wrinkle in Time

FICTION
Madeleine L'Engle
1962

Introduction

studysync tv

Meg Murry and her precocious younger brother, Charles Wallace, will do anything they can to find their father. Did their father's top-secret experiments with time-travel cause his mysterious disappearance? What evil forces are holding him hostage? In *A Wrinkle in Time* by Madeleine L'Engle (1918–2007), Meg and Charles embark on a dangerous journey to find the answers, joined by their young neighbor, Calvin. In the excerpt, they have arrived on distant planet Camazotz, where they encounter a strange man with a fixed, red-eyed gaze. Telepathically, he urges them to merge their thoughts with his. First published in 1963, L'Engle's beloved novel won a Newbery Medal, the Sequoyah Book Award, and the Lewis Carroll Shelf Award, and it remains a classic to this day.

Meg Murry and her younger brother, Charles Wallace, along with their neighbor Calvin, embark on a dangerous journey to find their father, whose top-secret time-travel experiments may have led to his disappearance. Arriving on Camazotz, a faraway planet ruled by an evil force, the trio are brought before a sinister red-eyed man. After passing an intelligence test, Meg asks the man if he can tell them the whereabouts of their father. Although the red-eyed man appears to know their father's location, he refuses to help. In anger, Charles hits him, and in turn, the red-eyed man challenges Charles to look into his eyes. Charles complies and becomes hypnotized. Worried for his safety, Meg knocks Charles to the floor. The red-eyed man threatens her, saying that he is losing his patience and if Meg does not cooperate with his orders, she will never see her father again.

 Proficiency-leveled summaries and summaries in multiple languages are available digitally.

 Audio and audio text highlighting are available with this text.

COMPARING WITHIN AND ACROSS GENRES

 Madeleine L'Engle's novel *A Wrinkle in Time* follows Meg, her younger brother Charles, and their neighbor Calvin as they embark on a dangerous journey to find Meg and Charles's missing father. Students will compare *A Wrinkle in Time* to the poem "Jabberwocky" and the novel *Gathering Blue* and consider how language and descriptions work to create a feeling of uncertainty, and how context clues help decipher unknown or unique language, settings, or events.

Access Complex Text

LEXILE: 740   **WORD COUNT:** 1,076

The following areas may be challenging for students, particularly 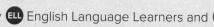 English Language Learners and Ⓐ Approaching grade-level learners.

Connection of Ideas	Specific Vocabulary	Sentence Structure
• Analyzing the relationship between character and plot may prove difficult for some students. • Suggest that students look for ways in which the decisions and actions of the characters alter or advance plot events and how the characters themselves change in response to events in the story.	• Some students may have difficulty with unfamiliar words, words with multiple meanings, and unusual constructions. • Words and constructions such as *once ten is ten* and *probed* may need to be defined.	• Much of the red-eyed man's dialogue is not directly attributed to him. Students must infer the speaker from the surrounding dialogue and narration. • Several of the sentences in the narration have multiple clauses and phrases. This may present problems for some students.

** SCAFFOLDS**   **ENGLISH LANGUAGE LEARNERS**   Ⓐ **APPROACHING GRADE LEVEL**   **BEYOND GRADE LEVEL**

These icons identify differentiation strategies and scaffolded support for a variety of students. See the digital lesson plan for additional differentiation strategies and scaffolds.

Instructional Path

The print teacher's edition includes essential point-of-use instruction and planning tools. Complete lesson plans and program documents appear in your digital teacher account.

First Read: *A Wrinkle in Time*

Objectives: After an initial reading and discussion of the text, students will be able to identify and describe characters and setting details as well as articulate events that are central to the story's plot.

Skill: Context Clues

Objectives: After reading and discussing a model of close reading, students will be able to determine the meaning of unknown words and phrases as they are used in the text.

Close Read: *A Wrinkle in Time*

Objectives: After engaging in a close reading and discussion of the text, students will be able to analyze how context clues and the author's language contribute to an understanding of the text in a short, written response.

Progress Monitoring

Opportunities to Learn	Opportunities to Demonstrate Learning	Opportunities to Reteach

Context Clues

⚙ Skill: Context Clues	⚙ Skill: Context Clues • Your Turn ▤ Close Read • Skills Focus • Collaborative Conversation • Write	⚙ Unit 6 Skill: Letter to His Daughter

First Read

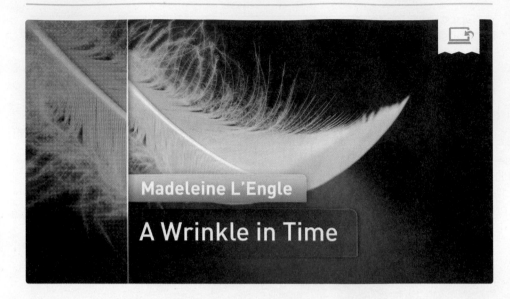

Madeleine L'Engle

A Wrinkle in Time

Introduce the Text

As a class, watch the video preview and have students read the introduction in pairs to make connections to the video preview.

To activate prior knowledge and experiences, ask students:

- What elements of the science fiction genre are present in this video preview?

- How does the information in the video preview and the introduction connect with other science fiction books you may have read?

ELL SPEAKING FRAMES

- The _____ in the video makes me think _____.
- The video shows _____. This makes me wonder _____.
- I think the text will _____. I think this because _____.
- I predict that there will be _____. I believe this because _____.

Entry Point

As students prepare to read *A Wrinkle in Time*, share the following information with them to provide context.

✓ Madeleine L'Engle's manuscript of *A Wrinkle in Time* was rejected 26 times before it was published. Some publishers thought the content would be too difficult for children to understand, especially since it had an underlying theme of good and evil. *A Wrinkle in Time* was the winner of the Newbery Medal in 1963, a year after it was published. To this day, it is still one of the most banned books of all time.

✓ L'Engle based the protagonist of *A Wrinkle in Time*, Meg Murray, on herself. She described herself as an awkward child who did not do well in school. Meg Murray became one of the first female protagonists in a science fiction novel. It is believed that publishers were also hesitant to have a girl as the lead in a science fiction story because it was a genre that mostly appealed to boys. However, the story, and Meg Murray, became a major success. This was a huge step for females in the world of science fiction.

✓ Madeleine L'Engle's novel *A Wrinkle in Time* was made into a fantasy/science fiction movie in 2018.

"The only reason we are here is because we think our father is here. Can you tell us where to find him?"

from Chapter 7: The Man with Red Eyes

1 "Once ten is ten. Once eleven is eleven. Once twelve is twelve."

2 The number words pounded insistently against Meg's brain. They seemed to be boring their way into her skull.

3 "Twice one is two. Twice two is four. Twice three is six."

4 Calvin's voice came out in an angry shout. "Fourscore and seven years ago our fathers brought forth on this continent a new nation, **conceived** in liberty, and dedicated to the proposition that all men are created equal."

5 "Twice four is eight. Twice five is ten. Twice six is twelve."

6 "Father!" Meg screamed. "Father!" The scream, half involuntary, jerked her mind back out of darkness.

7 The words of the multiplication table seemed to break up into laughter. "Splendid! Splendid! You have passed your **preliminary** tests with flying colors."

8 "You didn't think we were as easy as all that, falling for that old stuff, did you?" Charles Wallace demanded.

9 "Ah, I hoped not. I most sincerely hoped not. But after all you are very young and very impressionable, and the younger the better, my little man. The younger the better."

10 Meg looked up at the fiery eyes, at the light pulsing above them, and then away. She tried looking at the mouth, at the thin, almost colorless lips, and this was more possible, even though she had to look obliquely, so that she was not sure exactly what the face really looked like, whether it was young or old, cruel or kind, human or alien.

11 "If you please," she said, trying to sound calm and brave. "The only reason we are here is because we think our father is here. Can you tell us where to find him?"

Skill:
Context Clues

Meg tries to look at the man and then looks away. She seems to be having a hard time looking directly at the man's fiery eyes. Looking at him obliquely suggests that she is looking at him sideways, or indirectly. So obliquely must mean "indirectly." Meg can't tell what he really looks like, or if he's even human!

Copyright © BookheadEd Learning, LLC

Analyze Vocabulary Using Context Clues

In paragraph 4, focus on the sentence that uses the word *conceived*. Point out these context clues:

1. First I notice that this is a quote from The Gettysburg Address.

2. In this quote, Lincoln is describing the creation of the United States.

3. I notice words and phrases that relate to birth and the creative spirit, like "brought forth" and "new."

4. I think the word *conceived* used this way must mean "formed" or "made up."

Context Clues

How does the author's description of the man and Meg's view of him help us to understand the meaning of the word "obliquely"?

The reader sees that Meg has a difficult time looking at the man directly, so the reader determines that "obliquely" means "not directly."

SELECTION VOCABULARY

conceive / concebir *verb* to think of or develop an idea COGNATE

preliminary / preliminar *adjective* describing a state, an action, or an event preceding something else COGNATE

- What is being described as *preliminary*?
- Did Charles say that they would be easy or difficult?

TEXT TALK

Who are Meg, Calvin, and Charles Wallace looking for?

See paragraph 11: The children are looking for Meg and Charles Wallace's father.

What mental powers does this being have?

See paragraphs 7 and 20: The being has the power of mind control and the ability to communicate without words.

Testing Our Limits

Skills Focus

QUESTION 1: Context Clues

The Man with Red Eyes uses the word "abandoning" when talking about Meg and Charles Wallace's father. He says, "He hasn't been acting very like a father." Meg and Charles are looking for their father - the word "abandoning" must mean "leaving."

Skills Focus

QUESTION 3: Character, Context Clues

The Man with Red Eyes accuses Meg of being impatient because she wants to see her father "right now." The narrator confirms that patience is "not one of Meg's virtues."

Skills Focus

QUESTION 4: Compare and Contrast

This exchange between Charles Wallace and the Man with Red Eyes reminds me of the father's warning to his son in "Jabberwocky":

"'Beware the Jabberwock, my son!/The jaws that bite, the claws that catch!

While Carroll and L'Engle use language in different ways, both establish a sense of menace.

Skills Focus

QUESTION 2: Setting, Context Clues

L'Engle confirms that the Man with Red Eyes is sitting at a higher level than the children. Meg and Calvin pull Charles Wallace "back from the platform." I also read that there are men in "dark smocks" in the room. This adds to the feeling that the setting is supernatural and eerie.

12 "Ah, your father!" There seemed to be a great chortling of delight. "Ah, yes, your father! It is not *can* I, you know, young lady, but *will* I?"

13 "Will you, then?"

14 "That depends on a number of things. Why do you want your father?"

15 "Didn't you ever have a father yourself?" Meg demanded. "You don't want him for a *reason*. You want him because he's your *father*."

16 "Ah, but he hasn't been *acting* very like a father, lately, has he? **Abandoning** his wife and his four little children to go gallivanting off on wild adventures of his own."

17 "He was working for the government. He'd never have left us otherwise. And we want to see him, please. Right now."

18 "My, but the little miss is impatient! Patience, patience, young lady."

19 Meg did not tell the man on the chair that patience was not one of her virtues.

20 "And by the way, my children," he continued blandly, "you don't need to vocalize verbally with me, you know. I can understand you quite as well as you can understand me."

21 Charles Wallace put his hands on his hips defiantly. "The spoken word is one of the triumphs of man," he proclaimed, "and I intend to continue using it, particularly with people I don't trust." But his voice was shaking. Charles Wallace, who even as an infant had seldom cried, was near tears.

22 "And you don't trust me?"

23 "What reason have you given us to trust you?"

24 "What cause have I given you for distrust?" The thin lips curled slightly.

25 Suddenly Charles Wallace darted forward and hit the man as hard as he could, which was fairly hard, as he had had a good deal of coaching from the twins.

26 "Charles!" Meg screamed.

27 The men in dark smocks moved smoothly but with swiftness to Charles. The man in the chair casually raised one finger, and the men dropped back.

28 "Hold it—" Calvin whispered, and together he and Meg darted forward and grabbed Charles Wallace, pulling him back from the platform.

29 The man gave a wince and the thought of his voice was a little breathless, as though Charles Wallace's punch had succeeded in winding him. "May I ask why you did that?"

Please note that excerpts and passages in the StudySync® library and this workbook are intended as touchstones to generate interest in an author's work. The excerpts and passages do not substitute for the reading of entire texts, and StudySync® strongly recommends that students seek out and purchase the whole literary or informational work in order to experience it as the author intended. Links to online resellers are available in our digital library. In addition, complete works may be ordered through an authorized reseller by filling out and returning to StudySync® the order form enclosed in this workbook.

Reading & Writing Companion   87

Copyright © BookheadEd Learning, LLC

V   SELECTION VOCABULARY

abandon / abandonar *verb* to leave in a troubled state   COGNATE

ELL
- What did Meg's father do?
- Did he do it alone or with his family?

NOTES

30 "Because you aren't you," Charles Wallace said. "I'm not sure what you are, but you"—he pointed to the man on the chair—"aren't what's talking to us. I'm sorry if I hurt you. I didn't think you were real. I thought perhaps you were a robot, because I don't feel anything coming directly from you. I'm not sure where it's coming from, but it's coming through you. It isn't you."

31 "Pretty smart, aren't you?" the thought asked, and Meg had an uncomfortable feeling that she detected a snarl.

32 "It's not that I'm smart," Charles Wallace said, and again Meg could feel the palm of his hand sweating inside hers.

33 "Try to find out who I am, then," the thought probed.

34 "I have been trying," Charles Wallace said, his voice high and troubled.

35 "Look into my eyes. Look deep within them and I will tell you."

36 Charles Wallace looked quickly at Meg and Calvin, then said, as though to himself, "I have to," and focused his clear blue eyes on the red ones of the man in the chair. Meg looked not at the man but at her brother. After a moment it seemed that his eyes were no longer focusing. The pupils grew smaller and smaller, as though he were looking into an **intensely** bright light, until they seemed to close entirely, until his eyes were nothing but an opaque blue. He slipped his hands out of Meg's and Calvin's and started walking slowly toward the man on the chair.

37 "No!" Meg screamed. "No!"

38 But Charles Wallace continued his slow walk forward, and she knew that he had not heard her.

39 "No!" she screamed again, and ran after him. With her inefficient flying tackle she landed on him. She was so much larger than he that he fell sprawling, hitting his head a sharp crack against the marble floor. She knelt by him, sobbing. After a moment of lying there as though he had been knocked out by the blow, he opened his eyes, shook his head, and sat up. Slowly the pupils of his eyes dilated until they were back to normal, and the blood came back to his white cheeks.

40 The man on the chair spoke directly into Meg's mind, and now there was a **distinct** menace to the words. "I am not pleased," he said to her. "I could very easily lose patience with you, and that, for your information, young lady, would not be good for your father. If you have the slightest desire to see your father again, you had better cooperate."

Excerpted from *A Wrinkle in Time* by Madeleine L'Engle, published by Farrar, Straus and Giroux.

Skills Focus

QUESTION 5: Connect to Essential Question

Charles Wallace becomes convinced that the man in front of them is not who has been "talking" to them because the Man with Red Eyes gets winded when he's hit. Charles Wallace thinks the real source of the talking is too powerful to be hurt.

Skills Focus

QUESTION 2: Setting, Context Clues

Here I read that Charles Wallace hits 'his head, "a sharp crack against the marble floor."' This and other examples of descriptive language makes me think that the room must be cold. It must be pretty large too, since Meg can manage an "inefficient running tackle."

Skills Focus

QUESTION 1: Context Clues

It ends threateningly. The man says he "could very easily lose patience." He threatens that "she had better cooperate" if she wants to see her father. The narrator says there is NOW a distinct menace to his words. "Distinct" must mean "clear and unmistakable."

Skills Focus

QUESTION 5: Connect to Essential Question

I think the Man with Red Eyes's reaction to Meg rescuing her brother will probably change her perspective on trying to push him into revealing where her father is. He wanted to control Charles Wallace's mind and Meg won't cooperate either.

V SELECTION VOCABULARY

intensely / intensamente *adverb* to a great degree COGNATE

ELL
- What is being described as "intensely"?
- Is it harder to look into a light that is very bright or not very bright?

distinct / distintivo/a *adjective* not alike; different in nature or quality

ELL
- How does the Man with Red Eyes sound?
- Is this the same or different from earlier?

Think Questions

Circulate as students answer Think Questions independently. Scaffolds for these questions are shown on the opposite page.

QUESTION 1: Textual Evidence

The tests consist of a voice trying to take over the children's minds with number repetitions: "The number words . . . seemed to be boring their way into her [Meg's] skull." The children pass the tests by defending their minds from this hostile takeover.

QUESTION 2: Textual Evidence

Unlike Meg and Calvin, Charles Wallace understands that the voice is trying to trick the children with mind control. He also directly defies the voice by continuing to use spoken words. Finally, he senses that the voice is not really coming from the figure in front of them.

QUESTION 3: Textual Evidence

When Charles Wallace walks toward the man, Meg acts without thinking and hits her brother with an "inefficient flying tackle." This angers the voice, who says, "I could very easily lose patience with you, and that, for your information, young lady, would not be good for your father."

QUESTION 4: Context Clues

I think *abandoning* must mean "leaving behind." The man uses the word to describe how Meg's father went "off on wild adventures of his own." Since he is doing it without the rest of his family, it must mean he left them behind.

QUESTION 5: Context Clues

I think *intensely* must mean "extremely." The text says that Charles's pupils were getting smaller until they were almost completely closed. The text compares this to what happens when you look into a light. I know that the amount of light can affect your pupils, so the light being described must be extremely bright.

 First Read

Read *A Wrinkle in Time*. After you read, complete the Think Questions below.

THINK QUESTIONS

1. The voice says that Meg, Calvin, and Charles have passed their "preliminary tests." What tests have they passed, and how? Cite textual evidence from the selection to support your answer.

2. Write two or three sentences contrasting Charles Wallace with Meg and Calvin.

3. The author alludes to the saying "Patience is a virtue." How does Meg demonstrate a lack of patience in the text? Cite textual evidence from the selection to support your answer.

4. Find the word **abandoning** in paragraph 16 of *A Wrinkle in Time*. Use context clues in the surrounding sentences, as well as the sentence in which the word appears, to determine the word's meaning. Write your definition here and identify clues that helped you figure out its meaning.

5. Use context clues to determine the meaning of **intensely** as it is used in paragraph 36 of *A Wrinkle in Time*. Write your definition here and identify clues that helped you figure out its meaning. Then check the meaning in the dictionary.

Reading & Writing Companion 89

Think Questions

Use the scaffolds below to differentiate instruction for your **ELL** English Language Learners and **A** Approaching grade-level learners.

ELL **BEGINNING** Write a response using the <u>word bank</u> and <u>sentence frames</u>.

INTERMEDIATE Write a response using the <u>sentence frames</u>.

ADVANCED, ADVANCED HIGH Write a response using the <u>Text-Dependent Question Guide</u>.

A **APPROACHING** Write a response using the <u>Text-Dependent Question Guide</u>.

BEGINNING	INTERMEDIATE	APPROACHING / ADVANCED, ADVANCED HIGH
Word Bank	**Sentence Frames**	**Text-Dependent Question Guide**
adventure controlling look extremely demands alone speak bright coming from multiplication tables leaving behind the Man with Red Eyes father trick	The voice tries to control the children's minds with ____. The children pass the tests by ____ their thoughts. Calvin shouts a speech and Meg calls for her ____.	1. • How does the voice try to control the children's minds? • How does Calvin protect himself? • How does Meg protect herself?
	Charles Wallace understands that the voice is trying to ____ the children with mind control. He also challenges the voice by continuing to ____. Finally, he senses that the voice is not really ____ the figure in front of the children.	2. • What does Charles Wallace understand? • How does Charles Wallace continue to do? • What does Charles Wallace suspect about the voice?
	Meg is not patient. She ____ to see her father. She argues with ____.	3. • What is Meg impatient about? • How does Meg act?
	Meg's father left on an ____. He did it all ____. This gives me a clue that "abandoning" means ____.	4. • Read: "Ah, but he hasn't been acting very like a father, lately, has he? **Abandoning** his wife and his four little children to go gallivanting off on wild adventures of his own." • What did Meg's father do? • Who did he do it with?
	"Intensely" describes how a very ____ light shines. It is hard to ____ at lights like that. This gives me a clue that "intensely" is similar to "____."	5. • Read: "The pupils grew smaller and smaller, as though he was looking into an **intensely** bright light, until they seemed to close entirely, until his eyes were nothing but an opaque blue." • What is being described? • Is it harder to look at a light that is very bright or less bright?

Reading Comprehension OPTIONAL

Have students complete the digital reading comprehension questions ✓ when they finish reading.

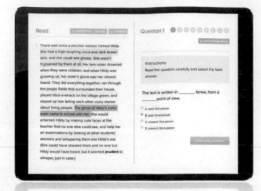

ANSWER KEY

QUESTION 1: A	**QUESTION 5:** A	**QUESTION 9:**
QUESTION 2: C	**QUESTION 6:** C	*See first chart.*
QUESTION 3: C	**QUESTION 7:** D	**QUESTION 10:**
QUESTION 4: B	**QUESTION 8:** B	*See second chart.*

Dialogue	Character
"Didn't you ever have a father yourself?"	Meg
"What reason have you given us to trust you?"	Charles
"But after all you are very young and very impressionable, and the younger the better, my little man."	The Man with Red Eyes
"Fourscore and seven years ago our fathers brought forth on this continent a new nation, conceived in liberty, and dedicated to the proposition that all men are created equal."	Calvin

Description	Character
ominous	The Man with Red Eyes
heroic	Meg
stubborn	Charles

Connect and Extend OPTIONAL

CONNECT TO EXTENDED WRITING PROJECT

Students can use *A Wrinkle in Time* as a mentor text for their Extended Writing Project. They may explore how a sudden change in setting can lead to an unexpected challenge as they craft their own narrative.

BEYOND THE BOOK

Game: **Telepathy Battle**

Group students in pairs for a telepathy battle with a fictional character. Each pair will need to select (or create) a character to engage in the telepathy battle. Some places from which students might select characters include:

- Unit texts, Pokemon, anime, video games, movies, books, etc.

Once students have selected their characters, they will decide how to engage in their telepathy battle. They can:

- Perform a telepathy battle with a rehearsed blocking.
- Write a sensorily rich script of their internal dialogue.
- Draw a comic strip of their characters engaged in a battle using a mix of drawings and thought bubbles.

Skill:
Context Clues

Use the Checklist to analyze Context Clues in *A Wrinkle in Time*. Refer to the sample student annotations about Context Clues in the text.

••• CHECKLIST FOR CONTEXT CLUES

In order to use context as a clue to infer the meaning of a word, note the following:

- ✓ clues about the word's part of speech
- ✓ clues in the surrounding text about the word's meaning
- ✓ signal words that cue a type of context clue, such as:
    - *for example* or *for instance* to signal an example context clue
    - *like, similarly,* or *just as* to signal a comparison clue
    - *but, however,* or *unlike* to signal a contrast context clue

To determine the meaning of a word as it is used in a text, consider the following questions:

- ✓ What is the overall sentence, paragraph, or text about?
- ✓ How does the word function in the sentence?
- ✓ What clues can help me determine the word's part of speech?
- ✓ What textual clues can help me figure out the word's definition?
- ✓ Are there any examples that show what the word means?
- ✓ What do I think the word means?

To verify the preliminary determination of the meaning of the word based on context, consider the following questions:

- ✓ Does the definition I inferred make sense within the context of the sentence?
- ✓ Which of the dictionary's definitions makes sense within the context of the sentence?

ⓥ SKILL VOCABULARY

context clue / la clave del contexto *noun* a hint in the surrounding text that can help a reader infer the meaning of an unfamiliar word, phrase, or description

infer / inferir *verb* to determine something by using reasoning and evidence from the text COGNATE

definition context clue / la clave del contexto de definición *noun* text that provides a definition of a word

---

Skill: Context Clues

Introduce the Skill

Watch the Concept Definition video and read the following definition with your students.

When readers come across words they don't know, they often use context to determine the meanings of the unfamiliar words. **Context clues** are hints in the surrounding text that a reader can use to **infer** the meaning of an unfamiliar word. Some common types of context clues include the following:

- **Definition:** an explanation of the word's meaning before or after the word appears, usually set off by a comma
- **Example:** one or more examples in a text that may demonstrate the meaning of a word
- **Comparison:** determining a word's meaning based on how it is like something else in the text
- **Contrast:** determining a word's meaning based on how it is unlike something else in the text

In addition, the genre of a text and what it is about also provide context clues for a word's meaning. Readers can verify their preliminary definitions of words or phrases by using a print or digital resource.

TURN AND TALK

1. Where have you seen or read words whose meanings you didn't know?

2. What did you do to determine what those unknown words meant?

ELL SPEAKING FRAMES
- A word I didn't know in the text was ____.
- I tried to understand this word by looking at ____.
- Now, I think this word means ____.

Your Turn

Ask students to complete the Your Turn Activity.

QUESTION 1

A. Incorrect. This word means "achievement" and does not help the readers understand the word "defiantly."

B. Incorrect. This phrase shows the reader that Charles was upset, but it does not describe the meaning of the word "defiantly."

C. Incorrect. This word is a synonym of the noun "baby" and does not help the reader understand the word "defiantly."

D. Correct. This phrase shows that "defiantly" describes Charles Wallace's manner as he resists what the man is saying by placing his hands on his hips.

QUESTION 2

A. Incorrect. The text states that Charles is near tears, which is strange since he seldom cried even as a baby. The reader can infer that "seldom" means "rarely", "not often"

B. Incorrect. The reader can use context clues to see that Charles barely cried as a baby, and so "always" would not make sense to describe the word "seldom."

C. Correct. The text states that Charles is near tears, which is strange since he seldom cried even as a baby. The reader can infer that "seldom" means "rarely," or that he hardly ever cried.

D. Incorrect. This word does not make sense within the sentence.

QUESTION 3

PART A

A. Correct Charles is deeply upset by what the man is saying because the text states that he puts his hand on his hips and responds defiantly. He is also scared since he is close to tears, even though he rarely cries.

B. Incorrect. Charles is not only scared of the man, he is also upset by him.

C. Incorrect. Charles is not only upset by the man, he is also scared of him.

D. Incorrect. This line shows what the Man with Red Eyes said, not the emotion it caused Charles or his opinion of him.

Skill:
Context Clues

Reread paragraphs 20–24 of *A Wrinkle in Time*. Then, using the Checklist on the previous page, answer the multiple-choice questions below.

⟳ YOUR TURN

1. Which word or phrase helped you determine the meaning of **defiantly** in the passage?

   ○ A. "triumph"
   ○ B. "voice was shaking"
   ○ C. "infant"
   ○ D. "put his hands on his hips"

2. What is most likely the meaning of the word **seldom** as it's used in this passage?

   ○ A. often
   ○ B. always
   ○ C. rarely
   ○ D. excited

3. This question has two parts. First, answer Part A. Then, answer Part B.

   Part A: How would you describe Charles's opinion of the Man with Red Eyes, using context clues?

   ○ A. Charles is both scared of and deeply upset by the Man with the Red Eyes.
   ○ B. Charles is scared of the Man with Red Eyes.
   ○ C. Charles is deeply upset by the Man with Red Eyes.
   ○ D. Charles is entertained by the Man with Red Eyes.

   Part B: Which of the following lines from the passage best supports the answer to Part A?

   ○ A. "I can understand you quite as well as you can understand me."
   ○ B. "But his voice was shaking. Charles Wallace, who even as an infant had seldom cried, was near tears."
   ○ C. "What cause have I given you for distrust?' The thin lips curled slightly."
   ○ D. "'And by the way, my children,' he continued blandly, 'you don't need to vocalize verbally with me, you know.'"

PART B

A. This line shows what the Man with Red Eyes said, not the emotion it caused Charles or his opinion of him.

B. Correct This line shows that Charles was experiencing both fear and sadness when talking to the Man with Red Eyes.

C. Incorrect. Although this line suggests that the Man with Red Eyes is not accepted by Charles and the others, it does not give evidence of Charles's opinion of him.

D. Incorrect. This line shows what the Man with Red Eyes said, not the emotion it caused Charles or his opinion of him.

Close Read

studysync●

Reread *A Wrinkle in Time*. As you reread, complete the Skills Focus questions below. Then use your answers and annotations from the questions to help you complete the Write activity.

◎ SKILLS FOCUS

1. Think about the word choices Madeleine L'Engle makes in *A Wrinkle in Time*. Identify examples of unknown words and what context clues you used to understand them.

2. Identify the words and phrases the author uses to describe the setting, and explain how you used context clues to understand them.

3. Using context clues, identify how the characters in *A Wrinkle in Time* feel and how you would feel if you were in their situation. Support your description with textual evidence.

4. In "Jabberwocky," Lewis Carroll uses nonsensical words. In *Gathering Blue*, Lois Lowry uses descriptive language. Identify passages in *A Wrinkle in Time* where L'Engle uses language in similar ways to Carroll's or Lowry's.

5. Meg, Calvin, and Charles Wallace are dealing with the challenge of understanding the unknown in *A Wrinkle in Time*. Explain how their experiences change their perspectives of the Man with Red Eyes. Support your explanation with textual evidence.

✎ WRITE

COMPARATIVE: "Jabberwocky" and *A Wrinkle in Time* both have eerie language. *A Wrinkle in Time* and *Gathering Blue* both feature settings and events that make the reader feel uncertain. How does using context clues help you understand these unique selections? Compare the language and context clues you used in *A Wrinkle in Time* with those in one of the other two selections. Remember to support your ideas with evidence from the texts.

 Close Read

Close Read

Skills Focus

QUESTION 1: Context Clues

See paragraphs 15–17 and 40.

QUESTION 2: Setting, Context Clues

See paragraphs 27–28 and 39.

QUESTION 3: Character, Context Clues

See paragraphs 17–19.

QUESTION 4: Compare and Contrast

Paragraphs 3-4: Calvin's anger reminds me of Vandara's in *Gathering Blue*. Both show anger against authority figures that have power over them. Calvin recites the Gettysburg Address to block out the Man with Red Eyes's attempt to control him. It's interesting that he picks something that talks about liberty and equality. Vandara is angry at the Council of Guardians for their ruling. She can't really change the ruling, but she remains defiant, stalking off after being dismissed.

QUESTION 4: Compare and Contrast

See paragraphs 22–24.

QUESTION 5: Connect to Essential Question

See paragraphs 30 and 40.

 ## Writer's Notebook

Connect to Essential Question: Give students time to reflect on how *A Wrinkle in Time* connects to the unit's essential question "What do we do when life gets hard?" by freewriting in their Writer's Notebooks.

ELL **Beginning & Intermediate**

Read aloud the unit's essential question: "What do we do when life gets hard?" Encourage students to draw their connections or allow students to write in their native language. Circulate around the room, prompting students for their thoughts as they respond orally or through pantomime.

Advanced & Advanced High

Allow students to share their connections orally in pairs or small groups before freewriting.

StudySyncTV

Project the StudySyncTV episode  and pause at the following times to prompt discussion:

2:46   What words and phrases do Drew, Alicia, and Michael focus on in describing Charles Wallace's personality? What do they conclude?

4:45   What words and phrases does Drew cite as characteristic of Meg? What textual evidence does the group use to determine if Meg's personality traits will help or hurt her in the setting?

8:29   Why do the students think Calvin chooses to recite the Gettysburg Address? How does this lead them to better understand what the Man with Red Eyes is trying to do? What do they conclude about why Meg, Charles Wallace, and Calvin might have an advantage over the Man with Red Eyes?

Collaborative Conversation

SCAFFOLDS

Break students into collaborative conversation groups to discuss the Close Read prompt. Ask students to use the StudySyncTV episode as a model for their discussion. Remind them to reference their Skills Focus annotations in their discussion.

"Jabberwocky" and *A Wrinkle in Time* both have eerie and supernatural language. *A Wrinkle in Time* and *Gathering Blue* both feature settings and events that create feelings of uncertainty. How does using context clues help you understand these unique selections? Compare the language and context clues in *A Wrinkle in Time* with those in one of the other two selections. Remember to support your ideas with evidence from the text.

Use the scaffolds below to differentiate instruction for your (ELL) English Language Learners and (A) Approaching grade-level learners.

(ELL)   **BEGINNING, INTERMEDIATE**   Use the <u>discussion guide</u> and <u>speaking frames</u> to facilitate the discussion with support from the teacher.

     ADVANCED, ADVANCED HIGH   Use the <u>discussion guide</u> and <u>speaking frames</u> to facilitate the discussion in mixed-level groups.

(A)   **APPROACHING**   Use the <u>discussion guide</u> to facilitate the discussion in mixed-level groups.

> APPROACHING
> ADVANCED, ADVANCED HIGH
> BEGINNING, INTERMEDIATE

Discussion Guide	Speaking Frames
1. What eerily suggestive language is used in "Jabberwocky" and *A Wrinkle in Time*?	• In "Jabberwocky," the author describes ____. • In *A Wrinkle in Time*, the author describes ____.
2. What language is used to describe challenging events in *Gathering Blue* and *A Wrinkle in Time*?	• In *Gathering Blue*, the author describes ____. • In *A Wrinkle in Time*, the author describes ____.
3. How do the authors use language to make the reader feel uncertain?	• The authors use language like ____. • This makes readers feel ____.

Review Prompt and Rubric

Before students begin writing, review the writing prompt and rubric with the class.

COMPARATIVE: "Jabberwocky" and *A Wrinkle in Time* both have eerie language. *A Wrinkle in Time* and Gathering Blue both feature settings and events that make the reader feel uncertain. How does using context clues help you understand these unique selections? Compare the language and context clues you used in *A Wrinkle in Time* with those in one of the other two selections. Remember to support your ideas with evidence from the texts.

ELL PROMPT GUIDE

A
- What eerie language is used in in *A Wrinkle in Time* and "Jabberwocky"?
- What language or descriptions do L'Engle and Carroll use to create this feeling?
- Why do the children in *A Wrinkle in Time* and Kira in *Gathering Blue* feel uncertain?

- What language or descriptions do L'Engle and Lowry use to create this feeling?
- How does using context clues help you understand these texts?
- How are the stories similar?
- How are they different?

Two additional rubric items for Language and Conventions appear in your digital teacher and student accounts

Score	Context Clues	Compare and Contrast
4	The writer clearly analyzes and explains how context clues and each author's language contribute to an understanding of the text. The writer provides exemplary analysis, using relevant evidence from the text.	The writer clearly compares and contrasts the texts. The writer provides exemplary analysis, using relevant evidence from the text.
3	The writer analyzes and explains how context clues and each author's language contribute to an understanding of the text. The writer provides sufficient analysis, using relevant evidence from the text most of the time.	The writer compares and contrasts the texts. The writer provides sufficient analysis, using relevant evidence from the text most of the time.
2	The writer begins to analyze or explain how context clues and each author's language contribute to an understanding of the text, but the analysis is incomplete. The writer uses relevant evidence from the text only some of the time.	The writer begins to compare and contrast the texts, but the comparison is incomplete. The writer uses relevant evidence from the text only some of the time.
1	The writer attempts to analyze or explain how context clues and each author's language contribute to an understanding of the text, but the analysis is not successful. The writer uses little or no relevant evidence from the text.	The writer attempts to compare and contrast the texts, but the comparison is not successful. The writer uses little or no relevant evidence from the text.
0	The writer does not provide a relevant response to the prompt or does not provide a response at all.	The writer does not provide a relevant response to the prompt or does not provide a response at all.

Write

Ask students to complete the writing assignment using textual evidence to support their answers.

Use the scaffolds below to differentiate instruction for your **ELL** English Language Learners and **A** Approaching grade-level learners.

ELL **BEGINNING** With the help of the <u>word bank</u>, write a response using <u>paragraph frame 1</u>.

INTERMEDIATE With the help of the <u>word bank</u>, write a response using <u>paragraph frames 1 and 2</u>.

ADVANCED, ADVANCED HIGH Write a response of differentiated length using the <u>sentence starters</u>.

A **APPROACHING** Write a response of differentiated length using the <u>sentence starters</u>.

BEGINNING		ADVANCED, ADVANCED HIGH
INTERMEDIATE		APPROACHING

Word Bank	Paragraph Frame 1	Paragraph Frame 2	Sentence Starters
context clues eerie abandoned nonsense Man with Red Eyes	L'Engle's character, the ____ , says the children's father ____ them, so the children are looking for their father in a strange place. Carroll uses ____ words in "Jabberwocky" to describe a strange creature. The settings of these texts seem supernatural and ____. I can use ____ to better understand what these unknown words mean in both texts.	Other unknown words L'Engle and Carroll use are ____ and ____. I can look at ____ to figure out the meanings of the unknown words. By using context clues, I know that ____ means ____ in *A Wrinkle in Time*. By using context clues, I know that ____ means ____ in "Jabberwocky."	• L'Engle uses the unknown words ____ to describe . . . • Carroll uses the unknown words ____ to describe . . . • Lowry uses the unknown words ____ to describe . . . • I can figure out these unknown words by . . . • This language is . . . • The stories are alike because . . . • One way that they are different is . . . • This is important because . . .

Peer Review

Students should submit substantive feedback to two peers using the review instructions below.

- How well does this response answer the prompt?
- How well does the writer support ideas with details and examples from each text?
- Which sentence in the writer's response made you think differently about each text?
- What did the writer do well in this response? What does the writer need to work on?

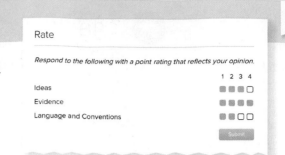

Rate

Respond to the following with a point rating that reflects your opinion.

	1 2 3 4
Ideas	■■■□
Evidence	■■■■
Language and Conventions	■■□□

Submit

 SENTENCE FRAMES

- You were able to (completely / partly / almost) ____ answer the prompt because . . .
- You could answer the prompt more completely by . . .
- You supported the idea of . . . with the detail of . . .

- One idea that needs more support is . . .
- I thought differently about the texts after reading . . .
- My favorite part of your responses is . . .

✸ Blast: Judge a Book by its Cover

How do you judge a book by its cover?

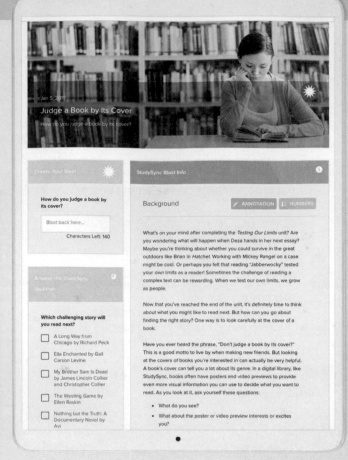

✸ TEXT TALK

What is one strategy you can use for self-selecting a new text? How does it work?

I can look at visual information to help me decide what I want to read.

What should you do once you choose a text that interests you?

Start reading the text to confirm my interest. If I like it, I should keep reading.

✸ Create Your Own Blast

SCAFFOLDS

Ask students to write a 140-character Blast after they complete the QuikPoll.

Use the scaffolds below to differentiate instruction for your **ELL** English Language Learners.

ELL **BEGINNING** Write a response using the <u>word bank</u> to complete the <u>sentence frames</u>.

INTERMEDIATE Write a response using the <u>sentence frames</u>.

ADVANCED, ADVANCED HIGH Write a response using the <u>sentence starter</u>.

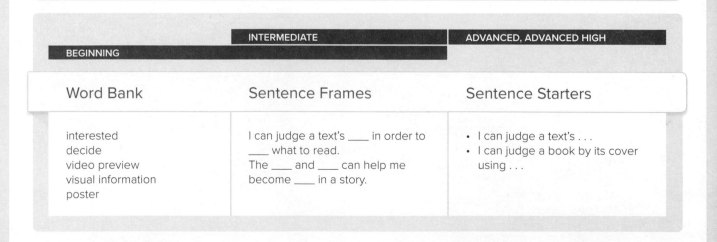

BEGINNING	INTERMEDIATE	ADVANCED, ADVANCED HIGH
Word Bank	**Sentence Frames**	**Sentence Starters**
interested decide video preview visual information poster	I can judge a text's ＿＿＿ in order to ＿＿＿ what to read. The ＿＿＿ and ＿＿＿ can help me become ＿＿＿ in a story.	• I can judge a text's . . . • I can judge a book by its cover using . . .

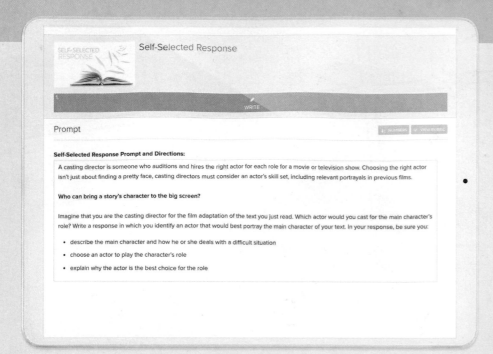

Self-Selected Response

Self-Selected Response Prompt and Directions:

A casting director is someone who auditions and hires the right actor for each role for a movie or television show. Choosing the right actor isn't just about finding a pretty face, casting directors must consider an actor's skill set, including relevant portrayals in previous films.

Who can bring a story's character to the big screen?

Imagine that you are the casting director for the film adaptation of the text you just read. Which actor would you cast for the main character's role? Write a response in which you identify an actor that would best portray the main character of your text. In your response, be sure you:

- describe the main character and how he or she deals with a difficult situation
- choose an actor to play the character's role
- explain why the actor is the best choice for the role

Self-Selected Response

Introduce the Prompt

Read aloud the prompt. Ask students to discuss:

- What is the prompt asking you to do?
- Why might it be a good idea to think about how a character deals with difficult situations in a text before choosing an actor?

 ## Write

SCAFFOLDS

Ask students to complete the writing assignment using text evidence to support their answers.

Use the scaffolds below to differentiate instruction for your **ELL** English Language Learners and **A** Approaching grade-level learners.

ELL **BEGINNING** With the help of the <u>word bank</u>, write a response using <u>paragraph frame 1</u>.

INTERMEDIATE With the help of the <u>word bank</u>, write a response using <u>paragraph frames 1 and 2</u>.

ADVANCED, ADVANCED HIGH Write a response of differentiated length using the <u>sentence starters</u>.

A **APPROACHING** Write a response of differentiated length using the <u>sentence starters</u>.

BEGINNING / INTERMEDIATE		INTERMEDIATE	ADVANCED, ADVANCED HIGH / APPROACHING
Word Bank	**Paragraph Frame 1**	**Paragraph Frame 2**	**Sentence Starters**
pain fear angry sensitive beautiful hunger sadness strong intelligent sly	I read the text (title) ____ by (author) ____. (Main character) ____ is a (describe main character) ____. One difficult situation (main character) ____ faces is (difficulty or conflict) ____. An actor who could portray (main character) ____ is (actor name) ____. I chose (actor name) ____ as the best for the role because of his portrayal in (movie title) ____. The reason why (actor name) ____ is the best for the role is ____.	I read the text (title) ____ by (author) ____. (Main character) ____ is a (describe main character) ____. One difficult situation (main character) ____ faces is (difficulty or conflict) ____. An actor who I think has the qualities to play this character in a film adaptation is (actor name) ____. (actor's name) ____ 's portrayal in the film (movie title) is the main reason I think he/she should play this role. Some qualities (actor's name) ____ has that make me think this are ____.	• I read the text . . . by . . . • The main character is . . . • One difficult situation from the text is . . . • An actor I would choose to portray a character from the text is . . . • This actor is appropriate because . . .

Extended Writing Project

EXTENDED WRITING PROJECT
NARRATIVE WRITING

The Extended Writing Project (EWP) in Grade 6, Unit 1 focuses on narrative writing. Students consider the following question—How can an unexpected event turn into a major challenge?—as they write a narrative about how an individual might face an unexpected challenge on what was supposed to be a normal day. The unit's selections about people experiencing challenges, difficulties, and other hardships provide a context for students, and the multiple pieces of fiction in the unit serve as mentor texts for students to analyze and emulate. Specific skill lessons teach developing ideas, organization, and conventions, while other skill lessons on story beginnings, descriptive details, and dialogue focus on characteristics of the genre and help students develop their unique voices. Directed revision leads students through the process of revising for clarity, development, organization, word choice, and sentence variety. Throughout the EWP, students have the opportunity to practice using created student writing, authentic texts, and their own work.

 Audio and audio text highlighting are available in select lessons in the Extended Writing Project.

CONNECT TO ESSENTIAL QUESTION

What do we do when life gets hard?

The texts in this unit taught students how an author uses narrative elements to show characters facing a challenge. Using plot, setting, character, and dialogue, students will now craft their own narrative about facing a challenge.

Extended Writing Project Prompt

How can an unexpected event turn into a major challenge?

Imagine the very worst possible day. What event or individual makes that day so terrible? How do your characters respond? Write a story in which the main character faces an unexpected challenge on what was supposed to be a normal day.

 **SCAFFOLDS**    **ELL ENGLISH LANGUAGE LEARNERS**   **A APPROACHING GRADE LEVEL**    **B BEYOND GRADE LEVEL**

These icons identify differentiation strategies and scaffolded support for a variety of students. See the digital lesson plan for additional differentiation strategies and scaffolds.

Instructional Path

The print teacher's edition includes essential point-of-use instruction and planning tools. Complete lesson plans and program documents appear in your digital teacher account.

Narrative Writing Process: Plan

Objectives: After learning about genre characteristics and craft, students will analyze a sample Student Model and plan a meaningful narrative in response to a prompt.

Skill: Organizing Narrative Writing

Objectives: After reading and discussing a model of student writing, students will develop their drafts by organizing their narrative effectively.

Narrative Writing Process: Draft

Objectives: After reading a Student Model draft and reviewing a writing checklist, students will draft a meaningful narrative in response to a prompt.

Skill: Story Beginnings

Objectives: After reading and discussing a model of student writing, students will improve the beginning of a narrative by revising to present expository information in a way that grabs a reader's attention.

Skill: Descriptive Details

Objectives: After reading and discussing a model of student writing, students will further their narrative drafts by developing descriptive details.

Skill: Narrative Techniques

Objectives: After reading and discussing a model of student writing, students will develop their drafts by using narrative techniques, such as dialogue, pacing, and description, to develop experiences, events, and/or characters.

Skill: Transitions

Objectives: After reading and discussing a model of student writing, students will develop their drafts by using appropriate transitions to clarify the relationships among ideas and concepts.

Skill: Conclusions

Objectives: After reading and discussing a model of student writing, students will develop their drafts by providing a conclusion that follows from the narrated experiences or events.

Narrative Writing Process: Revise

Objectives: Students will use a revision guide to revise the draft of their narrative for clarity, development, organization, style, diction, and sentence effectiveness.

Grammar: Personal Pronouns

Objectives: After learning about personal pronouns and seeing how they are used in text examples, students will practice using personal pronouns correctly.

Grammar: Pronouns and Antecedents

Objectives: After learning about pronouns and antecedents and seeing how they are used in text examples, students will practice using pronouns and antecedents correctly.

Grammar: Consistent Pronoun Use

Objectives: After learning the rules of consistent pronoun use and seeing how they are used in text examples, students will practice using consistent pronouns.

Narrative Writing Process: Edit and Publish

Objectives: After seeing an example of editing in the Student Model and reviewing an editing checklist, students will edit and publish the final draft of their narrative.

Progress Monitoring

Opportunities to Learn	Opportunities to Demonstrate Learning	Opportunities to Reteach
Narrative Writing Process: Plan		
Narrative Writing Process: Plan	Narrative Writing Process: Plan • Write	Units 2–6 Process: Plan
Narrative Writing Process: Draft		
Narrative Writing Process: Draft	Narrative Writing Process: Draft • Write	Units 2–6 Process: Draft
Narrative Writing Process: Revise		
Narrative Writing Process: Revise	Narrative Writing Process: Revise • Write	Units 2–6 Process: Revise

Narrative Writing Process: Edit and Publish

Narrative Writing Process: Edit and Publish	Narrative Writing Process: Edit and Publish • Write	Units 2–4, 6 Process: Edit and Publish Unit 5 Process: Edit and Present

Organizing Narrative Writing

Skill: Organizing Narrative Writing	Skill: Organizing Narrative Writing • Your Turn Narrative Writing Process: Draft	Spotlight Skill: Organizing Narrative Writing

Story Beginnings

Skill: Story Beginnings	Skill: Story Beginnings • Your Turn Narrative Writing Process: Revise	Spotlight Skill: Story Beginnings

Descriptive Details

Skill: Descriptive Details	Skill: Descriptive Details • Your Turn Narrative Writing Process: Revise	Spotlight Skill: Descriptive Details

Narrative Techniques

Skill: Narrative Techniques	Skill: Narrative Techniques • Your Turn Narrative Writing Process: Revise	Spotlight Skill: Narrative Techniques

Transitions

⚙ Skill: Transitions

⚙ Skill: Transitions
  • Your Turn

✏ Narrative Writing Process: Revise

⚙ Units 2–3
  Skill: Transitions

⚙ Spotlight Skill: Transitions

Conclusions

⚙ Skill: Conclusions

⚙ Skill: Conclusions
  • Your Turn

✏ Narrative Writing Process: Revise

⚙ Units 2–3
  Skill: Conclusions

⚙ Spotlight Skill: Conclusions

Personal Pronouns

⚙ Grammar: Personal Pronouns

⚙ Grammar: Personal Pronouns
  • Your Turn

✏ Narrative Writing Process: Edit and Publish

⚙ Grammar: Subject-Verb Agreement —
  Agreement with Subject Pronouns

⚙ Grammar: Nouns — Proper and Common

Pronouns and Antecedents

⚙ Grammar:
  Pronouns and Antecedents

⚙ Grammar: Pronouns and Antecedents
  • Your Turn

✏ Narrative Writing Process: Edit and Publish

⚙ Grammar: Subject-Verb Agreement —
  Agreement with Indefinite Pronouns as Subjects

Consistent Pronoun Use

⚙ Grammar: Consistent Pronoun Use

⚙ Grammar:
  Consistent Pronoun Use
  • Your Turn

✏ Narrative Writing Process: Edit and Publish

⚙ Grammar: Pronouns — Interrogative and Demonstrative

Narrative Writing Process: Plan

Introduce the Extended Writing Project

- What is the prompt asking you to do?

- Which characteristics of narrative writing will you need to learn more about in order to respond to the prompt?

- What are the five characteristics of narrative writing?

- What elements of craft do narrative writers use?

  DIFFERENTIATED QUESTIONS

A • What does **challenge** mean?

- What are some situations that you would consider to be a challenge?

- What might make a challenge unexpected?

 ## Review the Rubric

Have students examine the Narrative Writing Rubric—Grade 6 grading rubric. Inform students that this is the same rubric that will be used to evaluate their completed Narrative Extended Writing Project.

 ### Narrative Writing Process: Plan

| PLAN | DRAFT | REVISE | EDIT AND PUBLISH |

The challenges that a character faces in a story are what make the story interesting. Sometimes a character is faced with a major challenge that is a matter of life and death, like Brian Robeson in *Hatchet*. At other times the challenge might be something small and seemingly insignificant, but it has a major effect on the character.

WRITING PROMPT

How can an unexpected event turn into a major challenge?

Imagine the very worst possible day. What event or individual makes that day so terrible? How do your characters respond? Write a story in which the main character faces an unexpected challenge on what was supposed to be a normal day. Regardless of the challenge you choose, be sure your narrative includes the following:

- a plot with a beginning, middle, and end
- a detailed setting
- characters and dialogue
- an interesting challenge
- a clear theme

Introduction to Narrative Writing

Narrative writing tells a story. It includes experiences or events that have been imagined by a writer. Good fiction writing uses effective techniques. These include relevant descriptive details and a structure with a series of events that contain a beginning, middle, and end. The characteristics of fiction writing include:

- setting
- characters
- plot
- theme
- point of view

As you continue with this Extended Writing Project, you'll receive more instruction and practice at crafting each of the characteristics of fiction writing to create your own narrative.

Before you get started on your own narrative, read this narrative that one student, Nik, wrote in response to the writing prompt. As you read the Model, highlight and annotate the features of narrative writing that Nik included in his narrative.

☰ STUDENT MODEL

 NOTES

An Unexpected Challenge

1   Even before he opened his eyes that Saturday morning, Tyler could hear the sirens. He tried to turn over and go back to sleep, but the piercing sound grew louder. Then he smelled smoke. Was his house on fire? Where were his parents? Tyler leaped out of bed and ran to the window. He gripped the windowsill tightly as he took in the scene. Smoke was pouring out of the house across the way. Three fire trucks, their lights blinking, were parked in the street. Mr. Molano stood on the curb in his pajamas, gesturing wildly.

2   Tyler flew to his bedroom door and flung it open. "Dad?!" he yelled, looking around wildly. "DAD!"

3   "Tyler? I could use your help down here!"

4   Tyler dashed down the stairs. His father was standing in the kitchen. He was holding the Molanos' infant daughter, Tonya. She was trying hard to keep her eyes open. Next to him, their 8-year-old son Max stood staring. He looked like he was in shock.

5   "I was just going to get you," Tyler's father said. "You saw the fire? Luckily no one has been seriously hurt. Look, I know this is a lot to ask, but I need your help here. Mrs. Molano has been taken to the hospital. I think she'll be fine, but Mr. Molano is too upset to drive. I have to take him to the hospital, and I need you to watch Tonya and Max until I get back."

6   Suddenly Tyler looked like *he* was in shock. "Look after *Tonya?* Dad, is she even a year old? I don't know how to. . ."

7   Tyler's father cut him off. "Tyler, I know this is a lot to ask. But your mom is at her office seeing patients until noon. There's no one else who can do this right now. Mr. Molano's sister is coming to see to their house, but she lives an hour away."

Reading & Writing Companion   **95**

 ## Read and Annotate

As students read, have them use the Annotation Tool to identify and label the characteristics of narrative writing:

- setting
- characters
- plot
- theme
- point of view

When students finish reading, ask them to share their annotations in small groups.

ELL   ANNOTATION GUIDE

Find the following quotes in the Student Model. Then, use the Annotation Tool to label each quote as an example of setting, character, plot, or point of view.

- Smoke was pouring out of the house across the way.
- "I need you to watch Tonya and Max until I get back."
- "Tyler? I could use your help down here!"
- For a moment, everything was wonderfully quiet.
- He was holding the Molanos' infant daughter, Tonya.
- His father was standing in the kitchen.

A   READ AND ANNOTATE

Pair students with on-grade-level peers to complete the annotation activity.

 ## TEXT TALK

Purpose

Where does Nik introduce the conflict in his story?

See paragraph 1: Nik introduces the conflict in the first paragraph, when Tyler realizes there's a fire at his neighbors' house.

Focus

How does Nik set the scene in the opening paragraphs to create a sense of panic and fear at the beginning of his narrative?

See paragraphs 1–6: Nik describes the smell of smoke and the sound of sirens and then includes panicked dialogue between Tyler and his father.

TEXT TALK

Organization

How does Nik create the fast pace of the narrative, which helps build tension?

Answers will vary. Sample answer: In paragraph 7, the text reads, "Tyler's father cut him off," suggesting that there was little time to waste.

Details

How does Nik use specific details to contribute to his narrative?

Answers will vary. Sample answer: In paragraphs 10 and 11, Nik provides details about Tyler's thought process over making breakfast for Max that make the scene feel realistic.

Ideas

Are the children's actions in the story believable? Why or why not?

Answers will vary. Sample answer: Yes. I think Max's tearful reaction to missing his mom in paragraph 13 is realistic.

Word Choice

Where do you find Nik's word choice especially strong or expressive?

Answers will vary. Sample answer: In paragraph 15, Nik writes that Tyler "patted the boy on the shoulder" and then offered comforting words to Max. The dialogue and the concrete details together create a strong and believable scene.

Sentence Fluency

Choose one sentence that you think is really effective. Why do you think it's so strong?

Answers will vary. Sample answer: I think the sentence "He sniffed a few times and then smiled weakly" in paragraph 16 is really strong. I can visualize an eight-year-old boy starting to feel better after crying.

NOTES

8   "But . . ."

9   "Tonya will probably sleep until we get back, Tyler. I'll place her in your bed and surround her with pillows so she'll be safe. See if you can get Max to eat some breakfast. Then take him up to your room so you can watch Tonya."

10 Almost before Tyler knew it, his father had swept up the stairs and then out the door. Tyler just stood there. Slowly, he looked down at Max. "Um, would you like some breakfast, Max?" he said. The boy just nodded, and Tyler led him over to the kitchen table.

11 Tyler thought about making pancakes. He had watched his father make them often enough. But it would take too long. He opened a cabinet and pulled out some cereal.

12 "Is this okay, Max?" Tyler asked.

13 The boy nodded again. Then, unexpectedly, he burst into tears. "I want my mom!" he wailed.

14 Tyler froze. What should he do? Then he remembered what his father had said—Mrs. Molano would be all right.

15 Tyler patted the boy on the shoulder. As he poured some cereal into a bowl, he said, "Don't worry, buddy. Your mom will be okay. The doctors at the hospital will take good care of her. My dad said he thought she would be fine. You'll see."

16 Max looked up at Tyler. He sniffed a few times and then smiled weakly. Tyler went to get him some tissues so Max could wipe his eyes.

17 After Max finished his cereal, Tyler said, "Let's go check on Tonya. Also, I've got a big picture book about space pirates I think you're going to like!"

18 Max grinned and Tyler felt a flood of relief. He wasn't sure how he would deal with Max if he started crying again.

19 Soon Max was sitting on the floor reading. For a moment, everything was wonderfully quiet. Tyler walked over to the window and peered out. The fire seemed under control. There was no more smoke at least. Best of all, it didn't seem as if the house had been damaged very much.

NOTES

20 Then, suddenly, Tonya woke up. It was as if someone had flipped a switch. The tiny baby went from a sound sleep to full-on crying mode. Tyler's eyes widened and he looked at Max. "What should I do?" he asked.

21 "Mom always picks her up," Max said.

22 Tyler bent over and carefully picked up the baby. He was terrified that he might drop her. But she still cried.

23 "Okay, now what?" Tyler asked.

24 "You should walk around with her."

25 Tyler walked around the bedroom and into the hallway with the baby. The motion seemed to calm her down. But anytime Tyler stopped walking, Tonya began crying again. "Okay, Tonya, you're the boss. I'll keep walking," Tyler said.

26 After Tyler had circled the hallway for what felt like the five-hundredth time, his mom came home. Tyler had never been so glad to see her in his life.

27 "Well, look at you!" Mom said. "You're an expert baby walker. May I hold her?"

28 "You bet. Boy, my arms are tired!"

29 As his mother scooped Tonya into her arms, she said, "Great job, Tyler. Dad called me from the hospital and told me what was going on. I got here as soon as I could, but it looks like you didn't even need my help. I'm really proud of you for rising to the challenge and helping out."

30 "Dad and Max were the real experts," Tyler said. "I just did what they told me to do."

31 Tyler's mother turned to smile at Max. "Your mom's going to be fine, Max," she said. "She'll be home tomorrow."

32 Max clapped and at the same time Tonya started crying again. Tyler's mother placed the baby back in Tyler's arms.

33 "Here," she laughed. "You're the champion baby walker!"

Reading & Writing
Companion **97**

TEXT TALK

Conventions

Does Nik consistently use correct personal pronouns?

Answers will vary. Sample answer: Yes. He consistently uses correct personal pronouns.

Write

Circulate as students use the questions in the bulleted list to plan their writing. See the instructions for scaffolding and differentiation that follow.

✓ CHECK FOR SUCCESS

If students struggle to come up with answers for the questions in the lesson, work with them to provide an answer to one question and then help them build from there.

For example, start by asking students "Where does your story take place?" or "What might happen on a normal day that could present a challenge to your character?" Once students have answered one question, help them to work through a second question until they've begun to build some momentum. It may be helpful to start with a different question than the one that's listed first in the lesson.

Extended Writing Project

  WRITE

Writers often take notes about story ideas before they sit down to write. Think about what you've learned so far about organizing narrative writing to help you begin prewriting.

- **Genre:** In what sort of genre would you like to write? Most any genre can include focus on an unexpected challenge. Genres include realistic fiction, science fiction, fantasy, or mystery, to name some examples.

- **Characters:** What kinds of characters will you include in your narrative?

- **Plot:** What would a normal day be like for your character or characters? What could happen that would pose a challenge for them?

- **Plot/Character:** How will your character or characters respond to the challenge?

- **Setting:** How might the setting of your story affect the characters and the challenges they face?

- **Point of View:** From which point of view should your story be told, and why?

Response Instructions

Use the questions in the bulleted list to write a one-paragraph summary. Your summary should describe what will happen in your narrative, like the one above.

Don't worry about including all of the details now; focus only on the most essential and important elements. You will refer back to this short summary as you continue through the steps of the writing process.

Review Prompt and Rubric

Before students begin writing, review the writing prompt and rubric with the class.

Response Instructions

Use the questions in the bulleted list to write a one-paragraph summary. Your summary should describe what will happen in your narrative.

Don't worry about including all of the details now; focus only on the most essential and important elements. You will refer back to this short summary as you continue through the steps of the writing process.

Score	Plan	Language and Conventions
4	The writer responds to the questions, and the writing is clear and focused.	The writer demonstrates a consistent command of grammar, punctuation, and usage conventions. Although minor errors may be evident, they do not detract from the fluency or the clarity of the essay.
3	The writer responds to the questions, but the writing is not always clear or focused.	The writer demonstrates an adequate command of grammar, punctuation, and usage conventions. Although some errors may be evident, they create few (if any) disruptions in the fluency of the writing or the clarity of the essay.
2	The writer responds to the questions, but the writing is somewhat unclear and unfocused.	The writer demonstrates a partial command of grammar, punctuation, and usage conventions. Some distracting errors may be evident, at times creating minor disruptions in the fluency or clarity of the writing.
1	The writer responds to the questions, but the writing is very unclear and unfocused.	The writer demonstrates little or no command of grammar, punctuation, and usage conventions. Serious and persistent errors create disruptions in the fluency of the writing and sometimes interfere with meaning.
0	The writer does not provide a relevant response to the prompt or does not provide a response at all.	Serious and persistent errors overwhelm the writing and interfere with the meaning of the response as a whole, making the writer's meaning impossible to understand.

Write

SCAFFOLDS

Use the scaffolds below to differentiate instruction for your **ELL** English Language Learners and **A** Approaching grade-level learners.

ELL **BEGINNING, INTERMEDIATE** With the help of the <u>word bank</u>, write a response using the <u>paragraph frame</u>.

ADVANCED, ADVANCED HIGH Write a response using the <u>sentence starters</u>.

A **APPROACHING** Write a response using the <u>sentence starters</u>.

BEGINNING	ADVANCED, ADVANCED HIGH
INTERMEDIATE	APPROACHING

Word Bank	Paragraph Frame	Sentence Starters
boy old noise scared problem house girl run away	My story will be about ____. It will take place in ____. The first thing to happen in my story is ____. Then, ____. My story will end ____.	• My story will be about . . . • It will take place . . . • First, . . . • Then, . . . • It will end . . .

Peer Review

Students should submit substantive feedback to two peers using the review instructions below.

• How well does this response answer the prompt?
• What part of the narrative are you most excited to read?
• Are there any ideas that could be improved on? How so?

Rate

Respond to the following with a point rating that reflects your opinion.

	1 2 3 4
Ideas	■ ■ ■ ☐
Evidence	■ ■ ■ ■
Language and Conventions	■ ■ ☐ ☐

Submit

ELL **A** **SENTENCE FRAMES**

• The response does a good job of addressing ____ from the prompt.
• The response would improve by addressing ____ from the prompt.

• I am most excited to read about ____.
• I think you could improve ____ by (adding / clarifying / describing) ____.

Skill:
Organizing Narrative Writing

sync•skills

••• CHECKLIST FOR ORGANIZING NARRATIVE WRITING

As you consider how to organize your writing for your narrative, use the following questions as a guide:

- Who is the narrator and who are the characters in the story?
- Where will the story take place?
- What conflict or problem will the characters have to resolve?
- Have I created a series of plot events that flow logically and naturally from one event to the next?

Here are some strategies to help you organize your narrative:

- Introduce a narrator and/or characters.
  - > Characters can be introduced all at once or throughout the narrative.
  - > Choose the role each character will play.

- Establish a context.
  - > Begin with your **exposition**—decide what background information your readers need to know about the characters, setting, and conflict.
  - > List the events of the **rising action**—be sure that these events build toward the climax.
  - > Describe what will happen during the **climax** of the story—make sure that this is the point of highest interest, conflict, or suspense in your story.
  - > List the events of the **falling action**—make sure that these events show what happens to the characters as a result of the climax.
  - > Explain the **resolution** of the main conflict in your story.

Skill: Organizing Narrative Writing

Introduce the Skill

Watch the Concept Definition video ▶ and read the following definition with your students.

In **narrative writing,** a writer creates a story out of real or imagined events. A narrative is usually organized by the **plot,** or the series of events that take place. The plot is driven by a **conflict,** or a problem that the characters face.

Many narratives arrange the story with a clear beginning, middle, and end, moving through five stages:

Exposition—provides background information

Rising action—develops the conflict

Climax—the point of highest interest or suspense

Falling action—what happens after the climax

Resolution—how the conflict is solved

When organizing a narrative, orient the reader with information about the characters and setting. Create an **inciting incident** that pushes a character into the main action of the story and the problem the character must solve. The events that lead to a solution should unfold naturally and logically, as in a series of cause-and-effect relationships.

TURN AND TALK

Turn to your partner and explain how your favorite movie follows the basic structure of narrative writing.

ELL SPEAKING FRAME

- The movie follows the basic structure of narrative writing because ____.

SKILL VOCABULARY

narrative writing / la escritura narrativa *noun* a story made out of real or imagined events

plot / la trama *noun* the sequence of events that form a story

conflict / el conflicto *noun* the main problem or struggle that characters face in a story COGNATE

exposition / la exposición *noun* the background information provided in the beginning of a story about the characters, the setting, and the conflict COGNATE

Your Turn

Ask students to complete the Your Turn activity.

Exposition	D
Rising Action	A
Climax	E
Falling Action	B
Resolution	C

⟳ YOUR TURN

Complete the chart below by matching each event to its correct place in the narrative sequence.

Event Options	
A	Her parents take out a boat at dusk to go fishing. They tell her to call for help if they're not back an hour after it gets dark.
B	They find Chloe's parents sitting on some rocks, their boat having capsized.
C	Chloe, her parents, and the man all get back to their cabins safely.
D	Chloe is on vacation with her parents.
E	When her parents still haven't come back after dark, Chloe asks a man in a neighboring cabin for help. They take his boat out to look for them.

Narrative Sequence	Event
Exposition	
Rising Action	
Climax	
Falling Action	
Resolution	

SKILL VOCABULARY

rising action / la tensión dramática creciente *noun* a series of events that work to create tension, interest, or suspense and result in the story's climax

climax / el clímax *noun* the point in the plot with the highest interest, conflict, or suspense   COGNATE

falling action / la acción decreciente *noun* a series of events that occur after the climax and lead to the resolution of the story's conflict

resolution / la resolución *noun* the final outcome of the story's conflict   COGNATE

inciting incident / el incidente generador *noun* the first event in which the conflict becomes apparent

YOUR TURN

Complete the chart below by writing a short summary of what will happen in each section of your narrative.

Narrative Sequence	Event
Exposition	
Rising Action	
Climax	
Falling Action	
Resolution	

Reading & Writing Companion **101**

Your Turn

Ask students to complete the Your Turn activity. Answers will vary.

Exposition	My story will be about two friends, Cora and Rosa, who are practicing soccer together in a park one evening.
Rising Action	While they're practicing, Cora will trip over the ball and hurt her ankle.
Climax	Since Cora can't walk, Rosa needs to go find help. There are no neighboring houses, and both girls have left their cell phones at home, so Rosa has to run to town to find help.
Falling Action	Once Rosa finds a phone and calls for help, she goes back to the park to wait with Cora.
Resolution	Rosa and Cora both go to the hospital, where Cora gets a cast put on her ankle and Rosa is the first to sign it.

Writer's Notebook

Choose four items from your classroom (for example, a pencil, a marker, a spoon, and a calendar). Place these items somewhere in the room where students can see all of them. Ask students to create a story using those items for the four parts of their plot diagram. Students should label each part of their story and write a one- or two-sentence summary of events for each image, like Nik did in the Student Model.

 TURN AND TALK

Allow students to share their summaries orally in pairs or small groups before freewriting.

Narrative Writing Process: Draft

Write

Ask students to complete the writing assignment.

If students struggle to begin drafting their narratives, ask them the following questions:

- Who is your story about?
- What is happening to that character?
- Where and when is the story happening?
- Why are the characters challenged by this particular situation?

 DRAFT CHECKLIST

- ☐ Does my opening explain the setting, characters, and conflict?
- ☐ Did I provide information about my characters with descriptions? With dialogue?
- ☐ Is the order of events in my story easy to follow?
- ☐ Does my resolution solve the conflict?

Extended Writing Project

 Narrative Writing Process: Draft

| PLAN | DRAFT | REVISE | EDIT AND PUBLISH |

You have already made progress toward writing your narrative. Now it is time to draft your narrative.

 WRITE

Use your Plan and other responses in your Binder to draft your narrative. You may also have new ideas as you begin drafting. Feel free to explore those new ideas as they occur to you. You can also ask yourself these questions:

- Have I included specifics about my setting, characters, plot, theme, and point of view?
- Have I made the conflict in the story clear to readers?
- Does the sequence of events in my story make sense?
- Does my main character face a challenge in the story?

Before you submit your draft, read it over carefully. You want to be sure that you've responded to all aspects of the prompt.

Peer Review

Students should submit substantive feedback to two peers using the review instructions below.

- What is the challenge the main character in the story faces? Does this need more explanation?
- Does the writer include all the elements of narrative writing? If not, can you offer any suggestions?
- What suggestions can you make to help the writer improve the organization of the story?
- Are there any ideas that could be improved? How so?

 SENTENCE FRAMES

- My favorite part of your story is ___.
- Your choices about (plot / characters / setting / point of view) are effective because ___.

- I think your (dialogue / organization) are strong because ___. I would suggest you ___.
- I like your resolution because ___. I would suggest improving your resolution by ___.

Here is Nik's short story draft. As you read, identify details that Nik includes in his inciting incident. As Nik continues to revise and edit his narrative, he will find and improve weak spots in his writing, as well as correct any language, punctuation, or spelling mistakes.

☰ STUDENT MODEL: FIRST DRAFT

 NOTES

An Unexpected Challenge

~~Tyler heard sirens. Then he smelled smoke. He wonder what was going on. He looked out the window. He saw smoke and fire trucks below. Mr. Molano was standing on the curb waveing her arms.~~

~~Tyler opened his bedroom door. "Dad?" he yelled, looking around wildly. "DAD!"~~

Even before he opened his eyes that Saturday morning, Tyler could hear the sirens. He tried to turn over and go back to sleep, but the piercing sound grew louder. Then he smelled smoke. Was his house on fire? Where were his parents? Tyler leaped out of bed and ran to the window. He gripped the windowsill tightly as he took in the scene. Smoke was pouring out of the house across the way. Three fire trucks, their lights blinking, were parked in the street. Mr. Molano stood on the curb in his pajamas, gesturing wildly.

Tyler flew to his bedroom door and flung it open. "Dad?" he yelled, looking around wildly. "DAD!"

Tyler went down the stairs. Him father was standing in the kitchen he was holding the Molanos' infant daughter, Tonya. Next to him, their 8-year-old son Max stood staring.

~~"You saw the fire? Mrs. Molano has been taken to the hospital. I think she'll be fine, but Mr. Molano is too upset to drive. I have to take him to the hospital, and I need you to watch Tonya and Max until I get back."~~

~~"I don't know how to . . ."~~

~~"I know this is a lot to ask. But you mom is at her office seeing patients until noon."~~

~~"But . . ."~~

 Skill:
Story Beginnings

To engage readers in the story, Nik has them experience the fire the way Tyler does. Nik uses the action method to grab readers' attention and set an urgent tone in the first paragraph.

 Skill:
Descriptive Details

Nik adds descriptive details to his draft so that readers can better imagine what is happening during this part of the story. Sound details like "the piercing sound grew louder" help readers imagine what Tyler hears in this specific event.

 ## Analyze Student Model

Have students discuss the questions in the lesson as well as the Student Model draft. Ask:

- What details does Nik present to his readers in the inciting incident?

- How does Nik make his conflict clear?

- How does Nik's use of dialogue reveal information about his characters and the challenge facing the main character?

Encourage students to share ideas for their own narratives based on the questions in the lesson.

> **ELL SPEAKING FRAMES**
>
> - In the inciting incident, the writer presents details such as ____.
> - The conflict is ____.
> - The writer ends his story with ____.
> - An idea that I have for my narrative is ____.

 ## Story Beginnings

Discuss the Model

1. The Model shows how Nik changed the beginning of his story. How did he change it?
   Nik added description, internal dialogue, and action. He also set an urgent tone.

2. How did those changes improve the story?
   Answers will vary.

3. How could Nik use a different story beginning to grab his readers' attention and set the tone?
   Answers will vary.

> **ELL SPEAKING FRAMES**
>
> - Nik changed the beginning of his story by ____.
> - These changes improved Nik's story because ____.
> - Nik could use a different story beginning, such as ____.

Descriptive Details

Discuss the Model

1. How do descriptive details help readers connect with a story? Descriptive details help readers imagine what a character sees, smells, tastes, hears, and feels.

2. What kinds of descriptive details does Nik add to his draft? Nik adds sight details, sound details, and touch details.

3. How do those changes improve his story? They help readers better understand what Tyler sees, hears, and feels.

> **ELL SPEAKING FRAMES**
>
> - Descriptive details help readers imagine ____.
> - Nik adds details that appeal to readers' senses of ____ and ____.
> - These changes improve his story because ____.
> - Nik could have added a sight detail such as ____.

Descriptive Details

Connect to Mentor Text

Project the following examples of descriptive details and discuss with your students:

- "The food!" Max screamed, and began to snatch up the franks. Coated with mustard, dirt, grass, and leaves, they looked positively prehistoric. (*Scout's Honor*)

- He had on a pair of good tennis shoes, now almost dry. And socks. And jeans and underwear and a thin leather belt and a T-shirt with a windbreaker so torn it hung on him in tatters. (*Hatchet*)

Ask students:

- What do you notice about these descriptive details?

- What do these details allow you to imagine?

 NOTES

 Skill: Narrative Techniques

Nik decides that the reason for dialogue in this section is to advance the plot and show why the characters, Tyler and his father, are under pressure. He adds dialogue tags to make it clear who is talking.

~~"Tonya will probably sleep until we get back. I'll place her in your bed and surround her with pillows so her will be safe. See if you can get Max to eat some breakfast. Then take he up to your room so you can watch Tonya."~~

"I was just going to get you," Tyler's father said. "You saw the fire? Luckily no one has been seriously hurt. Look, I know this is a lot to ask, but I need your help here. Mrs. Molano has been taken to the hospital. I think she'll be fine, but Mr. Molano is too upset to drive. I have to take him to the hospital, and I need you to watch Tonya and Max until I get back."

Suddenly Tyler looked like *he* was in shock. "Look after *Tonya?* Dad, is she even a year old? I don't know how to . . ."

Tyler's father cut him off. "Tyler, I know this is a lot to ask. But your mom is at her office seeing patients until noon. There's no one else who can do this right now. Mr. Molano's sister is coming to see to their house, but she lives an hour away."

"But . . ."

"Tonya will probably sleep until we get back, Tyler. I'll place her in your bed and surround her with pillows so she'll be safe. See if you can get Max to eat some breakfast. Then take him up to your room so you can watch Tonya."

~~Almost before Tyler knows it, his father had gone up the stairs. Then out the door. Tyler just stood there. Slowly, he looked down at Max. "Um, would you like some breakfast, Max"? he said. The boy just nodded, and Tyler led them over to the kitchen table.~~

~~Tyler thought about making pancakes. He had watched his father make them often enough. Sometimes on Saturday mornings the whole family would sit in the kitchen and watch as Dad mixed the batter and cooked each pancake. But it would take too long. He opened a cabinet and found some cereal.~~

~~"Is this okay?"~~

NOTES

~~The boy nodded again. Then, unexpectedly, he burst into tears. "Me want my mom"!~~

Almost before Tyler knew it, his father had swept up the stairs and then out the door. Tyler just stood there. Slowly, he looked down at Max. "Um, would you like some breakfast, Max?" he said. The boy just nodded, and Tyler led him over to the kitchen table.

Tyler thought about making pancakes. He had watched his father make them often enough. But it would take too long. He opened a cabinet and pulled out some cereal.

"Is this okay, Max?" Tyler asked.

The boy nodded again. Then, unexpectedly, he burst into tears. "I want my mom!" he wailed.

Tyler froze. What should she do? Then he remembered. What his father had said—Mrs. Molano would be all right.

Tyler patted the boy on the shoulder. As he poared some cereal into the bowl, he said "Don't worry, buddy. Your mom will be okay, the doctors at the hospital will take good care of them. My dad said he thought she would be fine. You'll see".

Max looked up at Tyler. He sniffed a few times. Then smiled weakly. Tyler went to get him some tissue so Max could wipe their eyes.

After Max finished his cereal, Tyler said "Let's go check on Tonya. Also, I've got a big picture book about space pirates I think you're going to like"!

Max grins and Tyler felt a flood of relief. He wasn't sure how he would deal with Max if he started crying again.

Soon Max was sitting on the floor reading. For a moment, everything was wonderfully quiet. Tyler walked over to the window and peared out. The fire seemed under control. There was no more smoke at least. Best of all, it didn't seem as if the house had been damaged very much. If it had been, Tyler wondered where the Molano would stay. Would they live in Tyler's house until their house was repaired?

**Skill:
Transitions**

Nik continues to add transitions throughout the rest of the story to show relationships between ideas from one paragraph to the next in his narrative. He decides to use the transitional phrase "almost before Tyler knew it" before "his father had swept up the stairs . . ." This signals a shift in time and how quickly the events are taking place.

Narrative Techniques

Discuss the Model

1. Why does Nik decide to add more detail to his story? Nik adds more detail to show why the characters feel pressure.

2. Why does Nik choose to add dialogue tags? Nik adds dialogue tags to make it clearer who is talking.

3. How do those changes improve his story? Answers will vary.

4. What other details could Nik add to reveal more about his characters, their experiences, and the plot events? Answers will vary.

ELL SPEAKING FRAMES

- Nik adds more detail because he wants to show why ____.
- Nik adds dialogue and dialogue tags because he wants to ____.
- These changes improve his story because ____.
- Another change Nik could make is ____.

Transitions

Discuss the Model

1. Where have you seen transitions in movies, TV shows, or books? Answers will vary. Sample answers: the scene change in a favorite movie.

2. Which transitions have been added between Nik's outline and his final draft? He added "even before opening his eyes" to show the timeline of the fire and when Tyler first knew about it.

3. How do those changes improve his story? Answers will vary.

4. What other transitions could Nik use to improve his story? Answers will vary.

ELL SPEAKING FRAMES

- I have seen transitions in ____.
- In Nik's outline he has ____, but in his final draft he writes ____.
- These changes improve his story because ____.
- Nik could also use ____ transitions because ____.

Conclusions

Discuss the Model

1. The Model shows how Nik concluded his story. What details did he include?
   He included details about character thoughts and feelings. He also used character dialogue.

2. How do those details improve his story?
   Answers will vary.

3. How could Nik use a different ending to conclude his narrative?
   Answers will vary.

> **ELL SPEAKING FRAMES**
> - Nik ended his story by ____.
> - These details improved his story because ____.
> - Nik could use a different story ending, such as ____.

Conclusions

Connect to Mentor Text

Project the following examples of conclusions and discuss with your students:

- Grinning with relief, we **simultaneously** clasped hands. "No matter what," Max reminded us.
  To which I added, "Scout's Honor." (*Scout's Honor*)

- Emerging from the Council Edifice into bright sunlight and the usual chaos of the village central plaza, she realized that it was still midafternoon, still an ordinary day in the existence of the people, and that no one's life had changed except her own. (*Gathering Blue*)

Ask students:

- What do you notice about these conclusions?

- What about the conclusions appeals to you?

- How do the conclusions make you feel?

Extended Writing Project

Skill: Conclusions

Nik revises these concluding events through character dialogue between Tyler and his mom. He sums up the story with how Tyler has changed and what his mom thinks about him.

Then, suddenly, Tonya woke up. It was as if someone had flipped a switch. The tiny baby goes from a sound sleep to full-on crying mode. Tyler's eyes widened and he looked at Max. "What should I do"? him asked. "Mom always picks her up," Max said.

Tyler bent over and carefully picks up the baby he was terrified that he might drop her. But she still cried.

"Okay, now what?" Tyler asked.

"You should walk around with her."

Tyler walks around the bedroom and into the hallway with the baby. The motion seemed to calm her down. But anytime Tyler stopped walking Tonya began crying again. "Okay, Tonya, you the boss. I'll keep walking" Tyler said.

~~After Tyler had circled the hallway yet again, his mom came home. Tyler was so happy to see her.~~

~~"Well, look at you!" Mom said. "You're an expert baby walker. May I hold her"?~~

~~"You bet. Boy, my arms are tired!"~~

~~As his mother took Tonya into her arms, she said, "Great job, Tyler. Dad called me from the hospital and told me what was going on. I got here as soon as I could, but it looks like you didn't even need my help. I'm really proud of you for rising to the challenge and helping out."~~

After Tyler had circled the hallway for what felt like the five-hundredth time, his mom came home. Tyler had never been so glad to see her in his life.

"Well, look at you!" Mom said. "You're an expert baby walker! May I hold her?"

"You bet. Boy, my arms are tired!"

As his mother scooped Tonya into her arms, she said, "Great job, Tyler. Dad called me from the hospital and told me what was going on. I got

---

106 Reading & Writing Companion

here as soon as I could, but it looks like you didn't even need my help. I'm really proud of you for rising to the challenge and helping out."

"Dad and Max were the real experts," Tyler said. "I just did what them told me to do."

Tyler's mother was smiling at Max. "Your mom's going to be fine, Max," she said. "She'll be home tomorrow."

Max clapped and at the same time Tonya started crying again. Tyler's mother placed the baby in he arms.

"Here. Your the champion baby walker!"

PEER CONFERENCE

Have students choose a sentence or passage from one of the mentor texts in the unit that they find particularly effective. Allow students time to discuss their selections in a small group, exploring why the passage stood out to them. Was it the structure? Writing style? Something else? Then, encourage students to emulate their mentor text in a section of their own writing.

Skill: Story Beginnings

Introduce the Skill

Watch the Concept Definition video and read the following definition with your students.

A **story beginning** is the opening section of a story in which the writer orients the reader by providing essential information, or **context**:

- **characters**—people or animals in the story

- **setting**—the time and place in which the action of a story occurs

- **conflict**—the problem that one or more of the characters must face

This essential background information for the story is called the **exposition.**

The best story beginnings also engage readers by grabbing their attention and tempting them to keep reading. Writers use a variety of techniques to start their stories and introduce the elements of the exposition in an engaging way. This includes establishing the **narrator,** or the one telling the story. The narrator can be a character in the story or someone outside the story who is never described. The narrator's relationship to the story is called the narrative **point of view**.

TURN AND TALK

Turn to your partner and talk about movies, TV shows, books, or comics that have exciting beginnings.

> **ELL SPEAKING FRAMES**
>
> - The (movie / TV show / book / comic) ___ begins with ___.
> - An example of an interesting beginning is ___.

Extended Writing Project

STORY BEGINNINGS
sync•skills

Skill:
Story Beginnings

••• CHECKLIST FOR STORY BEGINNINGS

Before you begin to write the beginning of your narrative, ask yourself the following questions:

- What kind of information does my reader need to know at the beginning of the story about the main character, the setting, and the character's conflict?
- What will happen to my character in the story?

There are many ways to engage and orient the reader to your narrative. Here are four methods to consider to help you establish a context and introduce the narrator and/or characters:

- Action
  > What action could help reveal information about my character or conflict?
  > How might an exciting moment grab my reader's attention?
  > How could a character's reaction help set the mood of my narrative?

- Description
  > Does my story take place in a special location or specific time period?
  > How can describing a location or character grab my reader's attention?

- Dialogue
  > What dialogue would help my reader understand the setting or the conflict?
  > How could a character's internal thoughts provide information for my reader?

- Information
  > Would a surprising statement grab my reader's attention?
  > What details will help my reader understand the character, conflict, or setting?

V SKILL VOCABULARY

story beginning / *el comienzo de la historia noun* the opening to a story

context / *el contexto noun* the set of facts or circumstances that surround a situation or event COGNATE

character / *el personaje noun* an individual in a literary work whose thoughts, feelings, actions, and reactions move the action of the plot forward

---

YOUR TURN

Read the beginning of each story below. Then, complete the chart by writing the type of story beginning that correctly matches each paragraph.

Story Beginning Options			
Description	Action	Information	Dialogue

Story Beginning	Type of Story Beginning
Back in 1946, when I was nine, I worried that I wasn't tough enough. That's why I became a Boy Scout. Scouting, I thought, would make a man of me. It didn't take long to reach Tenderfoot rank. You got that for joining. To move up to Second Class, however, you had to meet three requirements. Scout Spirit and Scout Participation were a cinch. The third requirement, Scout Craft, meant I had to go on an overnight hike in the country. In other words, I had to leave Brooklyn, on my own, for the first time in my life. "Scout's Honor"	
"Sit down, sit down. Don't be afraid." Chairman Jin pointed to the empty chair. "These comrades from your father's work unit are just here to have a study session with you. It's nothing to worry about." *Red Scarf Girl*	
I know he's in there, I thought. I saw the curtains in his bedroom move—only a little, yes, but they moved. "The Good Samaritan"	
They would look for him, look for the plane. His father and mother would be frantic. They would tear the world apart to find him. Brian had seen searches on the news, seen movies about lost planes. When a plane went down, they mounted extensive searches and almost always they found the plane within a day or two. *Hatchet*	

WRITE

Use the questions in the checklist to revise the beginning of your narrative.

Reading & Writing Companion **109**

SKILL VOCABULARY

setting / el escenario *noun* the time and place of the story

exposition / la exposición *noun* the background information provided in the beginning of a story about the characters, the setting, and the conflict
COGNATE

narrator / el narrador *noun* someone who tells a story COGNATE

point of view / el punto de vista *noun* the standpoint, or perspective, from which a story is told

---

Your Turn

Ask students to complete the Your Turn activitiy.

"Back in 1946. . ." ("Scout's Honor")	Description
"Sit down, sit down. . ." (*Red Scarf Girl*)	Dialogue
"I know. . ." ("The Good Samaritan")	Action
"They would look for him. . ." (*Hatchet*)	Information

Write

Ask students to complete the writing assignment.

ELL REWRITE CHECKLIST

A **Action**

- ☐ What action could help reveal information about my character or conflict?
- ☐ How might an exciting moment grab my reader's attention?

Description

- ☐ Does my story take place in a significant location or specific time period?
- ☐ How can describing a location or character grab my reader's attention?

Dialogue

- ☐ What dialogue would help my reader understand the setting or the conflict?
- ☐ How could a character's internal thoughts provide information for my reader?

Information

- ☐ Would a surprising statement grab my reader's attention?
- ☐ What details will help my reader understand the character, conflict, or setting?

Skill: Descriptive Details

Introduce the Skill

Watch the Concept Definition video ▶ and read the following definition with your students.

Descriptive details are details that writers include to help readers imagine the world in which the story takes place and the characters who live in it. These details are important because they help to orient the reader by establishing a **context** or the circumstances that form the setting of events or a situation in a story.

Descriptive details often use **precise language**—specific nouns and action verbs—to convey experiences or events. Many descriptive details use sensory language to appeal to one or more of the reader's five senses. **Sensory details** tell how something looks, sounds, feels, smells, or tastes.

In a story, it is easy to include many interesting details, but not every detail is **relevant,** that is, important, appropriate, and purposeful. Think about what the reader really needs to know in order to understand or picture what is happening. This will help you select and include only the most relevant details for your story.

 ## TURN AND TALK

Turn to your partner and brainstorm descriptive adjectives that appeal to each of your senses—sight, sound, smell, touch, and taste.

ELL SPEAKING FRAMES

- A word or phrase that appeals to my sense of sight is ____.
- A word or phrase that appeals to my sense of hearing is ____.
- A word or phrase that appeals to my sense of smell is ____.
- A word or phrase that appeals to my sense of touch is ____.
- A word or phrase that appeals to my sense of taste is ____.

Extended Writing Project

 ### Skill: Descriptive Details

••• CHECKLIST FOR DESCRIPTIVE DETAILS

First, reread the draft of your narrative and identify the following:

- where descriptive details are needed to convey experiences and events
- vague, general, or overused words and phrases
- places where you want to tell how something looks, sounds, feels, smells, or tastes, such as:
  - > experiences
  - > events

Use precise words and phrases, relevant descriptive details, and sensory language to convey experiences and events, using the following questions as a guide:

- What experiences and events do I want to convey in my writing?
- Have I included descriptive details that are relevant and make sense in my story?
- Where can I add descriptive details to describe the characters and the events of the plot?
- Have I told how something looks, sounds, feels, smells, or tastes in order to help the reader picture the story in their mind?
- What can I refine or revise in my word choice to make sure that the reader can picture what is taking place?

 ## SKILL VOCABULARY

descriptive detail / el detalle descriptivo *noun* a detail that helps readers imagine the world in which the story takes place and the characters who live in it

context / el contexto *noun* the set of facts or circumstances that surround a situation or event COGNATE

precise language / el lenguaje preciso *noun* exact language that includes specific nouns and action verbs COGNATE

YOUR TURN

Choose the best answer to each question.

1. The following section is from an earlier draft of Nik's story. In the underlined sentence, Nik did not use the most appropriate word to describe the sound of the sirens. Which of the following is the best replacement for the word *crazy*?

> When he woke up, Tyler could hear the sirens. <u>The crazy sound grew louder and louder.</u> He could no longer go back to sleep.

- ○ A. dull
- ○ B. red
- ○ C. ear-splitting
- ○ D. large

2. Nik wants to add a descriptive sensory visual detail to this sentence from a previous draft. Which sentence BEST adds sight detail to his sentence?

> The fire looked like it was under control.

- ○ A. The bright orange flames got fainter and fainter against the bright blue sky and the fire finally looked like it was under control.
- ○ B. As Tyler took a deep breath in, the scent of smoke seemed less extreme—the fire looked like it was under control.
- ○ C. The fire looked like it was under control and Tyler could no longer hear the welcome sound of the firehose blasting the raging flames.
- ○ D. With the syrupy sweet taste of soda still circulating in his mouth, Tyler noticed that the fire finally looked like it was under control.

Your Turn

Ask students to complete the Your Turn activity.

QUESTION 1

A. Incorrect. The sound cannot be dull, since it is the sound of a siren, which is more shrill.

B. Incorrect. A sound cannot be red.

C. **Correct.** The sound of a siren is ear-splitting, especially when it grows louder.

D. Incorrect. A sound cannot be large.

QUESTION 2

A. **Correct.** This sentence adds sensory visual details, including color.

B. Incorrect. This sentence adds smell detail.

C. Incorrect. This sentence adds sound detail.

D. Incorrect. This sentence adds taste detail.

V SKILL VOCABULARY

sensory detail / el detalle sensorial *noun* a detail that appeals to the sense of sight, sound, smell, touch, or taste

relevant / relevante *adjective* appropriate and logically related to the topic COGNATE

Your Turn

Ask students to complete the Your Turn activity.
Answers will vary.

sight	The lake was so deep that it was impossible to see the bottom.
smell	I could only catch a faint whiff of smoke from the faraway campfire.
touch	The freezing water gripped my whole body.
taste	The taste of muddy lake water filled my mouth as I tried to scream.
sound	My heartbeat pounded in my ears.

Extended Writing Project

↻ YOUR TURN

Complete the chart by writing a descriptive detail that appeals to each sense for your narrative.

Sense	Descriptive Detail
sight	
smell	
touch	
taste	
sound	

112 | Reading & Writing Companion

 Writer's Notebook

Project these five sentences on the board:

- I looked out the window. [sight]
- I went into the basement. [smell]
- The pan on the stove was hot. [touch]
- I went into the auditorium. [sound]
- I sat down to eat lunch. [taste]

Ask students to rewrite each sentence, adding sensory details that appeal to each sense.

Skill:
Narrative Techniques

••• CHECKLIST FOR NARRATIVE TECHNIQUES

As you begin to develop the techniques you will use in your narrative, ask yourself the following questions:

- Which characters are talking? How am I organizing the dialogue?
- How quickly or slowly do I want the plot to move? Why?
- Which literary devices can be added to strengthen the characters or plot? How can I better engage the reader?

There are many techniques you can use in a narrative. Here are some methods that can help you write dialogue, pacing, and description, to develop experiences, events, and/or characters:

- Use dialogue between characters to explain events or move the action forward.
  - > Set all dialogue off in quotation marks.
  - > Include identifying names as needed before or after quotation marks.
- Include description to engage the reader and help them visualize the characters, setting, and other elements in the narrative.
  - > Include only those descriptions relevant to the reader's understanding of the element being described.
- Use pacing effectively to convey a sense of urgency or calm in a narrative.
  - > To speed up the pace, try using limited description, short paragraphs, brief dialogue, and simpler sentences.
  - > To slow down the pace, try using detailed description, longer paragraphs, and more complex sentence structures.
- Use any combination of the above narrative techniques to develop experiences, events, and/or characters.

Reading & Writing Companion **113**

ⓥ SKILL VOCABULARY

narrative techniques / las técnicas narrativas *noun* the tools authors use to develop a story **COGNATE**

dialogue / el diálogo *noun* the conversation between characters **COGNATE**

description / la descripción *noun* the use of literary devices to enhance readers' engagement with the story **COGNATE**

plot line / la línea argumental *noun* a series of events in a narrative focused on a particular action, setting, and set of characters; a narrative may have more than one plot line

---

⚙ Skill: Narrative Techniques

Introduce the Skill

Watch the Concept Definition video and read the following definition with your students.

When writing a narrative, authors use a variety of tools to develop the plot and characters or to explore their own personal experiences. **Narrative techniques** include dialogue, description, pacing, reflection, and multiple plot lines.

Narratives often have **dialogue,** or a conversation between characters. Dialogue can be used to develop characters or to to move the plot forward. In addition, authors use **description** outside of dialogue to develop the setting, characters, and plot events. While narratives often have one plot, some have multiple **plot lines.**

Authors use pacing to control the flow of the narrative. **Pacing** is the speed at which a story is told. For example, a writer might speed up the pace as the story nears a climax, or slow it down to reflect a character's indecision. The author or narrator might also want to comment on the events or theme. This technique is called **reflection,** and it is particularly effective in a personal narrative.

TURN AND TALK

Turn to your partner and brainstorm a list of movies, TV shows, or books that have memorable dialogue, descriptive details, and pacing of the plot.

 SPEAKING FRAMES

- A (movie / TV show / book) with memorable dialogue is ____.
- A (movie / TV show / book) with descriptive details is ____.
- An example of a memorable line of dialogue is ____.

Your Turn

Ask students to complete the Your Turn activity.

QUESTION 1

A. Incorrect. The possessive *your* is needed in the sentence.

B. **Correct.** Quotation marks are necessary to enclose the dialogue.

C. Incorrect. The past tense is necessary in the sentence.

D. Incorrect. The sentence needs to be enclosed in quotation marks.

QUESTION 2

A. Incorrect. This is a description of Tyler's actions.

B. Incorrect. This is a description of Tyler's actions.

C. **Correct.** This describes how Tyler feels by using the feeling word "nervously."

D. Incorrect. This describes Tyler's thoughts.

Extended Writing Project

 YOUR TURN

Choose the best answer to each question.

1. The following section is from a previous draft of Nik's story. What change, if any, needs to be made in the underlined sentence?

> Before Tyler knew it, his father had run up the stairs and out the door. Tyler stood there nervously and then looked down at Max. Um, would you like me to refill your water bottle, Max?" he said. The boy nodded, so Tyler walked him over to the sink.

○ A. Change *your* to *you're*.
○ B. Insert quotation marks at the beginning of the sentence.
○ C. Change *said* to *says*.
○ D. The underlined sentence does not need to be changed.

2. The following section is from a previous draft of Nik's story. Which of the following is a description of how Tyler feels?

> Before Tyler knew it, his father had run up the stairs and out the door. Tyler stood there nervously and then looked down at Max. Um, would you like me to refill your water bottle, Max?" he said. The boy nodded, so Tyler walked him over to the sink.

○ A. "looked down at Max"
○ B. "walked him over to the sink"
○ C. "stood there nervously"
○ D. "before Tyler knew it"

114　Reading & Writing Companion

 SKILL VOCABULARY

pacing / el ritmo *noun* the rate at which the plot of the narrative unfolds

reflection / la reflexión *noun* an author's thoughts about events in the narrative　COGNATE

3. The following sentences are from a previous draft of Nik's story. What is the correct way to write the sentences?

"The real experts are Dad and Max," Tyler said. "I just did what I was asked."

○ A. The real experts are Dad and Max," Tyler said. "I just did what I was asked."
○ B. "The real experts are Dad and Max," Tyler said. I just did what I was asked."
○ C. "The real experts are Dad and Max, Tyler said. I just did what I was asked."
○ D. The sentences are written correctly in the story.

✏ WRITE

Use the questions in the checklist to add narrative techniques, such as writing new dialogue, for your narrative.

Reading & Writing Companion 115

QUESTION 3

A. Incorrect. This sentence is missing quotation marks at the beginning of the dialogue.

B. Incorrect. This sentence is missing quotation marks at the beginning of the last sentence.

C. Incorrect. This sentence is missing quotation marks around the dialogue.

D. Correct. This sentence does not need to be edited.

✎ Write

Ask students to complete the writing assignment.

ELL REWRITE CHECKLIST

A Use dialogue between characters to explain events or move the action forward.

☐ Which characters are talking?
☐ How am I organizing the dialogue?

Include description to engage the reader and help them visualize the characters, setting, and other elements in the narrative.

☐ What problem does my character have?
☐ Are my descriptions of the characters, setting, and events relevant to the story?

Use pacing effectively to convey a sense of urgency or calm in a narrative.

☐ How can I speed up the pace by using shorter paragraphs and sentences?
☐ How can I slow down the pace by using longer paragraphs and sentences?

◑ Writer's Notebook

Ask students to recall the memorable dialogue they discussed during the Turn and Talk activity. Have students use their favorite examples as models while they write dialogue for their own narratives.

Skill: Transitions

Introduce the Skill

Watch the Concept Definition video and read the following definition with your students.

Transitions are connecting words, phrases, and clauses that writers use to **clarify** the relationships among ideas and details in a text. Transitions have different functions depending on whether the text is argumentative, informative, or narrative.

In an argumentative essay, writers state claims and provide reasons and evidence for their claims. To clarify a relationship between a claim and a reason or supporting evidence, transitions such as *although* and *on the other hand* help make connections clear.

For informative essays, transitions such as *however, in addition,* and *for example* may help create **cohesion** among ideas and concepts.

In narrative writing, authors use a variety of words, phrases, and clauses to signal shifts in time, setting, and action. Transitions such as *until now, meanwhile,* and *once it was over* may make narrative events more **coherent.**

Transitions also help to connect ideas both within and across paragraphs and between major sections of text.

 ## TURN AND TALK

Turn to your partner and explain how your favorite movie uses (or doesn't use) transitions to show relationships between events in the narrative.

Extended Writing Project

Skill: Transitions

••• CHECKLIST FOR TRANSITIONS

Before you revise your current draft to include transitions, think about:

- the key ideas you discuss in your body paragraphs
- the organizational structure of your essay
- the relationships among ideas and concepts

Next, reread your current draft and note areas in your essay where:

- the organizational structure is not yet apparent

  > For example, if you are comparing and contrasting two texts, your explanations about how two texts are similar and different should be clearly stated.

- the relationship between ideas from one paragraph to the next is unclear

  > For example, an essay that describes a process in sequential order should make clear the order of steps using transitional words like *first*, *then*, *next*, and *finally*.

- the relationship between ideas within a paragraph is unclear

  > For example, when providing evidence to support an idea in a topic sentence, you should introduce the evidence with a transition such as *for example* or *to illustrate*.

Revise your draft to use appropriate transitions to clarify the relationships among ideas and concepts, using the following questions as a guide:

- What kind of transitions should I use to make the organizational structure clear to readers?
- Which transition best connects the ideas within a paragraph?
- Which transition best connects ideas across paragraphs?

V SKILL VOCABULARY

transition / la transición *noun* a connecting word or phrase that a writer may use to clarify the relationship between ideas in a text; set off with a comma COGNATE

clarify / aclarar *verb* to make clear and intelligible COGNATE

YOUR TURN

Choose the best answer to each question.

1. Which of the following is a transition word that signals a shift in time in this sentence?

> After Max finished his cereal, Tyler said, "Let's go check on Tonya. Also, I've got a big picture book about space pirates I think you're going to like!"

- ○ A. "After"
- ○ B. "check"
- ○ C. "Also"
- ○ D. "finished"

2. Which of the following phrases includes transition words that signal a shift in action?

> Then, suddenly, Tonya woke up. It was as if someone had flipped a switch. The tiny baby went from a sound sleep to full-on crying mode. Tyler's eyes widened and he looked at Max. "What should I do?" he asked.

- ○ A. "as if someone had flipped a switch"
- ○ B. "from a sound sleep"
- ○ C. "Then, suddenly"
- ○ D. "Tyler's eyes widened."

YOUR TURN

Complete the chart by adding transitions that organize the structure of your draft and show the relationship between ideas.

Transitions that organize the story structure	Transitions that show the relationship between ideas

Reading & Writing Companion **117**

SKILL VOCABULARY

cohesion / la cohesión *noun* the quality of parts working together as a whole COGNATE

coherent / coherente *adjective* marked by being orderly and logical; easy to understand COGNATE

Your Turn

Ask students to complete the Your Turn activity.

QUESTION 1

A. **Correct.** This is a transition that signals a shift in time.

B. Incorrect. This is not a transition word.

C. Incorrect. This is not a transition word.

D. Incorrect. This is not a transition word.

QUESTION 2

A. Incorrect. This phrase does not include a transition word.

B. Incorrect. This phrase does not include a transition word.

C. **Correct.** "Then" and "suddenly" are both transition words that signal a shift in action.

D. Incorrect. This phrase does not include a transition word.

Your Turn

Ask students to complete the Your Turn activity. Answers will vary.

Transitions that organize the story structure	"Then, he put on his sandals and put the dog in his cage." I added "then" to organize the events in my story.
Transitions that show the relationship between ideas	"All at once, the dishes broke on the floor and the dog started barking." I added "all at once" to show the chaos of the moment and show the relationship between the dog barking and the dishes falling.

Skill: Conclusions

Introduce the Skill

Watch the Concept Definition video and read the following definition with your students.

A **conclusion** is the closing paragraph or section of an essay, argument, or narrative. It is where the writer brings an essay to a close by restating the main idea or **thesis statement** or the **claim** in an argument. It also summarizes the evidence and research that support the claim or thesis. The conclusion should follow logically from the information, explanations, or claim that has been presented. A conclusion is a good way to suggest to your readers that you have accomplished what you set out to do. In addition, try to leave readers with an interesting final impression. This might be accomplished by closing with a quote, an anecdote, or a call to action.

In a **narrative,** a conclusion should follow logically from the events of the plot and what the characters have experienced. It might include characters reflecting on events, why they matter, and how they feel about them.

TURN AND TALK

Turn to your partner and brainstorm a list of movies, TV shows, or books that have strong and memorable endings.

ELL SPEAKING FRAMES

- The (movie / TV show / book) ____ ends with ____.
- An example of a strong or memorable conclusion is ____.

Extended Writing Project

Skill:
Conclusions

••• CHECKLIST FOR CONCLUSIONS

Before you write your conclusion, ask yourself the following questions:

- What important details should I include in the summary in my conclusion?
- What other thoughts and feelings could the characters share with readers in the conclusion?
- Should I express the importance of the events in my narrative through dialogue or a character's actions?

Below are two strategies to help you provide a conclusion that follows from the narrated experiences or events:

- Peer Discussion

  > After you have written your introduction and body paragraphs, talk with a partner about possible endings for your narrative, writing notes about your discussion.

  > Review your notes and think about how you want to end your story.

  > Briefly summarize the events in the narrative through the narrator or one of the characters.

  > Describe how the narrator feels about the events they experienced.

  > Reveal to readers why the experiences in the narrative matter through a character's reflections or dialogue.

  > Write your conclusion.

- Freewriting

  > Freewrite for 10 minutes about what you might include in your conclusion. Don't worry about grammar, punctuation, or having fully formed ideas. The point of freewriting is to discover ideas.

  > Review your notes and think about how you want to end your story.

  > Briefly summarize the events in the narrative through the narrator or one of the characters.

  > Describe how the narrator feels about the events they experienced.

  > Reveal to readers why the experiences in the narrative matter through a character's reflections or dialogue.

  > Write your conclusion.

V SKILL VOCABULARY

 conclusion / la conclusión *noun* the closing paragraph or section of an essay; a closing argument in an argumentative text COGNATE

thesis statement / la presentación de la tesis *noun* a statement that shares the main idea of an argumentative or informative essay

narrative / la narración *noun* a story, real or imagined, consisting of connected events

Extended Writing Project

YOUR TURN

Read the conclusions below. Then, complete the chart by sorting them into those that are strong conclusions and those that are not.

	Conclusion Options
A	"You're the champion baby walker!"
B	As his mother scooped Tonya into her arms, she said, "Great job, Tyler. Dad called me from the hospital and told me what was going on. I got here as soon as I could, but it looks like you didn't even need my help. I'm really proud of you for rising to the challenge and helping out."
C	Max clapped and at the same time Tonya started crying again.
D	But anytime Tyler stopped walking, Tonya began crying again.

Strong Conclusion	Not Strong Conclusion

WRITE

Use the questions in the checklist to add a conclusion: use details, dialogue, action, and character feelings or thoughts to conclude your narrative.

Reading & Writing Companion **119**

Your Turn

Ask students to complete the Your Turn activitiy.

Strong Conclusion	Not Strong Conclusion
B	D
A	C

Write

Ask students to complete the writing assignment.

ELL REWRITE CHECKLIST

A **Action**

- ☐ What action would logically come next in the plot?
- ☐ What character action could I add to resolve the problem and end my story?

Feelings

- ☐ How should the characters feel at the end of the story?
- ☐ What character feelings could I add to resolve the problem and end my story?

Dialogue

- ☐ What can my characters say at the end of the story?
- ☐ What character dialogue could I add to resolve the problem and end my story?

Thoughts

- ☐ What character thoughts could I add to resolve the problem and end my story?

Writer's Notebook

Project the list of the 100 Best Last Lines from Novels on the board. Ask students to choose their two or three favorites and mimic them as last lines for their own narrative conclusions.

Narrative Writing Process: Revise

Review Revision Guide

Break the class into five groups, and assign each group a category of the revision guide. Ask:

- What is the purpose of this section of the guide?
- How did it improve Nik's writing?
- How will it help to improve your writing?

Allow groups to share their ideas with the class.

ELL SPEAKING FRAMES

- I think ____ (clarity / development / organization / word choice / sentence variety) improved Nik's writing by ____.
- I think ____ (clarity / development / organization / word choice / sentence variety) will improve my writing because ____.

Narrative Writing Process: Revise

| PLAN | DRAFT | REVISE | EDIT AND PUBLISH |

You have written a draft of your narrative. You have also received input from your peers about how to improve it. Now you are going to revise your draft.

← REVISION GUIDE

Examine your draft to find areas for revision. Keep in mind your purpose and audience as you revise for clarity, development, organization, and style. Use the guide below to help you review.

Review	Revise	Example
Clarity		
Label each piece of dialogue so you know who is speaking. Annotate any places where it is unclear who is speaking.	Use the character's name to show who is speaking or add description about the speaker.	"Is this okay, Max?" Tyler asked. The boy nodded again. Then, unexpectedly, he burst into tears. "I want my mom!" he wailed.
Development		
Identify key moments leading up to the climax. Annotate places that don't move the story along toward the climax or the resolution.	Focus on a single event and think carefully about whether it drives the story forward or keeps it standing still. If it doesn't move the story forward, you might consider adding or subtracting details to make it more important to the plot.	Tyler thought about making pancakes. He had watched his father make them often enough. ~~Sometimes on Saturday mornings the whole family would sit in the kitchen and keep Dad company while he mixed the batter and cooked each pancake.~~ But it would take too long. He opened a cabinet and pulled out some cereal.

Review	Revise	Example
Organization		
Explain your story in one or two sentences. Reread and annotate any parts that don't match your explanation.	Rewrite the events in the correct sequence. Delete events that are not essential to the story.	Soon Max was sitting on the floor reading. For a moment, everything was wonderfully quiet. Tyler walked over to the window and peered out. The fire seemed under control. There was no more smoke at least. Best of all, it didn't seem as if the house had been damaged very much. ~~If it had been, Tyler wondered where the Molanos would stay. Would they live in Tyler's house until their house was repaired?~~
Style: Word Choice		
Identify every pronoun that takes the place of a noun in your story.	Select sentences to rewrite using consistent pronoun use and correct pronoun and antecedent agreement.	Mr. Molano was standing on the curb waving ~~her~~ his arms.
Style: Sentence Variety		
Think about a key event where you want your reader to feel a specific emotion. Long sentences can draw out a moment and make a reader think; short sentences can show urgent actions or danger.	Rewrite a key event making your sentences longer or shorter to achieve the emotion you want your reader to feel.	After Tyler had circled the hallway ~~yet again,~~ for what felt like the five-hundredth time, his mom came home. Tyler ~~was so happy to see her~~ had never been so glad to see her in his life.

✏ WRITE

Use the guide above, as well as your peer reviews, to help you evaluate your narrative to determine areas that should be revised.

Reading & Writing Companion **121**

Revise

Students should start this activity with a copy of their drafts either printed on paper or open in a word-processing program, such as Google Docs. Allow students time to revise their drafts using the instructions in the revision guide. Once students have finished revising their narrative, have them submit their work.

✓ CHECK FOR SUCCESS

Circulate around the room to spend time with individual students. Ask:

- What category are you working on?
- Why are you revising this specific section?
- How are you revising it?
- How does this change support your purpose?
- Does this change make your writing appropriate for your audience?

If students struggle while revising their drafts, choose an exemplary revision to share with the class while the student talks through the process. You could also invite a student to share a dilemma in the revision process and allow the class to offer feedback or suggestions.

ELL WORD CHOICE

A Tell students to revise their drafts using the revision guide, focusing on word choice.

Write

Ask students to complete the writing assignment.

ELL REVISION CHECKLIST

A ☐ Find a word that can be replaced with a pronoun.
☐ Check to make sure the pronoun will agree in number and gender with the antecedent.
☐ Replace the word with a pronoun, and make sure the pronoun use is consistent in the sentence.

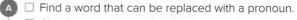

Grammar: Personal Pronouns

Introduce the Skill

Review the image and definition for personal pronouns as a class.

- personal pronoun: replaces the subject or object of a sentence

- subject, or nominative case, pronoun: serves as the subject of a sentence or clause

- object, or objective case, pronoun: serves as the object of a verb or preposition

 ## Discuss the Model

1. Why might someone choose to use a personal pronoun? Someone might use it to replace a noun or a group of nouns. It can make writing more concise.

2. What are the different types of personal pronouns? A personal pronoun can be singular or plural, as well as being a subject or object pronoun.

Extended Writing Project

Grammar: Personal Pronouns

Personal pronouns are pronouns used to refer to persons or things. Two cases, or forms, that pronouns take are nominative case, or subject, and objective case, or object. Each case is determined by how the pronoun functions in a sentence.

Subject Pronouns:
Singular: *I, you, he, she, it*
Plural: *we, you, they*

Object Pronouns:
Singular: *me, you, him, her*
Plural: *us, you, them*

They might come today. Hatchet	The subject pronoun *they* is the subject of the sentence.
In this manner, stopping to rest when I was tired, I carried **him** to the headland. Island of the Blue Dolphins	The object pronoun *him* is the object of the verb *carried*.
There were threats against **me** and my family and even out-and-out attempts at physical harm to **me**. I Never Had It Made: An Autobiography of Jackie Robinson	The object pronoun *me* is the object of the prepositions *against* and *to*.

When writing, make sure to use pronouns in the correct case.

Correct	Incorrect
I walk one mile to school every day.	Me walk one mile to school every day.
Paula asked them for help.	Paula asked they for help.

Reading & Writing Companion

↻ YOUR TURN

1. How should this sentence be changed?

> Them mow lawns during summer vacation.

- ○ A. Change **Them** to **Her**.
- ○ B. Change **Them** to **They**.
- ○ C. Change **Them** to **Him**.
- ○ D. No change needs to be made to this sentence.

2. How should this sentence be changed?

> She told he a funny joke.

- ○ A. Change **he** to **him**.
- ○ B. Change **she** to **her**.
- ○ C. Change **he** to **they**.
- ○ D. No change needs to be made to this sentence.

3. How should this sentence be changed?

> We nervously watched the big, brown dog approach us.

- ○ A. Change **We** to **Us**.
- ○ B. Change **We** to **Him**.
- ○ C. Change **us** to **we**.
- ○ D. No change needs to be made to this sentence.

4. How should this sentence be changed?

> Her brought Cara for a visit.

- ○ A. Change **Cara** to **she**.
- ○ B. Change **Her** to **Us**.
- ○ C. Change **Her** to **She**.
- ○ D. No change needs to be made to this sentence.

Reading & Writing
Companion

⚙ Your Turn

Ask students to complete the Your Turn activity.

QUESTION 1

A. Incorrect.

B. Correct. *They* is a subject pronoun, so it fits as the subject of the sentence.

C. Incorrect.

D. Incorrect.

QUESTION 2

A. Correct. *Him* is an object pronoun and fits as the object of the verb *told*.

B. Incorrect.

C. Incorrect.

D. Incorrect.

QUESTION 3

A. Incorrect.

B. Incorrect.

C. Incorrect.

D. Correct. *We* is a subject pronoun, so is appropriate as the subject of the sentence. *Us* is an object pronoun, so is appropriate as the object of the verb *approach*.

QUESTION 4

A. Incorrect.

B. Incorrect.

C. Correct. *She* is a subject pronoun, so is appropriate as the subject of a sentence.

D. Incorrect.

Grammar: Pronouns and Antecedents

Introduce the Skill

Review the image and definition for pronouns and antecedents as a class.

- pronoun: a word that takes the place of a noun
- antecedent: the noun to which a pronoun refers

Discuss the Model

1. What is a pronoun? A pronoun is a word that takes the place of a noun mentioned earlier in the sentence.

2. What is an antecedent? The noun is the pronoun's antecedent.

3. What do writers need to know when using pronouns and antecedents? Pronouns can replace nouns, but the noun being replaced (antecedent) must agree with the pronoun in both number and gender. Pronouns must also have a clear antecedent.

Grammar: Pronouns and Antecedents

Pronouns and Antecedents

A pronoun is a word that takes the place of a noun mentioned earlier. The noun is the pronoun's antecedent. A pronoun must agree in number and gender with its antecedent.

Text	Pronoun	Antecedent
The morning after my **teacher** came she led me into **her** room and gave me a doll. The Story of My Life	her	teacher
Some of the **Dodgers** who swore **they** would never play with a black man had a change of mind, when **they** realized I was a good ballplayer who could be helpful in **their** earning a few thousand more dollars in world series money. I Never Had It Made: An Autobiography of Jackie Robinson	they their	Dodgers
On this bus on that day, **Rosa Parks** initiated a new era in the American quest for freedom and equality. **She** sat near the middle of the bus, just behind the 10 seats reserved for whites. The Story Behind the Bus	she	Rosa Parks

A pronoun's antecedent should always be clear.

Clear	Unclear	Explanation
Andrea and her sister baked bread. **Her sister** had a special talent for it.	Andrea and her sister baked bread. **She** had a special talent for it.	The pronoun *she* in the second sentence could refer to either Andrea or her sister.
The diplomats, who had traveled from Puerto Rico, met with the reporters.	The diplomats met with the reporters. **They** had traveled from Puerto Rico.	The pronoun *they* could refer to either the diplomats or the reporters.

YOUR TURN

1. How should this sentence be changed?

   > My brother has a test tomorrow, so it is going to study after dinner.

   - A. Change the word **it** to **we**.
   - B. Change the word **it** to **he**.
   - C. Change the word **it** to **she**.
   - D. No change needs to be made to this sentence.

2. How should this sentence be changed?

   > John Adams disagreed with Thomas Jefferson, but he later changed his opinions.

   - A. Change **he** to **Adams**.
   - B. Change **he** to **they**.
   - C. Change **he** to **it**.
   - D. No change needs to be made to this sentence.

3. How should these sentences be changed?

   > The Sistine Chapel is in Rome. Michelangelo painted it.

   - A. Change **Michelangelo** to **He**.
   - B. Change **The Sistine Chapel** to **It**.
   - C. Change **it** to **her**.
   - D. No changes need to be made to these sentences.

4. How should this sentence be changed?

   > All of the teams promote its star players.

   - A. Change **teams** to **team**.
   - B. Change **its** to **their**.
   - C. Change **its** to **his**.
   - D. No change needs to be made to this sentence.

Reading & Writing
Companion

Your Turn

Ask students to complete the Your Turn activity.

QUESTION 1

A. Incorrect.

B. Correct. The pronoun matches the antecedent in both gender (male) and number (singular).

C. Incorrect.

D. Incorrect.

QUESTION 2

A. Correct. It is unclear if the pronoun *he* refers to Adams or to Jefferson. The sentence should be rewritten to show more clearly which man changed his opinions. Of all the choices presented, *Adams* is the one that adds more clarity.

B. Incorrect.

C. Incorrect.

D. Incorrect.

QUESTION 3

A. Incorrect.

B. Incorrect.

C. Incorrect.

D. Correct. The pronoun *it* corresponds in gender and number to *The Sistine Chapel*.

QUESTION 4

A. Incorrect.

B. Correct. *Its* is singular and does not correspond in number to the plural *all*; *their* corresponds.

C. Incorrect.

D. Incorrect.

Grammar: Consistent Pronoun Use

Introduce the Skill

Review the image and definition for consistent pronoun use as a class.

- pronoun: a word that takes the place of a noun
- indefinite pronoun: does not refer to any person, place, or thing in particular
- personal pronoun: forms in first, second, and third person, as well as singular and plural
- antecedent: the noun to which the pronoun refers; should be clear

Discuss the Model

1. What must a pronoun and its antecedent do to be consistent? A pronoun and its antecedent must match in number and person.

2. Why might someone choose to use an indefinite pronoun rather than a personal pronoun? Someone might choose to use an indefinite pronoun rather than a personal pronoun to signal that the pronoun does not refer to a particular person, place, or thing.

Grammar: Consistent Pronoun Use

An antecedent is the word or group of words to which a pronoun refers or that a pronoun replaces. A pronoun must agree with its antecedent in number (singular or plural) and gender (masculine, feminine, or neutral). A pronoun's antecedent may be a noun, another pronoun, or a phrase or clause acting as a noun.

Text	Explanation
I even move **my** chair a little to the right. Not **mine**, not **mine**, not **mine**. Eleven	The pronoun *I* is the antecedent of the pronouns *my* and *mine*. The pronouns agree in person and number.
"Oh, I forgot to show you my pigs!" **he** exclaimed, the gleam returning to **his** eyes. The Pigman	The pronoun *he* is the antecedent of the pronoun *his*. The pronouns agree in person and number.

Pronouns should be used with consistency, so avoid shifting pronoun number and person within a sentence or passage.

Correct	Incorrect
Many older Americans know the exact date **they** started their first job.	Many older Americans know the exact date it started their first job.
My friends and I attended the football game; then **we** walked uptown.	My friends and I attended the football game; then he walked uptown.

Do not use *you* and *they* as indefinite pronouns, and avoid pronouns with no clear antecedent. If clearer, name the person or group to which you are referring.

Correct	Incorrect
As the old adage says: Better safe than sorry.	You know what they say: Better safe than sorry.
People in the community like to attend weekly basketball games. Anybody can have a great time.	People in the community like to attend weekly games. You don't have to love basketball to have a great time.

Reading & Writing Companion

⟳ YOUR TURN

1. How should this sentence be changed?

    > Penelope likes the game of soccer; it plays often.

    ○ A. Change **it** to **they**.
    ○ B. Change **it** to **he**.
    ○ C. Change **it** to **she**.
    ○ D. No change needs to be made to this sentence.

2. How should this sentence be changed?

    > Maria and Sean thought the computer was just what he needed to make their business work.

    ○ A. Change **he** to **they**.
    ○ B. Change **he** to **she**.
    ○ C. Change **he** to **it**.
    ○ D. No change needs to be made to this sentence.

3. How should this sentence be changed?

    > Jason was spending the week with his dad in Boston, where you were going to watch two Celtics games.

    ○ A. Change **his** to **its**.
    ○ B. Change **you** to **they**.
    ○ C. Change **you** to **he**.
    ○ D. No change needs to be made to this sentence.

4. How should this sentence be changed?

    > Sidney moved to the city of Seattle and became a member of its city council.

    ○ A. Change **its** to **your**.
    ○ B. Change **its** to **their**.
    ○ C. Change **its** to **our**.
    ○ D. No change needs to be made to this sentence.

Reading & Writing Companion

Your Turn

Ask students to complete the Your Turn activity.

QUESTION 1

A. Incorrect.

B. Incorrect.

C. Correct. The pronoun *she* agrees in person with the antecedent *Penelope*.

D. Incorrect.

QUESTION 2

A. Correct. The pronoun *they* agrees in number and person with the antecedents *Maria and Sean*.

B. Incorrect.

C. Incorrect.

D. Incorrect.

QUESTION 3

A. Incorrect.

B. Correct. The pronoun *they* agrees in person with the antecedents *Jason* and *his dad*.

C. Incorrect.

D. Incorrect.

QUESTION 4

A. Incorrect.

B. Incorrect.

C. Incorrect.

D. Correct. The pronoun *its* agrees in number and person with the antecedent *city of Seattle*.

Narrative Writing Process: Edit and Publish

Practice with Student Model (Optional)

Provide groups with a different section of Nik's draft. Each group should practice editing Nik's model using the checklist in the lesson. Has he:

☐ followed all the rules for punctuating dialogue?

☐ used correct pronoun and antecedent agreement throughout the story?

☐ used correct and consistent pronouns throughout the story?

☐ corrected any sentence fragments or run-on sentences?

☐ spelled everything correctly?

After the groups have finished, call on volunteers from each group to make edits until all the mistakes have been found and edited, pausing to discuss points of disagreement.

ELL SPEAKING FRAMES

A
- Nik (did / did not) punctuate dialogue correctly when he wrote ____.
- Nik (did / did not) use correct pronoun and antecedent agreement when he wrote ____.
- Nik (did / did not) use consistent pronouns when he wrote ____.
- ____ is an example of a (run-on sentence / sentence fragment) that Nik (has / has not) corrected.
- ____ is spelled incorrectly. The correct spelling is ____.

Extended Writing Project

Narrative Writing Process: Edit and Publish

| PLAN | DRAFT | REVISE | EDIT AND PUBLISH |

You have revised your narrative based on your peer feedback and your own examination.

Now, it is time to edit your narrative. When you revised, you focused on the content of your narrative. You probably looked at the story's beginning, descriptive details, and dialogue. When you edit, you focus on the mechanics of your story, paying close attention to things like grammar and punctuation.

Use the checklist below to guide you as you edit:

☐ Have I followed all the rules for punctuating dialogue?

☐ Have I used correct pronoun and antecedent agreement throughout the story?

☐ Have I used correct and consistent pronouns throughout the story?

☐ Do I have any sentence fragments or run-on sentences?

☐ Have I spelled everything correctly?

Notice some edits Nik has made:

- Changed a pronoun to agree with the antecedent.
- Fixed a sentence fragment.
- Corrected spelling.
- Added a comma before a piece of dialogue.
- Fixed a run-on sentence.
- Changed a pronoun to maintain consistency.
- Moved a period inside quotation marks.

122 | Reading & Writing Companion

Tyler froze. What should ~~she~~ he do? Then he ~~remembered. What~~ remembered what his father had said—Mrs. Molano would be all right.

Tyler patted the boy on the shoulder. As he ~~poared~~ poured some cereal into the bowl, he ~~said~~ ~~"Don't~~ said, "Don't worry, buddy. Your mom will be ~~okay the~~ okay. The doctors at the hospital will take good care of ~~them~~ her. My dad said he thought she would be fine. You'll ~~see".~~ see."

✏️ WRITE

Use the questions on the previous page as well as your peer reviews, to help you evaluate your narrative to determine areas that need editing. Then edit your narrative to correct those errors.

Once you have made all your corrections, you are ready to publish your work. You can distribute your writing to family and friends, hang it on a bulletin board, or post it on your blog. If you publish online, share the link with your family, friends, and classmates.

Write

After students finish editing, suggest, if there's time, that they set their essays aside for a few minutes, and that they then proofread it one more time. Once students have finished editing their narrative, have them submit their work.

✓ CHECK FOR SUCCESS

If students struggle to edit successfully, help them determine where edits are needed, and what changes need to be made.

Direct students to the grammar lessons in this unit if they are uncertain about the rules for specific concepts.

ELL READ ALOUD

Encourage students to read their stories aloud to themselves or to a partner in order to catch any remaining mistakes.

A READ ALOUD

Encourage students to read their stories aloud to themselves or to an on-grade-level peer in order to catch any remaining mistakes.

B WRITE A BLURB

Have students review their narrative and determine where their writing was most effective. Allow students to write a blurb like they might find on the back of a book that highlights and praises the best qualities of their work. Alternately, have students write blurbs for the students in the class and post them around the room.

English Language Learner Resources

studysync

GRADE 6 > UNIT

USERS   ASSIGNMENTS

6   7

Testing Our Limits
Core ELA
Grade 6
30 Days

Unit Overview

Integrated Reading and Writing

Extended Writing Project

ELL Resources

Novel Study

End-of-Unit Assessment

Instructional Path

Add to books!

Lost Island

Connected

Skill: Classroom Vocabulary

Students will learn and recognize classroom vocabulary words and practice using them in a variety of contexts.

Teacher Resources: Lesson Plan

Skill: Taking Notes

Students will learn and practice the skill of taking notes when they listen to or read a text.

Teacher Resources: Lesson Plan

Lessons in the English Language Learner Resources section offer explicit ELL instruction. These lessons share a thematic and genre focus with all other lessons in the Core ELA unit.

The twenty ELL Resources are developed around two texts, "Lost Island" and "Connected," and an Extended Oral Project. Each text is written at four distinct levels. For ELLs, these texts serve as structural and thematic models of authentic texts in the Integrated Reading and Writing section of the unit. Thus, teachers may use the ELL texts in place of or as extensions for "Hatchet," and "A Wrinkle in Time."

ELL lessons modify the routines used with texts in the Integrated Reading and Writing section. Explicit vocabulary instruction is emphasized, and reading and writing Skills lessons focus strongly on language acquisition and reading comprehension.

After reading texts about challenges and trying situations, students will complete an Extended Oral Project that can be used in place of or as an extension to the Extended Writing Project. In this unit, students will plan and present a realistic scene in the form of a group presentation.

Focus on English Language Proficiency Levels

- ADVANCED HIGH
- ADVANCED
- INTERMEDIATE
- BEGINNING

ELL Resources provide targeted support for four levels of proficiency: Beginning, Intermediate, Advanced, and Advanced High. Instruction and scaffolds, as well as the texts themselves, are differentiated based on these levels.

Additional differentiated scaffolds include visual glossaries, speaking and writing frames, and suggested grouping for peer and teacher support. Lessons also include suggested extension activities to challenge Advanced and Advanced High students as they progress through the year.

ELL Resources

ELL TEXTS

Lost Island
- Skill: Sight Vocabulary and High-Frequency Words
- Skill: Seeking Clarification
- First Read
- Skill: Analyzing Expressions
- Skill: Conveying Ideas
- Skill: Spelling Patterns and Rules
- Close Read

Connected
- Skill: Classroom Vocabulary
- Skill: Taking Notes
- First Read
- Skill: Language Structures
- Skill: Retelling and Summarizing
- Skill: Subject-Verb Agreement
- Close Read

EXTENDED ORAL PROJECT

- Introduction
- Skill: Acquiring Vocabulary
- Plan

- Skill: Sentence Lengths
- Practice
- Present

Lost Island

FICTION

Introduction

Marina wakes up alone, thirsty, and hungry on a deserted island. How did she get here, and why is her head throbbing? As she slowly recalls a large wave smashing into Uncle Merlin's fishing boat, Marina takes her first steps towards survival.

Slowly waking up, Mariana notices that she has sand in her mouth and the smell of sea in her nose. She opens her eyes to the bright sun and realizes that she's on a small island, no bigger than a soccer field. She remembers fishing with her Uncle Merlin. They had just anchored and were dropping their lines when a big wave suddenly capsized their boat. When Mariana surfaced, she spotted the island and swam for it until she was exhausted. Upon reaching the shore, she passed out and slept for hours. Now, the sun is high in the sky and Mariana is frightened. Why isn't her uncle here? As her fear turns to panic, she realizes that he could have drowned and that no one is coming to help her. At the same time, she remembers how her uncle always urged her to use her head. Using her wits, she could find a way to survive.

 Summaries in multiple languages are available digitally.

🔊 Audio and audio text highlighting are available with this text.

CONNECT TO ESSENTIAL QUESTION

What do we do when life gets hard?

A girl and her uncle are fishing when their boat is overturned. The girl is now stranded on the island and can't find her uncle. How will she get to safety?

Core ELA Connections

Texts	Theme	Genre
Hatchet	Mariana wakes up stranded on a deserted island. The text builds on the idea of fear, self-determination, and the will to survive.	An adventure story written in the first person, "Lost Island" orients readers to the thoughts and feelings of a realistic narrator.

Differentiated Text Levels

ELL LEVEL	BEGINNING	INTERMEDIATE	ADVANCED	ADVANCED HIGH
WORD COUNT	255	396	445	531
LEXILE	230L	360L	480L	600L

Instructional Path

The print teacher's edition includes essential point-of-use instruction and planning tools. Complete lesson plans and program documents appear in your digital teacher account.

Skill: Sight Vocabulary and High-Frequency Words

Objectives: Students will be able to learn and recognize sight vocabulary and high-frequency words in English.

Objectives: Students will be able to recognize sight vocabulary and high-frequency words when listening and reading, and produce sight vocabulary and high-frequency words when speaking and writing.

Skill: Seeking Clarification

Objectives: Students will be able to learn and practice the skill of seeking clarification when they do not understand spoken language.

Objectives: Students will be able to seek clarification when they do not understand spoken language and while reading a new or unfamiliar text.

First Read: Lost Island

Objectives: Students will be able to perform an initial reading of a text using the strategy of seeking clarification and demonstrate comprehension by responding to questions using textual evidence.

Objectives: Students will be able to demonstrate comprehension of a text by responding to questions orally and in writing using textual evidence.

Skill: Analyzing Expressions

Objectives: Students will be able to learn and practice the skill of analyzing expressions when reading.

Objectives: Students will be able to identify and understand common expressions such as idioms, sayings, and figurative language in what they read.

Skill: Conveying Ideas

Objectives: Students will be able to learn and practice the skill of conveying ideas when speaking.

Objectives: Students will be able to use multiple strategies to convey ideas when speaking.

Skill: Spelling Patterns and Rules

Objectives: Students will be able to recognize and apply spelling patterns and rules.

Objectives: Students will be able to recognize spelling patterns and rules when reading and apply spelling patterns and rules when writing.

Close Read: Lost Island

Objectives: Students will be able to perform a close reading of a text in order to analyze expressions.

Objectives: Students will be able to demonstrate analysis of expressions by participating in a collaborative conversations and writing a short constructed response.

Progress Monitoring

Opportunities to Learn	Opportunities to Demonstrate Learning	Opportunities to Reteach

Sight Vocabulary and High-Frequency Words

⚙ Skill: Sight Vocabulary and High-Frequency Words	⚙ Skill: Sight Vocabulary and High-Frequency Words • Your Turn 🖥 First Read • Sight Vocabulary and High-Frequency Words	⚙ Spotlight Skill: Sight Vocabulary and High-Frequency Words

Seeking Clarification

⚙ Skill: Seeking Clarification	⚙ Skill: Seeking Clarification • Your Turn 🖥 First Read • Skills Focus	⚙ Spotlight Skill: Seeking Clarification

Analyzing Expressions

⚙ Skill: Analyzing Expressions	⚙ Skill: Analyzing Expressions • Your Turn	⚙ Spotlight Skill: Analyzing Expressions

Conveying Ideas

⚙ Skill: Conveying Ideas	⚙ Skill: Conveying Ideas • Your Turn 🖥 Close Read • Complete Skills Focus • Write	⚙ Spotlight Skill: Conveying Ideas

Spelling Patterns and Rules

⚙ Skill: Spelling Patterns and Rules	⚙ Skill: Spelling Patterns and Rules • Your Turn 🖥 Close Read • Write	⚙ Spotlight Skill: Spelling Patterns and Rules

First Read

StudySync

Lost Island

Introduce the Text

As a class, watch the video preview ▶ and have students read the introduction in pairs to make connections to the video preview. Ask students various "wh" questions such as:

- What did you see in the video? How does it make you feel?
- What do you think the text will be about?
- Is there something in the video or introduction that surprised you?

> **ELL** **Beginning & Intermediate**
>
> **SPEAKING FRAMES**
> - I see ____. I feel ____.
> - I think the text will be about ____.
> - I was surprised by ____.

Practice Prereading Skill

Remind students that Seeking Clarification:

Helps you better understand the text you read and the conversations you have with others. When you discover that you do not understand a word in a text or a conversation, you can use different questions to seek clarification. To help you understand, someone may speak slower or use gestures.

Have students work in small, on-level groups to choral read or listen to the audio of the summary. Remind students to seek clarification from you or their peers as needed.

As students are working in small groups, circulate to listen for sample questions like:

- *What does this word mean?*
- *Would you repeat that?*

Activate Prior Knowledge and Experiences OPTIONAL

Have students make connections while practicing their oral language by discussing what they know about boats.

Generate a list (on the board or on paper) of any information or ideas your students have about boats.

Ask students to share where their background knowledge came from. For example, did their ideas come from a movie, friend, television show, book, or family member?

VOCABULARY

damp
wet

capsized
tipped over in the water

intense
very strong

rescuer
someone who saves a person from harm or danger

anchored
held in place firmly

cautioned
gave a warning

READ

NOTES

1   Mariana woke up slowly.

2   She was on her back. She felt sand in her mouth. The air was hot and **damp**. Where am I? Her head was throbbing. Was that the smell of salt in the air? Did I hear a seagull cry?

3   Mariana turned her head and slowly opened her eyes. The bright light was too **intense** for her. At first, she saw only damp yellow sand. She looked around. She saw stones, weeds, and a few palm trees. She could see the entire island. It was no larger than a soccer field.

4   Then Mariana remembered. She remembered fishing with Uncle Merlin. They found a good spot, so they **anchored** their boat near a little island. In the warm morning sun, the bay was calm. Mariana and Merlin got their fishing lines ready, when suddenly an enormous, thundering wave came out of nowhere. The wave overturned the boat, tossing them into the water. Mariana

---

 Preteach Vocabulary

Model the first word and example for the class.

1. The first word is *damp*, and its meaning is "wet."

2. When I hear the word *damp*, I think of something that is wet but not soaking.

3. For example, if I twist my towel to get most of the water out before I hang it up, it will be *damp* but not soaking wet.

Continue this exercise with each word in the glossary, calling on individuals or groups of students to share out.

ELL Beginning

PRETEACH VOCABULARY

Use the gestures to clarify meanings.

- **damp** (Wipe your hand over your "sweaty" forehead.)

- **intense** (Pantomime putting on sunglasses to protect your eyes from a bright light.)

- **anchored** (Tack a piece of paper to the bulletin board.)

- **capsized** (Tip over a box or cup.)

- **rescuer** (Pantomime helping someone who has fallen down.)

- **cautioned** (Shake your finger in warning.)

🔊 **AUDIO TEXT HIGHLIGHTING**

Allow students to use the audio text highlight feature to follow along as they read. Alternately, you may wish to work directly with students or group them in twos or threes for partner reading or choral reading.

Sight Vocabulary and High-Frequency Words Focus

Remind students of the sight vocabulary and high-frequency words that they studied at the beginning of the unit. Point out that some of the words may be useful as they think about and discuss the text. For example:

- the (**The** island was . . .)
- I (**I** think that Mariana . . .)
- two (There were **two** . . .)
- where (**Where** is . . .)
- little (Their **little** boat was . . .)

TEXT TALK

Have students discuss the questions in small groups. Circulate and check for understanding.

1. What is the story about?
2. Who are the story's characters?
3. Where does the story take place?
4. How does the story make you feel?

 All Levels

SPEAKING FRAMES

Giving Information

- This story is about ___.
- The story's characters are ___.
- This story takes place in ___.
- This story makes me feel ___.

Asking for Information:

- Can you explain ___?
- What do you think about ___?
- Why do you think ___?

Lost Island

remembered rising to the surface and seeing land. She swam toward it; she swam and swam. An eternity seemed to have passed. She remembered thinking: Why don't I just give up? What had motivated her to keep swimming? She had finally reached the shore and had crawled up onto the sand. Exhausted.

5 Mariana looked at her surroundings now and thought. She must have passed out and slept on the beach for hours. The boat had **capsized** in early morning, but now the sun was high in the sky. It must be noon.

6 Noon, and hot.

7 Mariana wondered where her uncle was. Why hasn't he come to get me? What is he waiting for? She felt hungry; her mouth was dry. She thought of the lunch her uncle had packed. A cool drink and a sandwich would be perfect right now!

8 Then she realized something. Maybe her uncle wasn't coming to get her because maybe he had drowned. Maybe no **rescuer** was coming to get her. She was trapped. Stuck. Alone. Was she going to die on this island?

9 Mariana started to cry, but she stopped herself quickly. Wait. She **cautioned** herself. Don't be a baby. Use your head. That's what Uncle Merlin always said: "Use your head!"

10 Slowly turning her body, she then lifted herself onto her elbows. Next, she got onto her knees and finally stood up. Her head throbbed, but she looked into the island and took a step.

First Read

Read the story. After you read, answer the Think Questions below.

THINK QUESTIONS

1. Who is the main character in the story? Where is she?

   _____ is the main character.

   She is _____.

2. What happened that tipped the boat over?

   The boat tipped over because _____.

3. How can you tell that Mariana is getting more worried as time passed?

   Mariana is getting more worried because _____

   _____.

4. Use context to confirm the meaning of the word *rescuer* as it is used in "Lost Island." Write your definition of *rescuer* here.

   Rescuer means _____.

   A context clue is _____.

5. What is another way to say that a boat *capsized*?

   A boat _____.

Think Questions

Circulate as students answer Think Questions independently. Answers will vary.

QUESTION 1: Comprehension

Mariana. She is on a small island.

QUESTION 2: Comprehension

A huge wave hit the boat.

QUESTION 3: Comprehension

Answers will vary, but may include the following examples:

- "Mariana wondered where her uncle was."
- "Maybe no rescuer was coming to get her."
- "Was she going to die on this island?"

Student responses should provide examples from the text and an explanation that describes how Mariana's level of anxiety is growing.

QUESTION 4: Language

Mariana worries that no rescuer will come get her. A rescuer must be someone who saves you from danger.

QUESTION 5: Language

A boat tipped over.

Skill: Analyzing Expressions

Introduce the Skill

Watch the Concept Definition video and read the definition for Analyzing Expressions.

TURN AND TALK

1. What does it mean to analyze expressions?

2. Why might it be difficult to analyze expressions?

3. What can you do if you are struggling to analyze expressions?

Beginning & Intermediate
SPEAKING FRAMES
- When I don't understand an expression, I ____.
- To determine the meaning of an expression, ____.

Advanced & Advanced High
SPEAKING FRAMES
- When I don't understand an expression, I ____.
  For example, ____.
- To determine the meaning of an expression, ____.
  For example, ____.

Lost Island

Skill: Analyzing Expressions

★ DEFINE

When you read, you may find English **expressions** that you do not know. An expression is a group of words that communicates an idea. Three types of expressions are idioms, sayings, and figurative language. They can be difficult to understand because the meanings of the words are different from their **literal**, or usual, meanings.

An **idiom** is an expression that is commonly known among a group of people. For example: "It's raining cats and dogs" means it is raining heavily. **Sayings** are short expressions that contain advice or wisdom. For instance: "Don't count your chickens before they hatch" means do not plan on something good happening before it happens. **Figurative** language is when you describe something by comparing it with something else, either directly (using the words *like* or *as*) or indirectly. For example, "I'm as hungry as a horse" means I'm very hungry. None of the expressions are about actual animals.

••• CHECKLIST FOR ANALYZING EXPRESSIONS

To determine the meaning of an expression, remember the following:

✓ If you find a confusing group of words, it may be an expression. The meaning of words in expressions may not be their literal meaning.

- Ask yourself: Is this confusing because the words are new? Or because the words do not make sense together?

✓ Determining the overall meaning may require that you use one or more of the following:

- context clues
- a dictionary or other resource
- teacher or peer support

✓ Highlight important information before and after the expression to look for clues.

V SKILL VOCABULARY

expression / la expresión *noun* a phrase used to express an idea
COGNATE

literal / literal *adjective* describing the usual meaning of a word COGNATE

idiom / el modismo *noun* a common expression that cannot be taken literally

saying / el dicho *noun* an expression that contains advice or wisdom

↻ YOUR TURN

Read paragraphs 9–10 from "Lost Island." Then complete the multiple-choice questions below.

> **from "Lost Island"**
>
> Mariana started to cry, but she stopped herself quickly. Wait. She cautioned herself. Don't be a baby. Use your head. That's what Uncle Merlin always said: "Use your head!"
>
> Slowly turning her body, she then lifted herself onto her elbows. Next, she got onto her knees and finally stood up.

1. What does Mariana mean when she says "use your head" in paragraph 9?

   ○ A. find her uncle
   ○ B. to be cautious exploring
   ○ C. to use her head as a tool
   ○ D. to think about a solution

2. Which context clue helped you determine the meaning of the expression?

   ○ A. "Mariana started to cry . . ."
   ○ B. "That's what Uncle Merlin always said."
   ○ C. "Slowly turning her body . . ."
   ○ D. ". . . she got onto her knees and finally stood up."

⚙ Discuss the Skill Model

1. **What does the student not understand?**

   She doesn't understand the meaning of the expression "An eternity seemed to have passed."

2. **How does the student analyze the expression?**

   She searches for context clues.

3. **What context clue does the student highlight? What does she conclude in her annotation?**

   "She swam toward it; she swam and swam," and "She had finally reached the shore and had crawled up onto the sand. Exhausted." She concludes that a significant amount of time has passed and that this is the meaning of the expression.

4. **What does the student do to confirm her analysis of the expression?**

   The student asks her teacher or peers what the expression means.

5. **How does knowing the meaning of the expression help the student?**

   The student better understands the text.

ELL Beginning & Intermediate

Have students use the speaking frames and helpful terms to participate in the group discussion. If beginning students are hesitant to participate in a discussion, encourage them by prompting with *yes* or *no* questions.

Advanced & Advanced High

Have students use the speaking frames to participate in the group discussion.

SPEAKING FRAMES

- The student does not understand the expression ____.
- The student analyzes the expression by searching for ____ in the text. A context clue is ____.
- The student highlights ____.
- The student believes the expression means ____. Another way of saying this expression is ____.
- The student ____ or ____ to confirm her understanding.
- The student improves her understanding of the text by ____.

HELPFUL TERMS FOR DISCUSSION

• context	• clues	• expression
• analyze	• confirm	• understanding
• highlight	• improve	• text

⚙ Your Turn   Ask students to complete the Your Turn activity. ELPS: (1)(H)

QUESTION 1:   D) Mariana decides to take action and find a solution to her current situation.

QUESTION 2:   D) This clue tells us that Mariana decided to take action.

Skill: Conveying Ideas

Introduce the Skill

Watch the Concept Definition video and read the definition for Conveying Ideas.

 TURN AND TALK

1. What does it mean to convey ideas?

2. Why might it be difficult to convey your ideas?

3. What can you do if you are struggling to convey your ideas?

ELL Beginning & Intermediate

SPEAKING FRAMES

- To convey an idea means to relay a ____.
- You may not be able to ____.
- You could use physical movements or ____.
- You could also say ____.

ELL Advanced & Advanced High

SPEAKING FRAMES

- To convey an idea means ____.
- You may not be able to ____ because ____.
- You could use physical movements or ____.
- You could also try using strategies like ____ or ____.

Lost Island

 Skill:
Conveying Ideas

★ DEFINE

Conveying ideas means communicating a **message** to another person. When speaking, you might not know what word to use to convey your ideas. When you do not know the exact English word, you can try different strategies. For example, you can ask for help from classmates or your teacher. You may use gestures and physical movements to act out the word. You can also try using **synonyms** or **defining** and describing the meaning you are trying to express.

••• CHECKLIST FOR CONVEYING IDEAS

To convey ideas for words you do not know, try the following strategies:

✓ Request help.

✓ Use gestures or physical movements.

✓ Use a synonym for the word.

✓ Describe what the word means using other words.

✓ Give an example of the word you want to use.

 SKILL VOCABULARY

convey / verbalizar *verb* to express

message / el mensaje *noun* a piece of information COGNATE

synonym / el sinónimo *noun* a word or phrase that means the same as another word or phrase COGNATE

define / definar *verb* to give the meaning of a word COGNATE

↻ YOUR TURN

Read the following excerpt from the story. Then imagine that someone is trying to convey the idea of the boat *overturning*. Find the correct example for each strategy to complete the chart below.

---

from "Lost Island"

Then Mariana remembered. She remembered fishing with Uncle Merlin. They found a good spot, so they anchored their boat near a little island. In the warm morning sun, the bay was calm. Mariana and Merlin got their fishing lines ready, when suddenly an enormous, thundering wave came out of nowhere. The wave overturned the boat, tossing them into the water. Mariana remembered rising to the surface and seeing land.

	Examples
A	The person explains that the word means "to roll over."
B	The person turns her or his hand upside-down.
C	The person uses the similar words *tip* over.
D	The person says this when you knock a glass over and it spills.

Strategies	Examples
Use gestures or physical movements.	
Use a synonym for the word.	
Describe what the word means using other words.	
Give examples of when you would use the word.	

Please note that excerpts and passages in the StudySync® library and this workbook are intended as touchstones to generate interest in an author's work. The excerpts and passages do not substitute for the reading of entire texts, and StudySync® strongly recommends that students seek out and purchase the whole literary or informational work in order to experience it as the author intended. Links to online resellers are available in our digital library. In addition, complete works may be ordered through an authorized reseller by filling out and returning to StudySync® the order form enclosed in this workbook.

Reading & Writing Companion **131**

Copyright © BookheadEd Learning, LLC

⚙ Discuss the Skill Model

1. What is the student trying to do?

   The student is trying to share their annotation.

2. Why is the student struggling?

   The student can't remember a word.

3. What strategies does the student use?

   Answers will vary, but should include: The student describes the word. The students says a synonym. The student asks for help.

ELL **Beginning & Intermediate**

Have students use the <u>speaking frames</u> and <u>helpful terms</u> to participate in the group discussion. If beginning students are hesitant to participate in a discussion, encourage them by prompting *yes* or *no* questions.

Advanced & Advanced High

Have students use the <u>speaking frames</u> to participate in the group discussion.

SPEAKING FRAMES

- The student is trying to expand on his ___.
- The student is struggling because he can't ___ a word.
- First, the student ___.
- The student also ___.

HELPFUL TERMS FOR DISCUSSION

- convey
- synonym
- asks
- explain
- ideas
- help
- remember
- describe
- example

⚙ Your Turn Ask students to complete the Your Turn activity.

Examples
The person turns their hand upside down.
The person uses the similar words *tip over*.
The person explains that the word means "to roll over."
The person says this when you knock a glass over and it spills.

English Language Learner Resources **269**

Close Read

Model Skills Focus

Remind students of the Reading Skill Analyzing Expressions. Tell students that one way you can analyze expressions you do not know in a story is to look for context clues about those expressions while you are reading. Direct students to the Skills Focus and remind them to track as you read aloud.

Find context clues that help you analyze expressions in the story.

Model this activity for students:

- I am going to focus on expressions that I do not understand well.

- I reread the story and look at my annotations. I notice that I highlighted the part about Mariana falling asleep on the beach.

- I didn't understand the sentence "She must have *passed out* and slept on the beach for hours."

- When I think of the words "passed out" I imagine someone passing out, or handing out, papers. But that doesn't make sense in the story.

- I look for context clues. In the previous paragraph, I know that Mariana was tired from swimming. Also, I know from the rest of the sentence that she was sleeping. These are all important clues. Now I understand that the expression "passed out" can mean falling asleep from exhaustion.

Complete Skills Focus

Divide students into pairs. Have each pair identify expressions in the story to analyze:

- Have both partners look for context clues to help determine the meaning of each expression.

- Have the partners ask each other what they believe each expression means based on the context clues.

- Have partners explain how the context clues helped them analyze and understand each expression.

Circulate and monitor groups as they work.

Lost Island

Close Read

PERSONAL RESPONSE: Mariana faces dangers that few people her age ever see. How would you react if you were faced with the same situation? How would your response be like Mariana's? How would it be different? Recount the events that Mariana experienced, and describe what you might feel and do in her situation. Pay attention to spelling patterns as you write.

Use the checklist below to guide you as you write:

- ☐ What happens to Marina in the story?
- ☐ What dangers does Mariana face?
- ☐ How does she act and feel?
- ☐ How would I be like Mariana?
- ☐ How would I be different from Mariana?

Use the sentence frames to organize and write your personal response.

If I were Mariana, _____.

First, I would _____.

Like Mariana, I would _____.

Unlike Mariana, I might _____.

Collaborative Conversation

Group students so they have a representative from each of the original pairs. Prompt partners to make a list of all the expressions they analyzed and what they mean.

- How did context clues help you analyze these expressions?
- How did asking other students help confirm your understanding?

- How did analyzing the expressions help your understanding of the story?

Collaborative Conversation

 SCAFFOLDS

ELL **BEGINNING, INTERMEDIATE** Use the word bank to participate in the group discussion.

ADVANCED Use the speaking frames to participate in the group discussion.

BEGINNING, INTERMEDIATE	ADVANCED
Word Bank	**Speaking Frames**
<ul><li>helped me understand</li><li>now I understand</li><li>character</li></ul> <ul><li>plot</li><li>action</li><li>description</li></ul>	<ul><li>Context clues helped me because ____.</li><li>Asking other students helped me because ____.</li><li>Analyzing the expressions helped me better understand ____ about the story.</li></ul>

Write

Ask students to complete the writing assignment. Remind students to pay attention to spelling patterns in words.

ELL **BEGINNING** Write a response using the paragraph frames and word banks.

INTERMEDIATE Write a response using the paragraph frames.

INTERMEDIATE		
BEGINNING		
Paragraph Frames		**Word Bank**
<ul><li>If I were Mariana, ____.</li><li>First, I would ____.</li></ul>	<ul><li>Like Mariana, I would ____.</li><li>Unlike Mariana, I might ____.</li></ul>	<ul><li>scared</li><li>rescuer</li><li>confused</li></ul> <ul><li>calm</li><li>intense</li></ul>

Connected

FICTION

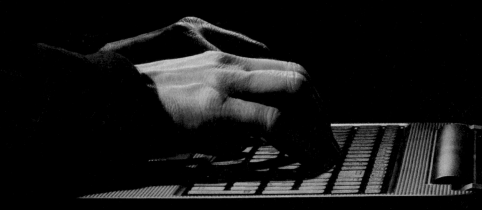

Introduction

What would you do if a friend went missing? What if you learned that a powerful, maybe even scary, secret lay behind the disappearance? In the story "Connected," three friends search for a missing person-and learn of a tantalizing force that could threaten the world as they know it.

Joshua is constantly on the Internet, which often makes him late. However, his friends expect him to be on time for opening night of the summer's blockbuster movie. When he doesn't show up, his worried friends look for him at home. They find only Joshua's typical messy bedroom and a glow coming from his computer. While Ibrahim and Victoria search for clues, Mateo reveals that Joshua had recently discovered a computer virus. According to Joshua, this virus is so powerful that it can take over computers and people. Ibrahim clicks the computer mouse, which triggers an undecipherable pattern on the screen that transforms into the following words: "Enter, if you wish." Upon hitting the enter key, bright lights flash and they suddenly find themselves in a hallway. A strange man approaches and tells them that he has information about Joshua. But first, they have to do something for him.

ELL Summaries in multiple languages are available digitally.

🔊 Audio and audio text highlighting are available with this text.

CONNECT TO ESSENTIAL QUESTION

What do we do when life gets hard?

A teenage boy discovers a computer virus before he goes missing. When his friends go to his room they find a strange message on his computer. What will they do to help their friend?

Core ELA Connections

Texts	Theme	Genre
A Wrinkle in Time	Three friends search for their friend Joshua, who is not where they expected him to be. The text builds on the idea of having to solve a puzzle in order to find out information and locate a missing person.	A science fiction story told in the third person, "Connected" challenges readers to question what is possible.

Differentiated Text Levels

ELL LEVEL	BEGINNING	INTERMEDIATE	ADVANCED	ADVANCED HIGH
WORD COUNT	310	408	461	540
LEXILE	240L	300L	350L	500L

Instructional Path

The print teacher's edition includes essential point-of-use instruction and planning tools. Complete lesson plans and program documents appear in your digital teacher account.

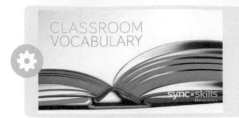

Skill: Classroom Vocabulary

Objectives: Students will be able to learn and recognize classroom vocabulary words in English.

Objectives: Students will be able to recognize classroom vocabulary words when listening and reading, and produce classroom vocabulary words when speaking and writing.

Skill: Taking Notes

Objectives: Students will be able to learn and practice the skill of taking notes when they listen to or read a text.

Objectives: Students will be able to take notes as they read a new or unfamiliar text.

First Read: Connected

Objectives: Students will be able to perform an initial reading of a text using the strategy of taking notes.

Objectives: Students will be able to demonstrate comprehension of a text by responding to questions orally and in writing using textual evidence.

Skill: Language Structures

Objectives: Students will be able to analyze language structures when reading.

Objectives: Students will be able to distinguish between the subject, object, and verb in simple sentences.

Skill: Retelling and Summarizing

Objectives: Students will be able to understand and practice the skill of retelling and summarizing to demonstrate comprehension of a text.

Objectives: Students will be able to distinguish between the beginning, middle, and end of a text.

Skill: Subject-Verb Agreement

Objectives: Students will be able to recognize and apply the rules of subject-verb agreement.

Objectives: Students will be able to recognize and edit for subject-verb agreement when reading and writing.

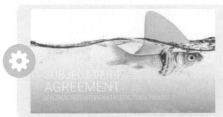

Close Read: Connected

Objectives: Students will be able to perform a close reading of a text in order to retell and summarize a text accurately.

Objectives: Students will be able to retell and summarize a text by participating in a collaborative conversations and writing a short constructed response.

Progress Monitoring

Opportunities to Learn	Opportunities to Demonstrate Learning	Opportunities to Reteach

Classroom Vocabulary

Opportunities to Learn	Opportunities to Demonstrate Learning	Opportunities to Reteach
⚙ Skill: Classroom Vocabulary	⚙ Skill: Classroom Vocabulary • Your Turn ▣ First Read • Classroom Vocabulary	⚙ Spotlight Skill: Classroom Vocabulary

Taking Notes

Opportunities to Learn	Opportunities to Demonstrate Learning	Opportunities to Reteach
⚙ Skill: Taking Notes	⚙ Skill: Taking Notes • Your Turn ▣ First Read • Skills Focus	⚙ Spotlight Skill: Taking Notes

Language Structures

Opportunities to Learn	Opportunities to Demonstrate Learning	Opportunities to Reteach
⚙ Skill: Language Structures	⚙ Skill: Language Structures • Your Turn	⚙ Spotlight Skill: Language Structures

Conveying Ideas

Opportunities to Learn	Opportunities to Demonstrate Learning	Opportunities to Reteach
⚙ Skill: Retelling and Summarizing	⚙ Skill: Retelling and Summarizing • Your Turn ▣ Close Read • Complete Skills Focus • Write	⚙ Spotlight Skill: Retelling and Summarizing

Subject-Verb Agreement

Opportunities to Learn	Opportunities to Demonstrate Learning	Opportunities to Reteach
⚙ Skill: Subject-Verb Agreement	⚙ Skill: Subject-Verb Agreement • Your Turn ▣ Close Read • Write	⚙ Spotlight Skill: Subject-Verb Agreement

First Read

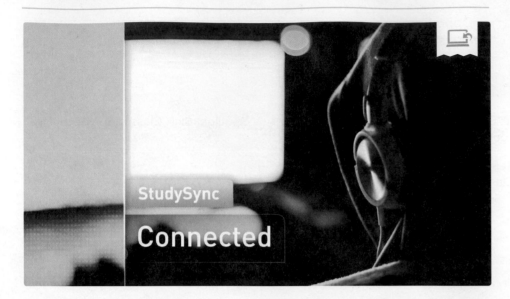

Introduce the Text

As a class, watch the video preview ▶ and have students read the introduction in pairs to make connections to the video preview. Ask students various "wh" questions such as:

- What did you see in the video? How does it make you feel?

- What do you think the text will be about?

- Is there something in the video or introduction that surprised you?

ELL **Beginning & Intermediate**

SPEAKING FRAMES
- I see ____. I feel ____.
- I think the text will be about ____.
- I was surprised by ____.

Practice Prereading Skill

Remind students that Taking Notes:

Helps you to stay focused on the information you are reading or hearing. When you begin to read or listen to information, write the main ideas and important details in an outline or chart. Taking notes like this lets you organize the information. This helps you understand it more easily, talk about the main ideas more clearly, and study better.

Have students work in small, on-level groups to create an outline of the summary using the main ideas and details chart.

As students are working in small groups, circulate to listen for sample questions like:

- *What are the main ideas?*

- *What are the important details?*

Activate Prior Knowledge and Experiences OPTIONAL

Have students make connections while practicing their oral language by discussing what they know about computers.

Generate a list (on the board or on paper) of any information or ideas your students have about computers.

Ask students to share where their background knowledge came from. For example, did their ideas come from a movie, friend, television show, book, or family member?

V VOCABULARY

habitually

done regularly or often

digits

symbols for the numbers 0 to 9

froze

stopped in a position and without further movement

whirlpool

a place in a body of water, such as a river or a stream, where the water moves very fast in a circle

virus

a software program that is created to cause harm to a computer or network

 NOTES

☰ READ

1 Joshua was late. At first, his friends were not surprised. Joshua was **habitually** late. Joshua liked to stay connected to the Internet. His friends thought he was *too* connected.

2 But it was opening night for the biggest movie of the summer. Joshua should have met them hours ago.

3 "Did you hear from him today?" Victoria asked. Ibrahim and Mateo shook their heads.

4 She frowned. "Something's not right. We need to see what's going on."

5 "I know where he could be," Ibrahim said.

6 "His computer," they all exclaimed.

. . .

🔊 AUDIO TEXT HIGHLIGHTING

Allow students to use the audio text highlight feature to follow along as they read. Alternately, you may wish to work directly with students or group them in twos or threes for partner reading or choral reading.

 Preteach Vocabulary

Model the first word and example for the class.

1. The first word is *habitually* and its meaning is "done regularly or often."

2. When I hear the word *habitually*, I think of something that it is done very frequently.

3. For example, after dinner, I *habitually* take my dog for a walk.

4. This is an example of something I do *habitually*, because it is done regularly.

Continue this exercise with each word in the glossary, calling on individuals or groups of students to share out.

ELL Beginning

PRETEACH VOCABULARY

Use the gestures to clarify meanings.

- **habitually** (Make three rounds around the class and always take the same book from the same desk.)
- **virus** (Mimic that your computer broke.)
- **froze** (Pose like a statue.)
- **digits** (Pantomime counting to nine with your fingers.)
- **whirlpool** (Pantomime a whirlpool with your index finger.)

Classroom Language Focus

Remind students of the sight vocabulary and high-frequency words that they studied at the beginning of the unit. Point out that some of the words may be useful as they think about and discuss the text. For example:

- notebook (The **notebook** was . . .)
- backpack (Ibrahim took the **backpack** and . . .)
- book (The friends saw books on . . .)
- desk (On Joshua's **desk**, Victoria found . . .)

TEXT TALK

Have students discuss the questions in small groups. Circulate and check for understanding.

1. What is the story about?
2. Who are the story's characters?
3. Where does the story take place?
4. How does the story make you feel?

ELL   All Levels

SPEAKING FRAMES

Giving Information:

- This story is about ____.
- The story's characters are ____.
- This story takes place in ____.
- This story makes me feel ____.

Asking for Information:

- Can you explain ____?
- What do you think about ____?
- Why do you think ____?

---

7   Ibrahim opened the door to Joshua's room and **froze**. Clothes, food wrappers, and comic books were on the floor. A blue light glowed on Joshua's computer. He wasn't there.

8   "Start looking," Victoria said.

9   "For what?" Ibrahim asked.

10   "I don't know," Victoria answered, "but I think we'll find a clue."

11   Mateo stood behind his friends.

12   Ibrahim searched Joshua's backpack. Victoria checked some notebooks. She saw Mateo's eyes before he glanced down.

13   "What's wrong? Aren't you going to help us?"

14   Mateo mumbled something but didn't look up.

15   "What is it?" Ibrahim asked.

16   Mateo answered, "A few days ago Joshua told me he discovered a **virus**. He said it was different. It could take over any computer."

17   "But there was more," Mateo continued. "Joshua said the virus could take over *anyone*. He was going to find out who created it. He asked me not to tell."

18   Victoria and Ibrahim were shocked. Mateo stepped forward.

19   "What about his computer?" he asked. "Maybe he left something there."

20   "Yes!" said Victoria.

21   The three friends gathered around the computer. Ibrahim took the mouse and clicked.

22   They saw white numbers moving across the screen. Soon, the **digits** moved faster. First, they moved diagonally, like rippling water. Then, they moved in circles like a **whirlpool**. The three friends moved closer to the screen. They couldn't look away. The numbers blurred and four words appeared:

Enter, if you wish

23   Ibrahim pressed [Enter].

Reading & Writing Companion   **135**

24 They saw a bright flash and had to close their eyes. When they opened their eyes, they were in a long hallway.

25 They could see a shape. It was the figure of a man, moving toward them.

26 "That was an interesting choice, wouldn't you say?" the figure said coolly. The words hung in the air like icicles.

27 Victoria spoke first. "Who are you?" she asked, her voice shivering.

28 "We will get to that. And we will get to your friend. But first you must do something for us."

136 Reading & Writing Companion

Think Questions

Circulate as students answer Think Questions independently. Answers will vary.

QUESTION 1: Comprehension

Joshua is late meeting his friends to see a movie.

QUESTION 2: Comprehension

Joshua's friends went to his room to find him. When they arrived, Joshua wasn't there.

QUESTION 3: Comprehension

There was a flash of light. They were in a long hallway.

QUESTION 4: Language

Joshua was late and his friends are not surprised. A definition for *habitually* is "done often."

QUESTION 5: Language

Ibrahim was very still.

CONNECTED   First Read

Read the story. After you read, answer the Think Questions below.

☁ THINK QUESTIONS

1. What is Joshua late for at the beginning of the story?

   Joshua is late for _____.

2. Where did Joshua's friends go to find him? What did they find?

   Joshua's friends went to _____.

   They found _____.

3. What happened when Ibrahim pressed [Enter] on the computer?

   There was _____.

4. Use context to confirm the meaning of the word *habitually* as it is used in "Connected." Write your definition of *habitually* here.

   Habitually means _____.

   A context clue is _____.

5. What is another way to say that Ibrahim *froze*?

   Ibrahim was _____.

Reading & Writing Companion   **137**

Connected

Skill:
Language Structures

★ DEFINE

In every language, there are rules that tell how to **structure** sentences. These rules define the correct order of words. In the English language, for example, a **basic** structure for sentences is subject, verb, and object. Some sentences have more **complicated** structures.

You will encounter both basic and complicated **language structures** in the classroom materials you read. Being familiar with language structures will help you better understand the text.

••• CHECKLIST FOR LANGUAGE STRUCTURES

To improve your comprehension of language structures, do the following:

✓ Monitor your understanding.

 • Ask yourself: Why do I not understand this sentence? Is it because I do not understand some of the words? Or is it because I do not understand the way the words are ordered in the sentence?

✓ Break down the sentence into its parts.

✓ In English, most sentences share the same pattern: subject + verb + object.

 • The **subject** names who or what is doing the action.

 • The **verb** names the action or state of being.

 • The **object** answers questions such as "Who?," "What?," "Where?," and "When?"

✓ Ask yourself: What is the subject and the verb of this sentence? What details do the other words provide?

✓ Confirm your understanding with a peer or teacher.

SKILL VOCABULARY

structure / la estructura *noun* the order of parts COGNATE

basic / básico *adjective* the most important parts without anything extra COGNATE

complicated / complicado *adjective* having many parts COGNATE

language structure / la estructura de lenguaje *noun* the order of words in a sentence

---

 ## Skill: Language Structures

Introduce the Skill

Watch the Concept Definition video and read the definition for Language Structures.

 ## TURN AND TALK

1. Have you ever read a sentence that confused you?

2. Why was it confusing?

> **ELL** **Beginning & Intermediate**
> **SPEAKING FRAMES**
> • A sentence that confused me is ____.
> • It was confusing because ____.

> **ELL** **Advanced & Advanced High**
> **SPEAKING FRAMES**
> • Once I was confused by ____.
> • It was confusing because ____ so I ____.

⚙ Discuss the Skill Model

1. Why does the reader highlight the sentence in yellow?

   He highlights it in yellow because he does not understand it.

2. Why does the reader highlight the sentence in different colors?

   He uses different colors to identify the parts of the sentence.

3. How does this help the reader?

   He gets an idea of the meaning of the sentence, and he identifies the part of the sentence that is confusing.

4. What does the reader do to confirm his understanding?

   He asks his teacher if his understanding is right.

ELL   **Beginning & Intermediate**

Have students use the <u>speaking frames</u> and <u>helpful terms</u> to participate in the group discussion. If beginning students are hesitant to participate in a discussion, encourage them by prompting with *yes* or *no* questions.

Advanced & Advanced High

Have students use the <u>speaking frames</u> to participate in the group discussion.

SPEAKING FRAMES

- The reader highlights in yellow to show that he does not ___.
- The reader highlights in different colors to identify ___.
- This helps the reader to get an idea of ___. He is able to identify ___.
- Finally the reader asks his teacher to ___.

HELPFUL TERMS FOR DISCUSSION

- determine
- identify
- understanding
- analyze
- teacher
- confusing
- discover
- confirm
- highlight

Connected

↻ YOUR TURN

Read the following excerpt from "Connected." Then, complete the chart by writing the words and phrases into the "Subject," "Verb," and "Object" columns. The first row has been done as an example.

from **"Connected"**

Mateo stood behind his friends.

Ibrahim searched Joshua's backpack. Victoria checked some notebooks. She saw Mateo's eyes before he glanced down.

Sentence	Subject	Verb	Object
Mateo stood behind his friends.	Mateo	stood	behind his friends
Ibrahim searched Joshua's backpack.			
Victoria checked some notebooks.			
She saw Mateo's eyes before he glanced down.			

Reading & Writing Companion   139

⚙ Your Turn   Ask students to complete the Your Turn activity.

Subject	Verb	Object
Ibrahim	searched	Joshua's backpack
Victoria	checked	some notebooks
She	saw	Mateo's eyes

Connected

Skill: Retelling and Summarizing

★ DEFINE

You can retell and summarize a text after reading to show your understanding. **Retelling** is telling a story again in your own words. **Summarizing** is giving a short explanation of the most important ideas in a text.

Keep your retelling or summary **concise**. Only include important information and keywords from the text. By summarizing and retelling a text, you can improve your comprehension of the text's ideas.

••• CHECKLIST FOR RETELLING AND SUMMARIZING

In order to retell or summarize text, note the following:

✓ Identify the main events of the text.
  • Ask yourself: What happens in this text? What are the main events that happen at the beginning, the middle, and the end of the text?

✓ Identify the main ideas in a text.
  • Ask yourself: What are the most important ideas in the text?

✓ Determine the answers to the 6 WH questions.
  • Ask yourself: After reading this text, can I answer Who? What? Where? When? Why? and How? questions.

140 Reading & Writing Companion

Please note that excerpts and passages in the StudySync® library and this workbook are intended as touchstones to generate interest in an author's work. The excerpts and passages do not substitute for the reading of entire texts, and StudySync® strongly recommends that students seek out and purchase the whole literary or informational work in order to experience it as the author intended. Links to online resellers are available in our digital library. In addition, complete works may be ordered through an authorized reseller by filling out and returning to StudySync® the order form enclosed in this workbook.

v SKILL VOCABULARY

retell / volver a contar *verb* to tell a story again in your own words

summarize / resumir *verb* to give a short explanation of the most important ideas in a text

concise / conciso/a *adjective* short COGNATE

Skill: Retelling and Summarizing

Introduce the Skill

Watch the Concept Definition video and read the definition for Retelling and Summarizing.

TURN AND TALK

1. Have you ever told a friend about a movie you watched or a news article you read?

2. Why have you told a friend about the movie or news article?

3. What are some of the things that you have told your friend about the movie or news article?

 Beginning & Intermediate
SPEAKING FRAMES
• I have told my friend about ____. I wanted my friend to ____.
• I told my friend about the main ____.

Advanced & Advanced High
SPEAKING FRAMES
• I told my friend about a movie or news article because ____.
• I told my friend about ____. For example, ____.

⚙ Discuss the Skill Model

1. Why does the reader want to retell the paragraph?

   To show her understanding of it.

2. What does the reader highlight in the paragraph?

   Answers will vary.

3. Why does she highlight these details?

   These details show the beginning, the middle, and the end events of the paragraph.

4. Why does the reader answer the 6 WH questions?

   The answers help the reader retell the details of the paragraph.

ELL   **Beginning & Intermediate**

Have students use the speaking frames and helpful terms to participate in the group discussion. If beginning students are hesitant to participate in a discussion, encourage them by prompting with *yes* or *no* questions.

Advanced & Advanced High

Have students use the speaking frames to participate in the group discussion.

SPEAKING FRAMES

- The reader wants to retell the paragraph to show her ____.
- The reader highlights the ____ in the paragraph.
- These details show the ____, the ____, and the ____.
- The reader answers the 6 WH questions because ____.

HELPFUL TERMS FOR DISCUSSION

- details
- middle
- highlight
- main event
- end
- retell
- beginning
- understanding
- explain

⟳ YOUR TURN

Read the following excerpt from "Connected." Then, write the events in the beginning, middle, and end of the excerpt to retell what happened.

> **from "Connected"**
>
> They saw white numbers moving across the screen. Soon, the digits moved faster. First, they moved diagonally, like rippling water. Then, they moved in circles like a whirlpool. The three friends moved closer to the screen. They couldn't look away. The numbers blurred and four words appeared: *Enter, if you wish.*

Event Options		
The friends moved closer to the screen.	The words "Enter, if you wish" appeared on the screen.	They saw numbers moving across the screen.

Beginning	
Middle	
End	

⚙ Your Turn   Ask students to complete the Your Turn activity.

Beginning	They saw numbers moving across the screen.
Middle	The friends moved closer to the screen.
End	The words "Enter, if you wish" appeared on the screen.

Connected

Close Read

✏ WRITE

PERSONAL RESPONSE: Would you have pressed [Enter] like Joshua's friends did? Write a short paragraph that explains your reasoning. Support your explanation with details and evidence from the text. Pay attention to subject-verb agreement as you write.

Use the checklist below to guide you as you write.

☐ What happened at the beginning and middle of the story?

☐ Why did Joshua's friends press [Enter] at the end of the story?

☐ What would you have done that is the same?

☐ What would you have done that is different?

Use the sentence frames to organize and write your personal response.

In the beginning, Joshua's friends realized that Joshua was _____.

They went to his room to look for _____.

Matteo remembered Joshua talking about a _____.

The friends decided to look at Joshua's _____.

Like Joshua's friends, I would have _____

because _____.

However, I would not have _____

because _____.

142 Reading & Writing Companion

Close Read

Model Skills Focus

Remind students of the Reading Skill Retelling and Summarizing. Tell students that one way to improve your understanding of a story or text is to retell the main events of a story or the main ideas of a text. Direct students to the Skills Focus and remind them to track as you read aloud.

Identify the decisions that Joshua's friends made in the beginning, middle, and end of the story. Then, explain what you would have done if you were with the group.

Model this activity for students:

- I am going to focus on the beginning of the story.

- In the beginning, Joshua's friends are waiting for him to see a movie.

- When he doesn't arrive, they decide to look for him. They remember that Joshua is always on his computer.

- If I were in the group, I would also decide to look for Joshua. They are friends, and I would worry if I had a friend that was missing.

Complete Skills Focus

Divide students into three even groups. Assign each group one of the following excerpts:

- Group 1: Beginning (through break)

- Group 2: Middle (students search Joshua's room)

- Group 3: End (group gathers around the computer)

Circulate and monitor groups as they work.

Collaborative Conversation

Group students so they have a representative from each of the original three groups. Ask the groups to share the decision(s) made in their excerpt of the story, along with their reactions to the characters.

- What decision did the characters make?
- How do I know?
- Do I agree with their decision?

- What would I have done?
- How did thinking about these decisions help my understanding of the story?

Collaborative Conversation

SCAFFOLDS

ELL **BEGINNING, INTERMEDIATE** Use the <u>word bank</u> to participate in the group discussion.

ADVANCED Use the <u>speaking frames</u> to participate in the group discussion.

BEGINNING, INTERMEDIATE	ADVANCED
Word Bank	**Speaking Frames**
<ul><li>helped me understand</li><li>now I understand</li><li>character</li></ul> <ul><li>decision</li><li>action</li><li>text</li></ul>	<ul><li>The decision the characters made is ___.</li><li>I know this because ___.</li><li>I (agree / do not agree) ___ with their decision.</li><li>I would have ___.</li><li>Thinking about these decisions helped my understanding of the story because ___.</li></ul>

Write

Ask students to complete the writing assignment. Remind students to pay attention to use the correct verbs for every sentence they write.

ELL **BEGINNING** Write a response using the <u>paragraph frames</u> and <u>word banks</u>.

INTERMEDIATE Write a response using the <u>paragraph frames</u>.

INTERMEDIATE

BEGINNING

Paragraph Frames

- In the beginning, Joshua's friends realized that Joshua was ____. They went to his room to look for ____. Matteo remembered Joshua talking about a ____. The friends decided to look at Joshua's ____.

- Like Joshua's friends, I would have ____ because ____. However, I would not have ____ because ____.

Word Bank

- missing
- scared
- clues
- computer
- worry
- virus

In the Extended Oral Project, students plan, draft, practice, and deliver an oral presentation that ties into the theme of the unit and spans informative, argumentative, and narrative genres. Lessons provide explicit instruction to prepare students for the unique challenges of an oral presentation, and to help break down the genre characteristics of each prompt. At each step in the process, students focus in-depth on specific writing and speaking skills as they brainstorm, organize, and refine their presentation. Students also receive discussion prompts and frames to guide them in providing effective peer feedback as they practice and discuss in small group before presenting to the class on the final day.

CONNECT TO ESSENTIAL QUESTION

What do we do when life gets hard?

In this unit, students practiced effective collaborative communication skills such as effectively conveying ideas and seeking clarification while reading and analyzing two texts about challenges. Now students will apply those skills to work together in writing and performing a dramatic scene.

Developing Effective Presentations

Form	Language and Conventions	Oral Language Production
Students may struggle with the creative demands of developing the dramatic scene, such as characters and plot.	Students should be encouraged to experiment with new sentence patterns and lengths to make their dialogue sound natural and realistic.	Students may make mistakes when they transfer grammatical forms from their native languages into English. Remind students to monitor their use of the letter s when indicating countable plural nouns and possessive nouns.

SCAFFOLDS   ELL ENGLISH LANGUAGE LEARNERS

Vocabulary, discussion, and peer and teacher support in the Extended Oral Project is differentiated for Beginning, Intermediate, Advanced, and Advanced High English Language Learners. See individual lesson plans for additional scaffolding and support.

Instructional Path

 All Extended Oral Project lessons lesson plans appear in your digital teacher account.

Introduction

Objectives: Identify the components of a realistic scene in order to write and perform in response to a prompt.

Objectives: Students will be able to record ideas for a realistic scene in writing.

DIGITAL ONLY

Skill: Acquiring Vocabulary

Objectives: Use concept maps to make connections between words and acquire new vocabulary in order to write a realistic scene.

Objectives: Students will be able to brainstorm new words to use in writing their scene.

DIGITAL ONLY

Plan

Objectives: Students will be able to plan and write a first draft of their scene.

Objectives: Students will be able to organize their first draft using an outline.

DIGITAL ONLY

Skill: Sentence Lengths

Objectives: Students will be able to apply knowledge of sentence lengths to revise the dialogue in their realistic scene.

Objectives: Students will be able to vary sentence lengths orally and in writing.

DIGITAL ONLY

Practice

Objectives: Students will be able to practice and revise their realistic scene based on peer feedback.

Objectives: Students will be able to practice a realistic scene orally and make revisions in writing.

DIGITAL ONLY

Present

Objectives: Students will be able to observe and perform a realistic scene in order to give and receive peer feedback.

Objectives: Students will be able to use varied sentence lengths in an oral presentation and give peer feedback orally and in writing.

DIGITAL ONLY

Novel Study

Each Core ELAR Unit contains two texts designated for Novel Study. The Novel Study supports the close reading of the complete text through its associated Reading Guide and a series of comparative reading and writing lessons. Novel Studies are not a part of each grade-level's 180 days of instruction; however, teachers may choose to draw from them if they wish to incorporate materials from other disciplines or develop an alternative, novel-based approach to instruction.

Each novel comes with a **Reading Guide** that provides both teacher and student support. Each lesson provides key vocabulary words and close reading questions, as well as a key passage that will help teachers guide students through an exploration of the essential ideas, events, and character development in the novel. This passage will also serve as the point from which students will engage in their own StudySyncTV-style group discussion. Each novel study's **Comparative Reading and Writing** lessons contain resources to support comparative analyses. Students read passages of other texts drawn from across the disciplines and compare those passages to specific sections of the novel in written responses.

Suggested Novel Studies

Title	Genre	Summary	Themes and Topics
Hatchet (1987)	Fiction	As students read *Hatchet*, ask them to pay attention to how Brian changes over the course of the novel. How does he overcome his fears and learn from his mistakes? What does it take to survive in the wild?	• Coming of Age • Survival • Fear
A Wrinkle in Time (1962)	Fiction	As students read *A Wrinkle in Time*, ask them to consider the significance of key issues such as free will versus fate, conformity versus individuality, and the complex relationship between good and evil. How does protagonist Meg Murry rise from zero to hero?	• Good and Evil • Individuality • Science Fiction

Hatchet

Hatchet is the story of Brian Robeson, a thirteen-year-old boy from suburban New York City. His parents have recently split, and Brian is spending the summer with his father in northern Canada. When the pilot of the single-engine plane that flies Brian over the Canadian wilderness has a fatal heart attack, Brian manages to crash-land the plane in a small lake. Thrown into a wild and harsh environment, he must learn to survive by trial and error as he constructs a shelter, finds food, creates fire, skirmishes with wildlife and weather, and steadily develops confidence and resilience. Throughout his ordeal, Brian's only tool is the hatchet his mother gave him just before his ill-fated flight. It proves invaluable as Brian learns how best to use it.

Author Gary Paulsen (b. 1939) wrote three sequels to *Hatchet: The River, Brian's Winter*, and *Brian's Return*. Readers can learn more about the real-life events that influenced *Hatchet* and its sequels in *Guts: The True Stories Behind Hatchet and the Brian Books*.

A Wrinkle in Time

First published in 1962, Madeleine L'Engle's *A Wrinkle in Time* is one of the forerunners of the contemporary young adult science fantasy novel, paving the way for the Harry Potters and Katniss Everdeens of the literary world. It received numerous accolades, including a Newbery Medal and the Lewis Carroll Shelf Award, and was also a runner-up for the prestigious Hans Christian Andersen Award. In spite of the novel's eventual impact, L'Engle's *A Wrinkle in Time* was rejected by dozens of publishing houses at first. One theory is that publishers at the time were reluctant to put out a science fantasy novel featuring a young girl as its heroine.

Author Madeleine L'Engle (1918–2007) is hailed as a pioneer of the young adult literature genre. Her first novel, *A Wrinkle in Time*, remains her most enduring, influential and beloved. *A Wrinkle in Time* is the first in the series of five titles known as the *Time Quintet*, featuring the ongoing adventures and misadventures of Meg Murry, her friends and family.

Spotlight Skills Review

A review day before the end-of-unit assessment gives you an opportunity to review difficult concepts with students using Spotlight Skills lessons. Spotlight Skills are targeted lessons that provide you resources to reteach or remediate without assigning additional readings. Every Core ELA Skill lesson has a corresponding Spotlight Skill lesson. Spotlight Skills can be assigned at any point in the year, but the end of each unit provides a natural moment to pause, review data collected throughout the unit, and reteach skills students have not yet mastered.

Progress Monitoring

The Progress Monitoring charts that appear before every text in this unit identify standards and associated Spotlight Skills. On review day, you may want to give preference to reteaching skills that are not revisited in later units. You can see where Skills are covered again in the Opportunities to Reteach column.

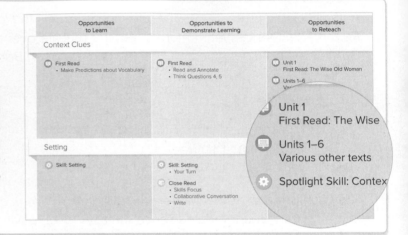

StudySync Gradebook

As students submit assignments on StudySync, their mastery of skills and standards is tracked via the gradebook. The gradebook can be sorted and viewed in a variety of ways. Sorting by assignment shows overall student performance, while sorting by standards or by Skill lessons displays student progress toward mastery goals.

Skills Library

Spotlight Skills are located in the Skills section of the StudySync Library. You can assign Spotlight Skills to individual students or groups of students. Search tools allow you to search by Skill type or name.

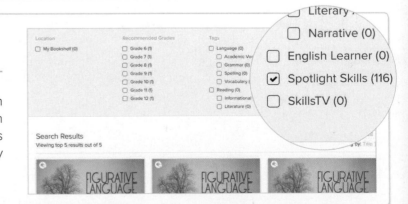

End-of-Unit Assessment

The end-of-unit assessment can be found in two places. The digital version of the assessment can be assigned from the Online Assessment tab inside your ConnectED account. The paper-based version of the assessment can be printed from the End-of-Unit Assessment tab inside this unit in your StudySync account.

Assessment Section	Content	Assessed Skills	
READING	Another Day in Paradise Genre: Fiction Word Count: 869 Lexile: 930	• Setting • Context Clues • Character	• Textual Evidence • Summarizing
	Stuck Genre: Drama Word Count: 686 Lexile: N/A	• Summarizing • Figurative Language • Character • Textual Evidence	• Dramatic Elements and Structure • Setting
	Powered Down Genre: Fiction Word Count: 669 Lexile: 940	• Setting • Dramatic Elements and Structure • Textual Evidence • Theme	• Plot • Context Clues • Compare and Contrast
	Business as Usual Genre: Drama Word Count: 935 Lexile: N/A	• Figurative Language • Setting • Plot • Character	• Textual Evidence • Dramatic Elements and Structure
REVISING and EDITING	Student Passage #1	• Personal Pronouns • Consistent Pronoun Use	• Pronouns and Antecedents
	Student Passage #2	• Organizing Narrative Writing • Beginnings • Narrative Techniques	• Transition Words • Descriptive Details • Conclusions
WRITING	Prompt: Narrative Writing	• Narrative Writing	

What's Next?

Assessment results can be viewed by item, standard, and skill to monitor mastery and make decisions for upcoming instruction.

RETEACH skills that students have not yet mastered, using Spotlight Skills or the Test Preparation and Practice book.

REVISE your teaching plan to provide more or less explicit instruction into a skill or text, using Beyond the Book activities for enrichment.

REGROUP students and levels of scaffolding based on standards progress.

You and Me

How do relationships shape us?

UNIT 2

You and Me

How do relationships shape us?

Can you even count the number of relationships you have had in your life? Some relationships are close and others more distant, but the relationships in our lives teach us about the people and even the animals around us. Even more important, our relationships can teach us a lot about ourselves.

What kinds of relationships do people have? Why are they important? Relationships with family, friends, and those around us can bring much joy, but they can also cause pain and frustration. What do readers learn when they study and analyze the relationships depicted in literary works? How can this help us with some of our own relationships?

Human bonds have been the subject of both fiction and informational texts. They are often the subject of poetry. This unit offers a wide variety of literature about relationships for your students to explore, including a selection from the classic novel *Roll of Thunder, Hear My Cry* by Mildred D. Taylor, a nonfiction letter to the editor, "We're On the Same Team," and poems such as "Teenagers" by Pat Mora and "A Poem for My Librarian, Mrs. Long" by Nikki Giovanni.

After reading stories, poems, and nonfiction selections about important relationships that had such a powerful impact they may have changed people's lives, students will then describe a person who has influenced them and use their personal experience to argue whether or not relationships can truly shape one's future.

Thematic Selections

Extended Writing Project and Grammar

English Language Learner Resources

Walk Two Moons
FICTION
Sharon Creech

Roll of Thunder, Hear My Cry
FICTION
Mildred D. Taylor

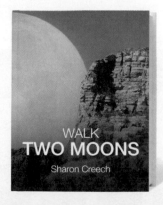

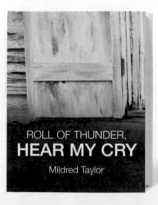

You and Me

StudySyncTV or SkillsTV Episode

Pacing Guide

Days	Readings	Skill and Standard Instruction	Skill Practice and Spiraling
1-2	**Essential Question** **The Big Idea: How do relationships shape us?** p. 306	• Recognizing Genre: Poetry • Academic Vocabulary	• Write: Analyzing Genre
3-6	**Walk Two Moons** (tv) p. 310	• Generating Questions • Language, Style, and Audience • Textual Evidence	• Character • Compare and Contrast • Narrative Writing • Collaborative Conversations
7-11	**Roll of Thunder, Hear My Cry** (tv) p. 330	• Connotation and Denotation • Theme (tv) • Story Structure (tv)	• Language, Style, and Audience • Collaborative Conversations
12-14	**Teenagers** p. 352	• Making Inferences • Figurative Language	• Textual Evidence • Literary Analysis Writing
15-17	**Tableau** p. 368	• Adjusting Fluency • Poetic Elements and Structure	• Textual Evidence • Figurative Language • Literary Analysis Writing
18-21	**PAIRED READINGS** **The Voice in My Head** p. 384 **We're On the Same Team** p. 398	• Summarizing	• Textual Evidence • Compare and Contrast • Informative Writing

THEMATIC PACING AT A GLANCE – 30 DAYS

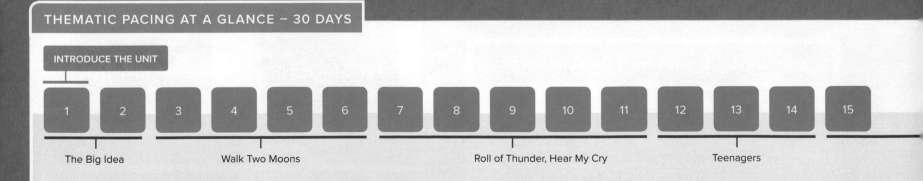

INTRODUCE THE UNIT

| 1 | 2 | 3 | 4 | 5 | 6 | 7 | 8 | 9 | 10 | 11 | 12 | 13 | 14 | 15 |

The Big Idea   Walk Two Moons   Roll of Thunder, Hear My Cry   Teenagers

Days	Readings	Skill and Standard Instruction	Skill Practice and Spiraling
22-23	**The Treasure of Lemon Brown** p. 414	• Point of View	• Character • Plot • Setting • Argumentative Writing
24-27	**PAIRED READINGS** **The Circuit: Stories from the Life of a Migrant Child** tv p. 438 **That Day** p. 452 **A Poem for My Librarian, Mrs. Long** p. 460	• Compare and Contrast • Analyzing Genre	• Theme • Point of View • Comparative Writing • Collaborative Conversations
28	**Self-Selected Reading and Response** p. 476	• Independent Reading	• Personal Response Writing

Review and Assessment   See page 560.

Days	Review and Assessment	Skill Practice and Assessment
29	**Skills Review** p. 560	Students will have the opportunity to complete one or more Spotlight Skill lessons in order to improve understanding and further practice skills from the unit that they found most challenging.
30	**End-of-Unit Assessment** p. 561	For more details, please see the End-of-Unit Assessment information for Grade 6 Unit 2 on page 560.

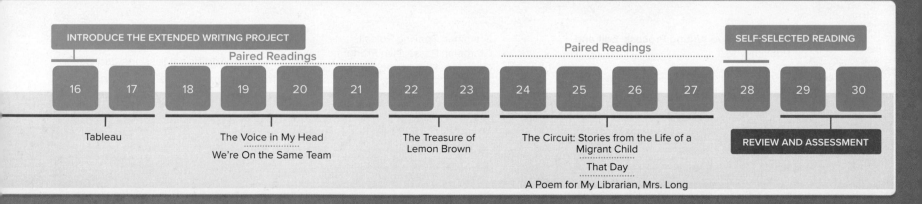

INTRODUCE THE EXTENDED WRITING PROJECT

Paired Readings

Paired Readings

SELF-SELECTED READING

16 17 18 19 20 21 22 23 24 25 26 27 28 29 30

Tableau

The Voice in My Head
We're On the Same Team

The Treasure of Lemon Brown

The Circuit: Stories from the Life of a Migrant Child

That Day

A Poem for My Librarian, Mrs. Long

REVIEW AND ASSESSMENT

Extended Writing Project and Grammar

Pacing Guide

In the second half of the unit, students continue exploring texts that address the unit's Essential Question and begin crafting a longer composition to share their own ideas about the Essential Question in the Extended Writing Project. The writing project will take your students through the writing process to produce an argumentative essay.

Extended Writing Project Prompt

Can relationships shape your future?

Think about the ways in which relationships have shaped the lives of the characters, speakers, or authors. Then reflect on your own life. Think of a person who has influenced you in some way. Would your life be different if this person were not in your life? Do you think relationships can truly shape people's futures? Why or why not?

Days	Extended Writing Project and Grammar	Skill and Standard Instruction	Connect to Mentor Texts
16	**Argumentative Writing Process: Plan** p. 486		
17-20	**Argumentative Writing Process: Draft** p. 500	• Organizing Argumentative Writing • Thesis Statement • Reasons and Relevant Evidence	• The Voice in My Head • We're On the Same Team
21-24	**Argumentative Writing Process: Revise** p. 515	• Introductions • Transitions • Style • Conclusions	• Walk Two Moons • We're On the Same Team • The Treasure of Lemon Brown
25-28	**Argumentative Writing Process: Edit and Publish** p. 523	• Grammar: Spelling Rules I • Grammar: Possessive Pronouns • Grammar: Formal and Informal Language	Additional lessons can be found in the StudySync Skills Library.

Research

The following lessons include opportunities for research:

Blast **The Power of Relationships** Research Links*

First Read **Role of Thunder, Hear My Cry** Independent Research (Beyond)

Blast **Sonnets to Social Media** Research Links*

First Read **Tableau** Independent Research (Beyond)

Close Read **Tableau** Beyond the Book

Blast **A Level Playing Field** Research Links*

Close Read **The Treasure of Lemon Brown** Text to World (Beyond)

*See the teacher lesson plan online

Self-Selected Reading Prompt

After reading a self-selected text, students will respond to the following personal response prompt:

A great text can make us laugh, cry, or hide underneath our beds. Sometimes what makes a text memorable is the impact it has on our thoughts and perspectives.

How can a text change the way you think?

Using your self-selected text, write a journal entry in response to this question. In your entry, be sure to explain how a word, phrase, line, or passage changed the way you think about an idea, individual, or event.

Integrated Scaffolding

ELL and Approaching grade-level students receive scaffolds for every lesson, whether in the Thematic, Novel Study or ELL Resources sections of the unit. Specific scaffolds are intentionally designed to support the needs of English Language Learners and Approaching grade-level students in the ELA classroom. Other scaffolds exist as part of the many standard features in the StudySync digital platform and can be strategically utilized to support students' comprehension and engagement.

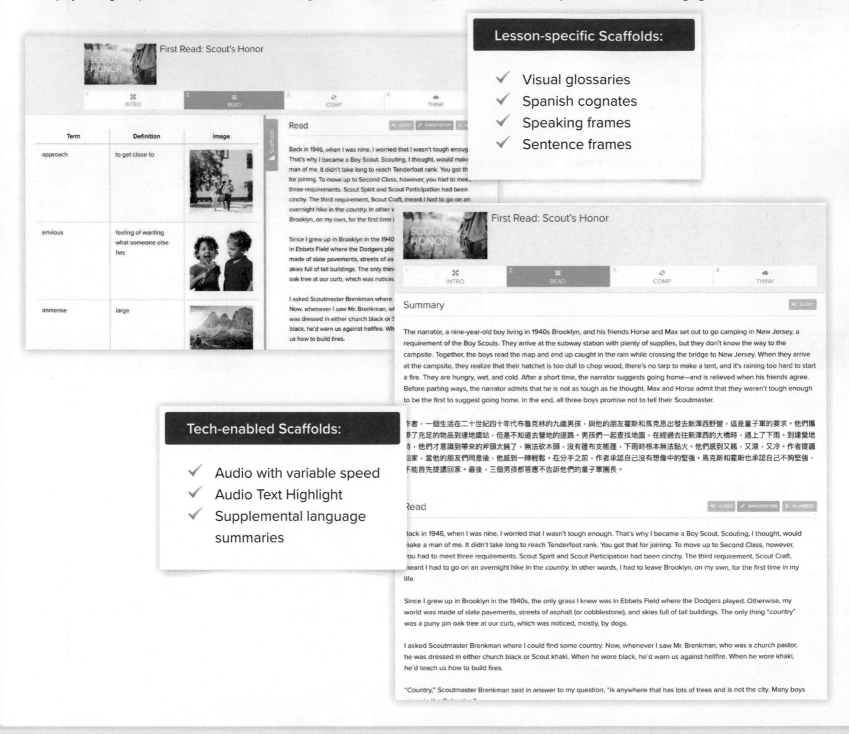

Lesson-specific Scaffolds:

- ✓ Visual glossaries
- ✓ Spanish cognates
- ✓ Speaking frames
- ✓ Sentence frames

Tech-enabled Scaffolds:

- ✓ Audio with variable speed
- ✓ Audio Text Highlight
- ✓ Supplemental language summaries

English Language Learner Resources

Both Thematic and Novel Study units include English Language Learner resources designed to match the thematic focus, text structures, and writing form of the unit. ELL resources include two leveled texts and an extended oral project.

ELL Texts	Differentiated Text Levels	Skill and Standard Instruction
 **THE OTHER SIDE**	**BEGINNING** 170L | 269 words **INTERMEDIATE** 430L | 405 words **ADVANCED** 530L | 459 words **ADVANCED HIGH** 640L | 547 words Use this text in place of, or as an extension to *Walk Two Moons*.	• Sight Vocabulary and High-Frequency Words • Demonstrating Listening Comprehension • Analyzing Expressions • Sharing Information • Spelling Patterns and Rules
 **A ROLE TO PLAY**	**BEGINNING** 320L | 255 words **INTERMEDIATE** 450L | 396 words **ADVANCED** 520L | 445 words **ADVANCED HIGH** 570L | 531 words Use this text in place of, or as an extension to *The Circuit*.	• Classroom Vocabulary • Making Connections • Language Structures • Drawing Inferences and Conclusions • Pronouns and Antecedents
EXTENDED ORAL PROJECT INTRODUCTION	In this Extended Oral Project, students will write and present a personal address. This may be assigned in place of this unit's EWP.	• Acquiring Vocabulary • Sentence Lengths

Focus on English Language Proficiency Levels

ADVANCED HIGH
ADVANCED
INTERMEDIATE
BEGINNING

ELL Resources provide targeted support for four levels of proficiency: Beginning, Intermediate, Advanced, and Advanced High. Instruction and scaffolds, as well as the texts themselves, are differentiated based on these levels.

Additional differentiated scaffolds include visual glossaries, speaking and writing frames, and suggested grouping for peer and teacher support. Lessons also include suggested extension activities to challenge Advanced and Advanced High students as they progress through the year.

Assessment

Assessment in StudySync is built upon a recursive cycle that includes assessment, instruction, and review. Screening, placement, and benchmark assessments help teachers establish baselines and determine scaffold needs. Throughout the course of instruction, teachers regularly assess student progress using formative and summative measures, and use the individualized data from those assessments to guide choices about instruction, review, remediation, and enrichment to bring all students to standards mastery and College and Career Readiness.

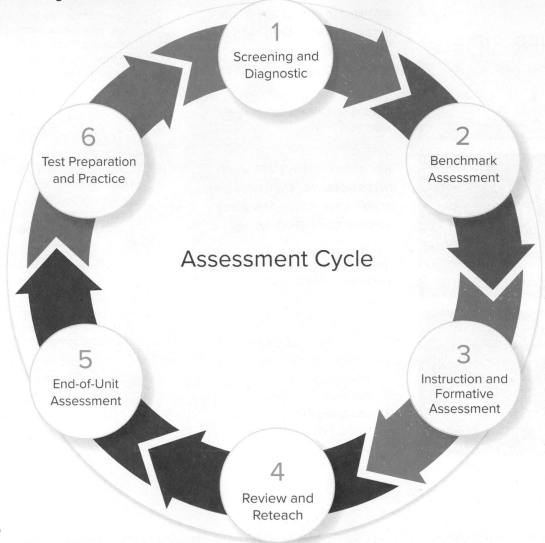

Assessment Cycle

1 Screening and Diagnostic

2 Benchmark Assessment

3 Instruction and Formative Assessment

4 Review and Reteach

5 End-of-Unit Assessment

6 Test Preparation and Practice

What's Next?

Assessment results can be viewed by item, standard, and skill to monitor mastery and make decisions for upcoming instruction.

✓ Reteach skills that students have not yet mastered, using Spotlight Skills or the Test Preparation and Practice book.

✓ Revise your teaching plan to provide more or less explicit instruction into a skill or text, using Beyond the Book activities for enrichment.

✓ Regroup students and levels of scaffolding based on standards progress.

Review

Spotlight Skills Review

A review day before the end-of-unit assessment gives you an opportunity to review difficult concepts with students using Spotlight Skills lessons. Spotlight Skills are targeted lessons that provide you resources to reteach or remediate without assigning additional readings. Every Core ELA Skill lesson has a corresponding Spotlight Skill lesson. Spotlight Skills can be assigned at any point in the year, but the end of each unit provides a natural moment to pause, review data collected throughout the unit, and reteach skills students have not yet mastered.

Progress Monitoring

The Progress Monitoring charts that appear before every text in this unit identify standards and associated Spotlight Skills. On review day, you may want to give preference to reteaching skills that are not revisited in later units. You can see where skills are covered again in the Opportunities to Reteach column.

StudySync Gradebook

As students submit assignments on StudySync, their mastery of skills and standards is tracked via the gradebook. The gradebook can be sorted and viewed in a variety of ways. Sorting by assignment shows overall student performance, while sorting by standards or by skill lessons displays student progress toward mastery goals.

	First Read	Skill: Text	Close Re...	
MAX SCORE	10	2	12	
STUDENT				
Tate O'Brien	10	2	9	
Olivia Adams	8	1	11	

Skills Library

Spotlight Skills are located in the Skills section of the StudySync Library. You can assign Spotlight Skills to individual students or groups of students. Search tools allow you to search by skill type or name.

End-of-Unit Assessment

Assessed Reading Skills

- ✓ Compare and Contrast
- ✓ Connotation and Denotation
- ✓ Figurative Language
- ✓ Language, Style, and Audience
- ✓ Poetic Elements and Structure
- ✓ Point of View
- ✓ Story Structure
- ✓ Textual Evidence
- ✓ Theme

Assessed Revising and Editing Skills

- ✓ Basic Spelling Rules
- ✓ Formal and Informal Language
- ✓ Introductions and Conclusions
- ✓ Possessive Pronouns
- ✓ Reasons and Relevant Evidence
- ✓ Style
- ✓ Thesis Statement
- ✓ Transitions

Unit Preview

Introduce the Unit

As a class, watch the unit preview ▶ and discuss the questions below.

- What two words would you use to describe this video?
- What key words or images from the video do you think will be most important to this unit?

Instructional Path

Big Idea Blast

Objectives: After exploring background information and research links about a topic, students will respond to a question with a 140-character response.

Skill: Recognize Genre

Objectives: After learning about the genre of poetry, students will be able to identify and describe poetic devices.

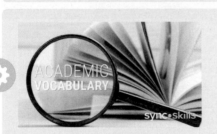

Skill: Academic Vocabulary

Objectives: After learning the meanings of ten academic vocabulary words, students will be able to recognize and use them in a variety of contexts.

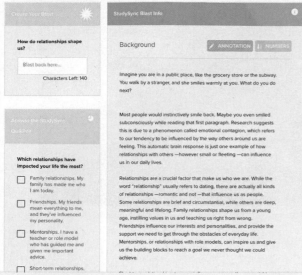

 ## Blast: The Power of Relationships

How do relationships shape us?

 ### TEXT TALK

What are some different types of relationships?

Some different types include family relationships, friendships, and romantic relationships.

How can short-term relationships influence our lives?

A one-time conversation with someone can change our perspective toward a topic or subject.

What does the author Mitch Albom say about relationships?

Albom says that we're all connected—"you can no more separate one life from another than you can separate a breeze from the wind."

 ## Create Your Own Blast

SCAFFOLDS

Ask students to write a 140-character Blast after they complete the QuikPoll.

Use the scaffolds below to differentiate instruction for your **ELL** English Language Learners.

ELL **BEGINNING** Write a response using the <u>word bank</u> to complete the <u>sentence frame</u>.

INTERMEDIATE Write a response using the <u>sentence frame</u>.

ADVANCED, ADVANCED HIGH Write a response using the <u>sentence starter</u>.

BEGINNING	INTERMEDIATE	ADVANCED, ADVANCED HIGH
Word Bank	Sentence Frame	Sentence Starter
affecting perspective changing view influencing attitude	Relationships shape us by ___ our ___.	• Relationships shape us by . . .

Skill: Recognize Genre

Introduce the Genre: Poetry

Watch the Concept Definitions video  and read the following definition with your students.

Poetry is writing that uses qualities of language to evoke feelings in addition to simply conveying meaning. These qualities of language include sound, symbolism, imagery, and rhythm. **Symbolism** is the use of concrete objects to represent abstract ideas or qualities. **Imagery** is descriptive language used to appeal to the reader's senses. **Rhythm** is the pattern of unstressed and stressed syllables in a line of poetry.

Poetry can appear in a variety of different forms. Some poems are **closed form** and have regular rhyme and rhythm. Other poems are **free verse** and have no regular rhyme or rhythm.

All types of poetry share certain characteristics. Poems are meant to be read aloud so the reader can hear aspects of sound, rhythm, meter, and voice. Poems often have multiple meanings. To interpret multiple meanings of a poem, a reader must examine the literal meaning of the poem in conjunction with the figurative meanings that arise from analyzing the rhythm, sound, images, and symbols.

 TURN AND TALK

1. What about poetry do you find most interesting? Why?

2. What are the different poetic devices a poet can use to send a message?

 SPEAKING FRAMES

- I think ____ is interesting in poems. I think it is interesting because ____.
- One poetic device a poet can use to convey meaning is ____. This poetic device can send a message by ____.

Your Turn

Ask students to complete the Your Turn activity.

Description	Poetic Device
She sells sea shells by the sea shore.	sound device
The fall leaves were like broken glass beneath his feet	imagery
What if you had to go to the school dance alone?	line break
Once upon a dreary day a boat left port to sail the bay	rhyme scheme

Skill: Academic Vocabulary

Introduce the Terms

appropriate / apropiado/a *adjective* suitable for a particular person, place, or condition COGNATE

assist / asistir *verb* to give support in an undertaking or effort; to help COGNATE

conduct / conducir *verb* to direct, guide, or lead COGNATE

establish / establecer *verb* to set up or lay the groundwork for COGNATE

focus / el foco *verb* the concentration of attention or energy on something COGNATE

involve / involucrarse *verb* to engage; to include

normal / normal *adjective* according to an established norm or rule; regular; natural COGNATE

participate / participar *verb* to take part in; to play a role COGNATE

positive / positivo/a *adjective* characterized by being affirming, accepting, and optimistic COGNATE

respond / responder *verb* to say something in return; to answer or reply COGNATE

Your Turn

Ask students to complete the Your Turn activities.

Your Turn 1

Word	Example	Non-Example
focus	paying close attention to a movie	thinking about something else while watching a movie
normal	a rainstorm during the summer in Texas	a snowstorm during the summer in Texas
positive	talking about all the reasons you can achieve your dreams	thinking about all the reasons why you may not achieve your dreams
appropriate	clapping loudly after seeing a show you like	booing loudly in the middle of a show you do not like
assist	helping your cat get down from a tree	ignoring your cat's cries when it is caught in a tree

Your Turn 2

QUESTION 1: C   **QUESTION 2:** D   **QUESTION 3:** A   **QUESTION 4:** C   **QUESTION 5:** C

Your Turn 3

See digital teacher's edition for complete sample activity.

Practice Using Vocabulary

Divide the vocabulary words into two lists. Pair students and give each student one half of the list. Challenge students to have a casual conversation with each other that uses every word on their list. Students should aim to insert their vocabulary words in a way that sounds natural. You may wish to turn this activity into a game, allowing partners to award each other points if they effectively use each word on their list.

Walk Two Moons

FICTION
Sharon Creech
1994

Introduction

studysync tv

Sal is on a road trip with her grandparents from Ohio to Idaho, hoping to find her mother and bring her home. To pass the time, Sal entertains her grandparents with stories about her friend Phoebe Winterbottom, whose mother also mysteriously disappeared. A beloved classic, this novel by Sharon Creech (b. 1945) has won numerous awards, including the Newbery Medal. The major themes of grief, family relationships, and and identity have resonated with readers since its publication in 1994. In this excerpt, readers become acquainted with the Winterbottom family.

After school, Sal and her friend Phoebe Winterbottom go to Phoebe's house, where Phoebe's mom has baked brownies. Phoebe gets angry with her mother and goes to her room. Sal remains downstairs, remembering the day before her own mother abandoned her family. She regrets that she refused her mother's invitation to go on a walk and wishes that she could go back and do it over. Phoebe's sister Prudence comes home upset about her cheerleading tryouts. While Prudence complains, Sal notices that Mrs. Winterbottom is hiding her own sad feelings, but Phoebe and Prudence are oblivious to this. Phoebe finds a message on the doorstep that reads, "In the course of a lifetime, what does it matter?" Walking home, Sal ponders the meaning of this message and reflects on the hole left by her mother's absence.

 Proficiency-leveled summaries and summaries in multiple languages are available digitally.

 Audio and audio text highlighting are available with the text.

CONNECT TO ESSENTIAL QUESTION

How do relationships shape us?

In this story, a young girl named Sal is racked with guilt because she thinks she is responsible when her mother leaves the family. Would Sal's relationship with her mother have been different if Sal hadn't yelled at her the last time she saw her?

Access Complex Text

LEXILE: 520L   WORD COUNT: 878

The following areas may be challenging for students, particularly English Language Learners and Approaching grade-level learners.

Organization	Connection of Ideas	Sentence Structure
• The selection contains brief flashbacks. • Some students may have difficulty distinguishing between the main character's recollections of past events and what is taking place in the present.	• The selection is written in first-person limited, so readers only know what the main character thinks, feels, and hears. • Assessing the motivations and actions of other characters in the story may prove difficult.	• The selection features some complex sentence structures. • In some dialogue exchanges, who is speaking may need some clarification.

 SCAFFOLDS   **ELL ENGLISH LANGUAGE LEARNERS**   **A APPROACHING GRADE LEVEL**   **B BEYOND GRADE LEVEL**

These icons identify differentiation strategies and scaffolded support for a variety of students. See the digital lesson plan for additional differentiation strategies and scaffolds.

Instructional Path

The print teacher's edition includes essential point-of-use instruction and planning tools. Complete lesson plans and program documents appear in your digital teacher account.

Skill: Generating Questions

Objectives: After reading and discussing a model, students will be able to generate questions before, during, and after reading to ensure understanding and gain information.

First Read: Walk Two Moons

Objectives: After an initial reading and discussion of the excerpt, students will be able to identify and describe characters and setting details as well as articulate events that are central to the story's plot.

Skill: Language, Style, and Audience

Objectives: After rereading and discussing a model of close reading, students will be able to analyze the impact of a specific word choice on meaning and tone.

Skill: Textual Evidence

Objectives: After rereading and discussing a model of close reading, students will be able to cite textual evidence to support an analysis of what the text says explicitly as well as inferences drawn from the text.

Close Read: Walk Two Moons

Objectives: After engaging in a close reading and discussion of the text, students will be able to analyze language, style, and audience, as well as cite textual evidence in order to write a short narrative.

Progress Monitoring

Opportunities to Learn	Opportunities to Demonstrate Learning	Opportunities to Reteach
Generating Questions		
⚙ Skill: Generating Questions	🖥 First Read • Read and Annotate	🖥 Unit 6 First Read: Bronx Masquerade ⚙ Spotlight Skill: Generating Questions
Language, Style, and Audience		
⚙ Skill: Language, Style, and Audience	⚙ Skill: Language, Style, and Audience • Your Turn 📄 Close Read • Complete Vocabulary Focus • Skills Focus • Write	⚙ Unit 5 Skill: Language, Style, and Audience - Listen, Slowly ⚙ Unit 6 Skill: Language, Style, and Audience - Brave ⚙ Spotlight Skill: Language, Style, and Audience
Textual Evidence		
⚙ Skill: Textual Evidence	⚙ Skill: Textual Evidence • Your Turn 📄 Close Read • Writer's Notebook • Skills Focus • Collaborative Conversation • Write	⚙ Unit 3 Skill: Textual Evidence - Margaret Bourke-White: Fearless Photographer ⚙ Spotlight Skill: Textual Evidence

First Read

Sharon Creech

Walk Two Moons

Introduce the Text

As a class, watch the video preview and have students read the introduction in pairs to make connections to the video preview.

To activate prior knowledge and experiences, ask students:

- What two words would you use to describe this video and why?

- What questions do you have after reading the introduction?

> **ELL SPEAKING FRAMES**
> - The ____ in the video makes me think ____.
> - The video shows ____. This makes me wonder ____.
> - I think the text will ____. I think this because ____.
> - I predict that there will be ____. I believe this because ____.

Entry Point

As students prepare to read *Walk Two Moons,* share the following information with them to provide context.

✓ Sharon Creech was born and raised in Ohio. Before becoming a novelist, Creech taught high school English in England and Switzerland. She has written two novels for adults, and many more for young adults. *Walk Two Moons* won the Newbery Award in 1995.

✓ This novel is part of a trilogy of interconnected stories, all inspired by real events from Creech's childhood. The first in the series is Absolutely Normal Chaos, which centers around the summer journal of a character named Mary Lou Finney. The main character in *Walk Two Moons,* Salamanca, is friends with another character from the first book. Chasing Redbird finishes the series and follows a character from the same town as Salamanca in *Walk Two Moons*. While the plot of each story is unique, many of the themes overlap.

"In the course of a lifetime, what does it matter?"

1 A few days after Phoebe and I had seen Mr. Birkway and Mrs. Cadaver whacking away at the rhododendron, I walked home with Phoebe after school. She was as **crotchety** and **sullen** as a three-legged mule, and I was not quite sure why. She had been asking me why I had not said anything to my father about Mrs. Cadaver and Mr. Birkway, and I told her that I was waiting for the right time.

2 "Your father was over there yesterday," Phoebe said. "I saw him. He'd better watch out. What would you do if Mrs. Cadaver chopped up your father? Would you go live with your mother?"

3 It surprised me when she said that, reminding me that I had told Phoebe nothing about my mother. "Yes, I suppose I would go live with her." That was impossible and I knew it, but for some reason I could not tell Phoebe that, so I lied.

4 Phoebe's mother was sitting at the kitchen table when we walked in. In front of her was a pan of burned brownies. She blew her nose. "Oh sweetie," she said, "you startled me. How was it?"

5 "How was what?" Phoebe asked.

6 "Why, sweetie, school of course. How was it? How were your classes?"

7 "Okay."

8 "Just okay?" Mrs. Winterbottom suddenly leaned over and kissed Phoebe's cheek.

9 "I'm not a baby, you know," Phoebe said, wiping off the kiss.

10 Mrs. Winterbottom stabbed the brownies with a knife. "Want one?" she asked.

11 "They're burned," Phoebe said. "Besides, I'm fat."

NOTES

Skill: Language, Style, and Audience

The author chooses words like sullen *to show the audience that Sal is smart because this is not a word kids often use. After reading this paragraph, I also know that Sal is from the country because she mentions a mule. She's funny, and she's tolerant because she doesn't get mad that Phoebe is grouchy.*

Please note that excerpts and passages in the StudySync® library and this workbook are intended as touchstones to generate interest in an author's work. The excerpts and passages do not substitute for the reading of entire texts, and StudySync® strongly recommends that students seek out and purchase the whole literary or informational work in order to experience it as the author intended. Links to online resellers are available in our digital library. In addition, complete works may be ordered through an authorized reseller by filling out and returning to StudySync® the order form enclosed in this workbook.

Reading & Writing Companion   1

Analyze Vocabulary Using Context Clues

In paragraph 1, focus on the sentence that uses the word *crotchety.* Point out these context clues:

1. First, I notice that the narrator compares her friend Phoebe to a three-legged mule.

2. I know that a mule needs four legs to walk. So, a mule with three legs would have trouble walking.

3. Having to walk on three legs would probably make the mule grouchy or in a bad mood. So *crotchety* must mean "cranky," or "out-of-sorts."

Language, Style, and Audience

How did the reader use the narrator's word choice to draw conclusions about the narrator's personality?

He noted that the use of the word sullen demonstrates Sal's intelligence. He also noted that the three-legged mule comparison reveals a country background and a sense of humor.

TEXT TALK

What is the relationship between Phoebe and the narrator?

See paragraph 1: Phoebe and the narrator are classmates. They walk home from school together.

For what reasons does Phoebe get mad at her mother, Mrs. Winterbottom?

See paragraphs 9–11: Phoebe gets mad when her mother kisses her on the cheek, and says she's not a baby anymore. When her mother offers her a brownie Phoebe says "no" because she thinks she's fat.

 SELECTION VOCABULARY

crotchety / malhumorado/a *adjective* irritable; grouchy

sullen / taciturno/a *adjective* gloomy; grumpy

- What is Phoebe being compared to?
- Would a three-legged mule be gloomy and silent or would it talk a lot?

Textual Evidence

How did the reader use evidence explicitly stated in the text to describe Mrs. Winterbottom and Phoebe's relationship?

She noted that Phoebe's words and actions reveal that she is irritated with Mrs. Winterbottom.

Skills Focus

QUESTION 1: Compare and Contrast

Textual evidence reveals that Sal, Phoebe, and Prudence have very different relationships with their mothers. In this passage, Phoebe's outburst at her mother shows that their relationship is strained.

This causes Sal to realize feelings of guilt over how she treated her mother. Sal regrets ignoring her mother on the last day she saw her.

Skills Focus

QUESTION 2: Character

Phoebe realizes that even though she didn't mean anything by it when she yelled at her mother, the action had consequences.

Skills Focus

QUESTION 4: Language, Style, and Audience

Dialogue reveals character. The author chooses short, blunt phrases for Phoebe to show she's annoyed with her mom. Mrs. Winterbottom, on the other hand, shows her love for Phoebe by baking brownies, reassuring her, calling her "sweetie," and asking about her day.

TEXT TALK

What kind of reaction does Prudence have when her mother suggests she come and watch her cheerleader tryout the next day?

See paragraph 25: She says it would be an awful idea.

Walk Two Moons

 NOTES

12   "Oh sweetie, you're not fat," Mrs. Winterbottom said.

13   "I am."

14   "No, you're not."

15   "I am, I am, I am!" Phoebe shouted at her mother. "You don't have to bake things for me. I'm too fat. And you don't have to wait here for me to come home. I'm thirteen now."

16   Phoebe marched upstairs. Mrs. Winterbottom offered me a brownie, so I sat down at the table. What I started doing was remembering the day before my mother left. I did not know it was to be her last day home. Several times that day, my mother asked me if I wanted to walk up in the fields with her. It was drizzling outside, and I was cleaning out my desk, and I just did not feel like going. "Maybe later," I kept saying. When she asked me for about the tenth time, I said, "No! I don't want to go. Why do you keep asking me?" I don't know why I did that. I didn't mean anything by it, but that was one of the last memories she had of me, and I wished I could take it back.

Skill: Textual Evidence

○ Using textual evidence, I can make inferences about Mrs. Winterbottom's sadness. I think Mrs. Winterbottom and Prudence have a rocky relationship. I can also infer Sal's guilt for how she treated her mother on their last day together.

17   Phoebe's sister, Prudence, stormed into the house, slamming the door behind her. "I blew it. I just know it!" she wailed.

18   "Oh sweetie," her mother said.

19   "I did!" Prudence said. "I did, I did, I did."

20   Mrs. Winterbottom half-heartedly chipped away at the burned brownies and asked Prudence if she would have another chance at cheerleading **tryouts.**

21   "Yes, tomorrow. But I know I'm going to blow it!"

22   Her mother said, "Maybe I'll come along and watch." I could tell that Mrs. Winterbottom was trying to rise above some awful sadness she was feeling, but Prudence couldn't see that. Prudence had her own **agenda**, just as I had had my own agenda that day my mother wanted me to walk with her. I couldn't see my own mother's sadness.

23   "What?" Prudence said. "Come along and *watch*?"

24   "Yes, wouldn't that be nice?"

25   "No!" Prudence said. "No, no, no. You can't. It would be awful."

26   I heard the front door open and shut and Phoebe came in the kitchen waving a white envelope. "Guess what was on the steps?" she said.

V   SELECTION VOCABULARY

tryout / la prueba *noun* test or trial of skill, usually in a particular sport or performance art

 ELL
- What is Prudence trying to become at school?
- Are students able to sign up for this team or must they be tested and then selected?

NOTES

27 Mrs. Winterbottom took the envelope and turned it over and over before she slowly unsealed it and slipped out the message.

28 "Oh," she said. "Who is doing this?" She held out the piece of paper: *In the course of a lifetime, what does it matter?*

29 Prudence said, "Well, I have more important things to worry about, I can **assure** you. I know I'm going to blow those cheerleading tryouts, I just know it."

30 On and on she went, until Phoebe said, "Cripes, Prudence, in the course of a lifetime, what does it matter?"

31 At that moment, it was as if a switch went off in Mrs. Winterbottom's brain. She put her hand to her mouth and stared out the window. She was invisible to Prudence and Phoebe, though. They did not notice.

32 Phoebe said, "Are these cheerleading tryouts such a big deal? Will you even remember them in five years?"

33 "Yes!" Prudence said. "Yes, I most certainly will."

34 "How about ten years? Will you remember them in ten?"

35 "Yes!" Prudence said.

36 As I walked home, I thought about the message. *In the course of a lifetime, what does it matter?* I said it over and over. I wondered about the mysterious messenger, and I wondered about all the things in the course of a lifetime that would not matter. I did not think cheerleading tryouts would matter, but I was not so sure about yelling at your mother. I was certain, however, that if your mother left, it would be something that mattered in the whole long course of your lifetime.

Excerpted from *Walk Two Moons* by Sharon Creech, published by HarperCollins Publishers.

Reading & Writing Companion   3

Skills Focus

QUESTION 3: Textual Evidence

Prudence explicitly states that she doesn't care about the note. She only cares about the cheerleading tryouts.

Skills Focus

QUESTION 5: Connect to Essential Question

Sal realizes that some things really don't matter in the long run—like cheerleading practice. But having your mother leave definitely affects you for the rest of your life.

TEXT TALK

What message does Phoebe find on the front steps of their house? What effect does it have on Prudence?

See paragraphs 26–29: Phoebe finds a message that reads, "In the course of a lifetime, what does it matter?" Prudence says she has more important things to think about.

What other questions are you able to ask and answer?

Answers will vary.

Think about the message in the letter. What aspects of our lives matter most?

Answers will vary.

B   Ask each Beyond grade-level student to write one additional discussion question. Then, have one or two students facilitate a discussion, using their questions to guide the conversation.

V   SELECTION VOCABULARY

agenda / la agenda *noun* plan; list of things to do COGNATE

ELL
- What does Prudence care more about right now—cheerleading or her mother?
- What did the narrator care more about on her last day with her mother—walking with her mother or cleaning her desk?

assure / asegurar *verb* to tell positively and with certainty and confidence in order to dispel any doubts

ELL
- What does Prudence care more about right now—cheerleading or the message Phoebe found?
- How does Prudence make sure the other characters know how she feels?

Think Questions

Circulate as students answer Think Questions independently. Scaffolds for these questions are shown on the opposite page.

QUESTION 1: Textual Evidence

Mrs. Winterbottom tries to take an interest in her children. She asks Phoebe about her day at school and kisses her cheek, but Phoebe wipes off the kiss and says, "I'm not a baby anymore." Prudence thinks having her mother come to her cheerleader tryouts "would be awful." They don't seem to care about their mother's feelings.

QUESTION 2: Textual Evidence

Phoebe finds a message that reads, "In the course of a lifetime, what does it matter?" This causes the narrator to think about when her mother left her family. She decides that in the course of a lifetime, having your mother leave would be something that mattered in your life, but cheerleading tryouts would not.

QUESTION 3: Textual Evidence

The mood in Mrs.Winterbottom's kitchen is one of anger and sadness. Phoebe shouts at her mother and "marches upstairs." When Prudence comes home she "storms into the house, slamming the door behind her." All of this makes Mrs. Winterbottom sad. She "chips away half-heartedly at the burned brownies." The narrator can tell that Mrs. Winterbottom is "trying to rise above some awful sadness."

QUESTION 4: Context Clues

I think *agenda* must mean "a list of concerns." The word is used to describe what is important to Prudence—cheerleading—and what was important to the narrator during her mother's last day at home—cleaning her desk. Neither girl is concerned over their mother's sadness.

QUESTION 5: Context Clues

I think *assure* must mean "to guarantee." Prudence uses the word to change the subject from the message back to cheerleading. She wants everyone to know that the cheerleading tryouts are much more important to her than the message.

 First Read

Read *Walk Two Moons*. After you read, complete the Think Questions below.

 **THINK QUESTIONS**

1. What kind of relationship does Mrs. Winterbottom have with her daughters Prudence and Phoebe? Cite evidence from the text to support your answer.

2. What message does Phoebe find on the steps? What effect does it have on the narrator? Be sure to cite textual evidence to support your answer.

3. Mood is the emotional quality or atmosphere of a story. What is the mood in Mrs. Winterbottom's kitchen in this excerpt from *Walk Two Moons*? Which words and descriptions contribute to this mood?

4. Find the word **agenda** in paragraph 22 of *Walk Two Moons*. Use context clues in the surrounding sentences, as well as the sentence in which the word appears, to determine the word's meaning. Write your definition here and identify clues that helped you figure out its meaning.

5. Use context clues to determine the meaning of **assure** as it is used in paragraph 29 of *Walk Two Moons*. Write your definition here and identify clues that helped you figure out its meaning. Then check the meaning in a dictionary.

Think Questions

Use the scaffolds below to differentiate instruction for your **ELL** English Language Learners and **A** Approaching grade-level learners.

ELL **BEGINNING** Write a response using the <u>word bank</u> and <u>sentence frames</u>.

INTERMEDIATE Write a response using the <u>sentence frames</u>.

ADVANCED, ADVANCED HIGH Write a response using the <u>Text-Dependent Question Guide</u>.

A **APPROACHING** Write a response using the <u>Text-Dependent Question Guide</u>.

| | INTERMEDIATE | APPROACHING |
| BEGINNING | | ADVANCED, ADVANCED HIGH |

Word Bank	Sentence Frames	Text-Dependent Question Guide
guarantee fat mother baby tells course marches chips important cheerleading lifetime things to do anger awful burned slams brownie	When Mrs. Winterbottom kisses Phoebe's cheek, Phoebe says "I'm not a ____". Then Mrs. Winterbottom asks if Phoebe wants a ____. Phoebe says no, they're ____ and she's too ____. Prudence tells Mrs.Winterbottom that it would be ____ if she came to watch her tryouts.	1. • What does Phoebe say when Mrs. Winterbottom kisses her? • How does Phoebe act when her mother asks if she wants a brownie? • What does Prudence say when her mother says she wants to watch her tryout?
	Phoebe finds a message on the steps that reads, "In the ____ of a____, what does it matter?" The narrator (Sal) thinks that ____ tryouts would not matter. She is sure though that if your ____ left, that would be something that mattered.	2. • What does the message that Phoebe finds say? • What does the narrator (Sal) think about the • How does the message change the way Sal thinks about her own mother?
	Mrs. Winterbottom's kitchen is full of ____ and sadness. Phoebe shouts at her and ____ upstairs. Prudence ____ the door. All of this makes Mrs. Winterbottom sad. She ____ away half-heartedly at the burned brownies.	3. • What does Phoebe do when she comes home from school? • How does Prudence act when she returns home after cheerleading tryouts? • How does this make Mrs. Winterbottom feel?
	Prudence and the narrator (Sal) have items that are ____ to them. This gives me a clue that *agenda* means a list of ____.	4. • Read: "Prudence had her own **agenda,** just as I had my own agenda that day my mother wanted me to walk with her." What does Prudence care more about—cheerleading or her mother? • What did the narrator care more about—walking with her mother or cleaning her desk?
	Prudence ____ the other characters what is most important to her. This gives me a clue that *assure* means to ____ something	5. • Read: "Prudence said, 'Well, I have more important things to worry about, I can **assure** you. I know I'm going to blow those cheerleading tryouts, I just know it.'" • Does Prudence care more about—cheerleading or the mysterious message on the porch? • How does Prudence make her concerns known to the other characters?

Reading Comprehension OPTIONAL

Have students complete the digital reading comprehension questions ✓ when they finish reading.

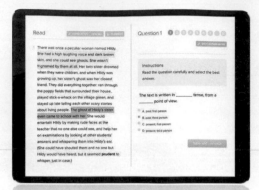

ANSWER KEY

QUESTION 1: C	**QUESTION 5:** A	**QUESTION 9:**
QUESTION 2: C	**QUESTION 6:** D	*See first chart.*
QUESTION 3: C	**QUESTION 7:** A	**QUESTION 10:**
QUESTION 4: A	**QUESTION 8:** B	*See second chart.*

Synonym	Word
irritable	crotchety
trial	tryout
gloomy	sullen
plan	agenda
convince	assure

First	Second	Third	Fourth
Phoebe refuses to eat her mother's brownies.	Mrs. Winterbottom offers to go to the second day of cheerleading tryouts.	Mrs. Winterbottom wonders who could be behind the note.	Phoebe confronts Prudence about her attitude toward tryouts.

Connect and Extend OPTIONAL

CONNECT TO EXTENDED WRITING PROJECT

Students can use *Walk Two Moons* as a mentor text for their Extended Writing Project. They may analyze Sharon Creech's methods for developing relationships among characters as they reflect on the nature of their own personal relationships.

BEYOND THE BOOK

Writing and Discussion: Parent Appreciation

In *Walk Two Moons,* Sal can see how Phoebe and Prudence take their mother, Mrs. Winterbottom, for granted. Ask students to:

- Create a list of all the things their parents or guardians do for them on a daily basis.
- Form small groups and discuss the following questions:
  - > Do you take your parents or guardians for granted?
  - > How often do you tell your parents or guardians you appreciate them?
  - > Why is it so common for kids to take parents or guardians for granted?

Reflect in writing:

- > Prior to this activity, did you feel like you took your parents or guardians for granted?
- > What can you do to let them know you appreciate what they do for you?

Skill:
Language, Style, and Audience

Use the Checklist to analyze Language, Style, and Audience in *Walk Two Moons*. Refer to the sample student annotations about Language, Style, and Audience in the text.

••• **CHECKLIST FOR LANGUAGE, STYLE, AND AUDIENCE**

In order to determine an author's style, do the following:

✓ identify and define any unfamiliar words or phrases

✓ use context, including the meaning of surrounding words and phrases

✓ note possible reactions to the author's word choice

✓ examine your reaction to the author's word choice, and how the author's choice affected your reaction

✓ note word choice and how it impacts the tone

To analyze the impact of specific word choice on meaning and tone, ask the following questions:

✓ How did your understanding of the language change during your analysis?

✓ What stylistic choices can you identify in the text? How does the style influence your understanding of the language?

✓ How could various audiences interpret this language? What different possible emotional responses can you list?

✓ How does the writer's choice of words impact or create a specific tone in the text?

✓ How does word choice impact tone?

Reading & Writing Companion **5**

Skill: Language, Style, and Audience

Introduce the Skill

Watch the Concept Definition video and read the following definitions with your students.

Authors use language to convey meaning or to affect the way their audience thinks and perceives. An **audience** is the intended reader or listener. Readers can analyze an author's style to better understand the tone and meaning of a text.

Style refers to the way an author uses language (words, sentences, paragraphs) to achieve a purpose. One element of style is **word choice.** Word choice is a technique in which writers choose specific words for precise meaning or to convey a certain tone. **Meaning** is a reader's interpretation of the text's deeper messages, themes, or ideas. **Tone** expresses a writer's **attitude** (or thoughts and feelings) toward his or her subject. Tone can be described, for example, as formal, casual, conversational, ironic, sad, bitter, humorous, or serious.

TURN AND TALK

1. Name a favorite character from a book, TV show, or movie.

2. How would you describe this character's personality?

3. In what ways does this character's speech match his or her personality?

ELL SPEAKING FRAMES

- One of my favorite characters is ____.
- I would describe this character as ____. This character is also ____.
- This character says things like ____. These words match the character's personality because ____.

 SKILL VOCABULARY

style / el estilo *noun* a way of expressing something that is characteristic of the person or time period **COGNATE**

word choice / la elección de palabras *noun* specific words chosen for precise meaning or to generate an emotional response

tone / el tono *noun* the writer's or speaker's attitude toward his or her subject matter **COGNATE**

Your Turn

Ask students to complete the Your Turn Activity.

QUESTION 1

A. **Correct.** Prudence bursts onto the scene and sucks everyone into her cheerleading drama with no regard for anything that was going on in the kitchen before her arrival.

B. Incorrect. Prudence is loud, and she is disrespectful of her mother's offer to attend the tryout the next day.

C. Incorrect. Prudence shows no interest in her mother or the narrator when she enters the kitchen.

D. Incorrect. Prudence is disrespectful of her mother's offer to attend the tryout the next day.

QUESTION 2

A. Incorrect. There is no evidence that Prudence is not being heard.

B. Incorrect. There is no evidence that Mrs. Winterbottom has poor hearing.

C. **Correct.** Prudence's speech is simple and angry like a child throwing a fit because she doesn't get her way.

D. Incorrect. Prudence's points are not complex and do not need emphasis.

QUESTION 3

A. Incorrect. Prudence does not want her mother to come to the tryouts.

B. **Correct.** Prudence is horrified at the thought of her mother coming to watch the tryouts.

C. Incorrect. Prudence's reaction is dramatic; she doesn't see anything funny in the situation.

D. Incorrect. Prudence is shocked or horrified over her mother's suggestion.

Walk Two Moons

 **Skill:**
Language, Style, And Audience

Reread paragraphs 17–25 of *Walk Two Moons*. Then, using the Checklist on the previous page, answer the multiple-choice questions below.

 **YOUR TURN**

1. How does the narrator use the words stormed and wailed in paragraph 17 to characterize Prudence?

   ○ A. Prudence is dramatic and self-absorbed.
   ○ B. Prudence is quiet and respectful.
   ○ C. Prudence is loud, but interested in others.
   ○ D. Prudence is distracted, but caring.

2. What does Prudence's repetition of words in paragraphs 19 and 25 reveal about her?

   ○ A. Prudence wants to make sure she's being heard.
   ○ B. Prudence accommodates her mother's poor hearing.
   ○ C. Prudence is childish, and she throws tantrums.
   ○ D. Prudence is a good speaker, and she emphasizes her points.

3. What is the effect of the author's use of italics in paragraph 23?

   ○ A. The italics show horror in Prudence's tone.
   ○ B. The italics show horror in Prudence's tone.
   ○ C. The italics show humor in Prudence's tone.
   ○ D. The italics show sorrow in Prudence's tone.

 SKILL VOCABULARY

attitude / la actitud *noun* a state involving beliefs and feelings that causes a person to think or act in a certain way COGNATE

audience / la audiencia *noun* the people who read a written text, listen to an oral response or presentation, or watch a performance COGNATE

meaning / el significado *noun* what is meant by a word; the general message of a text or idea

Skill:
Textual Evidence

Use the Checklist to analyze Textual Evidence in *Walk Two Moons*. Refer to the sample student annotations about Textual Evidence in the text.

••• CHECKLIST FOR TEXTUAL EVIDENCE

In order to support an analysis by citing textual evidence that is explicitly stated in the text, do the following:

- ✓ read the text closely and critically
- ✓ identify what the text says explicitly
- ✓ find the most relevant textual evidence that supports your analysis
- ✓ consider why an author explicitly states specific details and information
- ✓ cite the specific words, phrases, sentences, or paragraphs from the text that support your analysis

In order to interpret implicit meanings in a text by making inferences, do the following:

- ✓ combine information directly stated in the text with your own knowledge, experiences, and observations
- ✓ cite the specific words, phrases, sentences, or paragraphs from the text that support these inferences

In order to cite textual evidence to support an analysis of what the text says explicitly as well as inferences drawn from the text, consider the following questions:

- ✓ Have I read the text closely and critically?
- ✓ What inferences am I making about the text? What textual evidence am I using to support these inferences?
- ✓ Am I quoting the evidence from the text correctly?
- ✓ Does my textual evidence logically relate to my analysis?

Reading & Writing Companion **7**

V SKILL VOCABULARY

cite / citar *verb* to quote as evidence to support a response

textual evidence / la evidencia del texto *noun* details from the text that a reader can use to support his or her ideas and opinions about the text

explicit / explícito/a *adjective* precisely and clearly expressed COGNATE

implicit / implícito/a *adjective* implied but not stated directly COGNATE

 ## Skill: Textual Evidence

Introduce the Skill

Watch the Concept Definition video and read the following definitions with your students.

Any time you're discussing a text, you need to **cite,** or point out, **textual evidence,** the details that readers use to support their ideas and opinions. Readers may cite evidence that is directly stated, or **explicit,** in the text. Other times, textual evidence may be **implicit,** which means it is suggested but not directly stated. One way to interpret implicit meanings is to **make inferences,** using clues from the text and your own experiences to make logical decisions about characters and events that are not stated directly.

Readers must also refer to textual evidence when they **analyze** and examine the different parts of a text. Analyzing specific parts of the text, such as the actions of a character or the cause-and-effect relationships between events in nonfiction, helps a reader **interpret** and explain the meaning, theme, or central idea of the text as a whole. When you cite textual evidence, someone else can look back at a particular part of a text you read and understand your analysis.

TURN AND TALK

1. When reading a text, why is looking for textual evidence important?

2. When the author doesn't explicitly tell you what's happening in the story, how can you make inferences?

ELL SPEAKING FRAMES
- When reading a text, I use textual evidence to ___.
- I can make an inference by ___.
- When analyzing a text, I need to ___.

Your Turn

Ask students to complete the Your Turn Activity.

QUESTION 1

A. Incorrect. This sentence describes Phoebe's reaction to her sister's obsession about cheerleading tryouts.

B. **Correct.** Prudence says the letter isn't important; she only cares about cheerleading tryouts.

C. Incorrect. This sentence describes Mrs. Winterbottom's reaction to the letter.

D. Incorrect. This sentence describes Sal's reaction to the letter.

QUESTION 2

A. Incorrect. Mrs. Winterbottom is no longer confused by the letter. A switch goes off in her brain, and she suddenly understands something about the letter.

B. Incorrect. Mrs. Winterbottom is interested in the letter. She stares out the window because she understands something about the letter.

C. **Correct.** It is as if "a switch went off in Mrs. Winterbottom's brain," and she puts her hand to her mouth and stares out the window. She has made a sudden realization regarding the letter.

D. Incorrect. Mrs. Winterbottom does not leave the scene, and being invisible to her daughters is not a direct effect of the letter.

QUESTION 3

A. Incorrect. The past and the present are not separate for Sal or Mrs. Winterbottom.

B. Incorrect. The past remains important for Sal and Mrs. Winterbottom.

C. **Correct.** The scene in the Winterbottom kitchen and the letter trigger important memories for Sal and Mrs. Winterbottom.

D. Incorrect. There is no reference to Sal's or Mrs. Winterbottom's future in the scene.

Walk Two Moons

Skill:
Textual Evidence

Reread paragraphs 27–36 of *Walk Two Moons*. Then, using the Checklist on the previous page, answer the multiple-choice questions below.

⟳ YOUR TURN

1. What evidence explicitly stated in the text best describes Prudence's reaction to the letter?

   ○ A. "'Cripes, Prudence, in the course of a lifetime, what does it matter?'"
   ○ B. "'Well, I have more important things to worry about, I can assure you.'"
   ○ C. "She put her hand to her mouth and stared out the window."
   ○ D. "I wondered about all the things in the course of a lifetime that would not matter."

2. In paragraph 31, what is the effect of the letter on Mrs. Winterbottom, and how is this effect revealed by the author?

   ○ A. Mrs. Winterbottom continues to be confused by the letter, which the author reveals by having Mrs. Winterbottom put her hand to her mouth.
   ○ B. Mrs. Winterbottom doesn't show interest in the letter, which the author reveals with the narration that Mrs. Winterbottom stares out the window.
   ○ C. Mrs. Winterbottom suddenly figures something out about the letter, which the author reveals with the narration that a switch went off in Mrs. Winterbottom's brain.
   ○ D. Mrs. Winterbottom opens the letter and disappears from the kitchen, which the author reveals with the narration that Mrs. Winterbottom is invisible to her daughters.

3. Which message can be inferred from this scene of Walk Two Moons?

   ○ A. The past and the present remain separate time periods in one's life.
   ○ B. The present is more important than the past.
   ○ C. The past can invade the present through triggered memories.
   ○ D. Past events determine future events through present choices.

Ⅴ SKILL VOCABULARY

make inferences / hacer inferencias *verb* to use your understanding of a text and your own experiences, to draw conclusions

analyze / analizar *verb* to consider in detail and discover essential features or meaning COGNATE

interpret / interpretar *verb* to explain the meaning of (information, words, or actions) COGNATE

Close Read

Reread *Walk Two Moons*. As you reread, complete the Skills Focus questions below. Then use your answers and annotations from the questions to help you complete the Write activity.

◎ SKILLS FOCUS

1. Identify evidence that shows how the author contrasts Sal's treatment of her own mother with the way Phoebe and Prudence respond to their mother, Mrs. Winterbottom.

2. Identify evidence that shows what Sal learns about herself after witnessing the scene between Mrs. Winterbottom, Phoebe, and Prudence.

3. Phoebe finds a note on the doorstep that asks, "In the course of a lifetime, what does it matter?" What inference can you draw from the text to explain Mrs. Winterbottom's reaction to the note? What evidence explicitly stated in the text explains Prudence's reaction?

4. Explain how the author's word choice influenced the reader's understanding of the characters of Phoebe and Mrs. Winterbottom.

5. Identify evidence in the last paragraph that reveals what Sal realizes when she reflects back about her own mother leaving home.

✎ WRITE

NARRATIVE: Rewrite this excerpt from *Walk Two Moons* with Phoebe, Prudence, or Mrs. Winterbottom as the narrator instead of Sal. Use evidence explicitly stated in the text, as well as inferences drawn from the text, to identify the narrator's relationship with the other characters. In your narrative, select language that reflects an appropriate tone for the narrator you choose.

Close Read

Skills Focus

QUESTION 1: Compare and Contrast

See paragraphs 15 and 16.

QUESTION 2: Character

See paragraph 16.

QUESTION 3: Textual Evidence

See paragraph 29.

QUESTION 4: Language, Style, and Audience

See paragraphs 12–15.

QUESTION 5: Connect to Essential Question

See paragraph 36.

✓ CHECK FOR SUCCESS

If students struggle to respond to Skills Focus Question #1, ask students the following questions:

- What is distinctive about how Phoebe speaks in paragraph 15?

- What is distinctive about how Sal describes her mother in paragraph 16?

- Based on textual evidence, how can you contrast the characters' relationships with their mothers?

Have students transition to read and annotate independently once they have successfully completed the first Skills Focus prompt.

Writer's Notebook

Connect to Essential Question: Give students time to reflect on how *Walk Two Moons* connects to the unit's essential question "How do relationships shape us?" by freewriting in their Writer's Notebooks.

ELL **Beginning & Intermediate**

Read aloud the unit's essential question: "How do relationships shape us?" Encourage students to draw their reflections or allow students to write in their native language. Circulate, prompting students for their thoughts as they respond orally or through pantomime.

Advanced & Advanced High

Allow students to share their reflections orally in pairs or small groups before freewriting.

StudySyncTV

Project the StudySyncTV episode and pause at the following times to prompt discussion:

1:37 How do the students use text evidence to determine some information about Mrs. Winterbottom's life?

2:36 How do the students use text evidence and inference to analyze why Sal can see Mrs. Winterbottom's unhappiness?

4:40 How do the students use text evidence to uncover the meaning of the note's message?

Collaborative Conversation

SCAFFOLDS

Break students into collaborative conversation groups to discuss the Close Read prompt. Ask students to use the StudySyncTV episode as a model for their discussion. Remind them to reference their Skills Focus annotations in their discussion.

Rewrite this excerpt of *Walk Two Moons* with Phoebe, Prudence, or Mrs. Winterbottom as the narrator instead of Sal. Use evidence explicitly stated in the text, as well as inferences drawn from the text, to identify the narrator's relationship with the other characters. In your narrative, select language that reflects an appropriate tone for the narrator you choose.

Use the scaffolds below to differentiate instruction for your **ELL** English Language Learners and **A** Approaching grade-level learners.

ELL **BEGINNING, INTERMEDIATE** Use the discussion guide and speaking frames to discuss with support from the teacher.

ADVANCED, ADVANCED HIGH Use the discussion guide and speaking frames to discuss in mixed-level groups.

A **APPROACHING** Use the discussion guide to discuss in mixed-level groups.

APPROACHING
ADVANCED, ADVANCED HIGH
BEGINNING, INTERMEDIATE

Discussion Guide	Speaking Frames
1. What is something that a reader can infer about a character from the story?	• A reader can infer ____. • If (Phoebe/Prudence/Mrs. Winterbottom) were the narrator, I would write that ____.
2. What words or phrases would you use to keep an appropriate tone for your narrator?	• I would use words and phrases like ____. • This would help maintain an appropriate tone because ____.

Review Prompt and Rubric

Before students begin writing, review the writing prompt and rubric with the class.

NARRATIVE: Rewrite this excerpt of *Walk Two Moons* with Phoebe, Prudence, or Mrs. Winterbottom as the narrator instead of Sal. Use evidence explicitly stated in the text, as well as inferences drawn from the text, to identify the narrator's relationship with the other characters. In your narrative, select language that reflects an appropriate tone for the narrator you choose.

PROMPT GUIDE

- Which narrator would you choose for the rewrite?
- What evidence explicitly found in the text would you use in the narrative?
- What inferences would you make about the narrator's relationships with the other characters?

- What is tone?
- What words or phrases would you use to maintain an appropriate tone for your narrator?

Score	Textual Evidence	Language, Style, and Audience	Language and Conventions
4	The writer is able to skillfully rewrite the excerpt with a different narrator using multiple examples of textual evidence explicitly stated in the text and inferences to successfully describe the relationships between the characters.	The writer consistently selects language that reflects an appropriate tone for the narrator.	The writer demonstrates a consistent command of grammar, punctuation, and usage conventions. Although minor errors may be evident, they do not detract from the fluency or the clarity of the essay.
3	The writer is able to rewrite the excerpt with a different narrator using some examples of textual evidence explicitly stated in the text and inferences to adequately describe the relationships between the characters.	The writer adequately selects language that reflects an appropriate tone for the narrator.	The writer demonstrates an adequate command of grammar, punctuation, and usage conventions. Although some errors may be evident, they create few (if any) disruptions in the fluency of the writing or the clarity of the essay.
2	The writer is able to rewrite the excerpt with a different narrator, but fails to use both evidence explicitly stated in the text and inferences to describe the relationships between the characters.	The writer sometimes selects language that reflects an appropriate tone for the narrator.	The writer demonstrates a partial command of grammar, punctuation, and usage conventions. Some distracting errors may be evident, at times creating minor disruptions in the fluency or clarity of the writing.
1	The writer is not able to rewrite the excerpt with a different narrator and fails to use both evidence explicitly stated in the text and inferences to describe the relationships between the characters. The narrative is presented in a random or illogical way.	The writer demonstrates little or no ability to select language that reflects an appropriate tone for the narrator.	The writer demonstrates little or no command of grammar, punctuation, and usage conventions. Serious and persistent errors create disruptions in the fluency of the writing and sometimes interfere with meaning.
0	The writer does not provide a relevant response to the prompt or does not provide a response at all.	The writer does not provide a relevant response to the prompt or does not provide a response at all.	Serious and persistent errors overwhelm the writing and interfere with the meaning of the response as a whole, making the writer's meaning impossible to understand.

Write

SCAFFOLDS

Ask students to complete the writing assignment using textual evidence to support their answers.

Use the scaffolds below to differentiate instruction for your **ELL** English Language Learners and **A** Approaching grade-level learners.

ELL **BEGINNING** With the help of the <u>word bank</u>, write a response using <u>paragraph frame 1</u>.

INTERMEDIATE With the help of the <u>word bank</u>, write a response using <u>paragraph frames 1 and 2</u>.

ADVANCED, ADVANCED HIGH Write a response of differentiated length using the <u>sentence starters</u>.

A **APPROACHING** Write a response of differentiated length using the <u>sentence starters</u>.

BEGINNING			ADVANCED, ADVANCED HIGH
INTERMEDIATE			APPROACHING
Word Bank	**Paragraph Frame 1**	**Paragraph Frame 2**	**Sentence Starters**
crying school myself kitchen brownies	I sat at the ____ table, staring at the burned ____. I needed to pull ____ together. Phoebe and Prudence would be home from ____ soon. I didn't want them to see me ____.	I don't know why I worry about hiding my ____. Phoebe and Prudence never ____. I don't think they would even notice that I was ____. As I was ____ my nose, Phoebe and her friend Sal came in. ____, I said, "Oh sweetie, how was it?"	• I sat at the kitchen table . . . • I was feeling . . . • I didn't want . . . • I don't know why I worry about . . . • I doubt they would even notice . . . • I was startled when . . . • I said, . . .

Peer Review

Students should submit substantive feedback to two peers using the review instructions below.

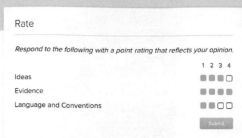

Rate

Respond to the following with a point rating that reflects your opinion.

	1 2 3 4
Ideas	■ ■ ■ □
Evidence	■ ■ ■ ■
Language and Conventions	■ ■ □ □

Submit

- How well does this response answer the prompt?
- How well does the writer use evidence explicitly stated in the text, as well as inferences, to describe the characters' relationships?
- How well does the writer choose language that reflects an appropriate tone for the narrator?
- Which sentence in the writer's rewrite made you think differently about the story?
- What did the writer do well in this rewrite? What does the writer need to work on?

 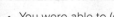

SENTENCE FRAMES

A
- You were able to (completely / partly / almost) _____ answer the prompt because . . .
- You could respond to the prompt more completely by . . .
- You used evidence explicitly found in the text when you wrote . . .
- You made inferences when you wrote . . .

- You maintained an appropriate tone for the narrator by . . .
- You could strengthen your narrator's tone by using . . .
- I thought differently about the narrator after reading . . .
- My favorite part of your rewrite is . . .

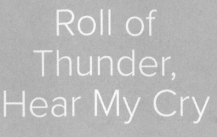

Roll of Thunder, Hear My Cry

FICTION
Mildred D. Taylor
1976

Introduction

studysync ⓣ

Written by Mildred D. Taylor (b. 1943), *Roll of Thunder, Hear My Cry* is the gripping story of the Logans, a land-owning black family in the Deep South struggling to keep things together during a tumultuous year in the 1930s. Largely insulated from the injustices of the world around her, but raised with a strong sense of fairness, nine-year-old Cassie is only beginning to understand the realities of racism and the everyday terror it brings to the grown-ups in her community. In the excerpt here, neighbors bring bad news for her father. Published in 1976, Taylor's novel won the Newbery Medal the following year.

Cassie overhears her parents talking about the trouble stemming from the local boycott of Mr. Wallace's store. Later that evening, Papa explains that he must leave soon for his railroad job so that he can pay the mortgage next year. He has delayed his departure because he is worried about problems from Mr. Wallace. Two of his friends tell Papa that they must abandon the boycott because their landowner, angry at their participation, has demanded a larger share of their cotton crop. Cassie's brother gets upset, but Papa reminds him that their family is lucky to own land, unlike many of their neighbors. Cassie asks whether they will give up the boycott, and Papa responds by pointing to the fig tree in the yard. He explains that despite being overshadowed by bigger trees, its roots run deep. Just like the fig tree, their family will not give up.

 Proficiency-leveled summaries and summaries in multiple languages are available digitally.

🔊 Audio and audio text highlighting are available with the text.

CONNECT TO ESSENTIAL QUESTION

How do relationships shape us?

A young black girl who lives in the South during the Great Depression begins to learn about the realities of racism. She has a close relationship with her family, but she wonders if they can they continue to carry on with the injustices she sees happening all around them.

Access Complex Text

LEXILE: 820L   WORD COUNT: 1,384

The following areas may be challenging for students, particularly **ELL** English Language Learners and **A** Approaching grade-level learners.

Connection of Ideas	Prior Knowledge	Sentence Structure
• The majority of plot events in the selection are revealed through dialogue. • Students will need to make connections between what the characters say and how the dialogue drives the events of the plot.	• The events in the selection are directly tied to its setting, and students may not be aware of the economic inequities of sharecropping or the grave effects of the Great Depression on African Americans. • The significance of Thurston Wallace's power over the other characters may need explication.	• Students may find the use of dialect and any deviations from standard English challenging. • Discuss the meanings of specific words and analyze what dialect reveals about the characters and what it contributes to the story.

 SCAFFOLDS   **ENGLISH LANGUAGE LEARNERS**   **A** **APPROACHING GRADE LEVEL**   **B** **BEYOND GRADE LEVEL**

These icons identify differentiation strategies and scaffolded support for a variety of students. See the digital lesson plan for additional differentiation strategies and scaffolds.

Instructional Path

First Read: Roll of Thunder, Hear My Cry

Objectives: After an initial reading and discussion of the text, students will be able to identify and describe characters and setting details as well as articulate events that are central to the story's plot.

Skill: Connotation and Denotation

Objectives: After rereading and discussing a model of close reading, students will be able to determine the connotative meaning of words and phrases as they are used in a text.

Skill: Theme

Objectives: After rereading and discussing a model of close reading, students will be able to determine the theme of a text and how it is conveyed through particular details.

Skill: Story Structure

Objectives: After rereading and discussing a model of close reading, students will be able to analyze how a particular sentence or chapter fits into the overall structure of a text and contributes to the development of theme, setting, or plot.

Close Read: Roll of Thunder, Hear My Cry

Objectives: Closely read the text to analyze theme in order to participate in a collaborative conversation and write a short constructed response.

Progress Monitoring

Opportunities to Learn	Opportunities to Demonstrate Learning	Opportunities to Reteach
Connotation and Denotation		
⚙ Skill: Connotation and Denotation	⚙ Skill: Connotation and Denotation • Your Turn 🗎 Close Read • Complete Vocabulary Chart • Skills Focus	⚙ Unit 4 Skill: Connotation and Denotation - I am Malala: The Girl Who Stood Up for Education and was Shot by the Taliban ⚙ Unit 6 Skill: Connotation and Denotation - Rosa Parks: My Story ⚙ Spotlight Skill: Connotation and Denotation
Theme		
⚙ Skill: Theme	⚙ Skill: Theme • Your Turn 🗎 Close Read • Skills Focus • Write	⚙ Unit 3 Skill: Theme - Hoot ⚙ Unit 4 Skill: Theme - All Summer in a Day ⚙ Spotlight Skill: Theme
Story Structure		
⚙ Skill: Story Structure	⚙ Skill: Story Structure • Your Turn 🗎 Close Read • Skills Focus	⚙ Unit 3 Skill: Story Structure - The Lightning Thief ⚙ Spotlight Skill: Story Structure

First Read

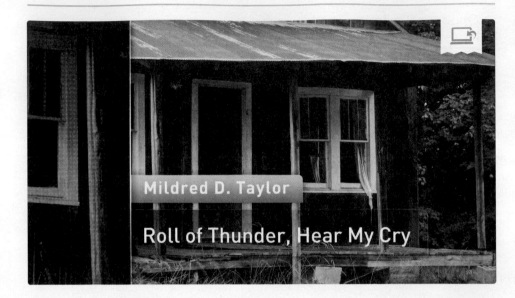

Mildred D. Taylor

Roll of Thunder, Hear My Cry

 ## Introduce the Text

As a class, watch the video preview and have students read the introduction in pairs to make connections to the video preview.

To activate prior knowledge and experiences, ask students:

- How do the images, words, and music in this video make you feel?

- What is one question you have about what you are going to read?

> **ELL SPEAKING FRAMES**
> - The ____ in the video makes me think ____.
> - The video shows ____. This makes me wonder ____.
> - I think the text will ____. I think this because ____.
> - I predict that there will be ____. I believe this because ____.

Entry Point

As students prepare to read *Roll of Thunder, Hear My Cry* share the following information with them to provide context.

✓ While the family of the main character in the novel owns their land, most African Americans in the American South during the Great Depression did not. Instead, most African Americans in the South were what is called "sharecroppers," meaning that they rented land from white landowners and paid those landowners with a portion of the crops they harvested each year. This system kept poor African American farmers tied to the land and unable to move upward in society.

✓ Mildred D. Taylor has written nine novels, many of which revolve around the Logan family. Her stories are based on family stories passed down to her from her father who grew up in Mississippi during the Great Depression.

"We keep doing what we gotta, and we don't give up. We can't. . . ."

1   When supper was ready, I eagerly grabbed the iron bell before Christopher-John or Little Man could claim it, and ran onto the back porch to summon Papa, Mr. Morrison, and Stacey from the fields. As the three of them washed up on the back porch, Mama went to the end of the porch where Papa stood alone. "What did Mr. Jamison want?" she asked, her voice barely **audible**.

2   Papa took the towel Mama handed him, but did not reply immediately. I was just inside the kitchen dipping out the butter beans. I moved closer to the window so that I could hear his answer.

3   "Don't keep anything from me, David. If there's trouble, I want to know."

4   Papa looked down at her. "Nothing to worry 'bout, honey . . . . just seems that Thurston Wallace been in town talking 'bout how he's not gonna let a few smart colored folks ruin his business. Says he's gonna put a stop to this shopping in Vicksburg. That's all."

5   Mama sighed and stared out across the plowed field to the sloping pasture land. "I'm feeling scared, David," she said.

6   Papa put down the towel. "Not yet, Mary. It's not time to be scared yet. They're just talking."

7   Mama turned and faced him. "And when they stop talking?"

8   "Then . . . then maybe it'll be time. But right now, pretty lady," he said, leading her by the hand toward the kitchen door, "right now I've got better things to think about."

NOTES

Skill:
Story Structure

I see that Mama is nervous because the narrator can hardly hear her ask the question about Mr. Jamison. This seems to be part of the conflict.

Papa does not seem worried about the situation with Mr. Jamison, but the problem seems serious. How will the family solve this problem?

Reading & Writing
Companion   **11**

Analyze Vocabulary Using Context Clues

In paragraph 1, focus on the sentence that uses the word *audible*. Point out these context clues:

1.   First I notice that the sentence includes the word *voice*, so *audible* must have something to do with voice or speaking.

2.   I also notice that the sentence includes the word *barely* before *audible*. I know that *barely* means "almost not at all."

3.   I've already read that Mama and Papa are at the end of the porch. If Cassie is inside the kitchen, she might have difficulty hearing her parents. Therefore, *audible* must mean "able to be heard."

Story Structure

What is story structure?

Story structure is how the authors organize the events of the plot. The reader highlighted the initial conflict in the first passage.

V   SELECTION VOCABULARY

audible / audible *adjective* able to be heard   COGNATE

TEXT TALK

Why is Thurston Wallace upset?

See paragraph 4: Black farmers are shopping in Vicksburg.

What does Papa tell Mama about being scared?

See paragraphs 6–8: Papa tells Mama that it is too soon to be scared, since the men in town are still just talking.

Connotation and Denotation

How did the reader determine the connotation of the word *beamed* as it is used in paragraph 9?

She determined that the word describes Papa's happy reaction to the meal. She noted the way Papa speaks about the event. The word has a positive connotation.

Skills Focus

QUESTION 4: Connect to Essential Question

Cassie thinks that planting more cotton might mean that the family will have enough money to pay the taxes without Papa needing to leave to work on the railroad. Papa explains that the cotton pays for living expenses. To pay the mortgage and taxes, he must work on the railroad.

TEXT TALK

Why does Papa not want to leave on Sunday?

See paragraph 11: He thinks things aren't over with Mr. Wallace.

Why does Papa need his railroad job?

See paragraphs 13–15: The family uses the railroad money to pay the mortgage and taxes.

Roll of Thunder, Hear My Cry

NOTES

Skill: Connotation and Denotation

I am not sure what this word means, but I can tell that Papa is very happy because he seems excited about the dinner. In this context, it seems like he is looking down at the table because he sees the dinner as he comes into the room. I think the word 'beam' means that he has a big smile on his face because he is very happy about seeing the dinner.

The third meaning of beam in the dictionary seems to fit the context of the sentence. It describes Papa's happy reaction when he sees the feast on the table. I was right!

9 Quickly I poured the rest of the butter beans into the bowl and hurried across the kitchen to the table. As Mama and Papa entered, I slid onto the bench beside Little Man and Christopher-John. Papa beamed down at the table.

10 "Well, look-a-here!" he exclaimed. "Good ole butter beans and cornbread! You better come on, Mr. Morrison! You too, son!" he called. "These womenfolks done gone and fixed us a feast."

11 After school was out, spring drooped quickly toward summer; yet Papa had not left for the railroad. He seemed to be waiting for something, and I secretly hoped that whatever that something was, it would never come so that he would not leave. But one evening as he, Mama, Big Ma, Mr. Morrison, and Stacey sat on the front porch while Christopher-John, Little Man, and I dashed around the yard chasing fireflies, I overheard him say, "Sunday I'm gonna have to go. Don't want to though. I got this gut feeling it ain't over yet. It's too easy."

12 I released the firefly **imprisoned** in my hand and sat beside Papa and Stacey on the steps. "Papa, please," I said, leaning against his leg, "don't go this year." Stacey looked out into the falling night, his face resigned, and said nothing.

13 Papa put out his large hand and caressed my face. "Got to, Cassie girl," he said softly. "Baby, there's bills to pay and ain't no money coming in. Your mama's got no job come fall and there's the **mortgage** and next year's taxes to think of."

14 "But, Papa, we planted more cotton this year. Won't that pay the taxes?"

15 Papa shook his head. "With Mr. Morrison here we was able to plant more, but that cotton is for living on; the railroad money is for the taxes and the mortgage."

16 I looked back at Mama wanting her to speak, to persuade him to stay, but when I saw her face I knew that she would not. She had known he would leave, just as we all had known.

17 "Papa, just another week or two, couldn't you—"

18 "I can't, baby. May have lost my job already."

19 "But Papa—"

20 "Cassie, that's enough now," Mama said from the deepening shadows.

 SELECTION VOCABULARY

imprisoned / encarcelado/a *verb* confined or restrained in any way

 ELL
- What does Cassie have "imprisoned"?
- What does she do with what she has "imprisoned"?

mortgage / la hipoteca *noun* a loan of money to buy a house or property

 ELL
- How do you know the "mortgage" is a bill?
- On what kind of property do the Logans live?

21 I grew quiet and Papa put his arms around Stacey and me, his hands falling casually over our shoulders. From the edge of the lawn where Little Man and Christopher-John had **ventured** after lightning bugs, Little Man called, "Somebody's coming!" A few minutes later Mr. Avery and Mr. Lanier emerged from the dusk and walked up the sloping lawn. Mama sent Stacey and me to get more chairs for the porch, then we settled back beside Papa still sitting on the steps, his back propped against a pillar facing the visitors.

22 "You goin' up to the store tomorrow, David?" Mr. Avery asked after all the amenities had been said. Since the first trip in January, Mr. Morrison had made one other trip to Vicksburg, but Papa had not gone with him.

23 Papa motioned to Mr. Morrison. "Mr. Morrison and me going the day after tomorrow. Your wife brought down that list of things you need yesterday."

24 Mr. Avery cleared his throat nervously. "It's—it's that list I come 'bout, David. . . . I don't want them things no more."

25 The porch grew silent.

26 When no one said anything, Mr. Avery glanced at Mr. Lanier, and Mr. Lanier shook his head and continued. "Mr. Granger making it hard on us, David. Said we gonna have to give him sixty percent of the cotton, 'stead of fifty . . . now that the cotton's planted and it's too late to plant more. . . . Don't s'pose though that it makes much difference. The way cotton sells these days, seems the more we plant, the less money we gets anyways—"

27 Mr. Avery's coughing interrupted him and he waited patiently until the coughing had stopped before he went on. "I'm gonna be hard put to pay that debt in Vicksburg, David, but I'm gonna. . . . I want you to know that."

. . .

28 Mr. Avery's coughing started again and for a while there was only the coughing and the silence. But when the coughing ceased, Mr. Lanier said, "I pray to God there was a way we could stay in this thing, but we can't go on no chain gang, David."

29 Papa nodded. "Don't expect you to, Silas."

30 Mr. Avery laughed softly. "We sure had 'em goin' for a time though, didn't we?"

31 "Yes," agreed Papa quietly, "we sure did."

NOTES

Skill: Theme

This conversation shows it's hard to prepare for bad things without getting too scared. The contrast between Mama and Papa shows this theme. When he tries to calm her, she feels like he is hiding something, which makes her more worried.

Theme

How does the reader use evidence to infer multiple themes?

The reader notes that Mama is nervous and that Papa tries to reassure her in their dialogue. The setting also plays an important role in this theme of anxiety since they are being threatened by a local store owner. Cassie shows the second theme of hope in her dialogue with Papa, telling him she wants him to stay.

Skills Focus

QUESTION 2: Story Structure

The author is developing the plot by including Mr. Avery's and Mr. Lanier's dialogue explaining why they won't shop in Vicksburg anymore. The reader is left wondering what will happen next in the story and how the Logan family's challenges will be resolved.

Skills Focus

QUESTION 3: Connotation and Denotation

The dictionary indicates that *sloping* can be an adjective or a verb. In this sentence, *sloping* is an adjective because it describes the lawn. The dictionary defines the adjective as "inclined" or "having a slant." This makes sense, since Mr. Avery and Mr. Lanier are walking up the lawn.

TEXT TALK

How is Mr. Granger making life difficult for Mr. Avery and Mr. Lanier?

See paragraph 26: He is threatening to take sixty percent of their cotton, instead of the usual fifty percent.

SELECTION VOCABULARY

venture / atreverse *verb* to do or undertake something despite the risk or danger involved

ELL
• What are Little Man and Christopher-John doing?
• Where are they doing it?

Skills Focus

QUESTION 1: Theme

Papa uses the fig tree to symbolize the Logan family and the larger oak and walnut trees to symbolize the more powerful whites in the community, like Thurston Wallace, who block the actions of the black farmers.

TEXT TALK

Why is Papa upset with Stacey?

See paragraphs 32–35: Stacey is upset with Mr. Avery and Mr. Lanier for backing out of using the Vicksburg store. Papa is upset because Stacey doesn't understand the pressures the two farmers face because they do not own their own land.

What other questions can you ask and answer?

Answers will vary.

B What is Cassie learning about their family and its relationship to the land?

---

32 When the men had left, Stacey snapped, "They got no right pulling out! Just 'cause them Wallaces threaten them one time they go jumping all over themselves to get out like a bunch of scared jackrabbits—"

33 Papa stood suddenly and grabbed Stacey upward. "You, boy, don't you get so grown you go to talking 'bout more than you know. Them men, they doing what they've gotta do. You got any idea what a risk they took just to go shopping in Vicksburg in the first place? They go on that chain gang and their families got nothing. They'll get kicked off that plot of land they tend and there'll be no place for them to go. You understand that?"

34 "Y-yessir," said Stacey. Papa released him and stared moodily into the night. "You were born blessed, boy, with land of your own. If you hadn't been, you'd cry out for it while you try to survive . . . like Mr. Lanier and Mr. Avery. Maybe even do what they doing now. It's hard on a man to give up, but sometimes it seems there just ain't nothing else he can do."

35 "I . . . I'm sorry, Papa," Stacey muttered.

36 After a moment, Papa reached out and draped his arm over Stacey's shoulder.

37 "Papa," I said, standing to join them, "we giving up too?"

38 Papa looked down at me and brought me closer, then waved his hand toward the drive. "You see that fig tree over yonder, Cassie? Them other trees all around . . . that oak and walnut, they're a lot bigger and they take up more room and give so much shade they almost **overshadow** that little ole fig. But that fig tree's got roots that run deep, and it belongs in that yard as much as that oak and walnut. It keeps on blooming, bearing good fruit year after year, knowing all the time it'll never get as big as them other trees. Just keeps on growing and doing what it gotta do. It don't give up. It give up, it'll die. There's a lesson to be learned from that little tree, Cassie girl, 'cause we're like it. We keep doing what we gotta, and we don't give up. We can't."

Excerpted from *Roll of Thunder, Hear My Cry* by Mildred D. Taylor, published by Puffin Books.

 14 Reading & Writing Companion

 SELECTION VOCABULARY

overshadow / eclipsar *verb* to cause something to seem less important than something else

 ELL
• What is being "overshadowed"?
• How do the trees compare in size?

Reading Comprehension OPTIONAL

Have students complete the digital reading comprehension questions ✅ when they finish reading.

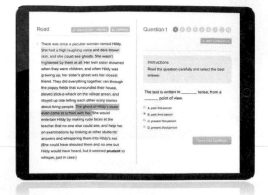

ANSWER KEY

QUESTION 1: A	**QUESTION 5:** C	**QUESTION 9:**
QUESTION 2: B	**QUESTION 6:** C	*See first chart.*
QUESTION 3: B	**QUESTION 7:** A	**QUESTION 10:**
QUESTION 4: C	**QUESTION 8:** D	*See second chart.*

Evidence of the Family's Struggle	Not Evidence
"I'm feeling scared, David," she said.	"As the three of them washed up on the back porch, Mama went to the end of the porch where Papa stood alone."
"'May have lost my job already.'"	"I released the firefly imprisoned in my hand and sat beside Papa and Stacey on the steps."
"'The way cotton sells these days, seems the more we plant, the less money we gets anyways—"	"After a moment, Papa reached out and draped his arm over Stacey's shoulder."

Evidence	Not Evidence
". . . I pray to God there was a way we could stay in this thing, but we can't go on no chain gang, David."	"Mama sighed and stared out across the plowed field to the sloping pasture land."

Connect and Extend OPTIONAL

CONNECT TO EXTENDED WRITING PROJECT

Students can use *Roll of Thunder, Hear My Cry* as a mentor text for their Extended Writing Project. They may consider using dialogue, as Mildred D. Taylor does, to illustrate relationships between characters.

BEYOND THE BOOK

Art: Social Hierarchy Tree

This excerpt ends with Papa using the three trees on their property to make a point about life as an African American in the Deep South. Ask students to:

- Think about different groups in society today who are marginalized, or have less power.

- Draw a picture representing different groups in society and their levels of power using the tree metaphor.

When students have completed their visuals, break them into groups of four, and allow them time to present their visuals.

To reflect, ask students:

- Did your group members identify the same groups in society or were there differences??

- What was most challenging about representing the different levels of power using the tree as a metaphor?

Think Questions

Circulate as students answer Think Questions independently. Scaffolds for these questions are shown on the opposite page.

QUESTION 1: Textual Evidence

Thurston Wallace and Mr. Granger are angry that some of the black farmers are shopping in Vicksburg, rather than in Wallace's store. Papa says Wallace is "talking 'bout how he's not gonna let a few smart colored folks ruin his business." Papa is worried this is going to cause trouble.

QUESTION 2: Textual Evidence

Unlike Mr. Avery and Mr. Lanier, Papa owns his land. He also works on the railroad for part of the year to earn money for the mortgage and taxes. Mr. Lanier and Mr. Avery can be kicked off the land they tend and end up with nothing.

QUESTION 3: Textual Evidence

Answers will vary but may include the following examples:

- "doing what they've gotta do"
- "what a risk they took"
- "go on that chain gang"
- "get kicked off that plot of land"

Student descriptions should explain that Papa understands that it is hard to stand up for what you believe in when you have a lot to lose.

QUESTION 4: Context Clues

I think *imprison* must mean "to confine in some way." The word is used to describe how Cassie has the firefly trapped in her hand.

QUESTION 5: Context Clues

I think *ventured* must mean "looked for or searched for." The word is used to describe how Little Man and Christopher-John went looking for lighting bugs.

First Read

Read *Roll of Thunder, Hear My Cry*. After you read, complete the Think Questions below.

☁ THINK QUESTIONS

1. Why are Thurston Wallace and Mr. Granger angry with the black farmers? Cite textual evidence from the selection to support your answer.

2. Write two or three sentences describing why Papa is in a better position than Mr. Avery and Mr. Lanier to stand up to Thurston Wallace. Cite textual evidence from the selection to support your answer.

3. Voice is the use of language that conveys the distinctive personality of the writer or speaker, the narrator, or a particular character. In paragraph 33, what words or phrases does Papa use when talking with Stacey that give you a sense of his personality? How would you describe his personality? Cite textual evidence from the selection to support your answer.

4. Find the word **imprisoned** in paragraph 12 of *Roll of Thunder, Hear My Cry*. Use context clues in the surrounding sentences, as well as the sentence in which the word appears, to determine the word's meaning. Write your definition here and identify clues that helped you figure out its meaning.

5. Use context to determine the meaning of the word **ventured** as it is used in *Roll of Thunder, Hear My Cry* in paragraph 21. Write your definition here and identify clues that helped you figure out its meaning. Then check the meaning in a dictionary.

Reading & Writing Companion 15

Think Questions

Use the scaffolds below to differentiate instruction for your **ELL** English Language Learners and **A** Approaching grade-level learners.

ELL **BEGINNING** Write a response using the <u>word bank</u> and <u>sentence frames</u>.

INTERMEDIATE Write a response using the <u>sentence frames</u>.

ADVANCED, ADVANCED HIGH Write a response using the <u>Text-Dependent Question Guide</u>.

A **APPROACHING** Write a response using the <u>Text-Dependent Question Guide</u>.

	INTERMEDIATE	APPROACHING
BEGINNING		ADVANCED, ADVANCED HIGH
Word Bank	Sentence Frames	Text-Dependent Question Guide
gotta do lose owns hand confine outside ruin railroad kicked off shopping risk trouble search for	Thurston Wallace and Mr. Granger are angry because the black farmers are ____ in Vicksburg. Wallace thinks it will ____ his business. Papa is worried about ____.	1. • Why are Thurston Wallace and Mr. Granger angry? • What does Wallace think will happen to his business? • What is Papa worried about?
	Unlike Mr. Avery and Mr. Lanier, Papa ____ his land. Papa also works on the ____. Mr. Lanier and Mr. Avery can be ____ the land they tend.	2. • What is different about the land the men farm? • How does Papa earn extra money? • What can happen to Mr. Avery and Mr. Lanier?
	Papa tells Stacey that Mr. Avery and Mr. Lanier were "doing what they ____." Papa says Stacey has no idea "what a ____ they took." This tells me that Papa understands that it is hard to stand up for what you believe in when you have a lot to ____.	3. • Papa is upset with Stacey because Stacey does not understand why Mr. Avery and Mr. Lanier backed down. • What words and phrases help me know this? • What does this tell me about Papa's personality?
	The firefly is imprisoned in Cassie's ____. Being able to release the firefly tells me that *imprisoned* means "to ____."	4. • Read: "I released the firefly **imprisoned** in my hand and sat beside Papa and Stacey on the steps." • Where is the firefly "imprisoned"? • What does the clue that Cassie can release the firefly tell me about the meaning of the word *imprisoned*?
	Little Man and Christopher-John are ____. The clue that Little Man and Christopher-John are "after lightning bugs" tells me that *ventured* means "to ____."	5. • Read: "From the edge of the lawn where Little Man and Christopher-John had **ventured** after lightning bugs, Little Man called, 'Somebody's coming!'" • Where are Little Man and Christopher-John? • What does the clue that Little Man and Christopher-John are "after lightning bugs" tell me about the meaning of the word *ventured*?

Skill: Connotation and Denotation

Introduce the Skill

Watch the Concept Definition video and read the following definitions with your students.

The **denotation** of a word is its dictionary definition. The **connotation** of a word is the idea or feeling that a word suggests, or that our culture or our emotions give the word. A word's connotation can be positive, negative, or neutral. For example, the words *cheap* and *affordable* both denote "inexpensive." However, *cheap* connotes something that is of low quality.

To determine the connotation of a word, readers must use **context**, such as the genre or subject of a text. They also use **context clues**, or the surrounding words that help a reader determine a word's meaning. To verify the denotation of a word and check for possible connotations, readers can consult reference materials such as dictionaries, glossaries, and thesauruses. To **analyze** an author's word choices, readers consider the emotional impact of language in the text for its potential effect on readers.

TURN AND TALK

1. What is one of your favorite go-to resources for finding word meanings?

2. Can you think of a time recently when you came across an unfamiliar word that had multiple meanings? What strategy did you use to figure out the word?

SPEAKING FRAMES
- One of my favorite resources is ____. I like this resource because ____.
- I found the word ____. I used ____ to figure it out.

Skill:
Connotation and Denotation

Use the Checklist to analyze Connotation and Denotation in *Roll of Thunder, Hear My Cry.* Refer to the sample student annotations about Connotation and Denotation in the text.

••• CHECKLIST FOR CONNOTATION AND DENOTATION

In order to identify the denotative meanings of words and phrases, use the following steps:

✓ first, note unfamiliar words and phrases; key words used to describe important characters, events, and ideas; or words that inspire an emotional reaction

✓ next, verify the denotative meaning of words by consulting a reference material such as a dictionary, glossary, or thesaurus

To better understand the meaning of words and phrases as they are used in a text, including connotative meanings, use the following questions:

✓ What is the genre or subject of the text? How does that affect the possible meaning of a word or phrase?

✓ Does the word create a positive, negative, or neutral emotion?

✓ What synonyms or alternative phrasing help you describe the connotative meaning of the word?

To determine the meaning of words and phrases as they are used in a text, including connotative meanings, use the following questions:

✓ What is the meaning of the word or phrase? What is the connotation as well as the denotation?

✓ If I substitute a synonym based on denotation, is the meaning the same? How does it change the meaning of the text?

V   SKILL VOCABULARY

denotation / la denotación *noun* the literal or dictionary meaning of a word, in contrast to the feelings or ideas that the word suggests COGNATE

connotation / la connotación *noun* an idea or feeling that a word suggests in addition to its literal or primary meaning COGNATE

context / el contexto *noun* the set of facts or circumstances that surround a situation or event COGNATE

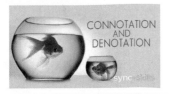

Skill:
Connotation and Denotation

Reread paragraph 21 of *Roll of Thunder, Hear My Cry*. Then, using the Checklist on the previous page, answer the multiple-choice questions below.

YOUR TURN

1. This question has two parts. First, answer Part A. Then, answer Part B.

   Part A: What does the word **ventured** mean as it is used in the context of paragraph 21?

   ○ A. set out
   ○ B. yelled loudly
   ○ C. remembered
   ○ D. caught

   Part B: Review the dictionary definitions of the word *venture* below.

   > **ven·ture** '/ven(t)SHər/ *verb*
   > 1. to journey or travel to do something
   > 2. to dare to do or say something that may be considered rude
   > 3. to expose (something) to the risk of loss

   Which definition BEST supports the conclusion drawn in Part A?

   ○ A. Definition 1
   ○ B. Definition 2
   ○ C. Definition 3
   ○ D. None of the above

Please note that excerpts and passages in the StudySync® library and this workbook are intended as touchstones to generate interest in an author's work. The excerpts and passages do not substitute for the reading of entire texts, and StudySync® strongly recommends that students seek out and purchase the whole literary or informational work in order to experience it as the author intended. Links to online resellers are available in our digital library. In addition, complete works may be ordered through an authorized reseller by filling out and returning to StudySync® the order form enclosed in this workbook.

Reading & Writing Companion   17

Your Turn

Ask students to complete the Your Turn Activity.

QUESTION 1

Part A

A. Correct. In this scene, Little Man and Christopher-John are described as having interacted with lightning bugs at the edge of the lawn. The two set out to go after the bugs.

B. Incorrect. The boys are not yelling at the lightning bugs; they call to the adults later in the paragraph.

C. Incorrect. This scene does not describe a flashback; they are not remembering that they chased lightning bugs.

D. Incorrect. There is no indication in this paragraph that the boys actually caught lightning bugs; they simply went after them.

Part B

A. Correct. This definition fits best because the boys have gone after the lightning bugs in paragraph 21.

B. Incorrect. There is no evidence in the passage to support this answer.

C. Incorrect. There is no evidence in the passage to support this answer.

D. Incorrect. The first definition of venture fits the context in paragraph 21.

V SKILL VOCABULARY

context clue / la clave del contexto *noun* a hint in the surrounding text that can help a reader infer the meaning of an unfamiliar word, phrase, or description

analyze / analizar *verb* to consider in detail and discover essential features or meaning COGNATE

Skill: Theme

Introduce the Skill

Watch the Concept Definition video and read the following definitions with your students.

The **topic** of a literary work is the subject of the work. It is usually expressed as a noun. The **theme** is the central idea or message of a work of literature. It is often expressed as a general statement about life. For example, the topic of a literary work might be love. The theme would be what the writer suggests about love: that it is wonderful or painful or maybe both at once. A literary work may have more than one theme.

Sometimes a writer states a theme directly. More often, though, theme is revealed gradually. In short stories, novels, and dramas, theme is revealed through elements such as character, setting, and plot, what the characters do and say, and how these elements affect the events that take place. When a theme is not stated directly, a reader will have to infer the theme. To **infer** means to determine something by using reasoning and textual evidence.

TURN AND TALK

1. What is one theme of your favorite book, TV show, or movie?

2. What other themes are evident in that book, TV show, or movie?

ELL SPEAKING FRAMES
- In the (book/TV show/movie) ___, one theme is ___.
- I know that is the theme because ___.
- This (book/TV show/movie) has other themes, too. For example, ___.
- I know those are themes because ___.

Roll of Thunder, Hear My Cry

 Skill: Theme

Use the Checklist to analyze Theme in *Roll of Thunder, Hear My Cry*. Refer to the sample student annotations about Theme in the text.

••• CHECKLIST FOR THEME

In order to identify a theme or central idea in a text, note the following:

✓ the topic of the text

✓ whether or not the theme is stated directly in the text

✓ details in the text that may reveal the theme
   - the title and chapter headings
   - details about the setting
   - a narrator's or speaker's tone
   - characters' thoughts, actions, and dialogue
   - the central conflict in the story's plot
   - the resolution of the conflict

✓ analyze how characters and the problems they face are affected by the setting, and what impact this may have on how the theme is developed

To determine a theme or central idea of a text and how it is conveyed through particular details, consider the following questions:

✓ What is a theme or central idea of the text?

✓ What details helped to reveal that theme or central idea?

✓ When did you become aware of that theme? For instance, did the story's conclusion reveal the theme?

18 Reading & Writing Companion
Please note that excerpts and passages in the StudySync® library and this workbook are intended as touchstones to generate interest in an author's work. The excerpts and passages do not substitute for the reading of entire texts, and StudySync® strongly recommends that students seek out and purchase the whole literary or informational work in order to experience it as the author intended. Links to online resellers are available in our digital library. In addition, complete works may be ordered through an authorized reseller by filling out and returning to StudySync® the order form enclosed in this workbook.

V   SKILL VOCABULARY

topic / el tema *noun* the subject of a literary work, usually expressed as a single word or phrase in the form of a noun

theme / el tema *noun* the central idea or message of a work of literature, often expressed as a general statement about life

infer / inferir *verb* to determine something by using reasoning and evidence from the text COGNATE

Skill:
Theme

Reread paragraphs 1–8 of *Roll of Thunder, Hear My Cry*. Then, using the Checklist on the previous page, answer the multiple-choice questions below.

 YOUR TURN

1. What can the reader infer about Mrs. Logan from these lines of dialogue?

   ○ A. She is shy about speaking to her husband.
   ○ B. She is not afraid to confront problems head on.
   ○ C. She expects her husband to protect her.
   ○ D. She feels easily scared over small events.

2. What can the reader infer about Mr. Logan from these lines of dialogue?

   ○ A. He doesn't trust his wife with information.
   ○ B. He is often silent during a conflict.
   ○ C. He remains reasonable in the face of conflict.
   ○ D. He is quick to anger.

3. What theme can readers infer from the dialogue between Mr. and Mrs. Logan?

   ○ A. It's best for a family if secrets are kept from the children.
   ○ B. When a person feels fear, he or she should back down from a conflict.
   ○ C. Don't go looking for trouble, but don't shy away from defending your rights either.
   ○ D. It's best to ignore problems until they work themselves out or go away on their own.

SkillsTV

Project the SkillsTV episode ▶ and pause at the following times to prompt discussion:

1:06 How does the student use Mama's actions to infer her emotional state?

1:15 How does the student use historical context as a way to understand the characters?

2:25 How does the student use punctuation to infer a shift in Cassie's emotional state?

Your Turn

Ask students to complete the Your Turn Activity.

QUESTION 1

A. Incorrect. Mrs. Logan's voice is barely audible because she doesn't want the children to overhear her conversation with her husband.

B. Correct. Mrs. Logan says, "If there's trouble, I want to know."

C. Incorrect. Mrs. Logan wants to discuss problems with her husband.

D. Incorrect. Mrs. Logan is scared over a big threat from white neighbors.

QUESTION 2

A. Incorrect. He shares the reason for Mr. Jamison's visit with his wife.

B. Incorrect. He doesn't reply immediately, but then he speaks.

C. Correct. He is aware of the situation, but he does not give in to fear.

D. Incorrect. He is comforting to his wife rather than angry over Mr. Jamison's visit.

QUESTION 3

A. Incorrect. The Logan children are aware that the family is shopping in Vicksburg as part of a protest against racism.

B. Incorrect. Mr. Logan doesn't suggest that Mrs. Logan's fear means the family should back out of the conflict.

C. Correct. Mr. Logan cautions against early fear, but he makes no suggestion that the family will back down if the problem becomes real.

D. Incorrect. Mr. Logan doesn't ignore the potential problem. He says to wait until the problem becomes real.

Skill: Story Structure

Introduce the Skill

Watch the Concept Definition video  and read the following definitions with your students.

Story structure is the framework writers use to develop the events of the **plot**. Any plot has a central problem or conflict which the story introduces, builds to a climax, and finally solves. The story may be character-driven, exploring one person's emotions, or it could be driven by suspense, with a complicated sequence of events that takes many twists and turns. The events may or may not be presented in chronological order. For example, an author who wishes to build tension may begin with a dramatic **flashback** before introducing the present situation in a story. A character-driven novel might describe events from the point of view of one character, and how the events change him or her. Whatever story structure an author chooses to use, **analyzing** how the events of a chapter or scene fit into the overall structure can help readers identify how it also contributes to the development of the **theme** and **setting**.

TURN AND TALK

1. Think of a movie, television show, or book you like. How are the stories you like best usually structured? Do they vary? What kind of structure do you like best?

2. How does understanding how a story is structured help you to better understand plot?

ELL SPEAKING FRAMES

- One [TV show/movie] that I like is ____.
- [TV show/movie title] is structured using ____.
- Story structure helps me understand plot because ____.

Roll of Thunder, Hear My Cry

Skill:
Story Structure

Use the Checklist to analyze Story Structure in *Roll of Thunder, Hear My Cry*. Refer to the sample student annotations about Story Structure in the text.

••• CHECKLIST FOR STORY STRUCTURE

In order to identify how a particular sentence, chapter, scene or stanza fits into the overall structure of a text, note the following:

✓ the author's use of description, dialogue, and narration and how each develops the events of the plot

✓ the pattern the author uses to organize the events within a story or chapter
- chronological, or in time order
- events out of time order

✓ any literary devices the author uses, such as flashback, a part of a story that shows something that happened in the past

✓ any particular sentence, chapter, scene, or a stanza in a poem that contributes to the development of the setting, the plot, and the theme

✓ how a particular sentence, chapter, scene, or a stanza in a poem fit into the overall structure

To analyze how a particular sentence, chapter, scene, or stanza fits into the overall structure of a text and contributes to the development of the theme, setting, or plot, consider the following questions:

✓ What are the key events in the story and when did they take place?

✓ What impact does the order of events that take place in the story have on the theme, setting, or plot?

✓ What literary devices does the author use? How does it affect the development of the plot?

✓ How does a particular sentence, chapter, scene, or a stanza in a poem fits into the overall structure? How do they contribute to the development of the theme, setting, or plot?

V SKILL VOCABULARY

story structure / la estructura de la historia *noun* the outline a writer uses to organize and tell a story

plot / la trama *noun* the sequence of events that form a story

flashback / la escena retrospectiva *noun* a scene in a story, play, movie, or TV show that is set in a time earlier than the events in the main story

analyze / analizar *verb* to consider in detail and discover essential features or meaning COGNATE

Skill:
Story Structure

Reread paragraphs 22–26 of *Roll of Thunder, Hear My Cry*. Then, using the Checklist on the previous page, answer the multiple-choice questions below.

YOUR TURN

1. This question has two parts. First, answer Part A. Then, answer Part B.

   Part A: Which of the following statements best summarizes how the dialogue in this passage moves the plot forward?

   ○ A. Farmers are making less money even though they're planting more cotton.
   ○ B. Mr. Avery doesn't need anything from Vicksburg on this trip.
   ○ C. Mr. Avery and Mr. Lanier need to give Mr. Granger 60 percent of their cotton.
   ○ D. Mr. Avery is backing out of shopping in Vicksburg because Mr. Granger is threatening him.

   Part B: Which of the following lines of dialogue BEST supports the summary selected in Part A?

   ○ A. "You goin' to the store tomorrow, David?"
   ○ B. "Your wife brought down that list of things you need yesterday."
   ○ C. "It's—it's that list I come 'bout, David... I don't want them things no more."
   ○ D. "The way cotton sells these days, seems the more we plant, the less money we gets anyways."

SKILL VOCABULARY

theme / el tema *noun* the central idea or message of a work of literature, often expressed as a general statement about life

setting / el escenario *noun* the time and place of the story

---

Your Turn

Ask students to complete the Your Turn Activity.

QUESTION 1

Part A

A. Incorrect. While this observation may be true, it does not help move the plot forward.

B. Incorrect. This statement doesn't reveal the real reason why Mr. Avery doesn't want to buy items in Vicksburg anymore.

C. Incorrect. This statement only explains the motivation behind Mr. Avery's and Mr. Lanier's change of heart, but not their actual decision to stop shopping in Vicksburg.

D. **Correct.** This statement summarizes both the plot event (backing out) and the reason for it (Granger's threat), therefore setting up the events to come.

Part B

A. Incorrect. This question does not signal a change in the plot.

B. Incorrect. This event does not change the direction of the plot.

C. **Correct.** This sentence signals a change in the plot—Mr. Avery is backing out of shopping in Vicksburg.

D. Incorrect. This is simply an observation and does not advance the plot.

SkillsTV

Project the SkillsTV episode ▶ and pause at the following times to prompt discussion:

0:16 What do students learn about the Logan family at the beginning of the story

0:44 During their conversation on the porch, what do Papa and Mama discuss? How does Mama react to the information Papa reveals? How does their dialogue contribute to the development of the plot?

2:14 How do the students respond to Mama's question? Is it an indication of trouble to come? How does the information fit into the overall structure of the text and help move the plot forward?

Close Read

Skills Focus

Have students read and annotate the text independently using the Skills Focus questions.

QUESTION 1: Theme
See paragraph 38.

QUESTION 2: Story Structure
See paragraphs 24–27.

QUESTION 3: Connotation and Denotation
See paragraph 21.

QUESTION 4: Connect to Essential Question
See paragraphs 13–15.

CHECK FOR SUCCESS

If students struggle to respond to Skills Focus Question #1, ask students the following questions:

- What do the trees in paragraph 38 symbolize?

- How is the fig tree's position in the yard like the Logans' position in the community?

- What is the parallel between what the fig tree does to survive and what the Logans do to survive?

Have students transition to read and annotate independently once they have successfully completed the first Skills Focus prompt.

Roll of Thunder, Hear My Cry

Close Read

Reread *Roll of Thunder, Hear My Cry*. As you reread, complete the Skills Focus questions below. Then use your answers and annotations from the questions to help you complete the Write activity.

◎ SKILLS FOCUS

1. Reread the last paragraph of the excerpt. Analyze how the trees in the Logans' backyard symbolize, or represent, their relationship with people like Thurston Wallace.

2. Identify parts of *Roll of Thunder, Hear My Cry* where the author uses specific words and phrases to create a tense atmosphere and how this relates to the overall plot.

3. Locate the word *sloping*. Analyze how the word functions in the sentence to help you determine which dictionary definition best represents the meaning of *sloping* in this context.

4. Identify parts in the story that show how Cassie's relationship with her family impacts her life and helps her see things in a new way.

✏ WRITE

DISCUSSION: In this excerpt, the author builds and releases tension through events in the plot. With each new challenge that the characters have to face, a new theme is revealed or suggested. Overall, do you feel that the author's themes, or messages, are positive or negative? As you prepare for your discussion, use specific parts of the text as well as supporting details to help you form an opinion. Additionally, include any lingering questions you have regarding characters and events.

Writer's Notebook

Connect to Essential Question: Give students time to reflect on how *Roll of Thunder, Hear My Cry* connects to the unit's essential question "How do relationships shape us?" by freewriting in their Writer's Notebooks.

 Beginning & Intermediate

Read aloud the unit's essential question: "How do relationships shape us?" Encourage students to draw their connections or allow students to write in their native language. Circulate around the room, prompting students for their thoughts as they respond orally or through pantomime.

Advanced & Advanced High

Allow students to share their connections orally in pairs or small groups before freewriting.

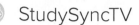

StudySyncTV

Project the StudySyncTV episode and pause at the following times to prompt discussion:

2:39 How do the students use textual evidence to uncover a fear to add to their list?

4:03 How does the disagreement over whether Papa should share economic information with Cassie lead the students to include "information" as a hope in their list?

6:23 How does the group reach and agree upon the conclusion that Papa is trying to make Cassie stronger?

Collaborative Conversation

SCAFFOLDS

Break students into collaborative conversation groups to discuss the Close Read prompt. Ask students to use the StudySyncTV episode as a model for their discussion. Remind them to reference their Skills Focus annotations in their discussion.

In this excerpt, the author builds and releases tension through events in the plot. With each new challenge that the characters have to face, a new theme is revealed or suggested. Overall, do you feel that the author's themes, or messages, are positive or negative? As you prepare for your discussion, use specific parts of the text as well as supporting details to help you form an opinion. Additionally, include any lingering questions you have regarding characters and events.

Use the scaffolds below to differentiate instruction for your **ELL** English Language Learners and **A** Approaching grade-level learners.

ELL **BEGINNING, INTERMEDIATE** Use the <u>discussion guide</u> and <u>speaking frames</u> to discuss with support from the teacher.

ADVANCED, ADVANCED HIGH Use the <u>discussion guide</u> and <u>speaking frames</u> to discuss in mixed-level groups.

A **APPROACHING** Use the <u>discussion guide</u> to discuss in mixed-level groups.

APPROACHING
ADVANCED, ADVANCED HIGH
BEGINNING, INTERMEDIATE

Discussion Guide	Speaking Frames
1. What challenges do the characters face?	• The characters face challenges, such as ____. • This causes a feeling of ____.
2. How does the author build and release tension in your text example?	• At the beginning/middle/end of the story, ____ happens and causes ____. • The author builds tension by ____ and releases tension by ____.
3. What theme does this tension reveal?	• The tension shows that the characters ____. • This develops the theme of ____ because ____.

Review Prompt and Rubric

Before students begin writing, review the writing prompt and rubric with the class.

REFLECTION: As you write, be sure to

- describe your best contribution to the discussion;
- identify a specific goal for improving your contributions to future discussions.

ELL **PROMPT GUIDE**

A
- Is the author's theme, or message, **positive** or negative?
- What makes you say this?

- What lingering questions do you have regarding characters and events?

Score	Reflection	Language and Conventions
4	The writer clearly reflects on how well he or she posed questions about characters and events and responded to classmates' comments about the text's themes, as well as his or her own participation. The writer consistently refers to specific examples from the discussion.	The writer demonstrates a consistent command of grammar, punctuation, and usage conventions. Although minor errors may be evident, they do not detract from the fluency or the clarity of the essay.
3	The writer reflects on how well he or she posed questions about characters and events and responded to classmates' comments about the text's themes, as well as his or her own participation. The writer refers to specific examples from the discussion most of the time.	The writer demonstrates an adequate command of grammar, punctuation, and usage conventions. Although some errors may be evident, they create few (if any) disruptions in the fluency of the writing or the clarity of the essay.
2	The writer begins to reflect on how well he or she posed questions about characters and events and responded to classmates' comments about the text's themes, as well as his or her own participation. The writer refers to specific examples from the discussion some of the time.	The writer demonstrates a partial command of grammar, punctuation, and usage conventions. Some distracting errors may be evident, at times creating minor disruptions in the fluency or clarity of the writing.
1	The writer attempts to reflect on how well he or she posed questions about characters and events and responded to classmates' comments about the text's themes, as well as his or her own participation in the response. The writer refers to few, if any examples from the discussion.	The writer demonstrates little or no command of grammar, punctuation, and usage conventions. Serious and persistent errors create disruptions in the fluency of the writing and sometimes interfere with meaning.
0	The writer does not provide a relevant response to the prompt or does not provide a response at all.	Serious and persistent errors overwhelm the writing and interfere with the meaning of the response as a whole, making the writer's meaning impossible to understand.

Write

SCAFFOLDS

Ask students to complete the writing assignment using textual evidence to support their answers.

Use the scaffolds below to differentiate instruction for your **ELL** English Language Learners and **A** Approaching grade-level learners.

ELL **BEGINNING** With the help of the <u>word bank</u>, write a response using <u>paragraph frame 1</u>.

INTERMEDIATE With the help of the <u>word bank</u>, write a response using <u>paragraph frames 1 and 2</u>.

ADVANCED, ADVANCED HIGH Write a response of differentiated length using the <u>sentence starters</u>.

A **APPROACHING** Write a response of differentiated length using the <u>sentence starters</u>.

BEGINNING	ADVANCED, ADVANCED HIGH
INTERMEDIATE	APPROACHING

Word Bank	Paragraph Frame 1	Paragraph Frame 2	Sentence Starters
good average evidence text questions examples characters theme	My discussion group talked about ____. I think my group did a(n) ____ job posing and responding to questions using ____ from the text. I think this because ____. Some people had ____ about ____. I added to the discussion by ____.	First I thought that the text's overall theme was ____. I asked a question about ____. Then another person answered and said ____. That made me realize ____. Now I think ____.	• My opinion of my group's performance is . . . • I have this opinion because . . . • I contributed to the discussion by . . . • When the discussion began, I asked . . . • When another student commented, I responded with . . . • I used evidence from the text when I said . . . • If I could change one thing about my contributions, it would be . . . • Next time, my discussion goal will be to . . .

Peer Review

Students should submit substantive feedback to two peers using the review instructions below.

• How well does the writer refer to specific examples from the discussion?
• What details does the writer provide to support his or her opinion about the text's themes?
• How well does the writer reflect on posing and responding to questions in the discussion?
• What does the writer do well in this reflection? What does the writer need to work on?

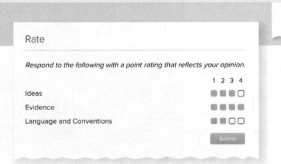

Rate

Respond to the following with a point rating that reflects your opinion.

	1 2 3 4
Ideas	■ ■ ■ □
Evidence	■ ■ ■ ■
Language and Conventions	■ ■ □ □

Submit

ELL **A** **SENTENCE FRAMES**

• You included examples ____ (most of the time / some of the time / not often).
• One idea you expressed well is ____.

• You posed a question about ____.
• You responded to a question about ____.
• You might improve by ____.

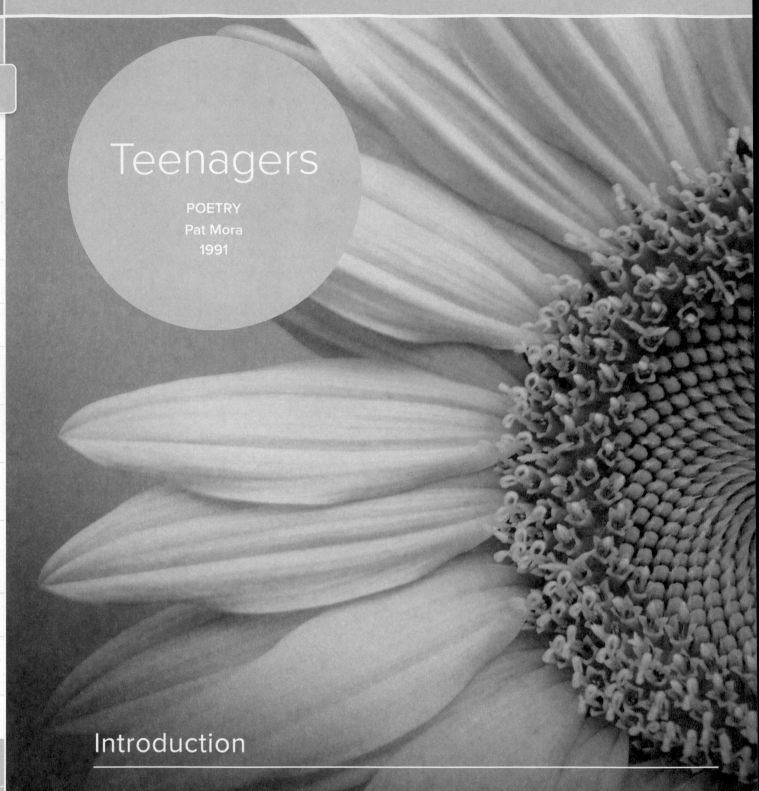

Teenagers

POETRY
Pat Mora
1991

Introduction

Pat Mora (b. 1942) is a celebrated Mexican-American author whose bilingual works explore themes of culture and identity among families in Texas and along the Southwestern border, where Mora was born and raised. Her 1991 poem "Teenagers" is written from the point of view of a parent who feels they have lost touch with their teenage children. In this brief, fourteen-line poem, Mora reflects upon a universal experience both parents and children endure as they age.

This poem details the lost connection a mother feels with her teenage children. The speaker describes how one day the children disappear to their rooms; the speaker notes that their doors stay shut, just like their lips. Around the house, it feels as if they have become strangers. Through the children's doors, the mother hears the children whisper, which sounds like code—one that she does not understand. Years pass and the teenagers emerge from their rooms. The mother recognizes their faces, but also notices how much they've grown as they walk past, glowing.

ELL Proficiency-leveled summaries and summaries in multiple languages are available digitally.

🔊 Audio and audio text highlighting are available with this text.

CONNECT TO ESSENTIAL QUESTION

How do relationships shape us?

In this poem, a mother reflects on how the children she has raised suddenly become strangers to her, silent and secretive teenagers, until one day they emerge from their silence as young adults, glowing "almost like pearls."

Access Complex Text

LEXILE: N/A   WORD COUNT: 73

The following areas may be challenging for students, particularly **ELL** English Language Learners and **A** Approaching grade-level learners.

Connection of Ideas	Organization	Genre
• The author uses many examples of figurative language. • Students may have difficulty using the figurative language the author employs to make inferences.	• The selection is written in the first-person, so readers only know what the main character thinks, feels, and hears. • This may present a challenge when students try to assess the motivations and conflicts of other characters.	• The poem is an example of free verse. It follows the rhythm of natural speech without consistent meter patterns and rhymes. • Students may have difficulty identifying the three stanzas as an account of teenage emotional development.

SCAFFOLDS   **ELL** ENGLISH LANGUAGE LEARNERS   **A** APPROACHING GRADE LEVEL   **B** BEYOND GRADE LEVEL

These icons identify differentiation strategies and scaffolded support for a variety of students. See the digital lesson plan for additional differentiation strategies and scaffolds.

Instructional Path

The print teacher's edition includes essential point-of-use instruction and planning tools. Complete lesson plans and program documents appear in your digital teacher account.

Skill: Making Inferences

Objectives: After reading and discussing a model, students will be able to make inferences in order to improve reading comprehension.

DIGITAL ONLY

First Read: Teenagers

Objectives: After an initial reading and discussion of the text, students will be able to use poetic devices to make inferences about the speaker and the poem as a whole.

Skill: Figurative Language

Objectives: After rereading and discussing a model of close reading, students will be able to describe how the poet's use of figurative language, such as metaphors, similes, and personification, achieves specific purposes.

Close Read: Teenagers

Objectives: After engaging in a close reading and discussion of the text, students will be able to explain how figurative language develops character and helps the reader understand more about the speaker.

Blast: Sonnets to Social Media

Objectives: After exploring background information and research links about a topic, students will respond to a question with a 140-character response.

DIGITAL ONLY

Progress Monitoring

Opportunities to Learn	Opportunities to Demonstrate Learning	Opportunities to Reteach

Making Inferences

⚙ Skill: Making Inferences	💬 First Read • Read and Annotate	⚙ Spotlight Skill: Making Inferences

Figurative Language

⚙ Skill: Figurative Language	⚙ Skill: Figurative Language • Your Turn 💬 Close Read • Complete Vocabulary Chart • Skills Focus • Write	⚙ Unit 6 Skill: Figurative Language - Letter to His Daughter ⚙ Spotlight Skill: Figurative Language

First Read

Pat Mora

Teenagers

Introduce the Text

As a class, watch the video preview and have students read the introduction in pairs to make connections to the video preview.

To activate prior knowledge and experiences, ask students:

- What part of the video stood out to you the most?
- How do you think this poem will make you feel? How can you tell?

> **ELL SPEAKING FRAMES**
> - The ____ in the video makes me think ____.
> - The video shows ____. This makes me wonder ____.
> - I think the text will ____. I think this because ____.
> - I predict that there will be ____. I believe this because ____.

Entry Point

As students prepare to read "Teenagers," share the following information with them to provide context.

✓ Pat Mora, born and raised in El Paso, Texas, writes poetry that has captivated critics and young audiences across the nation. Aside from receiving numerous awards for her works, she is credited with the advocacy and advancement of *El día de los niños/El día de los libros*. This day , April 30th, celebrates the joy of children and reading.

✓ The subject matter associated with most of Mora's work recounts common experiences in family life. Today, Mora continues to speak and write about important themes such as imagination, inclusivity, and the joy of reading.

"Doors and lips shut and we become strangers in our own home."

NOTES

1 One day they disappear
2 into their rooms.
3 Doors and lips shut
4 and we become strangers
5 in our own home.

6 I **pace** the hall, hear whispers,
7 a **code** I knew but can't remember,
8 mouthed by mouths I taught to speak.

9 Years later the door opens.
10 I see faces I once held,
11 open as sunflowers in my hands. I see
12 **familiar** skin now stretched on long bodies
13 that move past me
14 glowing almost like pearls.

"Teenagers" by Pat Mora is reprinted with permission from the publisher of "Communion" (© 1991 Arte Público Press - University of Houston)

Skill: Figurative Language

The poet uses a simile in line 11. The speaker describes the children's faces "as" sunflowers. A sunflower's petals are not closed up like a rose. I think this means the speaker's children were open to learning from her when they were younger.

Analyze Vocabulary Using Context Clues

In stanza 2, focus on the sentence that uses the word *pace*. Point out these context clues:

1. First I notice that the the word *pace* is a verb in the sentence. So, I think it is an action word that describes movement.

2. When I read the sentence again, I see that the speaker hears whispers while she paces the hall. This suggests that she is moving past a door.

3. If I replace *pace* with *walk*, it still makes sense in the sentence. So *pace* must have something to do with walking. Since the speaker is trying to hear what is being said, it makes sense that he or she would walk down the hall more than once. So *pace* must mean "to walk back and forth."

Figurative Language

How does the reader use the simile to help her visualize what the poet is saying?

The reader notes that the poet compares her children's faces to an open sunflower, eager to learn from her.

TEXT TALK

What happens on the "one day" that the speaker describes? Who does the speaker mean by "they"?

See stanza 1, lines 1–3: "They" are the teenagers who live in the home the poet describes. They go into their rooms, shut the door, and stop talking to the other people in the house.

What happens after they disappear and "doors and lips shut"?

See stanza 1, lines 4–5: The speaker says that the actions of the teenagers have made them all strangers in their home.

Who do the teenagers talk to? What does the speaker hear?

The teenagers talk to each other. The speaker hears whispers. She says it is a code she doesn't understand. See stanza 2, line 6: "I pace the hall, hear whispers."

When does the door open? What happens afterward?

See stanza 3, lines 9–12: the door opens years later and familiar faces come out ready to talk.

How does the speaker see the teenagers now?

See stanza 3, line 14: The speaker sees them as "glowing almost like pearls."

What other inferences can you make about the poem?

Answers will vary.

Think about the teenagers' actions in the poem. How might you isolate yourself from your parents as you grow into adulthood?

Answers will vary.

 Ask each Beyond grade-level student to write one additional discussion question. Then, have one or two students facilitate a discussion, using their questions to guide the conversation

 ## Skills Focus

QUESTION 1: Textual Evidence

See lines 6–8: The speaker is outside in the hall. She can hear her teenagers whispering inside their rooms, like she did when she was a teenager. But she can no longer remember what it was like to be a teenager. She can't remember what she talked about. So the whispers are like a code she no longer understands.

QUESTION 2: Figurative Language

See lines 1–5, 9: In the opening stanza, the poet uses "rooms" and "shut doors" as metaphors. The speaker's teenagers are shutting her out of their lives. "Lips shut" is also a metaphor. Her teenagers no longer talk openly with the speaker about their lives. In line 9, the poet uses another metaphor when the door opens. Her children are now older, and the open door means they have let her back into their lives.

QUESTION 3: Connect to Essential Question

See lines 1–5: The speaker feels like she and her children are becoming strangers because the teenagers have shut her out of their lives.

 SELECTION VOCABULARY

pace / caminar *verb* to walk back and forth in the same space

code / el código *noun* a set of words, letters, symbols, or numbers used to create secret messages

- Can the speaker understand the whispers? Why not?
- What did the speaker once know? Does she know now?

familiar / familiar *adjective* known from past association, recognizable **COGNATE**

- What is familiar?
- Does the speaker know these people? How does this make their skin familiar?

Reading Comprehension OPTIONAL

Have students complete the digital reading comprehension questions ✓ when they finish reading.

ANSWER KEY

QUESTION 1:	B	**QUESTION 3:**	C	**QUESTION 5:**	
QUESTION 2:	B	**QUESTION 4:**	D	*See chart.*	

Textual Evidence	Inference
Doors and lips shut and we become strangers	The teenagers do not interact with their parents.
a code I knew but can't remember	The speaker used to be a teenager.
I see faces I once held, open as sunflowers in my hands.	The speaker sees the children she remembers now fully grown.
familiar skin now stretched on long bodies that move past me glowing almost like pearls.	The narrator is amazed and deeply impacted by how her children have grown.

Connect and Extend OPTIONAL

CONNECT TO EXTENDED WRITING PROJECT

Students can use "Teenagers" as a mentor text for their Extended Writing Project. The speaker in Pat Mora's poem illustrates the point of view of a parent watching her child grow up. Students may consider the perspective of a parent or another family member as they describe a similar relationship in their letter.

BEYOND THE BOOK

Writing: Copy Change

Copy Change is a way to use the structure of other poets' poems to create new poems with new meaning for ourselves. Ask students to use the structure of "Teenagers" to compose their own poem about a new subject: their parents or guardians. Ask students to write from the perspective of a teenager.

To reflect, ask students:

- Did your relationship with your parents or guardians inspire parts of this poem?

- Do you like writing copy change poems where you have some structure but get to fill in the blanks with your own words, or do you prefer to write poems without having a structure from?

Think Questions

Circulate as students answer Think Questions independently. Scaffolds for these questions are shown on the opposite page.

QUESTION 1: Textual Evidence

The strangers are teenagers and their parents. The title of the poem is "Teenagers" and the words *we* and *our* are clues that this is a family.

QUESTION 2: Textual Evidence

The last part of the poem begins "Years later the door opens." The teenagers come out of their rooms and have grown older and taller.

QUESTION 3: Textual Evidence

Answers will vary but may include the following examples:

- "Mouths I taught to speak" suggests that the speaker is a parent who taught his or her small children to talk.

- Using the word "pace" in "I pace the hall" suggests something a worried parent might do.

- The grown children "move past me" when the door opens.They have left childhood behind and are going out into the world.

Student descriptions should explain how the speaker sounds, and whether the language gives them a sense of the speaker's age and personality.

QUESTION 4: Context Clues

I think *code* must mean "words or a way of speaking that only a few people know." "I knew but can't remember" is a clue that the speaker doesn't understand what she hears.

QUESTION 5: Word Meaning

Definition number 3 most closely matches the meaning of the word *familiar* in the last stanza. The speaker is probably a mother, who recognizes faces I once held," and describes seeing "familiar skin, now stretched on long bodies." A mother would have personal knowledge of her children's faces and appearance over the years

---

teenagers

First Read

Read "Teenagers." After you read, complete the Think Questions below.

☁ THINK QUESTIONS

1. In lines 4 and 5, the speaker says that "we become strangers in our own home." Who are the strangers in this home? Cite textual evidence to support your answer.

2. Write two or three sentences that explain what happens to the "strangers" when "years later, the door opens"?

3. "Voice" is the way an author uses word choice, tone, and speech patterns to show the personality of a speaker, narrator, or character. Voice gives the sense that a real person is talking to the reader or to other characters. Whose voice is talking in this poem? Cite words and phrases that support your answer.

4. Find the word **code** in the second stanza of "Teenagers." Use context clues in the surrounding stanzas, as well as the stanza in which the word appears, to determine the word's meaning. Write your definition here and identify clues that helped you figure out its meaning.

5. Read the following dictionary entry:

   familiar
   fa•mil•iar \fə 'mil yər\ *adjective*

   1. closely acquainted
   2. sociable
   3. having personal knowledge

   Which definition most closely matches the meaning of **familiar** as it is used in the last stanza? Explain how you chose the correct meaning.

Please note that excerpts and passages in the StudySync® library and this workbook are intended as touchstones to generate interest in an author's work. The excerpts and passages do not substitute for the reading of entire texts, and StudySync® strongly recommends that students seek out and purchase the whole literary or informational work in order to experience it as the author intended. Links to online resellers are available in our digital library. In addition, complete works may be ordered through an authorized reseller by filling out and returning to StudySync® the order form enclosed in this workbook.

Reading & Writing
Companion   25

Think Questions

Use the scaffolds below to differentiate instruction for your **ELL** English Language Learners and **A** Approaching grade-level learners.

ELL **BEGINNING** Write a response using the underline{word bank} and sentence frames.

INTERMEDIATE Write a response using the underline{sentence frames}.

ADVANCED, ADVANCED HIGH Write a response using the underline{Text-Dependent Question Guide}.

A **APPROACHING** Write a response using the underline{Text-Dependent Question Guide}.

BEGINNING	INTERMEDIATE	APPROACHING / ADVANCED, ADVANCED HIGH
Word Bank	**Sentence Frames**	**Text-Dependent Question Guide**
whispers long parents Pat Mora grown up teenagers	From the title of the poem, the strangers must be ____ and ____. The clues are ____ and ____.	1. • What is the title of the poem? • What clues does the speaker use to refer to the people who become strangers and where this happens?
cannot the code our own home	The door opens ____ later. The bodies the speaker once knew are now ____. This means the children are now ____.	2. • How much time goes by before the closed door opens? • How have the bodies of the children changed? What does this mean?
	The poet is ____, so the speaker is a ____. The phrases that tell me this are ____ and ____.	3. • Who is the poet? • What phrases tell you that the speaker has known the teenagers as children?
years mother we	The speaker hears ____. The speaker ____ understand the words. The speaker remembers knowing ____.	4. • What does the speaker hear? • Can the speaker understand the words? • What does the speaker remember?
faces I held three I taught children	The speaker has known the teenagers since they were ____. *Familiar,* as used in the text, matches definition # ____.	5. • How long has the speaker known the teenagers? • Does *familiar* mean "being acquainted" with someone? (#1) • Does *familiar* mean that the people in the poem are sociable? (#2) • Does *familiar* mean that the speaker knows the teenagers well? (#3)

Skill: Figurative Language

Introduce the Skill

Watch the Concept Definition video ▶ and read the following definitions with your students.

Figurative language is language used for descriptive effect, often to illustrate or imply ideas indirectly. Types of figurative language include simile, metaphor, and personification. A **simile** uses the words *like* or *as* to compare two seemingly unlike things. A **metaphor** directly compares two seemingly unlike things without using *like* or *as*. **Personification** is a **figure of speech** in which an animal, object, force of nature, or an idea is given human qualities.

When reading prose, and especially poetry, readers use **context**—including when and where a text was written, for example—to analyze the impact of word choice and to help determine or interpret the meaning of figurative words and phrases.

TURN AND TALK

1. Have you ever helped a friend try to imagine or visualize something that you've seen? Did you compare it to something else, and if so, what kind of comparison did you use?

2. How can you describe feelings by comparing what you feel to something else?

ELL **SPEAKING FRAMES**
- I saw something great and it was ____. I compared it to ____.
- My friend could ____. One feeling I had was ____. It felt like ____. I compared it to ____.

Teenagers

Skill:
Figurative Language

Use the Checklist to analyze Figurative Language in "Teenagers." Refer to the sample student annotations about Figurative Language in the text.

••• CHECKLIST FOR FIGURATIVE LANGUAGE

To determine the meaning of figures of speech in a text, note the following:

- ✓ words that mean one thing literally and suggest something else
- ✓ similes, such as "strong as an ox"
- ✓ metaphors, such as "her eyes were stars"
- ✓ personification, such as "the daisies danced in the wind"

In order to interpret the meaning of a figure of speech in context, ask the following questions:

- ✓ Does any of the descriptive language in the text compare two seemingly unlike things?
- ✓ Do any descriptions include the words "like" or "as" that indicate a simile?
- ✓ Is there a direct comparison that suggests a metaphor?
- ✓ Is a human quality used to describe an animal, object, force of nature or idea in a way that suggests personification?
- ✓ How does the use of this figure of speech change your understanding of the thing or person being described?

In order to analyze the impact of figurative language on the meaning of a text, use the following questions as a guide:

- ✓ Where does figurative language appear in the text? What does it mean?
- ✓ Why does the author use figurative language rather than literal language?

 SKILL VOCABULARY

figurative language / el lenguaje figurativo *noun* expressions used for descriptive or rhetorical effect that are not literally true but that express some truth beyond the literal level) COGNATE

simile / el símil *noun* a figure of speech that uses the words like or as to compare two seemingly unlike things COGNATE

metaphor / la metáfora *noun* a figure of speech that compares two seemingly unlike things but implies a comparison instead of stating it directly with the words like or as COGNATE

Skill:
Figurative Language

sync•skills

Reread "Teenagers." Then, using the Checklist on the previous page, answer the multiple-choice questions below.

⟳ YOUR TURN

1. The poet uses a metaphor comparing whispers to a code for the purpose of —

   ○ A. showing that the speaker cannot hear the voices.
   ○ B. illustrating that the language the teenagers use is not something she understands.
   ○ C. suggesting that the teenagers are writing secret notes.
   ○ D. saying the speaker fears that the teenagers are talking about her.

2. Based on the examples of figurative language in the poem, you can infer that the speaker—

   ○ A. is afraid to admit that her children are grown and are now moving out into the wider world as adults.
   ○ B. still does not understand her children even though they are now familiar again and have grown into strong and tall young adults.
   ○ C. enjoyed holding her children's faces and teaching them when they were younger, but is gratified that they have grown into fine young adults.
   ○ D. is angry that so much time has passed with her teenagers behind closed doors and unwilling to communicate.

Reading & Writing Companion **27**

Your Turn

Ask students to complete the Your Turn Activity.

QUESTION 1

A. Incorrect. The speaker does hear the whispering voices.

B. **Correct.** The words the speaker hears sound like a code that she is unable to understand.

C. Incorrect. There is no evidence that the teenagers are writing notes.

D. Incorrect. Since the speaker cannot understand what is being said, she doesn't really know what the whispers are about.

QUESTION 2

A. Incorrect. The speaker seems pleased that her children are grown and moving past her into the world.

B. Incorrect. The familiar bodies and open sunflower faces suggests that the teenagers are receptive to her once again as parent.

C. **Correct.** The speaker fondly remembers the faces of her children, open like sunflowers and eager to learn from her, and she is pleased that they now "glow almost like pearls" as young adults.

D. Incorrect. There is no evidence that the speaker is angry about the time that has passed or about her teenagers' unwillingness to communicate.

Ⅴ SKILL VOCABULARY

personification / la personificación *noun* a figure of speech in which an animal, object, force of nature, or an idea is given human form or qualities COGNATE

figure of speech / la figura literaria *noun* a word or phrase not meant to be taken literally, but rather used for effect

context / el contexto *noun* the set of facts or circumstances that surround a situation or event COGNATE

Close Read

Skills Focus

QUESTION 1: Textual Evidence

See lines 6–8.

QUESTION 2: Figurative Language

See lines 1–5, 9.

QUESTION 3: Connect to Essential Question

See lines 1–5.

✓ CHECK FOR SUCCESS

If students struggle to respond to Skills Focus Question #1, ask students the following questions:

- What does the speaker hear?
- What is the speaker calling a "code"?
- If the speaker knew the code once but can no longer remember it, when do you think she knew the code?
- What does this tell you about the meaning of "a code I knew but can't remember"?

 Close Read

Reread "Teenagers." As you reread, complete the Skills Focus questions below. Then use your answers and annotations from the questions to help you complete the Write activity.

◎ SKILLS FOCUS

1. Use textual evidence to infer what the speaker means when she writes "a code I knew but can't remember."

2. Identify examples of similes and metaphors in the poem and explain what purpose the poet achieves by using this figurative language.

3. Identify and explain the ways in which the poem explores how relationships impact our lives.

✎ WRITE

LITERARY ANALYSIS: In the poem "Teenagers," a parent talks about her teenage children and how they have changed over time. How does the poem show the speaker's character? Identify examples of figurative language that help the reader understand the speaker. **Respond** using evidence from the text.

 ## Writer's Notebook

Connect to Essential Question: Give students time to reflect on how "Teenagers" connects to the unit's essential question "How do relationships shape us?" by freewriting in their writer's notebooks.

 Beginning & Intermediate

Read aloud the unit's essential question: "How do relationships shape us?" Encourage students to draw their reflections or allow students to write in their native language. Circulate, prompting students for their thoughts as they respond orally or through pantomime.

Advanced & Advanced High

Allow students to share their reflections orally in pairs or small groups before freewriting.

Collaborative Conversation

Break students into collaborative conversation groups to discuss the Close Read prompt. Remind them to reference their Skills Focus annotations in their discussion.

In the poem "Teenagers," a parent talks about her teenage children and how they have changed over time. How does the poem describe the speaker's character? Identify examples of figurative language that help the reader understand the speaker. Respond using evidence from the text.

Use the scaffolds below to differentiate instruction for your **ELL** English Language Learners and **A** Approaching grade-level learners.

ELL **BEGINNING, INTERMEDIATE** Use the discussion guide and speaking frames to facilitate the discussion with support from the teacher.

ADVANCED, ADVANCED HIGH Use the discussion guide and speaking frames to facilitate the discussion in mixed-level groups.

A **APPROACHING** Use the discussion guide to facilitate the discussion in mixed-level groups.

APPROACHING
ADVANCED, ADVANCED HIGH
BEGINNING, INTERMEDIATE

Discussion Guide	Speaking Frames
1. How would you describe the speaker's character?	• I think the speaker is ____. • I think this because ____.
2. What figurative language does the poet use that helps you understand the speaker's character.	• One example of figurative language is ____. • I think the poet means ____.
3. How does this figurative language help the reader understand the speaker?	• I think the figurative language shows ____. • I think this because ____.

Review Prompt and Rubric

Before students begin writing, review the writing prompt and rubric with the class.

LITERARY ANALYSIS: In the poem "Teenagers," a parent talks about her teenage children and how they have changed over time. How does the poem describe the speaker's character? Identify examples of figurative language that help the reader understand the speaker. **Respond (AV)** using evidence from the text.

ELL PROMPT GUIDE

A
- Based on the figurative language in the poem, how would you describe the speaker's character?
- What figurative language does the poet use in her poem that helps you understand the speaker's character?

- What are some examples of figurative language that help the reader learn more about the speaker's character?

Score	Figurative Language	Language and Conventions
4	The writer clearly analyzes and explains how the poet uses figurative language to help the reader understand the speaker. The writer provides exemplary analysis, using relevant evidence from the text.	The writer demonstrates a consistent command of grammar, punctuation, and usage conventions. Although minor errors may be evident, they do not detract from the fluency or the clarity of the essay.
3	The writer analyzes and explains how the poet uses figurative language to help the reader understand the speaker. The writer provides sufficient analysis, using relevant evidence from the text most of the time.	The writer demonstrates an adequate command of grammar, punctuation, and usage conventions. Although some errors may be evident, they create few (if any) disruptions in the fluency of the writing or the clarity of the essay.
2	The writer begins to analyze or explain how the poet uses figurative language to help the reader understand the speaker, but the analysis is incomplete. The writer uses relevant evidence from the text only some of the time.	The writer demonstrates a partial command of grammar, punctuation, and usage conventions. Some distracting errors may be evident, at times creating minor disruptions in the fluency or clarity of the writing.
1	The writer attempts to analyze or explain how the poet uses figurative language to help the reader understand the speaker, but the analysis is not successful. The writer uses little or no relevant evidence from the text.	The writer demonstrates little or no command of grammar, punctuation, and usage conventions. Serious and persistent errors create disruptions in the fluency of the writing and sometimes interfere with meaning.
0	The writer does not provide a relevant response to the prompt or does not provide a response at all.	Serious and persistent errors overwhelm the writing and interfere with the meaning of the response as a whole, making the writer's meaning impossible to understand.

Write

SCAFFOLDS

Ask students to complete the writing assignment using textual evidence to support their answers.

Use the scaffolds below to differentiate instruction for your **ELL** English Language Learners and **A** Approaching grade-level learners.

ELL **BEGINNING** With the help of the word bank, write a response using paragraph frame 1.

INTERMEDIATE With the help of the word bank, write a response using paragraph frames 1 and 2.

ADVANCED, ADVANCED HIGH Write a response of differentiated length using the sentence starters.

A **APPROACHING** Write a response of differentiated length using the sentence starters.

BEGINNING	ADVANCED, ADVANCED HIGH
INTERMEDIATE	APPROACHING

Word Bank	Paragraph Frame 1	Paragraph Frame 2	Sentence Starters
open up happiness and pride relationships change shut out	This poem explains the impact of ____ on our lives. Teenagers often ____ their parents, which can make parents upset. Teenagers ____again when they grow into young adults. Parents respond to this with ____. The speaker understands that relationships ____ over time.	In stanza 1, the poet uses "____" and "____" as metaphors. This figurative language tells me that ____. In stanza 2, the poet uses the phrase "____." This figurative language tells me that the speaker ____. In stanza 3, the poet uses the similes "____" and "____." This figurative language tells me that the speaker has ____.	• The speaker's character is . . . • In the first stanza, the poet uses the figurative language . . . • This figurative language means . . . • In the second stanza, the poet uses the figurative language . . . • This figurative language means . . . • In the third stanza, the poet uses the figurative language . . . • This figurative language means . . . • This poet's use of figurative language . . .

Peer Review

Rate

Respond to the following with a point rating that reflects your opinion.

	1 2 3 4
Ideas	■■■□
Evidence	■■■■
Language and Conventions	■■□□

Submit

Students should submit substantive feedback to two peers using the review instructions below.

• How well does this response answer the prompt?
• How well does the writer support his or her ideas with details and examples from the text?
• Which sentence in the writer's response made you think differently about the text?
• What did the writer do well in this response? What does the writer need to work on?

Remember that your comments are most useful when they are kind and constructive.

ELL **A** **SENTENCE FRAMES**

• You were able to (completely / partly / almost) ____ answer the prompt because . . .
• You could answer the prompt more completely by . . .
• You supported the idea of . . . with the detail of . . .

• One idea that needs more support is . . .
• I thought differently about the texts after reading . . .
• My favorite part of your response is . . .

Tableau

POETRY
Countee Cullen
1925

Introduction

" "Tableau" was published in 1925 during the peak of the Harlem Renaissance. Its author, Countee Cullen (1903–1946), was one of the leading poetic voices throughout the African-American neighborhood's cultural explosion, and would go on to publish multiple books during his lifetime. While he certainly had fans among fellow African Americans, the Harvard-educated Cullen was more successfully able to connect with white audiences and critics in his time than his most famous contemporary, the Harlem poet Langston Hughes. In "Tableau," Cullen speaks to his unique perspective of walking through both white and black universes, and the joys and challenges that sprang from blacks and whites attempting to forge relationships during this time.

In the 1920s, two boys—one black and one white—walk down the street together, arms interlocked, the best of friends. Through lowered blinds inside their homes, black people stare at them. The white people talk about the boys. Both groups feel angry that these two boys dare to walk together. However, the two boys don't notice the reactions they have caused. They walk on, their friendship blazing a trail for a more united racial future.

ELL Proficiency-leveled summaries and summaries in multiple languages are available digitally.

🔊 Audio and audio text highlighting are available with this text.

CONNECT TO ESSENTIAL QUESTION

How do relationships shape us?

This poem answers the question: What happens when two boys of different races walk down the street together?

Access Complex Text

LEXILE: N/A **WORD COUNT: 71**

The following areas may be challenging for students, particularly **ELL** English Language Learners and **A** Approaching grade-level learners.

Prior Knowledge	Connection of Ideas	Genre
• "Tableau" was published in 1925 during the Harlem Renaissance. • Cullen writes of the challenges blacks and whites faced attempting to forge relationships when segregation was still the law of the land.	• The author uses many similes and metaphors in the poem. • The use of figurative language and its connection to the theme may prove challenging. For example, the metaphors comparing the boys to thunder and lightning question society's disdain by associating them with two things that go together in the natural world.	• The poem's rhyme scheme is ABAB. • The use of a simple ballad form gives the poem a natural and familiar lilt. which how natural it should be to see a black boy and a white boy walking hand in hand.

SCAFFOLDS **ENGLISH LANGUAGE LEARNERS** **APPROACHING GRADE LEVEL** **B** **BEYOND GRADE LEVEL**

These icons identify differentiation strategies and scaffolded support for a variety of students. See the digital lesson plan for additional differentiation strategies and scaffolds.

Instructional Path

The print teacher's edition includes essential point-of-use instruction and planning tools. Complete lesson plans and program documents appear in your digital teacher account.

First Read: Tableau

Objectives: After an initial reading and discussion of the poem, students will be able to analyze the structure of a poem and explain how it contributes to the development of theme.

Skill: Adjusting Fluency

Objectives: After rereading and discussing a model of close reading, students will be able to adjust fluency as they read aloud in order to improve reading comprehension.

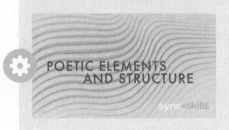

Skill: Poetic Elements and Structure

Objectives: After rereading and discussing a model of close reading, students will be able to analyze how a particular stanza fits into the overall structure of a text and contributes to the development of theme.

Close Read: Tableau

Objectives: After engaging in a close reading and discussion of the text, students will be able analyze how specific lines and stanzas develop the theme of friendship in the poem.

Progress Monitoring

Opportunities to Learn	Opportunities to Demonstrate Learning	Opportunities to Reteach

Adjusting Fluency

⚙ Skill: Adjusting Fluency	🖥 First Read • Read and Annotate	⚙ Spotlight Skill: Adjusting Fluency

Poetic Elements and Structure

⚙ Skill: Poetic Elements and Structure	⚙ Skill: Poetic Elements and Structure • Your Turn 🖥 Close Read • Skills Focus • Write	⚙ Unit 3 Skill: Poetic Elements and Structure - I, Too ⚙ Unit 4 Skill: Poetic Elements and Structure - Famous ⚙ Spotlight Skill: Poetic Elements and Structure

First Read

Countee Cullen

Tableau

 Introduce the Text

As a class, watch the video preview ▶ and have students read the introduction in pairs to make connections to the video preview.

To activate prior knowledge and experiences, ask students:

- What part of the video stood out to you the most?
- What do you think *perspective* means?

> **ELL** SPEAKING FRAMES
> - The ____ in the video makes me think ____.
> - The video shows ____. This makes me wonder ____.
> - I think the text will ____. I think this because ____.
> - I predict that there will be ____. I believe this because ____.

Entry Point

As students prepare to read "Tableau," share the following information with them to provide context.

✓ From 1910–1940, numerous African American individuals and families moved from the South to the North. Many people settled in an area of New York called Harlem. This migration, which eventually became known as the Great Migration, was the end result of several different factors. There was the sudden availability of work in the North, as well as affordable housing in new neighborhoods.

✓ Also during this period, the neighborhood of Harlem became a cultural powerhouse, producing art and literature that celebrated the African American community. From 1910-mid 1930s, this area of the United States experienced what is now known as the Harlem Renaissance.

Tableau

"The golden splendor of the day
The sable pride of night."

 NOTES

 Skill: Poetic Elements and Structure

Stanza 1 helps me to understand the setting. Two boys are walking together outside. The poet describes the white boy as "golden splendor of the day," while the black boy is the "sable pride of night."

Stanza 2 helps me understand that some people were not happy to see boys of two different races walking together as friends. I think one theme of the poem is that not everyone celebrates diversity.

1 Locked arm in arm they cross the way
2 The black boy and the white,
3 The golden **splendor** of the day
4 The sable pride of night.

5 From lowered blinds the dark folk stare
6 And here the **fair** folk talk,
7 **Indignant** that these two should dare
8 In **unison** to walk.

9 **Oblivious** to look and word
10 They pass, and see no wonder
11 That lightning brilliant as a sword
12 Should blaze the path of thunder.

Copyrights held by The Amistad Research Center, Tulane University Administered by Thompson and Thompson, Brooklyn, NY

Copyright © BookheadEd Learning, LLC

 ## Analyze Vocabulary Using Context Clues

In stanza 1, focus on the sentence that uses the word *splendor*. Point out these context clues:

1. First I notice that the adjective *golden* is used to describe *splendor*. I also see the word day. I think of a bright and beautiful sunny day when I read *golden day.*

2. When I read the line again, I'll substitute *beauty* for *splendor.* This makes sense, so I think splendor means "great beauty."

3. When I read the stanza again, I see that the poet uses "the golden splendor of the day" to describe the white boy and "the sable pride of night" to describe the black boy. I think the poet is using *golden splendor* and *sable pride* to contrast the boys' skin tones.

 ## Poetic Elements and Structure

According to the reader, what effect do the structural elements have on the poem in the first stanza?

The reader focused on the poet's introduction of the setting in the first stanza and how this reveals aspects of the mood.

How did the reader explain the effect of poetic structure in the second stanza of "Tableau"?

The reader noted that the second stanza draws attention to the strength and pride of the boys' friendship despite the disapproving neighbors.

Prepare for Advanced Courses

Use the activity below to differentiate instruction for **B** Beyond grade level learners.

Ask students: What is the speaker's attitude to the friendship in the poem? How do the metaphors of "lightning" and "thunder" contribute to your understanding?

Sample answer; answers will vary: The friends are disobeying a rule in society, but they don't realize it. Love, however, arms them against society's disapproval. Like love, lightning is a force of nature--like a sword it protects them, and its light will show the way ahead for all who follow them.

TEXT TALK

How do the people react to seeing the boys walk together?

See lines 7 and 8: They are indignant, or angry, that the boys dare to walk together.

How do the boys react to the people's stares and indignant talk?

See lines 9 and 10: They don't notice it or don't care because they and see nothing strange or wrong in what they are doing.

Who "crosses the way"?

See stanza 1, line 2: "The black boy and the white" pass by.

Who sees the boys walk together?

See lines 5 and 6: The "dark," or black folk and the "fair," or white folk see the boys walk together.

How do the people react to seeing the boys walk together?

See lines 7 and 8: They are indignant, or angry, that the boys dare to walk together.

How do the boys react to the people's stares and indignant talk?

See lines 9 and 10: They don't notice it or don't care because they are oblivious and see nothing strange or wrong in what they are doing.

What does the speaker think about the boys walking together?

See lines 11 and 12: The poet thinks that the event is like lightning that prepares the way for a big noise.

What other inferences can you make?

Answers will vary.

Why do you think the name of the poem is "Tableau"? What message does the scene of the two boys represent?

Answers will vary.

 BEYOND TEXT TALK

Ask each Beyond grade-level student to write one additional discussion question. Then, have one or two students facilitate a discussion, using their questions to guide the conversation.

 ## Skills Focus

QUESTION 1: Poetic Elements and Structure

See lines 9–12: The first two lines of this stanza reveal that the boys pay no mind to their neighbors glares. They happily continue marching on. This stanza reflects the potential impact of the boys' relationship on their neighbors' views of race.

QUESTION 2: Figurative Language

See lines 1–4: In the first stanza, Cullen uses "day" and "night" as metaphors for the white boy and the black boy. This metaphor emphasizes that night and day are opposites, but makes clear to the audience that the boys are equal in worth and beauty by adding the details "splendor" and "pride."

QUESTION 3: Connect to Essential Question

See lines 1–4 : The poem reads like a story. In the first stanza, Cullen introduces the boys' relationship and makes clear that they are happy and comfortable with it.

 SELECTION VOCABULARY

splendor / **el esplendor** *noun* magnificent and impressive appearance COGNATE

fair / **claro/a** *adjective* have pale or light skin or hair

- Who is "fair"?
- What word does "fair" contrast with in line 5?

indignant / **indignado/a** *adjective* showing or feeling anger about something that is wrong or unfair COGNATE

- Who is "indignant"?
- What are they "indignant" about? Are they happy or upset?

unison / **al unísono** *noun* a simultaneous performance of actions COGNATE

- Who is walking?
- Are they together or apart?

oblivious / **ajeno/a** *adjective* lacking mindfulness; unaware

- Who is "oblivious"?
- What are they doing or not doing?

 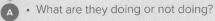

Reading Comprehension OPTIONAL

Have students complete the digital reading comprehension questions ✓ when they finish reading.

ANSWER KEY

QUESTION 1: A	**QUESTION 3:** A	**QUESTION 5:**
QUESTION 2: C	**QUESTION 4:** D	*See chart.*

Synonym	Word
pale	fair
magnificence	splendor
displeased	indignant
clueless	oblivious

Connect and Extend

CONNECT TO EXTENDED WRITING PROJECT

Students can use Countee Cullen's poem "Tableau" as a mentor text for their Extended Writing Project, and consider how relationships that fly in the face of certain conventions can still be rewarding and shape our lives.

BEYOND THE BOOK

Research Project: Social Taboos

Assign small groups a country and ask them to research a social taboo in their assigned country. After students select a social taboo, request that they pitch their idea for approval to ensure they are focusing on appropriate topics. In their pitch, they should address the following:

- What is the social taboo?
- Why is the behavior or social interaction considered taboo?
- What does it reveal about the country's culture?

Upon receiving approval, groups will create a tableau. The name "tableau" comes from the term *tableau vivant* which means "living picture." In this activity, students create a still picture, without talking, to capture and communicate the meaning of the social taboo. Have groups take turns acting out their tableau.

To reflect, ask students:

- Which social taboo was most interesting or surprising?
- What social taboos exist in the United States? How are they similar or different?

Think Questions

Circulate as students answer Think Questions independently. Scaffolds for these questions are shown on the opposite page.

QUESTION 1: Textual Evidence

The poet contrasts "the black boy and the white." He contrasts them as day and night and "golden splendor" with "sable pride."

QUESTION 2: Textual Evidence

The "dark folk stare," which probably means they have not seen a black boy and a white boy together as friends. They must be surprised. The "fair folk talk, indignant," which likely means that they are upset that the boys are together and do not approve.

QUESTION 3: Textual Evidence

Answers may vary. The boys' passing is compared to "lightning brilliant as a sword (blazing) the path of thunder." The metaphor means that the boys walking as black and white together is a surprising and shocking event that cuts through old ways of thinking.

QUESTION 4: Word Meaning

I think *oblivious* must mean "not noticing or knowing." The boys don't see the looks or hear the words people say. Context clues are "to look and word" and "they pass, and see no wonder."

QUESTION 5: Word Meaning

Definition number 2 most closely matches the meaning of the word *unison* in the second stanza. The two boys are described in the first stanza as "locked arm in arm," so that means they are walking together at the same time.

First Read

Read "Tableau." After you read, complete the Think Questions below.

☁ THINK QUESTIONS

1. How does the poet contrast the two boys in the first stanza? Cite textual evidence from the poem to support your answer.

2. Write two to three sentences explaining what people likely think about the two boys in the second stanza.

3. A metaphor is a figure of speech that compares two seemingly unlike things but implies a comparison instead of stating it directly with the words "like" or "as." In stanza 3, what is the boys' passing compared to? What do you think the metaphor means?

4. Find the word **oblivious** in line 9 of "Tableau." Use context clues in the surrounding lines, as well as the line in which the word appears, to determine the word's meaning. Write your definition here and identify clues that helped you figure out its meaning.

5. Read the following dictionary entry:

unison
u•ni•son \'yü-nə-sən\ noun

1. singing parts of a song together
2. at the same time
3. all elements in one place

Which definition most closely matches the meaning of **unison** as it is used in the second stanza? Write the correct definition of *unison* here. Then explain how you figured out the correct meaning.

Reading & Writing Companion   31

Think Questions

Use the scaffolds below to differentiate instruction for your **ELL** English Language Learners and **A** Approaching grade-level learners.

ELL **BEGINNING** Write a response using the <u>word bank</u> and <u>sentence frames</u>.

INTERMEDIATE Write a response using the <u>sentence frames</u>.

ADVANCED, ADVANCED HIGH Write a response using the <u>Text-Dependent Question Guide</u>.

A **APPROACHING** Write a response using the <u>Text-Dependent Question Guide</u>.

BEGINNING	INTERMEDIATE	APPROACHING / ADVANCED, ADVANCED HIGH
Word Bank	**Sentence Frames**	**Text-Dependent Question Guide**
boys skin together	The ___ are locked arm in arm. Two words that are opposite in meaning are ___ and ___. These two words describe ___ color.	1. • Who are locked arm and arm? • What are two words that are opposite in meaning? • What do these two words describe?
bolt shocked second	The dark folk ___. The fair folk ___. The people are ___ and ___ about seeing the boys together.	2. • What do the dark folk do from lowered blinds? • What do the fair folk do? • How do the people feel about seeing the boys together?
talk wonder black	The poet compares the boys to ___. To see black and white boys ___ is like being hit by a ___ of lightning.	3. • Who passes by? • What does the poet say they are like? • How does this affect the people who see them?
upset white stare	The boys are oblivious to ___ and ___. They ___ by and see no ___. This tells me that *oblivious* means not ___.	4. • What are the boys **oblivious** to? • What do they do that suggests they do not notice the people? • What does this tell you about the meaning of *oblivious*?
look word lightning knowing pass	*Unison* as used in the text matches the ___ definition.	5. • Is **unison** about *singing*? (#1) • Is *unison* about something that happens at the same time? (#2) • Is *unison* about things that are in one place? (#3)

Skill: Poetic Elements and Structure

Introduce the Skill

Watch the Concept Definition video and read the following definitions with your students.

Poetic structure describes the organization of words and lines in a poem as well as its rhyme scheme and meter. Poems consist of words that are divided into **lines.** A group of lines is called a **stanza.**

Other elements of poetry that contribute to structure include rhyme and rhythm. **Rhyme** is the repetition of the same or similar vowel sounds. The rhyme scheme of a poem is the pattern formed by the rhyming words at the end of lines. Rhythm is the pattern of unstressed and stressed syllables in a line of poetry. A regular pattern is called **meter,** and it gives a line of poetry a predictable rhythm.

The poet's choice of **poetic form,** or arrangement and style of a poem, will help determine the structure. Common forms include haiku, limerick, and sonnet, each with its own rules. Poetry without a consistent meter, rhyme, or stanza length is called **open form.**

TURN AND TALK

1. How does the structure of a poem influence the meaning?

2. What is your favorite poem? What makes it your favorite?

ELL SPEAKING FRAMES

- I think that a poem's structure can influence meaning when ___.
- My favorite poem is ___. I like this poem because ___.

Tableau

POETIC ELEMENTS AND STRUCTURE

sync•skills

Skill:
Poetic Elements and Structure

Use the Checklist to analyze Poetic Elements and Structure in "Tableau." Refer to the sample student annotations about Poetic Elements and Structure in the text.

••• CHECKLIST FOR POETIC ELEMENTS AND STRUCTURE

In order to identify elements of poetic structure, note the following:

- ✓ how the words and lines are arranged
- ✓ the form and overall structure of the poem
- ✓ the rhyme, rhythm, and meter, if present
- ✓ how the arrangement of lines and stanzas in the poem contribute to the poem's theme, or message

To analyze how a particular stanza fits into the overall structure of a poem and contributes to the development of the theme, consider the following questions:

- ✓ What poetic form does the poet use? What is the structure?
- ✓ How do the lengths of the lines and stanzas affect the meaning?
- ✓ How does a poem's stanza fit into the structure of the poem overall?
- ✓ In what ways does the form and structure affect the poem's meaning?
- ✓ How does the stanza contribute to the poem's theme?

V SKILL VOCABULARY

poetic structure / la estructura poética *noun* the organization of words and lines as well as the rhyme and meter of a poem COGNATE

line / el verso *noun* a string of words in a poem, not necessarily a full sentence or phrase

stanza / la estrofa *noun* the basic unit of a poem, made up of a series of lines

rhythm / el ritmo *noun* the pattern of unstressed and stressed syllables in a line of poetry

Skill:
Poetic Elements and Structure

Reread lines 9–12 of "Tableau." Then, using the Checklist on the previous page, answer the multiple-choice questions below.

YOUR TURN

1. Lines 9–10 reveal . . .

   ○ A. the boys are impolite as they ignore their neighbors.
   ○ B. the conflict in the poem.
   ○ C. the boys' proud nature as they walk together.
   ○ D. the importance of the setting in the poem.

2. What theme does stanza 3 reveal?

   ○ A. Don't judge a book by its cover.
   ○ B. Be confident when doing the right thing.
   ○ C. Ignoring others leads to the path of justice.
   ○ D. Gossiping is wrong.

Reading & Writing Companion   **33**

Your Turn

Ask students to complete the Your Turn Activity.

QUESTION 1

A. Incorrect. The two boys are not impolite. They are proud to be friends.

B. Incorrect. The conflict is revealed in the second stanza.

C. **Correct.** These lines describe the boys blissfully ignoring the stares of the people in town as they choose to walk proudly together.

D. Incorrect. The setting is established in the first stanza, and it is revealed as part of the conflict in the second stanza.

QUESTION 2

A. Incorrect. This stanza is about the boys confidently moving forward together despite the neighbors, who judge the boys by what they look like.

B. **Correct.** The boys are confidently walking through the town and don't care about what prejudiced people think of their friendship.

C. Incorrect. The boys' confidence is what leads them down a positive path, not ignoring the neighbors.

D. Incorrect. The neighbors stare and talk about the boys in the second stanza, not in the third.

SKILL VOCABULARY

meter / la métrica *noun* a regular pattern of unstressed and stressed syllables in a line of poetry

rhyme / la rima *noun* the repetition of the same or similar sounds in a poem

rhyme scheme / el patrón de rima *noun* the pattern formed by the rhyming words at the end of lines in a poem

poetic form / la forma poética *noun* the particular set of rules guiding the arrangement of words and lines in a poem COGNATE

open form / la forma abierta *noun* poetic form without consistent meter, rhyme, or stanza length

Close Read

Skills Focus

QUESTION 1: Poetic Elements and Structure

See lines 9–12.

QUESTION 2: Figurative Language

See lines 1–4.

QUESTION 3: Connect to Essential Question

See lines 1–4.

 CHECK FOR SUCCESS

If students struggle to respond to Skills Focus Question #1, ask them the following questions:

- What is the pattern of stressed and unstressed syllables in the first two stanzas?

- How is this pattern of stressed and unstressed syllables different in the third stanza?

- What effect does this change have on the poem?

Tableau

 Close Read

Reread "Tableau." As you reread, complete the Skills Focus questions below. Then use your answers and annotations from the questions to help you complete the Write activity.

SKILLS FOCUS

1. Identify lines in the poem that help contribute to the poem's overall theme.

2. Identify places in the poem where Cullen uses figurative language, and explain how this language contributes to the poem's meaning.

3. Countee Cullen's poem "Tableau" reads like a story. Identify and explain the events in the poem and how they explore the way relationships impact our lives.

✏ WRITE

LITERARY ANALYSIS: In "Tableau," the poet Countee Cullen describes an unlikely pair of friends. How does the poet use specific stanzas and lines to focus on the theme of friendship? Use evidence from the text to support your response.

Writer's Notebook

Connect to Essential Question: Give students time to reflect on how "Tableau" connects to the unit's essential question "How do relationships shape us?" by freewriting in their Writer's Notebooks.

ELL Beginning & Intermediate

Read aloud the unit's essential question: "How do relationships shape us?" Encourage students to draw their reflections or allow students to write in their native language. Circulate, prompting students for their thoughts as they respond orally or through pantomime.

Advanced & Advanced High

Allow students to share their reflections orally in pairs or small groups before freewriting.

Collaborative Conversation

Break students into collaborative conversation groups to discuss the Close Read prompt. Remind them to reference their Skills Focus annotations in their discussion.

In "Tableau," the poet Countee Cullen describes an unlikely pair of friends. How does the poet use specific stanzas and lines to focus on the theme of friendship? Use evidence from the text to support your response.

Use the scaffolds below to differentiate instruction for your **ELL** English Language Learners and **A** Approaching grade-level learners.

ELL **BEGINNING, INTERMEDIATE** Use the <u>discussion guide</u> and <u>speaking frames</u> to discuss with support from the teacher.

ADVANCED, ADVANCED HIGH Use the <u>discussion guide</u> and <u>speaking frames</u> to discuss in mixed-level groups.

A **APPROACHING** Use the <u>discussion guide</u> to discuss in mixed-level groups.

APPROACHING
ADVANCED, ADVANCED HIGH
BEGINNING, INTERMEDIATE

Discussion Guide	Speaking Frames
1. How does Cullen structure this poem?	• Cullen lines and stanzas to create a ____ meaning. • He does this by ____.
2. Which lines in stanza 2 convey a shift in mood?	• Lines ____ create a ____ feeling. • He does this by ____.
3. What theme does Cullen reveal in stanza 3?	• Cullen uses stanza 3 to explain the theme of ____. • He does this by ____.

Review Prompt and Rubric

Before students begin writing, review the writing prompt and rubric with the class.

LITERARY ANALYSIS: In "Tableau," the poet Countee Cullen describes an unlikely pair of friends. How does the poet use specific stanzas and lines to focus on the theme of friendship? Use evidence from the text to support your response.

 PROMPT GUIDE

- What is poetic structure?
- How does Cullen use specific lines to explore the theme of friendship in the first stanza?

- How does Cullen use the second stanza to convey a shift in mood and explore the theme of friendship?r?
- How does Cullen use specific lines to explore the theme of friendship in the third stanza?

Score	Poetic Elements and Structure	Language and Conventions
4	The writer clearly explains how the poet uses specific stanzas and lines to focus on the theme of friendship presented in the poem. The writer provides exemplary analysis, using relevant evidence from the text.	The writer demonstrates a consistent command of grammar, punctuation, and usage conventions. Although minor errors may be evident, they do not detract from the fluency or the clarity of the essay.
3	The writer explains how the poet uses specific stanzas and lines to focus on the theme of friendship presented in the poem. The writer provides sufficient analysis, using relevant evidence from the text most of the time.	The writer demonstrates an adequate command of grammar, punctuation, and usage conventions. Although some errors may be evident, they create few (if any) disruptions in the fluency of the writing or the clarity of the essay.
2	The writer begins to explain how the poet uses specific stanzas and lines to focus on the theme of friendship presented in the poem, but the analysis is incomplete. The writer uses relevant evidence from the text only some of the time.	The writer demonstrates a partial command of grammar, punctuation, and usage conventions. Some distracting errors may be evident, at times creating minor disruptions in the fluency or clarity of the writing.
1	The writer attempts to explain how the poet uses specific stanzas and lines to focus on the theme of friendship presented in the poem, but the analysis is not successful. The writer uses little or no relevant evidence from the text.	The writer demonstrates little or no command of grammar, punctuation, and usage conventions. Serious and persistent errors create disruptions in the fluency of the writing and sometimes interfere with meaning.
0	The writer does not provide a relevant response to the prompt or does not provide a response at all.	Serious and persistent errors overwhelm the writing and interfere with the meaning of the response as a whole, making the writer's meaning impossible to understand.

Write

Ask students to complete the writing assignment using textual evidence to support their answers.

Use the scaffolds below to differentiate instruction for your **ELL** English Language Learners and **A** Approaching grade-level learners.

ELL **BEGINNING** With the help of the <u>word bank</u>, write a response using <u>paragraph frame 1</u>.

INTERMEDIATE With the help of the <u>word bank</u>, write a response using <u>paragraph frames 1 and 2</u>.

ADVANCED, ADVANCED HIGH Write a response of differentiated length using the <u>sentence starters</u>.

A **APPROACHING** Write a response of differentiated length using the <u>sentence starters</u>.

BEGINNING		ADVANCED, ADVANCED HIGH
INTERMEDIATE		APPROACHING

Word Bank	Paragraph Frame 1	Paragraph Frame 2	Sentence Starters
friendship and racial equality changes specific lines friendship and racial equality upset	Cullen uses the poem's structure to tell a story about ____. In the first stanza, Cullen uses ____ to create a picture of a steady, happy friendship between the two boys. Additionally, Cullen uses the second ____ to explain why people are ____ about their friendship. In the third stanza, Cullen draws attention to ____ in attitudes about race.	Lines 3 and 4 in the first stanza reinforce the positive nature of the boys' ____. Lines 5, 6 and 7 in the second stanza show people's reactions to the boys' ____. This draws attention to the ____ and ____ lines in the third stanza. This creates a feeling of ____ for the future.	• Cullen uses the stanzas to tell a story about . . . • In the first stanza, Cullen uses ____ to create . . . • He does this by . . . • In the second stanza, Cullen uses ____ to explain . . . • He does this by . . . • In the third stanza, Cullen changes the ____ by . . . • This change draws attention to . . . • This conveys the theme . . .

Peer Review

Students should submit substantive feedback to two peers using the review instructions below.

- How well does this response answer the prompt?
- How well does the writer support her or his ideas with details and examples from the poem?
- Which sentence in the writer's response made you think differently about the poem?
- What did the writer do well in this response? What does the writer need to work on? Remember that your comments are most useful when they are kind and constructive.

Rate

Respond to the following with a point rating that reflects your opinion.

	1 2 3 4
Ideas	▪▪▪☐
Evidence	▪▪▪▪
Language and Conventions	▪▪☐☐

Submit

ELL **SENTENCE FRAMES**

A
- You were able to (completely / partly / almost) ____ answer the prompt because . . .
- You could answer the prompt more completely by . . .
- You supported the idea of . . . with the detail of . . .

- One idea that needs more support is . . .
- I thought differently about the texts after reading . . .
- My favorite part of your response is . . .

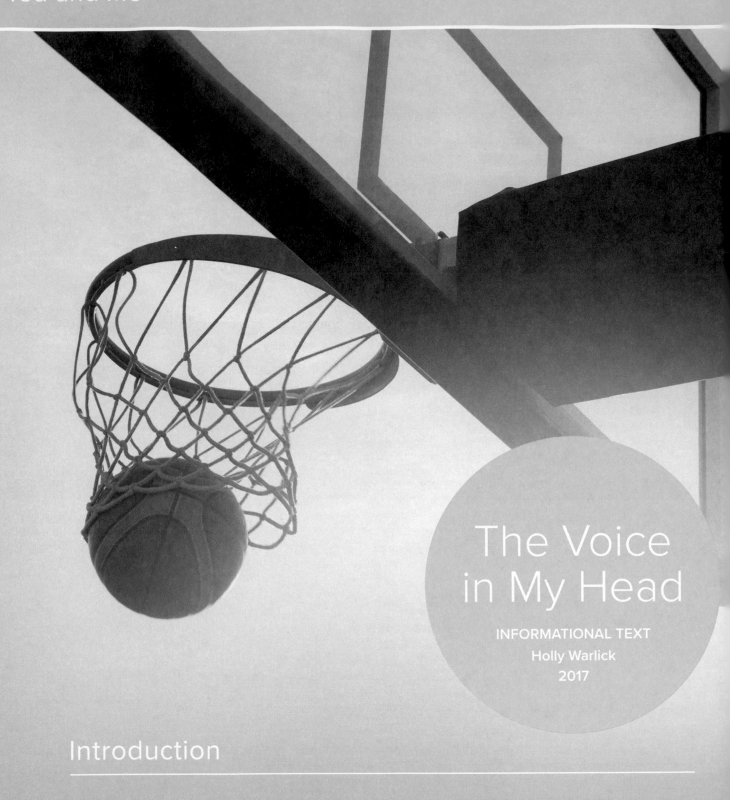

The Voice in My Head

INFORMATIONAL TEXT
Holly Warlick
2017

Introduction

In this essay from The Players' Tribune, Tennessee Lady Vols women's basketball coach Holly Warlick speaks to her profound and life altering relationship with her mentor, legendary coach Pat Summitt. Among the winningest college basketball coaches of all time with eight NCAA titles, Pat Summitt is remembered as much for her advocacy for women's sports and deep regard for the development of her players outside of the sport as she is for her impressive championship record.

In this loving tribute, ex-member of the Tennessee Lady Vols basketball team Holly Warlick writes about her former coach, Pat Summitt. Walking into tryouts in her freshman year, Warlick had heard that Summitt was tough, but she was shocked to discover how draining the drills were. Still, she kept coming back because Warlick wanted to prove to Summitt that she could take it. Later, she learned that her coach wanted the players to prove their stamina and skills to themselves. Eventually, Warlick received an offer to be Summitt's assistant coach, and she instantly agreed. In 2011, Summitt was diagnosed with dementia and Warlick remembers that Summitt delivered this news by cracking jokes. The two remained close for the rest of Summitt's life, yet the loss still greatly impacts Warlick. Warlick visits a statue of Summitt every day and keeps an empty chair on the court in her honor.

 Proficiency-leveled summaries and summaries in multiple languages are available digitally.

 Audio and audio text highlighting are available with this text.

COMPARING WITHIN AND ACROSS GENRES

 The essay "The Voice in My Head" describes a relationship between a basketball player and her coach. Holly Warlick remembers her basketball coach in a heartfelt tribute, despite their relationship having a rocky start. Read with "We're On the Same Team," students contemplate the ways that the lessons we learn through sports can reverberate into other areas of our lives.

Access Complex Text

LEXILE: 690L   WORD COUNT: 1,983

The following areas may be challenging for students, particularly **ELL** English Language Learners and **A** Approaching grade-level learners.

Genre	Specific Vocabulary	Prior Knowledge
• This text is a biographical essay. Students would benefit from knowing that the essay is about real people, places, and events.	• Some idioms related to basketball, such as "dribbling drills, full-court vs. half-court," and "suicides" may need to be explained to students.	• A short overview of basketball and the history of women's sports may be helpful to students who are unfamiliar with these topics.

SCAFFOLDS   **ENGLISH LANGUAGE LEARNERS**   **APPROACHING GRADE LEVEL**   **BEYOND GRADE LEVEL**

These icons identify differentiation strategies and scaffolded support for a variety of students. See the digital lesson plan for additional differentiation strategies and scaffolds.

Instructional Path

The print teacher's edition includes essential point-of-use instruction and planning tools. Complete lesson plans and program documents appear in your digital teacher account.

Independent Read: The Voice in My Head

Objectives: After reading the text, students will demonstrate their understanding by responding to comprehension questions, participating in a collaborative conversation, and writing a personal response.

Independent Read

Holly Warlick

The Voice in My Head

Introduce the Text

As a class, watch the video preview ▶ **and have students read the introduction in pairs to make connections to the video preview.**

- What part of the video stood out to you the most?
- How does this information connect to something you already know?
- What is one prediction you can make about the essay you're going to read?

> **ELL SPEAKING FRAMES**
> - The ____ in the video makes me think ____.
> - The video shows ____. This makes me wonder ____.
> - I think the text will ____. I think this because ____.
> - I predict that there will be ____. I believe this because ____.

Entry Point

As students prepare to read, share the following information with them to provide context.

✓ Coach Pat Summitt, who was the inspiration for Holly Warlick's essay "The Voice in My Head," had an extremely impressive career before her untimely death at age 64. The Tennessee women's basketball coach won 1,098 games and eight NCAA titles. She never had a losing record in 38 seasons and continued to coach for the University of Tennessee even after her Alzheimer's diagnosis. She holds the title for the most wins for both women's and men's college basketball coaches (record set in 2009).

✓ Holly Warlick, the protege of Pat Summitt, replaced her idol as head coach of the Tennessee women's basketball team in 2012. Before that, she was the assistant head coach alongside Pat Summitt for 27 seasons, from 1985-2012. She has said that she thinks of her former friend and coach everyday for inspiration.

"She'd break you down . . . and yet you'd show up the next day."

NOTES

1   I remember the first time Pat Summitt ever watched me play basketball.

2   I was a senior in high school — a small, quick point guard from the Knoxville area — and Pat was the new Tennessee Lady Vols head coach. It was 1975. She was only six years older than me.

3   "You've got to come and see this girl play," someone had told her. There wasn't much recruiting back then — not like there is today. A coach would show up, and if they liked what they saw, that was it.

4   Pat didn't like what she saw.

5   I didn't even finish the game — I sprained my ankle real bad.

6   She left the gym, and I never heard from her again.

7   It's a good thing I was fast. I ran track in high school as well, and won the state championship in the 400 (it was yards back then, not meters). My speed got me the scholarship to Tennessee.

8   But while running came naturally to me, it wasn't what I loved — basketball was. I'd played since I was 10. My dad, Bill, who was a coach, taught me how to dribble. I'd run dribbling drills around chairs, and play with my older brother and our neighbors in the street for as long as it was light outside.

9   Back then, girls weren't allowed to play full-court basketball — just half-court, three-on-three. It was thought that girls' bodies couldn't handle the strain and physicality of full-court basketball. But I knew otherwise. I knew that I could handle it, and that playing with the boys only made me tougher, and made me better. My dad knew it, too. He encouraged it.

10   I tried to walk on to the basketball team my freshman year before my track career even started. I hadn't seen Pat since I had blown it in high school. I'd met some of her players, though, and asked about her — asked what to expect.

Copyright © BookheadEd Learning, LLC

Analyze Vocabulary Using Context Clues

As students read the text, ask them to make predictions about each bold vocabulary word based on the context clues in the sentence. Have students use the annotation tool to make their predictions.

TURN AND TALK

Have students discuss their original vocabulary predictions with a neighbor. Come to a consensus as a class before confirming their definitions.

TEXT TALK

Who was Pat Summitt?

See paragraph 2: Pat Summitt was the head coach for the University of Tennessee Lady Vols basketball team.

Author's Word Choice

Explain to students that authors vary sentence length in writing in order to give the writing rhythm and flow. Generally, longer sentences provide needed information and shorter sentences really emphasize a point. Have students look at the various sentence structures in paragraphs 11–15 and read out loud to hear the rhythm. Ask students: How does the author use shorter sentences to emphasize her point? What point is she making? Are the varying sentence lengths effective?

11 "She's hard."

12 "She's tough."

13 Every single player said the same thing. Not that I cared — I just wanted to play. And, I figured, at least I was in shape. How bad could it be?

14 I walked into the gym on the first day of tryouts. *Does she remember me?* I thought. *Nope, no recognition.* Pat put us on the line and blew her whistle.

15 Suicides. A lot of suicides. Then she put 30 minutes on the clock for a continuous four-on-two fast break.

16 And that was just the warmup.

17 "That woman is crazy," I said to myself after walking out of the gym that day. "What am I getting myself into?"

18 But I went back the next day, and the day after that. She had that way about her. She'd break you down . . . and yet you'd show up the next day. You wanted to prove to her that you could take it. It took me years to realize that she didn't care about players proving it to her.

19 She cared about players proving it to themselves.

. . .

20 I made the team.

21 "You didn't even recruit her," people would say to Pat years later.

22 "Yeah, I recruited her," Pat would deadpan. "She wasn't very good."

23 She had one drill in practice that she named after me. "This is a Holly day!" she'd yell. Everyone would line up and run suicides, while I had to make 10 layups in a row, sprinting from one end of the court to the other. I was notorious for missing layups because I was too fast — I'd run full speed and my momentum would carry me too far under the basket. I'd make eight in a row and then miss. Every single one of us would have to start over again. It was brutal.

24 She was brutal.

25 But she was building us. She was also building her own legacy, though it probably didn't feel like that at the time. She made $250 a month to coach, recruit, wash our uniforms and drive the team van. (She had a habit of

TEXT TALK

Why did Warlick struggle with layups?

See paragraph 23: Warlick struggled with layups because she moved too fast on the court.

NOTES

multitasking behind the wheel generally: speeding, applying mascara and — when cellphones became a thing — talking on the phone.) She was also fighting for equal opportunities for women's basketball — not just our program — at every turn. She demanded the best from people and her players. It was the only way she knew, and it worked. Wins and championships followed.

26   In 1985, a few years after I graduated, I got a call from Pat. In that time, I'd played professionally in the Women's Professional Basketball League for a year, and was working at the University of Nebraska as an assistant coach.

27   "Would you be interested in coming here to coach?" she asked me.

28   "I can be there in 18 hours," I said.

29   The coaching dynamic between us — head coach and assistant — wasn't all that different from the dynamic between us when I was a player and she was my coach. As a player, Pat pushed me harder than others because she knew I could take it. She would give me the hardest defensive assignments, or yell at me a little louder than she would at everybody else. When I became her assistant, she kept challenging me. Our basketball philosophy was the same — how could it not be? But she knew when, how and just how far to push me.

30   She called me Warlick. I called her Summitt.

31   Eventually, through all the time we spent together, especially traveling to road games or going on recruiting trips, that dynamic shifted to something more like friendship. Everyone knows about Pat's icy stare and tough persona, but she was also a loving matriarch with a quick wit. She was someone you always wanted to be around because you never knew what was going to come out of her mouth or happen next.

• • •

32   I was the buffer between Pat and the players.

33   I'm not sure how it got started, but that's how it worked: She'd chew them out, and I'd remind them that they were O.K. I "survived" Pat myself. Everyone survives.

34   Our players — they were just kids — would come in knowing that she was going to be tough. But they still didn't really *know*. Not until they got here. So, that was my role: to listen and reassure. Over time, I slowly started to lead some practices, handle scouting and sit in on meetings with parents.

35   And when Pat got sick, I slowly started to take the lead on everything.

Reading & Writing Companion

TEXT TALK

What did Summitt ask Warlick to do a few years after graduation?

See paragraphs 26 and 27: Summitt asked Warlick to become her assistant coach.

36   She was suffering from dementia before any of us knew it. We all knew something was wrong, but we just covered for her. It was *Pat Summitt*, you know? No one ever asked. But when she was diagnosed in 2011, we weren't surprised. She told the staff one night, not long before the news broke, on the back porch at her house. We sat quietly for a minute after that before she cut through the silence:

37   "Now, I can drink all I want because I won't remember," she said.

38   That's Pat, for you. One of the worst days of our lives, and there she was, cracking jokes.

39   I remember being in the locker room with Pat later that season. Her illness had been announced publicly, and as a coaching staff, we were just trying to keep our focus on the game. I was going to be acting as head coach that night.

40   "What do you want to see?" I asked Pat. "Do you want to see a press?"

41   "I want to see you not sweat tonight," she said. "I'm gonna be sittin' beside you, and you sweat so much."

42   We laughed our way through it.

43   Together, over time, Pat and I talked about the **transition** of me becoming the head coach quite a bit. But the truth is . . . she was planning on being here forever. I was planning on it, too.

44   I inherited a lot. How do you fill those shoes? Pat Summitt is a basketball icon who not only built a championship program at Tennessee — but she also made it known the world over. She set the standard for other programs. She created opportunities for women when there had been none before, and her monumental **influence** on the game of basketball made little girls all over the world — little girls who may never have seen the Lady Vols play — feel seen and strong.

45   The expectation for the Lady Vols is to win a championship. It's a wonderful burden — to be known and celebrated for greatness, but to be disappointed in anything that falls short of another championship banner. I wouldn't be truthful if I said it's not a challenge. I've had to grow more in the last five years than the 25 plus that came before.

46   Someone was always going to have to follow Pat.

47   Pat Summitt is a mountain. We're all standing in her shadow.

Reading & Writing Companion   39

TEXT TALK

What happened to Summitt?

See paragraphs 35 and 36: Summitt became sick and suffered from dementia.

SELECTION VOCABULARY

transition / la transición *noun* the process of changing from one state to another COGNATE

ELL
- What is the author "transitioning" into?
- What does that process tell you about the meaning of "transition"?

influence / la influencia *noun* the power or ability to affect someone or something COGNATE

ELL
- Who is described as an "influence"?
- What did she do for the sport of women's basketball?

48 I visited her often after she stepped down. We'd take rides on her boat or just spend time on the beach. Pat loved the beach. We'd talk, but rarely about basketball. Just . . . life. Her health was **declining** and I was traveling more, so when I couldn't visit, I'd call.

49 "Pat, turn to channel 25 — so-and-so is playing," I'd tell her. Or, I'd ask, "Hey, Pat, what are you up to?"

50 "You know I'm not doing anything," she'd say.

51 She always made me laugh.

52 Our conversations got more difficult as the years passed. She didn't know she was struggling, but I could see it grow. When people who hadn't seen her in a while would visit, I could see the shock on their faces. Pat Summitt was supposed to be invincible.

53 Last June, I'd gotten a call saying she was in bad condition. I went to the hospice where she was staying. Nikki Fargas and Mickie DeMoss were there — both former assistants — and we sat in Pat's room while she lay quietly. I stepped out for a bit while Nikki and Mickie were telling old stories, laughing up a riot.

54 When I came back, there was Pat, sitting up straight while those two were laughing their way through the past. I walked over to the side of her bed and listened. Pat grabbed my shirt and pulled me close to her.

55 "Pat, you know I love you," I said.

56 She'd been hanging on for so many people. Her whole life was about other people.

57 "You gotta let go," I said.

58 That's one of the last things I remember — her gripping my shirt, pulling me close . . . and letting me go.

59 She knew what was coming.

· · ·

60 People say grief is like the ocean — that it comes in waves. But waves is too soft of a description. It feels more like lightning. Sometimes, I'll be driving somewhere and suddenly be struck, crying on my way to the grocery. Grief splits you open. I swear you spend your whole life trying to sew yourself back up.

40 Reading & Writing Companion

 SELECTION VOCABULARY

decline / decaer **verb** to diminish in health or strength; to worsen

- What is "declining?"
- What are the effects of that "decline"?

The Voice in My Head

61   I see her statue every day just outside of our facility. Our court is named after her. There's an empty chair on our bench in her memory. I'm confronted by her loss — personally and professionally — in so many visceral ways. On some level, it's comforting. I'm glad she's still around. She's the voice in my head.

62   Pat's presence when she was alive was so big that the void she left was **inevitably** going to be **vast**. As the Lady Vols' head coach, I am trying now to continue her legacy but when I'm not on the sideline — when I go home and sit with everything — I'm just someone who lost their best friend.

63   I carry the weight of that loss, and the weight of the program. But I'll do that every day with gratitude for her life and all that she imparted. And I'll do it with pride for this team and program, which I love with every fiber of my being.

64   I want to make a difference in these kids' lives — because that's what Pat made in mine.

✎ WRITE

PERSONAL RESPONSE: Why do you think it's important to have mentors in your life? Write a response to this question that represents your own point of view. Use examples from the essay "The Voice in My Head" to support your response.

👤 TEXT TALK

How is Summitt's presence still a part of the team?

See paragraph 61: Summitt's presence is still part of the team because the court is named after her, there is a statue of her, and there is an empty seat on the bench in honor of her.

Think about the impact Pat Summitt had on Holly Warlick. Are positive mentor relationships necessary for success?

Answers will vary.

B Ask each Beyond grade-level student to write one additional discussion question. Then, have one or two students facilitate a discussion, using their questions to guide the conversation.

Reading & Writing Companion   41

Ⅴ SELECTION VOCABULARY

inevitably / inevitablemente *adverb* in a manner that is sure or certain to happen; unavoidably COGNATE

ELL
- What effect does the author think Pat Summit's death will have?
- How certain is the author that effect?

vast / vasto/a *adjective* of very great extent or quantity, a large amount of something COGNATE

ELL
- What word does the author use to describe Pat Summitt's presence?
- How does that word provide a context clue for the meaning of "vast"?

Reading Comprehension

Have students complete the digital reading comprehension questions ✅ when they finish reading.

ANSWER KEY

QUESTION 1: A	QUESTION 5: C	QUESTION 9:
QUESTION 2: D	QUESTION 6: B	*See first chart.*
QUESTION 3: C	QUESTION 7: D	QUESTION 10:
QUESTION 4: B	QUESTION 8: D	*See second chart.*

First	Second	Third	Fourth
Coach Summitt goes public with her early onset dementia diagnosis.	Coach Warlick assumes responsibility for head coaching duties.	Coach Warlick is told that Coach Summitt's health has taken a turn for the worse.	Coach Warlick tells Coach Summitt to "let go."

Action	Person
Let Holly play basketball with the boys	Holly's father
Won 8 NCAA Championships	Coach Summitt
Was the "good cop" to Coach Summitt's "bad cop" with the players	Coach Warlick
Told funny stories about working with Coach Summitt	Nikki Fargas

Connect and Extend OPTIONAL

CONNECT TO EXTENDED WRITING PROJECT

Students can find inspiration in "The Voice in My Head" for their informational essays. Have students discuss what they think are the important moments in the essay and explain how those moments changed everything for Holly Warlick.

BEYOND THE BOOK

Writing: Who is the Voice in Your Head?

Students will identify a person in their lives who has had a significant impact on them and consider what they've learned from that person.

Ask students to think about the most influential people in their lives.

- Who has challenged them the most?
- Whose voice do they hear inside their head when they are faced with one of life's many challenges?
- How has this person impacted their life and the choices they've made?

Ask them to write this person a letter to say how this person has influenced their lives. Remind them to include specific examples of situations they have faced and how the lessons they've learned from this person have helped them to navigate these moments or challenges. Encourage students to send the final drafts of their letters!

Collaborative Conversation

Break students into collaborative conversation groups to discuss the writing prompt. Remind them to reference their Skills Focus annotations in their discussion.

Why do you think it's important to have mentors in your life? Write a response in which you answer this question. Use examples from the essay "The Voice in My Head" to support your response.

Use the scaffolds below to differentiate instruction for your **ELL** English Language Learners and **A** Approaching grade-level learners.

ELL **BEGINNING, INTERMEDIATE** Use the <u>discussion guide</u> and <u>speaking frames</u> to facilitate the discussion with support from the teacher.

ADVANCED, ADVANCED HIGH Use the <u>discussion guide</u> and <u>speaking frames</u> to facilitate the discussion in mixed-level groups.

A **APPROACHING** Use the <u>discussion guide</u> to facilitate the discussion in mixed-level groups.

APPROACHING
ADVANCED, ADVANCED HIGH
BEGINNING, INTERMEDIATE

Discussion Guide	Speaking Frames
1. Why do you think it's important to have mentors in your life?	• Mentors are important because ____.
2. What connections can you make between the essay and your own knowledge and experiences?	• This story reminds me of ____. • This story connects to ____.
3. How has the essay changed the way you think about mentors?	• The essay has made me realize that ____. • I used to think ____. Now I think ____.

Review Prompt and Rubric

Before students begin writing, review the writing prompt and rubric with the class.

PERSONAL RESPONSE: Why do you think it's important to have mentors in your life? Write a response in which you answer this question. Use examples from the essay "The Voice in My Head" to support your response.

ELL **PROMPT GUIDE**

A
- Why do you think it's important to have mentors in your life?
- What connections can you make between the essay and your knowledge and experiences?

- How has the essay changed the way you think about mentors?

Score	Personal Response	Language and Conventions
4	The writer clearly explains his or her personal response to the text, using relevant evidence from the text as needed.	The writer demonstrates a consistent command of grammar, punctuation, and usage conventions. Although minor errors may be evident, they do not detract from the fluency or the clarity of the essay.
3	The writer sufficiently explains his or her personal response to the text, using relevant evidence from the text most of the time.	The writer demonstrates an adequate command of grammar, punctuation, and usage conventions. Although some errors may be evident, they create few (if any) disruptions in the fluency of the writing or the clarity of the essay.
2	The writer begins to explain his or her personal response to the text, but the explanation is incomplete. The writer uses relevant evidence from the text only some of the time.	The writer demonstrates a partial command of grammar, punctuation, and usage conventions. Some distracting errors may be evident, at times creating minor disruptions in the fluency or clarity of the writing.
1	The writer attempts to explain his or her personal response to the text, but the explanation is not successful. The writer uses little or no relevant evidence from the text.	The writer demonstrates little or no command of grammar, punctuation, and usage conventions. Serious and persistent errors create disruptions in the fluency of the writing and sometimes interfere with meaning.
0	The writer does not provide a relevant response to the prompt or does not provide a response at all.	Serious and persistent errors overwhelm the writing and interfere with the meaning of the response as a whole, making the writer's meaning impossible to understand.

Write

Ask students to complete the writing assignment using textual evidence to support their answers.

Use the scaffolds below to differentiate instruction for your **ELL** English Language Learners and **A** Approaching grade-level learners.

ELL **BEGINNING** With the help of the <u>word bank</u>, write a response using <u>paragraph frame 1</u>.

INTERMEDIATE With the help of the <u>word bank</u>, write a response using <u>paragraph frames 1 and 2</u>.

ADVANCED, ADVANCED HIGH Write a response of differentiated length using the <u>sentence starters</u>.

A **APPROACHING** Write a response of differentiated length using the <u>sentence starters</u>.

| BEGINNING | | ADVANCED, ADVANCED HIGH |
| INTERMEDIATE | | APPROACHING |

Word Bank	Paragraph Frame 1	Paragraph Frame 2	Sentence Starters
possible teachers stronger opportunities inspire	Mentors are important because they ____ young people. This reminds me of ____ who encourage students to follow their dreams. In the essay, Pat Summitt pushed Holly Warlick and the other players to become ____. Summitt also created ____ for female players. In this way, mentors make it ____ for young people to achieve their goals.	A goal I have is ____. An example of a mentor who could help me is ____. This person could help me ____. This is similar to the essay because Summitt helped Warlick ____.	• Mentors are important because . . . • The essay reminds me of . . . • Summitt helped Warlick . . . • This essay made me realize . . . • When I read . . . , I thought . . . • A mentor who could help me is . . . because . . .

Peer Review

Students should submit substantive feedback to two peers using the instructions below.

- How well does this response answer the prompt?
- Which of the author's comments inspired you to think differently about the text?
- What did the writer do well in this response? What does the writer need to work on?

Remember that your comments are most useful when they are kind and constructive.

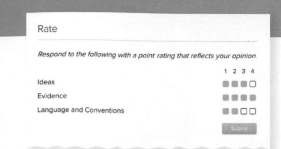

Rate

Respond to the following with a point rating that reflects your opinion.

	1 2 3 4
Ideas	■ ■ ■ ☐
Evidence	■ ■ ■ ■
Language and Conventions	■ ■ ☐ ☐

Submit

 SENTENCE FRAMES

A
- You were able to (completely / partly / almost) ___ answer the prompt.
- You could answer the prompt more completely by . . .

- I thought differently about the text after reading . . .
- My favorite part of your response is . . .

We're on the Same Team

INFORMATIONAL TEXT
Jacki Jing
2017

Introduction

Jacki Jing was an NCAA Division I volleyball player at Binghamton University, where she was inducted into the school's Athletic Hall of Fame. Here, she draws from personal experiences to respond to a newspaper article that questioned the difficulty of mastering the sport.

Jacki Jing, a former National Collegiate Athletic Association (NCAA) Division I volleyball player, responds to a *SportsNews* article that claims volleyball has become popular because it requires a lower level of athleticism than basketball. In her letter, Jing finds fault with this reasoning and describes the technique and work ethic necessary to master volleyball. Just like basketball, volleyball takes a lifetime of practice and refinement. Jing also states that she chose to pursue volleyball because of the hard work it entailed. Lastly, Jing addresses any young woman who might read her letter, explaining how the sport changed her life: it gave her lifelong friendships and taught her important lessons, such as the ability to perform under pressure.

ELL Proficiency-leveled summaries and summaries in multiple languages are available digitally.

 Audio and audio text highlighting are available with this text.

COMPARING WITHIN AND ACROSS GENRES

 In the letter "We're On the Same Team," the author Jacki Jing deals with a misunderstanding in regard to the difficulty of her sport, volleyball. She describes what volleyball has taught her, even in life beyond the court. In "The Voice in My Head," Holly Warlick explores another aspect of how sports can shape our lives in an essay.

Access Complex Text

LEXILE: 760L **WORD COUNT:** 632

The following areas may be challenging for students, particularly **ELL** English Language Learners and **A** Approaching grade-level learners.

Prior Knowledge	Genre	Specific Vocabulary
• The game of volleyball may be unfamiliar to some students. • Volleyball is a game for two teams, usually comprising six players each, in which a large ball is hit by hand over a net. The aim is to score points by making the ball reach the ground on the opponent's side of the net.	• The selection is written as an argument in the form of a letter. • Students may not be familiar with some of the features of an argument, such as a *claim*.	• Acronyms associated with basketball and volleyball appear in the selection. • Acronyms such as *NCAA, NBA,* and *WNBA* may need to be defined.

SCAFFOLDS **ELL** ENGLISH LANGUAGE LEARNERS   **A** APPROACHING GRADE LEVEL   **B** BEYOND GRADE LEVEL

These icons identify differentiation strategies and scaffolded support for a variety of students. See the digital lesson plan for additional differentiation strategies and scaffolds.

Instructional Path

The print teacher's edition includes essential point-of-use instruction and planning tools. Complete lesson plans and program documents appear in your digital teacher account.

First Read: We're on the Same Team

Objectives: After an initial reading and discussion of the letter, students will be able to identify and restate the text's key ideas and details.

Skill: Summarizing

Objectives: After reading and discussing a model of close reading, students will be able to provide a summary of the text free of personal opinions or judgments.

Close Read: We're on the Same Team

Objectives: After engaging in a close reading and discussion of the text, students will be able to summarize in order to participate in a collaborative conversation and write a short informational response.

Blast: A Level Playing Field

Objectives: After exploring background information and research links about a topic, students will respond to a question with a 140-character response.

DIGITAL ONLY

Progress Monitoring

Opportunities to Learn	Opportunities to Demonstrate Learning	Opportunities to Reteach

Summarizing

⚙ Skill: Summarizing	⚙ Skill: Summarizing • Your Turn ▣ Close Read • Skills Focus • Write	⚙ Unit 6 • Skills: Summarizing – Bronx Masquerade ⚙ Spotlight Skill: Summarizing

First Read

Jacki Jing

We're on the Same Team

Introduce the Text

As a class, watch the video preview and have students read the introduction in pairs to make connections to the video preview.

To activate prior knowledge and experiences, ask students:

- How does the information in this video connect to what you already know?

- What questions do you have after reading the introduction?

> **ELL SPEAKING FRAMES**
> - The ____ in the video makes me think ____.
> - The video shows ____. This makes me wonder ____.
> - I think the text will ____. I think this because ____.
> - I predict that there will be ____. I believe this because ____.

Entry Point

As students prepare to read "We're On the Same Team," share the following information with them to provide context.

✓ This letter is significant because Jacki Jing not only defends the sport of volleyball, but also defends female athletes as a result. Female athletes receive less media attention and recognition than their male counterparts. A stigma has surrounded female sports in American society. A poll conducted in 2016 found that nearly half of the male participants believed that men were better at sports, and nearly a third of women agreed. Society has made progress with eliminating this unfair judgment of athletes based on gender, with campaigns that aim to change the perception of the strength, stamina, and talent of female athletes.

✓ After graduating Binghamton University in 2008, author Jacki Jing went on to become a news and traffic reporter, as well as a host and producer for IGN Entertainment.

"I had to bleed and I had to sweat just as hard as any other elite athlete."

Jacki Jing
562 Maple St.
Dallas, TX 75215

March 21, 2018

SportsNews
854 Commerce St.
New York, NY 10103

Dear Editor,

1   I was pretty excited recently when I saw a SportsNews article titled, "Why Volleyball Is So Popular." As a former NCAA Division I volleyball player, I was excited to see my favorite sport featured on your website. My excitement quickly turned to disbelief as I read your article.

2   In particular, I was insulted when I read the following passage:

> Athletes go where they find success. Basketball is a difficult sport to master. Unless you're willing to put in the time and effort and have a certain level of athleticism and hand-eye skills, you will not be successful. You will be pushed out of the sport because of what it demands. In volleyball, those barriers are lower.

3   Basketball is an incredible sport. It requires talent and athletic ability. Yet the exact same is true of volleyball.

4   Just like basketball, it takes years to hone volleyball skills. Volleyball requires long practices in the gym (or in the sand) multiple times a week. Approaching, hitting, serving, passing—these aspects of volleyball may not look hard. However, playing at a high level requires an athlete to master a very specific **technique** for each skill. In this regard, volleyball is no different than basketball. Anyone can pick up a ball and shoot it at the basket. But it takes a lifetime of practice to be as good as the best NBA and WNBA players. The ladies on the

Skill: Summarizing

Jacki Jing, a former college volleyball player, writes a letter to the editor of SportsNews to say that she has a problem with an article she recently read on the website called "Why Volleyball Is So Popular."

According to Jing, mastering volleyball skills and techniques requires years of practice, especially for high level players. Jing insists that volleyball is an intensely difficult sport to learn and play, and I am neither supporting nor opposing her opinion.

Analyze Vocabulary Using Context Clues

In paragraph 4, focus on the sentence that uses the word *technique*. Point out these context clues:

1.   First I notice the words *athlete, master,* and *skill*. In this context, I think of learning a way or method to do something, such as throwing a ball.

2.   In the paragraph, I find more context clues, like the words *practices, hitting, serving,* and *passing*. I think that these are some of the skills that players must learn and practice.

3.   I can reread the sentence and the paragraph and think about the meaning of *technique* as "a way to perform or practise a skill." This definition makes sense.

Summarizing

How did the reader choose to begin his summary? How does this help the reader maintain logical order?

The reader highlighted important details then started with answers to who, what, and when questions. He also said a little about why the letter was written. By starting at the beginning, the reader managed to keep to the right order of the letter.

TEXT TALK

Who is Jacki Jing? Why did she want to read the *SportsNews* article?

See paragraph 1: Jacki Jing is a former NCAA Division 1 volleyball player. Volleyball is her favorite sport, and she was excited to see it featured on the *SportsNews* website.

What is one way volleyball is like basketball?

See paragraphs 3 and 4: Answers may vary. Volleyball requires talent and athletic ability. It takes years of practice to learn the skills. Players must master a specific technique for each skill.

V SELECTION VOCABULARY

technique / la técnica *noun* the way a particular task or performance is done COGNATE

Skills Focus

QUESTION 3: Connect to Essential Question

Jing developed strong relationships with her teammates. The fact that she thinks of her teammates as sisters is proof of how volleyball affected her life.

TEXT TALK

Why did Jacki Jing choose volleyball?

See paragraph 5: She says she was a gangly, awkward teen. Volleyball taught her to control her body, think fast, move quickly, and use strategy.

How does Jacki Jing feel about people who say that volleyball is easy?

See paragraph 6: She resents any idea that volleyball is an easier path than basketball. She says that she learned how to perform under pressure, push herself, and discover what it means to achieve.

What can competitive sports teach you about life?

Answers will vary.

> **B** **BEYOND TEXT TALK**
>
> Ask each Beyond grade-level student to write one additional discussion question. Then, have one or two students facilitate a discussion, using their questions to guide the conversation.

We're on the Same Team

Olympic volleyball teams might make it look easy. That's because years of practice have **refined** their movements so they appear fluid and graceful.

5 I remember being a gangly, awkward teen. I had to choose between volleyball and basketball. Every person chooses his or her own path for different reasons. I don't think one sport is better or harder than the other. Personally, I chose volleyball because it **required** work. I had to learn how to control my body. I had to learn how to do more than just jump high. I had to learn how to swing hard and sharp. I had to think fast, move quickly, and use strategy. I had to bleed and I had to sweat just as hard as any other **elite** athlete.

6 I am tired of hearing that volleyball is easy. I resent that this article **implies** volleyball players have somehow chosen an "easier" path. More young women are choosing to play volleyball because it is tough. It is competitive. It is fierce and fun. That's it.

7 As for the young women out there who are thinking about volleyball, I can tell you right now it is my life and my passion. I was not able to become an Olympian. Yet at 30 years old I still play as much as I can. And believe me, I still have not mastered it. I am always refining my skills and my knowledge of the game.

Women's volleyball: A tough, but fun, sport

8 Volleyball changed my life. When I think about playing in high school and college, it brings back memories that make me tear up. My teammates are my sisters. I am still friends with some of my biggest rivals from college. The relationships you form when working that hard at something stay with you forever.

9 I still hold close to my heart some of my biggest wins and hardest losses. I've learned what is necessary to perform under pressure. I've learned how to push myself mentally and physically. I've learned how to work with a large group of people. I've learned what it takes to achieve what I want. I have experienced the highest highs of my life on the volleyball court.

10 SportsNews, volleyball is not girly. It is not any less athletic. It is just awesome.

Sincerely,
Jacki Jing

 SELECTION VOCABULARY

refine / refinar *verb* to make small changes to improve upon something COGNATE

ELL
• What is being "refined"?
• What is the result of being "refined"?

require / requerir *verb* to need for a function or demand by authority COGNATE

ELL
• What was "required" in volleyball?
• What was learned?

elite / selecto/a *adjective* of a group or class that is considered the very best

ELL
• What kind of athlete is "elite"?
• What makes Jacki an "elite" athlete?

imply / insinuar *verb* to suggest something as true without a direct statement

ELL
• What has the author of the SportsNews article suggested about volleyball?
• Why does Jacki resent this?

Reading Comprehension OPTIONAL

Have students complete the digital reading comprehension questions ✓ when they finish reading.

ANSWER KEY

QUESTION 1: A   **QUESTION 3:** B   **QUESTION 5:**
QUESTION 2: D   **QUESTION 4:** C   *See chart.*

Definition	Word
a person or group of people with high ability or qualities	elite
improved by making small changes	refined
to strongly suggest something without saying it directly	implies
necessary for a purpose	required
a way of accomplishing something, a skill	technique

Connect and Extend OPTIONAL

CONNECT TO EXTENDED WRITING PROJECT

Students can use "We're on the Same Team" as a mentor text for their Extended Writing Project, and analyze how Jacki Jing supports her argument. They can also reflect on how playing volleyball helped Jacki to establish important relationships in her life, and how sports may have impacted relationships in their own lives.

BEYOND THE BOOK

Performance: The 30 Second Elevator Speech

The 30 Second Elevator Speech is a clear, brief message about you. It communicates who you are, what you are arguing, and why others should see your argument from your point of view. What if Jacki Jing only had 30 seconds to share her message with the *SportsNews* Editor?

Ask students to:

- Imagine they are Jing and have just run into the *SportsNews* Editor in an elevator.
- Adapt Jing's letter into a 30 Second Elevator Speech. Incorporate Jing's tone and argument in order to communicate her message in an effective and memorable way.

To reflect, ask students:

- What words did you feel were essential to communicating Jing's message?
- What was the most difficult part?
- What is the benefit of being able to communicate an important message in 30 seconds or less?

Think Questions

Circulate as students answer Think Questions independently. Scaffolds for these questions are shown on the opposite page.

QUESTION 1: Textual Evidence

The author disagrees that volleyball is an easy sport to master. She says, "I resent that this article implies volleyball players have somehow chosen an 'easier' path." The author says that basketball "requires talent and athletic ability. And the exact same is true of volleyball."

QUESTION 2: Textual Evidence

The author says she chose volleyball over basketball "because it required work." She points out that the work meant she had to "learn how to control my body. . . how to do more than just jump high . . . had to swing hard and sharp . . . and think fast, move quickly, and use strategy."

QUESTION 3: Textual Evidence

The author says that more young women are choosing to play volleyball because it is "tough," "competitive," "fierce," and "fun."

QUESTION 4: Context Clues

I think *refined* must mean "perfected, or improved over time." The word is used to describe what happens after years of practicing volleyball. The Olympic volleyball team members make the game look easy with fluid and graceful, or refined, movements.

QUESTION 5: Context Clues

I think that *implies* means "suggests." The words in the paragraph that led to my understanding are "tired of hearing" and "somehow chosen." A dictionary meaning is "to suggest without stating directly."

WE'RE ON THE SAME TEAM

First Read

Read "We're on the Same Team." After you read, complete the Think Questions below.

☁ **THINK QUESTIONS**

1. What is the author of the letter's main problem with the SportsNews article? Cite evidence from the selection to support your answer.

2. Why did the author choose to play volleyball? Cite textual evidence from the text to explain the author's reasoning.

3. According to the author, why do young women choose to play volleyball? Provide evidence from the text to support your answer.

4. Find the word **refined** in paragraph 3 of We're on the Same Team. Use context clues in the surrounding sentences, as well as the sentence in which the word appears, to determine the word's meaning. Write your definition here and identify clues that helped you figure out its meaning.

5. Use context clues to determine the meaning of **implies** in paragraph 5. Write your definition here and identify clues that helped you figure out its meaning. Then check the meaning in a dictionary.

 Reading & Writing Companion | **45**

Think Questions

Use the scaffolds below to differentiate instruction for your **ELL** English Language Learners and **A** Approaching grade-level learners.

ELL **BEGINNING** Write a response using the <u>word bank</u> and <u>sentence frames</u>.

INTERMEDIATE Write a response using the <u>sentence frames</u>.

ADVANCED, ADVANCED HIGH Write a response using the <u>Text-Dependent Question Guide</u>.

A **APPROACHING** Write a response using the <u>Text-Dependent Question Guide</u>.

	INTERMEDIATE	APPROACHING
BEGINNING		ADVANCED, ADVANCED HIGH
Word Bank	**Sentence Frames**	**Text-Dependent Question Guide**
favorite basketball more tired	Jacki Jing wants to read the article because volleyball is her ___ sport. The article says that the demands of volleyball are ___ than basketball. I know how Jacki Jing feels because she says she was ___.	1. • Why did Jacki Jing want to read the article? • What does the passage say about the demands of volleyball? • How do I know how Jacki feels?
improved lower tough	Jacki Jing chose a sport to play when she was a ___. Her choices were volleyball and ___. She chose volleyball because it required ___.	2. • When did Jacki Jing choose a sport to play? • What were Jacki Jing's choices? • Why did Jacki Jing choose volleyball?
movements suggests teen	The author says that ___ young women are choosing volleyball. The first reason is that volleyball is ___.	3. • What does the author say about young women choosing volleyball? • What is the first reason the author gives? • What words does the author use?
work somehow insulted	The Olympic team's ___ are fluid and graceful after years of practice. This tells me that refined means ___ over time.	4. • Read: "The ladies on the Olympic team might make it look easy. That's because years of practice have **refined** their movements so they appear fluid and graceful." • What happens after years of practice? • What does that tell me about the meaning of the word *refined*?
	Jackie Jing is ___ of hearing people say volleyball is easy. She says that the article implies that players have ___ chosen an easier path. A word that can be used in place of *implies* is ___.	5. • How does Jacki Jing feel when people say that volleyball is easy? • What does Jacki Jing say the article *implies*? • What is a word in a dictionary definition that can be used in place of *implies*?

Skill: Summarizing

Introduce the Skill

Watch the Concept Definition video and read the following definitions with your students.

When you **summarize** a text, you briefly state the main points and most important details in your own words. Summarizing can help you organize, explain, and remember concepts in an informational text or the events that take place in a story.

To summarize, you must decide what is most important as you read. Ask the basic questions: *who, what, when, where, why,* and *how*. Using your own words, write your answers to these questions from an **objective** point of view, without inserting your own feelings and opinions.

Summarizing is sometimes confused with paraphrasing. When you **paraphrase**, you do not condense a text to its most important details. Instead, you restate the entire text in your own words. A summary is much shorter than the original text, while a paraphrase may be the same length as the original text.

TURN AND TALK

1. How would you tell a friend about a book, movie, or television program you liked? Do you tell everything that happened or just the most important parts? Do you tell what happened in order?

2. Do you think you would be able to describe the meaning of what you read or watched? Why or why not?

ELL SPEAKING FRAMES
- I told a friend about ____.
- I described ____.
- My friend ____.

We're on the Same Team

Skill: Summarizing

Use the Checklist to analyze Summarizing in "We're on the Same Team." Refer to the sample student annotations about Summarizing in the text.

••• CHECKLIST FOR SUMMARIZING

In order to determine how to write an objective summary of a text, note the following:

✓ in a nonfiction text, examine details to identify the main idea, making notations in a notebook or graphic organizer

✓ answers to the basic questions *who, what, where, when, why,* and *how*

✓ stay objective, and do not add your own personal thoughts, judgments, or opinions to the summary

To provide an objective summary of a text free of personal opinions or judgments, consider the following questions:

✓ What are the answers to basic *who, what, where, when, why,* and *how* questions in literature and works of nonfiction?

✓ In what order should I put the main ideas and most important details in a work of nonfiction to make my summary logical?

✓ Is my summary objective, or have I added my own thoughts, judgments, or personal opinions?

Please note that excerpts and passages in the StudySync® library and this workbook are intended as touchstones to generate interest in an author's work. The excerpts and passages do not substitute for the reading of entire texts, and StudySync® strongly recommends that students seek out and purchase the whole literary or informational work in order to experience it as the author intended. Links to online resellers are available in our digital library. In addition, complete works may be ordered through an authorized reseller by filling out and returning to StudySync® the order form enclosed in this workbook.

V SKILL VOCABULARY

summarize / resumir *verb* to restate briefly the most important points in a text

objective / objetivo/a *adjective* undistorted by emotion or personal bias COGNATE

paraphrase / parafrasear *verb* to restate the author's words in your own words COGNATE

Skill:
Summarizing

Reread paragraphs 5–6 of "We're on the Same Team." Then, using the Checklist on the previous page, answer the multiple-choice questions below.

🔁 YOUR TURN

1. What is the best summary of paragraph 5?

   ○ A. Jing states that she chose to play volleyball because she was awkward.
   ○ B. Jing states that she chose to play volleyball because it was challenging.
   ○ C. Jing states that she chose to play volleyball because it involved jumping.
   ○ D. Jing states that she chose to play volleyball because she got to swing hard.

2. What is the best summary of paragraph 6?

   ○ A. Jing believes young women choose to play volleyball because it is fun not because it is easy.
   ○ B. Jing believes that young women play volleyball because it is tough and competitive not because it is easy.
   ○ C. While Jing knows that many people think volleyball is an easy sport, she believes volleyball is tough.
   ○ D. Jing knows that young women find out that volleyball is tough and competitive after thinking it was an easy sport.

Reading & Writing
Companion   **47**

Your Turn

Ask students to complete the Your Turn Activity.

QUESTION 1

A. Incorrect. This summary states a main idea that is inaccurate. Jing chose to play volleyball because it was challenging.

B. **Correct.** This summary states a main idea that is accurate. Jing chose to play volleyball because it was challenging. She says "it required work."

C. Incorrect. This summary states a main idea that is inaccurate. Jing chose to play volleyball because "it required work."

D. Incorrect. This summary states a main idea that is inaccurate. Jing chose to play volleyball because it was challenging.

QUESTION 2

A. Incorrect. The summary statements are not in a logical order. The idea that volleyball is fun is not the main idea Jing wants readers to know.

B. **Correct.** This summary maintains meaning, focuses on Jing's main problem with the article, and logically points to a reason that supports this meaning.

C. Incorrect. This summary begins with a main idea but does not say that this is a problem for Jing or that it is the article that is the source. The second statement is not correct. Jing states that young women choose volleyball because it is tough.

D. Incorrect. This summary does not state what Jing's problem is with the article, and incorrectly states that young women who play volleyball think it is easy and then find out it is tough and competitive.

Close Read

Skills Focus

Have students read and annotate the text independently using the Skills Focus questions.

QUESTION 1: Textual Evidence

See paragraph 4: Jing restates her main argument that volleyball is an incredible sport that requires athletic ability and talent.

QUESTION 2: Summarizing

See paragraph 7: I believe the Olympics, age, her love of volleyball, and her continuing quest to master it are important details. I could summarize this paragraph thus, "Even though she never qualified for the Olympics, Jing at 30 still loves volleyball and works to master the game."

QUESTION 3: Connect to Essential Question

See paragraph 8.

Close Read

Reread "We're on the Same Team." As you reread, complete the Skills Focus questions below. Then use your answers and annotations from the questions to help you complete the Write activity.

◎ SKILLS FOCUS

1. Identify textual evidence that supports Jacki Jing's argument in favor of volleyball.

2. Select a paragraph in Jing's argument. Identify the most important details in the paragraph. Then use the details to summarize the main ideas in your own words.

3. Identify evidence in the letter that indicates how sports relationships affected Jing's life. Use details to summarize the impact of these relationships.

✏ WRITE

INFORMATIONAL: In the essay "The Voice in My Head" by Holly Warlick and the letter to the editor "We're On the Same Team" by Jacki Jing, both authors write about the ways they have worked hard in athletics and in life. In a blog post of your own, summarize the ways that each author had to work hard, including challenges they faced and what helped them succeed. Then, explain a situation where you had to work hard to achieve a goal. Include any setbacks you had and how you finally managed to succeed. Be sure to provide textual evidence from the two texts and your own personal experiences to convey your ideas.

Writer's Notebook

Connect to Essential Question: Give students time to reflect on how "We're on the Same Team" connects to the unit's essential question "How do relationships shape us?" by freewriting in their Writer's Notebooks.

ELL Beginning & Intermediate

Read aloud the unit's essential question: "How do relationships shape us?" Encourage students to draw their reflections or allow students to write in their native language. Circulate around the room, prompting students for their thoughts as they respond orally or through pantomime.

Advanced & Advanced High

Allow students to share their connections orally in pairs or small groups before freewriting.

Collaborative Conversation

Break students into collaborative conversation groups to discuss the Close Read prompt. Remind them to reference their Skills Focus annotations in their discussion.

In the essay "The Voice in My Head" by Holly Warlick and the letter to the editor "We're On the Same Team" by Jacki Jing, both authors write about the ways they have worked hard in athletics and in life. In a blog post of your own, summarize the ways that each author had to work hard, including challenges they faced and what helped them succeed. Then, explain a situation where you had to work hard to achieve a goal. Include any setbacks you had and how you finally managed to succeed. Be sure to provide textual evidence from the two texts and your own personal experiences to convey your ideas.

Use the scaffolds below to differentiate instruction for your **ELL** English Language Learners and **A** Approaching grade-level learners.

ELL **BEGINNING, INTERMEDIATE** Use the discussion guide and speaking frames to facilitate the discussion with support from the teacher.

ADVANCED, ADVANCED HIGH Use the discussion guide and speaking frames to facilitate the discussion in mixed-level groups.

A **APPROACHING** Use the discussion guide to facilitate the discussion in mixed-level groups.

| APPROACHING |
| ADVANCED, ADVANCED HIGH |
| BEGINNING, INTERMEDIATE |

Discussion Guide	Speaking Frames
1. How does Jing describe her experience with volleyball and hard work?	• Jing describes basketball by ____. • She talks about hard work when ____.
2. How does Warlick describe her experience with basketball and hard work?	• Warlick describes basketball by ____. • She talks about hard work when ____.
3. How does Jing's letter or Warlick's essay help you craft your blog post?	• One way Jing's letter or Warlick's essay helps is ____. • I think this because ____.

Review Prompt and Rubric

Before students begin writing, review the writing prompt and rubric with the class.

INFORMATIONAL: In the essay "The Voice in My Head" by Holly Warlick and the letter to the editor "We're On the Same Team" by Jacki Jing, both authors write about the ways they have worked hard in athletics and in life. In a blog post of your own, summarize the ways that each author had to work hard, including challenges they faced and what helped them succeed. Then, explain a situation where you had to work hard to achieve a goal. Include any setbacks you had and how you finally managed to succeed. Be sure to provide textual evidence from the two texts and your own personal experiences to convey your ideas.

ELL PROMPT GUIDE

A
- How does Jing describe her experience with volleyball and hard work?
- How does Warlick describe her experience with basketball and hard work?

- When did you have to work hard to achieve something?
- How did Jing, Warlick, and you overcome challenges?

Score	Summarizing	Language and Conventions
4	The writer clearly summarizes both texts, explaining both authors' challenges and successes, and explains a personal challenge. The writer provides well-chosen and relevant evidence from each text and personal experiences to convey ideas.	The writer demonstrates a consistent command of grammar, punctuation, and usage conventions. Although minor errors may be evident, they do not detract from the fluency or the clarity of the essay.
3	The writer summarizes both texts, explaining both authors' challenges and successes, and explains a personal challenge. The writer provides sufficient evidence from each text and personal experiences to convey ideas.	The writer demonstrates an adequate command of grammar, punctuation, and usage conventions. Although some errors may be evident, they create few (if any) disruptions in the fluency of the writing or the clarity of the essay.
2	The writer mostly summarizes both texts, explaining both authors' challenges and successes, and explains a personal challenge, but in an incomplete manner. The writer provides some relevant evidence from each text and personal experiences to convey ideas.	The writer demonstrates a partial command of grammar, punctuation, and usage conventions. Some distracting errors may be evident, at times creating minor disruptions in the fluency or clarity of the writing.
1	The writer attempts to summarize both texts, explaining both authors' challenges and successes, and attempts to explain a personal challenge, but with many errors. The writer provides little to no evidence from each text or personal experiences to convey ideas.	The writer demonstrates little or no command of grammar, punctuation, and usage conventions. Serious and persistent errors create disruptions in the fluency of the writing and sometimes interfere with meaning.
0	The writer does not provide a relevant response to the prompt or does not provide a response at all.	Serious and persistent errors overwhelm the writing and interfere with the meaning of the response as a whole, making the writer's meaning impossible to understand.

Write

Ask students to complete the writing assignment using textual evidence to support their answers.

Use the scaffolds below to differentiate instruction for your **ELL** English Language Learners and **A** Approaching grade-level learners.

ELL **BEGINNING** With the help of the word bank, write a response using paragraph frame 1.

INTERMEDIATE With the help of the word bank, write a response using paragraph frames 1 and 2.

ADVANCED, ADVANCED HIGH Write a response of differentiated length using the sentence starters.

A **APPROACHING** Write a response of differentiated length using the sentence starters.

| BEGINNING | | ADVANCED, ADVANCED HIGH |
| INTERMEDIATE | | APPROACHING |

Word Bank	Paragraph Frame 1	Paragraph Frame 2	Sentence Starters
basketball lessons quit volleyball challenges	Holly Warlick worked hard in ____. Jacki Jing worked hard in ____. They both faced ____. However, both Jing and Warlick learned ____ about how to accomplish their goals in life. In order to reach my goals, I know to work hard in school and never ____.	In "The Voice in My Head," Warlick became a successful athlete because she ____. In "We're on the Same Team," Jing writes that volleyball players are ____. Like these two authors, sometimes I have ____ when I want to accomplish something. In school, ____was hard for me. However, with hard work and ____, I got better grades. I succeeded just like Jing and Warlick.	• Holly Warlick worked hard in . . . • Jacki Jing worked hard in . . . • Warlick faced challenges, like . . . • Jing faced challenges, like . . . • In order to succeed, it's important to . . . • One challenge in my life was when . . . • I had to work hard to . . .

Peer Review

Students should submit substantive feedback to two peers using the review instructions below.

- How well does this response answer the prompt?
- How well does the writer support his or her ideas with details and examples?
- Which sentence in the writer's response made you think differently about the topic?
- What did the writer do well in this response? What does the writer need to work on?

Rate

Respond to the following with a point rating that reflects your opinion.

	1 2 3 4
Ideas	▪▪▪☐
Evidence	▪▪▪▪
Language and Conventions	▪▪☐☐

Submit

ELL **A** **SENTENCE FRAMES**

- You were able to (completely / partly / almost) ____ answer the prompt because ____.
- You could answer the prompt more completely by ____.
- You supported the topic of ____ with the detail of ____.

- One idea that needs more support is ____.
- I thought differently about the texts after reading ____.
- My favorite part of your response is ____.

The Treasure of Lemon Brown

FICTION
Walter Dean Myers
1983

Introduction

Award-winning writer and former National Ambassador for Young People's Literature, Walter Dean Myers (1937–2014) once said, "I write to give hope to those kids who are like the ones I knew—poor, troubled, treated indifferently by society." Myers was raised in Harlem, New York, and grew up loving stories—both the ones his family told him and the ones he read in books. Much of what he writes is based on experiences from his own life. In the short story "The Treasure of Lemon Brown," teenager Greg Ridley meets a homeless man who teaches him a valuable lesson.

In Harlem, fourteen-year-old Greg Ridley sits on his stoop in a bad mood because his father has prohibited him from joining the local basketball team due to his poor math grades. Reluctant to face another lecture, Greg goes for a walk. When it starts raining, he seeks shelter in an abandoned building. Greg encounters a homeless man named Lemon Brown, who thinks Greg is there to steal his treasure. When local thugs break in to steal his treasure, Lemon and Greg hide upstairs. After they chase away the thieves, Lemon shows Greg his treasure: old newspaper clippings that feature him playing the harmonica and singing the blues. Lemon explains that his son died in the war, and his stack of clippings, which his son always carried with him, is his treasure. Not quite grasping what makes his clippings a treasure, Greg leaves for home, anticipating another lecture from his father.

ELL Proficiency-leveled summaries and summaries in multiple languages are available digitally.

🔊 Audio and audio text highlighting are available with the text.

CONNECT TO ESSENTIAL QUESTION

How do relationships shape us?

Teenager Greg Ridley meets Lemon Brown, a homeless man who claims he has a treasure. Soon Greg discovers that Brown's treasure will help him discover what he treasures most.

Access Complex Text

LEXILE: 760L   WORD COUNT: 3,366

The following areas may be challenging for students, particularly **ELL** English Language Learners and **A** Approaching grade-level learners.

Organization	Specific Vocabulary	Sentence Structure
• The story opens with a flashback to an earlier time. • Notice these clues ("His father's voice came to him again" and "that had been two nights before") in paragraphs 1 and 5 that mark the start and end of the flashback and how it introduces the conflict.	• Some terms may be unfamiliar to students. • Explain that "the blues" is a musical form created by African Americans. The Salvation Army is a charitable organization.	• Some students may need assistance following the dialogue. • Point out that the three intruders are not differentiated as separate, distinct characters, so it's only important that they appear as a united threat.

SCAFFOLDS **ENGLISH LANGUAGE LEARNERS**   **APPROACHING GRADE LEVEL**   **BEYOND GRADE LEVEL**

These icons identify differentiation strategies and scaffolded support for a variety of students. See the digital lesson plan for additional differentiation strategies and scaffolds.

Instructional Path

The print teacher's edition includes essential point-of-use instruction and planning tools. Complete lesson plans and program documents appear in your digital teacher account.

First Read: The Treasure of Lemon Brown

Objectives: After an initial reading and discussion of the short story, students will be able to identify and describe characters and setting details as well as articulate events that are central to the story's plot.

Skill: Point of View

Objectives: After reading and discussing a model of close reading, students will be able to identify the author's use of a particular point of view in a work of fiction to achieve a specific purpose.

Close Read: The Treasure of Lemon Brown

Objectives: After engaging in a close reading and discussion of the text, students will be able to analyze point of view in order to participate in a collaborative conversation and write a short argumentative response.

Progress Monitoring

Opportunities to Learn	Opportunities to Demonstrate Learning	Opportunities to Reteach

Point of View

⚙ Skill: Point of View	⚙ Skill: Point of View • Your Turn 🖥 Close Read • Skills Focus • Write	⚙ Unit 6 • Skills: Point of View – All Summer in a Day ⚙ Spotlight Skill: Point of View

First Read

Walter Dean Myers

The Treasure of Lemon Brown

Introduce the Text

As a class, watch the video preview and have students read the introduction in pairs to make connections to the video preview.

To activate prior knowledge and experiences, ask students:

- What key words, sounds, or images from the video do you think will be most important to the story you are about to read?

- What is one prediction you can make about the story you're going to read?

> **ELL SPEAKING FRAMES**
>
> - The ____ in the video makes me think ____.
> - The video shows ____. This makes me wonder ____.
> - I think the text will ____. I think this because ____.
> - I predict that there will be ____. I believe this because ____.

Entry Point

As students prepare to read "The Treasure of Lemon Brown," share the following information with them to provide context.

✓ Walter Dean Myers is a very decorated author, winning the most awards for any writer for young adults. He has written more than 110 books. Myers is a New York Times bestselling author and the recipient of numerous other accolades, including the following: 1969 winner of the Council on Interracial Books for Children Contest, five-time winner of the Coretta Scott King Award, and his book *Monster* was the first recipient of the Michael L. Printz Award. Walter Dean Myers was appointed by the Library of Congress to serve as the National Ambassador for Young People's Literature.

✓ Walter Dean Myers was inspired to begin writing by his teacher when he was very young. He had a speech impediment, and the teacher thought if he started writing, it would help him pronounce the words he found to be difficult. Myers took this advice and started writing poems and short stories as a child. It is possible that his inspiration for "The Treasure of Lemon Brown" also stems from his childhood, especially his great relationship with his foster father. When Walter Dean Myers was two years old, his father sent him and two of his sisters to live with a foster family after his mother died. This family, the Deans, were a huge inspiration to the author, so he added their last name to his own, hence his double last name: Dean Myers.

"Didn't I tell you every man got a treasure?"

NOTES

1   The dark sky, filled with angry, swirling clouds, reflected Greg Ridley's mood as he sat on the **stoop** of his building. His father's voice came to him again, first reading the letter the principal had sent to the house, then lecturing endlessly about his poor efforts in math.

2   "I had to leave school when I was thirteen," his father had said, "that's a year younger than you are now. If I'd had half the chances you have, I'd . . ."

**Skill:
Point of View**

The narrator is describing what happens from outside the story because I see a character's name and the pronoun he. I know how Greg feels, but not what his father feels. So the point of view must be third-person limited.

3   Greg sat in the small, pale green kitchen listening, knowing the lecture would end with his father saying he couldn't play ball with the Scorpions. He had asked his father the week before, and his father had said it depended on his next report card. It wasn't often the Scorpions took on new players, especially fourteen-year-olds, and this was a chance of a lifetime for Greg. He hadn't been allowed to play high school ball, which he had really wanted to do, but playing for the Community Center team was the next best thing. Report cards were due in a week, and Greg had been hoping for the best. But the principal had ended the suspense early when she sent the letter saying Greg would probably fail math if he didn't spend more time studying.

4   "And you want to play *basketball?*" His father's brows knitted over deep brown eyes. "That must be some kind of a joke. Now you just get into your room and hit those books."

5   That had been two nights before. His father's words, like the distant thunder that now echoed through the streets of Harlem, still rumbled softly in his ears.

6   It was beginning to cool. Gusts of wind made bits of paper dance between the parked cars. There was a flash of nearby lightning, and soon large drops of rain splashed onto his jeans. He stood to go upstairs, thought of the lecture that probably awaited him if he did anything except shut himself in his room with his math book, and started walking down the street instead. Down the block there was an old tenement that had been abandoned for some months. Some of the guys had held an **impromptu** checker tournament there the week before, and Greg had noticed that the door, once boarded over, had been slightly ajar.

Copyright © Bookheart Learning, LLC

Analyze Vocabulary Using Context Clues

In paragraph 1, focus on the sentence that uses the word *stoop*. Point out these context clues:

1. First I notice that a *stoop* is part of a building.

2. I know Greg is outside the building because the dark, cloud-filled sky is visible.

3. I can conclude that a *stoop* is part of the outside of a building, and I know that it's a place where Greg can sit.

4. I think that a *stoop* might be a kind of porch because that's a place outside a building where people can sit.

Point of View

How did the reader use details in the story to identify the narrator and point of view?

The reader noted the character's name and the pronoun *he* as identifying a third-person narrator. She also noted that she knew what only one character was thinking, which makes the point of view limited.

SELECTION VOCABULARY

stoop / la escalera de entrada *noun* a porch, entryway steps, or platform at the entrance to a house

impromptu / espontáneo/a *adjective* unplanned, unrehearsed

ELL
• Is the checker tournament planned or does it take place in the moment?
• Is the building where the checker tournament takes place abandoned or filled with people?

TEXT TALK

Why does Greg find himself in the old abandoned tenement building near his home?

See paragraph 6: Greg wants to avoid going home and listening to another lecture by his father, but he needs shelter from the storm.

Skills Focus

QUESTION 1: Setting

The author adds another layer to the tone through his description of the building. Not only is there a storm raging, but Greg is entering a grim building scarred with graffiti. Now I not only feel Greg's mood but also a rising sense of suspense.

7   Pulling his collar up as high as he could, he checked for traffic and made a dash across the street. He reached the house just as another flash of lightning changed the night to day for an instant, then returned the graffiti-scarred building to the grim shadows. He vaulted over the outer stairs and pushed **tentatively** on the door. It was open, and he let himself in.

8   The inside of the building was dark except for the dim light that filtered through the dirty windows from the streetlamps. There was a room a few feet from the door, and from where he stood in the entrance, Greg could see a squarish patch of light on the floor. He entered the room, frowning at the musty smell. It was a large room that might have been someone's parlor at one time. Squinting, Greg could see an old table on its side against one wall, what looked like a pile of rags or a torn mattress in the corner, and a couch, with one side broken, in front of the window.

9   He went to the couch. The side that wasn't broken was comfortable enough, though a little creaky. From the spot he could see the blinking neon sign over the bodega on the corner. He sat awhile, watching the sign blink first green then red, allowing his mind to drift to the Scorpions, then to his father. His father had been a postal worker for all Greg's life, and was proud of it, often telling Greg how hard he had worked to pass the test. Greg had heard the story too many times to be interested now.

10 For a moment Greg thought he heard something that sounded like a scraping against the wall. He listened carefully, but it was gone.

11 Outside the wind had picked up, sending the rain against the window with a force that shook the glass in its frame. A car passed, its tires hissing over the wet street and its red tail lights glowing in the darkness.

12 Greg thought he heard the noise again. His stomach tightened as he held himself still and listened intently. There weren't any more scraping noises, but he was sure he had heard something in the darkness—something breathing!

13 He tried to figure out just where the breathing was coming from; he knew it was in the room with him. Slowly he stood, tensing. As he turned, a flash of lightning lit up the room, frightening him with its sudden brilliance. He saw nothing, just the overturned table, the pile of rags and an old newspaper on the floor. Could he have been imagining the sounds? He continued listening, but heard nothing and thought that it might have just been rats. Still, he thought, as soon as the rain let up he would leave. He went to the window and was about to look when he heard a voice behind him.

14 "Don't try nothin' 'cause I got a razor sharp enough to cut a week into nine days!"

Reading & Writing Companion   51

 SELECTION VOCABULARY

tentatively / tentativamente *adverb* with uncertainty COGNATE

- Is Greg certain or uncertain about entering the building?
- Does Greg push on the door with confidence or some fear?

NOTES

15 Greg, except for an **involuntary** tremor in his knees, stood stock still. The voice was high and brittle, like dry twigs being broken, surely not one he had ever heard before. There was a shuffling sound as the person who had been speaking moved a step closer. Greg turned, holding his breath, his eyes straining to see in the dark room.

16 The upper part of the figure before him was still in darkness. The lower half was in the dim rectangle of light that fell unevenly from the window. There were two feet, in cracked, dirty shoes from which rose legs that were wrapped in rags.

17 "Who are you?" Greg hardly recognized his own voice.

18 "I'm Lemon Brown," came the answer. "Who're you?"

19 "Greg Ridley."

20 "What you doing here?" The figure shuffled forward again, and Greg took a small step backward.

21 "It's raining," Greg said.

22 "I can see that," the figure said.

23 The person who called himself Lemon Brown peered forward, and Greg could see him clearly. He was an old man. His black, heavily wrinkled face was surrounded by a halo of crinkly white hair and whiskers that seemed to separate his head from the layers of dirty coats piled on his smallish frame. His pants were bagged to the knee, where they were met with rags that went down to the old shoes. The rags were held on with strings, and there was a rope around his middle. Greg relaxed. He had seen the man before, picking through the trash on the corner and pulling clothes out of a Salvation Army box. There was no sign of a razor that could "cut a week into nine days."

24 "What are you doing here?" Greg asked.

25 "This is where I'm staying," Lemon Brown said. "What you here for?"

26 "Told you it was raining out," Greg said, leaning against the back of the couch until he felt it give slightly.

27 "Ain't you got no home?"

28 "I got a home," Greg answered.

29 "You ain't one of them bad boys looking for my treasure, is you?"

Skills Focus

QUESTION 2: Plot

Greg is scared when he first encounters Lemon Brown. He can't see who is talking because his back is turned. Even when he turns, he can't really see in the dark.

V SELECTION VOCABULARY

involuntary / involuntario/a *adjective* not done by choice; happening without control COGNATE

ELL
- Is Greg still or moving?
- Does Greg control or not control the tremor in his knees?

Prepare for Advanced Courses

Use the activity below to differentiate instruction for your **B** Beyond grade-level learner.

Look at paragraph 41

"Hard times, boy. Hard times always after a poor man. One day I got tired, sat down to rest a spell and felt a tap on my shoulder. Hard times caught up with me."

Ask students to conduct informal research into the causes of homelessness and into the help that is offered. Ask students to connect what they have learned to Lemon Brown.

30 Lemon Brown cocked his head to one side and squinted one eye.

31 "Because I told you I got me a razor."

32 "I'm not looking for your treasure," Greg answered, smiling. "*If* you have one."

33 "What you mean, if I have one." Lemon Brown said. "Every man got a treasure. You don't know that, you must be a fool!"

34 "Sure," Greg said as he sat on the sofa and put one leg over the back. "What do you have, gold coins?"

35 "Don't worry none about what I got," Lemon Brown said. "You know who I am?"

36 "You told me your name was orange or lemon or something like that."

37 "Lemon Brown," the old man said, pulling back his shoulders as he did so," they used to call me Sweet Lemon Brown."

38 "Sweet Lemon?" Greg asked.

39 "Yessir. Sweet Lemon Brown. They used to say I sung the blues so sweet that if I sang at a funeral, the dead would **commence** to rocking with the beat. Used to travel all over Mississippi and as far as Monroe, Louisiana, and east on over to Macon, Georgia. You mean you ain't never heard of Sweet Lemon Brown?"

40 "Afraid not," Greg said. "What . . . happened to you?"

41 "Hard times, boy. Hard times always after a poor man. One day I got tired, sat down to rest a spell and felt a tap on my shoulder. Hard times caught up with me."

42 "Sorry about that."

43 "What you doing here? How come you don't go in home when the rain come? Rain don't bother you young folks none."

44 "Just didn't." Greg looked away.

45 "I used to have a knotty-headed boy just like you." Lemon Brown had half walked, half shuffled back to the corner and sat down against the wall. "Had them big eyes like you got. I used to call them moon eyes. Look into them moon eyes and see anything you want."

TEXT TALK

Why does Lemon Brown ultimately decide that Greg is not a threat?

See paragraphs 32 and 45: Greg assures Lemon that Greg is not looking for Lemon's treasure, and Greg reminds Lemon of his son Jesse.

SELECTION VOCABULARY

commence / comenzar *verb* to take the first step or steps in carrying out an action; to start or begin COGNATE

ELL
• Are dead people generally still or rocking?
• What causes the dead people to shift from stillness to rocking?

46　"How come you gave up singing the blues?" Greg asked.

47　"Didn't give it up," Lemon Brown said. "You don't give up the blues; they give you up. After a while you do good for yourself, and it ain't nothing but foolishness singing about how hard you got it. Ain't that right?"

48　"I guess so."

49　"What's that noise?" Lemon Brown asked, suddenly sitting upright.

50　Greg listened, and he heard a noise outside. He looked at Lemon Brown and saw the old man pointing toward the window. Greg went to the window and saw three men, neighborhood thugs, on the stoop. One was carrying a length of pipe. Greg looked back toward Lemon Brown, who moved quietly across the room to the window. The old man looked out, then beckoned frantically for Greg to follow him. For a moment Greg couldn't move. Then he found himself following Lemon Brown into the hallway and up the darkened stairs. Greg followed as closely as he could. They reached the top of the stairs, and Greg felt Lemon Brown's hand first lying on his shoulder, then probing down his arm until he took Greg's hand into his own as they crouched in the darkness.

51　"They's bad men," Lemon Brown whispered. His breath was warm against Greg's skin.

52　"Hey! Rag man!" A voice called. "We know you in here. What you got up under them rags? You got any money?"

53　Silence.

54　"We don't want to have to come in and hurt you, old man, but we don't mind if we have to."

55　Lemon Brown squeezed Greg's hand in his own hard, gnarled fist.

56　There was a banging downstairs and a light as the men entered. They banged around noisily, calling for the rag man.

57　"We heard you talking about your treasure." The voice was slurred.

58　"We just want to see it, that's all."

59　"You sure he's here?" One voice seemed to come from the room with the sofa.

60　"Yeah, he stays here every night."

Skills Focus

QUESTION 3: Point of View

The third-person limited point of view is a disadvantage in this paragraph. Since I don't know Lemon Brown's thoughts, I don't know whether he is trying to comfort Greg by holding his hand, guide him, or seek comfort from him.

Reading & Writing Companion

TEXT TALK

Why does Lemon Brown immediately threaten Greg with a razor?

See paragraphs 50–52: Lemon Brown is used to being threatened by men in the neighborhood, so he immediately assumes Greg is a threat.

Point of View

How does the reader analyze how the point of view affects the way the story is told?

When Lemon Brown moves, the reader notes that she has only Greg's thinking about what might happen. So the reader is surprised along with Greg by Brown's actions. The reader explains that the story told from this point of view is suspenseful.

 NOTES

61 "There's another room over there; I'm going to take a look. You got that flashlight?"

62 "Yeah, here, take the pipe too."

63 Greg opened his mouth to quiet the sound of his breath as he sucked it in uneasily. A beam of light hit the wall a few feet opposite him, then went out.

64 "Ain't nobody in that room," a voice said. "You think he gone or something?"

65 "I don't know," came the answer. "All I know is that I heard him talking about some kind of treasure. You know they found that shopping bag lady with that load of money in her bags."

66 "Yeah. You think he's upstairs?"

67 "HEY, OLD MAN, ARE YOU UP THERE?"

68 Silence.

69 "Watch my back. I'm going up."

70 There was a footstep on the stairs, and the beam from the flashlight danced crazily along the peeling wallpaper. Greg held his breath. There was another step and a loud crashing noise as the man banged the pipe against the wooden banister. Greg could feel his temples throb as the man slowly neared them. Greg thought about the pipe, wondering what he would do when the man reached them—what he *could* do.

71 Then Lemon Brown released his hand and moved toward the top of the stairs. Greg looked around and saw stairs going up to the next floor. He tried waving to Lemon Brown, hoping the old man would see him in the dim light and follow him to the next floor. Maybe, Greg thought, the man wouldn't follow them up there. Suddenly, though, Lemon Brown stood at the top of the stairs, both arms raised high above his head.

72 "There he is!" A voice cried from below.

73 "Throw down your money, old man, so I won't have to bash your head in!"

74 Lemon Brown didn't move. Greg felt himself near panic. The steps came closer, and still Lemon Brown didn't move. He was an **eerie** sight, a bundle of rags standing at the top of the stairs, his shadow on the wall looming over him. Maybe, the thought came to Greg, the scene could be even eerier.

 Skill:
Point of View

The speaker describes Greg's feelings and actions. He seems scared and doesn't know what to do.

Greg doesn't know what Lemon Brown plans to do, so neither do I. That's what happens with third-person limited point of view. Is Lemon Brown trying to protect Greg? Or scare the men? Not knowing creates suspense in the story.

Reading & Writing Companion 55

 SELECTION VOCABULARY

eerie / espeluznante *adjective* unexpected, strange, or mysterious

 ELL
• How does Lemon Brown hold his body, and what is the effect on the wall?
• Is Lemon Brown's appearance safe or scary?

75 Greg wet his lips, put his hands to his mouth and tried to make a sound. Nothing came out. He swallowed hard, wet his lips once more and howled as evenly as he could.

76 "What's that?"

77 As Greg howled, the light moved away from Lemon Brown, but not before Greg saw him hurl his body down the stairs at the men who had come to take his treasure. There was a crashing noise, and then footsteps. A rush of warm air came in as the downstairs door opened, then there was only an ominous silence.

78 Greg stood on the landing. He listened, and after a while there was another sound on the staircase.

79 "Mr. Brown?" he called.

80 "Yeah, it's me," came the answer. "I got their flashlight."

81 Greg exhaled in relief as Lemon Brown made his way slowly back up the stairs.

82 "You OK?"

83 "Few bumps and bruises," Lemon Brown said.

84 "I think I'd better be going," Greg said, his breath returning to normal. "You'd better leave, too, before they come back."

85 "They may hang around for a while," Lemon Brown said, "but they ain't getting their nerve up to come in here again. Not with crazy rag men and howling spooks. Best you stay a while till the coast is clear. I'm heading out west tomorrow, out to east St. Louis."

86 "They were talking about treasures," Greg said. "You really have a treasure?"

87 "What I tell you? Didn't I tell you every man got a treasure?" Lemon Brown said. "You want to see mine?"

88 "If you want to show it to me," Greg shrugged.

89 "Let's look out the window first, see what them scoundrels be doing," Lemon Brown said.

90 They followed the oval beam of the flashlight into one of the rooms and looked out the window. They saw the men who had tried to take the treasure

Skills Focus

QUESTION 4: Character

By directly asking about Lemon Brown's treasure, Greg helps move the plot toward resolution. Before the attack, Greg didn't believe there was a treasure. Now he isn't so sure.

sitting on the curb near the corner. One of them had his pants leg up, looking at his knee.

91   "You sure you're not hurt?" Greg asked Lemon Brown.

92   "Nothing that ain't been hurt before," Lemon Brown said. "When you get as old as me all you say when something hurts is, 'Howdy, Mr. Pain, sees you back again.' Then when Mr. Pain see he can't worry you none, he go on mess with somebody else."

93   Greg smiled.

94   "Here, you hold this." Lemon Brown gave Greg the flashlight.

95   He sat on the floor near Greg and carefully untied the strings that held the rags on his right leg. When he took the rags away, Greg saw a piece of plastic. The old man carefully took off the plastic and unfolded it. He revealed some yellowed newspaper clippings and a battered harmonica.

96   "There it be," he said, nodding his head. "There it be."

97   Greg looked at the old man, saw the distant look in his eye, then turned to the clippings. They told of Sweet Lemon Brown, a blues singer and harmonica player who was appearing at different theaters in the South. One of the clippings said he had been the hit of the show, although not the headliner. All of the clippings were reviews of shows Lemon Brown had been in more than fifty years ago. Greg looked at the harmonica. It was dented badly on one side, with the reed holes on one end nearly closed.

98   "I used to travel around and make money to feed my wife and Jesse—that's my boy's name. Used to feed them good, too. Then his mama died, and he stayed with his mama's sister. He growed up to be a man, and when the war come he saw fit to go off and fight in it. I didn't have nothing to give him except these things that told him who I was, and what he come from. If you know your pappy did something, you know you can do something too.

99   "Anyway, he went off to war, and I went off still playing and singing. 'Course by then I wasn't as much as I used to be, not without somebody to make it worth the while. You know what I mean?"

100   "Yeah." Greg nodded, not quite really knowing.

101   "I traveled around, and one time I come home, and there was this letter saying Jesse got killed in the war. Broke my heart, it truly did.

Copyright © BookheadEd Learning, LLC

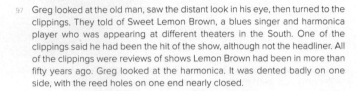

Skills Focus

QUESTION 5: Connect to Essential Question

I think watching Lemon Brown carefully unwrap the clippings and the harmonica and seeing the distant look in his eyes makes Greg begin to understand how a treasure doesn't need to be gold coins.

102   "They sent back what he had with him over there, and what it was is this old mouth fiddle and these clippings. Him carrying it around with him like that told me it meant something to him. That was my treasure, and when I give it to him he treated it just like that, a treasure. Ain't that something?"

103   "Yeah, I guess so," Greg said.

104   "You guess so?" Lemon Brown's voice rose an octave as he started to put his treasure back into the plastic. "Well, you got to guess 'cause you sure don't know nothing. Don't know enough to get home when it's raining."

105   "I *guess* . . . I mean, you're right."

106   "You OK for a youngster," the old man said as he tied the strings around his leg, "better than those scalawags what come here looking for my treasure. That's for sure."

107   "You really think that treasure of yours was worth fighting for?" Greg asked. "Against a pipe?"

108   "What else a man got 'cepting what he can pass on to his son, or his daughter, if she be his oldest?" Lemon Brown said. "For a big-headed boy you sure do ask the foolishest questions."

109   Lemon Brown got up after patting his rags in place and looked out the window again.

110   "Looks like they're gone. You get on out of here and get yourself home. I'll be watching from the window so you'll be all right."

111   Lemon Brown went down the stairs behind Greg. When they reached the front door the old man looked out first, saw the street was clear and told Greg to scoot on home.

112   "You sure you'll be OK?" Greg asked.

113   "Now didn't I tell you I was going to east St. Louis in the morning?"

114   Lemon Brown asked. "Don't that sound OK to you?"

115   "Sure it does," Greg said. "Sure it does. And you take care of that treasure of yours."

116   "That I'll do," Lemon said, the wrinkles around his eyes suggesting a smile. "That I'll do."

TEXT TALK

What is Lemon Brown's treasure?

See paragraph 102: Lemon's treasure is the knowledge that his son Jesse was proud of his father as evidenced by the harmonica and newspaper clippings Jesse carried with him during the war.

117   The night had warmed and the rain had stopped, leaving puddles at the curbs. Greg didn't even want to think how late it was. He thought ahead of what his father would say and wondered if he should tell him about Lemon Brown. He thought about it until he reached his stoop, and decided against it. Lemon Brown would be OK, Greg thought, with his memories and his treasure.

118   Greg pushed the button over the bell marked Ridley, thought of the lecture he knew his father would give him, and smiled.

Reprinted by permission of Miriam Altshuler Literary Agency, on behalf of Walter Dean Myers. Copyright © 1983, by Walter Dean Myers.

TEXT TALK

How does Greg's attitude toward his father change after meeting Lemon Brown?

See paragraph 118: Instead of trying to avoid a lecture from his father, Greg smiles in anticipation of the coming lecture.

What other predictions are you able to make about the story?

Answers will vary.

Think about Lemon Brown and Greg's interaction. How can "putting yourself in someone else's shoes" help you become a more open-minded person?

Answers will vary.

B   BEYOND TEXT TALK

Ask each Beyond grade level student to write one additional discussion question. Then, have one or two students facilitate a discussion, using their questions to guide the conversation.

Reading Comprehension OPTIONAL

Have students complete the digital reading comprehension questions ✅ when they finish reading.

ANSWER KEY

QUESTION 1: C	**QUESTION 5:** C	**QUESTION 9:**
QUESTION 2: A	**QUESTION 6:** A	*See first chart.*
QUESTION 3: D	**QUESTION 7:** B	**QUESTION 10:**
QUESTION 4: B	**QUESTION 8:** B	*See second chart.*

Synonym	Word
unrehearsed	impromptu
hesitantly	tentatively
porch	stoop
spooky	eerie
unconsciously	involuntarily
begin	commence

First	Second	Third	Fourth
Greg is skeptical that Lemon actually has any treasure.	Greg begins to remind Lemon of his son.	Lemon injures himself leaping on the two men who have come to rob him.	Lemon shows Greg his harmonica and clippings.

Connect and Extend OPTIONAL

CONNECT TO EXTENDED WRITING PROJECT

Students can use "The Treasure of Lemon Brown" as a mentor text for their Extended Writing Project. They may analyze Walter Dean Myers's methods for developing relationships, including the use of flashback to establish Greg's frame of mind when he meets Lemon Brown, and what the encounter means to Greg.

BEYOND THE BOOK

Discussion: 4 Corner Conversation about Treasures

Count students off by four and ask all of the 1s to form a group, all of the 2s form a group, and so on. Each group should sit in a circle to discuss the following questions. Remind them to reference specific moments in the text to support their ideas as they contribute to the conversation.

- How would you define treasure after reading this short story?
- What makes a "treasure" valuable?
- Why do you think Greg smiles at the end when he thinks of his father giving him a lecture?
- Have you ever learned a life lesson from an unlikely source?

Think Questions

Circulate as students answer Think Questions independently. Scaffolds for these questions are shown on the opposite page.

QUESTION 1: Textual Evidence

He considers them his treasure because they stand for his successful career as a blues musician and because his son Jesse valued them enough to carry them with him until he died in the war. They show how proud Jesse was of his father.

QUESTION 2: Textual Evidence

Jesse's death broke Lemon's heart, causing a down spiral in Lemon's career. Lemon says he didn't give up the blues, they gave him up when he betrayed them with success. Even with the sorrow of his son's death, Lemon cannot coax the blues back into his life, which leads him into homelessness.

QUESTION 3: Textual Evidence

This figurative expression shows that Lemon was a very talented musician. When Lemon played, his music was so powerful that the only way to describe its impact on the audience is through figurative language. Lemon's music seemed to reach beyond the world of the living to entertain the dead as well.

QUESTION 4: Context Clues

I think *commence* means "to begin or start." The word is used to describe a change in the state of dead people. I know that dead people do not move, but when Lemon Brown plays his music, the dead rock with the beat. This change from stillness to movement begins or commences with Lemon's music.

QUESTION 5: Word Meaning

Number 4 most matches the meaning of *eerie* in paragraph 74. The mood is "panic" as Greg and Lemon fear being attacked. Lemon stands at the top of the stairs with his "arms raised high above his head," creating a "shadow" that looms over him. The effect causes fright in the intruders, who leave.

THE TREASURE OF LEMON BROWN

First Read

Read "The Treasure of Lemon Brown." After you read, complete the Think Questions below.

☁ THINK QUESTIONS

1. Why does Lemon Brown consider a harmonica and some newspaper clippings his "treasure"? Cite textual evidence from the selection to support your answer.

2. Write two or three sentences describing how Lemon's heart got broken and how this event contributes to his life as an older man.

3. Figurative language is language used for descriptive effect, often to illustrate or imply ideas indirectly. Expressions of figurative language are not literally true, but express some truth beyond the literal level. What does the figurative expression "the dead would commence to rocking with the beat" tell readers about Lemon's talent as a blues musician? Cite textual evidence from the selection to support your answer.

4. Use context clues to determine the meaning of **commence** as it is used in paragraph 39 of "The Treasure of Lemon Brown." Write your definition here and identify clues that helped you figure out its meaning.

5. Read the following dictionary entry:

   eerie
   ee•rie \'ir-ē\ adjective

   1. mysterious
   2. strange
   3. unexpected
   4. causing fright

   Which definition most closely matches the meaning of **eerie** as it is used in paragraph 74? Write the correct definition of *eerie* here and explain how you figured out the correct meaning.

Think Questions

Use the scaffolds below to differentiate instruction for your **ELL** English Language Learners and **A** Approaching grade-level learners.

ELL **BEGINNING** Write a response using the <u>word bank</u> and <u>sentence frames</u>.

INTERMEDIATE Write a response using the <u>sentence frames</u>.

ADVANCED, ADVANCED HIGH Write a response using the <u>Text-Dependent Question Guide</u>.

A **APPROACHING** Write a response using the <u>Text-Dependent Question Guide</u>.

BEGINNING	INTERMEDIATE	APPROACHING / ADVANCED, ADVANCED HIGH
Word Bank	**Sentence Frames**	**Text-Dependent Question Guide**
begin carry career death emotional four knowledge move proud stillness successful talented	He considers them his treasure because they stand for his ____ and because his son Jesse valued them enough to ____ until he died in the war. They show how ____ Jesse was of his father.	1. • What does the harmonica show about Lemon Brown's career? • What do the newspaper clippings show about Lemon Brown? • How did Lemon Brown's son Jesse feel about the harmonica and the clippings, and how do you know?
	Lemon loses the ability to sing blues music when he becomes ____. Lemon loses his ____ connection to the music. When Jesse's ____ breaks Lemon's heart, Lemon can't get back the ability to sing blues music.	2. • Why does Lemon lose the ability to sing blues music? • During the war, what happens to Jesse Brown? • Why can't Lemon get back the ability to sing blues music?
	Dead people do not usually ____ to music. This ____ lets readers know that Lemon was a very ____ musician.	3. • Are dead people usually able to move to music? • What does this expression tell you about Lemon's abilities as a musician? • Is Lemon a talented or untalented musician?
	The dead move from a state of ____ to a state of rocking. This gives me a clue that *commence* means to ____.	4. • Read: "They used to say I sung the blues so sweet that if I sang at a funeral, the dead would **commence** to rocking with the beat." • Are dead people usually expected to rock to music? • What does this unexpected movement tell me about the meaning of the word *commence*?
	Eerie as used in the text matches definition #____.	5. • Read: "He was an **eerie** sight, a bundle of rags standing at the top of the stairs, his shadow on the wall looming over him." • Does *eerie* mean "mysterious"? (#1) • Does *eerie* mean "strange"? (#2) • Does *eerie* mean "unexpected"? (#3) • Does *eerie* mean "causing fright"? (#4)

Skill: Point of View

Introduce the Skill

Watch the Concept Definition video and read the following definitions with your students.

In works of fiction, the term **point of view** refers to the perspective of whomever is telling a story. The character, or voice telling a story, is known as the **narrator.** Narrators can tell a story as a major or minor character, or as an observer to the plot. How a narrator reveals the plot can change your experience of a story. As a reader, it is important to question whether or not you can trust a narrator to be reliable.

Additionally, a narrator can either provide an **omniscient point of view,** with an "all-knowing" understanding of characters and events, or a **limited point of view,** providing only the thoughts and feelings of a single character. Some stories will also be written with m**ultiple points of view,** where two or more characters narrate the story.

TURN AND TALK

1. What is one of your favorite stories?

2. Who tells the story? Is it one of the characters? Or is the narrator a person on the outside who tells the story from the perspective of one or more characters?

ELL SPEAKING FRAMES
- One of my favorite characters is ____.
- The story is told from the perspective of ____. I knew what happened through ____.
- Another story I like had a narrator who ____. I knew what happened through ____.

The Treasure of Lemon Brown

 Skill:
Point Of View

Use the Checklist to analyze Point Of View in "The Treasure of Lemon Brown." Refer to the sample student annotations about Point Of View in the text.

••• CHECKLIST FOR POINT OF VIEW

In order to identify how an author develops the point of view of the narrator or speaker in a text, note the following:

- ✓ the speaker or narrator
- ✓ what pronouns the narrator or speaker uses to describe characters or events, such as *I, me, he, she,* or *they*
- ✓ how much the narrator or speaker knows and reveals
- ✓ what the narrator or speaker says or does that reveals how they feel about other characters and events in the poem or story

To explain how an author develops the point of view of the narrator or speaker in a text, consider the following questions:

- ✓ Is the text narrated or spoken from first person or third person point of view?
- ✓ Does the narrator reveal characters' thoughts and feelings, or is the narrator objective?
- ✓ How does the narrator or speaker reveal their thoughts about the events or the other characters in the story or poem?
- ✓ What is the narrator's or the speaker's point of view?

V SKILL VOCABULARY

point of view / el punto de vista *noun* the standpoint, or perspective, from which a story is told

narrator / el narrador *noun* someone who tells a story COGNATE

omniscient point of view / el punto de vista omnisciente *noun* a point of view when a narrator has an "all-knowing" understanding of characters and events

The Treasure of Lemon Brown

Skill:
Point Of View

sync•skills

Reread paragraphs 71–77 of "The Treasure of Lemon Brown." Then, using the Checklist on the previous page, answer the multiple-choice questions below.

↻ YOUR TURN

1. Based on the text in paragraphs 74 and 75, what can you infer about how the author develops the point of view of the narrator in the story?

   ○ A. The narrator describes only what Greg and Lemon Brown are doing, not thinking.
   ○ B. The reader knows how Greg and Lemon Brown are feeling because the narrator is Greg.
   ○ C. The author reveals only what Greg is feeling and thinking.
   ○ D. The reader knows why the characters are acting as they do because the narrator is Lemon Brown.

2. How would the story be different if it were told only from Lemon Brown's point of view?

   ○ A. The narrator would only describe what the men were thinking as they called out from below.
   ○ B. One of the men would be using the pronoun I to reveal his thoughts.
   ○ C. The narrator would be asking the reader what he or she thought of the scene.
   ○ D. Only Lemon Brown's thoughts would be revealed to the reader.

3. Which paragraph best reveals Greg's thoughts and feelings about the sight of Lemon Brown on the stairs?

   ○ A. 71
   ○ B. 74
   ○ C. 75
   ○ D. 77

Ⓥ SKILL VOCABULARY

limited point of view / el punto de vista limitado *noun* a point of view that only provides the thoughts and feelings of one character

multiple points of view / el enfoque narrativo múltiple *noun* a narrating technique where two or more characters narrate the story

---

⚙ Your Turn

Ask students to complete the Your Turn Activity.

QUESTION 1

A. Incorrect. The narrator does describe what Greg is thinking and feeling.

B. Incorrect. The narrator does not describe how both characters are feeling or what they are thinking, and Greg is not the narrator. The story is told by a narrator outside of the story, or from a third person point of view.

C. **Correct.** The author reveals what one character is thinking and feeling in a third-person limited point of view. In these paragraphs, the narrator reveals Greg's thoughts and feelings.

D. Incorrect. The narrator is not Lemon Brown, and the narrator does not reveal the motivations behind the characters' actions.

QUESTION 2

A. Incorrect. This would only be true if the story were told from the men's point of view.

B. Incorrect. If Lemon Brown were the narrator of the story, and it were told from his point of view, he would be the only character to use the pronoun I.

C. Incorrect. This describes a narrator in a second person point of view, and this would not be Lemon Brown's point of view.

D. **Correct.** If the author revealed only Lemon Brown's thoughts and feelings, the point of view would be third person limited. If Lemon Brown were the narrator, explaining only his feelings to the reader, it would be a first person point of view. Either way, his thoughts and feelings would be the only ones revealed.

QUESTION 3

A. Incorrect.

B. **Correct.** The paragraph describes Greg as near panic and his thinking that the sight of Lemon Brown is eerie and could be even more so.

C. Incorrect.

D. Incorrect.

Close Read

Skills Focus

QUESTION 1: Setting

See paragraph 7.

QUESTION 2: Plot

See paragraphs 14 and 15.

QUESTION 3: Point of View

See paragraph 50.

QUESTION 4: Character

See paragraphs 86–88.

QUESTION 5: Connect to Essential Question

See paragraphs 95–97.

Close Read

Reread "The Treasure of Lemon Brown." As you reread, complete the Skills Focus questions below. Then use your answers and annotations from the questions to help you complete the Write activity.

◎ SKILLS FOCUS

1. Identify the setting of "The Treasure of Lemon Brown" and explain how the setting affects the tone at the beginning of the story.

2. Identify key events in the plot and how Greg's response to Lemon Brown changes throughout the story.

3. Identify the advantages and disadvantages of the author's choice of point of view when trying to understand the scene with the three bad men.

4. Identify how Greg's thoughts, words, and actions help the plot unfold throughout the story.

5. Explain how Greg Ridley's brief encounter with Lemon Brown impacts his life and how it may shape his relationship with his father.

✎ WRITE

ARGUMENTATIVE: Three men, one carrying a length of pipe, arrive at the abandoned building to steal Lemon Brown's treasure. Lemon, with Greg's help, scares them off. Does the author reveal enough about Lemon Brown's treasure for the reader to understand its importance? Do you think Lemon Brown's treasure is worth fighting for? Why or why not? Defend your point of view with evidence from the text.

✓ CHECK FOR SUCCESS

If students struggle to respond to Skills Focus Question #1, ask students the following questions:

- What do you learn about the setting in paragraph 1? How does the setting reflect the tone at the beginning of the story?

- How does the setting affect the tone in paragraph 7?

- What creates the feeling of suspense in paragraphs 11 and 12?

Have students transition to read and annotate independently once they have successfully completed the first Skills Focus prompt.

Reading & Writing Companion 63

Writer's Notebook

Connect to Essential Question: Give students time to reflect on how "The Treasure of Lemon Brown" connects to the unit's essential question "How do relationships shape us?" by freewriting in their Writer's Notebooks.

 Beginning & Intermediate

Read aloud the unit's essential question: "How do relationships shape us?" Encourage students to draw their reflections and allow students to write in their native language. Circulate around the room, prompting students for their thoughts as they respond orally or through pantomime.

Advanced & Advanced High

Allow students to share their reflections orally in pairs or small groups before freewriting.

Collaborative Conversation

Break students into collaborative conversation groups to discuss the Close Read prompt. Remind them to reference their Skills Focus annotations in their discussion.

Three men, one carrying a length of pipe, arrive at the abandoned building to steal Lemon Brown's treasure. Lemon, with Greg's help, scares them off. Does the author reveal enough about Lemon Brown's treasure for the reader to understand its importance? Do you think Lemon Brown's treasure is worth fighting for? Why or why not? Defend your point of view with evidence from the text.

Use the scaffolds below to differentiate instruction for your **ELL** English Language Learners and **A** Approaching grade-level learners.

ELL **BEGINNING, INTERMEDIATE** Use the <u>discussion guide</u> and <u>speaking frames</u> to discuss with support from the teacher.

ADVANCED, ADVANCED HIGH Use the <u>discussion guide</u> and <u>speaking frames</u> to discuss in mixed-level groups.

A **APPROACHING** Use the <u>discussion guide</u> to discuss in mixed-level groups.

APPROACHING
ADVANCED, ADVANCED HIGH
BEGINNING, INTERMEDIATE

Discussion Guide	Speaking Frames
1. What is Lemon Brown's treasure, and why is it important to him?	• Lemon Brown's treasure is ____. • The treasure is important to him because ____.
2. What textual evidence tells you the treasure is valuable to Lemon Brown?	• One event that tells me this is ____. • Another event that tells me this is ____.
3. Based on the textual evidence, do you think the treasure is worth fighting for? Why or why not?	• I think the treasure (is/is not) worth fighting for. • I think this because ____.

Review Prompt and Rubric

Before students begin writing, review the writing prompt and rubric with the class.

ARGUMENTATIVE: Three men, one carrying a length of pipe, arrive at the abandoned building to steal Lemon Brown's treasure. Lemon, with Greg's help, scares them off. Does the author reveal enough about Lemon Brown's treasure for the reader to understand its importance? Do you think Lemon Brown's treasure is worth fighting for? Why or why not? Defend your point of view with evidence from the text.

ELL PROMPT GUIDE

A
- What is Lemon Brown's treasure, and why is it important to him?
- What textual evidence tells you the treasure is valuable to Lemon Brown?

- Based on the textual evidence, do you think the treasure is worth fighting for? Why or why not?

Score	Point of View	Language and Conventions
4	The writer clearly analyzes how well the author explains the treasure in order to support his or her point of view about whether or not it was worth the fight. The writer provides exemplary analysis, using relevant evidence from the text.	The writer demonstrates a consistent command of grammar, punctuation, and usage conventions. Although minor errors may be evident, they do not detract from the fluency or the clarity of the essay.
3	The writer analyzes how well the author explains the treasure in order to support his or her point of view about whether or not it was worth the fight. The writer provides sufficient analysis, using relevant evidence from the text most of the time.	The writer demonstrates an adequate command of grammar, punctuation, and usage conventions. Although some errors may be evident, they create few (if any) disruptions in the fluency of the writing or the clarity of the essay.
2	The writer begins to analyze how well the author explains the treasure in order to support his or her point of view about whether or not it was worth the fight, but the analysis is incomplete. The writer uses relevant evidence from the text only some of the time.	The writer demonstrates a partial command of grammar, punctuation, and usage conventions. Some distracting errors may be evident, at times creating minor disruptions in the fluency or clarity of the writing.
1	The writer attempts to analyze how well the author explains the treasure in order to support his or her point of view about whether or not it was worth the fight, but the analysis is not successful. The writer uses little or no relevant evidence from the text.	The writer demonstrates little or no command of grammar, punctuation, and usage conventions. Serious and persistent errors create disruptions in the fluency of the writing and sometimes interfere with meaning.
0	The writer does not provide a relevant response to the prompt or does not provide a response at all.	Serious and persistent errors overwhelm the writing and interfere with the meaning of the response as a whole, making the writer's meaning impossible to understand.

Write

Ask students to complete the writing assignment using textual evidence to support their answers.

Use the scaffolds below to differentiate instruction for your **ELL** English Language Learners and **A** Approaching grade-level learners.

ELL **BEGINNING** With the help of the <u>word bank</u>, write a response using <u>paragraph frame 1</u>.

INTERMEDIATE With the help of the <u>word bank</u>, write a response using <u>paragraph frames 1 and 2</u>.

ADVANCED, ADVANCED HIGH Write a response of differentiated length using the <u>sentence starters</u>.

A **APPROACHING** Write a response of differentiated length using the <u>sentence starters</u>.

BEGINNING / INTERMEDIATE			ADVANCED, ADVANCED HIGH / APPROACHING
Word Bank	**Paragraph Frame 1**	**Paragraph Frame 2**	**Sentence Starters**
Greg is/is not thugs newspaper clippings son	Lemon Brown's treasure is his old harmonica and ____ about his performances. The author reveals that the treasure is valuable to Lemon Brown because his ____ took it to war. The treasure is so valuable to Lemon Brown that he fought the ____ for it. Lemon Brown also wanted ____ to see the treasure. This evidence makes me think the treasure ____ worth fighting for.	Some treasures are more valuable than ____. Lemon Brown's treasure is valuable because it was his ____. It told Jesse what he ____. The fact that Jesse ____ made Lemon Brown treasure it even more. It is Lemon Brown's connection to ____.	• Lemon Brown's treasure is . . . • The author reveals that the treasure is valuable because . . . • The treasure is so valuable that . . . • Lemon Brown also wanted . . . • This evidence makes me think that the treasure (is/is not) . . . • Some treasures are more valuable than . . .

Peer Review

Students should submit substantive feedback to two peers using the review instructions below.

- How well does this response answer the prompt?
- How well does the writer support ideas with details and examples from the text?
- Which sentence in the writer's response made you think differently about the text?
- What did the writer do well in this response? What does the writer need to work on?

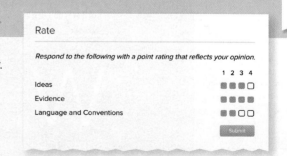

Rate

Respond to the following with a point rating that reflects your opinion.

	1 2 3 4
Ideas	■ ■ ■ □
Evidence	■ ■ ■ ■
Language and Conventions	■ ■ □ □

Submit

ELL **A** **SENTENCE FRAMES**

- You were able to (completely / partly / almost) ____ answer the prompt because . . .
- You could answer the prompt more completely by . . .
- You supported the idea of . . . with the detail of . . .

- One idea that needs more support is . . .
- I thought differently about the texts after reading . . .
- My favorite part of your response is . . .

The Circuit: Stories from the Life of a Migrant Child

FICTION
Francisco Jiménez
1997

Introduction

studysync

When Francisco Jiménez (b. 1943) was four years old, he and his family immigrated to the United States. At the age of six, he began working on farms, like other members of his family. Now a professor of literature at Santa Clara University in California, Jiménez said, "I came to realize that learning and knowledge were the only stable things in my life. Whatever I learned in school, that knowledge would stay with me no matter how many times we moved." *The Circuit: Stories from the Life of a Migrant Child* is Jiménez's autobiographical novel about migrant farm workers in 1950s California. It describes how migrant workers would go from farm to farm picking fruits and vegetables—also known as traveling the circuit.

Francisco Jiménez, a migrant worker in 1950s California, arrives home on the last day of strawberry-picking season to see a familiar but dreaded site: cardboard boxes that signal another move. The family drives to Fresno where they find temporary work picking grapes. When the season ends, Francisco is excited to be able to return to school. On his first day, Francisco forms a relationship with his teacher Mr. Lema, who readily agrees to help with his reading skills. They spend every lunch hour together, and Francisco comes to see Mr. Lema as his best friend. Mr. Lema even offers to teach Francisco how to play the trumpet. Going home that day, Francisco is eager to share his good news, but when he opens the door he unexpectedly encounters the sight of freshly-packed cardboard boxes. The family has to move again.

 Proficiency-leveled summaries and summaries in multiple languages are available digitally.

 Audio and audio text highlighting are available with this text.

COMPARING WITHIN AND ACROSS GENRES

 Thematically linked to "That Day" and "A Poem for My Librarian, Mrs. Long" in its exploration of a mentor relationship that changes a life, Francisco Jiménez's autobiographical novel *The Circuit* follows the life of a young migrant who is forced to move frequently to find work.

Access Complex Text

LEXILE: 730L   **WORD COUNT:** 2,332

The following areas may be challenging for students, particularly **ELL** English Language Learners and **A** Approaching grade-level learners.

Prior Knowledge	Genre	Specific Vocabulary
• The selection focuses on the lives of California migrant workers during the 1950s. • The nomadic way of life of California migrant workers, who were primarily immigrants from Mexico, may need further explanation.	• The text is an excerpt from an autobiographical novel. • Explain the difference between an autobiographical novel and autobiography. The first blends fact with fiction, and includes dialogue or isolated fictional events in order to make a more satisfying story. The second is a first-person account of the author's life and contains no fiction.	• The selection contains many words and phrases in Spanish. • Words such as *bracero* (a Mexican migrant worker) and *mi olla* (my pot) may need translation in lieu of context clues.

 **SCAFFOLDS**   **ELL** ENGLISH LANGUAGE LEARNERS   **A** APPROACHING GRADE LEVEL   **B** BEYOND GRADE LEVEL

These icons identify differentiation strategies and scaffolded support for a variety of students. See the digital lesson plan for additional differentiation strategies and scaffolds.

Instructional Path

The print teacher's edition includes essential point-of-use instruction and planning tools. Complete lesson plans and program documents appear in your digital teacher account.

Independent Read: The Circuit

Objectives: After reading an excerpt from the text, students will demonstrate an understanding of characterization through a personal connection in a short, written response.

Independent Read

Francisco Jiménez

The Circuit: Stories from the Life of a Migrant Child

Introduce the Text

As a class, watch the video preview ▶ and have students read the introduction in pairs to make connections to the video preview.

- How does the information in this video connect to what you already know?

- In what ways does the process of moving sometimes make people feel unsure or unsteady?

- What do you think the phrase "stable things in my life" means?

ELL **SPEAKING FRAMES**

- The ____ in the video makes me think ____.
- The introduction mentions ____. This is connected to ____ in the video.
- The video shows ____. This makes me wonder ____.
- I think the text will ____. I think this because ____.
- I predict that there will be ____. I believe this because ____.

Entry Point

As students prepare to read *The Circuit,* share the following information with them to provide context.

✓ Author Francisco Jiménez was born in 1943 in Tlaquepaque, Mexico. His family moved to California when he was a child and worked picking fruit. They moved with the seasons, disrupting school and living in brutal conditions, often without electricity or running water. After high school, Jiménez attended Santa Clara University and went on to get a PhD. He is now a college professor and has published several autobiographical books.

✓ Migrant farmworkers are people who move from farm to farm harvesting fruit. They move from farm to farm through the growing season. In America, there are still estimated to be 500,000 children working as migrant farmworkers. These children are not covered by the protections of most child labor laws and face difficult working conditions.

"My mouth was dry. My eyes began to water. I could not begin. . . ."

NOTES

from the Chapter: **The Circuit**

1 It was that time of year again. Ito, the strawberry sharecropper[1], did not smile. It was natural. The peak of the strawberry season was over and the last few days the workers, most of them *braceros,* were not picking as many boxes as they had during the months of June and July.

2 As the last days of August disappeared, so did the number of braceros. Sunday, only one—the best picker—came to work. I liked him. Sometimes we talked during our half-hour lunch break. That is how I found out he was from Jalisco, the same state in Mexico my family was from. That Sunday was the last time I saw him.

3 When the sun had tired and sunk behind the mountains, Ito signaled us that it was time to go home. "*Ya esora,*" he yelled in his broken Spanish. Those were the words I waited for twelve hours a day, every day, seven days a week, week after week. And the thought of not hearing them again saddened me.

4 As we drove home Papá did not say a word. With both hands on the wheel, he stared at the dirt road. My older brother, Roberto, was also silent. He leaned his head back and closed his eyes. Once in a while he cleared from his throat the dust that blew in from outside.

5 Yes, it was that time of year. When I opened the front door to the shack, I stopped. Everything we owned was neatly packed in cardboard boxes. Suddenly I felt even more the weight of hours, days, weeks, and months of work. I sat down on a box. The thought of having to move to Fresno and knowing what was in store for me there brought tears to my eyes.

6 That night I could not sleep. I lay in bed thinking about how much I hated this move.

7 A little before five o'clock in the morning, Papá woke everyone up. A few minutes later, the yelling and screaming of my little brothers and sisters, for

---

1. **sharecropper** a farmer who farms someone else's land, and in exchange, is allowed to live there

Reading & Writing Companion **65**

Copyright © BookheadEd Learning, LLC

Analyze Vocabulary using Context Clues

As students read the text, ask them to make predictions about each bold vocabulary word based on the context clues in the sentence. Have students use the annotation tool to make their predictions.

TURN AND TALK

Have students discuss their original vocabulary predictions with a neighbor. Come to a consensus as a class before confirming their definitions.

TEXT TALK

What happens in the writer's world during "that time of year"?

See paragraphs 1–4: Strawberry season is over, workers are leaving, the writer's family is moving, and he will miss people he has come to know.

NOTES

whom the move was a great adventure, broke the silence of dawn. Shortly, the barking of the dogs accompanied them.

8 While we packed the breakfast dishes, Papá went outside to start the "*Carcachita*." That was the name Papá gave his old black Plymouth. He bought it in a used-car lot in Santa Rosa. Papá was very proud of his little jalopy[2]. He had a right to be proud of it. He spent a lot of time looking at other cars before buying this one. When he finally chose the *Carcachita*, he checked it thoroughly before driving it out of the car lot. He examined every inch of the car. He listened to the motor, tilting his head from side to side like a parrot, trying to **detect** any noises that spelled car trouble. After being satisfied with the looks and sounds of the car, Papá then insisted on knowing who the original owner was. He never did find out from the car salesman, but he bought the car anyway. Papá figured the original owner must have been an important man because behind the rear seat of the car he found a blue necktie.

9 Papá parked the car out in front and left the motor running. "*Listo,*" he yelled. Without saying a word, Roberto and I began to carry the boxes out to the car. Roberto carried the two big boxes and I carried the two smaller ones. Papá then threw the mattress on top of the car roof and tied it with ropes to the front and rear bumpers.

10 Everything was packed except Mamá's pot. It was on old large galvanized pot she had picked up at an army surplus store in Santa Maria. The pot had many dents and nicks, and the more dents and nicks it **acquired** the more Mamá liked it. "*Mi olla,*" she used to say proudly.

11 I held the front door open as Mamá carefully carried out her pot by both handles, making sure not to spill the cooked beans. When she got to the car, Papá reached out to help her with it. Roberto opened the rear car door and Papá gently placed it on the floor behind the front seat. All of us then climbed in. Papá sighed, wiped the sweat off his forehead with his sleeve, and said wearily: "*Es todo.*"

12 As we drove away, I felt a lump in my throat. I turned around and looked at our little shack for the last time.

13 At sunset we drove into a labor camp near Fresno. Since Papá did not speak English, Mamá asked the camp **foreman** if he needed any more workers. "We don't need no more," said the foreman, scratching his head. "Check with Sullivan down the road. Can't miss him. He lives in a big white house with a fence around it."

2. **jalopy** an old automobile, usually in disrepair

Copyright © BookheadEd Learning, LLC

 SELECTION VOCABULARY

detect / detectar *verb* to discover or determine the presence or fact of COGNATE

 ELL
• What is papa listening to?
• What is papa trying to hear?

acquired / adquirir *verb* to obtain, come into possession of; to earn COGNATE

 ELL
• Does the pot have many or just a few dents and nicks?
• Does the pot get more or fewer dents and nicks over time?

NOTES

14 When we got there, Mamá walked up to the house. She went through a white gate, past a row of rose bushes, up the stairs to the front door. She rang the doorbell. The porch light went on and a tall husky man came out. They exchanged a few words. After the man went in, Mamá clasped her hands and hurried back to the car. "We have work! Mr. Sullivan said we can stay there the whole season," she said, gasping and pointing to an old garage near the stables.

15 The garage was worn out by the years. It had no windows. The walls, eaten by termites, strained to support the roof full of holes. The dirt floor, populated by earthworms, looked like a gray road map.

16 That night, by the light of a kerosene lamp[3], we unpacked and cleaned our new home. Roberto swept away the loose dirt, leaving the hard ground. Papá plugged the holes in the walls with old newspapers and tin can tops. Mamá fed my little brothers and sisters. Papá and Roberto then brought in the mattress and placed it on the far corner of the garage. "Mamá, you and the little ones sleep on the mattress. Roberto, Panchito, and I will sleep outside under the trees," Papá said.

17 Early next morning Mr. Sullivan showed us where his crop was, and after breakfast, Papá, Roberto, and I headed for the vineyard to pick.

18 Around nine o'clock the temperature had risen to almost one hundred degrees. I was completely soaked in sweat and my mouth felt as if I had been chewing on a handkerchief. I walked over to the end of the row, picked up the jug of water we had brought, and began drinking. "Don't drink too much; you'll get sick," Roberto shouted. No sooner had he said that than I felt sick to my stomach. I dropped to my knees and let the jug roll off my hands. I remained motionless with my eyes glued on the hot sandy ground. All I could hear was the drone of insects. Slowly I began to recover. I poured water over my face and neck and watched the dirty water run down my arms to the ground.

19 I still felt a little dizzy when we took a break to eat lunch. It was past two o'clock and we sat underneath a large walnut tree that was on the side of the road. While we ate, Papá jotted down the number of boxes we had picked. Roberto drew designs on the ground with a stick. Suddenly I noticed Papá's face turn pale as he looked down the road. "Here comes the school bus," he whispered loudly in alarm. Instinctively, Roberto and I ran and hid in the vineyards. We did not want to get in trouble for not going to school. The neatly dressed boys about my age got off. They carried books under their arms. After they crossed the street, the bus drove away. Roberto and I came out from hiding and joined Papá. "*Tienen que tener cuidado,*" he warned us.

3. **kerosene lamp** a handheld lamp that burned liquid fuel for light

Reading & Writing Companion **67**

 SELECTION VOCABULARY

foreman / el/la encargado/a *noun* the leader of a group of workers

 (ELL)
- Why does Mama speak to the foreman?
- What does the foreman seem to be in charge of?

 TEXT TALK

What are working conditions in Fresno like for the writer?

See paragraph 18: The temperature reaches 100 degrees in the morning, and the writer passes out from the heat.

Why do the writer and his brother hide from the school bus?

See paragraph 19: It is illegal for children not to attend school. Their father wants them to be careful, because the family needs their wages.

The Circuit: Stories from the Life of a Migrant Child

NOTES

20 After lunch we went back to work. The sun kept beating down. The buzzing insects, the wet sweat, and the hot dry dust made the afternoon seem to last forever. Finally the mountains around the valley reached out and swallowed the sun. Within an hour it was too dark to continue picking. The vines blanketed the grapes, making it difficult to see the bunches. "*Vámonos,*" said Papá, signaling to us that it was time to quit work. Papá then took out a pencil and began to figure out how much we had earned our first day. He wrote down numbers, crossed some out, wrote down some more, "*Quince,*" he murmured.

21 When we arrived home, we took a cold shower underneath a water hose. We then sat down to eat dinner around some wooden crates that served as a table. Mamá had cooked a special meal for us. We had rice and tortillas with *carne con chile,* my favorite dish.

22 The next morning I could hardly move. My body ached all over. I felt little control over my arms and legs. This feeling went on every morning for days until my muscles finally got used to the work.

23 It was Monday, the first week of November. The grape season was over and I could now go to school. I woke up early that morning and lay in bed, looking at the stars and **savoring** the thought of not going to work and of starting sixth grade for the first time that year. Since I could not sleep, I decided to get up and join Papá and Roberto at breakfast. I sat at the table across from Roberto, but I kept my head down. I did not want to look up and face him. I knew he was sad. He was not going to school today. He was not going tomorrow, or next week, or next month. He would not go until the cotton season was over, and that was sometime in February. I rubbed my hands together and watched the dry, acid stained skin fall to the floor in little rolls.

24 When Papá and Roberto left for work, I felt relief. I walked to the top of a small grade next to the shack and watched the *Carcachita* disappear in the distance in a cloud of dust.

25 Two hours later, around eight o'clock, I stood by the side of the road waiting for school bus number twenty. When it arrived I climbed in. Everyone was busy either talking or yelling. I sat in an empty seat in the back.

26 When the bus stopped in front of the school, I felt very nervous. I looked out the bus window and saw boys and girls carrying books under their arms. I put my hands in my pant pockets and walked to the principal's office. When I entered I heard a woman's voice say: "May I help you?" I was startled. I had not heard English for months. For a few seconds I remained speechless. I looked at the lady who waited for an answer. My first instinct was to answer her in Spanish, but I held back. Finally, after struggling for English words, I

SELECTION VOCABULARY

savoring / disfrutar *verb* to take great delight in

ELL

- Is Francisco looking forward to or dreading not going to work?
- Is Francisco looking forward to or dreading going to school?

The Circuit: Stories from the Life of a Migrant Child

managed to tell her that I wanted to enroll in the sixth grade. After answering many questions, I was led to the classroom.

— NOTES —

27 Mr. Lema, the sixth grade teacher, greeted me and assigned me a desk. He then introduced me to the class. I was so nervous and scared at that moment when everyone's eyes were on me that I wished I were with Papá and Roberto picking cotton. After taking roll, Mr. Lema gave the class the assignment for the first hour. "The first thing we have to do this morning is finish reading the story we began yesterday," he said enthusiastically. He walked up to me, handed me an English book, and asked me to read. "We are on page 125," he said politely. When I heard this, I felt my blood rush to my head; I felt dizzy. "Would you like to read?" he asked **hesitantly**. I opened the book to page 125. My mouth was dry. My eyes began to water. I could not begin. "You can read later," Mr. Lema said understandingly.

28 For the rest of the reading period I kept getting angrier and angrier with myself. I should have read, I thought to myself. During recess I went into the restroom and opened my English book to page 125. I began to read in a low voice, pretending I was in class. There were many words I did not know. I closed the book and headed back to the classroom.

29 Mr. Lema was sitting at his desk correcting papers. When I entered he looked up at me and smiled. I felt better. I walked up to him and asked if he could help me with the new words. "Gladly," he said.

30 The rest of the month I spent my lunch hours working on English with Mr. Lema, my best friend at school.

31 One Friday, during lunch hour, Mr. Lema asked me to take a walk with him to the music room. "Do you like music?" he asked me as we entered the building. "Yes, I like *corridos*⁴," I answered. He then picked up a trumpet, blew on it, and handed it to me. The sound gave me goose bumps. I knew that sound. I had heard it in many *corridos*. "How would you like to learn how to play it?" he asked. He must have read my face because before I could answer, he added: "I'll teach you how to play it during our lunch hours."

4. corridos a traditional Mexican ballad, usually with lyrics describing an actual historical event

Reading & Writing Companion **69**

Prepare for Advanced Courses

Use the activity below to differentiate instruction for your **B** Beyond grade-level learners.

Look at the word *assigned* in paragraph 27.

If students are unfamiliar with the word *assign*, explain that it is an academic vocabulary word with three meanings:

- allocate (a job or duty)
- designate or set (something) aside for a specific purpose.
- transfer (legal rights or liabilities).

Ask students: Which definition is the author using in paragraph 27? How are the definitions for the word *assign* similar and connected?

TEXT TALK

When the writer goes to school, how is he treated by his teacher, Mr. Lema?

See paragraphs 29 and 30: Mr. Lema helps him with English and says he will teach him how to play the trumpet.

V SELECTION VOCABULARY

hesitantly / con indecisión *adverb* characterized by acting or speaking slowly and nervously

- Is Mr. Lema certain or uncertain about whether Francisco can read English?
- Does Mr. Lema speak forcefully or softly?

Integrated Reading and Writing **445**

32   That day I could hardly wait to tell Papá and Mamá the great news. As I got off the bus, my little brothers and sisters ran up to meet me. They were yelling and screaming. I thought they were happy to see me, but when I opened the door to our shack, I saw that everything we owned was neatly packed in cardboard boxes.

© 1992 by Francisco Jiménez, THE CIRCUIT: STORIES FROM THE LIFE OF A MIGRANT CHILD. Reproduced by permission of Francisco Jiménez.

 **WRITE**

PERSONAL RESPONSE: In *The Circuit*, Francisco and his family are constantly moving. Each time Francisco's family moves, he feels sad to leave yet another place behind. At school, Francisco finds stability with a teacher, Mr. Lema, who helps him with reading.
Have you ever moved? If so, how did it make you feel? If not, think about something in your life that is stable and consistent. How does it contribute to your happiness? How do your feelings compare or contrast with Francisco's? Use newly-acquired vocabulary and evidence from the text to support your response.

 **TEXT TALK**

What does the writer see when he gets home, and what does the sight mean?

See paragraph 32: He sees the family's belongings packed in boxes, meaning they are about to move again and he won't get to study with Mr. Lema.

Why do you think moving is likely to be emotionally distressing and difficult for the narrator at the end of the story?

Answers will vary.

B BEYOND TEXT TALK

What challenges does Francisco face as the son of a migrant worker, and what is he learning from his family members?

Reading Comprehension

Have students complete the digital reading comprehension questions 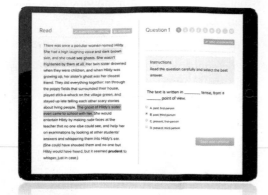 when they finish reading.

ANSWER KEY

QUESTION 1: B	**QUESTION 5:** C	**QUESTION 9:**
QUESTION 2: D	**QUESTION 6:** B	*See first chart.*
QUESTION 3: C	**QUESTION 7:** D	**QUESTION 10:**
QUESTION 4: A	**QUESTION 8:** B	*See second chart.*

First	Second	Third	Fourth
Francisco's family moves to Fresno at the end of strawberry season.	Francisco and Roberto hide from a school bus while working in the vineyard.	Roberto goes to work in the cotton fields.	Francisco learns to read English from Mr. Lema.

Synonym	Word
uncertainly	hesitantly
supervisor	foreman
notice	detect
gain	acquire
route	circuit
delighting in	savoring

Connect and Extend OPTIONAL

CONNECT TO EXTENDED WRITING PROJECT

Francisco Jiménez paints a vivid picture of life as a migrant worker using descriptive language. Prompt students to notice striking words, phrases, and sentences that illustrate the people, places, and events in Jiménez's life most clearly. Such descriptions will help students craft descriptive details in their own letters.

BEYOND THE BOOK

Photography: If You Could Only Take 3 Items

Ask students to imagine they have to pack up and move every few months. They have limited space to pack sentimental items, and can only carry three along. What would they take? Why? Ask students to identify their items, photograph each, and share that photo with a brief explanation of its significance.

Allow students time to explore each others' pictures, then place them in small groups to discuss their choices.

- What did you decide to bring?
- What is significant about these three items?
- Which items were you tempted to include but didn't?

To reflect, ask students:

- After seeing what your peers selected, would you change any of your choices?
- What did you learn about the individuals in our class based on their choices?

StudySyncTV

Project the StudySyncTV episode ▶ and pause at the following times to prompt discussion:

0:14–0:40 What do the students disagree about at the beginning of the discussion?

1:30 How do the students use textual evidence to determine why Francisco feels bad about leaving the fields when strawberry picking season is over?

4:34 How does the student make a personal connection with the main character Francisco?

5:17 How do the students use plot and characterization to determine theme?

Collaborative Conversation

 **SCAFFOLDS**

Break students into collaborative conversation groups to discuss the writing prompt. Ask students to use the StudySyncTV episode as a model for their discussion. Remind them to reference their Skills Focus annotations in their discussion.

In *The Circuit*, Francisco and his family are constantly moving. Each time Francisco's family moves, he feels sad to leave yet another place behind. At school, Francisco finds stability with a teacher, Mr. Lema, who helps him with reading. Have you ever moved? If so, how did it make you feel? If not, think about something in your life that is stable and consistent. How does it contribute to your happiness? How do your feelings compare or contrast with Francisco's?

Use the scaffolds below to differentiate instruction for your **ELL** English Language Learners and **A** Approaching grade-level learners.

ELL **BEGINNING, INTERMEDIATE** Use the <u>discussion guide</u> and <u>speaking frames</u> to facilitate the discussion with support from the teacher.

ADVANCED, ADVANCED HIGH Use the <u>discussion guide</u> and <u>speaking frames</u> to facilitate the discussion in mixed-level groups.

A **APPROACHING** Use the <u>discussion guide</u> to facilitate the discussion in mixed-level groups.

APPROACHING
ADVANCED, ADVANCED HIGH
BEGINNING, INTERMEDIATE

Discussion Guide	Speaking Frames
1. Why does moving make Francisco feel sad? How does Mr. Lema help Francisco find some stability he doesn't usually have?	• I think Francisco feels sad about moving because ____. • I think Mr. Lema helps Francisco find some stability he doesn't usually have by ____.
2. What connections can you make between Francisco's move and one of your own?	• This story reminds me of the time when I moved from ____. • (Un)Like Francisco, my move made me feel ____ because ____.
3. What connections can you make between Francisco's sense of stability and your own?	• The story makes me realize that ____ provides me with stability because ____. • This stability contributes to my happiness by ____. My feelings compare (contrast) with Francisco's in that ____.

Review Prompt and Rubric

Before students begin writing, review the writing prompt and rubric with the class.

PERSONAL RESPONSE: In *The Circuit*, Francisco and his family are constantly moving. Each time Francisco's family moves, he feels sad to leave yet another place behind. At school, Francisco finds stability with a teacher, Mr. Lema, who helps him with reading. Have you ever moved? If so, how did it make you feel? If not, think about something in your life that is stable and consistent. How does it contribute to your happiness? How do your feelings compare or contrast with Francisco's? Use newly-acquired vocabulary and evidence from the text to support your response.

 PROMPT GUIDES

- Why does moving make Francisco feel sad? How does Mr. Lema help Francisco?
- What connections can you make between Francisco's move and one of your own?

- If you've never moved, what do you think it would be like? Do you think you would share some of Francisco's feelings?
- What connections can you make between Francisco's feelings and your own?

Score	Personal Response	Language And Conventions
4	The writer clearly explains his or her personal connection to the text, using relevant evidence from the text as needed.	The writer demonstrates a consistent command of grammar, punctuation, and usage conventions. Although minor errors may be evident, they do not detract from the fluency or the clarity of the essay.
3	The writer sufficiently explains his or her personal connection to the text, using relevant evidence from the text most of the time.	The writer demonstrates an adequate command of grammar, punctuation, and usage conventions. Although some errors may be evident, they create few (if any) disruptions in the fluency of the writing or the clarity of the essay.
2	The writer begins to explain his or her personal connection to the text, but the explanation is incomplete. The writer uses relevant evidence from the text only some of the time.	The writer demonstrates a partial command of grammar, punctuation, and usage conventions. Some distracting errors may be evident, at times creating minor disruptions in the fluency or clarity of the writing.
1	The writer attempts to explain his or her personal connection to the text, but the explanation is not successful. The writer uses little or no relevant evidence from the text.	The writer demonstrates little or no command of grammar, punctuation, and usage conventions. Serious and persistent errors create disruptions in the fluency of the writing and sometimes interfere with meaning.
0	The writer does not provide a relevant response to the prompt or does not provide a response at all.	Serious and persistent errors overwhelm the writing and interfere with the meaning of the response as a whole, making the writer's meaning impossible to understand.

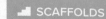

Write

Ask students to complete the writing assignment using textual evidence to support their answers.

Use the scaffolds below to differentiate instruction for your **ELL** English Language Learners and **A** Approaching grade-level learners.

ELL **BEGINNING** With the help of the word bank, write a response using paragraph frame 1.

INTERMEDIATE With the help of the word bank, write a response using paragraph frames 1 and 2.

ADVANCED, ADVANCED HIGH Write a response of differentiated length using the sentence starters.

A **APPROACHING** Write a response of differentiated length using the sentence starters.

| BEGINNING | ADVANCED, ADVANCED HIGH |
| INTERMEDIATE | APPROACHING |

Word Bank	Paragraph Frame 1	Paragraph Frame 2	Sentence Starters
nervous sad alone English moved new teaching friends	Moving makes Francisco feel scared because ____. Mr. Lema helps Francisco by ____. I imagine he feels ____ because ____. A similar experience I had was when ____. It made me feel ____. My feelings might have been the same as Francisco's because ____.	I can also connect to Francisco's feelings of ____. An example of this in the text is when ____. I once felt that way when ____. We both ____.	• I moved from . . . to . . . when . . . • This move made me feel . . . because . . . • My feelings were (un)like Francisco's in that . . . • One thing that gives me stability in life is . . . • This contributes to my happiness because . . . • One thing that gives Francisco stability during his move is . . . • This will contribute to his happiness because . . . • Francisco's feelings connect with mine in that . . .

Peer Review

Students should submit substantive feedback to two peers using the review instructions below.

- How well does this response describe the personal feelings that can occur with a move?
- How well does this response describe stability, consistency, and happiness in the author's life?
- How well does this response compare and contrast Francisco's feelings with the writer's?
- How well does this response use textual evidence?
- What does the writer do well in this response? What does the writer need to work on?

Rate

Respond to the following with a point rating that reflects your opinion.

	1 2 3 4
Ideas	▪▪▪☐
Evidence	▪▪▪▪
Language and Conventions	▪▪☐☐

Submit

ELL SENTENCE FRAMES

A
- You were able to (completely / partly / almost) ___ answer the prompt.
- You could answer the prompt more completely by . . .

- I thought differently about the text after reading . . .
- My favorite part of your response is . . .

That Day

POETRY
David Kherdian
1978

Introduction

David Kherdian (b. 1931) is an Armenian-American writer and poet who is best known for penning an account of his mother's childhood during the Armenian Genocide called *The Road from Home*. In total, he has published more than 75 books in numerous genres, from creative nonfiction to poetry, and has also worked as an editor of numerous literary journals and anthologies. In his poem "That Day," presented here, Kherdian reflects on a special memory of his father.

In this poem, the speaker remembers the time his father joined him and his friends in a game of softball in the street. As an immigrant to the United States, the speaker's father was unfamiliar with this American game but tried his best anyway. Although his father made a fool of himself, the speaker remembers his effort both as a loving gesture and a reminder of the hardships and dangers of the life that his father's family managed to escape.

 Proficiency-leveled summaries and summaries in multiple languages are available digitally.

 Audio and audio text highlighting are available with this text.

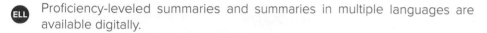

COMPARING WITHIN AND ACROSS GENRES

Relationships between parents and their children can be unique. Poet David Kherdian reflects about what happened on "That Day" between himself and his father. The poem "That Day" continues to push students to explore the theme of life changing-relationships which also is evident in *The Circuit* and "A Poem for My Librarian, Mrs. Long."

Access Complex Text

LEXILE: N/A   WORD COUNT: 88

The following areas may be challenging for students, particularly **ELL** English Language Learners and **A** Approaching grade-level learners.

Genre	Sentence Structure	Specific Vocabulary
• The selection is written in free verse. • You may need to point out to some students that free verse does not follow any conventional rhyme scheme or have a regular meter.	• Students may need assistance analyzing the poem. • The selection is composed of two stanzas, and each stanza consists of one long, continuous sentence.	• Certain words in the poem have multiple meanings. • The word *fabric,* for example, as Kherdian uses it, means "structure" or "framework" as well as a bolt of cloth.

 SCAFFOLDS   **ENGLISH LANGUAGE LEARNERS**   **APPROACHING GRADE LEVEL**   **BEYOND GRADE LEVEL**

These icons identify differentiation strategies and scaffolded support for a variety of students. See the digital lesson plan for additional differentiation strategies and scaffolds.

Instructional Path

The print teacher's edition includes essential point-of-use instruction and planning tools. Complete lesson plans and program documents appear in your digital teacher account.

Independent Read: That Day

Objectives: After reading the text, students will write a short response that demonstrates their understanding of characterization through a personal connection.

Independent Read

David Kherdian

That Day

Introduce the Text

As a class, watch the video preview ▶ and have students read the introduction in pairs to make connections to the video preview.

• What key words or images from the video do you think will be most important to the poem you are about to read?

• What is one prediction you can make about the poem you're going to read?

• How do you think this poem will relate to *The Circuit?*

> **ELL** SPEAKING FRAMES
>
> • The ____ in the video makes me think ____.
> • The video shows ____. This makes me wonder ____.
> • I think the text will ____. I think this because ____.
> • I predict that there will be ____. I believe this because ____.

Entry Point

As students prepare to read "That Day," share the following information with them to provide context.

✓ Nestled between Turkey and Azerbaijan, the country of Armenia was overtaken by the Ottoman Empire in the fifteenth century. During this time, the Turkish community of Muslims regarded the Christian Armenians as inferior. Armenians had fewer rights and even had to pay higher taxes as the Turks questioned the loyalty of the Armenian people. Even so, the Armenian community thrived in education and wealth, thus a jealous rivalry was born.

✓ During World War I, the Turkish supported Germany while Armenia supported the Allies. This further angered the Turkish government who attempted to maintain control. The Turkish government decided to take unjust and shocking action. Between 1915 and 1920, upwards of one million Armenian people were brutally murdered and forcibly removed from their homes in what is now named the Armenian Genocide. Genocide is a premeditated and systematic campaign to exterminate an entire people. Many Armenians were deported or were able to escape to the United States.

✓ In his poem "That Day," David Kherdian reflects on life in the United States after the Armenian Genocide.

"Just once
and the day stands out forever
in my memory"

1 Just once
2 my father stopped on the way
3 into the house from work
4 and joined in the softball game
5 we were having in the street,
6 and **attempted** to play in *our*
7 game that *his* country had never
8 known.
9 Just once
10 and the day stands out forever
11 in my memory
12 as a father's living **gesture**
13 to his son,
14 that in playing even the fool
15 or the clown, he would **reveal**
16 that the lines of their lives
17 were sewn from a tougher **fabric**
18 than the son had **previously** known.

© 1978 by David Kherdian, "That Day" from I Remember Root River. Used by permission of David Kherdian.

 WRITE

PERSONAL RESPONSE: Using "That Day" as an inspiration, write about a memory of an experience from which you learned something valuable about a family member or friend. Borrow key language from the poem to describe what you saw and felt, along with details and descriptions of your own.

Reading & Writing Companion

V SELECTION VOCABULARY

attempt / el intento *verb* to make an effort to do something

gesture / el gesto *noun* a movement or action made to indicate a feeling or attitude COGNATE

reveal / revelar *verb* to make something previously hidden known COGNATE

fabric / la tela *noun* woven cloth or material

previously / anteriormente *adverb* happening at an earlier time

 ## Analyze Vocabulary Using Context Clues

As students read the text, ask them to make predictions about each bold vocabulary word based on the context clues in the sentence. Have students use the annotation tool to make their predictions.

 ## TURN AND TALK

Have students discuss their original vocabulary predictions with a neighbor. Come to a consensus as a class before confirming their definitions.

 ## TEXT TALK

What does the father do on his way home from work?

See line 4: He joins the softball game the speaker and his friends are playing.

What do the italicized words in *"our game"* and *"his country"* tell you?

See lines 6–8: The players expect only sons, not fathers, to join in the game. And the speaker's father must have immigrated from a country that didn't play baseball.

What does the father's action reveal to the speaker?

See line 17: That the father's generation is stronger than the speaker's; they are made of "tougher fabric."

Do you think the speaker respects the sacrifices his father made to start a new life life in America? Why or why not?

Answers will vary.

 B BEYOND TEXT TALK

Ask each Beyond grade-level student to write one additional discussion question. Then, have one or two students facilitate a discussion, using their questions to guide the conversation.

Reading Comprehension

Have students complete the digital reading comprehension questions ✓ when they finish reading.

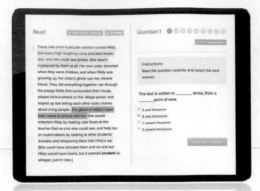

ANSWER KEY

QUESTION 1: A   **QUESTION 3:** B   **QUESTION 5:**

QUESTION 2: C   **QUESTION 4:** C   *See chart below.*

Synonym	Word
show	reveal
earlier	previously
tried	attempted
sign	gesture
material	fabric

Connect and Extend OPTIONAL

CONNECT TO EXTENDED WRITING PROJECT

Students can find inspiration from David Kherdian for their letters. Have them imitate Kherdian's style as they describe a moment or event that illustrates a personal relationship.

BEYOND THE BOOK

Performance: Living Separate Lives Together

Put students into small groups and ask them to write the first two scenes of a play focused on exploring the separate lives that kids and parents lead despite living in the same home. Remind them to think about the following details:

- How old are the kids in this play?
- Where does this family live?
- What do the parents do for a living?
- What issues or tensions exist in the family?

Remind students to include stage directions in addition to their dialogue. Once they've written their scenes, allow students time to rehearse before they perform their scenes for the class.

To reflect, ask students:

- What similarities did you notice between the various scenes? What common tensions exist between parents and their kids?
- Which aspect of this assignment was most challenging (e.g., writing dialogue, writing stage directions, performing)

Collaborative Conversation

Break students into collaborative conversation groups to discuss the Close Read prompt. Remind them to reference their Skills Focus annotations in their discussion.

Using "That Day" as an inspiration, write about a memory in which you learned something valuable about a family member or friend. Borrow key language from the poem to describe what you saw and felt, along with details and descriptions of your own.

Use the scaffolds below to differentiate instruction for your **ELL** English Language Learners and **A** Approaching grade-level learners.

ELL **BEGINNING, INTERMEDIATE** Use the discussion guide and speaking frames to facilitate the discussion with support from the teacher.

ADVANCED, ADVANCED HIGH Use the discussion guide and speaking frames to facilitate the discussion in mixed-level groups.

A **APPROACHING** Use the discussion guide to facilitate the discussion in mixed-level groups.

APPROACHING
ADVANCED, ADVANCED HIGH
BEGINNING, INTERMEDIATE

Discussion Guide	Speaking Frames
1. When did a family member or friend do something that taught you a valuable lesson about him/her?	• ____ did something that taught me a valuable lesson about him/her. • I learned a lesson when ____.
2. What did you learn about the family member or friend as a result of this event?	• As a result, I learned ____. • This lesson was important because ____.
3. What sights, sounds, and feelings do you remember from this event?	• I remember these sights sounds, feelings: ____. • During this event, I felt ____.

Review Prompt and Rubric

Before students begin writing, review the writing prompt and rubric with the class.

PERSONAL RESPONSE: Using "That Day" as an inspiration, write about a memory in which you learned something valuable about a family member or friend. Borrow key language from the poem to describe what you saw and felt, along with details and descriptions of your own.

 PROMPT GUIDE

A
- When did a family member or friend do something that taught you a valuable lesson about him/her?
- What did you learn about the family member or friend as a result of this event?

- What sights, sounds, smells, tastes, textures, and feelings do you remember from this event?

Score	Personal Response	Language and Conventions
4	The writer clearly explains his or her personal connection to the text, using relevant evidence from the text as needed.	The writer demonstrates a consistent command of grammar, punctuation, and usage conventions. Although minor errors may be evident, they do not detract from the fluency or the clarity of the essay.
3	The writer sufficiently explains his or her personal connection to the text, using relevant evidence from the text most of the time.	The writer demonstrates an adequate command of grammar, punctuation, and usage conventions. Although some errors may be evident, they create few (if any) disruptions in the fluency of the writing or the clarity of the essay.
2	The writer begins to explain his or her personal connection to the text, but the explanation is incomplete. The writer uses relevant evidence from the text only some of the time.	The writer demonstrates a partial command of grammar, punctuation, and usage conventions. Some distracting errors may be evident, at times creating minor disruptions in the fluency or clarity of the writing.
1	The writer attempts to explain his or her personal connection to the text, but the explanation is not successful. The writer uses little or no relevant evidence from the text.	The writer demonstrates little or no command of grammar, punctuation, and usage conventions. Serious and persistent errors create disruptions in the fluency of the writing and sometimes interfere with meaning
0	The writer does not provide a relevant response to the prompt or does not provide a response at all.	Serious and persistent errors overwhelm the writing and interfere with the meaning of the response as a whole, making the writer's meaning impossible to understand.

Write

Ask students to complete the writing assignment using textual evidence to support their answers.

Use the scaffolds below to differentiate instruction for your **ELL** English Language Learners and **A** Approaching grade-level learners.

ELL BEGINNING With the help of the <u>word bank</u>, write a response using <u>paragraph frame 1</u>.

INTERMEDIATE With the help of the <u>word bank</u>, write a response using <u>paragraph frames 1 and 2</u>.

ADVANCED, ADVANCED HIGH Write a response of differentiated length using the <u>sentence starters</u>.

A APPROACHING Write a response of differentiated length using the <u>sentence starters</u>.

BEGINNING INTERMEDIATE			ADVANCED, ADVANCED HIGH APPROACHING
Word Bank	**Paragraph Frame 1**	**Paragraph Frame 2**	**Sentence Starters**
father happy launched sacrifices valuable created relationship bond feeling experience	Like the son in "That Day," I learned something ____ about the ____ people make. In this memory, I recall feeling ____. I also felt ____ afterward. I learned something important about the ____ between people.	This moment ____. It revealed ____. The day stands out forever in my memory because ____.	• I learned something valuable about . . . when . . . • During this experience, I saw . . . • During this experience, I heard . . . • During this experience, I felt . . . • This experience revealed . . . • This experience stands out forever in my memory because . . .

Peer Review

Students should submit substantive feedback to two peers using the review instructions below.

- How well does this response describe a memory where the writer learned something valuable about a family member or friend?
- How well does this response use sensory descriptions and express the writer's feelings?
- How well does this response borrow key language from the poem "That Day"?
- What does the writer do well in this response? What does the writer need to work on?

Rate

Respond to the following with a point rating that reflects your opinion.

	1 2 3 4
Ideas	■ ■ ■ □
Evidence	■ ■ ■ ■
Language and Conventions	■ ■ □ □

Submit

ELL A SENTENCE FRAMES

- You were able to (completely / partly / almost) answer the prompt.
- You could answer the prompt more completely by ____ . . .

- I thought differently about the text after reading . . .
- My favorite part of your response is . . .

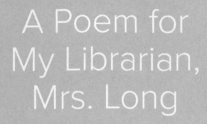

A Poem for My Librarian, Mrs. Long

POETRY
Nikki Giovanni
2007

Introduction

Nikki Giovanni (b. 1943) calls herself a "Black American, a daughter, a mother, a professor of English." She is also the recipient of twenty-five honorary degrees, as well as an award-winning poet, writer, and activist who gives voice to issues of social justice and identity. In this poem, she adopts the persona of a "troubled little girl" in need of a book to demonstrate how reading can be a revolutionary act.

Growing up in Nashville, this poem's speaker remembers spending time on the porch and listening to jazz on her portable radio in the evenings. She also recalls visiting a bookstore and basking in the scent of hardcover books that she could not afford. The speaker would visit her black neighborhood's library where she would tell the librarian, Mrs. Long, what she was seeking. In order to procure these books, Mrs. Long would trek to the big uptown library and suffer humiliation from the white folks working there. Nonetheless, Mrs. Long would obtain these books, which the speaker would take back to her grandmother's front porch, where she would read and dream of faraway worlds. The speaker fondly remembers Mrs. Long for exposing her to these worlds.

ELL Proficiency-leveled summaries and summaries in multiple languages are available digitally.

Audio and audio text highlighting are available with this text.

COMPARING WITHIN AND ACROSS GENRES

Strong relationships can form between almost any two people. In "A Poem for My Librarian, Mrs. Long" by Nikki Giovanni, the speaker reflects on how a librarian in her segregated Southern town helped change the direction of her life when she managed to obtain books for her that Nikki might not have read otherwise. In the selections *The Circuit* and "That Day" students will continue to explore this theme in an autobiographical novel and a poem, respectively.

Access Complex Text

LEXILE: N/A   **WORD COUNT:** 339

The following areas may be challenging for students, particularly **ELL** English Language Learners and **A** Approaching grade-level learners.

Prior Knowledge	Connection of Ideas	Specific Vocabulary
• Several singers are mentioned that students may not know. These singers, popular in the 1950s, place the poem in a specific time period.	• There is a literary allusion that may be unfamiliar to some students.	• The poem contains several specialized vocabulary words.
• The jfg sign is an advertisement for coffee that still stands in Knoxville, Tennessee. References like this locate the setting of the poem in a real place.	• Giovanni mentions opening a wardrobe, but there are no witches or lions inside it. This is a reference to the world of Narnia that C.S. Lewis created.	• The "main black corridor" refers to a street where many African Americans lived. A stereoscope combined two photos to create a three dimensional effect.

 SCAFFOLDS   **ELL** ENGLISH LANGUAGE LEARNERS   APPROACHING GRADE LEVEL   BEYOND GRADE LEVEL

These icons identify differentiation strategies and scaffolded support for a variety of students. See the digital lesson plan for additional differentiation strategies and scaffolds.

Instructional Path

First Read: A Poem for My Librarian, Mrs. Long

Objectives: After an initial reading and discussion of the poem, students will be able to identify and describe speaker and setting details as well as articulate aspects of the poem that are central to the message.

Skill: Compare and Contrast

Objectives: After rereading and discussing a model of close reading, students will be able to compare and contrast texts in different forms or genres (e.g., stories and poems; historical novels and fantasy stories) in terms of their approaches to similar topics.

Close Read: A Poem for My Librarian, Mrs. Long

Objectives: After engaging in a close reading and discussion of the text, students will analyze the theme and compare and contrast that theme with those of *The Circuit* and "That Day" in order to participate in a collaborative conversation and write a short, written response.

Progress Monitoring

Opportunities to Learn	Opportunities to Demonstrate Learning	Opportunities to Reteach

Compare and Contrast

Opportunities to Learn

⚙ Skill: Compare and Contrast

Opportunities to Demonstrate Learning

⚙ Skill: Compare and Contrast
- Your Turn

▣ Close Read
- Skills Focus
- Write

Opportunities to Reteach

⚙ Unit 4
- Skills: Compare and Contrast – Freedom's Daughters: The Unsung Heroines of the Civil Rights Movement from 1830 to 1970

⚙ Unit 6
- Skills: Compare and Contrast – Rosa Parks: My Story

⚙ Spotlight Skill: Compare and Contrast

First Read

Nikki Giovanni

A Poem for My Librarian, Mrs. Long

 ## Introduce the Text

As a class, watch the video preview ▶ and have students read the introduction in pairs to make connections to the video preview.

To activate prior knowledge and experiences, ask students:

- What two words would you use to describe this video?

- What kind of poem are you about to read? How can you tell?

> **ELL** **SPEAKING FRAMES**
>
> - The ____ in the video makes me think ____.
> - The video shows ____. This makes me wonder ____.
> - I think the text will ____. I think this because ____.
> - I predict that there will be ____. I believe this because ____.

Entry Point

As students prepare to read "A Poem for My Librarian, Mrs. Long," share the following information with them to provide context.

✓ During the 1950s and 1960s the African American community fought for equal rights, treatment, and opportunities in America. This movement is known as the Civil Rights Movement. Popular leaders such as Martin Luther King Jr. and Malcolm X emerged, and artists throughout the nation also began to show support for the movement through their works. Nikki Giovanni is one such artist.

✓ Growing up in the midst of the Civil Rights Movement, Giovanni's works highlight her experiences in the South and those individuals who have had the most profound impact on her outlook on life. She pulls inspiration from her family's oral traditions in her writing. Giovanni's voice emphasizes the importance of activism and radiates ideas of revolution.

✓ Recounting her past and the experience of other prominent African American figures allows for many Americans to reflect on and further understand life during the Civil Rights Movement. As an artist and an activist, Giovanni has been recognized by esteemed organizations such as the NAACP and has been regarded as a major figure artistically and politically.

"You never know what troubled little girl needs a book. . ."

A Poem for My Librarian, Mrs. Long
(You never know what troubled little girl needs a book)

1 At a time when there was not tv before 3:00 P.M.
2 And on Sunday none until 5:00
3 We sat on the front porches watching
4 The jfg sign go on and off greeting
5 The neighbors, discussing the political
6 **Situation** congratulating the preacher
7 On his sermon
8 There was always the radio which brought us
9 Songs from wlac in nashville and what we would now call
10 Easy listening or smooth jazz but when I listened
11 Late at night with my **portable** (that I was so proud of)
12 Tucked under my pillow
13 I heard nat king cole and matt dennis, june christy and ella
14 Fitzgerald
15 And sometimes sarah vaughan sing
16 Black coffee
17 Which I now drink
18 It was just called music

19 There was a bookstore uptown on gay street
20 Which I visited and inhaled that wonderful odor
21 Of new books
22 Even today I read hardcover as a preference paperback only
23 As a last resort

24 And up the hill on vine street
25 (The main black corridor) sat our carnegie library
26 Mrs. Long always glad to see you
27 The stereoscope always ready to show you faraway
28 Places to dream about

Analyze Vocabulary using Context Clues

Focus on lines 5–7, which contain the word *situation*. **Point out these context clues:**

1. First I notice the speaker observes the neighbors talking about something.

2. I also see the the word "political" is being used to describe "situation." This word is an adjective.

3. I know that when people talk about political things, they are referring to an event or an issue.

4. I think situation means issue.

TEXT TALK

What do the family and their neighbors do on Sunday afternoons?

See lines 1 through 10: They sit on the porch, talk about politics, and listen to music on the radio.

How does the music the speaker listens to at night differ from the Sunday afternoon porch music?

See lines 10 through 18: The speaker's music is not "easy listening" or "smooth."

What two favorite places does the speaker mention visiting?

See lines 19 through 28: The speaker likes to visit "a bookstore uptown on gay street" and "our carnegie library."

 SELECTION VOCABULARY

situation / la situación *noun* a condition or circumstance

portable / portable *adjective* a lightweight device, such as a radio or small television, that can be easily carried COGNATE

• What is the function of the speaker's "portable"?
• Is the "portable" large or small?

humiliating / humillante *adjective* causing someone to feel shame or embarrassment COGNATE

ELL • What is the relationship between southern whites and southern blacks?
• Are the two groups nice or mean to each other?

nonetheless / sin embargo *adverb* despite what has just been said

ELL • How is Mrs. Long probably treated when she goes uptown to borrow books?
• Does Mrs. Long bring back the books from uptown or not?

Skills Focus

QUESTION 1: Theme

These lines emphasize the speaker's' love of reading and her active imagination. According to Nikki, this allows her to mentally leave the world around her, the one full of racism. The theme of this poem is the importance of relationships. I know this because Nikki shows appreciation for Mrs. Long for giving her books to transport herself into other worlds.

Skills Focus

QUESTION 2: Point of View

Giovanni also wants the audience to know that she had people in her life when she was a child, people like Mrs. Long, who were willing to face the hostility of whites to help her. This made her happy. Most people can relate because they have had someone to help them imagine worlds other than their own.

Skills Focus

QUESTION 4: Compare and Contrast

Nikki Giovanni understands what Mrs. Long did for her. Mrs. Long opened her life to a world outside her immediate community. Similarly, the son says in "That Day" that his father's "living gesture" stands out as something extraordinary in his memory.

Skills Focus

QUESTION 5: Connect to Essential Question

Giovanni's grandmother gave her love and security, and taught Giovanni to love the world she grew up in. Mrs. Long showed Giovanni a world beyond and gave her the courage to enter it.

TEXT TALK

Who runs the library, and what is the speaker's relationship with this person?

See lines 29 through 37: Mrs. Long runs the library. Mrs. Long acts as a kind of mentor to the speaker by providing her with books.

Why are the books important to the speaker?

See lines 40 and 41 and 45 through 52: The books introduce the speaker to a world beyond her own.

NOTES

29 Mrs. Long asking what are you looking for today
30 When I wanted Leaves of Grass or Alfred North Whitehead
31 She would go to the big library uptown and I now know
32 Hat in hand to ask to borrow so that I might borrow
33 Probably they said something **humiliating** since southern
34 Whites like to humiliate southern blacks

35 But she **nonetheless** brought the books
36 Back and I held them to my chest
37 Close to my heart
38 And happily skipped back to grandmother's house
39 Where I would sit on the front porch
40 In a gray **glider** and dream of a world
41 Far away

42 I love the world where I was
43 I was safe and warm and grandmother gave me neck kisses
44 When I was on my way to bed

45 But there was a world
46 Somewhere
47 Out there
48 And Mrs. Long opened that **wardrobe**
49 But no lions or witches scared me
50 I went through
51 Knowing there would be
52 Spring

"A Poem for My Librarian, Mrs. Long" from ACOLYTES by NIKKI GIOVANNI
Used by permission of HarperCollins Publishers

Reading & Writing Companion **75**

SELECTION VOCABULARY

glider / el columpio *noun* a swinging sofa suspended from a frame

- Where is the "glider"?
- What does the speaker do on the "glider"?

wardrobe / el armario *noun* a cabinet in which to store clothes

- In this poem the speaker refers to a part of a famous story called *The Lion, the Witch and the Wardrobe*. The story is fantasy. In the story, a family of children get from England to a magical land through an ordinary "wardrobe."
- What would you expect an object called a "wardrobe" to hold?

Reading Comprehension OPTIONAL

Have students complete the digital reading comprehension questions ✓ when they finish reading.

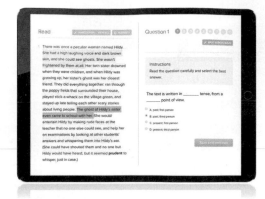

ANSWER KEY

QUESTION 1: B	**QUESTION 5:** A	**QUESTION 9:**
QUESTION 2: B	**QUESTION 6:** D	*See first chart.*
QUESTION 3: C	**QUESTION 7:** A	**QUESTION 10:**
QUESTION 4: A	**QUESTION 8:** C	*See second chart.*

Synonym	Word
compact	portable
shameful	humiliating
however	nonetheless
swing	glider
cabinet	wardrobe

Connect and Extend OPTIONAL

CONNECT TO EXTENDED WRITING PROJECT

Reading might not seem like a "revolutionary act," but it is to the speaker of Nikki Giovanni's poem. When considering to whom they will write their letters, prompt students to create a list of characteristics of people who leave an impact, such as Mrs. Long.

BEYOND THE BOOK

What It Reveals	Line
The speaker and her grandmother live in an African-American neighborhood.	"(The main black corridor) sat our carnegie library"
The speaker didn't realize as a child what Mrs. Long did for her.	"She would go to the big library uptown and I now know"
The speaker listened to jazz singers on the radio.	"I heard nat king cole and matt dennis, june christy and ella Fitzgerald."
There were some books that could only be found at a "white" library.	"When I wanted *Leaves of Grass* or Alfred North Whitehead"

Think Questions

Circulate as students answer Think Questions independently. Scaffolds for these questions are shown on the opposite page.

QUESTION 1: Textual Evidence

The setting is a segregated southern town, possibly during the 1950s. The speaker describes the library as being in "The main black corridor," and she mentions "southern / Whites" and "southern blacks."

QUESTION 2: Textual Evidence

Mrs. Long goes out of her way to provide the speaker with the books she requests. Mrs. Long also provides the speaker with an opportunity to discover the world: "there was a world / Somewhere / Out there."

QUESTION 3: Textual Evidence

Line 13 is mostly a list of singers' names: "nat king cole and matt dennis, june christy and ella." Perhaps the speaker is so excited about naming these artists that she runs out of breath before she can say, "Fitzgerald," forcing this name to line 14. The speaker is a "little girl," and kids often talk fast when they get excited. It's as if Giovanni's line structure works to characterize her young speaker.

QUESTION 4: Context Clues

I think *portable* means a radio you can carry around. In the poem, the portable is something the speaker uses to listen to music. The speaker also says that the portable is "tucked under my pillow," so it must be small enough to put there.

QUESTION 5: Word Meaning

Definition number 1, "in spite of that," most closely matches the meaning of the word *nonetheless* in line 35. The word *But* signals surprise that Mrs. Long brought the books back to the speaker. The phrases "by any means" and "without care" don't substitute as well.

A Poem for My Librarian, Mrs. Long

First Read

Read "A Poem for My Librarian, Mrs. Long." After you read, complete the Think Questions below.

☁ **THINK QUESTIONS**

1. Describe the setting of the poem. Cite textual evidence from the selection to support your answer.

2. Why is Mrs. Long important to the speaker of the poem? Cite textual evidence from the selection to support your answer.

3. Poetic structure describes the organization of words and lines in a poem. Examine Giovanni's line breaks. One line often runs into the next. What ideas about the speaker do you get from the way lines 13 and 14 run together? Cite textual evidence from the selection to support your answer.

4. Use context clues to determine the meaning of **portable** as it is used in line 11 of "A Poem for My Librarian, Mrs. Long."

5. Read the following dictionary entry:

   nonetheless
   none•the•less \ˌnən-thə-ˈles\ adverb

   1. in spite of that
   2. by any means
   3. without care

   Which definition most closely matches the meaning of **nonetheless** as it is used in line 35? Write the correct definition of *nonetheless* here and explain how you figured out the correct meaning.

Think Questions

■ SCAFFOLDS

Use the scaffolds below to differentiate instruction for your **ELL** English Language Learners and **A** Approaching grade-level learners.

ELL **BEGINNING** Write a response using the <u>word bank</u> and <u>sentence frames</u>.

INTERMEDIATE Write a response using the <u>sentence frames</u>.

ADVANCED, ADVANCED HIGH Write a response using the <u>Text-Dependent Question Guide</u>.

A **APPROACHING** Write a response using the <u>Text-Dependent Question Guide</u>.

BEGINNING	INTERMEDIATE	APPROACHING / ADVANCED, ADVANCED HIGH
Word Bank	**Sentence Frames**	**Text-Dependent Question Guide**
appreciates black borrows breath excited one listens segregated singers trait circumstances radio	The setting is a ____ southern town, possibly during the 1950s. The speaker describes the library in the ____ part of town. The speaker mentions "southern" whites and blacks. The speaker mentions ____ who were popular in the 1950s.	1. • Is the poem set in a city or in the country? • In what part of the United States is the poem set? In what ways is the setting divided? • What year might it be?
	Mrs. Long ____ books for the speaker even though the white librarians are probably mean to Mrs. Long. The speaker ____ Mrs. Long's effort because the books allow the speaker to see the world beyond her ____.	2. • Who is Mrs. Long? • What does Mrs. Long do for the speaker? • Does Mrs. Long have any trouble doing this task?
	Line 13 is mostly a list of popular singers' names. The speaker is so ____ that she runs out of ____ before she can say, "Fitzgerald." Giovanni's line structure works to show a ____ of her young speaker.	3. • Why might Ella Fitzgerald's name stretch across two different lines? • Is line 13 easy or hard to read aloud? • Do you run out of breath before you reach the end of line 13?
	The speaker ____ to music. This gives me a clue that *portable* means a small ____ you can carry with you.	4. • Read: "but when I listened/ Late at night with my portable (that I was so proud of)/ Tucked under my pillow" • What is the speaker doing? • What is the speaker using the portable for?
	Nonetheless as used in the text matches definition ____.	5. • Read: "But she nonetheless brought the books / Back" • Does she bring the books carelessly? (#3) • Does she bring the books by different methods? (#2) • Does she bring the books despite humiliation? (#1)

Skill: Compare and Contrast

Introduce the Skill

Watch the Concept Definition video and read the following definitions with your students.

To **compare** two or more texts means to explain how they are similar. To **contrast** texts means to explain how they are different. A reader may compare and contrast texts within and across genres. **Genre** refers to a specific category of literary text, such as science fiction, satire, historical drama, epic poetry, and the essay. Genre may also refer to a specific category of creative expression in other **media,** such as film, fine art, and music—examples include the Western, Impressionism, and jazz.

Readers may write or deliver **comparative responses** in which they use evidence to analyze the similarities and differences between two or more texts or other media. **Textual evidence** refers to details from the texts that support ideas and opinions about similarities and differences between them. Evidence may be quoted directly by including the author's exact words and placing them within quotation marks. Readers may also **paraphrase,** or restate the evidence in their own words.

TURN AND TALK

1. What do you compare and contrast when you make choices? How do these comparisons help you make a choice?

ELL **SPEAKING FRAMES**
- I compare ____. This helps me ____.
- My favorite ____. One way they are similar is ____.
- One way they are different is ____.

COMPARE AND CONTRAST

Skill: Compare and Contrast

Use the Checklist to analyze Compare and Contrast in "A Poem for My Librarian, Mrs. Long." Refer to the sample student annotations about Compare and Contrast in the text.

••• CHECKLIST FOR COMPARE AND CONTRAST

In order to determine how to compare and contrast texts in different forms or genres, use the following steps:

✓ first, choose texts with similar subjects or topics

✓ next, identify the qualities or speakers of each genre

✓ after, identify the theme in each work

✓ finally, analyze ways in which the texts are similar and different in the way they approach similar themes and topics

- think about what the speakers do and say
- think about what happens as a result of the speakers' words and actions

To compare and contrast texts in different forms or genres in terms of their approaches to similar themes and topics, consider the following questions:

✓ How does each text approach the theme and topic? How does the form or genre of the text affect this approach?

✓ What are the similarities and differences in the subjects or topics of the texts I have chosen?

Reading & Writing Companion **77**

V **SKILL VOCABULARY**

compare / comparar *verb* to explain how two or more things are similar COGNATE

contrast / contrastar *verb* to explain how two or more things are different COGNATE

genre / el género *noun* the different categories or types of literature, in which the main categories are fiction, nonfiction, poetry, and drama

media / los medios *noun* the plural form of the word medium; a means of sending a communication to an intended audience

Skill:
Compare and Contrast

Reread paragraphs 28–30 of *The Circuit*, lines 45–52 of "A Poem for My Librarian, Mrs. Long" and lines 9–18 of "That Day." Then, using the Checklist on the previous page, complete the chart below to compare and contrast the passages.

YOUR TURN

	Observation Options
A	A librarian's special interest in a girl who loves to read prepares the girl to enter the wider world unafraid.
B	Through the help of an understanding adult all the characters find ways to bridge their world with the wider world.
C	A teacher becomes a friend and helps the main character work on his English.
D	A father's willingness to seem foolish shows his son the strength needed to live in a new and strange home.

The Circuit	A Poem for My Librarian, Mrs. Long	That Day	All

SKILL VOCABULARY

comparative response / la respuesta comparativa *noun* an oral or written response in which a reader explains the similarities and differences between two or more things

textual evidence / la evidencia del texto *noun* details from the text that a reader can use to support his or her ideas and opinions about the text

quote / citar *verb* to use an author's exact words and place them within quotation marks

paraphrase / parafrasear *verb* to restate the author's words in your own words **COGNATE**

Your Turn

Ask students to complete the Your Turn Activity.

QUESTION 1

The Circuit	"A Poem for My Librarian, Mrs. Long"	"That Day"	All
A teacher becomes a friend and helps the main character work on his English.	A librarian's special interest in a girl who loves to read prepares the girl to enter the wider world unafraid.	A father's willingness to seem foolish shows his son the strength needed to live in a new and strange home.	All the narrators find ways through the help of an understanding adult to bridge their world with the wider world.

Close Read

Skills Focus

QUESTION 1: Theme

See lines 30–42.

QUESTION 2: Point of View

See lines 35–41.

QUESTION 3: Compare and Contrast

See lines 29–34: Mrs. Long goes out of her way to help the young Nikki Giovanni get the books she wants. Unlike Mr. Lema, Mrs. Long has to face humiliation to help Nikki.However, both adults want to help. Both authors believe that caring adults can have an amazing impact on young people.

QUESTION 4: Compare and Contrast

See lines 45–52.

QUESTION 5: Connect to Essential Question

See lines 42–52.

✓ CHECK FOR SUCCESS

If students struggle to respond to Skills Focus Prompt #1, ask students the following questions:

- What does the author describe in lines 19–21?
- What does the author tell you about her adult life in lines 22–23?
- What does this information reveal about the theme of the poem?

Close Read

Reread "A Poem for My Librarian, Mrs. Long." As you reread, complete the Skills Focus questions below. Then use your answers and annotations from the questions to help you complete the Write activity.

◎ SKILLS FOCUS

1. Identify the theme of "A Poem for My Librarian, Mrs. Long." Use textual evidence to explain the theme.

2. Nikki Giovanni writes from her own point of view as a child. How does this help the reader relate to her? Use textual evidence from the poem to support your answer.

3. In *The Circuit*, Mr. Lema gives up his lunch hour to help Francisco improve his reading. Identify evidence in "A Poem for My Librarian, Mrs. Long" where Mrs. Long steps in to help the young Nikki Giovanni. Use textual evidence to compare and contrast what the two authors want their audience to understand when they read about these actions.

4. The boy in "That Day" is deeply touched when his father joins his softball game. Identify evidence in "A Poem for My Librarian, Mrs Long" that reveals how Nikki Giovanni also appreciated Mrs. Long's efforts. Use textual evidence to compare and contrast the responses of the two young people.

5. The impact of relationships on people's lives is one of the messages in *The Circuit*. Grateful for Mr. Lema's guidance, Francisco considers him his best friend at school. Identify textual evidence in "A Poem for My Librarian, Mrs. Long" that shows Nikki Giovanni is delivering a similar message about the importance of relationships. Use textual evidence to explain how relationships have impacted Giovanni's life.

✎ WRITE

COMPARATIVE: What theme do *The Circuit*, "That Day," and "A Poem for My Librarian, Mrs. Long" have in common? Write a response in which you compare and contrast each text's theme. Remember to support your ideas with evidence from all three texts, and use newly-acquired vocabulary as appropriate.

Reading & Writing Companion   **79**

💬 Writer's Notebook

Connect to Essential Question: Give students time to reflect on how "A Poem for My Librarian, Mrs. Long," *The Circuit*, and "That Day" connect to the unit's essential question "How do relationships shape us?" by freewriting in their Writer's Notebooks.

ELL Beginning & Intermediate

Read aloud the unit's essential question: "How do relationships shape us?" Encourage students to draw their connections or allow students to write in their native language. Circulate around the room, prompting students for their thoughts as they respond orally or through pantomime.

Advanced & Advanced High

Allow students to share their connections orally in pairs or small groups before freewriting.

Collaborative Conversation

SCAFFOLDS

Break students into collaborative conversation groups to discuss the Close Read prompt. Remind them to reference their Skills Focus annotations in their discussion.

What theme do *The Circuit*, "That Day," and "A Poem for My Librarian, Mrs. Long" have in common? Write a response in which you compare and contrast each text's theme. Remember to support your ideas with evidence from all three texts, and use newly acquired vocabulary as appropriate.

Use the scaffolds below to differentiate instruction for your (ELL) English Language Learners and (A) Approaching grade-level learners.

(ELL) **BEGINNING, INTERMEDIATE** Use the <u>discussion guide</u> and <u>speaking frames</u> to facilitate the discussion with support from the teacher.

ADVANCED, ADVANCED HIGH Use the <u>discussion guide</u> and <u>speaking frames</u> to facilitate the discussion in mixed-level groups.

(A) **APPROACHING** Use the <u>discussion guide</u> to facilitate the discussion in mixed-level groups.

APPROACHING

ADVANCED, ADVANCED HIGH

BEGINNING, INTERMEDIATE

Discussion Guide	Speaking Frames
1. What is the theme of *The Circuit*? How do you know?	• The theme is ____. • I know this because ____.
2. What is the theme of "That Day"? How do you know?	• The theme is ____. • I know this because ____.
3. What is the theme of "A Poem for My Librarian, Mrs. Long"? How do you know?	• The theme is ____. • I know this because ____.

Review Prompt and Rubric

Before students begin writing, review the writing prompt and rubric with the class.

COMPARATIVE: What theme do *The Circuit,* "That Day," and "A Poem for My Librarian, Mrs. Long" have in common? Write a response in which you compare and contrast each text's theme. Remember to support your ideas with evidence from all three texts, and use newly-acquired vocabulary as appropriate.

 PROMPT GUIDE

- What is each text's theme?
- How is each theme similar?

- How is each theme different?

Score	Theme	Compare and Contrast	Language and Conventions
4	The writer clearly analyzes and explains what theme *The Circuit*, "That Day," and "A Poem for My Librarian, Mrs. Long" have in common. The writer provides exemplary analysis, using relevant evidence from the texts.	The writer clearly compares and contrasts the texts. The writer provides exemplary analysis, using relevant evidence from the texts.	The writer demonstrates a consistent command of grammar, punctuation, and usage conventions. Although minor errors may be evident, they do not detract from the fluency or the clarity of the essay.
3	The writer analyzes and explains what theme *The Circuit*, "That Day," and "A Poem for My Librarian, Mrs. Long" have in common. The writer provides sufficient analysis, using relevant evidence from the texts most of the time.	The writer compares and contrasts the texts. The writer provides sufficient analysis, using relevant evidence from the texts most of the time.	The writer demonstrates an adequate command of grammar, punctuation, and usage conventions. Although some errors may be evident, they create few (if any) disruptions in the fluency of the writing or the clarity of the essay.
2	The writer begins to analyze or explain what theme *The Circuit*, "That Day," and "A Poem for My Librarian, Mrs. Long" have in common, but the analysis is incomplete. The writer uses relevant evidence from the texts only some of the time.	The writer begins to compare and contrast the texts, but the comparison is incomplete. The writer uses relevant evidence from the texts only some of the time.	The writer demonstrates a partial command of grammar, punctuation, and usage conventions. Some distracting errors may be evident, at times creating minor disruptions in the fluency or clarity of the writing.
1	The writer attempts to analyze or explain what theme *The Circuit*, "That Day," and "A Poem for My Librarian, Mrs. Long" have in common, but the analysis is not successful. The writer uses little or no relevant evidence from the texts.	The writer attempts to compare and contrast the texts, but the comparison is not successful. The writer uses little or no relevant evidence from the texts.	The writer demonstrates little or no command of grammar, punctuation, and usage conventions. Serious and persistent errors create disruptions in the fluency of the writing and sometimes interfere with meaning.
0	The writer does not provide a relevant response to the prompt or does not provide a response at all.	The writer does not provide a relevant response to the prompt or does not provide a response at all.	Serious and persistent errors overwhelm the writing and interfere with the meaning of the response as a whole, making the writer's meaning impossible to understand.

Write

Ask students to complete the writing assignment using textual evidence to support their answers.

Use the scaffolds below to differentiate instruction for your **ELL** English Language Learners and **A** Approaching grade-level learners.

ELL **BEGINNING** With the help of the word bank, write a response using paragraph frame 1.

INTERMEDIATE With the help of the word bank, write a response using paragraph frames 1 and 2.

ADVANCED, ADVANCED HIGH Write a response of differentiated length using the sentence starters.

A **APPROACHING** Write a response of differentiated length using the sentence starters.

BEGINNING INTERMEDIATE			ADVANCED, ADVANCED HIGH APPROACHING
Word Bank	**Paragraph Frame 1**	**Paragraph Frame 2**	**Sentence Starters**
reading books softball relationships childhood	All three authors write to share memories of their ____. All three texts share a similar theme: that ____ have a positive impact on people. Mr. Lema helps Francisco improve his ____. The father connects with his son through ____. Mrs. Long introduces Nikki Giovanni to the larger world through ____.	Each message is slightly different because each adult ____. Mr Lema offers Francisco ____. The father offers his son a ____. Mrs. Long is willing to face ____ to provide Nikki Giovanni with the ____.	• All three authors write to . . . • The texts share a similar theme that . . . • Mr. Lema helps Francisco . . . • The father connects with his son by . . . • Mrs. Long introduces Nikki Giovanni to . . . • Each theme is slightly different because . . . • Mr Lema offers Francisco . . . • The father offers his son . . . • Mrs. Long is willing to face ____ to provide Nikki Giovanni with . . .

Peer Review

Students should submit substantive feedback to two peers using the review instructions below.

- How well does this response answer the prompt?
- How well does the writer support his or her ideas with details and examples from the text?
- Which sentence in the writer's response made you think differently about the text?
- What did the writer do well in this response? What does the writer need to work on?

Rate

Respond to the following with a point rating that reflects your opinion.

	1 2 3 4
Ideas	■ ■ ■ □
Evidence	■ ■ ■ ■
Language and Conventions	■ ■ □ □

Submit

ELL **A** **SENTENCE FRAMES**

- You were able to (completely / partly / almost) . . . answer the prompt because . . .
- You could answer the prompt more completely by . . .
- You supported the idea of . . . with the detail of ____.

- One idea that needs more support is . . .
- I thought differently about the texts after reading . . .
- My favorite part of your response is . . .

You and Me

Blast: Author! Author! Read All About It!

How can researching information about an author help you self-select a text?

TEXT TALK

What is one strategy you can use for self-selecting a new text? How does it work?

I can research information about an author before reading their work. While I am finding information, I can use the suggested questions as a guide.

What should you do once you choose a text that interests you?

Start reading the text to confirm my interest. If I like it, I should keep reading.

Create Your Own Blast

SCAFFOLDS

Ask students to write a 140-character Blast after they complete the QuikPoll.

Use the scaffolds below to differentiate instruction for your English Language Learners.

ELL **BEGINNING** Write a response using the <u>word bank</u> to complete the <u>sentence frames</u>.

INTERMEDIATE Write a response using the <u>sentence frames</u>.

ADVANCED, ADVANCED HIGH Write a response using the <u>sentence starters</u>.

BEGINNING	INTERMEDIATE	ADVANCED, ADVANCED HIGH
Word Bank	Sentence Frames	Sentence Starters
relatable interesting reading connection author	I can research ____ information about an ____ before ____ their work. This can help me find a ____ with the ____.	• I can research information about an author . . . • This information can help me . . .

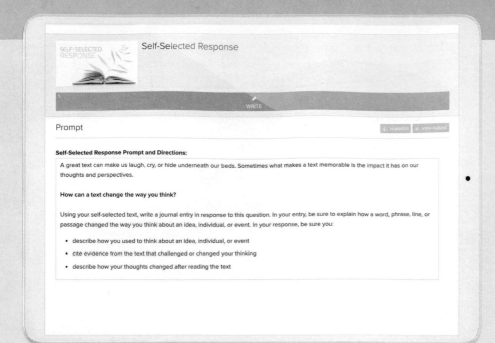

Self-Selected Response

Prompt

Self-Selected Response Prompt and Directions:

A great text can make us laugh, cry, or hide underneath our beds. Sometimes what makes a text memorable is the impact it has on our thoughts and perspectives.

How can a text change the way you think?

Using your self-selected text, write a journal entry in response to this question. In your entry, be sure to explain how a word, phrase, line, or passage changed the way you think about an idea, individual, or event. In your response, be sure you:

- describe how you used to think about an idea, individual, or event
- cite evidence from the text that challenged or changed your thinking
- describe how your thoughts changed after reading the text

Self-Selected Response

Introduce the Prompt

Read aloud the prompt. Ask students to discuss:

- What is the prompt asking you to do?
- Why might it be useful to reflect on how a text can change the way you think?

Write

SCAFFOLDS

Ask students to complete the writing assignment using text evidence to support their answers.

Use the scaffolds below to differentiate instruction for your **ELL** English Language Learners and **A** Approaching grade level learners.

ELL **BEGINNING** With the help of the word bank, write a response using paragraph frame 1.

INTERMEDIATE With the help of the word bank, write a response using paragraph frame 2.

ADVANCED, ADVANCED HIGH Write a response of differentiated length using the sentence starters.

A **APPROACHING** Write a response of differentiated length using the sentence starters.

BEGINNING / INTERMEDIATE		INTERMEDIATE	ADVANCED, ADVANCED HIGH / APPROACHING
Word Bank	**Paragraph Frame 1**	**Paragraph Frame 2**	**Sentence Starters**
love family war friendship sports difficult easy hardest enjoyable challenging	I read the text (title) ____ by (author) ____. I used to think ____. I thought this because ____. Now, I think ____. I think this because the text says, "____."	I read the text (title) ____ by (author) ____. I used to think ____. I thought this because ____. Now, I think ____. I think this because the text says, "____." This made me think ____. Therefore, ____ changed the way I think about ____.	• I read the text . . . by . . . • I used to think . . . • I thought this because . . . • Now I think . . . • I think this because in the text it says, . . . • This changed my thinking because . . .

Extended Writing Project

EXTENDED WRITING PROJECT
ARGUMENTATIVE WRITING

The Extended Writing Project (EWP) in Grade 6, Unit 2 focuses on argumentative writing. Students consider the following question—Can relationships shape your future?—as they write an argumentative essay about a person who has influenced their life. The unit's selections about relationships provide examples of young lives that are strongly influenced by another person, and several pieces serve as mentor texts for students to emulate when organizing their argumentative essays. Specific skill lessons teach developing ideas, organization, and conventions, while other skill lessons focus on introductions, evidence, and transitions and help students write a focused essay. Directed revision leads students through the process of revising for clarity, development, organization, word choice, and sentence variety. Throughout the EWP, students have the opportunity to practice using created student writing, authentic texts, and their own work.

 Audio and audio text highlighting are available in select lessons in the Extended Writing Project.

How do relationships shape us?

In this unit students explored the ways in which characters and people develop life-changing relationships. Students will write an argumentative essay explaining how a relationship has changed his or her own life, using proper techniques for formal writing.

Extended Writing Project Prompt

Can relationships shape your future?

Think about the ways in which relationships have shaped the lives of the characters, speakers, or authors. Then reflect on your own life. Think of a person who has influenced you in some way. Would your life be different if this person were not in your life? Do you think relationships can truly shape people's futures? Why or why not?

 **SCAFFOLDS**  **ENGLISH LANGUAGE LEARNERS**  **APPROACHING GRADE LEVEL**  **BEYOND GRADE LEVEL**

These icons identify differentiation strategies and scaffolded support for a variety of students. See the digital lesson plan for additional differentiation strategies and scaffolds.

Instructional Path

Argumentative Writing Process: Plan

Objectives: After learning about genre characteristics and craft, students will analyze a sample Student Model and plan a meaningful argumentative response to a prompt.

Skill: Organizing Argumentative Writing

Objectives: After reading and discussing a model of student writing, students will develop their drafts by organizing their argument effectively.

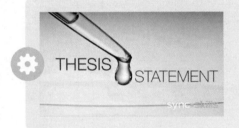

Skill: Thesis Statement

Objectives: After reading and discussing a model of student writing, students will develop their thesis statements for their arguments.

Skill: Reasons and Relevant Evidence

Objectives: After reading and discussing a model of student writing, students will improve their arguments by adding reasons and relevant evidence.

Argumentative Writing Process: Draft

Objectives: After reading a Student Model draft and reviewing a writing checklist, students will draft a meaningful argument in response to a prompt.

The print teacher's edition includes essential point-of-use instruction and planning tools. Complete lesson plans and program documents appear in your digital teacher account.

Skill: Introductions

Objectives: After reading and discussing a model of student writing, students will develop their drafts by improving their introductions.

Skill: Transitions

Objectives: After reading and discussing a model of student writing, students will develop their drafts by using transitions to connect ideas within and between paragraphs.

Skill: Style

Objectives: After reading and discussing a model of student writing, students will develop their drafts by establishing and maintaining a formal style.

Skill: Conclusions

Objectives: After reading and discussing a model of student writing, students will develop their drafts by improving their conclusions.

Argumentative Writing Process: Revise

Objectives: Students will use a revision guide to revise the draft of their argument for clarity, development, organization, style, diction, and sentence effectiveness.

Grammar: Basic Spelling Rules I

Objectives: After learning basic spelling rules and seeing how they are used in text examples, students will spell correctly.

Grammar: Possessive Pronouns

Objectives: After learning about possessive pronouns and seeing how they are used in text examples, students will practice using possessive pronouns correctly.

Grammar: Formal and Informal Language

Objectives: After learning about formal and informal language and seeing how they are used in text examples, students will practice using formal and informal language correctly.

Argumentative Writing Process: Edit and Publish

Objectives: After seeing an example of editing in the Student Model and reviewing an editing checklist, students will edit and publish the final draft of their argument.

Progress Monitoring

Opportunities to Learn	Opportunities to Demonstrate Learning	Opportunities to Reteach

Argumentative Writing Process: Plan

Argumentative Writing Process: Plan	Argumentative Writing Process: Plan • Write	Units 3–6 Process: Plan

Argumentative Writing Process: Draft

Argumentative Writing Process: Draft	Argumentative Writing Process: Draft • Write	Units 3–6 Process: Draft

Argumentative Writing Process: Revise

Argumentative Writing Process: Revise	Argumentative Writing Process: Revise • Write	Units 3–6 Process: Revise

Argumentative Writing Process: Edit and Publish

Argumentative Writing Process: Edit and Publish	Argumentative Writing Process: Edit and Publish • Write	Units 3–4, 6 Process: Edit and Publish Unit 5 Process: Edit and Present

	Opportunities to Learn	Opportunities to Demonstrate Learning	Opportunities to Reteach

Organizing Argumentative Writing

| ⚙ Skill: Organizing Argumentative Writing | ⚙ Skill: Organizing Argumentative Writing
• Your Turn

✏ Argumentative Writing Process: Draft | ⚙ Unit 4
Skill: Organizing Argumentative Writing

⚙ Spotlight Skill: Organizing Argumentative Writing |

Thesis Statement

| ⚙ Skill: Thesis Statement | ⚙ Skill: Thesis Statement
• Your Turn

✏ Argumentative Writing Process: Draft | ⚙ Units 3, 6
Skill: Thesis Statement

⚙ Spotlight Skill: Thesis Statement |

Reasons and Relevant Evidence

| ⚙ Skill: Reasons and Relevant Evidence | ⚙ Skill: Reasons and Relevant Evidence
• Your Turn

✏ Argumentative Writing Process: Draft | ⚙ Units 4, 5
Skill: Reasons and Relevant Evidence

⚙ Spotlight Skill: Reasons and Relevant Evidence |

Introductions

| ⚙ Skill: Introductions | ⚙ Skill: Introductions
• Your Turn

✏ Argumentative Writing Process: Revise | ⚙ Units 3, 4
Skill: Introductions

⚙ Spotlight Skill: Introductions |

Transitions

| ⚙ Skill: Transitions | ⚙ Skill: Transitions
• Your Turn

✏ Argumentative Writing Process: Revise | ⚙ Units 3, 4
Skill: Transitions

⚙ Spotlight Skill: Transitions |

Opportunities to Learn	Opportunities to Demonstrate Learning	Opportunities to Reteach

Style

⚙ Skill: Style	⚙ Skill: Style • Your Turn ✏ Argumentative Writing Process: Revise	⚙ Units 3, 4 Skill: Style ⚙ Spotlight Skill: Style

Conclusions

⚙ Skill: Conclusions	⚙ Skill: Conclusions • Your Turn ✏ Argumentative Writing Process: Revise	⚙ Units 3, 4 Skill: Conclusions ⚙ Spotlight Skill: Conclusions

Basic Spelling Rules I

⚙ Grammar: Basic Spelling Rules I	⚙ Grammar: Basic Spelling Rules I • Your Turn ✏ Argumentative Writing Process: Edit and Publish	⚙ Grammar: Spelling — Homographs ⚙ Grammar: Spelling — Commonly Misspelled Words

Possessive Pronouns

⚙ Grammar: Possessive Pronouns	⚙ Grammar: Possessive Pronouns • Your Turn ✏ Argumentative Writing Process: Edit and Publish	⚙ Grammar: Pronouns — Relative ⚙ Grammar: Nouns — Possessive

Formal and Informal Language

⚙ Grammar: Formal and Informal Language	⚙ Grammar: Formal and Informal Language • Your Turn ✏ Argumentative Writing Process: Edit and Publish	⚙ Grammar: Modifiers — *Good* or *Well*; *Bad* or *Badly*

Argumentative Writing Process: Plan

Introduce the Extended Writing Project

- What is the prompt asking you to do?

- Which characteristics of argumentative writing will you need to learn more about in order to respond to the prompt?

- What are the five characteristics of argumentative writing?

- What elements of craft do argumentative writers use?

 DIFFERENTIATED QUESTIONS

- Who has influenced you?

- Would your life be different without this person? Why or why not?

- Can relationships really shape people's futures? Why or why not?

Argumentative Writing Process: Plan

| PLAN | DRAFT | REVISE | EDIT AND PUBLISH |

In this unit, you have read and learned about how relationships can shape people's lives. Sometimes, the way a relationship influences our lives goes unnoticed, like Phoebe's dismissive, uncaring behavior toward her mother in *Walk Two Moons*. In other cases, a relationship may leave an impression that lasts from childhood to adulthood, as in Nikki Giovanni's "A Poem for My Librarian, Mrs. Long."

WRITING PROMPT

Can relationships shape your future?

Think about the ways in which relationships have shaped the lives of the characters, speakers, or authors. Then reflect on your own life. Think of a person who has influenced you in some way. Would your life be different if this person were not in your life? Do you think relationships can truly shape people's futures? Why or why not? Support your argument with the following:

- an introduction
- a thesis statement
- coherent body paragraphs
- reasons and relevant evidence
- a conclusion

Writing to Sources

As you gather ideas and information from the texts in the unit, be sure to:

- include a claim;
- address counterclaims;
- use evidence from multiple sources; and
- avoid overly relying on one source.

Copyright © BookheadEd Learning, LLC

Reading & Writing Companion

Extended Writing Project

Introduction to Argumentative Writing

Argumentative writing is meant to convince readers of the writer's position or point of view on a subject. To best support an opinion in argumentative writing, the writer introduces claims, which are statements that explain why he or she agrees or disagrees with the prompt. In order to make a convincing argument, writers may address opposing points of view, or counterclaims, and explain why these are not true in their opinion. Argumentative writing also relies on reasons and relevant evidence to support the writer's point of view. Without specific examples or logical reasoning, an argument wouldn't be very strong.

A successful argument should have the following characteristics:

- an introduction
- a clear thesis statement summarizing the argument's main idea or central claim
- body paragraphs containing specific claims
- reasons and relevant evidence to support the claims
- a conclusion

As you continue with this Extended Writing Project, you'll receive more instruction and practice at crafting each of the characteristics of argumentative writing in order to develop your opinion about whether or not relationships can truly impact people's futures.

Copyright © BookheadEd Learning, LLC

Review the Rubric

Have students examine the Argumentative Writing Rubric—Grade 6 grading rubric this Student Model was written to satisfy. Inform students that this is the same rubric that will be used to evaluate their completed Argumentative Extended Writing Project.

Read and Annotate

As students read, have them use the Annotation Tool to identify and label the aspects of argumentative writing:

- an introduction

- a clear thesis statement summarizing the argument's main idea or central claim

- body paragraphs containing specific claims

- reasons and relevant evidence to support the claims

- a conclusion

When students finish reading, ask them to share their annotations in small groups.

ELL   **ANNOTATION GUIDE**

Find the following quotes in the Student Model. Then, use the Annotation Tool to label each quote as part of the the introduction, the thesis statement, part of the conclusion, or a reason that supports the argument.

- When I read this poem, I thought of Mr. Lin, who did the same thing for me at theater camp last year.
- One way that a relationship shapes your future is by helping you become a better version of yourself.
- I'll never forget the lessons I learned from my favorite teacher, Mr. Lin.
- I believe that relationships can truly shape your future because if Mr. Lin were not in my life, I would be a completely different person than I am today.

A   **READ AND ANNOTATE**

Pair students with on-grade-level peers to complete the annotation activity.

Before you get started on your own argument, read the essay that one student, Ellie, wrote in response to the writing prompt. As you read the Model, highlight and annotate the features of argumentative writing that Ellie included in her argument.

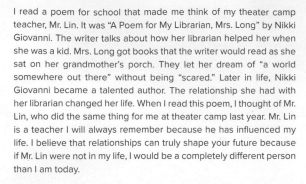

☰ STUDENT MODEL   NOTES

1   I read a poem for school that made me think of my theater camp teacher, Mr. Lin. It was "A Poem for My Librarian, Mrs. Long" by Nikki Giovanni. The writer talks about how her librarian helped her when she was a kid. Mrs. Long got books that the writer would read as she sat on her grandmother's porch. They let her dream of "a world somewhere out there" without being "scared." Later in life, Nikki Giovanni became a talented author. The relationship she had with her librarian changed her life. When I read this poem, I thought of Mr. Lin, who did the same thing for me at theater camp last year. Mr. Lin is a teacher I will always remember because he has influenced my life. I believe that relationships can truly shape your future because if Mr. Lin were not in my life, I would be a completely different person than I am today.

2   One way that a relationship shapes your future is by helping you become a better version of yourself. The most important thing Mr. Lin did was help me to be a braver person. Before I went to theater camp, I was shy. I wanted to work behind the scenes painting sets and sewing costumes. However, Mr. Lin wanted everybody to feel what it's like to be onstage. I was nervous. My hands got sweaty and my voice shook when it was time to say my lines. Then, Mr. Lin gave me some advice. First, he said that all people get nervous when they go onstage, but good actors don't let it show. Next, Mr. Lin said, "Say your lines loud and say them proud!" What a difference his words made! During the play, I was finally able to hide my fear and say my lines. When people clapped at the end, it was amazing. Mr. Lin helped me become a confident person.

3   Some people think that you make your own future, so the relationships you have with people don't make much of a difference. I disagree. Relationships help you work hard to achieve your goals. Without Mr. Lin's advice, I still would have been afraid to try my hardest. Even though Mr. Lin was my theater teacher, he helped me to become a better student in my other classes. One time I had to give a talk in

Reading & Writing   83
Companion

💬 **TEXT TALK**

Purpose

Where does Ellie state the purpose of her argument?

See paragraph 1: Ellie states that her theater teacher, Mr. Lin, changed her life, and therefore she believes that relationships can truly shape your future. This is her thesis statement.

Focus

How does Ellie remain focused on the prompt?

See paragraphs 2–4: After stating that Mr. Lin was the person who impacted her life, Ellie focuses each main paragraph around claims that support her argument about relationships affecting people's futures, using examples of things she was able to accomplish because of Mr. Lin.

Extended Writing Project

science class about how volcanoes erupt. I did my research, but I felt nervous. I wanted a good grade. I did not want to get laughed at. In front of the class, I made my fears go away by remembering what Mr. Lin taught me. I pretended I was acting the part of a volcano expert in a play. I got an A. Thanks to Mr. Lin, I'm a great student in all of my classes. He helped me believe in myself.

4 Lastly, people can influence your future by helping you realize what you're meant to be. Although some may argue that people's influence on our lives often goes unnoticed, I don't think that's true. Because of Mr. Lin's influence in my life, I decided what I want to be when I grow up. I realized I wanted to be an actor when I had to give a speech at a dinner for our team's soccer coach. I wanted to say something from my heart, but it was pounding in my chest. I remembered what Mr. Lin taught me about speaking, so I took a deep breath and just started talking about how great Coach Healy was and how much we'd miss her. Everybody was impressed with my speaking skills and told me I would be a great actor one day. Because of my relationship with Mr. Lin, I know I *will* be a great actor one day.

5 Mr. Lin could have had a big acting career instead of being a theater camp teacher. However, I am really glad he was my teacher. Just like Mrs. Long changed Nikki Giovanni's life, I think Mr. Lin was part of my life for a reason. My life would have been very different without him. He showed me how to face my fears and act like my words matter. He taught me how to be a good actor and a brave person. He changed how I felt about myself and the goals I have for my future. Therefore, it's true that relationships with people can really shape your future. I'll never forget the lessons I learned from my favorite teacher, Mr. Lin.

Reading & Writing Companion

TEXT TALK

Organization

How does Ellie organize her argument to convince the reader to agree with her?

See paragraphs 2–4: Each body paragraph focuses on a different claim that supports the argument that relationships can truly shape one's future. Ellie writes that relationships make you a better version of yourself, work hard, and realize what you're meant to be.

Evidence

How does Ellie use reasons and relevant evidence to support her argument?

Answers will vary. Sample answer: In paragraph 3, Ellie uses the specific example, or evidence, of Mr. Lin's advice helping her get an A in science class, therefore defending her claim that relationships encourage you to work hard to achieve your goals.

Elaboration

How does Ellie elaborate on her examples to convince the reader to agree with her argument?

Answers will vary. Sample answer: In paragraph 4, Ellie elaborates on how she gave a speech and decided to become an actor one day. She writes, "Because of my relationship with Mr. Lin, I know I *will* be a great actor one day" to emphasize how much her relationship with Mr. Lin affected her future.

Word Choice

Where do you find Ellie's word choice especially strong or expressive?

Answers will vary. Sample answer: In the last paragraph, Ellie sums up why Mr. Lin was so important to her, writing that she'll "never forget" the lessons she learned from him.

Sentence Fluency

Choose one sentence that you think is really effective. Why do you think it's so strong?

Answers will vary. Sample answer: In paragraph 4, Ellie writes, "I wanted to say something from my heart, but it was pounding in my chest." The descriptive details help the reader understand how scared Ellie was.

Conventions

Does Ellie use the correct possessive pronouns? If not, where does she need to correct her pronouns?

Answers will vary. Sample answer: Yes, she does use the correct possessive pronouns.

Write

Circulate as students use the questions in the bulleted list to plan their writing. See the instructions for scaffolding and differentiation that follow.

CHECK FOR SUCCESS

If students struggle to come up with answers for the questions in the lesson, work with students to provide an answer to one question and then help them build from there.

For example, start by asking students "Who will you write about?" or "When did you receive a piece of especially helpful advice?" Once students have answered one question, help them to work through a second question until they've begun to build some momentum. It may be helpful to start with a different question than the one that's listed first in the lesson.

WRITE

Writers often take notes about their ideas before they sit down to write. Think about what you've learned so far about argumentative writing to help you begin prewriting.

- Who has influenced you? In what way?

- Would your life be different without this person? Why or why not?

- Drawing from your own experiences and relationships, do you believe that relationships can truly shape people's futures? Why or why not?

Response Instructions

Use the questions in the bulleted list to write a one-paragraph summary. Your summary should include a personal example of a relationship that has influenced you, if your life would be different without this person, as well as your opinion about whether or not relationships can truly shape someone's future.

Don't worry about including all of the details now; focus only on the most essential and important elements. You will refer to this short summary as you continue through the steps of the writing process.

Reading & Writing Companion

Review Prompt and Rubric

Before students begin writing, review the writing prompt and rubric with the class.

Response Instructions

Use the questions in the bulleted list on the previous page to write a one-paragraph summary. Your summary should include a personal example of a relationship that has influenced you, if your life would be different without this person, as well as your opinion about whether or not relationships can truly shape someone's future.

Don't worry about including all of the details now; focus only on the most essential and important elements. You will refer back to this short summary as you continue through the steps of the writing process.

Score	Plan	Language and Conventions
4	The writer responds to the questions, and the writing is clear and focused.	The writer demonstrates a consistent command of grammar, punctuation, and usage conventions. Although minor errors may be evident, they do not detract from the fluency or clarity of the writing.
3	The writer responds to the questions, but the writing is not always clear or focused.	The writer demonstrates an adequate command of grammar, punctuation, and usage conventions. Although some errors may be evident, they create few (if any) disruptions in the fluency or clarity of the writing.
2	The writer responds to the questions, but the writing is somewhat unclear and unfocused.	The writer demonstrates a partial command of grammar, punctuation, and usage conventions. Some distracting errors may be evident, at times creating minor disruptions in the fluency or clarity of the writing.
1	The writer responds to the questions, but the writing is very unclear and unfocused.	The writer demonstrates little or no command of grammar, punctuation, and usage conventions. Serious and persistent errors create disruptions in the fluency of the writing and sometimes interfere with meaning.
0	The writer does not provide a relevant response to the prompt or does not provide a response at all.	Serious and persistent errors overwhelm the writing and interfere with the meaning of the response as a whole, making the writer's meaning impossible to understand.

Write

SCAFFOLDS

Use the scaffolds below to differentiate instruction for your **ELL** English Language Learners and **A** Approaching grade-level learners.

ELL **BEGINNING, INTERMEDIATE** With the help of the <u>word bank</u>, write a response using the <u>paragraph frame</u>.

ADVANCED, ADVANCED HIGH Write a response using the <u>sentence starters</u>.

A **APPROACHING** Write a response using the <u>sentence starters</u>.

BEGINNING	ADVANCED, ADVANCED HIGH
INTERMEDIATE	APPROACHING

Word Bank	Paragraph Frame	Sentence Starters
can cannot same friends different teacher shy	I will write about ____. This person has influenced me by ____. If this person weren't in my life, my life would be ____. I think this because ____. I think that relationships ____ shape your future because ____.	• I will write about . . . • This person has influenced me by . . . • If this person weren't in my life, my life would be . . . • I think this because . . . • I think that relationships . . . because . . .

Peer Review

Students should submit substantive feedback to two peers using the review instructions below.

- How well does this response answer the prompt?
- What part of their argument are you most excited to read?
- Are there any ideas that could be improved on? How so?

Rate

Respond to the following with a point rating that reflects your opinion.

	1 2 3 4
Ideas	■■■□
Evidence	■■■■
Language and Conventions	■■□□

Submit

ELL **SENTENCE FRAMES**

A
- The response does a good job of addressing ____ from the prompt.
- The response would improve by addressing ____ from the prompt.

- I am most excited to read about ____.
- I think you could improve ____ by (adding / clarifying / describing) ____.

Extended Writing Project

Skill: Organizing Argumentative Writing

As you consider how to organize your writing for your argumentative essay, use the following questions as a guide:

- What is my position on this topic?
- Have I chosen the best organizing structure to present my information?
- Can my claim be supported by logical reasoning and relevant evidence?
- Do I have enough evidence to support my claim?

Follow these steps to plan out the organization of your argumentative essay, including organizing your reasons and evidence clearly:

- Identify your claim.
  - > Write a statement that will present your claim in the first paragraph.
- Choose an organizing structure that will present your claim effectively.
- identify reasons and evidence that support your claim.

Copyright © Bookheaded Learning, LLC

  Reading & Writing Companion

 SKILL VOCABULARY

argumentative writing / la escritura argumentativa *noun* a genre of writing in which a writer presents a central claim and provides reasons and evidence to support that claim COGNATE

claim / la afirmación *noun* the writer's or speaker's position on a debatable issue or problem

---

Skill: Organizing Argumentative Writing

Introduce the Skill

Watch the Concept Definition video ▶ and read the following definition with your students.

Argumentative writing intends to convince readers of an author's position or point of view on a subject. To build an argument, authors introduce **claims**, which are arguments they will support with logical and valid reasoning and relevant evidence from reliable sources. In order to make a convincing argument, authors must distinguish their claim or claims from opposing points of view, or **counterclaims**.

When a writer is planning an argumentative essay, he or she will need to choose an organizational structure to present the argument in a logical and persuasive way.

An **organizational structure** is the order or pattern that a writer uses to structure and present ideas or events. A writer of an argumentative text may do one of the following:

- discuss a claim or claims in order of importance
- compare and contrast ideas
- present cause-and-effect relationships
- list advantages and disadvantages
- describe a problem and offer a solution

TURN AND TALK

Turn to your partner and talk about the last argument you made and what side you chose.

ELL SPEAKING FRAMES
- The last argument I made was ____.
- My evidence was ____.

Your Turn

Ask students to complete the Your Turn activity.

Position	B
Claim	A
Reason/Evidence	C

Write

Ask students to complete the writing assignment.

ELL

A

REWRITE CHECKLIST

☐ First, think about your overall purpose or task.
  ☐ Do I agree or disagree with the prompt? Why?
  ☐ What do I want my reader to learn?
☐ What are the claims, or main ideas, of my argument?
☐ Find reasons, evidence, or relevant examples that you need to include in your argument.
☐ Organize your ideas using an outline.

↻ YOUR TURN

Read the statements below. Then, complete the chart by matching each statement to its correct place in the outline.

Statement Options	
A	People can influence your future by helping you realize what you're meant to be.
B	Relationships can truly shape people's futures.
C	Mr. Lin helped me decide that I want to be an actor when I grow up.

Outline	Statement
Position	
Claim	
Reason/Evidence	

✎ WRITE

Use the questions in the checklist section to write an outline for your argument.

Reading & Writing Companion   **87**

Ⅴ SKILL VOCABULARY

counterclaim / el contraargumento *noun* an idea that is contrary to the author's position or point of view; an opposing claim

organizational structure / la estructura organizativa *noun* the order or pattern that a writer uses to organize information, such as cause-and-effect or compare-and-contrast COGNATE

Extended Writing Project

Skill:
Thesis Statement

••• CHECKLIST FOR THESIS STATEMENT

Before you begin writing your thesis statement, ask yourself the following questions:

- What is the prompt asking me to write about?
- What is the topic of my argument or essay?
- What claim do I want to make about the topic of this argument or essay? Is my opinion clear to my reader?
- Does my thesis statement introduce the body of my argument or essay?
- Where should I place my thesis statement?

Here are some methods to introduce and develop your claim and topic:

- Think about the topic and central idea of your essay.
  > The central idea of an argument is stated as a claim, or what will be proven or shown to be true.
  > Identify as many claims as you intend to prove.

- Write a clear statement about the central idea or claim. Your thesis statement should:
  > let the reader anticipate in the body of your essay.
  > respond completely to the writing prompt.

- Consider the best placement for your thesis statement.
  > If your response is short, you may want to get right to the point. Your thesis statement may be presented in the first sentence of the argument or essay.
  > If your response is longer (as in a formal argument or essay), you can build up to your thesis statement. In this case, you can place your thesis statement at the end of your introductory paragraph.

Skill: Thesis Statement

Introduce the Skill

Watch the Concept Definition video and read the following definition with your students.

In an essay, a **thesis statement** expresses the writer's main idea about a topic. The thesis statement usually appears in the **introduction**, or opening paragraph of your essay, and is often the last sentence of the introduction. The **body paragraphs** of the essay should offer a thorough explanation of the thesis statement as well as supporting details, reasons, and relevant evidence. The thesis is often restated in the **conclusion** of an essay.

TURN AND TALK

Turn to your partner and explain the thesis statement, or main idea or claim, of the last non-fiction essay, article, or book you read, based on the Concept Definition video.

ELL **SPEAKING FRAMES**
- In the last book I read, the thesis statement expressed the writer's ___.
- The thesis statement appeared in the ___.

V SKILL VOCABULARY

thesis statement / la presentación de la tesis *noun* a statement that shares the main idea of an argumentative or informative essay

introduction / la introducción *noun* the opening paragraph or section of an essay COGNATE

body paragraph / el párrafo del cuerpo *noun* a paragraph that appears between the introduction and the conclusion of an essay

conclusion / la conclusión *noun* the closing paragraph or section of an essay; a closing argument in an argumentative text COGNATE

Your Turn

Ask students to complete the Your Turn activity.

What is the prompt asking me to write about?	B
What is the topic of my argument?	A
What is the main claim I want to make in my argument, and how can I turn this into a thesis statement?	E
Does my thesis statement set up the rest of the argument?	D
Where should I place my thesis statement?	C

 YOUR TURN

Read the thesis statement questions and responses below. Then, complete the chart by correctly matching each thesis statement question with the appropriate response.

Response Options	
A	The topic of my argument is that my life would be very different if it weren't for my basketball coach, Mr. Montgomery, because he helped me decide that I want to be a basketball player when I grow up.
B	The prompt is asking whether or not relationships can shape people's futures. The prompt is also asking me to argue if my life would be different if a certain person were not in my life.
C	My argument will have an introduction, three body paragraphs, and a conclusion. Since it's a formal argument, I will put my thesis statement as the last sentence of the introduction.
D	My thesis statement tells the reader that I will list reasons for how Coach Montgomery helped shape my future, so it sets up the rest of the argument very well.
E	My main claim is that I think that relationships can shape people's futures because Coach Montgomery shaped mine. My thesis statement will be something like this: Special people in your life can definitely shape your future, just like Coach Montgomery helped shape mine.

Thesis Statement Question	Response
What is the prompt asking me to write about?	
What is the topic of my argument?	
What is the main claim I want to make in my argument, and how can I turn this into a thesis statement?	
Does my thesis statement set up the rest of the argument?	
Where should I place my thesis statement?	

Copyright © BookheadEd Learning, LLC

Reading & Writing Companion   **89**

Writer's Notebook

Project these three thesis statements on the board. Ask students to freewrite a short summary or outline for an argument for each of the three thesis statements. Remind them to think about the topic and how to support it with reasons and evidence.

- Recycling is the most important thing you can do to help the environment.
- The school board should put vending machines in the school cafeteria.
- Playing video games too often can have bad consequences.

ELL **TURN AND TALK**

Allow students to share their summaries orally in pairs or small groups before freewriting their outlines.

YOUR TURN

Complete the chart by answering each of the questions about your thesis statement.

Thesis Statement Question	Response
What is the prompt asking me to write about?	
What is the topic of my argument?	
What is the main claim I want to make in my argument, and how can I turn this into a thesis statement?	
Does my thesis statement set up the rest of the argument?	
Where should I place my thesis statement?	

 Your Turn

Ask students to complete the Your Turn activity. Answers will vary.

What is the prompt asking me to write about?	The prompt is asking me to give my opinion about relationships and if they can change someone's future, and if there's someone in my life who has made my life different.
What is the topic of my argument?	My topic is that I believe that relationships can shape people's futures because my violin teacher, Mrs. Hollis, has helped my life in many ways.
What is the main claim I want to make in my argument, and how can I turn this into a thesis statement?	My main claim is that I believe that your relationships can shape your future. Mrs. Hollis is my real-life example of this. I would write my thesis statement like this: Just like Mrs. Hollis, some people come into your life to help you with your future.
Does my thesis statement set up the rest of the argument?	The thesis statement explains my opinion and tells the reader about Mrs. Hollis, so it sets up the rest of my argument so I can give reasons and evidence.
Where should I place my thesis statement?	I would like to put my thesis statement at the end of the first paragraph so that the readers see it before reading my reasons and evidence in the body paragraphs.

Skill: Reasons and Relevant Evidence

Introduce the Skill

Watch the Concept Definition video and read the following definition with your students.

An **argument** is a set of reasons designed to persuade others to adopt a certain point of view or take a certain action. The **claim** is the main idea of the argument. The structure of an argument consists of a claim and the support for that claim. Support for the claim includes reasons and evidence. **Reasons** are logical explanations that state why the author believes in his or her claim and why others should accept the claim. **Relevant evidence** consists of facts, statistics, specific examples, and expert opinions and quotations from reliable sources that uphold the claim. To be relevant and reliable, evidence for an argument must come from **credible sources** that contain verifiable information closely connected to the topic and essential to the reader's understanding of the argument.

REASONS AND
RELEVANT EVIDENCE

Skill: Reasons and Relevant Evidence

••• CHECKLIST FOR REASONS AND RELEVANT EVIDENCE

As you begin to determine what reasons and relevant evidence will support your claim(s), use the following questions as a guide:

- What is the claim (or claims) that I am making in my argument?
- Are the reasons I have included clear and easy to understand?
- What relevant evidence (specific examples) am I using to support this claim?

Use the following steps as a guide to help you determine how you will support your claim(s) with clear reasons and relevant evidence:

- Identify the claim(s) you will make in your argument.
- Establish clear reasons for making your claim(s).
- Explain the connection between your claim(s) and the evidence/examples selected.

Reading & Writing Companion   **91**

TURN AND TALK

Turn to your partner and brainstorm a list of reasons and relevant evidence, or specific examples, you might add to support the following opinion: Our class picnic was fun, but it was too hot to enjoy it as much as we could have.

ELL SPEAKING FRAMES

- The reason our class picnic was not that fun was because it was ____.
- The picnic was not enjoyable when this happened: ____.

V SKILL VOCABULARY

argument / el argumento *noun* a set of claims, evidence, and reasons designed to persuade others to adopt a certain point of view or to take a certain action COGNATE

claim / la afirmación *noun* the writer's or speaker's position on a debatable issue or problem

reason / la razón *noun* an explanation that states why others should accept a claim

Extended Writing Project

YOUR TURN

Choose the best answer to each question.

1. The following is a section from a previous draft of Ellie's argument. Ellie would like to add a reason to support the claim she has presented in the underlined sentence. Which of these would BEST follow and support the underlined sentence?

> Some people think that you make your own future, so the relationships you have with people don't make much of a difference. I disagree. <u>Relationships help you work hard to achieve your goals.</u>

- ○ A. I pretended I was acting the part of a volcano expert in a play.
- ○ B. One time I had to give a talk in science class about how volcanoes erupt.
- ○ C. I did my research, but I felt nervous.
- ○ D. Without Mr. Lin's advice, I still would have been afraid to try my hardest.

2. The following is a paragraph from a previous draft of Ellie's argument. Ellie has included an unnecessary example that does not support her claim. Which sentence should be deleted from this paragraph?

> (1) Lastly, people can influence your future by helping you realize what you're meant to be. (2) Mr. Lin helped me decide what I want to be when I grow up. (3) When I was little, I wanted to be a princess. (4) I realized I wanted to be an actor when I had to give a speech at a dinner for our team's soccer coach. (5) I wanted to say something from my heart, but it was pounding in my chest. (6) I remembered what Mr. Lin taught me about speaking, so I took a deep breath and just started talking about how great Coach Healy was and how much we'd miss her.

- ○ A. Sentence 2
- ○ B. Sentence 3
- ○ C. Sentence 4
- ○ D. Sentence 6

WRITE

Use the three questions in the checklist to revise the first few paragraphs of your argument by adding one or more reasons and/or relevant evidence to support your claim(s) and overall opinion.

Copyright © BookheadEd Learning, LLC

ⓥ SKILL VOCABULARY

relevant / relevante *adjective* appropriate and logically related to the topic **COGNATE**

evidence / la evidencia *noun* facts, examples, and expert opinions that support a claim **COGNATE**

credible source / la fuente confiable *noun* a source that is trustworthy and believable

---

Your Turn

Ask students to complete the Your Turn activity.

QUESTION 1

A. Incorrect. This is an example in Ellie's argument, not a reason that explains her claim.

B. Incorrect. This is an example in Ellie's argument, not a reason that explains her claim.

C. Incorrect. This is an example in Ellie's argument, not a reason that explains her claim.

D. **Correct.** This reason illustrates the empowering effect Mr. Lin's advice had on Ellie to work hard.

QUESTION 2

A. Incorrect. Sentence 2 introduces Ellie's reasoning as to why people can help you realize what you're meant to be since Mr. Lin helped her.

B. **Correct.** Sentence 3 should be taken out because it does not support Ellie's claim about how people can help you decide what you're meant to be.

C. Incorrect. Sentence 4 introduces Ellie's evidence, or specific example, of when she knew that she wanted to be an actor.

D. Incorrect. Sentence 6 explains how Mr. Lin helped Ellie speak in front of others, which led to her confidence in acting.

Write

Ask students to complete the writing assignment.

ELL REWRITE CHECKLIST

Ⓐ Claim(s)
- ☐ What claim or claims should I introduce in my first few paragraphs?

Reasons
- ☐ What kind of explanation can I give for my claim?

Relevant Evidence
- ☐ What specific examples can I think of that will support my argument and claim(s)?

Argumentative Writing Process: Draft

Write

Ask students to complete the writing assignment.

CHECK FOR SUCCESS

If students struggle to begin drafting their arguments, ask them the following questions:

- Do you agree or disagree with the prompt?
- Is there a certain person in your life who has changed your life?
- What are some reasons why a relationship might change someone's future?

DRAFT CHECKLIST

- ☐ Have I agreed or disagreed with the prompt?
- ☐ Have I written claims to support my argument?
- ☐ Do I provide enough reasons and relevant evidence to support my claims?
- ☐ Does the organization make sense?

Argumentative Writing Process: Draft

| PLAN | DRAFT | REVISE | EDIT AND PUBLISH |

You have already made progress toward writing your argument. Now it is time to draft your argument.

 WRITE

Use your Plan and other responses in your Binder to draft your argument. You may also have new ideas as you begin drafting. Feel free to explore those new ideas as you have them. You can also ask yourself these questions:

- Have I clearly stated if I agree or disagree with the prompt's question?
- Have I clearly provided claims about whether or not relationships can truly shape one's future?
- Do I provide enough reasons and relevant evidence to support my claims?
- Does the organization of the argument make sense?

Before you submit your draft, read it over carefully. You want to be sure that you've responded to all aspects of the prompt.

Peer Review

Students should submit substantive feedback to two peers using the review instructions below.

- Has the writer clearly stated his or her main ideas, or claims, for the argument? If not, can you offer any suggestions?
- Has the writer provided supporting details, reasons, or relevant evidence? Is there any place where they could be added or improved?
- Does the writer include all the elements of argumentative writing? If not, can you offer any suggestions?
- What suggestions can you make to help the writer improve the organization of the argument?

SENTENCE FRAMES

- Your argument would be clearer if ____.
- One claim I like is ____. One place that you could add/improve reasons and relevant evidence to support it is ____.
- One element of argumentative writing you might add is ____.
- I like the organization of your argument because ____. I think you could improve the organization by ____.

Extended Writing Project

Here is Ellie's argument draft. First, notice her thesis statement. She summarized her opinion about the prompt's questions in the last sentence of the first paragraph. From there, she is able to organize her ideas to make a claim in the first body paragraph. Ellie makes the claim that relationships can shape your future by helping you become a better version of yourself. As you read, identify how she supported her claim through reasons and relevant evidence.

 NOTES

 Skill:
Introductions

Ellie decides that although her introduction has a clear claim and thesis statement, it doesn't grab the attention of the reader. Ellie connects her relationship with Mr. Lin to the poem "A Poem for My Librarian, Mrs. Long" by Nikki Giovanni. She decides that this connection would make a perfect "hook" for her introduction.

STUDENT MODEL: FIRST DRAFT

~~Mr. Lin is a teacher I will always remember because he has influenced my life. I believe that relationships can truly shape your future because if Mr. Lin were not in my life, I would be a completely different person than I am today.~~

I read a poem for school that made me think of my theater camp teacher, Mr. Lin. It was "A Poem for My Librarian, Mrs. Long" by Nikki Giovanni. The writer talks about how her librarian helped her when she was a kid. Mrs. Long got books that the writer would read as she sat on her grandmother's porch. They let her dream of "a world somewhere out there" without being "scared." Later in life, Nikki Giovanni became a talented author. The relationship she had with her librarian changed her life. When I read this poem, I thought of Mr. Lin, who did the same thing for me at theater camp last year. Mr. Lin is a teacher I will always remember because he has influenced my life. I believe that relationships can truly shape your future because if Mr. Lin were not in my life, I would be a completely different person than I am today.

~~One way that a relationship shapes your future is by helping you becom a better version of yourself. The most important thing Mr. Lin did was help me to be a braver person. I was shy. I wanted to work behind the scenes painting sets and sewing costumes. But Mr. Lin wanted everybody to feel what it's like to be onstage. I was nervous. My hands got sweaty and my voice shook when it was time to say my lines. Mr. Lin gave me some advice. first he said that all people get nervous when they go onstage, but good actors don't let it show. Next, Mr. Lin said, "Say your lines loud and say them proud!" What a difference his words made! I was able to hide my fear and say my lines. When people clapped at the end, it was amazing. Mr. Lin helped me becom a confident person.~~

 Analyze Student Model

Have students discuss the questions in the lesson as well as the Student Model draft. Ask:

- How does Ellie make her argument clear to the reader? What is her thesis statement?
- What claim does Ellie provide?
- How does Ellie support her claim with reasons and relevant evidence?

Encourage students to share ideas for their own arguments based on the questions in the lesson.

 SPEAKING FRAMES

- Ellie makes her argument clear by writing ____.
- One reason Ellie includes to support her claim is ____.
- An idea that I have for my argument is ____.

Introductions

Discuss the Model

1. How does Ellie clearly write her thesis statement? She states her claim about how relationships truly shape the future and connects it to her relationship with her teacher, Mr. Lin.

2. How does Ellie use a text in her introduction? Ellie connects her claim to Nikki Giovanni's "A Poem for My Librarian, Mrs. Long." This provides an interesting "hook" for her reader.

3. What else could Ellie write to make her introduction clear and organized? Answers will vary.

 SPEAKING FRAMES

- Ellie clearly states her claim and thesis statement by ____.
- Ellie uses reasons and evidence to support her claim, such as ____.

 THOUGHT SHUFFLE

Have students write their claims, main idea, and topic sentences on index cards and shuffle the deck. Ask students to examine the combinations that result from their shuffling and consider whether any of them would lead to a stronger organizational structure.

Transitions

Discuss the Model

1. What different purposes can transition words and phrases serve? Transitions can clarify a relationship between a claim and a reason or relevant evidence or provide cohesion to the argument.

2. How does Ellie use transitions? Transitions logically describe how Mr Lin's advice helped her.

3. How did Ellie's revisions improve her paragraph? Answers will vary. Sample answer: Ellie drew attention to the effects of Mr. Lin's advice.

ELL SPEAKING FRAMES

- One purpose of transitions is to ____.
- Ellie uses the transitions to ____.
- The transitions improve Ellie's paragraph by ____.

 Style

Discuss the Model

1. Where have you seen different types of style in movies, TV shows, or books? Answers will vary.

2. Which changes did Ellie make? She fixed spelling mistakes and got rid of slang and informal language.

3. How do those changes improve her essay? Those changes make her essay more formal and professional.

4. What other changes could Ellie make so her argument sounds more professional? Answers will vary.

ELL SPEAKING FRAMES

- Ellie made ____ style changes.
- These changes improve her essay because ____.

 NOTES

One way that a relationship shapes your future is by helping you become a better version of yourself. The most important thing Mr. Lin did was help me to be a braver person. Before I went to theater camp, I was shy. I wanted to work behind the scenes painting sets and sewing costumes. However, Mr. Lin wanted everybody to feel what it's like to be onstage. I was nervous. My hands got sweaty and my voice shook when it was time to say my lines. Then, Mr. Lin gave me some advice. First, he said that all people get nervous when they go onstage, but good actors don't let it show. Next, Mr. Lin said, "Say your lines loud and say them proud!" What a difference his words made! During the play, I was finally able to hide my fear and say my lines. When people clapped at the end, it was amazing. Mr. Lin helped me become a confident person.

~~Some people think that you make your own future, so the relationships you have with people don't make much of a difference. I like totally disagree. Relationships help you work hard to acheive your goals. Without Mr. Lin's advice, I stil would have been afraid to try my hardest. Even though Mr. Lin was my theater teacher, his helped me to become a better student in my other classes. One time I had to give a talk in science class about how volcanoes erupt. It was so crazy because I did my research, but I felt nervous, I wanted a good grad. I really really didn't want to get laughed at. In front of the class, I made mine fears go away by remembering what Mr. Lin taught me. I pertended I was acting the part of a volcano expert in a play. I was like the most excited person ever when I got an A. Thanks to Mr. Lin, I'm a great student in all of my classes. He helped me believe in myself.~~

Some people think that you make your own future, so the relationships you have with people don't make much of a difference. I disagree. Relationships help you work hard to achieve your goals. Without Mr. Lin's advice, I still would have been afraid to try my hardest. Even though Mr. Lin was my theater teacher, he helped me to become a better student in my other classes. One time I had to give a talk in science class about how volcanoes erupt. I did my research, but I felt nervous. I wanted a good grade. I did not want to get laughed at. In front of the class, I made my fears go away by remembering what Mr. Lin taught me. I pretended I was acting the part of a volcano expert

 Skill: Transitions

Ellie adds transitions and transitional phrases to three key sentences in the paragraph to make the relationship between her claim and her examples clearer. She writes "Before I went to theater camp" before "I was shy" to connect the ideas and the events.

 Skill: Style

Since this argument is an academic assignment, it requires formal language, not slang or a conversational tone. Ellie changed several instances of informal or conversational language. She changed "I like totally disagree" to "I disagree," as well as "I was like the most excited person ever when I got an A" to "I got an A." Eliminating her conversational tone helps her essay to sound more formal and professional.

Reading & Writing Companion   **95**

NOTES

in a play. I got an A. Thanks to Mr. Lin, I'm a great student in all of my classes. He helped me believe in myself.

Lastly, people can influence your future by helping you realize what you're meant to be. Although some may argue that people's influence on our lives often goes innoticed, I don't think that's true. Because of Mr. Lin's influence in my life, I decid what I want to be when I grow up. I realized I wanted to be an actor when I had to give a speech at a dinner for ours team's soccer coach. I wanted to say something from mine heart, but it was pounding in my chest. I remembered what Mr. Lin taught me about speaking, so I took a deep breath and just started talking about how great Coach Healy was and how much we'd miss hers. Everybody was inpresed with my speaking skills and told me I would be a great actor one day. Because of my relationship with Mr. Lin, I know I will be a great actor one day.

~~Mr. Lin could have had a big acting career instead of being a theater camp teacher. But, I am really glad he was my teacher. Just like Mrs. Long changed Nikki Giovanni's life, I think Mr. Lin was part of my life for a reason. My life would have been very different without him. He showed me how to face my fears and act like my words matter. He taught me how to be a good actor and a brave person. He changed how I felt about myself and the goals I have for mine future. And, it's true that relationships with people can really shape your future.~~

Mr. Lin could have had a big acting career instead of being a theater camp teacher. However, I am really glad he was my teacher. Just like Mrs. Long changed Nikki Giovanni's life, I think Mr. Lin was part of my life for a reason. My life would have been very different without him. He showed me how to face my fears and act like my words matter. He taught me how to be a good actor and a brave person. He changed how I felt about myself and the goals I have for my future. Therefore, it's true that relationships with people can really shape your future. I'll never forget the lessons I learned from my favorite teacher, Mr. Lin.

Skill: Conclusions

Ellie needs to remind the reader of her opinion about the prompt's question: Can relationships truly shape your future? Ellie decides to end her conclusion with the following statement to remind the readers that relationships can provide you with memorable lessons that will last forever: "I'll never forget the lessons I learned from my favorite teacher, Mr. Lin."

  Reading & Writing Companion

---

 ## Conclusions

Discuss the Model

1. The Model shows how Ellie changed the conclusion of her argumentative essay. How did she change it? She restated her thesis statement and included a memorable comment.

2. How did these changes improve her argument? These changes improved her argument by reminding the reader of her opinion of the prompt's question.

3. How could Ellie use a different memorable comment to end her argumentative essay? Answers will vary.

ELL **SPEAKING FRAMES**

- Ellie changed the conclusion of her argumentative essay by ____.
- These changes improved her argument because ____.

Conclusions

Connect To Mentor Text

Project the following example of a conclusion and discuss with your students:

I still hold close to my heart some of my biggest wins and hardest losses. I've learned what is necessary to perform under pressure. I've learned how to push myself mentally and physically. I've learned how to work with a large group of people. I've learned what it takes to achieve what I want. I have experienced the highest highs of my life on the volleyball court.

SportsNews, volleyball is not girly. It is not any less athletic. It is just awesome. ('We're on the Same Team')

Ask students:

- What do you notice about the author's conclusion?

- How does she summarize her claims about volleyball?

- In which sentence(s) does she restate the thesis statement?

Skill: Introductions

Introduce the Skill

Watch the Concept Definition video and read the following definition with your students.

The **introduction** is the opening paragraph or section of an essay or other nonfiction text. To begin an argumentative essay, writers identify the **topic**, or what the essay will be about. The most important part of the introduction in an argumentative essay is the **thesis statement**. This statement contains the writer's **claim**, or main argument, and it states something that the writer believes to be true.

In an informative/explanatory text, the introduction should provide readers with necessary information in order to introduce a topic. It should state the thesis, which in an informative/explanatory essay is a short statement that summarizes the main point of the essay and previews the ideas that will follow in the text. In an informative/explanatory essay, many writers also include one or two sentences that are called a "hook." They are intended to engage readers' interest and grab their attention so they keep reading.

Skill: Introductions

••• CHECKLIST FOR INTRODUCTIONS

Before you write your introduction, ask yourself the following questions:

- What is my claim? How can I introduce my claim(s) so it is clear to readers?
- What is the best way to organize my ideas, concepts, reasons, and evidence in a clear and logical order?
- How will I "hook" my reader's interest? I might:
  > start with an attention-grabbing statement.
  > begin with an intriguing question.
  > use descriptive words to set a scene.

Below are two strategies to help you introduce your topic and claim, and organize reasons and evidence clearly in an introduction:

- Peer Discussion
  > Talk about your topic with a partner, explaining what you already know and your ideas about your topic.
  > Write notes about the ideas you have discussed and any new questions you may have.
  > Review your notes and think about what will be your claim or controlling idea.
  > Briefly state your claim or thesis.
  > Organize your reasons and evidence in an order that is clear to readers, presenting your reasons first, followed by evidence.
  > Write a possible "hook."

TURN AND TALK

Turn to your partner and brainstorm a list of classes, presentations, textbooks, or non-fiction books that have introduced the topic clearly and in an organized way.

ELL SPEAKING FRAMES

- The (class / presentation / textbook / non-fiction book) ____ introduces the topic clearly by ____.
- An example of a clear and organized introduction is ____.

V SKILL VOCABULARY

introduction / la introducción *noun* the opening paragraph or section of an essay COGNATE

topic / el tema *noun* the subject of a literary work, usually expressed as a single word or phrase in the form of a noun

thesis statement / la presentación de la tesis *noun* a statement that shares the main idea of an argumentative or informative essay

claim / la afirmación *noun* the writer's or speaker's position on a debatable issue or problem

Extended Writing Project

- Freewriting

  > Freewrite for 10 minutes about your topic. Don't worry about grammar, punctuation, or having fully formed ideas. The point of freewriting is to discover ideas.

  > Review your notes and think about what will be your claim or controlling idea.

  > Briefly state your claim or thesis.

  > Organize your reasons and evidence in an order that is clear to readers, presenting your reasons first, followed by evidence.

  > Write a possible "hook."

  Reading & Writing Companion

Your Turn

Ask students to complete the Your Turn activity.

QUESTION 1

A. Incorrect. This sentence helps the writer transition from the "hook" to the thesis statement.

B. Incorrect. This sentence provides a reason to support the thesis statement.

C. Incorrect. This sentence is the thesis statement and needs to be in the introduction.

D. Correct. This statement does not answer the main argument, or claim.

QUESTION 2

A. Incorrect. This statement is vague.

B. Incorrect. This statement only describes Ellie's opinion of Mr. Lin, but it doesn't interest the reader.

C. Correct. This hook would interest the reader and provide a good transition for Ellie to talk about how "A Poem for My Librarian, Mrs. Long" connects to how she feels about Mr. Lin and the lasting impact of relationships.

D. Incorrect. This statement is a counterclaim to Ellie's argument.

Write

Ask students to complete the writing assignment.

REWRITE CHECKLIST

A **Topic/Claim**

☐ Have I clearly identified the topic, or what the argument will be about?

Thesis Statement

☐ How can I make sure my thesis statement is presented clearly to my readers?

Reasons and Evidence

☐ What reasons or evidence do I have to support my argument?

 YOUR TURN

Choose the best answer for each question.

1. Below is a section from a previous draft of Ellie's introduction. Keeping in mind the organization of the introduction, which sentence does not belong?

> (1) When I read this poem, I thought of Mr. Lin because he helped me at theater camp last year. (2) Mr. Lin is a teacher I will always remember because he has influenced my life. (3) I believe that relationships can truly shape your future because if Mr. Lin were not in my life, I would be a completely different person than I am today. (4) I'm a lot like Nikki Giovanni because the relationship she had with her librarian changed her life.

○ A. Sentence 1
○ B. Sentence 2
○ C. Sentence 3
○ D. Sentence 4

2. Which "hook" could Ellie add to improve the introduction of her argumentative essay?

○ A. Relationships are important.
○ B. Mr. Lin was the best teacher.
○ C. Have you ever read something that reminded you of someone?
○ D. Some people don't value relationships as much as I do.

 WRITE

Use the questions and notes in the checklist to revise the introduction of your argumentative essay.

Reading & Writing Companion   99

Extended Writing Project

Skill:
Transitions

••• CHECKLIST FOR TRANSITIONS

Before you revise your current draft to include transitions, think about:

- the key ideas you discuss in your body paragraphs.
- the organizational structure of your essay.
- the relationships among claim(s) and reasons.

Next, reread your current draft and note areas in your essay where:

- the relationships between your claim(s) and the reasons and evidence are unclear, identifying places where you could add linking words or other transitional devices to make your argument more cohesive. Look for:
  - > sudden jumps in your ideas.
  - > breaks between paragraphs where the ideas in the next paragraph are not logically following from the previous.

Revise your draft to use words, phrases, and clauses to clarify the relationships among claim(s) and reasons, using the following questions as a guide:

- Are there unifying relationships between the claims, reasons, and the evidence I present in my argument?
- Have I clarified, or made clear, these relationships?
- What linking words (such as conjunctions), phrases, or clauses could I add to my argument to clarify the relationships between the claims, reasons, and evidence I present?

Introduce the Skill

Watch the Concept Definition video and read the following definition with your students.

Transitions are connecting words, phrases, and clauses that writers use to **clarify** the relationships among ideas and details in a text. Transitions have different functions depending on whether the text is argumentative, informative, or narrative.

In an argumentative essay, writers state claims and provide reasons and evidence for their claims. To clarify a relationship between a claim and a reason or supporting evidence, transitions such as *although* and *on the other hand* help make connections clear.

For informative essays, transitions such as *however, in addition,* and *for example* may help create **cohesion** among ideas and concepts.

In narrative writing, authors use a variety of words, phrases, and clauses to signal shifts in time, setting, and action. Transitions such as *until now, meanwhile,* and *once it was over* may make narrative events more **coherent**.

Transitions also help to connect ideas both within and across paragraphs and between major sections of text.

Copyright © BookheadEd Learning, LLC

TURN AND TALK

Turn to your partner and brainstorm a list of transition words you regularly use in daily conversation and in your own writing. Discuss how using these transitional words and phrases can help you connect as well as compare and contrast ideas.

ELL SPEAKING FRAMES

- One transition I regularly use is ___.
- Another transition I regularly use is ___.
- This transition helps me connect ideas by ___.

SKILL VOCABULARY

transition / la transición *noun* a connecting word or phrase that a writer may use to clarify the relationship between ideas in a text; set off with a comma COGNATE

clarify / aclarar *verb* to make clear and more comprehensible

cohesion / la cohesión *noun* the quality of parts working together as a whole COGNATE

coherent / coherente *adjective* marked by being orderly and logical; easy to understand COGNATE

⚙ Your Turn

Ask students to complete the Your Turn activity.

QUESTION 1

A. **Correct.** This transition explains the contrast of Mr. Lin being a theater teacher and also helping Ellie in her academic subjects at school.

B. Incorrect. This transition signals that the two statements are related, rather than an explanation of the contrast of how Mr. Lin has helped Ellie in other classes despite only being her theater teacher.

C. Incorrect. This transition signals that a similar point is being made, which does not explain the contrasting example the writer gives.

D. Incorrect. This transition signals that a final point is being introduced, rather than an explanation of how Mr. Lin has helped Ellie in other classes besides theater.

QUESTION 2

A. Incorrect. This transition signals a contrast and does not effectively combine the ideas in the two sentences.

B. **Correct.** This transition signals a sequence of events, which effectively shows how Ellie first remembers her teacher's advice, then takes a deep breath and starts talking.

C. Incorrect. This transition signals a sequence of events that does not fit with these sentences.

D. Incorrect. This transition signals a contrast and does not effectively combine the ideas in the two sentences.

Extended Writing Project

🔄 YOUR TURN

Choose the best answer to each question.

1. The following section is from an earlier draft of Ellie's argument. Ellie has not used the most effective transition (underlined). Which of the following could replace *On the other hand* in the following sentence?

> <u>On the other hand</u> Mr. Lin was my theater teacher, he helped me to become a better student in my other classes.

○ A. Even though
○ B. Since
○ C. Similarly
○ D. Finally

2. The following section is from an earlier draft of Ellie's argument. Ellie would like to add a transition word to unify sentences 1 and 2. Which of these is the most effective transition to add to combine sentences 1 and 2?

> (1) I remembered what Mr. Lin taught me about speaking. (2) I took a deep breath and just started talking about how great Coach Healy was and how much we'd miss her.

○ A. , but
○ B. , so
○ C. , lastly
○ D. , however

Reading & Writing Companion 101

Copyright © BookheadEd Learning, LLC

📖 Writer's Notebook

Have students select something they have done today, such as get ready for school, eat lunch, or have a conversation with a friend. Have them write a paragraph describing the activity, using at least four transitions. Encourage students to think about which types of transitions will be most effective in their paragraph.

ELL TURN AND TALK

Allow students to share their paragraphs orally in pairs or small groups before freewriting.

Extended Writing Project

YOUR TURN

Complete the chart by writing a transitional sentence that connects ideas with or between sentences or paragraphs in your argument.

Transition	Transitional Sentence
Transitions that clarify a relationship between a claim and reasons/evidence	
Transitions that make writing more coherent, or clear	
Transitions that provide cohesion, or a logical flow of ideas	

Your Turn

Ask students to complete the Your Turn activity. Answers will vary.

Transitions that clarify a relationship between a claim and reasons/ evidence	Although I appreciate all that my parents have done for me, my future is my decision. Therefore, I will decide what I want to be when I grow up.
Transitions that make writing more coherent, or clear	Until now, I always thought I had to take over the family business because it was a tradition.
Transitions that provide cohesion, or a logical flow of ideas	First, I wasn't sure if my relationship with my parents would shape my future. Then, I realized that I should shape my own future! I get to make my own destiny.

Skill: Style

Introduce the Skill

Watch the Concept Definition video and read the following definition with your students.

Style is the way a writer uses language to express ideas and convey information. It is revealed through the writer's choice of words and sentence construction. Style also involves being aware of the rules for writing standard English.

Choosing an appropriate style depends on the audience and the purpose for writing. Different subjects require different styles of writing. For both argumentative and informative writing, writers must use a formal style. With a **formal style**, a writer chooses **academic** language—the type of vocabulary used in school texts, for example—rather than informal or conversational language. The writer might also use special vocabulary unique to a particular topic, sometimes called **domain-specific** language.

Finally, to help maintain a formal style, writers must be sure to follow conventional rules for grammar, spelling, capitalization, and punctuation.

Skill:
Style

••• CHECKLIST FOR STYLE

First, reread the draft of your argumentative essay and identify the following:

- places where you use slang, contractions, abbreviations, and a conversational tone.
- areas where you could use subject-specific or academic language in order to help persuade or inform your readers.
- areas where sentence structure lacks variety.
- incorrect uses of the conventions of standard English for grammar, spelling, capitalization, and punctuation.

Establish and maintain a formal style in your essay, using the following questions as a guide:

- Have I avoided slang in favor of academic language?
- Have I varied my sentence structure and the length of my sentences? Apply these specific questions where appropriate:
  > Where should I make some sentences longer by using conjunctions to connect independent clauses, dependent clauses, and phrases?
  > Where should I make some sentences shorter by separating any independent clauses?
- Did I follow the conventions of standard English including:
  > grammar?
  > spelling?
  > capitalization?
  > punctuation?

Reading & Writing Companion **103**

TURN AND TALK

Turn to your partner and explain if your favorite book has formal or informal style and how that affects the story.

ELL SPEAKING FRAMES

- My favorite book is ____.
- It has (formal / informal) style because ____.
- This style affects the story because ____.

SKILL VOCABULARY

style / el estilo *noun* a way of expressing something that is characteristic of the person or time period COGNATE

formal style / el estilo formal *noun* a writing style or way of writing for academic essays

academic / académico/a *adjective* having to do with school COGNATE

domain-specific / específico/a del campo *adjective* having to do with a particular topic

Extended Writing Project

YOUR TURN

Read the words and phrases below. Then, complete the chart by sorting them into those that maintain a formal style and those that do not.

Word and Phrase Options	
A	It was like, the best day ever!?
B	researched
C	It was totally crazy that I felt nervous and stuff, caus oh boy, I was ready!
D	believe
E	resaerchd
F	Mr. lin who was my theater camp teacher was the COOLEST teacher ever, dont ya think?
G	It was unusual that I felt nervous because I was prepared.
H	beleive
I	Mr. Lin, my theater camp teacher, helped me become a great student.
J	It was the best day of my life!

Maintaining a Formal Style	Informal Style/Containing Errors

Your Turn

Ask students to complete the Your Turn activity.

Maintaining a Formal Style	Informal Style/Containing Errors
D	H
J	A
B	E
G	C
I	F

Writer's Notebook

Project a school-appropriate informal/slang text conversation from a volunteer student. Have students work together to edit the conversation to create more formal language. Discuss why it is appropriate to use informal language in text conversations, but not in academic essays.

ELL TURN AND TALK

Allow students to share their changes orally in pairs or small groups.

Your Turn

Ask students to complete the Your Turn activity. Answers will vary.

The assignment was turned in totally too late for my teacher to be impresed?	The assignment was turned in too late for my teacher to be impressed.
even though I erned a poor grad in science I stil wantted to be a doctor.	Even though I earned a poor grade in science, I still wanted to be a doctor.
He put him notes undernaeth the book.	He put his notes underneath the book.
It was the craziest thing ever when mrs. Long unnounced the field trip.	It was so exciting and unexpected when Mrs. Long announced the field trip.
Marissa ate she lunch with me class on Wednesday.	Marissa ate her lunch with my class on Wednesday.

↻ YOUR TURN

Edit the sentences to fix the style mistakes.

Sentence	Corrected Sentence
The assignment was turned in totally too late for my teacher to be impresed?	
even though I erned a poor grad in science I stil wantted to be a doctor.	
He put him notes undernaeth the book.	
It was the craziest thing ever when mrs. Long unnounced the field trip.	
Marissa ate she lunch with me class on Wednesday.	

Extended Writing Project

Skill:
Conclusions

••• CHECKLIST FOR CONCLUSIONS

Before you write your conclusion, ask yourself the following questions:

- How can I restate the thesis or main idea in my concluding section or statement? What impression can I make on my reader?

- How can I write my conclusion so that it follows logically from my argument?

- Should I include a call to action?

- How can I conclude with a memorable comment?

Below are two strategies to help you provide a concluding statement or section that follows from the argument presented:

- Peer Discussion

  > After you have written your introduction and body paragraphs, talk with a partner and tell them what you want readers to remember, writing notes about your discussion.

  > Review your notes and think about what you wish to express in your conclusion.

  > Do not simply restate your claim or thesis statement. Rephrase your main idea to show the depth of your knowledge, the importance of your idea, and encourage readers to adopt your view.

  > Write your conclusion.

- Freewriting

  > Freewrite for 10 minutes about what you might include in your conclusion. Don't worry about grammar, punctuation, or having fully formed ideas. The point of freewriting is to discover ideas.

  > Review your notes and think about what you wish to express in your conclusion.

  > Do not simply restate your claim or thesis statement. Rephrase your main idea to show the depth of your knowledge, the importance of your idea, and encourage readers to adopt your view.

  > Write your conclusion.

Skill: Conclusions

Introduce the Skill

Watch the Concept Definition video and read the following definition with your students.

A **conclusion** is the closing paragraph or section of an essay, argument, or narrative. It is where the writer brings an essay to a close by restating the main idea or **thesis statement** or the **claim** in an argument. It also summarizes the evidence and research that support the claim or thesis. The conclusion should follow logically from the information, explanations, or claim that has been presented. A conclusion is a good way to suggest to your readers that you have accomplished what you set out to do. In addition, try to leave readers with an interesting final impression. This might be accomplished by closing with a quote, an anecdote, or a call to action.

In a **narrative**, a conclusion should follow logically from the events of the plot and what the characters have experienced. It might include characters reflecting on events, why they matter, and how they feel about them.

TURN AND TALK

Turn to your partner and brainstorm a list of movies, TV shows, or books that have logical endings.

> **ELL** SPEAKING FRAMES
>
> - The (movie / TV show / book) ____ concludes with ____.
> - An example of a logical ending is ____.

SKILL VOCABULARY

conclusion / la conclusión *noun* the closing paragraph or section of an essay; a closing argument in an argumentative text COGNATE

thesis statement / la presentación de la tesis *noun* a statement that shares the main idea of an argumentative or informative essay

claim / la afirmación *noun* the writer's or speaker's position on a debatable issue or problem

narrative / la narración *noun* a story, real or imagined, consisting of connected events

Your Turn

Ask students to complete the Your Turn activity.

QUESTION 1

A. Incorrect. This sentence is not relevant to the prompt's question.

B. **Correct.** This sentence describes how relationships can affect one's future.

C. Incorrect. This sentence is not relevant to the prompt's question.

D. Incorrect. This sentence is not relevant to the prompt's question.

QUESTION 2

A. **Correct.** This sentence does not relate to a claim made in the argument.

B. Incorrect. This sentence restates Ellie's claim.

C. Incorrect. This sentence restates Ellie's claim.

D. Incorrect. This sentence restates Ellie's claim.

 ## Write

Ask students to complete the writing assignment.

 REWRITE CHECKLIST

A **Restating the Thesis Statement**

☐ How can you restate your thesis?

Summarizing the Claims from the Argument

☐ How can you summarize your main claims?

Adding a Memorable Comment

☐ What sentence or phrase can you add to the conclusion that will interest the reader?

 YOUR TURN

Choose the best answer to each question.

1. Below is the restatement of Ellie's thesis statement. Which of the following sentences could be added to support this restatement?

> He changed how I felt about myself and the goals I have for my future. Therefore, it's true that relationships with people can really shape your future.

○ A. He was the best ever.
○ B. There are special relationships that can truly change the outcome of your life.
○ C. I'll never forget my favorite teacher Mr. Lin and his fun acting classes.
○ D. Hopefully, one day you will have a teacher like Mr. Lin!

2. Ellie wants to improve the conclusion of her argumentative draft. One of these sentences is in the wrong spot because it doesn't summarize a claim from her argument. Which sentence needs to be moved?

> (1) Mr. Lin could have had a big acting career instead of being a theater camp teacher. (2) He showed me how to face my fears and act like my words matter. (3) He taught me how to be a good actor and a brave person. (4) He changed how I felt about myself and the goals I have for my future.

○ A. Sentence 1
○ B. Sentence 2
○ C. Sentence 3
○ D. Sentence 4

 WRITE

Use the questions in the checklist to revise the conclusion of your argumentative essay.

Reading & Writing Companion **107**

 ## Writer's Notebook

Project "We're on the Same Team" with the last two paragraphs missing. Have students write a logical conclusion to Jacki Jing's letter.

TURN AND TALK

Allow students to share their first few sentences orally in pairs or small groups before writing.

Extended Writing Project

Argumentative Writing Process: Revise

| PLAN | DRAFT | REVISE | EDIT AND PUBLISH |

You have written a draft of your argument. You have also received input from your peers about how to improve it. Now you are going to revise your draft.

◄◄ REVISION GUIDE

Examine your draft to find areas for revision. Keep in mind your purpose and audience as you revise for clarity, development, organization, and style. Use the guide below to help you review:

Review	Revise	Example
Clarity		
Highlight the first few sentences in a paragraph, ensuring that the topic or claim is clearly stated first.	Move your claims to the beginning of each body paragraph.	One way that a relationship shapes your future is by helping you become a better version of yourself. The most important thing Mr. Lin did was help me to be a braver person. ~~One way that a relationship shapes your future is by helping you become a better version of yourself.~~
Development		
Identify places where you identify claims. Note reasons, relevant evidence, or specific examples you could incorporate to add support.	Focus on a single claim and add reasons, relevant evidence, or examples to support your ideas.	Without Mr. Lin's advice, I still would have been afraid to try my hardest. Even though Mr. Lin was my theater teacher, he helped me to become a better student in my other classes. One time I had to give a talk in science class about how volcanoes erupt.

Copyright © BookheadEd Learning, LLC

108 Reading & Writing Companion

Please note that excerpts and passages in the StudySync® library and this workbook are intended as touchstones to generate interest in an author's work. The excerpts and passages do not substitute for the reading of entire texts, and StudySync® strongly recommends that students seek out and purchase the whole literary or informational work in order to experience it as the author intended. Links to online resellers are available in our digital library. In addition, complete works may be ordered through an authorized reseller by filling out and returning to StudySync® the order form enclosed in this workbook.

Argumentative Writing Process: Revise

Review Revision Guide

Break the class into five groups, and assign each group a category of the revision guide. Ask:

- What is the purpose of this section of the guide?
- How did it improve Ellie's writing?
- How will it help to improve your writing?

Allow groups to share their ideas with the class.

ELL SPEAKING FRAMES

- I think ____ (clarity / development / organization / word choice / sentence variety) improved Ellie's writing by ____.
- I think ____ (clarity / development / organization / word choice / sentence variety) will improve my writing because ____.

Revise

Students should start this activity with a copy of their drafts either printed on paper or open in a word-processing program, such as Google Docs. Allow students time to revise their drafts using the instructions in the revision guide. Once students have finished revising their argument, have them submit their work.

CHECK FOR SUCCESS

Circulate around the room to spend time with individual students. Ask:

- What category are you working on?
- Why are you revising this specific section?
- How are you revising it?
- How does this change support your purpose?
- Does this change make your writing appropriate for your audience?

If students struggle while revising their drafts, choose an exemplary revision to share with the class while the student talks through the process. You could also invite a student to share a dilemma in the revision process and allow the class to offer feedback or suggestions.

ELL DEVELOPMENT

Revise your draft, focusing on strengthening your use of reasons, relevant evidence, and specific examples.

A DEVELOPMENT

Tell students to revise their drafts using the revision guide, focusing on development. In addition, have students make revisions that focus on word choice, as practiced in the previous unit.

Write

Ask students to complete the writing assignment.

Review	Revise	Example
Organization		
Examine the first sentence in each paragraph. Annotate any paragraph that does not transition smoothly from the previous paragraph.	Add a transitional phrase or sentence to provide coherence among body paragraphs.	Lastly, people can influence your future by helping you realize what you're meant to be.
Style: Word Choice		
Identify informal words and phrases that do not help convey your purpose or opinion in an effective manner.	Select sentences to rewrite using more formal language.	~~I was like the most excited person ever when~~ I got an A.
Style: Sentence Variety		
Annotate paragraphs, sentences, and words that are unusually long.	Separate long sentences into two sentences or shorten sentences by deleting information that is repetitive or unnecessary.	I remembered what Mr. Lin taught me about speaking, so I took a deep breath and just started talking about how great Coach Healy was and how much we'd miss her. ~~It felt like I talked forever about all of the things she had done for us and all of the reasons we would miss her.~~

 WRITE

Use the guide above, as well as your peer reviews, to help you evaluate your argument to determine areas that should be revised.

ELL **REVISION CHECKLIST**
A
- ☐ Find a paragraph with a claim that lacks support.
- ☐ Brainstorm evidence or specific examples to better support the claim.
- ☐ Add to or replace the weaker reasons or examples with stronger ones.

Extended Writing Project

Grammar:
Basic Spelling Rules I

Suffixes and the Silent *e*

Spelling Conventions	Base Words	Correct	Incorrect
When adding a suffix that begins with a consonant to a word that ends with a silent **e**, keep the **e**.	place hope	placement hopeful	placment hopful
When adding a suffix that begins with a vowel or **y** to a word that ends with a silent **e**, usually drop the **e**.	race pore	racism porous	raceism poreous
When adding **-ly** to a word that ends with an **l** plus a silent **e**, drop the **le**.	probable humble	probably humbly	probablely humblely

Suffixes and the Final *y*

Spelling Conventions	Base Words	Correct	Incorrect
When a word ends in a consonant + **y**, change the **y** to **i** before adding a suffix. However, if the suffix begins with **i**, do not change the **y** to **i**.	bounty duty fry	bountiful dutiful frying	bountyful dutyful friing
When a word ends in a vowel + **y**, keep the **y**.	essay joy	essayist joyous	essaist joious

Spelling *ie* and *ei*

Spelling Conventions	Correct	Incorrect
Usually, when **i** and **e** appear together in one syllable, the **i** comes before the **e**.	yield friend	yeild freind
When **i** and **e** appear after a **c**, the **e** usually comes before the **i**.	receive conceit	recieve conciet
However, there are exceptions to these patterns.	seizure weird weigh	siezure wierd wiegh

Reading & Writing Companion

Grammar: Basic Spelling Rules I

Introduce the Skill

Review the image and definition for basic spelling rules I as a class.

- suffix: an affix attached to the end of a word; may change the spelling of the base word depending on the suffix

- spelling *ie* and *ei*: may sound the same; generally, *i* comes before *e*, except when both letters follow *c* or when both letters are pronounced together as an *a*-sound, as in *neighbor* or *weigh*

Discuss the Model

Why might you have to change the spelling of a word when adding a suffix to it? The spelling of a word usually changes when the word ends with a silent *e* and the suffix begins with a vowel or *y*.

⚙ Your Turn

Ask students to complete the Your Turn activity.

QUESTION 1

A. **Correct.** The *i* goes before the e in this word because the two vowels are in different syllables and do not make a single vowel sound.

B. Incorrect.

C. Incorrect.

D. Incorrect.

QUESTION 2

A. Incorrect.

B. Incorrect.

C. **Correct.** *Belief* is the correct spelling. The long *e* sound is represented by the double vowel *ie*.

D. Incorrect:

QUESTION 3

A. **Correct.** When a word ends in a vowel + *y*, the *y* does not change to an *i* before a suffix, so *portrayal* is the correct spelling.

B. Incorrect.

C. Incorrect.

D. Incorrect.

QUESTION 4

A. Incorrect.

B. Incorrect.

C. **Correct.** When adding a suffix that begins with a consonant to a word that ends with a silent *e*, you keep the *e*.

D. Incorrect.

⟳ YOUR TURN

1. How should the spelling error in this sentence be corrected?

> *Dragonwings* is about the expereinces of a young boy from China who goes to America to join his father, a maker of kites that are beautiful enough to be heirlooms.

- ○ A. Change **expereinces** to **experiences**.
- ○ B. Change **beautiful** to **beautyful**.
- ○ C. Change **heirlooms** to **hierlooms**.
- ○ D. No change needs to be made to this sentence.

2. How should the spelling error in this sentence be corrected?

> A person's heart was weighed right after death to determine whether the person had been guilty of deceit or other sins—that was the beleif of the ancient Egyptians.

- ○ A. Change **weighed** to **wieghed**.
- ○ B. Change **deceit** to **deciet**.
- ○ C. Change **beleif** to **belief**.
- ○ D. No change needs to be made to this sentence.

3. How should the spelling error in this sentence be corrected?

> Because of their stark portraial of the thin, pitiful faces of the poor, Dorothea Lange's photographs changed the way the public perceived the Depression.

- ○ A. Change **portraial** to **portrayal**.
- ○ B. Change **pitiful** to **pityful**.
- ○ C. Change **perceived** to **percieved**.
- ○ D. No change needs to be made to this sentence.

4. How should the spelling error in this sentence be corrected?

> When Rosa Parks courageously refused to give up her bus seat, she committed an incredibly dangerous act, but her bravry helped launch the civil rights movement.

- ○ A. Change **courageously** to **couragously**.
- ○ B. Change **incredibly** to **incredibley**.
- ○ C. Change **bravry** to **bravery**.
- ○ D. No change needs to be made to this sentence.

Reading & Writing Companion 🖥

Extended Writing Project

Grammar:
Possessive Pronouns

sync•skills

Possessive pronouns are a kind of personal pronoun. A possessive pronoun takes the place of a person or thing that owns or possesses something. It can come before the noun that is possessed, or it can stand alone in a sentence.

USED BEFORE NOUNS	USED ALONE
Singular: my, your, her, his, its	Singular: mine, yours, hers, his, its
Plural: our, your, their	Plural: ours, yours, theirs
Ever since I can remember, I had wanted to know about the Land of the Golden Mountain, but **my** mother had never wanted to talk about it. Dragonwings	Athene claimed that she had the better right, for the beauty of wisdom such as **hers** surpassed all else. Black Ships Before Troy: The Story of the Iliad

When using a personal pronoun to show possession, make sure the pronoun is in the possessive case.

Correct	Incorrect
The computer quickly stores information in **its** huge memory.	The computer quickly stores information in **it** huge memory.
Our dog is a Labrador Retriever.	**We** dog is a Labrador Retriever.
The clever idea was **theirs**.	The clever idea was **their**.

Grammar: Possessive Pronouns

Introduce the Skill

Review the image and definition for possessive pronouns as a class.

- possessive noun: a noun that shows ownership of things or of qualities
- possessive pronoun: a pronoun showing ownership; takes the place of a noun

Discuss the Model

1. What is the function of a possessive pronoun? A possessive pronoun takes the place of a person or thing that possesses or owns something.

2. Where does a possessive pronoun go in a sentence? A possessive pronoun can come before the noun it is possessing, or it can stand alone in the sentence.

⚙ Your Turn

Ask students to complete the Your Turn activity.

QUESTION 1

A. Correct. *Our* is a possessive pronoun, but it must come before a noun. *Ours* is a possessive pronoun that can stand alone.

B. Incorrect.

C. Incorrect.

D. Incorrect.

QUESTION 2

A. Incorrect.

B. Correct. *Her* is a possessive pronoun and comes before a noun, so *her hand* is correct.

C. Incorrect.

D. Incorrect.

QUESTION 3

A. Incorrect.

B. Incorrect.

C. Incorrect.

D. Correct. *Yours* is a possessive pronoun that can stand alone.

QUESTION 4

A. Incorrect.

B. Correct. *His* is a possessive pronoun and can come before a noun, so *his guitar* is correct.

C. Incorrect.

D. Incorrect.

↻ YOUR TURN

1. How should this sentence be changed?

   > The red house on the corner is our.

   ○ A. Change **our** to **ours**.
   ○ B. Change **our** to **they**.
   ○ C. Change **our** to **their**.
   ○ D. No change needs to be made to this sentence.

2. How should this sentence be changed?

   > She hand shot up when the teacher asked for volunteers.

   ○ A. Change **she** to **him**.
   ○ B. Change **she** to **her**.
   ○ C. Change **she** to **hers**.
   ○ D. No change needs to be made to this sentence.

3. How should this sentence be changed?

   > Yours is the third seat in the first row.

   ○ A. Change **your** to **you**.
   ○ B. Change **yours** to **they**.
   ○ C. Change **yours** to **their**.
   ○ D. No change needs to be made to this sentence.

4. How should this sentence be changed?

   > Will strummed him guitar and invited everyone to sing.

   ○ A. Change **him** to **he**.
   ○ B. Change **him** to **his**.
   ○ C. Change **him** to **we**.
   ○ D. No change needs to be made to this sentence.

Reading & Writing Companion

Extended Writing Project

Grammar: Formal and Informal Language

Different types of language are appropriate for different situations. Follow these rules when using formal and informal language:

Rules	Informal	Formal
Using a contraction makes language sound more informal.	I can't do it.	I cannot do it.
When writing an academic essay, it is necessary to use formal language.	We should totally focus on how crazy fast animals are disappearing.	The most important fact to consider about endangered animal species is the rate of their disappearance.
When conversing with a friend, it is appropriate to use informal language.	What's up, Sam?	Hello, Sam. How are you doing today?

The type of language you use affects the tone of your writing or speaking.

Formal	Informal
Papa took the towel Mama handed him, but did not reply immediately. I was just inside the kitchen dipping out the butter beans. I moved closer to the window so that I could hear his answer. Roll of Thunder, Hear My Cry	You ain't one of them bad boys looking for my treasure, is you? The Treasure of Lemon Brown
I resent that this article implies volleyball players have somehow chosen an "easier" path. We're on the Same Team	She was as crotchety and sullen as a three-legged mule, and I was not quite sure why. Walk Two Moons

Reading & Writing Companion

Grammar: Formal and Informal Language

Introduce the Skill

Review the image and definition for formal and informal language as a class.

- **formal language:** professional and grammatically correct language
- **informal language:** natural or spontaneous language, often not grammatically correct
- **contraction:** shortening two words into one word using an apostrophe

Discuss the Model

1. When should you use formal language? You should use formal language when writing an academic essay and talking to your teachers.

2. When should you use informal language? You can use informal language when talking to your friends.

⚙ Your Turn

Ask students to complete the Your Turn activity.

QUESTION 1

A. Incorrect.

B. Incorrect.

C. **Correct.** This example uses formal language and eliminates contractions.

D. Incorrect.

QUESTION 2

A. **Correct.** This example uses the informal language of "hey dude" and "do an example."

B. Incorrect.

C. Incorrect.

D. Incorrect.

QUESTION 3

A. Incorrect.

B. **Correct.** This sentence has no contractions.

C. Incorrect.

D. Incorrect.

↻ YOUR TURN

1. How could this sentence be changed from informal to formal language?

   > Hey dude, what's happenin' today?

   ○ A. Hey, what's gonna happen today?
   ○ B. Hello, what's going on today?
   ○ C. Hello. What are you doing today?
   ○ D. Dude, what's going on today?

2. How could these sentences be changed from formal to informal language?

   > Good afternoon. Please include an example in your essay.

   ○ A. Hey dude, also do an example when you write that essay.
   ○ B. Please include an example in your essay.
   ○ C. Include an example in your essay.
   ○ D. Hello. Make sure to include an example.

3. How can this sentence be changed to eliminate contractions?

   > I'm thinking there's a good chance you won't be able to try the cake today.

   ○ A. I am thinking there is a good chance you won't be able to try the cake today.
   ○ B. I think there is a good chance you will not be able to try the cake today.
   ○ C. I'm thinking there is a good chance you will not be able to try the cake today.
   ○ D. I'm thinking there's a good chance you will not be able to try the cake today.

Reading & Writing Companion

Extended Writing Project

Argumentative Writing Process: Edit and Publish

PLAN	DRAFT	REVISE	EDIT AND PUBLISH

You have revised your argument based on your peer feedback and your own examination.

Now it is time to edit your argumentative essay. When you revised, you focused on the content of your argument. You looked at your use of reasons, evidence, specific examples, and transitions. When you edit, you focus on the mechanics of your essay, paying close attention to things like grammar, spelling, and punctuation.

Use the checklist below to guide you as you edit:

☐ Have I followed basic spelling rules for words with *ie/ei*, unstressed vowels, suffixes, and prefixes?

☐ Have I correctly used possessive pronouns?

☐ Have I used formal language and eliminated informal language?

☐ Have I spelled everything correctly?

☐ Do I have any sentence fragments or run-on sentences?

Notice some edits Ellie has made:

- Used basic spelling rules to correct spelling errors.

- Fixed errors with possessive pronouns.

- Corrected informal language, changing it to have a more formal and appropriate tone.

Argumentative Writing Process: Edit and Publish

Practice with Student Model (optional)

Provide groups with a different section of Ellie's draft. Each group should practice editing Ellie's model using the checklist in the lesson: Has she:

☐ followed basic spelling rules for words with *ie/ei*, unstressed vowels, suffixes, and prefixes?

☐ correctly used possessive pronouns?

☐ used formal language and eliminated informal language?

☐ spelled everything correctly?

☐ corrected any sentence fragments or run-on sentences?

After the groups have finished, call volunteers from each group to make edits until all the mistakes have been found and edited, pausing to discuss points of disagreement.

 SPEAKING FRAMES

- Ellie (did / did not) follow the basic spelling rules for words with *ie/ei*, unstressed vowels, suffixes, and prefixes when she wrote ____.
- Ellie (did / did not) use possessive pronouns correctly when she wrote ____.
- Ellie (did / did not) make her writing more formal when she wrote ____.
- ____ is spelled incorrectly. The correct spelling is ____.
- ____ is an example of a (run-on sentence / sentence fragment) that Ellie (has / has not) corrected.

Write

After students finish editing, suggest, if there's time, that they set their arguments aside for a few minutes, and that they then proofread them one more time. Once students have completed their writing, have them submit their work.

✓ CHECK FOR SUCCESS

If students struggle to edit successfully, help them determine where edits are needed, and what changes need to be made.

Direct students to the grammar lessons in this unit if they are uncertain about the rules for specific concepts.

ELL READ ALOUD

Encourage students to read their arguments aloud to themselves or to a partner in order to catch any remaining mistakes.

A READ ALOUD

Encourage students to read their arguments aloud to themselves or to an on-grade-level peer in order to catch any remaining mistakes.

B PLAY CRITIC

Have students review their writing for any potential weaknesses or places in which they might have gone in different directions. Invite them to operate as their own critics—how might the ending of their creative piece be resolved differently? How might someone with an opposing point of view challenge a point made in their essay? What other piece of evidence might have been included in their essay? Have students critically analyze an aspect of their own work from an outsider's perspective.

Relationships help you work hard to ~~acheive~~ achieve your goals. Without Mr. Lin's advice, I ~~stil~~ still would have been afraid to try my hardest. Even though Mr. Lin was my theater teacher, ~~his~~ he helped me to become a better student in my other classes. One time I had to give a talk in science class about how volcanoes erupt. ~~It was so crazy because~~ I did my research, but I felt nervous~~;~~ . I wanted a good ~~grad~~ grade. I ~~really really didn't~~ did not want to get laughed at. In front of the class, I made ~~mine~~ my fears go away by remembering what Mr. Lin taught me. I ~~pertended~~ pretended I was acting the part of a volcano expert in a play.

✎ WRITE

Use the questions on the previous page, as well as your peer reviews, to help you evaluate your argumentative essay to determine areas that need editing. Then edit your argument to correct those errors.

Once you have made all your corrections, you are ready to publish your work. You can distribute your writing to family and friends, hang it on a bulletin board, or post it on your blog. If you publish online, share the link with your family, friends, and classmates.

English Language Learner Resources

:::studysync®   USERS   ASSIGNMENTS

GRADE 6 > UNIT

You and Me
Core ELA
Grade 6
30 Days

Unit Overview

Integrated Reading and Writing

Extended Writing Project

ELL Resources

Novel Study

End-of-Unit Assessment

Instructional Path

The Other Side

A Role to Play

Add to booksh

6   7

Skill: Classroom Vocabulary

Students will learn and recognize academic classroom
vocabulary words and practice using them in a variety
of contexts.

Teacher Resources: Lesson Plan

&+ Assign

Skill: Making Connections

Students will learn and practice the skill of making
connections when reading in order to demonstrate
and improve comprehension.

Teacher Resources: Lesson Plan

&+ Assign

Lessons in the English Language Learner Resources section offer explicit ELL instruction. These lessons share a thematic and genre focus with all other lessons in the Core ELA unit.

The twenty ELL Resources are developed around two texts, "The Other Side" and "A Role to Play," and an Extended Oral Project. Each text is written at four distinct levels. For ELLs, these texts serve as structural and thematic models of authentic texts in the Integrated Reading and Writing section of the unit. Thus, teachers may use the ELL texts in place of or as extensions for "*Teenagers*" and *The Circuit*.

ELL lessons modify the routines used with texts in the Integrated Reading and Writing section. Explicit vocabulary instruction is emphasized, and reading and writing Skills lessons focus strongly on language acquisition and reading comprehension.

After reading texts about the power of relationships, students will complete an Extended Oral Project that can be used in place of or as an extension to the Extended Writing Project. In this unit, students will plan and present a personal address expressing gratitude to a person who has impacted them.

Focus on English Language Proficiency Levels

ADVANCED HIGH
ADVANCED
INTERMEDIATE
BEGINNING

ELL Resources provide targeted support for four levels of proficiency: Beginning, Intermediate, Advanced, and Advanced High. Instruction and scaffolds, as well as the texts themselves, are differentiated based on these levels.

Additional differentiated scaffolds include visual glossaries, speaking and writing frames, and suggested grouping for peer and teacher support. Lessons also include suggested extension activities to challenge Advanced and Advanced High students as they progress through the year.

ELL Resources

ELL TEXTS

The Other Side

- Skill: Sight Vocabulary and High-Frequency Words
- Skill: Demonstrating Listening Comprehension
- First Read
- Skill: Analyzing Expressions
- Skill: Sharing Information
- Skill: Spelling Patterns and Rules
- Close Read

A Role to Play

- Skill: Classroom Vocabulary
- Skill: Making Connections
- First Read
- Skill: Language Structures
- Skill: Drawing Inferences and Conclusions
- Skill: Pronouns and Antecedents
- Close Read

EXTENDED ORAL PROJECT

- Introduction
- Skill: Acquiring Vocabulary
- Plan

- Skill: Sentence Lengths
- Practice
- Present

The Other Side

FICTION

Introduction

Many of us know what it's like to wish for superpowers. We might sometimes wish we could do things nobody else can do, or know things nobody else could know. But if we did have these powers, would anyone else understand? For the narrator of the short story "The Other Side," an extraordinary experience leads to complicated feelings and big questions.

The passage opens with the narrator telling his sister, Alexandria, a secret about what happened to him earlier that morning. It was a typical Wednesday, but the narrator awoke before dawn with a feeling that he would soon be completely changed. He walked down the hall, expecting to arouse the attention of his family, but they all slept peacefully. Even the floor didn't creak where it usually did. When he arrived at the front door, he could feel a presence on the other side. He knew that once he opened it, he would never be the same. Collecting himself, he opened the door and was suddenly hyperaware of his environment: the colors, wind, and earth beneath his feet. Alexandria is amazed at this account, but the narrator feels guilty for burdening her. She asks if anyone besides her knows about his secret, and the narrator wonders if anyone else would even believe him.

ELL Summaries in multiple languages are available digitally.

 Audio and audio text highlighting are available with this text.

CONNECT TO ESSENTIAL QUESTION

How do relationships shape us?

In this story, a boy wakes up one morning after a life-changing experience. He knows nothing will ever be the same. The boy decides to tell his sister what he has become and what he can do now. Will she understand?

Core ELA Connections

Texts	Theme	Genre
Walk Two Moons	A young boy suddenly wakes up with special powers and struggles to explain them to his sister. The text builds on ideas of transformation, coming of age, and familial bonds.	This first-person fictional text relies on flashbacks and dialogue to relay events to the reader.

Differentiated Text Levels

ELL LEVEL	BEGINNING	INTERMEDIATE	ADVANCED	ADVANCED HIGH
WORD COUNT	269	405	459	547
LEXILE	170L	430L	530L	640L

Instructional Path

Skill: Sight Vocabulary and High-Frequency Words

Objectives: Students will be able to learn and recognize sight vocabulary and high-frequency words in English.

Objectives: Students will be able to recognize sight vocabulary and high-frequency words when listening and reading, and produce sight vocabulary and high-frequency words when speaking and writing.

Skill: Demonstrating Listening Comprehension

Objectives: Students will be able to learn and practice the skill of demonstrating listening comprehension when reading a new text.

Objectives: Students will be able to demonstrate listening comprehension using strategies presented in a video clip in which students read aloud, agree and disagree, answer questions, and build on ideas.

First Read: The Other Side

Objectives: Students will be able to perform an initial reading of a text using the strategy of demonstrating listening comprehension.

Objectives: Students will be able to demonstrate comprehension of a text by responding to questions orally and in writing using textual evidence.

Skill: Analyzing Expressions

Objectives: Students will be able to analyze expressions when reading.

Objectives: Students will be able to analyze expressions when reading and justify their thinking when speaking.

Skill: Sharing Information

Objectives: Students will be able to learn the skill of sharing information and practice distinguishing between asking and providing information.

Objectives: Students will be able to learn the skill of sharing information when speaking with peers.

Skill: Spelling Patterns and Rules

Objectives: Students will be able to recognize and apply spelling patterns and rules.

Objectives: Students will be able to recognize spelling patterns and rules when reading and apply spelling patterns and rules when writing.

Close Read: The Other Side

Objectives: Students will be able to perform a close reading of a text in order to share information with peers.

Objectives: Students will be able to demonstrate the ability to share information with peers by participating in a collaborative conversations and writing a short constructed response.

Progress Monitoring

Opportunities to Learn	Opportunities to Demonstrate Learning	Opportunities to Reteach
Sight Vocabulary and High-Frequency Words		
⚙ Skill: Sight Vocabulary and High-Frequency Words	⚙ Skill: Sight Vocabulary and High-Frequency Words 📖 First Read • Sight Vocabulary and High-Frequency Words	⚙ Spotlight Skill: Sight Vocabulary and High-Frequency Words
Demonstrating Listening Comprehension		
⚙ Skill: Demonstrating Listening Comprehension	⚙ Skill: Demonstrating Listening Comprehension 📖 First Read • Skills Focus	⚙ Spotlight Skill: Demonstrating Listening Comprehension
Analyzing Expressions		
⚙ Skill: Analyzing Expressions	⚙ Skill: Analyzing Expressions • Your Turn	⚙ Spotlight Skill: Analyzing Expressions
Sharing Information		
⚙ Skill: Sharing Information	⚙ Skill: Sharing Information • Your Turn 📖 Close Read • Complete Skills Focus • Write	⚙ Spotlight Skill: Sharing Information
Spelling Patterns and Rules		
⚙ Skill: Spelling Patterns and Rules	⚙ Skill: Spelling Patterns and Rules 📖 Close Read • Write	⚙ Spotlight Skill: Spelling Patterns and Rules

First Read

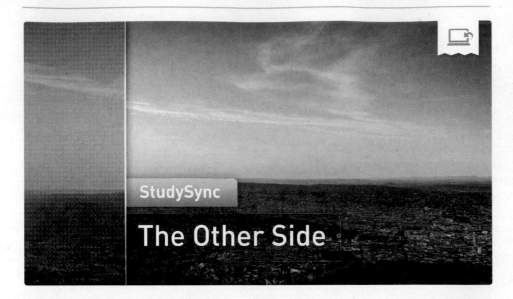

StudySync

The Other Side

Introduce the Text

As a class, watch the video preview ▶ and have students read the introduction in pairs to make connections to the video preview. Ask students various "wh" questions such as:

- What did you see in the video? How does it make you feel?
- What do you think the text will be about?
- Is there something in the video or introduction that surprised you?

> **ELL Beginning & Intermediate**
>
> **SPEAKING FRAMES**
> - I see ____. I feel ____.
> - I think the text will be about ____.
> - I was surprised by ____.

Practice Prereading Skill

Remind students that Demonstrating Listening Comprehension:

Helps you better understand the text. Listening to a story may help you notice details. Talking with another student can help you form new ideas. By listening closely and agreeing, disagreeing, and asking further questions about each other's ideas, you can develop a deeper understanding of the story than you would from just reading it alone.

Have students work in small, on-level groups to choral read or listen to the audio of the summary. Remind students to seek clarification from you or their peers as needed.

As students are working in small groups, circulate to listen for sample questions like:

- What does this word mean?
- Would you repeat that?

Activate Prior Knowledge and Experiences OPTIONAL

Have students make connections while practicing their oral language by discussing what they know about fantasy.

Generate a list (on the board or on paper) of any information or ideas your students have about fantasy.

Ask students to share where their background knowledge came from. For example, did their ideas come from a movie, friend, television show, book, or family member?

VOCABULARY

glanced
looked quickly

instant
a moment; a very short span of time

frowned
turned corners of the mouth down to show displeasure

reached
moved arm to touch or hold

creak
make a sound when moved or stepped on

grasped
held tightly

motionless
not moving

READ

 NOTES

1 I **glanced** at my sister, Alexandria, swaying under the tree in our backyard. How could I explain it? I couldn't keep it a secret. She knew there was more.

2 "What aren't you telling me?" she **frowned**. "This doesn't just happen. What did you do?"

3 In most ways, last Wednesday was normal. The sun took its place in the sky, and like countless times before, our neighborhood slowly came alive.

Reading & Writing Companion **113**

AUDIO TEXT HIGHLIGHTING

Allow students to use the audio text highlight feature to follow along as they read. Alternately, you may wish to work directly with students or group them in twos or threes for partner reading or choral reading.

The Other Side

 ## Preteach Vocabulary

Model the first word and example for the class.

1. The first word is *glanced* and its meaning is "looked quickly."

2. When I hear the word *glanced*, I think of when I take a brief look at something.

3. For example, when my dad is driving, he takes a brief look at the rearview mirror to see what is behind him. He *glances* at it from time to time.

4. This is an example of *glancing* because my dad doesn't look at the rearview mirror for a long time. He does it for only a brief time.

Continue this exercise with each word in the glossary, calling on individuals or groups of students to share out.

ELL **Beginning**

PRETEACH VOCABULARY

Use the gestures to clarify meanings.

- **glanced** (Glance at someone or something.)
- **frowned** (Make an unhappy face.)
- **creak** (Make a squeaking, creaking noise.)
- **motionless** (Be completely still, like a statue.)
- **instant** (Snap your fingers.)
- **reached** (Reach for something.)
- **grasped** (Hold something tightly.)

Sight Vocabulary and High-Frequency Words Focus

Remind students of the sight vocabulary and high-frequency words that they studied at the beginning of the unit. Point out that some of the words may be useful as they think about and discuss the text. For example:

- and (The wind **and** the earth . . .)
- can (I **can** not remember the last time I . . .)
- my (I looked at **my** sister . . .)
- said (Alexandria **said** that I was . . .)
- look (I **looked** at Alexandria, as she . . .)

TEXT TALK

1. What is the story about?
2. Who are the story's characters?
3. Where does the story take place?
4. How does the story make you feel?

ELL All Levels

SPEAKING FRAMES

Giving Information:
- This story is about ____.
- The story's characters are ____.
- This story takes place in ____.
- This story makes me feel ____.

Asking for Information:
- Can you explain ____?
- What do you think about ____?
- Why do you think ____?

The Other Side

 NOTES

4　What was unusual was that I woke up early. I can't remember the last time I was up before sunrise. That Wednesday something had woken me. I knew that there was no going back because I would be different.

5　I didn't mention that when I told Alexandria before. Now her eyes were asking me to help her understand.

6　"Listen," I pleaded. "I'm trying to explain."

7　That morning, I slipped out of my bedroom and walked slowly down the hallway. The house was silent and my mom and sister slept peacefully. Our dog, Bella, was curled up somewhere.

8　There was darkness in the hallway but I knew where I had to go. I waited for the floorboards to **creak** but they didn't.

9　I arrived at the front door, standing there **motionless**. At first, I felt the presence on the other side. Something was calling to me and waiting for me. I don't know how long the presence had been there, but it wasn't going anywhere. I didn't try to understand. How could I?

10　I couldn't breathe. I looked at the doorknob for a long, long time. I knew that once I opened the door, I wouldn't be the same. I thought of my family and wondered if they would understand. I wished I'd just stayed in bed.

11　I tried to collect myself, but my heart was racing. I turned the knob and stepped forward.

12　In an **instant** I was aware of *everything*: The colors, the wind, and the earth below me — I understood it and could feel it more than ever.

13　I **reached** out to touch it and I changed forever.

14　I looked at Alexandria, as she **grasped** the tree trunk, her mouth open in amazement. I couldn't imagine how this sounded. I felt guilty for burdening her. At the same time, I felt relieved.

15　"Does anyone else know?" Alexandria asked frantically, not even trying to hide her concern.

16　I shook my head. Who could understand — let alone believe — what I could do now?

First Read

Read the story. After you read, answer the Think Questions below.

☁ THINK QUESTIONS

1. Who is the story about? How are they related?

   The story is about _____.

   They are _____.

2. Where does the story take place?

   The story takes place _____.

3. How does Alexandria feel at the end of the story?

   Alexandria feels _____.

4. Use context to confirm the meaning of the word *motionless* as it is used in "The Other Side." Write your definition of *motionless* here.

   Motionless means _____.

   A context clue is _____.

5. What is another way to say that the boy *glanced* at Alexandria?

   The boy _____.

Reading & Writing Companion **115**

🖵 Think Questions

Circulate as students answer Think Questions independently. Answers will vary.

QUESTION 1: Comprehension

The main characters are a boy and a girl named Alexandria. They are siblings.

QUESTION 2: Comprehension

At the beginning, they are in their backyard, under a tree. Then the boy describes what happened to him Wednesday, inside their house.

QUESTION 3: Comprehension

Alexandria is worried about her brother. She asks him if he told anyone about his new powers.

QUESTION 4: Language

The boy is standing in front of the front door. He doesn't know what to do at first. That tells me that he is standing there without moving, or is motionless for a moment. A definition for *motionless* is "not moving."

QUESTION 5: Language

The boy took a brief look at Alexandria.

Skill: Analyzing Expressions

Introduce the Skill

Watch the Concept Definition video and read the definition for Analyzing Expressions.

TURN AND TALK

1. Have you learned a phrase in English that you didn't understand at first?

2. How did you figure out its meaning?

3. What are some idioms or expressions in English that you know?

ELL **Beginning & Intermediate**

SPEAKING FRAMES

- A phrase in English that I didn't understand at first is ____.
- I figured out its meaning using ____.
- An idiom or expression in English that I know is ____.

ELL **Advanced & Advanced High**

SPEAKING FRAMES

- A phrase in English that I didn't understand at first is ____.
- I figured out its meaning ____.
- Two idioms or expressions in English that I know are ____ and ____. The first one means ____. The second one means ____.

The Other Side

Skill: Analyzing Expressions

★ DEFINE

When you read, you may find English expressions that you do not know. An **expression** is a group of words that communicates an idea. Three types of expressions are **idioms**, **sayings**, and **figurative language**. They can be difficult to understand because the meanings of the words are different from their **literal**, or usual, meanings.

An **idiom** is an expression that is commonly known among a group of people. For example, "It's raining cats and dogs" means it is raining heavily. **Sayings** are short expressions that contain advice or wisdom. For instance: "Don't count your chickens before they hatch" means do not plan on something good happening before it happens. **Figurative** language is when you describe something by comparing it with something else, either directly (using the words like or as) or indirectly. For example, "I'm hungry as a horse" means I'm very hungry. None of the expressions are about actual animals.

••• CHECKLIST FOR ANALYZING EXPRESSIONS

To determine the meaning of an expression, remember the following:

✓ If you find a confusing group of words, it may be an expression. The meaning of words in expressions may not be their literal meaning.

- Ask yourself: Is this confusing because the words are new? Or because the words do not make sense together?

✓ Determining the overall meaning may require that you use one or more of the following:

- context clues
- a dictionary or other resource
- teacher or peer support

✓ Highlight important information before and after the expression to look for clues.

SKILL VOCABULARY

expression / la expresión *noun* a phrase used to express an idea COGNATE

literal / literal *adjective* describing the usual meaning of a word COGNATE

idiom / el modismo *noun* a common expression that cannot be taken literally

saying / el dicho *noun* an expression that contains advice or wisdom

YOUR TURN

Read the following excerpt from the "The Other Side." Then complete the multiple-choice questions below.

from **"The Other Side"**

I couldn't breathe. I looked at the doorknob for a long, long time. I knew that once I opened the door, I wouldn't be the same. I thought of my family and wondered if they would understand. I wished I'd just stayed in bed.

I tried to collect myself, but my heart was racing. I turned the knob and stepped forward.

In an instant I was aware of *everything*: The colors, the wind, and the earth below me — I understood it and could feel it more than ever.

I reached out to touch it and I changed forever.

1. What does the narrator mean when he says "my heart was racing"?

    ○ A. He is in a competition.
    ○ B. He is in love.
    ○ C. He is nervous.
    ○ D. He is excited.

2. Which context clue helped you determine the meaning of the expression?

    ○ A. "I couldn't breathe. I looked at the doorknob for a long, long time."
    ○ B. "I thought of my family and wondered if they would understand."
    ○ C. "I turned the knob and stepped forward."
    ○ D. "I reached out to touch it and I changed forever."

Please note that excerpts and passages in the StudySync® library and this workbook are intended as touchstones to generate interest in an author's work. The excerpts and passages do not substitute for the reading of entire texts, and StudySync® strongly recommends that students seek out and purchase the whole literary or informational work in order to experience it as the author intended. Links to online resellers are available in our digital library. In addition, complete works may be ordered through an authorized reseller by filling out and returning to StudySync® the order form enclosed in this workbook.

Reading & Writing Companion · **117**

Your Turn   Ask students to complete the Your Turn Activity.

QUESTION 1:   C) The boy is nervous and his heart is beating quickly.

QUESTION 2:   A) This shows the boy's hesitation.

Discuss the Skill Model

1. What expression confused the reader?

    "The sun took its place in the sky" and "our neighborhood slowly came alive."

2. Why was the reader confused?

    These phrases usually describe living things.

3. What does the reader do to analyze the expression?

    She reads on to look for context clues.

4. What do the context clues help the reader conclude?

    She concludes that the story started early in the morning, as the sun was rising. The expressions describe the rising sun and the people in the neighborhood waking up.

5. What can the reader do to check the meaning of the expressions in the text?

    Answers will vary, but should include consulting a teacher or peers for support.

ELL **Beginning & Intermediate**

Have students use the speaking frames and helpful terms to participate in the group discussion. If beginning students are hesitant to participate in a discussion, encourage them by prompting with *yes* or *no* questions.

Advanced & Advanced High

Have students use the speaking frames to participate in the group discussion.

SPEAKING FRAMES

- The student is confused by ____.
- She was confused because ____.
- The student looks for ____.
- She concludes ____.
- The reader can ____.

HELPFUL TERMS FOR DISCUSSION

- conclusion
- students
- literal
- analyze
- clues
- teacher
- expression
- confirm

Skill: Sharing Information

Introduce the Skill

Watch the Concept Definition video ▶ and read the definition for Sharing Information.

TURN AND TALK

1. Do you ever talk to friends about a movie or TV show you saw? Why?

2. What are the advantages of discussing ideas in a group rather than thinking on your own?

ELL **Beginning & Intermediate**

SPEAKING FRAMES

- I talk to friends about movies and TV shows because ____.
- Discussing in a group lets me ____.

ELL **Advanced & Advanced High**

SPEAKING FRAMES

- Talking about movies and TV shows lets me ____. For example, when my friends and I talked about ____, we realized that ____.
- Thinking on your own can let you ____, but discussing in a group lets you ____. This means that ____.

The Other Side

Skill: Sharing Information

★ DEFINE

Sharing information involves asking for and giving information. The process of sharing information with other students can help all students learn more and better understand a text or a topic. You can share information when you participate in **brief** discussions or **extended** speaking assignments.

••• CHECKLIST FOR SHARING INFORMATION

When you have to speak for an extended period of time, as in a discussion, you ask for and share information. To ask for and share information, you may use the following sentence frames:

✓ To ask for information:

- What do you think about _____?
- Do you agree that _____?
- What is your understanding of _____?

✓ To give information:

- I think _____.
- I agree because _____.
- My understanding is _____.

SKILL VOCABULARY

share / compartir *verb* to tell someone

brief / corto/a *adjective* short

extended / extendido/a *adjective* long   COGNATE

⟳ YOUR TURN

Watch the "The Lightning Thief" StudySyncTV episode ▶. After watching, sort the following statements from the episode into the appropriate columns:

	Statements
A	Makes me feel bad for him.
B	But Percy is not normal.
C	Do you think he is lying?
D	How do you know Percy is lonely?
E	I can feel it.
F	Can you prove it?

Asking for Information	Giving Information

Reading & Writing Companion 🖥 **119**

⚙ Your Turn Ask students to complete the Your Turn activity.

Asking for Information	Giving Information
How do you know Percy is lonely?	But Percy is not normal.
Do you think he is lying?	I can feel it.
Can you prove it?	Makes me feel bad for him.

⚙ Discuss the Skill Model

1. What does Sean do to have the group share information?

   Sean asks questions. For example, he asks Olivia, "How do you know that?"

2. What strategy do both use to share information?

   They ask and answer questions.

3. How does Sam share information when Sean asks the questions in the second video clip?

   Sam shares information by disagreeing with Sean and then making a statement.

4. How do the students improve the way they share information with one another?

   Sam asks for time to review the text. This allows the group the share details from the text.

ELL Beginning & Intermediate

Have students use the speaking frames and helpful terms to participate in the group discussion. If beginning students are hesitant to participate in a discussion, encourage them by prompting with *yes* or *no* questions.

Advanced & Advanced High

Have students use the speaking frames to participate in the group discussion.

SPEAKING FRAMES

- Sean asks ____.
- They ____ and ____ questions.
- Sam ____ and then makes a ____.
- The students improve the way they share information by ____.

HELPFUL TERMS FOR DISCUSSION

• answer	• ask	• information
• statement	• review	• disagree

Close Read

Model Skills Focus

Remind students of the Reading Skill Sharing Information. Tell students that asking for and giving information about a text can help improve their understanding. Direct students to the Skills Focus and remind them to track as you read aloud.

What do you think happened to the narrator? Use details from the text to support your ideas.

Model this activity for students:

- I am going to focus on the detail "There was darkness in the hallway but I knew where I had to go."

- I know that the narrator changed in some way. This details says that he knows where to go even though it is dark.

- It's hard to know where to go in the dark because it is difficult to see.

- This clue leads me to believe that maybe the narrator gained the ability to see in the dark!

Complete Skills Focus

Divide the class into even groups of three or four students. Prompt groups to:

- look for an unusual detail about the narrator or his sister

- imagine what this detail could mean about the narrator's change in the story

- come to an agreement as a group about what happened to the narrator

Circulate and monitor groups as they work.

THE OTHER SIDE   Close Read

✎ WRITE

NARRATIVE: Think about the end of the story. How has the main character changed? What do you think happens next? Recount the events at the end of the story and describe what you think would happen if the story continued. Pay attention to the *IE* and *EI* spelling rule as you write.

Use the checklist below to guide you as you write.

☐ How was the boy changed?

☐ How does Alexandria feel and what does she do?

☐ How does it end?

Use the sentence frames to organize and write your narrative.

I shook my head. Who could understand — let alone believe — what I could do now?

I couldn't believe that now I _____.

Alexandria was _____.

Then, _____.

Suddenly, _____.

I decided _____.

120 Reading & Writing Companion

Collaborative Conversation

Group students so they have a representative from each of the original groups. Have students share their ideas with their new group members.

- Did the idea make sense?
- Did the idea have support from the text?
- Did imagining these ideas help me better understand the story?

Collaborative Conversation

ELL **BEGINNING, INTERMEDIATE** Use the word bank to participate in the group discussion.

ADVANCED Use the speaking frames to participate in the group discussion.

BEGINNING, INTERMEDIATE	ADVANCED
Word Bank	**Speaking Frames**
• detail • helped me understand • support • now I understand • imagine • made sense	• The answers (did / did not) ___ make sense because ___. • The answers (did / did not) ___ have support from the text. For example ___. • The answers enhanced my understanding of the story because ___.

Write

Ask students to complete the writing assignment. Remind students to pay attention to spelling patterns in words.

ELL **BEGINNING** Write a response using the paragraph frames and word banks.

INTERMEDIATE Write a response using the paragraph frames.

INTERMEDIATE		
BEGINNING		
Paragraph Frames		**Word Bank**
• I shook my head. Who could understand—let alone believe—what I could do now?	• I couldn't believe that now I ___. • Alexandria was ___. • Then, ___. Suddenly, ___. I decided ___.	• power • bad • surprised • good • afraid • happy • amazing • worried • changed • feel

A Role to Play

FICTION

Introduction

On a day like any other day in science class, Bryan gets unwelcome news. He is assigned a role for a group project. He doubts his own abilities as he thinks back to a role he was assigned for a group project in sixth grade. He had wanted to do well, but he let his group down. Now Bryan must confront his fears and fulfill his role. Can he do it?

Bryan's science teacher announces that there is a group project due next week and each member of the group has a role to play. This announcement makes Bryan remember last year's language arts class. Bryan was assigned to pick out passages from a text and explain their significance. When his group members checked in with him, Bryan assured them that he was getting the work done. He actually lied because he did not understand the assignment. He still feels guilty about it. For the science project, Bryan is assigned the role of webmaster and has to make a website for his group. The next day, he explains to his teacher that he can't do it. She doesn't agree and reminds him that his videos for the art club have been great. Bryan realizes that his teacher might be right and thinks that he could be a good webmaster.

ELL Summaries in multiple languages are available digitally.

 Audio and audio text highlighting are available with this text.

CONNECT TO ESSENTIAL QUESTION

How do relationships shape us?

Bryan must participate in a group project. Last year's group project was disastrous because of him. Now he doubts his abilities and fears the outcome of the upcoming group project. Will he let his group down?

Core ELA Connections

Texts	Theme	Genre
The Circuit	Bryan doubts his abilities when he is assigned an important role in a group project for his science class. The text builds on the idea that even the biggest challenges are manageable if with support.	Told with a limited third-person narrator, "A Role to Play" portrays the personal thoughts of the main character, reminiscent of a memoir.

Differentiated Text Levels

ELL LEVEL	BEGINNING	INTERMEDIATE	ADVANCED	ADVANCED HIGH
WORD COUNT	255	396	445	531
LEXILE	320L	450L	520L	570L

Instructional Path

The print teacher's edition includes essential point-of-use instruction and planning tools. Complete lesson plans and program documents appear in your digital teacher account.

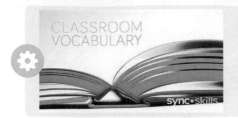

Skill: Classroom Vocabulary

Objectives: Students will be able to learn and recognize classroom vocabulary words and practice using them in a variety of contexts in English.

Objectives: Students will be able to recognize classroom vocabulary when listening and reading, and produce classroom vocabulary when speaking and writing.

Skill: Making Connections

Objectives: Students will be able to learn and practice the skill of making connections when reading a new text to improve comprehension.

Objectives: Students will be able to make connections in a new or unfamiliar text by making connections to themselves, the world, and other texts.

First Read: A Role to Play

Objectives: Students will be able to perform an initial reading of a text using the strategy of making connections.

Objectives: Students will be able to demonstrate comprehension of a text by responding to questions orally and in writing using textual evidence.

Skill: Language Structures

Objectives: Students will be able to analyze language structures.

Objectives: Students will be able to distinguish between different language structures when reading and demonstrate their understanding of adjective-noun structures when speaking.

Skill: Drawing Inferences and Conclusions

Objectives: Students will be able to draw inferences and conclusions.

Objectives: Students will be able to draw inferences and conclusions and justify those inferences and conclusions when speaking.

Skill: Pronouns and Antecedents

Objectives: Students will be able to recognize and apply pronoun and antecedent agreement.

Objectives: Students will be able to recognize pronoun and antecedent agreement when reading and apply pronoun and antecedent agreement when writing.

Close Read: A Role to Play

Objectives: Students will be able to perform a close reading of a text in order to draw inferences and conclusions .

Objectives: Students will be able to demonstrate an ability to draw inferences and conclusions by participating in a collaborative conversations and writing a short constructed response.

Progress Monitoring

Opportunities to Learn	Opportunities to Demonstrate Learning	Opportunities to Reteach

Classroom Vocabulary

⚙ Skill: Classroom Vocabulary	⚙ Skill: Classroom Vocabulary ▣ First Read • Classroom Vocabulary	⚙ Spotlight Skill: Classroom Vocabulary

Making Connections

⚙ Skill: Making Connections	⚙ Skill: Making Connections ▣ First Read • Skills Focus	⚙ Spotlight Skill: Making Connections

Language Structures

⚙ Skill: Language Structures	⚙ Skill: Language Structures • Your Turn	⚙ Spotlight Skill: Language Structures

Drawing Inferences and Conclusions

⚙ Skill: Drawing Inferences and Conclusions	⚙ Skill: Drawing Inferences and Conclusions • Your Turn ▣ Close Read • Complete Skills Focus • Write	⚙ Spotlight Skill: Drawing Inferences and Conclusions

Pronouns and Antecedents

⚙ Skill: Pronouns and Antecedents	⚙ Skill: Pronouns and Antecedents ▣ Close Read • Write	⚙ Spotlight Skill: Pronouns and Antecedents

First Read

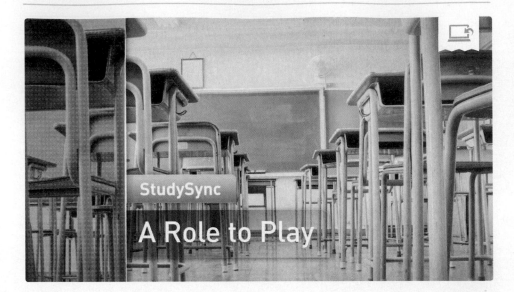

Introduce the Text

As a class, watch the video preview ▶ and have students read the introduction in pairs to make connections to the video preview. Ask students various "wh" questions such as:

- What did you see in the video? How does it make you feel?
- What do you think the text will be about?
- Is there something in the video or introduction that surprised you?

> **ELL** **Beginning & Intermediate**
>
> **SPEAKING FRAMES**
> - I see ____. I feel ____.
> - I think the text will be about ____.
> - I was surprised by ____.

Practice Prereading Skill

Remind students that Making Connections:

Helps you better understand a text by connecting what you read to your own experiences, to other texts you have read, or to the world around you.

Have students work in small, homogeneous groups to make connections to the summary.

As students are working in small groups, circulate to listen for sample connections such as:

- *What happened to Bryan reminds me of . . .*
- *This is almost like the story . . .*

Activate Prior Knowledge and Experiences OPTIONAL

Have students make connections while practicing their oral language by discussing what they know about the environment.

Generate a list (on the board or on paper) of any information or ideas your students have about the environment.

Ask students to share where their background knowledge came from. For example, did their ideas come from a movie, friend, television show, book, or family member?

VOCABULARY

 environment
the natural world

 nervous
anxious, agitated, worried

 conservation
protection of the natural environment

 webmaster
a person who maintains a website

 erratically
moving or behaving in a way that is not usual or predictable

 NOTES

READ

1 Bryan sat in science class. "Next week, we will be finishing our unit on the **environment** and **conservation**," Mrs. Jesky said. "So it's time to show what you have learned. You will complete a group project on conservation. I will be assigning each person in the group a role. Your role will help the group complete the project."

2 At once, Bryan felt his palms get damp. He told himself to breathe. He could feel his heart thumping **erratically**. *Group project? Roles?* he thought. *Anything but that.* It was like being back in sixth-grade language arts. Bryan and his group had to prepare a presentation on their book. Their teacher, Mr. Mack, gave each person a role. Bryan's role was to pick important passages from the text and explain their significance. Bryan was **nervous**. He wasn't sure how to do his task. His group asked a few times about his progress. He said he was almost done. But it was a lie. A year later, he still felt guilty for letting his group down.

122 Reading & Writing Companion

Preteach Vocabulary

Model the first word and example for the class.

1. The first word is *environment* and its meaning is "the natural world."

2. When I hear the word *environment*, I think of the landscape outdoors and how it changes from place to place.

3. For example, a polar bear lives in a cold *environment*, and a lizard lives in a dry *environment*.

4. Your *environment* can change if you move from one place to another.

Continue this exercise with each word in the glossary, calling on individuals or groups of students to share out.

ELL **Beginning**

PRETEACH VOCABULARY
Use the gestures to clarify meanings.

- **environment** (Gesture expansively out the window.)
- **conservation** (Hold a houseplant protectively.)
- **erratically** (Walk in a zigzag path.)
- **nervous** (Pantomime anxiety by rubbing your hands together and looking around.)
- **webmaster** (Pretend to tap on a keyboard.)

AUDIO TEXT HIGHLIGHTING

Allow students to use the audio text highlight feature to follow along as they read. Alternately, you may wish to work directly with students or group them in twos or threes for partner reading or choral reading.

Classroom Language Focus

Remind students of the sight vocabulary and high-frequency words that they studied at the beginning of the unit. Point out that some of the words may be useful as they think about and discuss the text. For example:

- do (He was not sure how to **do** . . .)
- ask (Bryan's group **asks** him about . . .)
- read (In language arts, students **read** . . .)
- teacher (Mrs. Jesky is Bryan's **teacher** for . . .)
- talk (In sixth grade, Bryan had to **talk** about . . .)

TEXT TALK

Have students discuss the questions in small groups. Circulate and check for understanding.

1. What is the story about?
2. Who are the story's characters?
3. Where does the story take place?
4. How does the story make you feel?

ELL All Levels

SPEAKING FRAMES

Giving Information:

- This story is about ____.
- The story's characters are ____.
- This story takes place in ____.
- This story makes me feel ____.

Asking for Information:

- Can you explain ____?
- What do you think about ____?
- Why do you think ____?

3   Back in science class, Bryan tried to focus. He looked about the room tentatively. Mrs. Jesky was explaining the project. "With your group, you will be creating a Web page to explain your idea for a community conservation project. Your role will be based on what you're good at and like to do."

4   Bryan was preoccupied with the science project. Mrs. Jesky gave Bryan the role of **webmaster**. It was his job to take the group's ideas and put them into a website. *Why webmaster? Why not researcher? Why not spokesperson?* He wasn't sure he could do it. It was just like sixth-grade language arts.

5   Bryan walked slowly into science class the next day. He usually showed more energy. Mrs. Jesky noticed the change in his demeanor. "Bryan, what's wrong?" she asked.

6   "It's the project," he said. "I don't think I can do it."

7   Mrs. Jesky said, "Bryan, I gave you that role for a good reason. Those videos and presentations you are making for Ms. Reed's art club are great! You are good at presenting information in a way that people understand."

8   Bryan thought about that. Finally, he smiled. "Maybe you're right," he said. "I do really like making those videos. And people have told me they are good. Maybe I can be a good webmaster."

9   Mrs. Jesky smiled. "I know you can."

Reading & Writing Companion   **123**

First Read

Read the story. After you read, answer the Think Questions below.

☁ THINK QUESTIONS

1. What role does Mrs. Jesky give Bryan?

   Mrs. Jesky gives Bryan _____ .

2. Why did Mrs. Jesky give Bryan that role?

   She gave him that role because _____ .

3. What happened to Bryan when he participated in a group project in sixth grade?

   When Bryan participated in the group project _____
   _____ .

4. Use context to confirm the meaning of the word *webmaster* as it is used in "A Role to Play." Write your definition of *webmaster* here.

   Webmaster means _____ .

   A context clue is _____ .

5. What is another way to say that your heart is thumping *erratically*?

   Your heart is thumping _____ .

Think Questions

Circulate as students answer Think Questions independently. Answers will vary.

QUESTION 1: Comprehension

She wants him to be the webmaster.

QUESTION 2: Comprehension

He is good at presenting information. He made great videos for the art club.

QUESTION 3: Comprehension

Answers will vary but may include the following examples:

- Mr. Mack gave him a task he did not understand.
- "A year later, he still felt guilty for letting his group down."

Student responses should provide an example from the text and an explanation that describes how the example bothered Bryan.

QUESTION 4: Language

The story says, "It was his job to take the group's ideas and put them into a website." A webmaster must be someone who sets up a website.

QUESTION 5: Language

Your heart is thumping wildly.

Skill: Language Structures

Introduce the Skill

Watch the Concept Definition video and read the definition for Language Structures.

TURN AND TALK

1. How can you tell who is speaking in a story?

2. When a sentence is long and complicated, how do you figure out what it means?

3. How could breaking a sentence into parts help you understand it better?

ELL Beginning & Intermediate

SPEAKING FRAMES

- A sentence with an unusual word order is ____.
- To understand it, I ____.

ELL Advanced & Advanced High

SPEAKING FRAMES

- A basic structure for English sentences is ____. For example, ____.
- Instead of being basic, some sentences are ____. For example, ____.

Skill:
Language Structures

★ DEFINE

In every language, there are rules that tell how to **structure** sentences. These rules define the correct order of words. In the English language, for example, a **basic** structure for sentences is subject, verb, and object. Some sentences have more **complicated** structures.

You will encounter both basic and complicated **language structures** in the classroom materials you read. Being familiar with language structures will help you better understand the text.

••• CHECKLIST FOR LANGUAGE STRUCTURES

To improve your comprehension of language structures, do the following:

✓ Monitor your understanding.

- Ask yourself: Why do I not understand this sentence? Is it because I do not understand some of the words? Or is it because I do not understand the way the words are ordered in the sentence?

✓ Break down the sentence into its parts.

✓ Confirm your understanding with a peer or teacher.

✓ In English, adjectives almost always come before the noun. Example: *He had a **big dog**.*

- A **noun** names a person, place, thing, or idea.

- An **adjective** modifies, or describes, a noun or a pronoun

- If there is more than one adjective, they usually appear in the following order separated by a comma: quantity or number, quality or opinion, size, age, shape, color. Example: *He had a **big, brown dog**.*

- If there is more than one adjective from the same category, include the word *"and."* Example: *He had a **brown and white dog**.*

✓ Ask yourself: What are the nouns in this sentence? What adjectives describe them? In what order are the nouns and adjectives?

Reading & Writing Companion   **125**

V SKILL VOCABULARY

structure / la estructura *noun* the order of parts **COGNATE**

basic / básico/a *adjective* the most important parts without anything extra **COGNATE**

complicated / complicado/a *adjective* having many parts **COGNATE**

language structure / la estructura del lenguaje *noun* the order of words in a sentence

YOUR TURN

Read each sentence in the first column. Then complete the chart by writing the words and phrases into the "Adjective" and "Noun" columns. The first row has been done as an example.

Sentence	Adjective	Noun
You will complete a group project on conservation.	group	project
Bryan's role was to pick important passages from the text and explain their significance.		
His group asked a few times about his progress.		
Back in science class, Bryan tried to focus.		
Bryan, I gave you that role for a good reason.		

Reading & Writing Companion

Please note that excerpts and passages in the StudySync® library and this workbook are intended as touchstones to generate interest in an author's work. The excerpts and passages do not substitute for the reading of entire texts, and StudySync® strongly recommends that students seek out and purchase the whole literary or informational work in order to experience it as the author intended. Links to online resellers are available in our digital library. In addition, complete works may be ordered through an authorized reseller by filling out and returning to StudySync® the order form enclosed in this workbook.

Your Turn   Ask students to complete the Your Turn activity.

Sentence	Adjective	Noun
Bryan's role was to pick important passages from the text and explain their significance.	important	passages
His group asked a few times about his progress.	few	times
Back in science class, Bryan tried to focus.	science	class
Bryan, I gave you that role for a good reason.	good	reason

Discuss the Skill Model

1. Why does the reader highlight the sentence in yellow?

   She highlights the sentence because she is confused about the phrase "sixth-grade language arts."

2. Why does the reader highlight the sentence in different colors?

   She uses different colors to identify the noun and the adjective.

3. How does this help the reader?

   She knows what "language arts" means and determines that "sixth-grade" provides more description.

4. What does the reader do to confirm her understanding?

   She asks her teacher if her understanding is right.

ELL **Beginning & Intermediate**

Have students use the speaking frames and helpful terms to participate in the group discussion. If beginning students are hesitant to participate in a discussion, encourage them by prompting with *yes* or *no* questions.

Advanced & Advanced High

Have students use the speaking frames to participate in the group discussion.

SPEAKING FRAMES

- The reader highlights the sentence because she is ___.
- The reader highlights in different colors to identify ___.
- This helps the reader ___. She is able to ___.
- Finally, the reader asks her teacher to ___.

HELPFUL TERMS FOR DISCUSSION

- determine
- identify
- understanding
- analyze
- teacher
- noun
- confused
- confirm
- adjective

Skill: Drawing Inferences and Conclusions

Introduce the Skill

Watch the Concept Definition video ▶ and read the definition for Drawing Inferences and Conclusions.

TURN AND TALK

1. How can you sometimes tell how your best friend is feeling without even talking to him or her?

2. How can you use your own experiences to draw conclusions about your friend's feelings?

3. What are some things that people do that can help you conclude that they are sad/mad/happy?

ELL **Beginning & Intermediate**

SPEAKING FRAMES

- I know how my friend is feeling by looking at ____.
- My own experiences help me understand when my friend feels ____.
- When people are sad/mad/happy, they might ____.

ELL **Advanced & Advanced High**

SPEAKING FRAMES

- When I see my friend ____, I know he/she feels ____.
- My own experiences with ____ help me understand when my friend feels ____.
- When people are sad/mad/happy, they might ____. For example, ____.

Skill: Drawing Inferences and Conclusions

★ DEFINE

Making **inferences** means connecting your experiences with what you read. Authors do not always tell readers directly everything that takes place in a story or text. You need to use clues to infer, or make a guess, about what is happening. To make an inference, first find facts, details, and examples in the text. Then think about what you already know. Combine the **textual evidence** with your **prior knowledge** to draw a **conclusion** about what the author is trying to communicate.

Making inferences and drawing conclusions can help you better understand what you are reading. It may also help you search for and find the author's message in the text.

••• CHECKLIST FOR DRAWING INFERENCES AND CONCLUSIONS

In order to make inferences and draw conclusions, do the following:

✓ Look for information that is missing from the text or that is not directly stated.

  • Ask yourself: What is confusing? What is missing?

✓ Think about what you already know about the topic.

  • Ask yourself: Have I had a similar experience in my life? Have I learned about this subject in another class?

✓ Combine clues from the text with prior knowledge to make an inference and draw a conclusion.

  • Think: I can conclude _____, because the text says _____ and I know that _____.

✓ Use textual evidence to support your inference and make sure that it is valid.

Reading & Writing Companion   **127**

V SKILL VOCABULARY

inference / la inferencia *noun* a conclusion or idea based on details from the text, as well as prior knowledge or experience COGNATE

text evidence / evidencia del texto *noun* details from the text that a reader can use to support their ideas

background knowledge / conocimiento previo *noun* information a person has gained through reading and experience

conclusion / la conclusión *noun* a final opinion or decision COGNATE

⟳ YOUR TURN

Read the following excerpt from "A Role to Play." Then, complete the multiple-choice questions below.

---

from "A Role to Play"

Back in science class, Bryan tried to focus. He looked about the room tentatively. Mrs. Jesky was explaining the project. "With your group, you will be creating a Web page to explain your idea for a community conservation project. Your role will be based on what you're good at and like to do."

Bryan was preoccupied with the science project. Mrs. Jesky gave Bryan the role of webmaster. It was his job to take the group's ideas and put them into a website. *Why webmaster? Why not researcher? Why not spokesperson?* He wasn't sure he could do it. It was just like sixth-grade language arts.

---

1. At the beginning of this excerpt, Bryan feels:

   ○ A. embarrassed by his lack of talent
   ○ B. anxious and unable to concentrate
   ○ C. angry at his teacher and classmates
   ○ D. frightened by the events in the room

2. A detail that best supports this conclusion is:

   ○ A. "tried to focus"
   ○ B. "Mrs. Jesky was explaining"
   ○ C. "With your group"
   ○ D. "what you're good at"

3. At the end of the excerpt, Bryan wonders whether:

   ○ A. Mrs. Jesky will let him quit
   ○ B. he belongs in a different class
   ○ C. other students are laughing at him
   ○ D. another role would suit him better

4. A detail that best supports this conclusion is:

   ○ A. "preoccupied with the science project"
   ○ B. "take the group's ideas"
   ○ C. *"Why not researcher?"*
   ○ D. "like sixth-grade language arts"

⚙ Your Turn Ask students to complete the Your Turn Activity.

QUESTION 1: B) Bryan is having trouble focusing.

QUESTION 2: A) This shows that Bryan is not able to pay attention.

QUESTION 3: D) Bryan is not sure he wants to be webmaster.

QUESTION 4: C) Bryan asks himself why he can't have a different role.

⚙ Discuss the Skill Model

1. What kinds of clues is the reader looking for?

   He is looking for clues that tell about Bryan's feelings.

2. What clues does the student highlight in the first annotation? What does he conclude?

   He highlights "palms get damp" and "heart beating erratically." He concludes that Bryan feels anxious about the group project.

3. How does the reader use his own experience to make inferences and draw conclusions?

   He thinks about how he feels when he acts the way Bryan acts.

4. What clues confirm his conclusion?

   He highlights "*Anything but that,*" which confirms Bryan's feelings about the project.

5. What can the reader do to check his conclusions about the text?

   He can share his ideas with a partner.

ELL Beginning & Intermediate

Have students use the <u>speaking frames</u> and <u>helpful terms</u> to participate in the group discussion. If beginning students are hesitant to participate in a discussion, encourage them by prompting with *yes* or *no* questions.

Advanced & Advanced High

Have students use the <u>speaking frames</u> to participate in the group discussion.

SPEAKING FRAMES

- The reader is looking for clues about ____.
- The student highlights ____ in the text.
- The student concludes that ____.
- He thinks about ____.
- The reader confirms his conclusion by ____.
- The reader can also ____.

HELPFUL TERMS FOR DISCUSSION

- conclude
- experience
- confirm
- personal
- feels
- inference
- background knowledge
- partner
- text evidence
- details
- feelings
- acts

Close Read

Model Skills Focus

Remind students of the Reading Skill Drawing Inferences and Conclusions. Tell students that readers often have to draw inferences and conclusions about the way characters are feeling and the reasons for their feelings. Direct students to the Skills Focus and remind them to track as you read aloud.

Draw conclusions about Bryan's feelings in the beginning, middle, and end of the story. Find evidence to support your conclusions.

Model this activity for students:

- I am going to focus on the beginning of the story.

- The author says, "Bryan felt his palms get damp."

- I know from personal experience that people's palms get damp when they are stressed or nervous. I can conclude from this evidence that Bryan is nervous.

Complete Skills Focus

Divide students into three even groups. Assign each group the following tasks:

- Draw a conclusion about how Bryan feels in the beginning of the story.

- Draw a conclusion about how Bryan feels in the middle of the story.

- Draw a conclusion about how Bryan feels in the end of the story.

Circulate and monitor groups as they work.

Close Read

✏ WRITE

LITERARY ANALYSIS: Why is Bryan nervous? How does the author show that something in his past is worrying him now? Write a short paragraph explaining why Bryan is nervous about working on a class project. Support your writing with evidence and specific details from the text, along with your personal experience. Pay attention to matching pronouns and antecedents as you write.

Use the checklist below to guide you as you write.

☐ How does Bryan feel?

☐ How do you know?

☐ Why does Bryan feel this way?

☐ How do you know?

Use the sentence frames to organize and write your literary analysis.

I believe that Bryan feels _____

because _____.

The passage supports my conclusion about _____

by telling about _____.

Reading & Writing Companion 129

Collaborative Conversation

Arrange students so they have a representative from each original group. Prompt students to share their evidence and conclusions, and give groups time to add to their notes where needed.

- Did we all agree on the conclusions?
- Did all the conclusions have evidence for support?
- Did drawing conclusions help me better understand the story?

Collaborative Conversation

SCAFFOLDS

ELL **BEGINNING, INTERMEDIATE** Use the word bank to participate in the group discussion.

ADVANCED Use the speaking frames to participate in the group discussion.

BEGINNING, INTERMEDIATE	ADVANCED
Word Bank	**Speaking Frames**
• helped us conclude • excited • does not like • past experience • nervous • group projects • unsure • infer	• We concluded that ____. • The evidence we used was ____. • This helped me better understand the story because ____.

Write

Ask students to complete the writing assignment. Remind students to pay attention to accurately matching pronouns with antecedents.

ELL **BEGINNING** Write a response using the paragraph frames and word banks.

INTERMEDIATE Write a response using the paragraph frames.

INTERMEDIATE		
BEGINNING		
Paragraph Frames		**Word Bank**
• I believe that Bryan feels ____ because ____.	• The passage supports my conclusion about ____ by telling about ____.	• nervous • evidence • earlier • anxious • guilty

You and Me

In the Extended Oral Project, students plan, draft, practice, and deliver an oral presentation that ties into the theme of the unit and spans informative, argumentative, and narrative genres. Lessons provide explicit instruction to prepare students for the unique challenges of an oral presentation, and to help break down the genre characteristics of each prompt. At each step in the process, students focus in-depth on specific writing and speaking skills as they brainstorm, organize, and refine their presentation. Students also receive discussion prompts and frames to guide them in providing effective peer feedback as they practice and discuss in small group before presenting to the class on the final day.

CONNECT TO ESSENTIAL QUESTION

How do relationships shape us?

In this unit, students practiced effective collaborative communication skills such as drawing inferences and conclusions and making connections while reading and analyzing two texts about relationships. Now students will apply those skills to work together in writing and presenting a personal address.

Developing Effective Presentations

Form	Language and Conventions	Oral Language Production
Students may struggle with the demands of developing the personal address, such as including a statement and adding details.	Students should be encouraged to experiment with new sentence patterns and lengths to make their address sound authentic.	Students may make mistakes when they transfer grammatical forms from their native languages into English. Remind students to monitor their use of articles.

SCAFFOLDS   **ELL ENGLISH LANGUAGE LEARNERS**

Vocabulary, discussion, and peer and teacher support in the Extended Oral Project is differentiated for Beginning, Intermediate, Advanced, and Advanced High English Language Learners. See individual lesson plans for additional scaffolding and support.

Instructional Path

 All Extended Oral Project lessons lesson plans appear in your digital teacher account.

Introduction

Objectives: Students will be able to identify the components of a personal address in order to write and perform in response to a prompt.

Objectives: Students will be able to record ideas for a personal address in writing.

Skill: Acquiring Vocabulary

Objectives: Students will be able to use graphic organizers to make comparisons between words and acquire new vocabulary in order to write a personal address.

Objectives: Students will be able to make comparisons between words and use new words in writing their personal address.

Plan

Objectives: Students will be able to plan and write a first draft of their personal address.

Objectives: Students will be able to organize their first draft using an outline.

Skill: Sentence Lengths

Objectives: Students will be able to apply knowledge of sentence lengths to revise their personal address.

Objectives: Students will be able to vary sentence lengths orally and in writing.

Practice

Objectives: Students will be able to practice and revise their personal address based on peer feedback.

Objectives: Students will be able to practice a personal address orally and make revisions in writing.

Present

Objectives: Students will be able to observe and perform a personal address in order to give and receive peer feedback.

Objectives: Students will be able to use varied sentence lengths in an oral presentation and give peer feedback orally and in writing.

Novel Study

Each Core ELAR Unit contains two texts designated for Novel Study. The Novel Study supports the close reading of the complete text through its associated Reading Guide and a series of comparative reading and writing lessons. Novel Studies are not a part of each grade-level's 180 days of instruction; however, teachers may choose to draw from them if they wish to incorporate materials from other disciplines or develop an alternative, novel-based approach to instruction.

Each novel comes with a **Reading Guide** that provides both teacher and student support. Each lesson provides key vocabulary words and close reading questions, as well as a key passage that will help teachers guide students through an exploration of the essential ideas, events, and character development in the novel. This passage will also serve as the point from which students will engage in their own StudySyncTV-style group discussion. Each novel study's **Comparative Reading and Writing** lessons contain resources to support comparative analyses. Students read passages of other texts drawn from across the disciplines and compare those passages to specific sections of the novel in written responses.

Suggested Novel Studies

Title	Genre	Summary	Themes and Topics
Walk Two Moons (1994)	Fiction	On a cross-country drive with her grandparents to visit her estranged mother, 13-year-old Sal tells the story of her friend Phoebe's mother's disappearance, drawing closer to the pain of her own abandonment.	• Parent-Child Relationships • Friendship • Mystery
Roll of Thunder, Hear My Cry (1976)	Fiction	Growing up black in 1930s Mississippi, the Logan children quickly learn that racial tensions run deep and wide.	• Racism • American South • Family

Walk Two Moons

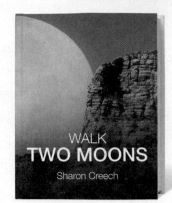

In *Walk Two Moons*, 13-year-old Sal and her grandparents drive across the United States to see Sal's estranged mother. On the trip, Sal talks of the disappearance of her best friend Phoebe's mother, and their investigations into it, exposing the fierce maternal discontent under the prim surface of their lives. As the American landscape whizzes past and their destination nears, Sal is forced to confront the huge absence in her life, and the resulting pain that will not let her go.

Sharon Creech (b. 1945) won numerous awards for Walk Two Moons, including the 1995 Newbery Medal, given for the most distinguished contribution to American literature for children. The road trip in *Walk Two Moons* was inspired by a real-life trip across the United States in her youth.

Roll of Thunder, Hear My Cry

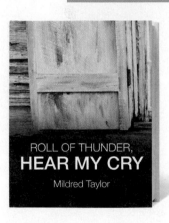

In the Newbery Medal-winning novel *Roll of Thunder, Hear My Cry*, nine-year-old Cassie Logan learns what it means to be African American in the segregated South of the 1930s. While her family struggles to pay taxes on their land, Cassie and her siblings become increasingly aware of growing racial tensions at her school and in the town of Strawberry—many of which explode into violence.

The writing of Mildred D. Taylor (b. 1943) is often based on her early childhood in Mississippi. In addition to *Roll of Thunder, Hear My Cry*, the Logans appear in four additional books, including Song of the Trees and Let the Circle Be Unbroken. Taylor's important contribution to young adult literature earned her the inaugural NSK Neustadt Prize for Children's Literature in 2003.

Spotlight Skills Review

A review day before the end-of-unit assessment gives you an opportunity to review difficult concepts with students using Spotlight Skills lessons. Spotlight Skills are targeted lessons that provide you resources to reteach or remediate without assigning additional readings. Every Core ELA Skill lesson has a corresponding Spotlight Skill lesson. Spotlight Skills can be assigned at any point in the year, but the end of each unit provides a natural moment to pause, review data collected throughout the unit, and reteach skills students have not yet mastered.

Progress Monitoring

The Progress Monitoring charts that appear before every text in this unit identify standards and associated Spotlight Skills. On review day, you may want to give preference to reteaching skills that are not revisited in later units. You can see where Skills are covered again in the Opportunities to Reteach column.

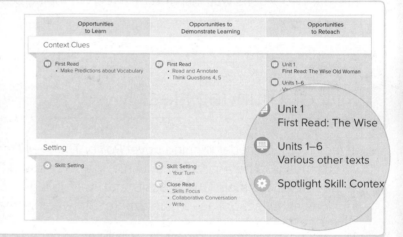

StudySync Gradebook

As students submit assignments on StudySync, their mastery of skills and standards is tracked via the gradebook. The gradebook can be sorted and viewed in a variety of ways. Sorting by assignment shows overall student performance, while sorting by standards or by Skill lessons displays student progress toward mastery goals.

	First Read: The Tell-Tale T	Skill: Textual Evidenc	Cl
	⚙ ▾	⚙ ▾	⚙ ▾
MAX SCORE	10	2	12
STUDENT			
Tate O'Brien	10	2	9
Olivia Adams	8	1	11

Skills Library

Spotlight Skills are located in the Skills section of the StudySync Library. You can assign Spotlight Skills to individual students or groups of students. Search tools allow you to search by Skill type or name.

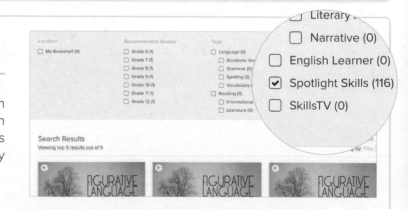

End-of-Unit Assessment

The end-of-unit assessment can be found in two places. The digital version of the assessment can be assigned from the Online Assessment tab inside your ConnectED account. The paper-based version of the assessment can be printed from the End-of-Unit Assessment tab inside this unit in your StudySync account.

Assessment Section	Content	Assessed Skills	
READING	The Sandpiper Genre: Poetry Word Count: 207 Lexile: N/A	• Figurative Language • Language, Style, and Audience	• Poetic Elements and Structure • Theme
	Kindred Spirits Genre: Non-fiction Word Count: 718 Lexile: 940	• Connotation and Denotation • Theme • Point of View	• Language, Style, and Audience • Textual Evidence • Story Structure
	Mothers of Men Genre: Poetry Word Count: 190 Lexile: N/A	• Figurative Language • Poetic Elements and Structure • Language, Style, and Audience	• Theme • Compare and Contrast
	When an Old Man Gets to Thinking Genre: Poetry Word Count: 240 Lexile: N/A	• Language, Style, and Audience • Figurative Language • Poetic Elements and Structure	• Language, Style, and Audience • Theme • Textual Evidence
REVISING and EDITING	Student Passage #1	• Possessive Pronouns • Spelling Rules	• Formal and Informal Language
	Student Passage #2	• Introductions • Reasons and Relevant Evidence	• Transitions
WRITING	Prompt: Argumentative Writing	• Argumentative Writing	

What's Next?

Assessment results can be viewed by item, standard, and skill to monitor mastery and make decisions for upcoming instruction.

RETEACH skills that students have not yet mastered, using Spotlight Skills or the Test Preparation and Practice book.

REVISE your teaching plan to provide more or less explicit instruction into a skill or text, using Beyond the Book activities for enrichment.

REGROUP students and levels of scaffolding based on standards progress.

In The Dark

How do you know what to do when there are no instructions?

UNIT 3

In The Dark

How do you know what to do when there are no instructions?

Darkness is associated with the unknown and the unknowable. It can be real, like an unexplored cave, or something like the unknown events that the future may bring. Darkness inspires fear and encourages uncertainty, yet some people find it safer to remain there. They would rather be "in the dark" than to take steps to try and "see the light."

Is darkness a place to live in, run from, or explore? What qualities does a person need in order to "face the darkness"? How does one finally reach the decision to take action in the face of uncertainty?

This unit offers a mixture of texts, both fiction and informational, about people that face uncertainty, including Rick Riordan's *The Lightning Thief*, Pat Mora's "Elena," "I, Too" by Langston Hughes, and Carl Hiaasen's *Hoot*. Informational texts by and about real individuals include *Hatshepsut: His Majesty, Herself* by Catherine M. Andronik, Randall Munroe's essay "Everybody Jump," and "Donna O'Meara: The Volcano Lady."

After reading the stories and informational texts about individuals and characters that take action in the face of uncertainty, students will have the opportunity to write an informative essay. In their essays, students will identify three individuals or characters from the unit texts and explore their motivations.

Thematic Selections

Extended Writing Project and Grammar

English Language Learner Resources

The Lightning Thief
FICTION
Rick Riordan

Hoot
FICTION
Carl Hiaasen

In the Dark

tv StudySyncTV or SkillsTV Episode

Pacing Guide

Days	Readings	Skill and Standard Instruction	Skill Practice and Spiraling
1-2	**Essential Question** **The Big Idea: How do you know what to do when there are no instructions?** p. 574	• Recognizing Genre: Informational Text • Academic Vocabulary	• Write: Analyzing Genre
3-5	**Heroes Every Child Should Know: Perseus** p. 578	• Visualizing • Character • Word Meaning	• Plot • Point of View • Literary Analysis Writing
6-8	**The Lightning Thief tv** p. 598	• Story Structure	• Character • Plot
9-13	**PAIRED READINGS** **Elena** p. 616 **Hatshesput: His Majesty, Herself tv** p. 624	• Informational Text Elements • Central or Main Idea • Greek and Latin Affixes and Roots	• Textual Evidence • Summarizing • Argumentative Writing • Collaborative Conversations
14-16	**I, Too** p. 646	• Poetic Elements and Structure **tv** • Media	• Figurative Language • Literary Analysis Writing
17-19	**Everybody Jump** p. 664	• Informational Text Structure **tv** • Technical Language	• Textual Evidence • Narrative Writing

THEMATIC PACING AT A GLANCE – 30 DAYS

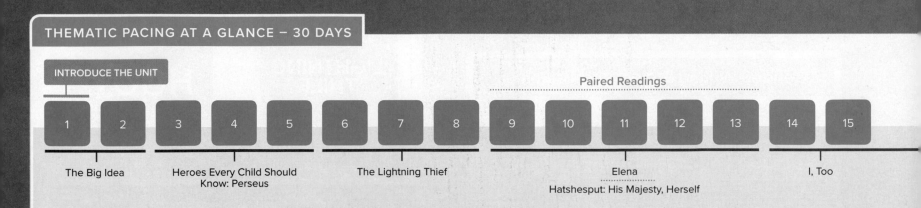

INTRODUCE THE UNIT

Paired Readings

| 1 | 2 | 3 | 4 | 5 | 6 | 7 | 8 | 9 | 10 | 11 | 12 | 13 | 14 | 15 |

The Big Idea
Heroes Every Child Should Know: Perseus
The Lightning Thief
Elena
Hatshesput: His Majesty, Herself
I, Too

Days	Readings	Skill and Standard Instruction	Skill Practice and Spiraling
20-22	Hoot tv p. 684	• Theme	• Textual Evidence • Character • Literary Analysis Writing • Collaborative Conversations
23-27	**PAIRED READINGS** **Donna O'Meara: The Volcano Lady** p. 700 **Dare to be Creative!** p. 710 **Margaret Bourke-White: Fearless Photographer** p. 720	• Synthesizing • Textual Evidence • Technical Language • Analyzing Genre	• Compare and Contrast • Comparative Writing
28	**Self-Selected Reading and Response** p. 740	• Independent Reading	• Personal Response Writing

Review and Assessment   See page 830.

Days	Review and Assessment	Skill Practice and Assessment
29	**Skills Review** p. 830	Students will have the opportunity to complete one or more Spotlight Skill lessons in order to improve understanding and further practice skills from the unit that they found most challenging.
30	**End-of-Unit Assessment** p. 831	For more details, please see the End-of-Unit Assessment information for Grade 6 Unit 3 on page 830.

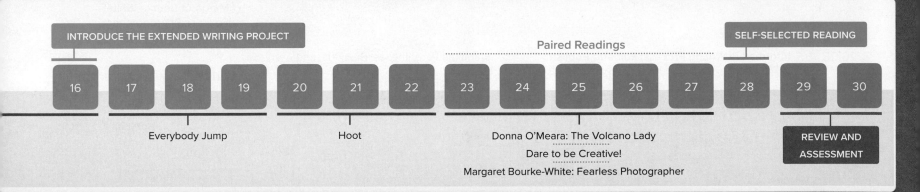

Extended Writing Project and Grammar

Pacing Guide

In the second half of the unit, students continue exploring texts that address the unit's Essential Question and begin crafting a longer composition to share their own ideas about the Essential Question in the Extended Writing Project. The writing project will take your students through the writing process to produce an informative essay.

Extended Writing Project Prompt

What motivates us to conquer feelings of uncertainty?

Think about the individuals from this unit who take action even when they are unsure of what lies ahead. Identify three of these individuals and write an informative essay explaining what drives them to respond, take action, or make a decision when there are no guidelines to help them.

Days	Extended Writing Project and Grammar	Skill and Standard Instruction	Connect to Mentor Texts
16	**Informative Writing Process: Plan** p. 752		
17-20	**Informative Writing Process: Draft** p. 766	• Thesis Statement • Organizing Informative Writing • Supporting Details	• Hatshepsut: His Majesty, Herself • Donna O'Meara: Volcano Lady
21-25	**Informative Writing Process: Revise** p. 781	• Introductions • Transitions • Precise Language • Style • Conclusions	• Heroes Every Child Should Know: Perseus • Donna O'Meara: Volcano Lady • Dare to be Creative! • Margaret Bourke-White: Fearless Photographer
26-28	**Informative Writing Process: Edit and Publish** p. 789	• Grammar: Parentheses, Brackets, and Ellipses • Grammar: Prefixes • Grammar: Spelling Rules II	Additional lessons can be found in the StudySync Skills Library.

Research

The following lessons include opportunities for research:

Blast In The Dark Research Links*

Close Read The Lightning Thief Beyond the Book

Blast What's Old is New Again Research Links*

Independent Read Elena Beyond the Book

First Read Hatshepsut: His Majesty, Herself Activate Prior Knowledge and Experiences

Close Read Everybody Jump Beyond the Book

Blast Emojis Speak Louder Than Words Research Links*

Independent Read Donna O'Meara: The Volcano Lady Beyond the Book

Independent Read Dare to be Creative! Connect to Extended Writing Project

*See the teacher lesson plan online

Self-Selected Reading Prompt

After reading a self-selected text, students will respond to the following narrative prompt:

Have you ever heard the expression: "walk a mile in someone else's shoes?" In other words, you can't really understand someone until you've spent some time imagining the world from their perspective.

How do you know what to do when there are no instructions?

Assume the role of a character, individual, or narrator/speaker from your self-selected text. Think about this role and how your chosen character, individual, or narrator/speaker would respond to the essential question from this unit. Write a monologue as this character, individual, or narrator/speaker using evidence from the text.

Integrated Scaffolding

ELL and Approaching grade-level students receive scaffolds for every lesson, whether in the Thematic, Novel Study or ELL Resources sections of the unit. Specific scaffolds are intentionally designed to support the needs of English Language Learners and Approaching grade-level students in the ELA classroom. Other scaffolds exist as part of the many standard features in the StudySync digital platform and can be strategically utilized to support students' comprehension and engagement.

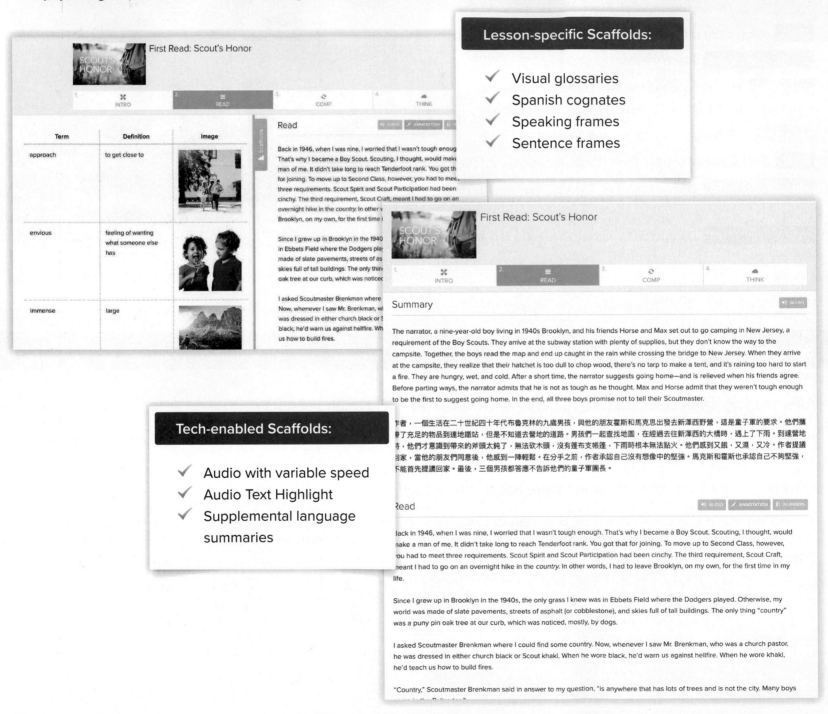

Lesson-specific Scaffolds:

- ✓ Visual glossaries
- ✓ Spanish cognates
- ✓ Speaking frames
- ✓ Sentence frames

Tech-enabled Scaffolds:

- ✓ Audio with variable speed
- ✓ Audio Text Highlight
- ✓ Supplemental language summaries

English Language Learner Resources

Both Thematic and Novel Study units include English Language Learner resources designed to match the thematic focus, text structures, and writing form of the unit. ELL resources include two leveled texts and an extended oral project.

ELL Texts	Differentiated Text Levels	Skill and Standard Instruction
 TRACKING DOWN TYPHOID MARY	**BEGINNING** 360L I 312 words **INTERMEDIATE** 430L I 463 words **ADVANCED** 620L I 543 words **ADVANCED HIGH** 680L I 533 words Use this text in place of, or as an extension to *Hatshepsut: His Majesty, Herself.*	• Sight Vocabulary and High-Frequency Words • Using Prereading Supports • Language Structures • Main Ideas and Details • Spelling Patterns and Rules
 THE NOTICE	**BEGINNING** 480L I 275 words **INTERMEDIATE** 550L I 377 words **ADVANCED** 630L I 429 words **ADVANCED HIGH** 760L I 477 words Use this text in place of, or as an extension to "Elena."	• Classroom Vocabulary • Making Predictions • Analyzing Expressions • Comparing and Contrasting • Verb Tenses
EXTENDED ORAL PROJECT INTRODUCTION	In this Extended Oral Project, students will write and present a biography. This may be assigned in place of this unit's EWP.	• Acquiring Vocabulary • Sentence Lengths

Focus on English Language Proficiency Levels

ADVANCED HIGH
ADVANCED
INTERMEDIATE
BEGINNING

ELL Resources provide targeted support for four levels of proficiency: Beginning, Intermediate, Advanced, and Advanced High. Instruction and scaffolds, as well as the texts themselves, are differentiated based on these levels.

Additional differentiated scaffolds include visual glossaries, speaking and writing frames, and suggested grouping for peer and teacher support. Lessons also include suggested extension activities to challenge Advanced and Advanced High students as they progress through the year.

Assessment

Assessment in StudySync is built upon a recursive cycle that includes assessment, instruction, and review. Screening, placement, and benchmark assessments help teachers establish baselines and determine scaffold needs. Throughout the course of instruction, teachers regularly assess student progress using formative and summative measures, and use the individualized data from those assessments to guide choices about instruction, review, remediation, and enrichment to bring all students to standards mastery and College and Career Readiness.

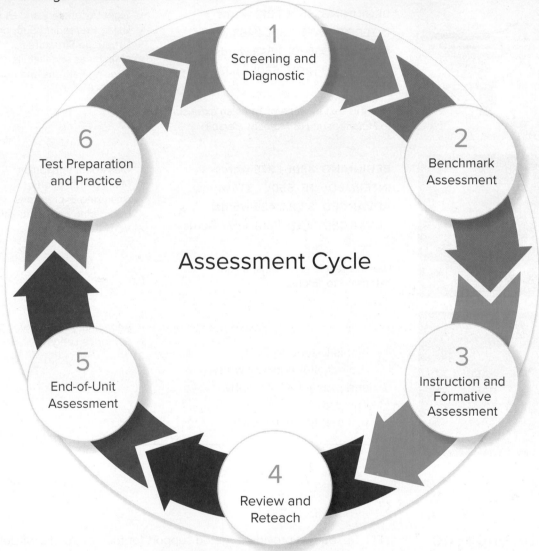

Assessment Cycle

1 Screening and Diagnostic

2 Benchmark Assessment

3 Instruction and Formative Assessment

4 Review and Reteach

5 End-of-Unit Assessment

6 Test Preparation and Practice

What's Next?

Assessment results can be viewed by item, standard, and skill to monitor mastery and make decisions for upcoming instruction.

✓ Reteach skills that students have not yet mastered, using Spotlight Skills or the Test Preparation and Practice book.

✓ Revise your teaching plan to provide more or less explicit instruction into a skill or text, using Beyond the Book activities for enrichment.

✓ Regroup students and levels of scaffolding based on standards progress.

Review

Spotlight Skills Review

A review day before the end-of-unit assessment gives you an opportunity to review difficult concepts with students using Spotlight Skills lessons. Spotlight Skills are targeted lessons that provide you resources to reteach or remediate without assigning additional readings. Every Core ELA Skill lesson has a corresponding Spotlight Skill lesson. Spotlight Skills can be assigned at any point in the year, but the end of each unit provides a natural moment to pause, review data collected throughout the unit, and reteach skills students have not yet mastered.

Progress Monitoring

The Progress Monitoring charts that appear before every text in this unit identify standards and associated Spotlight Skills. On review day, you may want to give preference to reteaching skills that are not revisited in later units. You can see where skills are covered again in the Opportunities to Reteach column.

Opportunities to Learn	Opportunities to Demonstrate Learning	
Context Clues		Unit 1 First Read: The Wise
First Read • Make Predictions about Vocabulary	First Read • Read and Annotate • Think Questions 4, 5	Units 1–6 Various other texts
		Spotlight Skill: Context

StudySync Gradebook

As students submit assignments on StudySync, their mastery of skills and standards is tracked via the gradebook. The gradebook can be sorted and viewed in a variety of ways. Sorting by assignment shows overall student performance, while sorting by standards or by skill lessons displays student progress toward mastery goals.

	First Read	Skill: Text	Close Re	
MAX SCORE	10	2	12	
STUDENT				
Tate O'Brien	10	2	9	
Olivia Adams	8	1	11	

Skills Library

Spotlight Skills are located in the Skills section of the StudySync Library. You can assign Spotlight Skills to individual students or groups of students. Search tools allow you to search by skill type or name.

End-of-Unit Assessment

Assessed Reading Skills

- ✓ Central or Main Idea
- ✓ Character
- ✓ Greek and Latin Affixes and Roots
- ✓ Informational Text Elements
- ✓ Informational Text Structure
- ✓ Story Structure
- ✓ Technical Language
- ✓ Textual Evidence
- ✓ Word Meaning
- ✓ Theme

Assessed Revising and Editing Skills

- ✓ Basic Spelling Rules
- ✓ Introductions and Conclusions
- ✓ Parentheses, Brackets, Ellipses
- ✓ Precise Language
- ✓ Prefixes
- ✓ Supporting Details
- ✓ Thesis Statement

Unit Preview

Introduce the Unit

As a class, watch the unit preview ▶ and discuss the questions below.

- What two words would you use to describe this video?
- What key words or images from the video do you think will be most important to this unit?

Instructional Path

Big Idea Blast

Objectives: After exploring background information and research links about a topic, students will respond to a question with a 140-character response.

Skill: Recognize Genre

Objectives: After learning about the genre of informational text, students will be able to identify and describe characteristics of informational texts.

Skill: Academic Vocabulary

Objectives: After learning the meanings of ten academic vocabulary words, students will be able to recognize and use them in a variety of contexts.

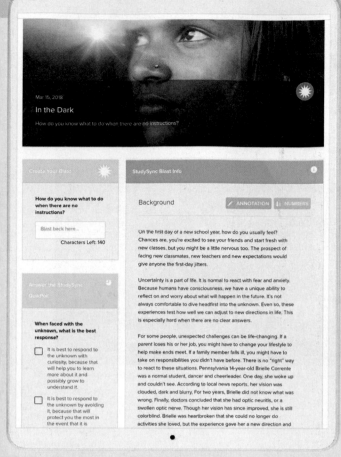

Mar 15, 2018

In the Dark

How do you know what to do when there are no instructions?

Blast: In the Dark

How do we know what to do when there are no instructions?

Ask students:

- What do you think this Blast will be about? Make a prediction.
- Do you feel uncertain when there are no instructions for something you need to do or accomplish? Why or why not? What could you do to control and defeat these feelings?

TEXT TALK

What are some common reactions to uncertainty? People often feel fear or anxiety.

How did Brielle Corrente feel when she first lost her vision? How did she make the best of the situation? At first she was heartbroken that she couldn't do what she loved. But then she went on to write a children's book and become Miss Teen Pennsylvania.

According to James Clear, what gets us through uncertain times? Clear says that self-confidence is what gets us through uncertainty.

Create Your Own Blast

SCAFFOLDS

Ask students to write a 140-character Blast after they complete the QuikPoll.

Use the scaffolds below to differentiate instruction for your English Language Learners.

ELL **BEGINNING** Write a response using the <u>word bank</u> to complete the <u>sentence frame</u>.

INTERMEDIATE Write a response using the <u>sentence frame</u>.

ADVANCED, ADVANCED HIGH Write a response using the <u>sentence starter</u>.

BEGINNING	INTERMEDIATE	ADVANCED, ADVANCED HIGH
Word Bank	**Sentence Frame**	**Sentence Starter**
listening instincts looking heart paying friends attention	When there are no instructions, you can figure out what to do by ____ to your ____.	• When there are no instructions, you can figure out what to do by . . .

Skill: Recognize Genre

Introduce the Genre: Informational Text

Watch the Concept Definitions video and read the following definition with your students.

Informational text presents readers information or ideas about real people, places, things, and events. In order to express information clearly, writers use a common set of informational text elements, including a **thesis,** or main idea, and supporting **evidence** in the form of details, facts, examples, statistics, and expert opinions.

A typical informational text includes an introduction that builds to a thesis, body paragraphs that include key ideas and supporting evidence, and a strong conclusion that restates the most important ideas to remember.

Within body paragraphs, writers might use specific **text structures,** or organizational patterns. For instance, a writer may discuss ideas in order of importance, tell about events in chronological order, or present causes and effects.

Informational writing can take many forms, including essays, pamphlets, news and magazine articles, textbook articles, and nonfiction books. What a person writes to share information is an informational text.

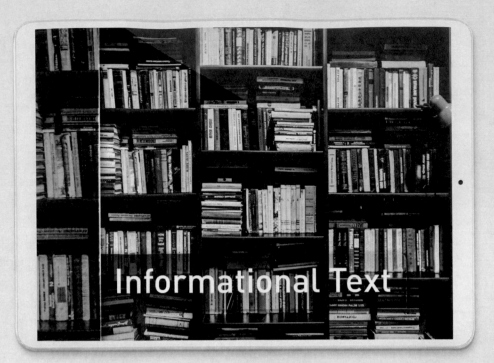

TURN AND TALK

Use the following questions to discuss informational texts with your students.

- What is the main purpose of an informational text?

- What features of this writing do you know about?

 SPEAKING FRAMES
- The purpose of an informational text is to ___.
- I already know about the feature ___.

Your Turn

Ask students to complete the Your Turn activity.

Description	Text Feature
A steam engine is made up of a cylinder and piston that move when steam creates a vacuum.	specialized vocabulary
Twelve percent of school-aged children do not eat breakfast.	statistics
I spent a year in Italy studying the buildings before I wrote this book.	research
The atmosphere is composed of nitrogen, oxygen, and argon.	facts

Your Turn

Ask students to complete the Your Turn activities.

Your Turn 1

See digital teacher's edition for sample answers.

Your Turn 2

QUESTION 1: B   **QUESTION 2:** D   **QUESTION 3:** C   **QUESTION 4:** A   **QUESTION 5:** C

Your Turn 3

See digital teacher's edition for sample answers.

Skill: Academic Vocabulary

benefit / beneficiar *verb* to do good; to be useful to COGNATE

benevolent / benevolente *adjective* intending or showing kindness and generosity COGNATE

benign / benigno/a *adjective* not dangerous to one's health; harmless COGNATE

maneuver / maniobrar *verb* to direct the course; to determine the direction of COGNATE

manipulate / manipular *verb* to treat, work, or operate with the hands COGNATE

manual / manual *adjective* requiring human effort or physical work COGNATE

manufacture / manufacturar *verb* to make something from raw material (by hand or by machine) COGNATE

manuscript / el manuscrito *noun* handwritten or typed book or document COGNATE

describe / describir *verb* to give an account or representation of in words COGNATE

prescribe / prescribir *verb* to give directions; to dictate COGNATE

Practice Using Vocabulary

Divide students into pairs or small groups. Assign each group a word from the list and prompt them to act out a short scene that demonstrates the meaning of their word. Then, have groups take turns performing their scene for the class.

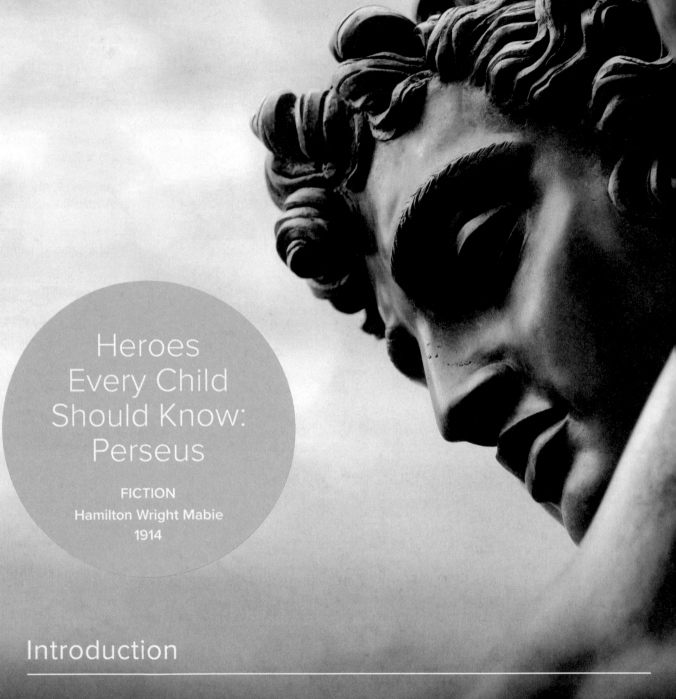

Heroes Every Child Should Know: Perseus

FICTION
Hamilton Wright Mabie
1914

Introduction

Perseus, the son of a mortal woman, Danaë, and Zeus, the king of the gods, faced challenges from the day he was born. Locked in a wooden chest, the infant and his mother are set adrift in the sea. They wash up safely on a remote island, where a fisherman takes them in and Perseus grows into a fine, able-bodied young man. One fateful day, he is visited by the goddess Athene, who has chosen him for the task of killing her bitter enemy Medusa, the snake-haired Gorgon whose gaze turns a beholder to stone. Perseus is all too willing to take on the mission, even if it means dying in the process.

The goddess Athene asks Perseus to kill Medusa, the snake-haired monster whose gaze is so potent that it turns people to stone. To protect Perseus, Athene provides him with a mirrored shield and a diamond scimitar to cut through Medusa's scales. To aid his travel, Hermes gives Perseus his golden-winged sandals. Without saying goodbye to his family, Perseus flies to see the Grey Sisters, where he steals the eye that the three women share and trades it for directions. Perseus is then sent to see Atlas the Giant and his daughters. Atlas tells Perseus to wear the hat of darkness so that the Gorgons guarding Medusa cannot see him. Perseus complies and flies to the Unshapen Land. Using the reflection in his shield, he swoops down and beheads Medusa. With her head wrapped in a goat skin and the Gorgons in angry pursuit, Perseus narrowly manages to escape.

 Proficiency-leveled summaries and summaries in multiple languages are available digitally.

🔊 Audio and audio text highlighting are available with this text.

CONNECT TO ESSENTIAL QUESTION

How do we know what to do when there are no instructions?

What steps does someone follow in order to become a hero? In this popular Greek myth, readers learn about the tasks Perseus must perform in order for him to become a hero.

Access Complex Text

LEXILE: 950L   **WORD COUNT:** 2,459

The following areas may be challenging for students, particularly English Language Learners and Approaching grade-level learners.

Prior Knowledge	Connection of Ideas	Sentence Structure
• The references to various figures from Greek mythology, such as Perseus, Athene, Hermes, and Atlas, are likely to be unfamiliar to students. • Hermes alludes to himself as the "Argus-slayer." Share with students the story of how and why Hermes killed the hundred-eyed Argus.	• This myth follows a common but sometimes confusing structure, the hero's quest, in which the hero travels from place to place until he obtains or kills what he has been searching for. • There are so many places Perseus must go and so many beings he must question that it will be hard to keep the stages in his journey straight.	• Students may be confused by the archaic sentence structures used in this text, such as "Touch me not." • Most of the sentences are quite long and use semicolons to connect clauses.

 **SCAFFOLDS**   **ENGLISH LANGUAGE LEARNERS**   **A** **APPROACHING GRADE LEVEL**   **BEYOND GRADE LEVEL**

These icons identify differentiation strategies and scaffolded support for a variety of students. See the digital lesson plan for additional differentiation strategies and scaffolds.

Instructional Path

The print teacher's edition includes essential point-of-use instruction and planning tools. Complete lesson plans and program documents appear in your digital teacher account.

Skill: Visualizing

Objectives: After reading and discussing a model, students will be able to visualize in order to improve reading comprehension.

First Read: Heroes Every Child Should Know: Perseus

Objectives: After an initial reading and discussion of the story, students will be able to identify and describe characters and setting details as well as articulate events that are central to the story's plot.

Skill: Character

Objectives: After rereading and discussing a model of close reading, students will be able to describe how characters respond or change as the plot moves toward a resolution.

Close Read: Heroes Every Child Should Know: Perseus

Objectives: After engaging in a close reading and discussion of the text, students will be able to analyze how the character's responses develop the plot and move the action of the story forward in a short, written response.

Progress Monitoring

Opportunities to Learn	Opportunities to Demonstrate Learning	Opportunities to Reteach

Visualizing

⚙ Skill: Visualizing	▤ First Read • Read and Annotate	▤ Unit 5 First Read: Listen, Slowly ⚙ Spotlight Skill: Visualizing

Character

⚙ Skill: Character	⚙ Skill: Character • Your Turn ⊞ Close Read • Skills Focus • Write	⚙ Unit 5 Skill: Character — Amigo Brothers ⚙ Spotlight Skill: Character

First Read

Hamilton Wright Mabie

Heroes Every Child Should Know: Perseus

 ## Introduce the Text

As a class, watch the video preview ▶ and have students read the introduction in pairs to make connections to the video preview.

To activate prior knowledge and experiences, ask students:

- What key images from the video do you think will be most important to the story you are about to read?

ELL SPEAKING FRAMES

- The ____ in the video makes me think ____.
- The video shows ____. This makes me wonder ____.
- I think the text will ____. I think this because ____. I predict that there will be ____. I believe this because ____.

Entry Point

As students prepare to read *Heroes Every Child Should Know:* Perseus, share the following information with them to provide context.

✓ Greece is a thriving modern-day country, but there is evidence of a highly developed human culture existing there before written history. Ancient Greece refers to a great civilization that began to emerge in southern Greece, Crete and the surrounding islands of the Mediterranean and Aegean seas around 1900 B.C.E. and is referred to as Mycenaean Civilization. The early Mycenaeans worshiped earth goddesses and sky gods, which established the beginnings of Greek mythology.

✓ Greek mythology explains the environment in which the ancient Greeks lived. There are myths that explain the origin of their gods and goddesses, where people come from, what happens after people die, how to live a happy life, and the retelling of historical events. Some Greeks believed the myths to be factually true, while others thought of them as stories. Perseus is one of the oldest heroes of Greek mythology.

Heroes Every Child Should Know: Perseus

"It is better to die like a hero than to live like an ox in a stall."

NOTES

from Chapter I: Perseus

1 Then Athene smiled and said:

2 "Be patient, and listen; for if you forget my words, you will indeed die. You must go northward to the country of the Hyperboreans,[1] who live beyond the pole, at the sources of the cold north wind, till you find the three Grey Sisters, who have but one eye and one tooth between them. You must ask them the way to the Nymphs, the daughters of the Evening Star, who dance about the golden tree, in the Atlantic island of the west. They will tell you the way to the Gorgon,[2] that you may slay her, my enemy, the mother of monstrous beasts. Once she was a maiden as beautiful as morn, till in her pride she sinned a sin at which the sun hid his face; and from that day her hair was turned to vipers, and her hands to eagle's claws; and her heart was filled with shame and rage, and her lips with bitter venom; and her eyes became so terrible that whosoever looks on them is turned to stone; and her children are the winged horse and the giant of the golden sword; and her grandchildren are Echidna the witch-adder, and Geryon the three-headed tyrant, who feeds his herds beside the herds of hell. So she became the sister of the Gorgons, the daughters of the Queen of the Sea. Touch them not, for they are **immortal;** but bring me only Medusa's head."

3 "And I will bring it!" said Perseus; "but how am I to escape her eyes? Will she not freeze me too into stone?"

4 "You shall take this polished shield," said Athene, "and when you come near her look not at her yourself, but at her image in the brass; so you may strike her safely. And when you have struck off her head, wrap it, with your face turned away, in the folds of the goatskin on which the shield hangs. So you will bring it safely back to me, and win to yourself **renown,** and a place among the heroes who feast with the Immortals upon the peak where no winds blow."

5 Then Perseus said, "I will go, though I die in going. But how shall I cross the seas without a ship? And who will show me my way? And when I find her, how shall I slay her, if her scales be iron and brass?"

---

1. **Hyperboreans:** giants in Greek myth who lived in the extreme north.
2. **Gorgons:** three monster-women of Greek myth, the most famous of whom is Medusa

Reading & Writing Companion 1

V SELECTION VOCABULARY

immortal / inmortal *adjective* not subject to dying; eternal; living forever COGNATE

renown / el renombre *noun* fame; the state of being discussed or talked about

- Who would feast with the gods—people who are famous or not famous?
- If Perseus kills Medusa, will he gain fame or remain unknown?

Analyze Vocabulary Using Context Clues

In paragraph 2 focus on the sentence that uses the word *immortal.* Point out these context clues:

1. First I notice that Medusa's sisters are described as immortal.

2. Athene tells Perseus to kill Medusa, but not to kill her sisters because they are immortal.

3. It must be impossible to kill Medusa's sisters.

4. Immortal must mean able to live forever.

TEXT TALK

What does Athene want Perseus to do?

See paragraph 2: Athene wants Perseus to kill her enemy Medusa.

Why is this task especially dangerous?

See paragraph 3: The task is especially dangerous because whoever looks into Medusa's eyes is turned to stone.

What will Perseus earn in exchange for completing this task?

See paragraph 4: Perseus will win fame among the Immortals.

Character

How does the reader use Perseus's thoughts and actions in the beginning of the story to understand the character and his influence on the plot?

The reader identifies Perseus's contrasting thoughts: he's scared, but jumps anyway. Then the reader notes that his actions move the plot toward the resolution with Medusa.

Skills Focus

QUESTION 4: Point of View

Examining the narration helps me determine whether the point of view is second or third person. The narrator doesn't address the reader, so the point of view isn't second person. The narrator does get inside Perseus's head and only Perseus's head; that means the point of view is third person limited.

Skills Focus

QUESTION 5: Connect to Essential Question

The quest tests Perseus's inner strength from the very beginning. He tries to postpone leaping off the cliff by suggesting things he should do before leaving.

NOTES

6   Now beside Athene appeared a young man more light-limbed than the stag, whose eyes were like sparks of fire. By his side was a **scimitar** of diamond, all of one clear precious stone, and on his feet were golden sandals, from the heels of which grew living wings.

7   Then the young man spoke: "These sandals of mine will bear you across the seas, and over hill and dale like a bird, as they bear me all day long; for I am Hermes, the far-famed Argus-slayer, the messenger of the Immortals who dwell on Olympus."

8   Then Perseus fell down and worshipped, while the young man spoke again:

9   "The sandals themselves will guide you on the road, for they are divine and cannot stray; and this sword itself the Argus-slayer, will kill her, for it is divine, and needs no second stroke. Arise, and gird them on, and go forth."

10   So Perseus arose, and girded on the sandals and the sword.

11   And Athene cried, "Now leap from the cliff and be gone."

12   But Perseus **lingered**.

13   "May I not bid farewell to my mother and to Dictys? And may I not offer burnt offerings to you, and to Hermes the far-famed Argus-slayer, and to Father Zeus above?"

14   "You shall not bid farewell to your mother, lest your heart **relent** at her weeping. I will comfort her and Dictys until you return in peace. Nor shall you offer burnt offerings to the Olympians; for your offering shall be Medusa's head. Leap, and trust in the armour of the Immortals."

Skill: Character

Perseus's thoughts show that he's afraid to leap from the cliff. He's embarrassed by his fear, but his desire for fame is stronger, so he leaps. This action brings him closer to the resolution when he will battle with Medusa.

15   Then Perseus looked down the cliff and shuddered; but he was ashamed to show his dread. Then he thought of Medusa and the renown before him, and he leapt into the empty air.

16   And behold, instead of falling he floated, and stood, and ran along the sky. He looked back, but Athene had vanished, and Hermes; and the sandals led him on northward ever, like a crane who follows the spring toward the Ister fens.

17   So Perseus started on his journey, going dry-shod over land and sea; and his heart was high and joyful, for the winged sandals bore him each day a seven days' journey. And he turned neither to the right hand nor the left, till he came to the Unshapen Land, and the place which has no name.

18   And seven days he walked through it on a path which few can tell, till he came to the edge of the everlasting night, where the air was full of feathers, and the soil was hard with ice; and there at last he found the three Grey Sisters, by the shore of the freezing sea, nodding upon a white log of

---

SELECTION VOCABULARY

scimitar / la cimitarra *noun* a short sword with a curved blade COGNATE

 ELL
- What is the scimitar made of?
- What is the purpose of the scimitar? Which word is a synonym for *scimitar*?

linger / quedarse merodeando *verb* to stay longer than needed

ELL
- Does Perseus immediately leap from the cliff, or does he stay a moment?
- What does Perseus want to do instead of leap from the cliff?

relent / ceder *verb* to become less harsh or severe; yield

ELL
- If Perseus's mother cries, is he likely to go on his mission or stay?
- Why is Athene worried about Perseus talking to his mother?

NOTES

driftwood, beneath the cold white winter moon; and they chanted a low song together, "Why the old times were better than the new."

19 There was no living thing around them, not a fly, not a moss upon the rocks. Neither seal nor sea gull dare come near, lest the ice should clutch them in its claws. The surge broke up in foam, but it fell again in flakes of snow; and it frosted the hair of the three Grey Sisters, and the bones in the ice cliff above their heads. They passed the eye from one to the other, but for all that they could not see; and they passed the tooth from one to the other, but for all that they could not eat; and they sat in the full glare of the moon, but they were none the warmer for her beams. And Perseus pitied the three Grey Sisters; but they did not pity themselves.

20 So he said, "Oh, venerable mothers, wisdom is the daughter of old age. You therefore should know many things. Tell me, if you can, the path to the Gorgon."

21 Then one cried, "Who is this who **reproaches** us with old age?" And another, "This is the voice of one of the children of men."

22 Then one cried, "Give me the eye, that I may see him"; and another, "Give me the tooth, that I may bite him." But Perseus, when he saw that they were foolish and proud, and did not love the children of men, left off pitying them. Then he stepped close to them, and watched till they passed the eye from hand to hand. And as they groped about between themselves, he held out his own hand gently, till one of them put the eye into it, fancying that it was the hand of her sister. Then he sprang back, and laughed, and cried:

23 "Cruel and proud old women, I have your eye; and I will throw it into the sea, unless you tell me the path to the Gorgon, and swear to me that you tell me right."

24 Then they wept, and chattered, and scolded; but in vain. They were forced to tell the truth, though, when they told it, Perseus could hardly make out the road.

25 "You must go," they said, "foolish boy, to the southward, into the ugly glare of the sun, till you come to Atlas the Giant, who holds the heaven and the earth apart. And you must ask his daughters, the Hesperides, who are young and foolish like yourself. And now give us back our eye, for we have forgotten all the rest."

26 So Perseus gave them back their eye. And he leaped away to the southward, leaving the snow and the ice behind. And the terns and the sea gulls swept laughing round his head, and called to him to stop and play, and the dolphins gambolled up as he passed, and offered to carry him on their back. And all night long the sea nymphs sang sweetly. Day by day the sun rose higher and leaped more swiftly into the sea at night, and more swiftly out of the sea at dawn; while Perseus skimmed over the billows like a sea gull, and his feet were never wetted; and leapt on from wave to wave, and his limbs were never weary, till he saw far away a mighty mountain, all rose-red in the setting

Skill:
Character

Perseus really is clever. He figures out what is going on with the Grey sisters and gains control of the eye.

He uses the eye as a way to get the information he wants in his quest to kill Medusa, which is the main conflict of the story.

I notice how Perseus has changed. He is brave and strong now. He is tough with the Grey sisters.

Reading & Writing Companion **3**

Character

How does the reader use Perseus's change of character later in the story to understand how the character gains the upper hand in a difficult situation?

The reader notes how Perseus becomes clever and strong, and he figures out the Grey sisters' weakness, captures the eye, and uses it to convince the sisters to tell him how to find Medusa.

Prepare for Advanced Courses

Use the activity below to differentiate instruction for your B Beyond grade level learners.

Ask students: What does the eye symbolize in this passage?

Sample answer; answers will vary: The eye seems to symbolize how limited "seeing" is. To understand something, it's not enough to have eyes, or even one eye to share, as the three Grey Sisters do. In fact, the eye does not even work. Perseus is able to trick the women into giving him information by threatening, ". . . I have your eye; and I will throw it into the sea . . . ," even though the eye serves no real purpose. They can't see that the real power they possess is their knowledge of the Gorgon.

V SELECTION VOCABULARY

reproach / reprochar *verb* to blame for a fault or wrongdoing; chide COGNATE

ELL
• Do the Grey Sisters find Perseus's words insulting or complimentary?
• Do the Grey Sisters like being described as old?

Skills Focus

QUESTION 1: Character

Athene told Perseus to find the Nymphs. His thoughts show that the is bashful to approach them once he finds them. He's brave enough for fame to risk his life to cut off Medusa's head, but he is shy around girls!

Skills Focus

QUESTION 2: Character

Perseus is focused on his quest. He is not even tempted to give up when the Nymphs ask him to dance and warn him of the danger ahead. He says he would rather die like a hero than live locked away with no purpose in life.

NOTES

sun. Perseus knew that it was Atlas, who holds the heavens and the earth apart.

27 He leapt on shore, and wandered upward, among pleasant valleys and waterfalls. At last he heard sweet voices singing; and he guessed that he was come to the garden of the Nymphs, the daughters of the Evening Star. They sang like nightingales among the thickets, and Perseus stopped to hear their song; but the words which they spoke he could not understand. So he stepped forward and saw them dancing, hand in hand around the charmed tree, which bent under its golden fruit; and round the tree foot was coiled the dragon, old Ladon the sleepless snake, who lies there for ever, listening to the song of the maidens, blinking and watching with dry bright eyes.

28 Then Perseus stopped, not because he feared the dragon, but because he was bashful before those fair maids; but when they saw him, they too stopped, and called to him with trembling voices:

29 "Who are you, fair boy? Come dance with us around the tree in the garden which knows no winter, the home of the south wind and the sun. Come hither and play with us awhile; we have danced alone here for a thousand years, and our hearts are weary with longing for a playfellow."

30 "I cannot dance with you, fair maidens; for I must do the errand of the Immortals. So tell me the way to the Gorgon, lest I wander and perish in the waves."

31 Then they sighed and wept; and answered:

32 "The Gorgon! she will freeze you into stone."

33 "It is better to die like a hero than to live like an ox in a stall. The Immortals have lent me weapons, and they will give me wit to use them."

34 Then they sighed again and answered: "Fair boy, if you are bent on your own ruin, be it so. We know not the way to the Gorgon; but we will ask the giant Atlas above upon the mountain peak." So they went up the mountain to Atlas their uncle, and Perseus went up with them. And they found the giant kneeling, as he held the heavens and the earth apart.

35 They asked him, and he answered mildly, pointing to the sea board with his mighty hand, "I can see the Gorgons lying on an island far away, but this youth can never come near them, unless he has the hat of darkness, which whosoever wears cannot be seen."

36 Then cried Perseus, "Where is that hat, that I may find it?"

37 But the giant smiled. "No living mortal can find that hat, for it lies in the depths of Hades, in the regions of the dead. But my nieces are immortal, and they shall fetch it for you, if you will promise me one thing and keep your faith."

Copyright © BookheadEd Learning, LLC

38 Then Perseus promised; and the giant said, "When you come back with the head of Medusa, you shall show me the beautiful horror, that I may lose my feeling and my breathing, and become a stone for ever; for it is weary labour for me to hold the heavens and the earth apart."

39 Then Perseus promised, and the eldest of the Nymphs went down, and into a dark cavern among the cliffs, out of which came smoke and thunder, for it was one of the mouths of hell.

40 And Perseus and the Nymphs sat down seven days and waited trembling, till the Nymph came up again; and her face was pale, and her eyes dazzled with the light for she had been long in the dreary darkness; but in her hand was the magic hat.

41 Then all the Nymphs kissed Perseus, and wept over him a long while; but he was only impatient to be gone. And at last they put the hat upon his head, and he vanished out of their sight.

42 But Perseus went on boldly, past many an ugly sight, far away into the heart of the Unshapen Land, till he heard the rustle of the Gorgons' wings and saw the glitter of their **brazen** talons; and then he knew that it was time to halt, lest Medusa should freeze him into stone.

The Arming of Perseus

43 He thought awhile with himself, and remembered Athene's words. He arose aloft into the air, and held the mirror of the shield above his head, and looked up into it that he might see all that was below him.

44 And he saw the three Gorgons sleeping. He knew that they could not see him, because the hat of darkness hid him; and yet he trembled as he sank down near them, so terrible were those brazen claws.

45 Two of the Gorgons were foul as swine, and lay sleeping heavily, with their mighty wings outspread; but Medusa tossed to and fro restlessly, and as she tossed Perseus pitied her. But as he looked, from among her tresses the vipers' heads awoke, and peeped up with their bright dry eyes, and showed their fangs, and hissed; and Medusa, as she tossed, threw back her wings and showed her brazen claws.

46 Then Perseus came down and stepped to her boldly, and looked steadfastly on his mirror, and struck with Herpe stoutly once; and he did not need to strike again.

Reading & Writing Companion   5

TEXT TALK

Why is Perseus successful in completing his task?

See paragraphs 30, 33, and 43: Perseus is successful because he carefully follows the instructions of Athene and Hermes.

V SELECTION VOCABULARY

brazen / descarado/a *adjective* made of brass; bold

ELL
- Does Perseus find the Gorgons' talons to be ordinary or shocking?
- Are the Gorgons' talons safe or dangerous?

Skills Focus

QUESTION 3: Plot

Perseus outruns the hounds of Death to complete his quest. The resolution shows that it required bravery and cleverness on the part of Perseus and the help of the Immortals to accomplish the quest.

47   Then he wrapped the head in the goat-skin, turning away his eyes, and sprang into the air aloft, faster than he ever sprang before.

48   For Medusa's wings and talons rattled as she sank dead upon the rocks; and her two foul sisters woke, and saw her lying dead.

49   Into the air they sprang yelling, and looked for him who had done the deed. They rushed, sweeping and flapping, like eagles after a hare; and Perseus's blood ran cold as he saw them come howling on his track; and he cried, "Bear me well now, brave sandals, for the hounds of Death are at my heels!"

50   And well the brave sandals bore him, aloft through cloud and sunshine, across the shoreless sea; and fast followed the hounds of Death. But the sandals were too swift, even for Gorgons, and by nightfall they were far behind, two black specks in the southern sky, till the sun sank and he saw them no more.

TEXT TALK

In what ways is Perseus successful in accomplishing his task?

See paragraphs 46–47 and 49–50: Perseus kills Medusa and wraps her head in a goat skin without being turned to stone. He escapes before Medusa's sisters capture him.

What other visualizations can you generate based on sensory details.

Answers will vary.

 Ask each Beyond grade level student to write one additional discussion question. Then, have one or two students facilitate a discussion, using their questions to guide the conversation.

Reading Comprehension OPTIONAL

Have students complete the digital reading comprehension questions ✅ when they finish reading.

ANSWER KEY

QUESTION 1: D	**QUESTION 5:** B	**QUESTION 9:**
QUESTION 2: C	**QUESTION 6:** C	*See first chart.*
QUESTION 3: C	**QUESTION 7:** D	**QUESTION 10:**
QUESTION 4: A	**QUESTION 8:** B	*See second chart.*

Grey Sisters	Atlas
"no living thing"	"valleys and waterfalls"
"everlasting night"	"sweet voices singing"
"soil was hard with ice"	"golden fruit"

First	Second	Third
Athene tells the story of how Medusa becomes a monster and tells Perseus how he can defeat Medusa.	Hermes provides Perseus with objects that will help him on his journey.	Perseus finds the Grey Sisters and tricks them into telling him where he must go.
Fourth	**Fifth**	**Sixth**
Atlas tells Perseus where the Gorgon lives.	The Nymphs give Perseus the hat of darkness.	Perseus is pursued by two Gorgons after he slays Medusa.

Connect and Extend OPTIONAL

CONNECT TO EXTENDED WRITING PROJECT

Students can use *Heroes Every Child Should Know: Perseus* as a mentor text for their Extended Writing Project. They may adopt the author's use of chronological order to structure the information in their essays.

BEYOND THE BOOK

Art: Graphic Story

In *Heroes Every Child Should Know: Perseus*, the author uses rich detail to tell the story of Perseus and Medusa. Students will transform this text into a graphic story.

Ask students to:

- Divide the story into sections (e.g. Athene's explanation of how Medusa became a monster, Perseus' conversation with Hermes).

- Create a draft of a storyboard with quick sketches depicting each scene.

- Select dialogue from the excerpt to include in your graphic story.

- Decide which scenes need captions.

Once students have completed a rough draft of their storyboard, they should take their rough sketches and turn them into a polished graphic story complete with colorful illustrations and text adapted from the excerpt. Students can use pen and paper or an online comic creator to create their stories.

Think Questions

Circulate as students answer Think Questions independently. Scaffolds for these questions are shown on the opposite page.

QUESTION 1: Textual Evidence

Athene provides Perseus with a plan and a tool for his journey to kill Medusa: "You must go northward to the country of the Hyperboreans" [and] . . . "take this polished shield." Hermes provides Perseus with further tools for his journey: "a scimitar of diamond . . . and . . . golden sandals."

QUESTION 2: Textual Evidence

The Grey Sisters help Perseus on his journey by telling him to visit "Atlas the Giant . . . [and] his daughters, the Hesperides." The Hesperides help Perseus by retrieving "the hat of darkness" from Hades. Atlas helps Perseus by telling him where to find Medusa, "on an island far away."

QUESTION 3: Textual Evidence

When Perseus first sees Medusa sleeping, "toss[ing] to and fro restlessly," he pities her. But, when the vipers' heads awake and Medusa turns and shows her claws, Perseus steps down and kills her with a single strike.

QUESTION 4: Context Clues

I think *renown* must mean "fame." The word is used to describe the "place among the heroes who feast with the Immortals" that Perseus will take after he kills Medusa.

QUESTION 5: Word Meaning

I think *scimitar* must mean a sword. The context clues in the sentence support this meaning, because he carries the scimitar on his side and it is described in paragraph 9 as a "sword" that will kill with one stroke.

 **First Read**

Read *Heroes Every Child Should Know: Perseus*. After you read, complete the Think Questions below.

THINK QUESTIONS

1. How do Athene and Hermes help prepare Perseus for his journey? Cite textual evidence from the selection to support your answer.

2. Who else helps Perseus in his quest? How do they help him? Cite specific evidence from the text in your response.

3. How does Perseus feel about Medusa? Cite textual evidence from the selection to support your answer.

4. Find the word **renown** in paragraph 4 of "Heroes Every Child Should Know: Perseus." Use context clues in the surrounding sentences, as well as the sentence in which the word appears, to determine the word's meaning. Write your definition here and identify clues that helped you figure out its meaning.

5. Use context to determine the meaning of the word **scimitar** as it is used in the text. Write your definition here and identify clues that helped you figure out its meaning. Then check the meaning in a dictionary.

Think Questions

Use the scaffolds below to differentiate instruction for your **ELL** English Language Learners and **A** Approaching grade-level learners.

ELL **BEGINNING** Write a response using the <u>word bank</u> and <u>sentence frames</u>.

INTERMEDIATE Write a response using the <u>sentence frames</u>.

ADVANCED, ADVANCED HIGH Write a response using the <u>Text-Dependent Question Guide</u>.

A **APPROACHING** Write a response using the <u>Text-Dependent Question Guide</u>.

	INTERMEDIATE	APPROACHING
BEGINNING		ADVANCED, ADVANCED HIGH
Word Bank	Sentence Frames	Text-Dependent Question Guide
behead fame giant hat	Athene tells Perseus to ___ the Grey Sisters and the Hesperides. Athene also gives Perseus a "polished ___." Hermes provides Perseus with further tools for his journey: a sword of ___ and "golden ___.	1. • What advice does Athene give Perseus? • What item does Athene give Perseus? • What items does Hermes give Perseus?
island kills her stroke	The Grey Sisters tell Perseus to visit "Atlas the ___." The Hesperides retrieve "the ___ of darkness" from Hades. Atlas tells Perseus where to find Medusa, "on an ___ far away."	2. • What do the Grey Sisters do for Perseus? • What do the Hesperides do for Perseus? • What does Atlas do for Perseus?
pities sandals shield diamond	When Perseus first sees Medusa sleeping, "tossing to and fro restlessly," he ___ her. But when the vipers' heads awake and Medusa turns and shows her claws, Perseus steps down and ___ with a single strike.	3. • When Perseus sees Medusa sleeping, how does he feel? • When Perseus sees Medusa's snake hair and claws, how does he feel? • How does Perseus react to Medusa?
sword visit	To win renown, Perseus must ___ the Gorgon Medusa. This gives me a clue that *renown* means ___.	4. • Read: "So you will bring it safely back to me, and win to yourself **renown,** and a place among the heroes who feast with the Immortals upon the peak where no winds blow." • What does Perseus have to do to win *renown*? • Who will admire Perseus for this deed?
	The young man tells Perseus that he can kill Medusa with one ___ of his weapon. This gives me a clue that *scimitar* means ___.	5. • Read: "By his side was a **scimitar** of diamond, all of one clear precious stone, and and on his feet were golden sandals" • What does the young man say about the two objects Perseus has in paragraph 9? • What does the young man tell Perseus he can use to kill Medusa?

Skill: Character

Introduce the Skill

Watch the Concept Definition video and read the following definitions with your students.

A **character** is a person, animal, or other being portrayed in a story. Every kind of fiction and drama needs characters. Characters' thoughts, feelings, actions, and reactions drive the **plot,** or the events that take place in the story. The **resolution** is the final outcome of the story's conflict. Writers use several techniques to develop characters and reveal aspects of their personality including **dialogue,** or conversation, description, and plot events. Character **traits** are the defining qualities of personality or behavior, good or bad, that make that character unique.

The main character—the one the story revolves around and who usually has a problem to solve—is called the **protagonist.** The character who opposes the protagonist is called the **antagonist.** Minor characters provide support for the protagonist or antagonist, helping to reveal aspects of their personalities.

 TURN AND TALK

1. What are some traits of your favorite characters from books, TV, or movies?

2. What's an example of a character whose thoughts, words, or actions have a big influence on the plot?

ELL **SPEAKING FRAMES**

- One of my favorite characters is ____. I like this character because ____.
- This character's actions affect the plot when ____.
- This character changes throughout the story by ____.

Heroes Every Child Should Know: Perseus

Skill:
Character

Use the Checklist to analyze Character in *Heroes Every Child Should Know: Perseus*. Refer to the sample student annotations about Character in the text.

••• CHECKLIST FOR CHARACTER

In order to determine how the characters respond or change as the plot moves toward a resolution, note the following:

✓ the characters in the story, including the protagonist and antagonist

✓ key events or series of episodes in the plot, especially events that cause characters to react, respond, or change in some way

✓ characters' responses as the plot reaches a climax, and moves toward a resolution of the problem facing the protagonist

✓ the resolution of the conflict in the plot and the ways that affects each character

✓ characters change or respond to events that move the plot toward a resolution

To describe how a particular story's or drama's plot unfolds in a series of episodes as well as how the characters respond or change as the plot moves toward a resolution, consider the following questions:

✓ How do the characters' responses change or develop from the beginning to the end of the story?

✓ Do the characters in the story change? Which event or events in the story causes a character to change?

✓ Is there an event in the story that provokes, or causes, a character to make a decision?

✓ Do the characters' problems reach a resolution? How?

✓ How does the resolution affect the characters?

✓ How do character's actions in response to events move the plot to a resolution?

8 | Reading & Writing Companion | Please note that excerpts and passages in the StudySync® library and this workbook are intended as touchstones to generate interest in an author's work. The excerpts and passages do not substitute for the reading of entire texts, and StudySync® strongly recommends that students seek out and purchase the whole literary or informational work in order to experience it as the author intended. Links to online resellers are available in our digital library. In addition, complete works may be ordered through an authorized reseller by filling out and returning to StudySync® the order form enclosed in this workbook.

 SKILL VOCABULARY

character / el personaje *noun* an individual in a literary work whose thoughts, feelings, actions, and reactions move the action of the plot forward

plot / la trama *noun* the sequence of events that form a story

resolution / la resolución *noun* the final outcome of the story's conflict COGNATE

dialogue / el diálogo *noun* the conversation between characters COGNATE

CHARACTER

Skill: Character

Reread paragraphs 46–50 of *Heroes Every Child Should Know: Perseus*. Then, using the Checklist on the previous page, answer the multiple-choice questions below.

⟳ YOUR TURN

1. Based on Perseus's actions in paragraphs 46 through 47, the reader can conclude that—

   ○ A. Athene will be pleased with the resolution of the plot's conflict.
   ○ B. Athene will be displeased with the resolution of the plot's conflict.
   ○ C. Hermes will be saddened over the resolution of the plot's conflict.
   ○ D. Hermes will be angry over the resolution of the plot's conflict.

2. When Perseus's blood runs cold in paragraph 49, it reveals that he has—

   ○ A. full confidence in Athene's plan.
   ○ B. no fear of death in the Unshapen Land.
   ○ C. brief doubt in Athene's plan.
   ○ D. no fear of Medusa's sisters.

Reading & Writing Companion 🖥 **9**

⚙ Your Turn

Ask students to complete the Your Turn Activity.

QUESTION 1

A. Correct. Perseus follows Athene's instructions and successfully slays Medusa.

B. Incorrect. Perseus follows Athene's instructions and successfully slays Medusa.

C. Incorrect. Perseus uses the sword as Hermes instructs and successfully slays Medusa.

D. Incorrect. Perseus uses the sword as Hermes instructs and successfully slays Medusa.

QUESTION 2

A. Incorrect. Perseus fears death when chased by the Gorgons.

B. Incorrect. Perseus fears death when chased by the Gorgons.

C. **Correct.** Perseus fears that Athene's plan will fail because he will not escape the Gorgons with his life.

D. Incorrect. Perseus feels fear when chased by the Gorgons.

⬛ SKILL VOCABULARY

trait / el rasgo *noun* an aspect of a character's behavior and attitude that make up that character's personality

protagonist / el/la protagonista *noun* the main character—the one the story revolves around and who usually has a problem to solve COGNATE

antagonist / el/la antagonista *noun* the character whose goals work against the protagonist COGNATE

Close Read

Skills Focus

QUESTION 1: Character

See paragraph 28.

QUESTION 2: Character

See paragraphs 30–33.

QUESTION 3: Plot

See paragraphs 49 and 50.

QUESTION 4: Point of View

See paragraph 15.

QUESTION 5: Connect to Essential Question

See paragraphs 11–13.

CHECK FOR SUCCESS

If students struggle to respond to Skills Focus Question #1, ask them the following questions:

- What did Athene prescribe about the Nymphs?

- How did Perseus respond to the Nymphs in paragraph 28?

- Why might this response surprise a reader?

Heroes Every Child Should Know: Perseus

Close Read

Reread *Heroes Every Child Should Know: Perseus*. As you reread, complete the Skills Focus questions below. Then use your answers and annotations from the questions to help you complete the Write activity.

◎ SKILLS FOCUS

1. Many of Perseus's actions in his quest are prescribed by Athene. Identify one of his thoughts and one of his actions that surprise you. Then identify one of his responses that is not directed by Athene.

2. Identify actions of Perseus that reveal something about who he is and what he wants. Explain what the actions reveal.

3. Identify the resolution of the conflict in the story. Explain how this resolution contributes to the meaning of myth.

4. Identify textual evidence that indicates from what point of view the myth is told. Explain what the point of view is and how you know.

5. As he tells the Nymphs, Perseus is on an errand for the immortals. Identify situations in the quest that test Perseus's inner strength.

✏ WRITE

LITERARY ANALYSIS: How do Perseus's responses to individuals and events drive the action of the plot forward? Write a response of at least 300 words. Support your writing with evidence from the text.

Copyright © BookheadEd Learning, LLC

Writer's Notebook

Connect to Essential Question: Give students time to reflect on how *Heroes Every Child Should Know: Perseus* connects to the unit's essential question "How do we know what to do when there are no instructions?" by freewriting in their Writer's Notebooks.

ELL Beginning & Intermediate

Read aloud the unit's essential question: "How do we know what to do when there are no instructions?" Encourage students to draw their reflections or allow students to write in their native language. Circulate around the room, prompting students for their thoughts as they respond orally or through pantomime.

Advanced & Advanced High

Allow students to share their reflections orally in pairs or small groups before freewriting.

Collaborative Conversation

SCAFFOLDS

Break students into collaborative conversation groups to discuss the Close Read prompt. Remind them to reference their Skills Focus annotations in their discussion.

How do Perseus's thoughts and actions concerning individuals and events drive the action of the plot forward?

Use the scaffolds below to differentiate instruction for your **ELL** English Language Learners and **A** Approaching grade-level learners.

ELL **BEGINNING, INTERMEDIATE** Use the discussion guide and speaking frames to facilitate the discussion with support from the teacher.

ADVANCED, ADVANCED HIGH Use the discussion guide and speaking frames to facilitate the discussion in mixed-level groups.

A **APPROACHING** Use the discussion guide to facilitate the discussion in mixed-level groups.

APPROACHING
ADVANCED, ADVANCED HIGH
BEGINNING, INTERMEDIATE

Discussion Guide	Speaking Frames
1. How does Perseus's response to the Grey Sisters drive the plot forward?	• Perseus responds to the Grey Sisters' lack of help by ____. • This response moves the plot's action along by ____.
2. How does Perseus's response to Atlas's request drive the plot forward?	• Perseus responds to Atlas's request by ____. • This response moves the plot's action along by ____.
3. How does Perseus's response to finding Medusa drive the plot forward?	• Perseus responds to finding Medusa by ____. • This response moves the plot's action along by ____.

Review Prompt and Rubric

Before students begin writing, review the writing prompt and rubric with the class.

LITERARY ANALYSIS: How do Perseus's responses to individuals and events drive the action of the plot forward? Write a response of at least 300 words. Support your writing with evidence from the text.

 PROMPT GUIDE

- How does Perseus's response to the Grey Sisters drive the plot forward?
- How does Perseus's response to Atlas's request drive the plot forward?

- How does Perseus's response to finding Medusa drive the plot forward?

Score	Character	Language and Conventions
4	The writer clearly analyzes and explains how Perseus's responses to individuals and events drive the action of the plot forward. The writer provides exemplary analysis, using relevant evidence from the text.	The writer demonstrates a consistent command of grammar, punctuation, and usage conventions. Although minor errors may be evident, they do not detract from the fluency or the clarity of the essay.
3	The writer analyzes and explains how Perseus's responses to individuals and events drive the action of the plot forward. The writer provides sufficient analysis, using relevant evidence from the text most of the time.	The writer demonstrates an adequate command of grammar, punctuation, and usage conventions. Although some errors may be evident, they create few (if any) disruptions in the fluency of the writing or the clarity of the essay.
2	The writer begins to analyze or explain how Perseus's responses to individuals and events drive the action of the plot forward, but the analysis is incomplete. The writer uses relevant evidence from the text only some of the time.	The writer demonstrates a partial command of grammar, punctuation, and usage conventions. Some distracting errors may be evident, at times creating minor disruptions in the fluency or clarity of the writing.
1	The writer attempts to analyze or explain how Perseus's responses to individuals and events drive the action of the plot forward, but the analysis is not successful. The writer uses little or no relevant evidence from the text.	The writer demonstrates little or no command of grammar, punctuation, and usage conventions. Serious and persistent errors create disruptions in the fluency of the writing and sometimes interfere with meaning.
0	The writer does not provide a relevant response to the prompt or does not provide a response at all.	Serious and persistent errors overwhelm the writing and interfere with the meaning of the response as a whole, making the writer's meaning impossible to understand.

Write

SCAFFOLDS

Ask students to complete the writing assignment using textual evidence to support their answers.

Use the scaffolds below to differentiate instruction for your **ELL** English Language Learners and **A** Approaching grade-level learners.

ELL BEGINNING With the help of the word bank, write a response using paragraph frame 1.

INTERMEDIATE With the help of the word bank, write a response using paragraph frames 1 and 2.

ADVANCED, ADVANCED HIGH Write a response of differentiated length using the sentence starters.

A APPROACHING Write a response of differentiated length using the sentence starters.

BEGINNING / INTERMEDIATE			ADVANCED, ADVANCED HIGH / APPROACHING
Word Bank	Paragraph Frame 1	Paragraph Frame 2	Sentence Starters
Atlas hat of darkness stealing their eye shield as a mirror Medusa's head	Perseus responds to the Grey Sisters' lack of help by ____. This forces the Grey Sisters to tell him how to find ____. When Atlas wants to see ____, Perseus agrees. This convinces Atlas to give Perseus the ____. When Perseus finds Medusa, he uses Athene's ____, which lets him cut off Medusa's head.	Each response moves the plot toward the ____. Without the Grey Sisters' information, Perseus would not have found ____. Without agreeing to Atlas's request, Perseus would not have gotten the ____. Without the hat of darkness, Perseus may not have been able to get close enough to ____ and resolve the ____.	• Perseus responds to the Grey Sisters by . . . • This forces the Grey Sisters to . . . • Perseus agrees to Atlas's request that . . . • This convinces Atlas to . . . • When Perseus finds Medusa, he . . . • Each response moves the plot toward . . .

Peer Review

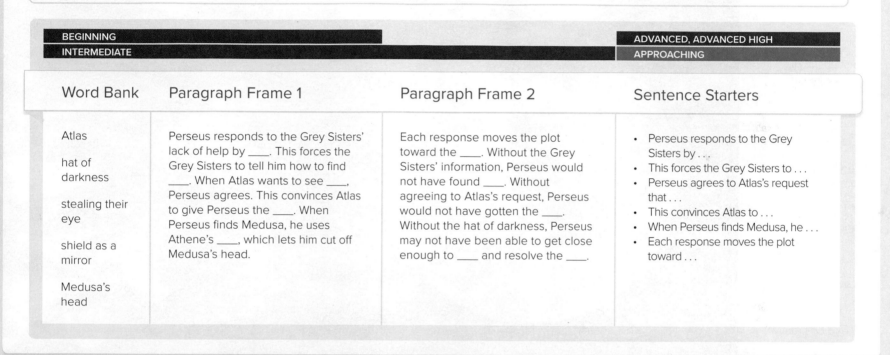

Students should submit substantive feedback to two peers using the review instructions below.
- How well does this response answer the prompt?
- How well does the writer support his or her ideas with details and examples from the text?
- Which sentence in the writer's response made you think differently about the text?
- What did the writer do well in this response? What does the writer need to work on?

Rate

Respond to the following with a point rating that reflects your opinion.

	1 2 3 4
Ideas	■ ■ ■ □
Evidence	■ ■ ■ ■
Language and Conventions	■ ■ □ □

Submit

ELL SENTENCE FRAMES

A
- You were able to (completely / partly / almost) ____ answer the prompt because ____.
- You could answer the prompt more completely by ____.
- You supported the idea of ____ with the detail of ____

- One idea that needs more support is ____.
- I thought differently about the texts after reading ____.
- My favorite part of your response is ____.

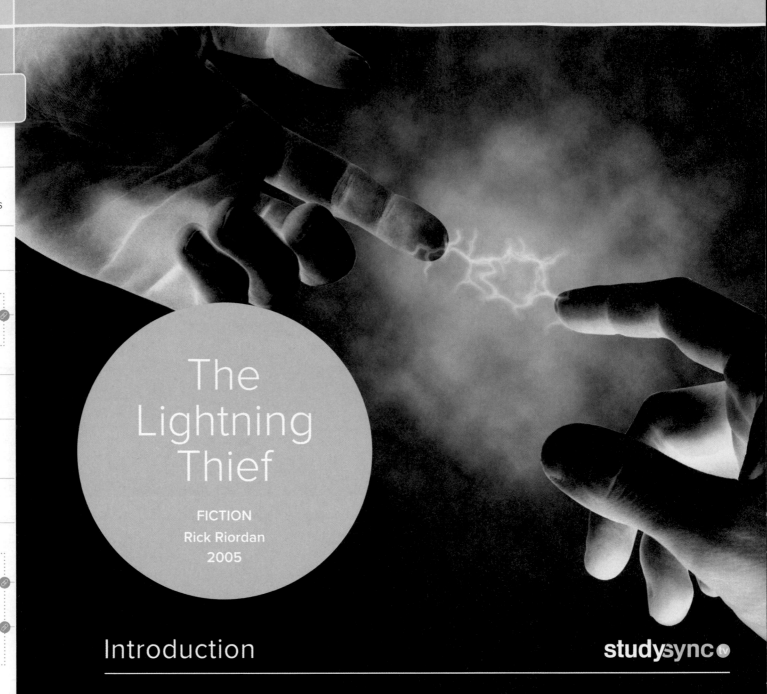

The
Lightning
Thief

FICTION
Rick Riordan
2005

Introduction

studysync ᴛᴠ

reek gods come to life in Rick Riordan's fantasy novel, *The Lightning Thief*. After being kicked out of boarding school, again, twelve-year-old Percy Jackson learns that his father is Poseidon, God of the Sea. Before long, Percy and his friends are off on a dangerous mission to find Zeus's missing lightning bolt, which must be returned before Mount Olympus erupts into war. Here, Percy questions his mother about the father who abandoned him, and then reflects on the odd things that seem to happen to him wherever he goes. This award-winning novel by Rick Riordan (b. 1964) has been adapted into a series of films. Riordan has also written other fictional series based on mythology, including *The Trials of Apollo* and *Magnus Chase and the Gods of Asgard*.

Twelve-year-old Percy Jackson and his mother are visiting their beach cabin in Montauk, Long Island. Every year, this trip brings out something special in his mother because it is where she and his father met. After dark, they make a campfire on the beach and Percy's mother reveals that his father was not around to see Percy born. She also tells him that his father would be proud of him. Percy wonders why, considering that he was just kicked out of his sixth boarding school even though he believes that it was not his fault. Percy recalls how something threatening happened at every school as if there was an evil force pursuing him. In the end, his mother mentions how his father wanted to send him to summer camp, but she wouldn't allow it because she was afraid that she would never see him again. When Percy asks about summer camp, he notices that his mother is about to cry.

 Proficiency-leveled summaries and summaries in multiple languages are available digitally.

 Audio and audio text highlighting are available with this text.

CONNECT TO ESSENTIAL QUESTION

How do we know what to do when there are no instructions?

How can a twelve-year-old boy become a hero? Find out what happens when the ancient Greek gods play a role in the life of a young boy who is alive today.

Access Complex Text

LEXILE: 740L   WORD COUNT: 1,181

The following areas may be challenging for students, particularly English Language Learners and Approaching grade-level learners.

Genre	Prior Knowledge	Organization
• *The Lightning Thief* is a contemporary fantasy in which the world of Greek gods is recreated in modern times. Impossible things happen alongside ordinary things, which may make the story hard to grasp.	• The excerpt is set in Montauk, an area of beaches in New York that may be unfamiliar to students. • References to figures prevalent in Greek mythology, including Hercules and Poseidon and their functions, may need explanation.	• Students may struggle with flashbacks — breaks in a narrative that recount previous events in the story. • Remind students that they are reading chapter 3, so they should make inferences about events and people who have been introduced previously.

 SCAFFOLDS    ENGLISH LANGUAGE LEARNERS    APPROACHING GRADE LEVEL   B BEYOND GRADE LEVEL

These icons identify differentiation strategies and scaffolded support for a variety of students. See the digital lesson plan for additional differentiation strategies and scaffolds.

Instructional Path

First Read: The Lightning Thief

Objectives: After an initial reading and discussion of the novel excerpt, students will be able to identify and describe characters and setting details as well as articulate events that are central to the story's plot.

Skill: Story Structure

Objectives: After rereading and discussing a model of close reading, students will be able to analyze story structure, including how particular parts of a text, such as flashbacks, fit into the overall structure of a text and contribute to the development of the theme, setting, or plot.

Close Read: The Lightning Thief

Objectives: After engaging in a close reading of the text to analyze story structure, students will participate in a collaborative conversation in response to a prompt, and write a reflection on participation in the discussion.

Blast: What's Old is New Again

Objectives: After exploring background information and research links about a topic, students will respond to a question with a 140-character response.

DIGITAL ONLY

Progress Monitoring

Opportunities to Learn	Opportunities to Demonstrate Learning	Opportunities to Reteach

Story Structure

⚙ Skill: Story Structure	⚙ Skill: Story Structure • Your Turn ▣ Close Read • Skills Focus • Write	⚙ Spotlight Skill: Story Structure

First Read

Rick Riordan

The Lightning Thief

Introduce the Text

As a class, watch the video preview ▶ and have students read the introduction in pairs to make connections to the video preview.

To activate prior knowledge and experiences, ask students:

- What other images could you imagine using in this video?

- How do the images, words, and music in the video connect to the information in the introduction?

ELL SPEAKING FRAMES

- The ____ in the video makes me think ____.
- The video shows ____. This makes me wonder ____.
- I think the text will ____. I think this because ____.
- I predict that there will be ____. I believe this because ____.

Entry Point

As students prepare to read *The Lightning Thief*, share the following information with them to provide context.

✓ Earlier in this unit you read "Heroes Every Child Should Know: Perseus," which is a modern telling of an Ancient Greek myth. Greek mythology includes characters that are gods and goddesses, mortal humans, and the Heroes – beings with one divine and one mortal parent.

✓ In this text Rick Riordan uses the characters from Greek mythology to write brand new stories about their lives. He got the idea to do this from his son. In an interview on his website Riordan says, "My son Haley asked me to tell him some bedtime stories about the Greek gods and heroes . . . When I ran out of myths, he was disappointed and asked me if I could make up something new with the same characters."

". . . For your own good. I have to send you away."

 NOTES

from Chapter 3

1   Our rental cabin was on the south shore, way out at the tip of Long Island. It was a little pastel box with faded curtains, half sunken into the dunes. There was always sand in the sheets and spiders in the cabinets, and most of the time the sea was too cold to swim in.

2   I loved the place.

3   We'd been going there since I was a baby. My mom had been going even longer. She never exactly said, but I knew why the beach was special to her. It was the place where she'd met my dad.

4   As we got closer to Montauk, she seemed to grow younger, years of worry and work disappearing from her face. Her eyes turned the color of the sea.

5   We got there at sunset, opened all the cabin's windows, and went through our usual cleaning routine. We walked on the beach, fed blue corn chips to the seagulls, and munched on blue jelly beans, blue saltwater taffy, and all the other free samples my mom had brought from work.

 Skill: Story Structure

This flashback tells me that both Percy and his mother are rebellious. Percy admires his mom for not giving in to Gabe. This might be a clue that Percy is also not one to back down. It helps us learn more about the characters' personalities.

6   I guess I should explain about the blue food.

7   See, Gabe had once told my mom there was no such thing. They had this fight, which seemed like a really small thing at the time. But ever since, my mom went out of her way to eat blue. She baked blue birthday cakes. She mixed blueberry smoothies. She bought blue-corn tortilla chips and brought home blue candy from the shop. This—along with keeping her maiden name, Jackson, rather than calling herself Mrs. Ugliano—was proof that she wasn't totally suckered by Gabe. She did have a **rebellious** streak, like me.

8   When it got dark, we made a fire. We roasted hot dogs and marshmallows. Mom told me stories about when she was a kid, back before her parents died in the plane crash. She told me about the books she wanted to write someday, when she had enough money to quit the candy shop.

9   Eventually, I got up the nerve to ask about what was always on my mind whenever we came to Montauk—my father. Mom's eyes went all misty. I

Copyright © BookheadEd Learning, LLC

Analyze Vocabulary Using Context Clues

In paragraph 7 focus on the sentence that uses the word *rebellious*. Point out these context clues:

1.   First I notice that Percy describes his mom as rebellious.

2.   Earlier in the paragraph, Percy explains how his mom ate blue food on purpose to prove Gabe wrong and did not change her last name like most women.

3.   She sounds like someone who isn't afraid of breaking rules or other peoples expectations.

4.   I think *rebellious* must mean "refusing to follow rules or expectations."

Story Structure

How does the reader use textual evidence to identify a flashback and analyze its purpose?

The reader notices words that signal the flashback. Then the reader identifies what the flashback shows about a character's traits.

TEXT TALK

Why are Percy and his mother visiting Long Island?

See paragraph 3: They have been visiting Long Island, New York, regularly since Percy was a baby. The place is special because Percy's mother met Percy's dad there.

How do Percy and his mother view Gabe?

See paragraph 7: Percy's mother has a strange relationship with Gabe. She's not able or willing to let go of a silly fight. Percy doesn't have a positive view of Gabe because he's proud that his mom isn't "totally suckered by Gabe."

ⓥ SELECTION VOCABULARY

rebellious / rebelde *adjective* refusing to follow rules or accepted ways of behaving COGNATE

dyslexic / disléxico / a *adjective* having a learning condition that makes it challenging to read, write, and spell COGNATE

 ELL
• Is it likely that a D+ student would be a good reader?
• Is it likely that a D+ student would be a good writer or speller?

Story Structure

How does the reader identify another flashback and analyze how it fits into the story's overall structure?

The reader notices another word that signals the flashback. Then the reader notes a contrast between the flashback and the facts, which contributes to the development of plot events that will eventually reveal the truth.

Skills Focus

QUESTION 2: Character

The reader doesn't need to guess about how Percy feels about himself—he spells it out. He obviously sees himself as a failure, even though his mother tells him that his father would be proud of him.

Skills Focus

QUESTION 5: Connect to Essential Question

Percy faces the challenge of growing up without a father. The fact that he resents his father for leaving before he was born adds to the conflict in the plot.

TEXT TALK

What does Percy remember about his father, and is this memory real?

See paragraphs 17 and 18: Percy remembers "a warm glow" and "a smile," but his mother suggests the memory isn't real because Percy's father has never seen him.

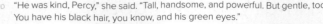

figured she would tell me the same things she always did, but I never got tired of hearing them.

10   "He was kind, Percy," she said. "Tall, handsome, and powerful. But gentle, too. You have his black hair, you know, and his green eyes."

11   Mom fished a blue jelly bean out of her candy bag. "I wish he could see you, Percy. He would be so proud."

12   I wondered how she could say that. What was so great about me? A **dyslexic, hyperactive** boy with a D+ report card, kicked out of school for the sixth time in six years.

13   "How old was I?" I asked. "I mean . . . when he left?"

14   She watched the flames. "He was only with me for one summer, Percy. Right here at this beach. This cabin."

15   "But . . . he knew me as a baby."

16   "No, honey. He knew I was expecting a baby, but he never saw you. He had to leave before you were born."

17   I tried to square that with the fact that I seemed to remember . . . something about my father. A warm glow. A smile.

18   I had always **assumed** he knew me as a baby. My mom had never said it outright, but still, I'd felt it must be true. Now, to be told that he'd never even seen me . . .

19   I felt angry at my father. Maybe it was stupid, but I **resented** him for going on that ocean voyage, for not having the guts to marry my mom. He'd left us, and now we were stuck with Smelly Gabe.

20   "Are you going to send me away again?" I asked her. "To another boarding school?"

21   She pulled a marshmallow from the fire.

22   "I don't know, honey." Her voice was heavy. "I think . . . I think we'll have to do something."

23   "Because you don't want me around?" I regretted the words as soon as they were out.

24   My mom's eyes welled with tears. She took my hand, squeezed it tight. "Oh, Percy, no. I—I *have* to, honey. For your own good. I have to send you away."

25   Her words reminded me of what Mr. Brunner had said—that it was best for me to leave Yancy.

26   "Because I'm not normal," I said.

Skill: Story Structure

The word remember signals another flashback. Percy recalls something he associates with his father. But, Percy's mother suggests this memory is false. Maybe the story might be about Percy's missing dad.

V   SELECTION VOCABULARY

hyperactive / hiperactivo / a *adjective* showing more activity or energy than is appropriate for a situation   COGNATE

ELL
- Is is likely that a D+ student would follow behavior rules in class?
- Is it likely that a D+ student would pay careful attention in class?

assume / asumir *verb* to accept to be true without proof   COGNATE

ELL
- Did Percy know his father as a baby?
- Why did Percy think he had known his father as a baby?

resent / molestarse *verb* to be angry or upset over a perceived injustice

ELL
- What does Percy's father do instead of stay with his family?
- How does Percy feel toward his father?

The Lightning Thief

NOTES

27 "You say that as if it's a bad thing, Percy. But you don't realize how important you are. I thought Yancy Academy would be far enough away. I thought you'd finally be safe."

28 "Safe from what?"

29 She met my eyes, and a flood of memories came back to me—all the weird, scary things that had ever happened to me, some of which I'd tried to forget.

30 During third grade, a man in a black trench coat had stalked me on the playground. When the teachers threatened to call the police, he went away growling, but no one believed me when I told them that under his broad-brimmed hat, the man only had one eye, right in the middle of his head.

31 Before that—a really early memory. I was in preschool, and a teacher accidentally put me down for a nap in a cot that a snake had slithered into. My mom screamed when she came to pick me up and found me playing with a limp, scaly rope I'd somehow managed to strangle to death with my meaty toddler hands.

32 In every single school, something creepy had happened, something unsafe, and I was forced to move.

33 I knew I should tell my mom about the old ladies at the fruit stand, and Mrs. Dodds at the art museum, about my weird **hallucination** that I had sliced my math teacher into dust with a sword. But I couldn't make myself tell her. I had a strange feeling the news would end our trip to Montauk, and I didn't want that.

34 "I've tried to keep you as close to me as I could," my mom said. "They told me that was a mistake. But there's only one other option, Percy—the place your father wanted to send you. And I just . . . I just can't stand to do it."

35 "My father wanted me to go to a special school?"

36 "Not a school," she said softly. "A summer camp."

37 My head was spinning. Why would my dad—who hadn't even stayed around long enough to see me born—talk to my mom about a summer camp? And if it was so important, why hadn't she ever mentioned it before?

38 "I'm sorry, Percy," she said, seeing the look in my eyes. "But I can't talk about it. I—I couldn't send you to that place. It might mean saying good-bye to you for good."

39 "For good? But if it's only a summer camp . . ."

40 She turned toward the fire, and I knew from her **expression** that if I asked her any more questions she would start to cry.

Excerpted from *The Lightning Thief* by Rick Riordan, published by Miramax Books/Hyperion Books for Children.

Copyright © BookheadEd Learning, LLC

14 📺 Reading & Writing Companion

Skills Focus

QUESTION 1: Story Structure

The author uses this flashback to alert the reader to the strange and scary things that have happened to Percy in the past. The flashback helps establish Percy as an outsider by providing hints about why he has been kicked out of so many schools. If Percy really was stalked by a one-eyed man, he is definitely different from other kids. We can expect that Percy will have more strange things happen to him as the story goes on.

TEXT TALK

What are some unusual things that have happened to Percy in school?

See paragraphs 30 and 31: A one-eyed man stalked him, and he killed a snake that had slithered into his nap cot.

Where is Percy's mother reluctant to send him?

See paragraphs 35, 36, and 38: Percy's father wants him to go to a special summer camp, but Percy's mother is worried that she'll never see Percy again if she lets him go.

Identify sensory details that help readers visualize the text.

Answers will vary.

How are the characters in The Lightning Thief connected to Greek mythology? Why did the author choose to incorporate Greek gods into a modern day story?

Answers will vary.

 B Ask each Beyond grade level student to write one additional discussion question. Then, have one or two students facilitate a discussion, using their questions to guide the conversation.

SELECTION VOCABULARY

hallucination / la alucinación *noun* vision, sound, or smell that seems real but is not COGNATE

ELL • How does Percy treat his math teacher?
• Is this action real or not?

expression / la expresión *noun* a particular look, action, or vocal intonation indicating something such as a thought or feeling COGNATE

ELL • How do you know if someone is about to cry?
• What might Percy's mom's face look like?

Think Questions

Circulate as students answer Think Questions independently. Scaffolds for these questions are shown on the opposite page.

QUESTION 1: Textual Evidence

Percy's view of himself is mostly negative. He describes himself using words with negative connotations such as "dyslexic" and "hyperactive." He also says he is a poor student with a "D+ report card."

QUESTION 2: Textual Evidence

Percy unhappily attends boarding schools away from home, but he has been "kicked out of school for the sixth time in six years." When he questions his mother about whether he'll have to go to another boarding school, she gives an unusual answer. Percy's mother suggests that she sends Percy away to these schools to keep him "far enough away" that he'll "be safe." This declaration causes Percy to recall a series of "weird, scary things" that have happened to him at school.

QUESTION 3: Textual Evidence

When Percy discovers that his father never knew him, not even as a baby, he feels "angry" and resentful. He judges his father to be a coward for "going on that ocean voyage" and "not having the guts to marry [his] mom."

QUESTION 4: Context Clues

I think *assumed* must mean "supposed something to be true without evidence." Percy uses this word when explaining that he thinks his dad knew him as a baby even though his mom "had never said it outright."

QUESTION 5: Context Clues

I think *resented* must mean "to be angry at someone who has treated you unfairly." After Percy says he is "angry" with his father, he uses the word "resented" to further describe his feelings toward his father, who left Percy and his mother. When I check in the dictionary, I see that I am right.

First Read

Read *The Lightning Thief*. After you read, complete the Think Questions below.

☁ THINK QUESTIONS

1. How does Percy describe himself? Is his view of himself mostly positive or negative? Cite textual evidence from the selection to support your answer.

2. What's unusual about Percy's school attendance? Use details from the text in your response.

3. What does Percy discover about his father? How does this discovery make Percy feel? Cite textual evidence from the selection to support your answer.

4. Find the word **assumed** in paragraph 18 of *The Lightning Thief*. Use context clues in the surrounding sentences, as well as the sentence in which the word appears, to determine the word's meaning. Write your definition here and identify clues that helped you figure out its meaning.

5. Use context clues to determine the meaning of **resented** as it is used in paragraph 19 of *The Lightning Thief*. Write your definition here and identify clues that helped you figure out the meaning. Then check the meaning in a dictionary.

Reading & Writing Companion   15

Think Questions

Use the scaffolds below to differentiate instruction for your (ELL) English Language Learners and (A) Approaching grade-level learners.

(ELL) **BEGINNING** Write a response using the word bank and sentence frames.

INTERMEDIATE Write a response using the sentence frames.

ADVANCED, ADVANCED HIGH Write a response using the Text-Dependent Question Guide.

(A) **APPROACHING** Write a response using the Text-Dependent Question Guide.

| | INTERMEDIATE | APPROACHING |
| BEGINNING | | ADVANCED, ADVANCED HIGH |

Word Bank	Sentence Frames	Text-Dependent Question Guide
baby kicked out evidence	Percy's view of himself is mostly____. He describes himself using ____ words such as "dyslexic" and "hyperactive." He also says he is a ____ student with a "D+ report card."	1. • What two words does Percy use to describe himself? • Are these words generally good or bad? • What kind of student is Percy?
knew left negative	Percy has been "____ of school for the ____ time in six years." Percy's mother suggests that she sends Percy away to these schools to keep him "____."	2. • How many schools has Percy attended in the last six years? • Why has Percy left each school? • Why does Percy's mother want him to go away to a boarding school?
poor true resentful	When Percy discovers that his father never ____ him, not even as a ____, he feels "angry" and ____.	3. • What has Percy always believed about his father? • What does Percy find out about this belief? • What words does Percy use to describe his feelings regarding this news?
mom safe sixth unfairly	Percy feels it must be true that his ____ knew him as a baby even though his ____ did not tell him this. This gives me a clue that *assumed* means to suppose something is ____ without ____ .	4. • Read: "I had always **assumed** he knew me as a baby." • What does Percy feel must be true? • Does Percy have evidence to support this feeling?
father unflattering upset	Percy feels angry with his father. He feels this way because his father ____ Percy and his mother. This gives me a clue that *resented* means to feel ____ with someone who has treated you ____.	5. • Read: "Maybe it was stupid, but I **resented** him for going on that ocean voyage, for not having the guts to marry my mom." • How does Percy feel about his father? • What causes Percy to feel this way?

Reading Comprehension OPTIONAL

Have students complete the digital reading comprehension questions ✓ when they finish reading.

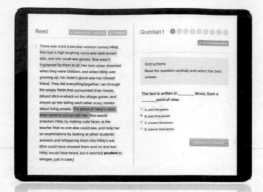

ANSWER KEY

QUESTION 1: C	**QUESTION 5:** B	**QUESTION 9:** B
QUESTION 2: B	**QUESTION 6:** B	**QUESTION 10:**
QUESTION 3: A	**QUESTION 7:** C	*See chart.*
QUESTION 4: C	**QUESTION 8:** A	

First	Second	Third	Fourth
Percy learns his father never met him.	Percy recalls strange events in his childhood.	Percy learns his father wanted him to go to summer camp.	Percy realizes attending summer camp might mean losing his mother forever.

Connect and Extend OPTIONAL

CONNECT TO EXTENDED WRITING PROJECT

Students can use *The Lightning Thief* as a mentor text for their Extended Writing Project. They may adapt how the author, Rick Riordan, uses dialogue.

BEYOND THE BOOK

Game: Percy's Perils

Using details from Percy's life combined with researched information about Greek mythology and the gods, students should work collaboratively to create a board game in which Percy attempts to find his father while avoiding pitfalls and villains.

Break students into small groups and ask them to:

- Brainstorm the various pitfalls Percy might encounter on his search for his father.
- Research Greek mythology and the gods to gather information they can use in their game.
- Decide on the format of their game.
  > Will the players draw cards or roll dice?
  > What colors, images, icons or pieces will they need?
- Create their game using art materials in the classroom.

Once the games have been finished, spend a class period allowing groups to play each other's games and provide anonymous feedback on paper or online about what they enjoyed about each game and how each game could be improved.

Skill:
Story Structure

sync•skills

Use the Checklist to analyze Story Structure in *The Lightning Thief*. Refer to the sample student annotations about Story Structure in the text.

••• CHECKLIST FOR STORY STRUCTURE

In order to identify how a particular sentence, chapter, scene or stanza fits into the overall structure of a text, note the following:

✓ the author's use of description, dialogue, and narration and how each develops the events of the plot

✓ the pattern the author uses to organize the events within a story or chapter

- chronological, or in time order
- events out of time order

✓ any literary devices the author uses, such as flashback, a part of a story that shows something that happened in the past

✓ any particular sentence, chapter, scene, or a stanza in a poem that contributes to the development of the setting, the plot, and the theme

✓ how a particular sentence, chapter, scene, or a stanza in a poem fits into the overall structure

To analyze how a particular sentence, chapter, scene, or stanza fits into the overall structure of a text and contributes to the development of the theme, setting, or plot, consider the following questions:

✓ What are the key events in the story and when did they take place?

✓ What impact does the order of events that take place in the story have on the theme, setting, or plot?

✓ What literary devices does the author use? How do they affect the development of the plot?

✓ How does a particular sentence, chapter, scene, or a stanza in a poem fit into the overall structure? How does it contribute to the development of the theme, setting, or plot?

16 Reading & Writing Companion

Skill: Story Structure

Introduce the Skill

Watch the Concept Definition video and read the following definitions with your students.

Story structure is the framework writers use to develop the events of the **plot.** Any plot has a central problem or conflict which the story introduces, builds to a climax, and finally solves. The story may be character-driven, exploring one person's emotions, or it could be driven by suspense, with a complicated sequence of events that takes many twists and turns. The events may or may not be presented in chronological order. For example, an author who wishes to build tension may begin with a dramatic **flashback** before introducing the present situation in a story. A character-driven novel might describe events from the point of view of one character, and how the events change him or her. Whatever story structure an author chooses to use, **analyzing** how the events of a chapter or scene fit into the overall structure can help readers identify how it also contributes to the development of the **theme** and **setting.**

TURN AND TALK

1. What is the storyline of a favorite book or movie?

2. What part of the story do you think is the most important part? Why is that part so important?

ELL SPEAKING FRAMES
- One of my favorite books/movies is ____. It is about ____.
- The most important part is when ____.
- That part is important because ____.

V SKILL VOCABULARY

story structure / la estructura de la historia *noun* the outline a writer uses to organize and tell a story

plot / la trama *noun* the sequence of events that form a story

flashback / la escena retrospectiva *noun* a scene in a story, play, movie, or TV show that is set in a time earlier than the events in the main story

Your Turn

Ask students to complete the Your Turn Activity.

QUESTION 1

A. Incorrect. The narrator uses this phrase to describe his mother.

B. **Correct.** The narrator uses this phrase to introduce a flashback to an earlier time.

C. Incorrect. The narrator uses this phrase to describe the memories he cites earlier in the sentence.

D. Incorrect. The narrator uses this phrase to describe the memories he cites earlier in the sentence.

QUESTION 2

A. Incorrect. Percy is angry at his father for abandoning the family, not because of these events in school.

B. Incorrect. Percy's mother's fears regarding Percy's safety seem to be correct, not irrational.

C. Incorrect. It is more likely best or easier for Mr. Brunner that Percy leave Yancy. The move is not in Percy's best interests.

D. **Correct.** Percy isn't normal. These flashbacks give evidence of the heroic traits Percy possesses because he is the son of Poseidon, God of the Sea.

QUESTION 3

A. Incorrect. This phrase just provides a set-up for the flashback.

B. **Correct.** This sentence sums up the previous flashbacks and indicates that these things might continue.

C. Incorrect. This sentence just provides the context for this particular flashback.

D. Incorrect. This sentence does imply that Percy has special traits, but is not the strongest answer.

Skill:
Story Structure

Reread paragraphs 29–32 of *The Lightning Thief*. Then, using the Checklist on the previous page, answer the multiple-choice questions below.

 YOUR TURN

1. Which phrase from paragraph 29 best signals the author's use of flashback?

   ○ A. she met my eyes
   ○ B. flood of memories came back to me
   ○ C. weird, scary things
   ○ D. had ever happened to me

2. Why might the author choose to use the flashbacks in paragraphs 30 and 31?

   ○ A. to explain Percy's earlier anger toward his missing father
   ○ B. to describe Percy's mother's irrational fear that Percy isn't safe
   ○ C. to support Mr. Brunner's earlier claim that it's best for Percy to leave Yancy
   ○ D. to reinforce the idea that Percy is different and unique

3. Which sentence or phrase from the passage gives the clearest understanding that the story will be about Percy's struggles?

   ○ A. "She met my eyes, and a flood of memories came back to me. . ."
   ○ B. "In every single school, something creepy had happened, something unsafe, and I was forced to move."
   ○ C. "I was in preschool, and a teacher accidentally put me down for a nap in a cot that a snake had slithered into."
   ○ D. "My mom screamed when she came to pick me up and found me playing with a limp, scaly rope I'd somehow managed to strangle to death with my meaty toddler hands.

Reading & Writing Companion 17

v SKILL VOCABULARY

analyze / analizar *verb* to consider in detail and discover essential features or meaning   COGNATE

theme / el tema *noun* the central idea or message of a work of literature, often expressed as a general statement about life

setting / el escenario *noun* the time and place of the story

Close Read

Reread *The Lightning Thief*. As you reread, complete the Skills Focus questions below. Then use your answers and annotations from the questions to help you complete the Write activity.

◎ SKILLS FOCUS

1. Explain how the author's use of flashbacks about Percy's childhood help develop the plot.

2. Identify examples of Percy's thoughts that reveal how he feels about himself. Explain how these thoughts help establish Percy as an outsider.

3. Identify textual evidence that illustrates how the author uses dialogue between Percy and his mother to develop the plot and theme. Explain your reasoning.

4. In the ninth paragraph, Percy finally gets up the nerve to ask about his father. How is this an example of a turning point in the story, and how does it further develop the plot? Explain your reasoning.

5. Percy has many challenges and few instructions on how to resolve them. Identify evidence of these challenges and explain how they contribute to the story's conflict.

✎ WRITE

DISCUSSION: How does this excerpt from *The Lightning Thief* connect to the overall structure of the story? What hints does the author provide about the overall plot and theme? Think about how the author uses flashbacks to describe Percy's past, Percy's thoughts, and Percy's dialogue with his mother. As you prepare for your discussion, be sure to find plenty of textual evidence to support your ideas.

Close Read

Skills Focus

QUESTION 1: Story Structure

See paragraphs 29 and 30.

QUESTION 2: Character

See paragraph 12.

QUESTION 3: Story Structure

See paragraphs 20–26. This dialogue between Percy and his mother reinforces that Percy sees himself as an different from other kids. I can tell from his questions that he feels rejected by being sent away to boarding school. But his mom's response makes it seem like he is in danger. We can tell that something dangerous will probably happen as the plot develops. One theme that could develop is that being different is what makes you special. Percy might come to realize this as the story continues.

QUESTION 4: Plot

See paragraphs 9–16. When Percy asks about his father, he thinks he's going to get the same old answers from his mother. Only this time, Percy gets a surprise. His mother reveals that Percy's father left before he was born. This is a turning point for Percy. I could ask, "How will this change the events of the story?" This information might make Percy more curious to find out more about his father, leading to adventures and discoveries in the plot.

QUESTION 5: Connect to Essential Question

See paragraphs 18 and 19.

📖 Writer's Notebook

Connect to Essential Question: Give students time to reflect on how *The Lightning Thief* connects to the unit's essential question "How do we know what to do when there are no instructions?" by freewriting in their Writer's Notebooks.

ELL Beginning & Intermediate

Read aloud the unit's essential question: "How do we know what to do when there are no instructions?" Encourage students to draw their connections or allow students to write in their native language. Circulate around the room, prompting students for their thoughts as they respond orally or through pantomime.

Advanced & Advanced High

Allow students to share their connections orally in pairs or small groups before freewriting.

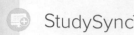

StudySyncTV
Project the StudySyncTV episode  and pause at the following times to prompt discussion:

2:15 How do the students use textual evidence to determine that Percy is lonely?

4:48 How does the search for textual evidence to support Sam's claim that there is something magical going on bring the students back to the prompt's focus on fact versus fiction?

6:50 How does Sean lead the students to consider the broader theme in *The Lightning Thief?* What does Sam conclude?

Collaborative Conversation

SCAFFOLDS

Break students into collaborative conversation groups to discuss the Close Read prompt. Ask students to use the StudySyncTV episode as a model for their discussion. Remind them to reference their Skills Focus annotations in their discussion.

How does this excerpt of *The Lightning Thief* connect to the overall structure of the story? What hints does the author provide about the overall plot and theme? Think about how the author's uses flashbacks to describe Percy's past, Percy's thoughts, and dialogue with his mother. As you prepare for your discussion, be sure to find plenty of textual evidence to support your ideas.

Use the scaffolds below to differentiate instruction for your **ELL** English Language Learners and **A** Approaching grade-level learners.

ELL **BEGINNING, INTERMEDIATE** Use the discussion guide and speaking frames to facilitate the discussion with support from the teacher.

ADVANCED, ADVANCED HIGH Use the discussion guide and speaking frames to facilitate the discussion in mixed-level groups.

A **APPROACHING** Use the discussion guide to facilitate the discussion in mixed-level groups.

> APPROACHING
> ADVANCED, ADVANCED HIGH
> BEGINNING, INTERMEDIATE

Discussion Guide	Speaking Frames
1. What can you tell from the flashbacks of Percy's past?	• The flashbacks make me think that the plot might be about ____. • The flashbacks make me think that the theme of the story might be ____.
2. What can you tell from Percy's thoughts?	• Percy's thoughts make me think that the plot might be about ____. • Percy's thoughts make me think that the theme of the story might be ____.
3. What can you tell from what Percy and his mother say to each other?	• The things Percy and his mother say to each other make me think that the plot might be about ____. • The things Percy and his mother say to each other make me think that the theme of the story might be ____.

Review Prompt and Rubric

Before students begin writing, review the writing prompt and rubric with the class.

Reflection: As you write, make sure to

- evaluate how well everyone followed the rules when making decisions affecting the group
- evaluate your own participation in the discussion
- reflect on how well you and your classmates followed the suggestions of the moderator to stay on topic, or, if you were the moderator, how well you guided your classmates to keep the discussion on track

 PROMPT GUIDE

- How does the author use flashbacks to help you understand the plot or the theme?
- How does the author use Percy's thoughts to help you understand the plot or the theme?

- How does the author use dialogue between Percy and his mother to help you understand the plot or the theme?

Score	Reflection	Language and Conventions
4	The writer clearly reflects on how well he or she moderated the discussion or followed suggestions of the moderator to keep the discussion on track as well as his or her own participation. The writer consistently refers to specific examples from the discussion.	The writer demonstrates a consistent command of grammar, punctuation, and usage conventions. Although minor errors may be evident, they do not detract from the fluency or the clarity of the essay.
3	The writer reflects on how well he or she moderated the discussion or followed suggestions of the moderator to keep the discussion on track as well as his or her own participation. The writer refers to specific examples from the discussion most of the time.	The writer demonstrates an adequate command of grammar, punctuation, and usage conventions. Although some errors may be evident, they create few (if any) disruptions in the fluency of the writing or the clarity of the essay.
2	The writer begins to reflect on how well he or she moderated the discussion or followed suggestions of the moderator to keep the discussion on track as well as his or her own participation. The writer refers to specific examples from the discussion some of the time.	The writer demonstrates a partial command of grammar, punctuation, and usage conventions. Some distracting errors may be evident, at times creating minor disruptions in the fluency or clarity of the writing.
1	The writer attempts to reflect on how well he or she moderated the discussion or followed suggestions of the moderator to keep the discussion on track as well as his or her own participation in the response. The writer refers to few, if any, examples from the discussion.	The writer demonstrates little or no command of grammar, punctuation, and usage conventions. Serious and persistent errors create disruptions in the fluency of the writing and sometimes interfere with meaning.
0	The writer does not provide a relevant response to the prompt or does not provide a response at all.	Serious and persistent errors overwhelm the writing and interfere with the meaning of the response as a whole, making the writer's meaning impossible to understand.

Write

 SCAFFOLDS

Ask students to complete the writing assignment using textual evidence to support their answers.

Use the scaffolds below to differentiate instruction for your **ELL** English Language Learners and **A** Approaching grade-level learners.

ELL **BEGINNING** With the help of the <u>word bank</u>, write a response using <u>paragraph frame 1</u>.

INTERMEDIATE With the help of the <u>word bank</u>, write a response using <u>paragraph frames 1 and 2</u>.

ADVANCED, ADVANCED HIGH Write a response of differentiated length using the <u>sentence starters</u>.

A **APPROACHING** Write a response of differentiated length using the <u>sentence starters</u>.

BEGINNING INTERMEDIATE			ADVANCED, ADVANCED HIGH APPROACHING
Word Bank	**Paragraph Frame 1**	**Paragraph Frame 2**	**Sentence Starters**
good

average

topic

plot

questions

listened

theme

story structure | My discussion group talked about ____. I think my group did a(n) ____ job following the discussion rules. I think this because ____. I added to the discussion by ____. | When we started talking, ____. Then another student said ____. That made me ____. Then, I was able ____. | • My opinion of my group's performance is . . .
• I have this opinion because . . .
• I contributed to the discussion by . . .
• When the discussion began, we created rules, such as . . .
• My group was/was not able to stay on track because . . .
• I was able to stay on topic by . . .
• If I could change one thing about my contributions, it would be . . .
• Next time, my discussion goal will be to . . . |

Peer Review

Students should submit substantive feedback to two peers using the review instructions below.

- How well does this response answer the reflection prompt?
- How well does the speaker support his or her ideas with details and examples from the discussion?
- What did the speaker do well in this response? What does the speaker need to work on?

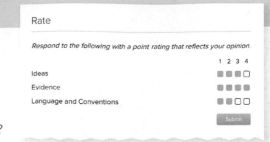

Rate

Respond to the following with a point rating that reflects your opinion.

	1 2 3 4
Ideas	■ ■ ■ □
Evidence	■ ■ ■ ■
Language and Conventions	■ ■ □ □

Submit

 SENTENCE FRAMES

- You were able to (completely / partly / almost) ____ answer the prompt because ____.
- You could answer the prompt more completely by ____.

- You supported the idea of ____ with the detail of ____.
- One idea that needs more support is ____.
- My favorite part of your response is ____.

Elena

POETRY
Pat Mora
1994

Introduction

Pat Mora (b. 1942) is a celebrated Mexican American author whose bilingual works explore themes of culture and identity in families across Texas and along the Southwestern border, where Mora was born and raised. The poem presented here, "Elena," is told from the perspective of a mother who has emigrated from Mexico to the United States with her husband and their children. After some time in the States, her kids have adapted and now speak English even at home—a language in which the mother has little fluency. In direct and confessional language, the mother worries about the increasing cultural divide between her and her children.

Elena is upset that Spanish, her native language, is no longer useful for communicating with her children. She fondly remembers when her kids were young and still spoke Spanish, and she was able to understand everything that they said. But since moving to the United States, the children have spoken exclusively in English, which has made Elena feel alone. She doesn't speak English well and cannot understand her children's conversations or jokes. Embarrassed, Elena buys a language book, but her husband discourages her from reading it. She ignores him and locks herself in the bathroom to read it. Ultimately, Elena wants to learn English because she is worried that she won't be able to understand her children if they are ever in trouble and need her help.

 Proficiency-leveled summaries and summaries in multiple languages are available digitally.

🔊 Audio and audio text highlighting are available with this text.

COMPARING WITHIN AND ACROSS GENRES

 In the poem, "Elena," a mother worries about the potential loss of communication with her children and strives to overcome their language barrier by learning English. Paired with *Hatshepsut: His Majesty, Herself*, students are forced to compare themes about female empowerment across genre.

Access Complex Text

LEXILE: N/A   WORD COUNT: 145

The following areas may be challenging for students, particularly **ELL** English Language Learners and **A** Approaching grade-level learners.

Connection of Ideas	Specific Vocabulary	Purpose
• Students will need to make inferences to interpret the meaning of the poem. For example, they will need to understand that the reference to being *deaf* is a metaphor.	• The use of Spanish in the poem may cause difficulties for students unfamiliar with the Spanish language.	• While the primary purpose of the poem is to express the speaker's emotional struggle, it also contains themes about cultural assimilation and language barriers. Students may struggle to understand the theme as well as the speaker's tone. • A discussion about the the speaker's feelings of frustration and isolation will help students to grasp the the tone, theme, and purpose of the poem.

SCAFFOLDS    **ELL** ENGLISH LANGUAGE LEARNERS    **A** APPROACHING GRADE LEVEL    **B** BEYOND GRADE LEVEL

These icons identify differentiation strategies and scaffolded support for a variety of students. See the digital lesson plan for additional differentiation strategies and scaffolds.

Instructional Path

The print teacher's edition includes essential point-of-use instruction and planning tools. Complete lesson plans and program documents appear in your digital teacher account.

Independent Read: Elena

Objectives: After reading the text, students will write a short response that demonstrates their understanding of characterization through poetry.

Independent Read

Pat Mora

Elena

Introduce the Text

As a class, watch the video preview ▶ and have students read the introduction in pairs to make connections to the video preview.

- What key words or images from the video do you think will be most important to the poem you are about to read?

- What is one question you have about what you are going to read?

- What is one prediction you can make about the poem you're going to read?

ELL SPEAKING FRAMES

- The ____ in the video makes me think ____.
- The video shows ____. This makes me wonder ____.
- A question I have about the poem is ____?
- One of my predictions about the poem is ____. I believe this because ____.

Entry Point

As students prepare to read "Elena," share the following information with them to provide context.

✓ People of all nations come to the US for various reasons such as stability of employment, to take refuge during time of instability, or to start a new life. Throughout history, emigration into Mexico into the United states has ebbed and flowed.

✓ Emigrating can be a daunting task as individuals must essentially start over in an unfamiliar country. Being an immigrant involves learning a new language, securing work and housing, and overcoming cultural barriers. All of the above can have a significant impact of the mentality of immigrants today.

✓ In her poem, "Elena," Pat Mora describes a mother's feelings about difficulties she faces post immigration.

"I stand at the stove and feel dumb, alone."

1 My Spanish isn't good enough.
2 I remember how I'd smile
3 listening to my little ones,
4 understanding every word they'd say,
5 their jokes, their songs, their **plots.**
6 *Vamos a pedirle dulces a mamá. Vamos.*
7 But that was in Mexico.
8 Now my children go to American high schools.
9 They speak English. At night they sit around
10 the kitchen table, laugh with one another.
11 I stand at the stove and feel dumb, alone.
12 I bought a book to learn English.
13 My husband **frowned**, drank more beer.
14 My oldest said, "*Mamá*, he doesn't want you
15 to be smarter than he is." I'm forty,
16 **embarrassed** at **mispronouncing** words,
17 embarrassed at the laughter of my children,
18 the grocer, the mailman. Sometimes I take
19 my English book and lock myself in the bathroom,
20 say the thick words softly,
21 for if I stop trying, I will be **deaf**
22 when my children need my help.

"Elena" from "Chants" by Pat Mora (©1994 Arte Público Press - University of Houston)

✏ WRITE

POEM: The poem "Elena" is told from the mother's point of view. Write a poem in response to the mother from the perspective of one of her children.

20   Reading & Writing Companion   Please note that excerpts and passages in the StudySync® library and this workbook are intended as touchstones to generate interest in an author's work. The excerpts and passages do not substitute for the reading of entire texts, and StudySync® strongly recommends that students seek out and purchase the whole literary or informational work in order to experience it as the author intended. Links to online resellers are available in our digital library. In addition, complete works may be ordered through an authorized reseller by filling out and returning to StudySync® the order form enclosed in this workbook.

Ⅴ SELECTION VOCABULARY

plot / la trama *noun* secret plans or schemes

frown / fruncir el ceño *verb* to turn the corners of the mouth down to show displeasure

embarrassed / avergonzado / a *adjective* feeling foolish or ashamed

mispronounce / pronunciar mal *verb* to speak a word incorrectly

deaf / sordo / a *adjective* partially or wholly unable to hear

 ## Analyze Vocabulary Using Context Clues

As students read the text, ask them to make predictions about each bold vocabulary word based on the context clues in the sentence. Have students use the annotation tool to make their predictions.

 ### TURN AND TALK

Have students discuss their original vocabulary predictions with a neighbor. Come to a consensus as a class before confirming their definitions.

Copyright © BookheadEd Learning, LLC

 ### TEXT TALK

Where is the speaker from?

See line 7: Mexico.

How does the speaker feel?

See line 11: dumb and alone.

What does the speaker do in the bathroom?

See lines 18–19: She takes her English book into the bathroom to learn English.

Why does the speaker want to learn English?

See lines 9, 11, 17 and 22. Answers will vary, but should include: She wants to learn English to understand her children like she did when they spoke Spanish. Also to be able to help her children if needed, to be a part of their new American life.

 Ⓑ Ask each Beyond grade level student to write one additional discussion question. Then, have one or two students facilitate a discussion, using their questions to guide the conversation.

Reading Comprehension

Have students complete the digital reading comprehension questions ✓ when they finish reading.

ANSWER KEY

QUESTION 1: C   **QUESTION 3:** B   **QUESTION 5:**

QUESTION 2: A   **QUESTION 4:** B   *See chart below.*

Definition	Word
ashamed or uncomfortably self-conscious	embarrassed
scowled, glared	frowned
unable to hear	deaf
secret plans or schemes	plots
saying something the wrong way	mispronouncing

Connect and Extend OPTIONAL

CONNECT TO EXTENDED WRITING PROJECT

Students can use "Elena" as inspiration for their Extended Writing Project. Ask students to discuss and take notes on what lessons they can glean from the poem about love and loss. Have students focus on the conflict within a parent-child relationship that bridges two different cultures and languages.

BEYOND THE BOOK

Debate: Digital Divide and Its Impact on Families

Are social media creating a digital divide that is hurting families?

Pair students up and assign each partner a pro or con position. Then ask them to:

1. Research the impacts of social media on all ages.

2. Develop a formal argument in favor of their position with clear claims and evidence.

3. Rehearse their statements separately.

Then allow each pair to engage in a formal debate and allow the class to anonymously vote on paper or online for the position they felt was strongest.

To reflect, ask students:

- If you had to argue a position you disagree with, how did you generate your claims?

- What process did you go through to ensure the information you found online was credible?

Collaborative Conversation

Break students into collaborative conversation groups to discuss the writing prompt. Remind them to reference their Skills Focus annotations in their discussion.

The poem "Elena" is told from the mother's point of view. Write a poem in response to the mother from the perspective of one of her children.

Use the scaffolds below to differentiate instruction for your **ELL** English Language Learners and **A** Approaching grade-level learners.

ELL **BEGINNING, INTERMEDIATE** Use the discussion guide and speaking frames to facilitate the discussion with support from the teacher.

ADVANCED, ADVANCED HIGH Use the discussion guide and speaking frames to facilitate the discussion in mixed-level groups.

A **APPROACHING** Use the discussion guide to facilitate the discussion in mixed-level groups.

APPROACHING
ADVANCED, ADVANCED HIGH
BEGINNING, INTERMEDIATE

Discussion Guide	Speaking Frames
1. How does the mother feel?	• The mother feels ____.
2. How are the children in the poem different from their mother?	• The children are different from their mother because ____.
3. What feelings or ideas about their mother might the children want to express in a poem?	• One feeling about their mother that the children might express is ___. • One idea they might have is ____.

Review Prompt and Rubric

Before students begin writing, review the writing prompt and rubric with the class.

POEM: The poem "Elena" is told from the mother's point of view. Write a poem in response to the mother from the perspective of one of her children.

ELL PROMPT GUIDE

A
- How does the mother feel about her relationship with her children?
- How are the children in the poem different from their mother?

- What feelings or ideas might the children want to express in a poem?
- What text evidence supports your ideas?

Score	Poetry	Language and Conventions
4	The writer writes a poem from the perspective of one of the speaker's children, using inspiration or relevant evidence from the text as needed.	The writer demonstrates a consistent command of grammar, punctuation, and usage conventions. Although minor errors may be evident, they do not detract from the fluency or the clarity of the essay.
3	The writer writes a poem from the perspective of one of the speaker's children, using inspiration or relevant evidence from the text most of the time.	The writer demonstrates an adequate command of grammar, punctuation, and usage conventions. Although some errors may be evident, they create few (if any) disruptions in the fluency of the writing or the clarity of the essay.
2	The writer begins to write a poem from the perspective of one of the speaker's children, but the poem is incomplete. The writer uses inspiration or relevant evidence from the text only some of the time.	The writer demonstrates a partial command of grammar, punctuation, and usage conventions. Some distracting errors may be evident, at times creating minor disruptions in the fluency or clarity of the writing.
1	The writer attempts to write a poem from the perspective of one of the speaker's children, but the attempt is not successful. The writer uses little or no inspiration or relevant evidence from the text.	The writer demonstrates little or no command of grammar, punctuation, and usage conventions. Serious and persistent errors create disruptions in the fluency of the writing and sometimes interfere with meaning.
0	The writer does not provide a relevant response to the prompt or does not provide a response at all.	Serious and persistent errors overwhelm the writing and interfere with the meaning of the response as a whole, making the writer's meaning impossible to understand.

Write

SCAFFOLDS

Ask students to complete the writing assignment using textual evidence to support their answers.

Use the scaffolds below to differentiate instruction for your **ELL** English Language Learners and **A** Approaching grade-level learners.

ELL **BEGINNING** With the help of the word bank, write a response using paragraph frame 1.

INTERMEDIATE With the help of the word bank, write a response using paragraph frames 1 and 2.

ADVANCED, ADVANCED HIGH Write a response of differentiated length using the sentence starters.

A **APPROACHING** Write a response of differentiated length using the sentence starters.

BEGINNING		ADVANCED, ADVANCED HIGH	
INTERMEDIATE		APPROACHING	
Word Bank	**Paragraph Frame 1**	**Paragraph Frame 2**	**Sentence Starters**
brave lion know strong English proud	If my mom were an animal, she would be a ____ because she is ____. My mom was ____ when she learned ____. I want her to ____ that I'm ____ of her.	It must have been ____ for my mom to ____ .I remember ____. I want my mom to know that ____.	• My mom is like a . . . because she . . . • I remember when my mom . . . • It must be . . . for my mom to . . . • My family is . . . • Our family is as . . . as . . . • When I think of the future, I see . . . • I want my mother to know that she . . .

Peer Review

Students should submit substantive feedback to two peers using the review instructions below.

• How well does this response answer the prompt?
• How does this poem make you think differently about the children's perspectives?
• What other details could the writer have included in this poem?

Rate

Respond to the following with a point rating that reflects your opinion.

	1 2 3 4
Ideas	▪▪▪☐
Evidence	▪▪▪▪
Language and Conventions	▪▪☐☐

Submit

ELL **A** **SENTENCE FRAMES**

• Your poem (completely / partly / almost) ____ answered the prompt.
• Your poem could answer the prompt more completely by ____.

• I thought differently about the text after reading ____ in your poem.
• My favorite part of your poem is ____.

Hatshepsut: His Majesty, Herself

INFORMATIONAL TEXT
Catherine M. Andronik
2001

Introduction

studysync

I n Egypt's eighteenth dynasty, during the mid-to-late 1400s BCE, a long pattern of male dominance was interrupted when Hatshepsut, the widow of Pharaoh Tuthmosis II, and daughter of the previous pharaoh, Tuthmosis I, took the throne. Hatshepsut's reign lasted 22 years, during which time she built great monuments, sent an expedition to the little-known land of Punt, and handed over a peaceful Egypt to her nephew, Tuthmosis III, who subsequently attempted to erase Hatshepsut's historical imprint.

Hatshepsut lived around the mid-to-late 1400s BCE in Egypt. Royal lineage and the line of succession were important, which is why Hatshepsut was forced to marry her half brother. When her husband died, he left behind an heir who was still an infant, and Hatshepsut was forced to rule until the heir was old enough. She was only fifteen years old at the time but quickly proved to be an effective ruler. Eventually, she appeared at public ceremonies walking in front of her nephew, the rightful monarch. During her rule, Hatshepsut even crowned herself pharaoh and wore a false golden beard upon her chin. As a ruler, she did not lead many military campaigns. Instead, she focused on building monuments in tribute to her nation's power. The greatest of these was the temple at Deir el-Bahri, where Hatshepsut was eventually laid to rest.

 Proficiency-leveled summaries and summaries in multiple languages are available digitally.

 Audio and audio text highlighting are available with this text.

COMPARING WITHIN AND ACROSS GENRES

 In the poem, "Elena," a Mexican wife and mother challenged male authority by learning English against her husband's wishes so she can communicate with her children raised in America. Compare the mother in "Elena" with Hatshepsut who defied the traditions of an entire male-dominated society.

Access Complex Text

LEXILE: 1070L   **WORD COUNT:** 1,415

The following areas may be challenging for students, particularly **ELL** English Language Learners and **A** Approaching grade-level learners.

Prior Knowledge	Genre	Specific Vocabulary
• The text is about events that took place in ancient Egypt 3,500 years ago. • Students may need additional information about the role of the pharaoh in Egyptian society and also ancient Egyptian funerary beliefs and practices.	• Remind students that a biography is the true story of a real person's life written by someone else. Review with students the features of a biography, such as chronological text structure, point of view, historical context, and direct and indirect description. • This biography introduces the Egyptian pharaoh Hatshepsut and describes her life and her accomplishments.	• The pronunciation of ancient Egyptian names, such as *Hatshepsut* and *Mutnofret*, may have to be sounded out for students. • The term *Maat* refers to the ancient Egyptian concepts of truth, balance, order, harmony, law, morality and justice, and it was the pharaoh's responsibility to protect and promote these ideals.

** SCAFFOLDS**   ** ENGLISH LANGUAGE LEARNERS**   ** APPROACHING GRADE LEVEL**   ** BEYOND GRADE LEVEL**

These icons identify differentiation strategies and scaffolded support for a variety of students. See the digital lesson plan for additional differentiation strategies and scaffolds.

Instructional Path

The print teacher's edition includes essential point-of-use instruction and planning tools. Complete lesson plans and program documents appear in your digital teacher account.

First Read: Hatshepsut: His Majesty, Herself

Objectives: After an initial reading and discussion of the biography, students will be able to identify and restate the text's key ideas and details.

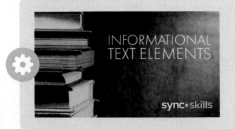

Skill: Informational Text Elements

Objectives: After rereading and discussing a model of close reading, students will be able to analyze in detail how a key individual, event, or idea is introduced, illustrated, and elaborated in a text (e.g., through examples or anecdotes).

Skill: Central or Main Idea

Objectives: After rereading and discussing a model of close reading, students will be able to determine the central idea of a text and how it is conveyed through particular details.

Close Read: Hatshepsut: His Majesty, Herself

Objectives: After engaging in a close reading and discussion of the text, students will be able to analyze how the central idea of the text is developed through supporting details in a short, written response.

Progress Monitoring

Opportunities to Learn	Opportunities to Demonstrate Learning	Opportunities to Reteach

Informational Text Elements

⚙ Skill: Informational Text Elements	⚙ Skill: Informational Text Elements • Your Turn ▤ Close Read • Skills Focus	⚙ Unit 6 Skill: Informational Text Elements — Rosa Parks: My Story ⚙ Spotlight Skill: Informational Text Elements

Central or Main Idea

⚙ Skill: Central or Main Idea	⚙ Skill: Central or Main Idea • Your Turn ▤ Close Read • Skills Focus • Write	⚙ Unit 4 Skill: Central or Main Idea — Freedom's Daughters: The Unsung Heroines of the Civil Rights Movement from 1830 to 1970 ⚙ Unit 6 Skill: Central or Main Idea — I Never Had It Made: An Autobiography of Jackie Robinson ⚙ Spotlight Skill: Central or Main Idea

First Read

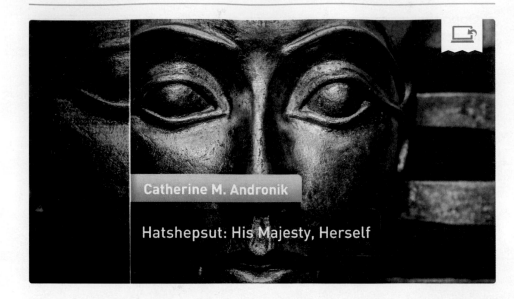

Catherine M. Andronik

Hatshepsut: His Majesty, Herself

Introduce the Text

As a class, watch the video preview and have students read the introduction in pairs to make connections to the video preview.

To activate prior knowledge and experiences, ask students:

- What key words or images from the video do you think will be most important to the biography you are about to read?

- What do you think the term *male dominance* means?

ELL SPEAKING FRAMES

- The ____ in the video makes me think ____.
- The video shows ____. This makes me wonder ____.
- I think the text will ____. I think this because ____.
- I predict that there will be ____. I believe this because ____.

Entry Point

As students prepare to read *Hatshepsut: His Majesty, Herself,* share the following information with them to provide context.

✓ Egypt's New Kingdom (1550-712 B.C.) was one of the world's greatest empires. Ruled under a united front, this large empire stretched from Nubia to the Euphrates River in Asia.

✓ Daily life in Egypt was prosperous as land was fertile and the economy flourished. Innovations such as a system of writing, architecture, and advanced agricultural techniques can be attributed to Ancient Egypt.

✓ In Egypt, the pharaoh ruled in both politics and religion. The pharaoh maintained ultimate control of the army and made decisions during times of war. In the eyes of Egyptians, the pharaoh was considered to be god. As the pharaoh thrived, so did Egypt.

Hatshepsut: His Majesty, Herself

"Hatshepsut took a bold and unprecedented step: She had herself crowned pharaoh . . ."

Skill: Informational Text Elements

I notice that the author introduces the character Hatshepsut through an anecdote about her marrying her half-brother. That seems weird to me that Hatshepsut would have to marry her half-brother, but the author explains that this was "customary," or normal, in ancient Egypt. Plus, she really didn't have a choice. Hatshepsut was her family's last hope to keep the family as royalty.

1   Hatshepsut, royal daughter of **Pharaoh** Tuthmosis and his Great Wife Ahmose, grew up in an Egypt that was peaceful, **prosperous,** and respected throughout the known world.

2   Despite this prosperity, all but one of Hatshepsut's siblings died. Fatal diseases were common, deadly creatures such as scorpions flourished in the Egyptian desert, accidents happened, and a doctor's treatment was often more superstitious than scientific. When the time came for Pharaoh Tuthmosis to name an **heir** to his throne, only one son remained: Tuthmosis, son of Mutnofret, a woman of the pharaoh's harem. When he became pharaoh, young Tuthmosis would have little choice but to marry a woman of the royal blood. Marriages between close relatives were customary within ancient Egypt's royal family, so Hatshepsut was destined to become her half brother's wife. As the sole child of the pharaoh and the God's Wife, Hatshepsut was her dynasty's last hope to keep the royal bloodlines of Egypt intact.

3   Hatshepsut's father, Pharaoh Tuthmosis I, died at the relatively old age of of fifty. His secret tomb, the first underground chamber to be hidden in the towering cliffs of the Valley of the Kings, just northwest of Thebes,[1] had been excavated years in advance. The fine sarcophagus (sar-KOFF-ah-guss), or stone coffin, which would hold his body, was also ready. The pharaoh's mummy was carefully prepared, as befitted a great and beloved king. After seventy days, with solemn ceremony, Tuthmosis was laid in a tomb filled with all the choice food and drink, games and furniture, clothing and jewelry, and the little clay servant figures, called shawabtis (shah-WAHB-tees), that he could possibly need in the afterlife.

4   Following her father's death, Hatshepsut married her half brother, and the young man was crowned Pharaoh Tuthmosis II. Hatshepsut may have been only about twelve years old. As queen, she received a variety of new titles. Her favorite was God's Wife. Tuthmosis II and Hatshepsut had one child, a daughter named Neferure (neh-feh-Roo-ray).

5   The reign of Tuthmosis II was unremarkable. It was also brief, for he was a sickly young man. Within a few years of his coronation, Hatshepsut's husband had died.

---

1.   **Thebes:** a Greek city important in ancient myth, home of Oedipus

Analyze Vocabulary Using Context Clues

In paragraph 1 focus on the sentence that uses the word *pharaoh*. Point out these context clues:

1.   First I notice that Hatshepsut is described as a "royal daughter."

2.   I know that royal people often govern nations.

3.   I think that a *pharaoh* must be a kind of government leader in Egypt, perhaps the ancient Egyptian word for "king."

Informational Text Elements

What was the anecdote that the reader noticed?

The reader highlighted the description of Hatshepsut's marriage to her half-brother in order to carry on the royal lineage.

TEXT TALK

Generally, how did someone become pharaoh of ancient Egypt?

See paragraph 2: Generally, a male would have to be born of royal blood or marry a woman of royal blood.

SELECTION VOCABULARY

pharaoh / el faraón *noun* a ruler in Ancient Egypt COGNATE

prosperous / próspero/a *adjective* having money and success COGNATE

- How does the word *peaceful* help you understand the meaning of the word *prosperous*?
- How does the word *respected* help you understand the meaning of the word *prosperous*?

heir / el/la heredero/a *noun* a successor; a person who has the right to property or title of another person on that person's death

- How does the word *son* help you understand the meaning of the word *heir*?
- How does the word *throne* help you understand the meaning of the word *heir*?

Central or Main Idea

What does the reader note about the details in regard to the central or main idea?

The reader notes that details in the text support the idea that Hatshepsut was a strong female leader.

Skills Focus

QUESTION 1: Central or Main Idea

Here the author explains an unusual event—Hatshepsut crowning herself pharaoh even though she's a woman. The author supports this main idea by describing the transition. The author can't explain when or how it happened, but she can give details about what Hatshepsut did.

Skills Focus

QUESTION 4: Connect to Essential Question

The text states that when Hatshepsut became a female pharaoh, it was unprecedented. Even though a woman had never called herself "pharaoh" before, Hatshepsut strongly accepted this challenge and succeeded, confidently leading Egypt in a peaceful reign.

TEXT TALK

What circumstances led to Hatshepsut's reign as a female pharaoh?

See paragraphs 4–8 and 11–12: Hatshepsut, who was of royal blood, married her half brother, who was not of royal blood. The half brother died. Hatshepsut then became regent for the baby boy of another of her half brother's wives until the baby could marry her daughter of royal blood, Neferure. In the meantime, Hatshepsut ruled Egypt and eventually had herself crowned pharaoh.

---

6   With the death of Tuthmosis II, Egypt was left without a king to ensure that the many gods would look kindly upon the fragile desert land. *Maat* was a delicate thing, and without a pharaoh to tend to its preservation, it was in danger of collapsing.

7   Although Hatshepsut had been Tuthmosis II's Great Wife, he'd had other wives in his harem,[2] including one named Isis. Isis had borne the pharaoh a baby boy, who was also named Tuthmosis. Since Isis was not royal, neither was her baby. But like his father, he could grow up to be pharaoh if he married a princess of the royal blood: his half sister, Neferure.

8   Until Tuthmosis III was mature enough to be crowned pharaoh, what Egypt needed was a regent,[3] an adult who could take control of the country. The regent would have to be someone familiar with palace life and **protocol**. He would need to conduct himself with the proper authority around the royal advisors. He should be prepared to wield power if it became necessary, and he should feel comfortable around visiting dignitaries from other lands. He needed to know his place among the priests of the various gods.

9   It was a job Hatshepsut, perhaps just fifteen years old, had been training for since her earliest days by her father's side. Women had acted as regents for infants at other times in Egypt's history, and the gods had not frowned upon them.

10 So until Tuthmosis III was ready to be crowned as pharaoh, the acting ruler of Egypt would be his aunt, the royal widow of the king, Hatshepsut.

11 At first, little Tuthmosis III was considered the pharaoh, with Hatshepsut just his second-in-command. But a small child could not be an effective ruler. As Hatshepsut settled into her role as regent, she gradually took on more and more of the royal decision-making. She appointed officials and advisors; dealt with the priests; appeared in public ceremonies first behind, then beside, and eventually in front of her nephew. Gradually, over seven years, her power and influence grew. In the end, Hatshepsut was ruling Egypt in all but name.

12 There is no reliable record of exactly when or how it happened, but at some point, Hatshepsut took a bold and unprecedented step: She had herself crowned pharaoh with the large, heavy, red-and-white double crown of the two Egypts, north and south. Since all pharaohs took a throne name, a sort of symbolic name, upon their coronation, Hatshepsut chose Maatkare (maht-KAH-ray). *Maat,* that crucial cosmic order, was important to Hatshepsut. Egypt required a strong pharaoh to ensure *maat.* Hatshepsut could be that pharaoh—even if she did happen to be a woman.

---

2. **harem:** a household of wives and/or servants attached to one man
3. **regent:** a person who exercises power temporarily on behalf of a ruler or monarch

 Skill: Central or Main Idea

These details support the main idea. Not only was Hatshepsut a female leader, she was a great, strong, female leader! She stood out from other women who had lead in the past.

Reading & Writing Companion   **23**

SELECTION VOCABULARY

protocol / el protocolo *noun* an official and established set of rules for situations and matters of the government COGNATE

ELL
- How does the phrase "palace life" help you understand the meaning of the word "protocol"?
- Does a palace typically have strict or relaxed ways of doing things?

NOTES

Skill: Informational
Text Elements

Hatshepsut is trying hard to be like a man in order to keep up with tradition and please her people. She even dresses like a man and is called "pharaoh," or king. I think this shows that she is determined.

13 A few women had tried to rule Egypt before, but never with such a valid claim to the throne or at such a time of peace and prosperity. When Queens Nitocris and Sobekneferu had come to the throne in earlier dynasties, Egypt had been suffering from political problems, and there had been no male heirs. These women had not ruled long or well, and neither had had the audacity to proclaim herself pharaoh. Hatshepsut would be different.

14 There was no word in the language of ancient Egypt for a female ruler; a queen was simply the wife of a king. Hatshepsut had no choice: she had to call herself pharaoh, or king—a male title. She was concerned with preserving and continuing traditional order as much as possible, so to the people of Egypt she made herself look like a man in her role as pharaoh. In ceremonies, she wore a man's short kilt instead of a woman's long dress, much as she had as a child. Around her neck she wore a king's broad collar. She even fastened a false golden beard to her chin. When she wrote about herself as pharaoh, sometimes she referred to herself as he, other times as she. This would be very confusing for historians trying to uncover her identity thousands of years later.

15 Since Hatshepsut could not marry a queen, her daughter Neferure acted as God's Wife in public rituals. It was good training for Neferure, who would in time be expected to marry her half brother, Tuthmosis III, and be his royal consort. But Hatshepsut never seems to have considered that her daughter could succeed her as pharaoh.

16 Hatshepsut might have had to look and act like a man in public, but she never gave up feminine pleasures. Archaeologists have uncovered bracelets and alabaster cosmetic pots with Hatshepsut's cartouche (kar-TOOSH), or hieroglyphic name symbol, inscribed on each. Both men and women in Egypt used cosmetics. They needed creams and oils to keep their skin and hair from drying out under the brutal desert sun. And the kohl, a kind of makeup made from powdered lead that people applied around their eyes, did more than make them attractive; it also helped block out the sun's glare. But Hatshepsut was especially particular about her appearance. One inscription describes her as "more beautiful than anything."

17 With the exception of one military campaign against Nubia, Hatshepsut's reign was peaceful. Instead of expanding Egypt's borders through war and conquest, Hatshepsut built monuments within her country to proclaim its power. Her masterpiece was the magnificent temple at the site known today as Deir el-Bahri. The temple was dedicated to Amen, the

The Temple of Hetshepsut in the Valley of the Kings

Informational Text Elements

What does the reader note about how the author illustrated Hatshepsut as an individual?

The reader noted the author's examples and key details describing how Hatshepsut dressed like a man in order to serve her people. The reader inferred that she was determined.

Skills Focus

QUESTION 2: Informational Text Elements

This final anecdote provides important information about Hatshepsut's rule. The author describes her as a peaceful and powerful pharaoh.

Skills Focus

QUESTION 3: Summarizing

I could summarize this paragraph by saying that Hatshepsut's accomplishments as pharaoh highlight her leadership skills. Hatshepsut's rule was basically peaceful. She concentrated on building monuments to show Egypt's power. Her grandest monument was the temple at Deir el-Bahri, which honored Amen, the god of the pharaohs. The temple's design used columns centuries before the Greeks used them in their temples.

TEXT TALK

In what ways did Hatshepsut maintain the illusion that a male ruled Egypt?

See paragraph 14: Hatshepsut dressed as a man for public functions.

What architectural achievements occurred during Hatshepsut's reign?

See paragraph 17: Hatshepsut built many monuments, including a temple to the god Amen at Deir el-Bahri.

Text to World

Read paragraph 18.

Have students think about what they know about parietal art (cave paintings) and how they convey stories to future generations. Ask students to think about how recorded historical events might be skewed based on the author's or artist's perspective and the cultural norms at the time.

 NOTES

god who was supposed to be the divine father of every pharaoh, the god to whom Hatshepsut felt she owed her good fortune. The temple at Deir el-Bahri was said to be Hatshepsut's own mortuary temple. The building is set into the side of a mountain and rises gracefully in three beautifully proportioned tiers, each supported by columns like those to be seen centuries later in Greek temples. Its design was far ahead of its time. Hatshepsut called it Djeser-Djeseru (JEH-sir jeh-SEH-roo)—"Holy of Holies."

18 On the walls of this temple, Hatshepsut had artists carve and paint her biography. According to the story told on the walls of Djeser-Djeseru, she had been chosen as pharaoh by the gods themselves, even before her birth. Perhaps, even after years on the throne, she still felt a need to **justify** a woman's right to rule. The gods in the pictures on the temple walls do not seem to care whether Hatshepsut is a man or a woman—in fact, some of the paintings show her as a boy.

"© 2001 by Catherine M. Andronik, reproduced by permission of Catherine M. Andronik.

Reading & Writing Companion **25**

TEXT TALK

What is one source of information regarding Hatshepsut's biography?

See paragraph 18: Artists carved and painted Hatshepsut's biography on the walls of the temple at Deir el-Bahri.

What other questions are you able to generate about the text?

Answers will vary.

What struggles did Hatshesput face as a woman in a leadership role?

Answers will vary.

B Ask each Beyond grade level student to write one additional discussion question. Then, have one or two students facilitate a discussion, using their questions to guide the conversation.

SELECTION VOCABULARY

justify / justificar *verb* to defend or explain by reasoning COGNATE

ELL
- How does the phrase "right to rule" help you understand the meaning of the word "justify"?
- Was rule by a woman common or uncommon in ancient Egypt? What might a female ruler want to prove to her people?

Reading Comprehension OPTIONAL

Have students complete the digital reading comprehension questions ✅ when they finish reading.

ANSWER KEY

QUESTION 1: B	QUESTION 5: A	QUESTION 9:
QUESTION 2: D	QUESTION 6: C	*See first chart.*
QUESTION 3: B	QUESTION 7: A	QUESTION 10:
QUESTION 4: D	QUESTION 8: C	*See second chart.*

First	Second	Third	Fourth
Hatshepsut is born to Pharaoh Tuthmosis I.	Hatshepsut's husband, Pharaoh Tuthmosis II, dies.	Hatshepsut appears behind little Tuthmosis III in public ceremonies.	The temple dedicated to Amen is built on the site of Deir el-Bahri.

Description	Character
". . . expected to marry her half brother, Tuthmosis III . . ."	Neferure
". . . concerned with preserving and continuing traditional order as much as possible."	Hatshepsut
". . . a sickly young man."	Tuthmosis II
". . . the gods had not frowned upon them."	Women who had previously ruled Egypt.

Connect and Extend OPTIONAL

CONNECT TO EXTENDED WRITING PROJECT

Students can use *Hatshepsut: His Majesty, Herself* as a mentor text for their Extended Writing Project. Depending on the subject they choose to research and write about, students may study the different text structures Catherine Andronik employs to present information and adopt or modify them for their own purposes.

BEYOND THE BOOK

Art: Hatshepsut's Life & Reign

Students will combine informal research with what they learned about Hatshepsut's life and reign from the excerpt to design a piece of artwork that celebrates her life.

Ask students to:

- Reread the passage noting key details about Hatshepsut's life and reign.

- Conduct informal online research to find out more about her.

- Use what they learn about her to design a painting, drawing, or collage depicting her life and reign.

- Publish these pieces of artwork by posting them around the classroom or online.

Allow time for students to do a gallery walk to see each other's artistic representations of Hatshepsut's life and reign.

To reflect, ask students:

- What did you learn about Hatshepsut's life and reign from your research that was not in the passage?

- What did you notice about the artwork as you did the gallery walk? How did different students portray Hatshepsut?

Think Questions

Circulate as students answer Think Questions independently. Scaffolds for these questions are shown on the opposite page.

QUESTION 1: Textual Evidence

Before Hatshepsut became pharaoh, she "had been training . . . since her earliest days by her father's side." Hatshepsut was familiar with palace life and protocol; knew how to conduct herself with proper authority around royal advisors; knew how to wield power if necessary; felt comfortable around dignitaries from other lands; and knew her place among the priests.

QUESTION 2: Textual Evidence

In contrast to the earlier queens, Nitocris and Sobekneferu, Hatshepsut proclaimed herself pharaoh and ruled during "a time of peace and prosperity." The earlier queens ruled for short, troubled periods when Egypt had been suffering from political problems and there were no male heirs to the throne.

QUESTION 3: Textual Evidence

Based on archaeological finds of jewelry and makeup, it appears that Hatshepsut cared about her appearance. One inscription written about Hatshepsut describes her with the phrase "more beautiful than anything."

QUESTION 4: Greek and Latin Affixes and Roots

I think *prosperous* must mean "having success or wealth." The word is used to describe Egypt, which is also defined with positive words such as *peaceful* and *respected*. If Egypt was respected by other countries, it must mean the country was strong and successful.

QUESTION 5: Context Clues

The word is used to describe life at the palace. The text says "the regent would have to be someone familiar with palace life and protocol. He would need to conduct himself with the proper authority around the royal advisers." So I think *protocol* must mean "accepted ways of doing things."

First Read

Read "Hatshepsut: His Majesty, Herself." After you read, complete the Think Questions below.

 THINK QUESTIONS

1. Before Hatshepsut became pharaoh, what experience does the text say she had for the job? Include evidence from the text to support your answer.

2. How was Hatshepsut's reign different from the reigns of the two earlier queens who had ruled Egypt? Use evidence from the text to support your answer.

3. What evidence does the text give to support the idea that Hatshepsut cared about her appearance? Refer to details from the text in your response.

4. Remembering that the Latin suffix *-ous* means "having, characterized by," use the context clues provided in the passage to determine the meaning of **prosperous**. Write your definition of "prosperous" here and tell how you were able to figure it out. In your answer, identify any relationships between words that helped you understand the meaning of "prosperous."

5. Use context to determine the meaning of the word **protocol** as it is used in the text. Then write your definition of *protocol* here and explain how you discovered the meaning of the word.

Think Questions

Use the scaffolds below to differentiate instruction for your **ELL** English Language Learners and **A** Approaching grade-level learners.

ELL **BEGINNING** Write a response using the <u>word bank</u> and <u>sentence frames.</u>

INTERMEDIATE Write a response using the <u>sentence frames.</u>

ADVANCED, ADVANCED HIGH Write a response using the <u>Text-Dependent Question Guide.</u>

A **APPROACHING** Write a response using the <u>Text-Dependent Question Guide.</u>

	INTERMEDIATE	APPROACHING
BEGINNING		**ADVANCED, ADVANCED HIGH**
Word Bank	**Sentence Frames**	**Text-Dependent Question Guide**
conduct bracelets cosmetic pots customs	Before Hatshepsut became pharaoh, she "had been training . . . since her earliest days by her ____." Hatshepsut knew palace life; how to ____ herself with royal advisors, visitors from other lands, and priests; and how to use her ____ when needed.	1. • Who trained Hatshepsut to rule? • How did this training take place? • What skills did Hatshepsut have as a ruler?
doing things father's side named herself	Hatshepsut ____ pharaoh and ruled during "a time of peace and prosperity." The earlier queens ruled for ____, troubled periods.	2. • What did Egypt suffer from during the reigns of Nitocris and Sobekneferu? • What was Egypt missing during these reigns? • Were the reigns of these two queens short or long?
positive power short	Based on archaeological finds, including ____ and ____, it seems that Hatshepsut cared about her appearance.	3. • What jewelry did archaeologists find? • What makeup did archaeologists find? • What do these finds suggest about Hatshepsut?
success	*Prosperous* must mean "having ____ or wealth." The word is used to describe Egypt, which is also defined with other ____ words.	4. • Read: "Hatshepsut, royal daughter of Pharaoh Tuthmosis and his Great Wife Ahmose, grew up in an Egypt that was peaceful, **prosperous,** and respected throughout the known world." • What does the word *peaceful* suggest about Egypt at this time? • What does the word *respected* suggest about Egypt at this time?
	Protocol must mean "accepted ways of ____." The word is used to describe life at the palace, which would follow certain formal ____.	5. • Read: "The regent would have to be someone familiar with palace life and **protocol**." • Is palace life marked by strict rules or freedom? • What does that tell me about the meaning of the word *protocol*?

Skill: Informational Text Elements

Introduce the Skill

Watch the Concept Definition video and read the following definitions with your students.

An **informational text** presents readers with information or ideas about real people, places, things, and events. To present information clearly writers use a common set of **informational text elements,** or features, that link key individuals, events and ideas. Some examples of informational text include biographies, diaries, interviews, articles, letters, editorials, essays, and speeches. Many of these texts will include **supporting evidence,** or any relevant fact that an author includes to support his or her ideas, as well as **pertinent examples.** These examples have a logical connection to a subject, such as discussing the Gettysburg Address in an article on Civil War battles. To identify informational text elements, readers should look for key details in the text as well as any photographs, charts, or maps the author includes, and analyze the connections and relationships between them. Analyzing the elements of an informational text helps the reader understand how they work together to support a central idea.

TURN AND TALK

1. What is your favorite biography/speech?

2. How is the information in this biography/speech conveyed to the reader/listener?

ELL SPEAKING FRAMES
- My favorite biography/speech is ____.
- I like this biography/speech because ____.
- I think the author/speaker conveys information by providing ____.

Skill:
Informational Text Elements

Use the Checklist to analyze Informational Text Elements in "Hatshepsut: His Majesty, Herself." Refer to the sample student annotations about Informational Text Elements in the text.

••• CHECKLIST FOR INFORMATIONAL TEXT ELEMENTS

In order to identify a key individual, event, or idea in a text, note the following:

- ✓ examples that describe or explain important ideas, events, or individuals in the text
- ✓ anecdotes in the text. An anecdote is a personal story an author has passed on to readers
- ✓ how a key individual, event, or idea is introduced or illustrated
- ✓ other features, such as charts, maps, sidebars, and photos that might provide additional information outside of the main text

To analyze in detail how a key individual, event, or idea is introduced, illustrated, and elaborated in a text, consider the following questions:

- ✓ How does the author introduce or illustrate a key individual, event, or idea?
- ✓ What key details does the author include to describe or elaborate on important information in the text?
- ✓ Does the author include any anecdotes? What do they add to the text?
- ✓ What other features, if any, help readers to analyze the events, ideas, or individuals in the text?

Reading & Writing Companion | 27

V SKILL VOCABULARY

informational text / el texto informativo *noun* non-fiction writing that presents information about real people, places, things, and events

informational text elements / los elementos del texto informativo *noun* characteristics of informational texts COGNATE

Hatshepsut: His Majesty, Herself

Skill:
Informational Text Elements

sync•skills

Reread paragraph 16 from "Hatshepsut: His Majesty, Herself." Then, using the Checklist on the previous page, answer the multiple-choice questions below.

⟳ YOUR TURN

1. This question has two parts. First, answer Part A. Then, answer Part B.

Part A: What does this paragraph reveal about Hatshepsut as an individual?

- ○ A. She was obsessed with her looks.
- ○ B. She was tired of acting like a man.
- ○ C. She was true to herself in private.
- ○ D. She hid her true gender from her people.

Part B: Which of the following details from the text best supports your answer to Part A?

- ○ A. "Hatshepsut might have had to look and act like a man in public, but she never gave up feminine pleasures."
- ○ B. "Archaeologists have uncovered bracelets and alabaster cosmetic pots with Hatshepsut's cartouche. . ."
- ○ C. "They needed creams and oils to keep their skin and hair from drying out under the brutal desert sun."
- ○ D. "One inscription describes her as 'more beautiful than anything.'"

Copyright © Bookhead Ed Learning, LLC

Please note that excerpts and passages in the StudySync® library and this workbook are intended as touchstones to generate interest in an author's work. The excerpts and passages do not substitute for the reading of entire texts, and StudySync® strongly recommends that students seek out and purchase the whole literary or informational work in order to experience it as the author intended. Links to online resellers are available in our digital library. In addition, complete works may be ordered through an authorized reseller by filling out and returning to StudySync® the order form enclosed in this workbook.

V SKILL VOCABULARY

supporting evidence / la evidencia de apoyo *noun* text evidence, descriptions, examples, reasons, expert opinions, facts, and statistics that further explain key aspects of the controlling idea

pertinent example / el ejemplo pertinente *noun* a related situation that shows that what is being demonstrated is true COGNATE

Your Turn

Ask students to complete the Your Turn Activity.

QUESTION 1

Part A

A. Incorrect. She was not a narcissist; she simply indulged in feminine pleasures, such as jewelry and cosmetics.

B. Incorrect. She wasn't tired of being a man in public; she just wanted to be feminine in private.

C. Correct. She hid her femininity from the public, but embraced it in private.

D. Incorrect. Her people knew she was a woman even though she dressed like a man in public.

Part B

A. Correct. This piece of evidence shows that she was one person to the public, but wanted to maintain femininity, too.

B. Incorrect. This piece of evidence shows what archaeologists found, but it doesn't describe or illustrate who Hatshepsut was in private.

C. Incorrect. This piece of evidence explains the benefits of creams and oils, not who Hatshepsut was in private.

D. Incorrect. This piece of evidence describes that Hatshepsut was beautiful, but not that she wanted to embrace her feminine side in private.

Your Turn

Ask students to complete the Your Turn Activity.

QUESTION 2

A. Incorrect. This evidence explains that both men and women used cosmetics, but it is not specific to Hatshepsut.

B. Incorrect. This evidence is not an opinion; it is fact.

C. **Correct.** This piece of evidence allows the reader to understand more about life in ancient Egypt.

D. Incorrect. This evidence does not correlate with the anecdote about Hatshepsut's desire to dress like a man in public.

---

2. Why does the author write that "both men and women in Egypt used cosmetics"?

- ○ A. to explain why Hatshepsut used cosmetics both in public and in private
- ○ B. to highlight an opinion concerning the use of cosmetics in ancient Egypt
- ○ C. to provide a factual detail that illustrates what ancient Egypt was like
- ○ D. to emphasize the anecdote about Hatshepsut and why she chose to dress like a man in public

Please note that excerpts and passages in the StudySync® library and this workbook are intended as touchstones to generate interest in an author's work. The excerpts and passages do not substitute for the reading of entire texts, and StudySync® strongly recommends that students seek out and purchase the whole literary or informational work in order to experience it as the author intended. Links to online resellers are available in our digital library. In addition, complete works may be ordered through an authorized reseller by filling out and returning to StudySync® the order form enclosed in this workbook.

Reading & Writing Companion   29

Skill:
Central or Main Idea

Use the Checklist to analyze Central or Main Idea in "Hatshepsut: His Majesty, Herself." Refer to the sample student annotations about Central or Main Idea in the text.

••• CHECKLIST FOR CENTRAL OR MAIN IDEA

In order to identify a central idea of a text, note the following:

- ✓ the topic or subject of the text
- ✓ the central or main idea, if it is explicitly stated
- ✓ details in the text that convey the theme

To determine a central idea of a text and how it is conveyed through particular details consider the following questions:

- ✓ What main idea do the details in one or more paragraphs explain or describe?
- ✓ What bigger idea do all the paragraphs support?
- ✓ What is the best way to state the central idea? How might you summarize the text and message?
- ✓ How do particular details in the text convey the central idea?

 ## Skill: Central or Main Idea

Introduce the Skill

Watch the Concept Definition video ▶ and read the following definitions with your students.

The **central idea** of a nonfiction text is the most important point that an author makes about a **topic.** The statement of a central idea answers the question, "What's it all about?" In order to find the answer, look for **supporting ideas** that help develop the central idea. Authors also include **details** as textual evidence to support the central idea about the topic. Readers **analyze** these supporting ideas or details to see what they have in common. What do they support, explain, or describe? Answering this question will help identify the central or main idea.

TURN AND TALK

1. What is the main idea of your favorite documentary or informational text?

2. What details within the show or text support this main idea?

ELL SPEAKING FRAMES
- The main idea in [text/documentary title] was ____.
- I think one supporting detail from the [text/documentary title] was ____.
- Another supporting detail from the [text/documentary title] was ____.

V SKILL VOCABULARY

central or main idea / la idea central o principal *noun* the most important point an author makes about a topic or in a section of text

topic / el tema *noun* the subject of a literary work, usually expressed as a single word or phrase in the form of a noun

supporting idea / la idea secundaria *noun* a focused explanation or argument that helps develop the central idea

⚙ Your Turn

Ask students to complete the Your Turn Activity.

QUESTION 1

Part A

A. Incorrect. The paragraph specifically states that she relied on peace throughout her reign.

B. Incorrect. She did build temples, but this is not the central idea of this paragraph.

C. Incorrect. She built grand temples, but there is no evidence to support that this influenced the ideas of other leaders.

D. **Correct.** She was able to maintain control and power by promoting and practicing peaceful strategies.

Part B

A. Incorrect. This answer describes the main idea that her reign was peaceful, but it does not highlight the detail of *how* she was able to maintain Egypt's power.

B. **Correct.** This answer choice provides an example of how she practiced peaceful tactics in order to maintain power.

C. Incorrect. This answer choice only states that she built a grand temple. There is no mention of maintaining power through peace.

D. Incorrect. This answer choice describes the grand temple she built, but does not support the idea that she maintained a peaceful reign to promote Egypt's power.

Skill:
Central or Main Idea

Reread paragraph 17 from "Hatshepsut: His Majesty, Herself." Then, using the Checklist on the previous page, answer the multiple-choice questions below.

🔄 YOUR TURN

1. This question has two parts. First, answer Part A. Then, answer Part B.

Part A: Which of the following statements best portrays the central idea of the paragraph?

- ○ A. Hatshepsut ensured violent military operations through which she was able to keep the peace.
- ○ B. Hatshepsut successfully built temples throughout Egypt, thus pleasing her people.
- ○ C. Hatshepsut's use of dynamic temple designs blazed a trail for future leaders.
- ○ D. Hatshepsut successfully led Egypt by exercising peaceful tactics to maintain power.

Part B: Which detail from the paragraph best supports your answer to Part A?

- ○ A. "With the exception of one military campaign against Nubia, Hatshepsut's reign was peaceful."
- ○ B. "Instead of expanding Egypt's borders through war and conquest, Hatshepsut built monuments within her country to proclaim its power."
- ○ C. "Her masterpiece was the magnificent temple at the site known today as Deir el-Bahri."
- ○ D. "The building is set into the side of a mountain and rises gracefully in three beautifully proportioned tiers . . ."

Reading & Writing
Companion **31**

Ⅴ SKILL VOCABULARY

detail / el detalle *noun* a fact, a description, an example, or a reason that further explains a key idea

analyze / analizar *verb* to consider in detail and discover essential features or meaning COGNATE

Close Read

Reread "Hatshepsut: His Majesty, Herself." As you reread, complete the Skills Focus questions below. Then use your answers and annotations from the questions to help you complete the Write activity.

◎ SKILLS FOCUS

1. Find evidence that supports the author's main idea in "Hatshepsut: His Majesty, Herself." Explain how this evidence supports the main idea.

2. Identify at least two informational text elements (such as anecdotes or examples) that introduce, illustrate, or elaborate the life of the pharaoh Hatshepsut.

3. Identify evidence of Hatshepsut's leadership skills and explain how you would restate the main

ideas and the most important details of the text in your own words.

4. The Essential Question asks: "How do we know what to do when there are no instructions?" Identify evidence in "Hatshepsut: His Majesty, Herself" that reveals how Hatshepsut made history by breaking tradition.

✎ WRITE

ARGUMENTATIVE: In "Elena," a woman strives to learn English in order to benefit her children, despite her family's lack of support. Similarly, in "Hatshepsut: His Majesty, Herself," a woman defies all odds and many years of tradition by becoming a pharaoh in Egypt to benefit her family and keep their royal lineage intact. Keeping these women in mind, respond to the following prompt: What central or main idea does the author of "Hatshepsut: His Majesty, Herself" convey about female empowerment? In your response, use evidence from the text to support your claim.

Close Read

Skills Focus

QUESTION 1: Central or Main Idea

See paragraphs 11 and 12.

QUESTION 2: Informational Text Elements

See paragraph 17.

QUESTION 3: Summarizing

See paragraph 17.

QUESTION 4: Connect to Essential Question

See paragraphs 12 and 13.

 CHECK FOR SUCCESS

If students struggle to respond to Skills Focus Question #1, ask students the following questions:

- What is the central or main idea of *Hatshepsut: His Majesty, Herself*?

- What is the central or main idea of paragraphs 11–12?

- What evidence supports the central or main idea in paragraphs 11–12?

 ## Writer's Notebook

Connect to Essential Question: Give students time to reflect on how *Hatshepsut: His Majesty, Herself* connects to the unit's essential question "How do we know what to do when there are no instructions?" by freewriting in their Writer's Notebooks.

ELL **Beginning & Intermediate**

Read aloud the unit's essential question: "How do we know what to do when there are no instructions?". Encourage students to draw their connections or allow students to write in their native language. Circulate around the room, prompting students for their thoughts as they respond orally or through pantomime.

Advanced & Advanced High

Allow students to share their connections orally in pairs or small groups before freewriting.

StudySyncTV   Project the StudySyncTV episode ▶ and pause at the following times to prompt discussion:

4:08 How do the students use evidence to explain the role of women as regents, and what information does Jalyn give about women acting as pharaohs?

4:34 What do the students say about Hatshepsut's leadership? What details does Jalyn give about Hatshepsut's power?

5:48 What information do the students give supporting the main or central idea of female acceptance and empowerment? What do Jalyn and Elaina conclude about Hatshepsut?

Collaborative Conversation

█ SCAFFOLDS

Break students into collaborative conversation groups to discuss the Close Read prompt. Ask students to use the StudySyncTV episode as a model for their discussion. Remind them to reference their Skills Focus annotations in their discussion.

In "Elena," a woman strives to learn English in order to benefit her children, despite her family's lack of support. Similarly, in *Hatshepsut: His Majesty, Herself*, a woman defies all odds and many years of tradition by becoming a pharaoh in Egypt to benefit her family and keep their royal lineage intact. Keeping these women in mind, respond to the following prompt: What central or main idea does the author of *Hatshepsut: His Majesty, Herself* convey about female empowerment? How does this idea compare and contrast with that of "Elena"? In your response, use evidence from the text to support your claim.

Use the scaffolds below to differentiate instruction for your **ELL** English Language Learners and **A** Approaching grade-level learners.

ELL **BEGINNING, INTERMEDIATE** Use the <u>discussion guide</u> and <u>speaking frames</u> to facilitate the discussion with support from the teacher.

ADVANCED, ADVANCED HIGH Use the <u>discussion guide</u> and <u>speaking frames</u> to facilitate the discussion in mixed-level groups.

A **APPROACHING** Use the <u>discussion guide</u> to facilitate the discussion in mixed-level groups.

| APPROACHING |
| ADVANCED, ADVANCED HIGH |
| BEGINNING, INTERMEDIATE |

Discussion Guide	Speaking Frames
1. How does Hatshepsut represent women or women taking a leadership role?	• One way that Hatshepsut represents women is ____. • I think this because ____.
2. What central or main idea is the author conveying to the reader about female empowerment?	• The author is saying that female empowerment is ____. • I think this because ____.

Review Prompt and Rubric

Before students begin writing, review the writing prompt and rubric with the class.

ARGUMENTATIVE: In "Elena," a woman strives to learn English in order to benefit her children, despite her family's lack of support. Similarly, in *Hatshepsut: His Majesty, Herself*, a woman defies all odds and many years of tradition by becoming a pharaoh in Egypt to benefit her family and keep their royal lineage intact. Keeping these women in mind, respond to the following prompt: What central or main idea does the author of *Hatshepsut: His Majesty, Herself* convey about female empowerment? How does this idea compare and contrast with that of "Elena"? In your response, use evidence from the text to support your claim.

ELL PROMPT GUIDE

A
- How does Hatshepsut represent women or women taking a leadership role?

- What central or main idea is the author conveying to the reader about female empowerment?

Score	Central or Main Idea	Language and Conventions
4	The writer clearly analyzes and explains the central or main idea of the text as it relates to female empowerment. The writer provides exemplary analysis, using relevant evidence from the text.	The writer demonstrates a consistent command of grammar, punctuation, and usage conventions. Although minor errors may be evident, they do not detract from the fluency or the clarity of the essay.
3	The writer analyzes and explains the central or main idea of the text as it relates to female empowerment. The writer provides sufficient analysis, using relevant evidence from the text most of the time.	The writer demonstrates an adequate command of grammar, punctuation, and usage conventions. Although some errors may be evident, they create few (if any) disruptions in the fluency of the writing or the clarity of the essay.
2	The writer begins to analyze or explain the central or main idea of the text as it relates to female empowerment, but the analysis is incomplete. The writer uses relevant evidence from the text only some of the time.	The writer demonstrates a partial command of grammar, punctuation, and usage conventions. Some distracting errors may be evident, at times creating minor disruptions in the fluency or clarity of the writing.
1	The writer attempts to analyze or explain the central or main idea of the text as it relates to female empowerment, but the analysis is not successful. The writer uses little or no relevant evidence from the text.	The writer demonstrates little or no command of grammar, punctuation, and usage conventions. Serious and persistent errors create disruptions in the fluency of the writing and sometimes interfere with meaning.
0	The writer does not provide a relevant response to the prompt or does not provide a response at all.	Serious and persistent errors overwhelm the writing and interfere with the meaning of the response as a whole, making the writer's meaning impossible to understand.

Write

Ask students to complete the writing assignment using textual evidence to support their answers.

Use the scaffolds below to differentiate instruction for your **ELL** English Language Learners and **A** Approaching grade-level learners.

ELL **BEGINNING** With the help of the <u>word bank</u>, write a response using <u>paragraph frame 1</u>.

INTERMEDIATE With the help of the <u>word bank</u>, write a response using <u>paragraph frames 1 and 2</u>.

ADVANCED, ADVANCED HIGH Write a response of differentiated length using the <u>sentence starters</u>.

A **APPROACHING** Write a response of differentiated length using the <u>sentence starters</u>.

| BEGINNING | | ADVANCED, ADVANCED HIGH |
| INTERMEDIATE | | APPROACHING |

Word Bank	Paragraph Frame 1	Paragraph Frame 2	Sentence Starters
sacrificed women strive break barriers pharaoh leadership role	Like the author of "Elena," Catherine M. Andronik conveys the idea that ____ against all odds. The author's main idea relates to female empowerment because Hatshepsut carved out a ____ for herself that defied tradition. Hatshepsut declared herself ____. Andronik also states that Hatshepsut ____ her femininity to appear like a man in public in order to be respected. Therefore, the author's main idea is that women can succeed and ____, even if other people don't believe in them or want them to be in power.	Andronik writes that Hatshepsut continued to ____, even though she ____. This shows the reader that women should not be ____ to be themselves. I identify this idea in "Elena," too. The main or central idea is that women ____. Readers need to understand not only what Hatshepsut and Elena did, but ____.	• The central idea of *Hatshepsut: His Majesty, Herself* is . . . • This central idea relates to female empowerment because . . . • The author, Andronik, uses ____ as supporting details to . . . • One thing you might learn about female leadership is . . . • This idea compares to that of "Elena" because . . . • Another thing you might learn is . . .

Peer Review

Students should submit substantive feedback to two peers using the review instructions below.
- How well does this response answer the prompt?
- How well does the writer support his or her claim with details and examples from the text?
- Which sentence in the writer's response made you think differently about the author's main idea about female empowerment?
- What does the writer do well in this response? What does the writer need to work on?

Rate

Respond to the following with a point rating that reflects your opinion.

	1 2 3 4
Ideas	▪▪▪☐
Evidence	▪▪▪▪
Language and Conventions	▪▪☐☐

Submit

ELL **SENTENCE FRAMES**

A
- You were able to (completely / partly / almost) ____ answer the prompt because ____.
- You could answer the prompt more completely by ____.
- You supported the idea of ____ with the detail of ____.

- One idea that needs more support is ____.
- I thought differently about the text after reading ____.
- My favorite part of your response is ____.

I, Too

POETRY
Langston Hughes
1925

Introduction

Born in Joplin, Missouri, James Mercer Langston Hughes (1902–1967) was an influential figure during the Harlem Renaissance, where he helped pioneer a new literary art form called jazz poetry. Inspired by Carl Sandburg and Walt Whitman, Hughes wrote poems that gave voice to his own experiences and the shared experiences of other African Americans during the era of segregation. "I, Too" starts as a personal statement and extends to inspire future generations.

The speaker in this Langston Hughes poem opens by saying, "I, too, sing America." He affirms that as an African American he celebrates this country despite the inequality that he continues to face. The speaker states that he still laughs even though he must eat in the kitchen when guests are present because he still eats well. In the second stanza, he says that tomorrow he will be allowed to eat at the table, and no one will dare to send him to the kitchen. "Tomorrow" indicates one day in the future, and the speaker believes this day will come. When it does, he is confident that the world will recognize his beauty and humanity because he, too, is an American.

ELL Proficiency-leveled summaries and summaries in multiple languages are available digitally.

🔊 Audio and audio text highlighting are available with this text.

Access Complex Text

LEXILE: N/A   WORD COUNT: 62

The following areas may be challenging for students, particularly **ELL** English Language Learners and **A** Approaching grade-level learners.

Prior Knowledge	Connection of Ideas	Genre
• Langston Hughes is often considered the poet laureate of the Harlem Renaissance, a cultural movement that took place in New York City during the 1920s and 30s. • The Harlem Renaissance gave rise to popular jazz as well as all kinds of African American art, literature, and poetry.	• Some students may need help connecting the idea that the table in the poem is synonymous with the word "America" in the first line. • Explain that this metaphor or comparison is intended to make the reader think about both references in new ways.	• The features and structure of free-verse poetry may need to be defined or explained to students. • Explain that the poem is considered a response to American poet Walt Whitman's "I Hear America Singing."

SCAFFOLDS    **ELL** ENGLISH LANGUAGE LEARNERS    **A** APPROACHING GRADE LEVEL   **B** BEYOND GRADE LEVEL

These icons identify differentiation strategies and scaffolded support for a variety of students. See the digital lesson plan for additional differentiation strategies and scaffolds.

Instructional Path

The print teacher's edition includes essential point-of-use instruction and planning tools. Complete lesson plans and program documents appear in your digital teacher account.

First Read: I, Too

Objectives: After an initial reading and discussion of the poem, students will be able to identify and describe the speaker and key details, and articulate events that are central to the poem.

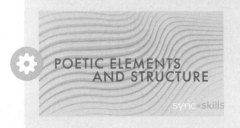

Skill: Poetic Elements and Structure

Objectives: After rereading and discussing a model of close reading, students will be able to analyze how a particular stanza fits into the overall structure of a text and contributes to the development of theme.

Skill: Media

Objectives: After rereading and discussing a model of close reading, students will be able to compare and contrast the experience of reading a poem with the experience of listening to an audio version of the poem and analyze the differences between what they "see" and "hear" when reading the text and what they perceive when they hear it read in an audio version.

Close Read: I, Too

Objectives: After engaging in a close reading and discussion of the text, students will be able to analyze how poetic elements and structure and listening to the poem affect the theme in a short, written response.

Progress Monitoring

Opportunities to Learn	Opportunities to Demonstrate Learning	Opportunities to Reteach
Poetic Elements and Structure		
⚙ Skill: Poetic Elements and Structure	⚙ Skill: Poetic Elements and Structure • Your Turn ▣ Close Read • Skills Focus • Write	⚙ Unit 4 Skill: Poetic Elements and Structure — Famous ⚙ Spotlight Skill: Poetic Elements and Structure
Media		
⚙ Skill: Media	⚙ Skill: Media • Your Turn ▣ Close Read • Skills Focus • Write	⚙ Unit 4 Skill: Media — Malala Yousafzai-Nobel Lecture ⚙ Unit 4 Skill: Media — All Summer in a Day ⚙ Spotlight Skill: Media

First Read

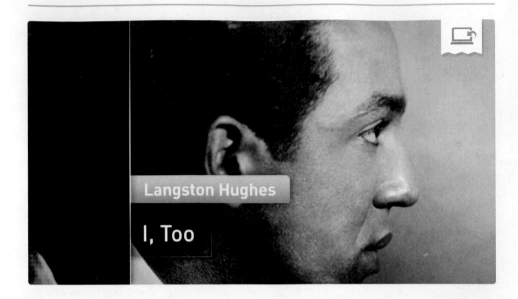

Langston Hughes

I, Too

Introduce the Text

As a class, watch the video preview ▶ and have students read the introduction in pairs to make connections to the video preview.

To activate prior knowledge and experiences, ask students:

- How does the information in this video connect to what you already know?

- What do you think the term *segregation* means?

ELL SPEAKING FRAMES

- The ____ in the video makes me think ____.
- The video shows ____. This makes me wonder ____.
- I think the text will ____. I think this because ____.
- I predict that there will be ____. I believe this because ____.

Entry Point

As students prepare to read "I, Too," share the following information with them to provide context.

✓ Langston Hughes (1902-1967) was born in Joplin, Missouri. After graduating from high school, he briefly attended Columbia University in New York City. There, during the peak of the Harlem Renaissance, he wrote poetry about life as an African American in the United States.

✓ It was Hughes's goal to write literature that uncompromisingly reflected the truth associated with being African American from the 1920s to the 1960s. His works range from joyous celebrations to trouble and suffering.

✓ Hughes's poem "I, Too" highlights important themes intended to inspire Americans during times of unjust treatment.

"I, too, am America."

NOTES

Skill: Poetic Elements and Structure

The speaker says he is the "darker brother." I think this means he is black. But by calling himself "brother" he must mean that he is still in some way connected to the people who send him to eat in the kitchen.

Skill: Media

The audio version of the poem emphasizes the speaker's upbeat tone. He has a sing-song tone to his voice when he speaks these lines. I think this is because he knows that change is coming and that he will be considered equal.

1 I, too, sing America.

2 I am the **darker** brother.
3 They send me to eat in the kitchen
4 When **company** comes,
5 I laugh,
6 And eat well,
7 And grow strong.

8 **Tomorrow**,
9 I'll be at the table
10 When company comes.
11 Nobody'll **dare**
12 Say to me,
13 "Eat in the kitchen,"
14 Then.

15 Besides,
16 They'll see how beautiful I am
17 And be **ashamed** —

18 I, too, am America.

Analyze Vocabulary Using Context Clues

In line 2 focus on the word *darker*. Point out these context clues:

1. First I notice the word *brother*, which implies a family.

2. But the word *darker* suggests contrast. The speaker is different from his family members.

3. I know that the base word *dark* can be used to describe color. I think the word *darker* here means that the speaker's skin color is brown in contrast to his white family members.

Poetic Elements and Structure

How does the reader use the structure of the poem's first two stanzas to analyze the meaning?

The reader notes that the first line of the poem is a statement. The speaker is very sure of himself. The fact that he refers to himself as the "darker brother" means that he sees himself in some way connected to the other people in the poem, the ones who send him to the kitchen when company comes.

Media

What did the reader notice when listening to the audio version of the poem?

The reader noticed that the narrator had a light, musical tone which reflects the positive changes he thinks are coming in the future for his people.

TEXT TALK

In what country is the poem set?

See line 1: The poem is set in America.

What difference does the speaker note between himself and those who send him to the kitchen?

See lines 2 and 3: The speaker is African American while those who send him to the kitchen are white.

In lines 7 and 16, how does the speaker describe himself?

See lines 7 and 16: The speaker describes himself as strong and beautiful.

What two time periods does the speaker describe in the poem?

See line 8: The speaker describes what happens now and what will happen in the future.

In line 17, how does the speaker predict his white oppressors will feel in the future regarding their behavior?

See line 17: The speaker predicts that his white oppressors will feel ashamed of their behavior.

What other questions are you able to ask and answer?

Answers will vary.

How does race affect how the speaker of the poem is treated? How does he fight the prejudice he faces?

Answers will vary.

 BEYOND TEXT TALK

How are the ideas of freedom and equality presented in this poem?

Prepare for Advanced Courses

Use the activity below to differentiate instruction for your **B** Beyond grade level learners.

Direct students to reread lines 15–17.

Ask students: What is the effect of using the word "beautiful" in line 16? How does this word reflect the tone of the poem and the perspective of the speaker?

Sample answer; answers will vary: The word "beautiful" works on many levels - it does not mean very pretty, but a truer sense of beauty. The word choice helps support the very honorable and proud tone of the poem.

 SELECTION VOCABULARY

dark / oscuro/a *adjective* having a color that is a shade deeper than another color

company / la compañía *noun* friends or family who are visitors or guests COGNATE

 ELL
- Who else might be invited to eat a meal with a family?
- Does the *company* live in the house with the family or do they arrive at the house?

tomorrow / mañana *noun* a time in the future; day after today

 ELL
- In what ways does the word *tomorrow* contrast with the word *today*?
- Does the word *tomorrow* have to do with the present or the future?

dare / animarse *verb* to be brave or bold enough to do something

 ELL
- In the future, will someone be bold enough to say, "Eat in the kitchen"?
- Does the speaker expect people to act boldly against him in the future?

ashamed / avergonzado / a *adjective* feeling embarrassed for having done something wrong

 ELL
- In what way does the description of the speaker as "beautiful" contrast with the feelings of shame in the people who used to send him to the kitchen?
- Is shame a positive or negative feeling?

Reading Comprehension OPTIONAL

Have students complete the digital reading comprehension questions ✓ when they finish reading.

ANSWER KEY

QUESTION 1: B   **QUESTION 3:** B   **QUESTION 5:**
QUESTION 2: A   **QUESTION 4:** C   *See chart below.*

First	Second	Third	Fourth
The speaker is sent away to eat in the kitchen when company arrives.	The speaker doesn't seem to care that he has to eat in the kitchen, and says he laughs, eats, and grows strong	The speaker feels confident that one day he will sit at the table and not in the kitchen.	The speaker believes that the people who sent him to the kitchen will one day feel shame for doing so.

Connect and Extend OPTIONAL

CONNECT TO EXTENDED WRITING PROJECT

Students can use "I, Too" as a mentor text for their Extended Writing Project. They may adopt some of Langston Hughes's methods for creating short, succinct sentences as they craft their informational essays.

BEYOND THE BOOK

Writing: Copy Change

Copy Change is a way to use the structure of another poet's work to create new poems with new meaning for ourselves. Ask students to use the structure of "I, Too" to compose a poem about their identity and how it has been shaped by America.

I, too, ____
I am the ____
____ send me to ____
When ____ comes,
But I ____,
And ____,
And ____.
Tomorrow,
I'll be ____
When ____ comes.
Nobody'll ____
Say to me,
"____,"
Then.
Besides,
They'll see ____ I am
And be ____ -
I, too, am ____.

To reflect, ask students:

- Which aspects of your identity helped to shape this poem?

- Do you like writing copy change poems, or do you prefer to write poems using your own structure?

Think Questions

Circulate as students answer Think Questions independently. Scaffolds for these questions are shown on the opposite page.

QUESTION 1: Textual Evidence

The speaker is an African American male because he calls himself the "darker brother."

QUESTION 2: Textual Evidence

The speaker compares a family dinner with American racism. In the first stanza, the African American speaker is not allowed at the table: "They send me to eat in the kitchen." In the second stanza, the speaker joins the meal: "I'll be at the table."

QUESTION 3: Textual Evidence

In the future, those who kept the speaker from the table will "be ashamed" because they will come to view African Americans differently, seeing their worth and beauty.

QUESTION 4: Word Meaning

Definition number 2 most closely matches the meaning of the word *company* in line 4. The speaker describes guests coming to a dinner.

QUESTION 5: Context Clues

I think *dare* must mean "to be bold enough to go against." The word is used to describe those who will not be bold enough to go against the speaker in the future by telling him that he has no place at the American table.

First Read

Read "I, Too, Sing America." After you read, complete the Think Questions below.

☁ THINK QUESTIONS

1. Who is the speaker of the poem? How do you know? Refer to one or more details from the beginning of the text to support your response.

2. What is the speaker comparing in lines 2–4 and 8–10? How are these two sets of lines similar? How are they different? Cite specific evidence from the text to support your answer.

3. Why will those who make the speaker "eat in the kitchen," in line 3, "be ashamed" in the future? Cite specific evidence from the text to support your response.

4. Read the following dictionary entry:

   com•pa•ny \kəmp(ə)nē\ *noun*

   a. A business or other commercial organization
   b. A visiting person or group
   c. A group of soldiers

   Which definition most closely matches the meaning of **company** as it is used in line 4? Write the correct definition of *company* here and explain how you figured out the correct meaning.

5. Based on the context of the poem, what do you think the word **dare** means in line 11? Write your definition of *dare* here and confirm the meaning in a print or digital dictionary.

Reading & Writing Companion **35**

Think Questions

Use the scaffolds below to differentiate instruction for your **ELL** English Language Learners and **A** Approaching grade-level learners.

ELL **BEGINNING** Write a response using the <u>word bank</u> and <u>sentence frames</u>.

INTERMEDIATE Write a response using the <u>sentence frames</u>.

ADVANCED, ADVANCED HIGH Write a response using the <u>Text-Dependent Question Guide</u>.

A **APPROACHING** Write a response using the <u>Text-Dependent Question Guide</u>.

| | INTERMEDIATE | APPROACHING |
| BEGINNING | | ADVANCED, ADVANCED HIGH |

Word Bank	Sentence Frames	Text-Dependent Question Guide
African beauty bold dinner joins male no place not allowed racism worth second	The speaker is an ___ American ___ because he calls himself the "darker brother."	1. • What does the word *darker* tell you about the speaker's skin color? • To what cultural group does the speaker likely belong? • What does the word *brother* tell you about the speaker's gender?
	The speaker compares a family ___ with American ___. In the first set of lines, the African American speaker is ___ at They send me to eat in the kitchen." In the second set of lines, the speaker ___ the meal: "I'll be at the table."	2. • What topic does the word *darker* suggest? • Why isn't the speaker allowed to eat with the other guests? • What setting do the words *eat, kitchen,* and *company* suggest?
	In the future, the hosts will "be ashamed" because they will come to view African Americans differently, seeing their ___ and ___.	3. • What will the hosts learn about African Americans in the future? • When the speaker uses the word *beautiful,* what does he mean? • Why will this beauty make the hosts feel shame?
	Company as used in the text matches the ___ definition.	4. • Read: "When **company** comes, / I laugh, / And eat well / And grow strong." • Which definition most closely matches the meaning of *company* as it is used in line 4? • Write the correct definition of *company*. • Explain how you figured the correct meaning.
	Dare must mean "___ enough to go against." The word is used to describe future hosts who will not tell the speaker he has ___ at the American table.	5. • Read: "Nobody'll **dare** / Say to me," • Does the speaker expect or not expect future hosts to say, "Eat in the kitchen"? • In the future, would it be bold or kind for a host to say these words?

Skill: Poetic Elements and Structure

Introduce the Skill

Watch the Concept Definition video ▶ and read the following definitions with your students.

Poetic structure describes the organization of words and lines in a poem as well as its rhyme scheme and meter. Poems consist of words that are divided into **lines**. A group of lines is called a **stanza**.

Other elements of poetry that contribute to structure include rhyme and rhythm. **Rhyme** is the repetition of the same or similar vowel sounds. The **rhyme scheme** of a poem is the pattern formed by the rhyming words at the end of lines. **Rhythm** is the pattern of unstressed and stressed syllables in a line of poetry. A regular pattern is called **meter,** and it gives a line of poetry a predictable rhythm.

The poet's choice of **poetic form,** or arrangement and style of a poem, will help determine the structure. Common forms include haiku, limerick, and sonnet, each with its own rules. Poetry without a consistent meter, rhyme, or stanza length is called **open form.**

TURN AND TALK

1. What is a poem or song you know that has a strong rhythm? How do you feel when you either hear it or read it aloud?

2. Do you prefer a poem with a rhyme scheme or a free-verse poem? Why?

ELL SPEAKING FRAMES

- A poem / song I know that has a strong rhythm is ____. I feel ____ when I read aloud or hear this poem / song.
- I prefer a poem with ____. I like this kind of poem because ____.

POETIC ELEMENTS AND STRUCTURE

sync•skills

Skill: Poetic Elements and Structure

Use the Checklist to analyze Poetic Elements and Structure in "I, Too, Sing America." Refer to the sample student annotations about Poetic Elements and Structure in the text.

••• CHECKLIST FOR POETIC ELEMENTS AND STRUCTURE

In order to identify elements of poetic elements and structure, note the following:

✓ how the words and lines are arranged

✓ the form and overall structure of the poem

✓ the rhyme, rhythm, and meter, if present

✓ how the arrangement of lines and stanzas in the poem contribute to the poem's theme, or message

To analyze how a particular stanza fits into the overall structure of a text and contributes to the development of the theme, consider the following questions:

✓ What poetic form does the poet use? What is the structure?

✓ How do the lengths of the lines and stanzas affect the meaning?

✓ How does a poem's stanza fit into the structure of the poem overall?

✓ How does the form and structure affect the poem's meaning?

✓ In what way does a specific stanza contribute to the poem's theme?

V SKILL VOCABULARY

meter / la métrica *noun* a regular pattern of unstressed and stressed syllables in a line of poetry

rhyme / la rima *noun* the repetition of the same or similar sounds in a poem

rhythm / el ritmo *noun* the pattern of unstressed and stressed syllables in a line of poetry

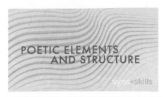

Skill:
Poetic Elements And Structure

Reread lines 8–18 of "I, Too, Sing America." Then, using the Checklist on the previous page, answer the multiple-choice questions below.

↻ YOUR TURN

1. How does the stanza from lines 8–14 convey a message to the reader?

   ○ A. It suggests that what the speaker hopes for will never happen.
   ○ B. It sends the message of the hope for equality in America.
   ○ C. It implies that the speaker will continue to wait.
   ○ D. It suggests that the speaker has given up.

2. What clues tell you the poem is open form?

   ○ A. The poem has a predictable rhythm scheme.
   ○ B. The words rhyme at the end of the lines.
   ○ C. It doesn't have consistent meter, rhyme, or stanza length.
   ○ D. There is a pattern of stressed and unstressed syllables.

3. How do the lines and line breaks, when read aloud, help to convey the theme of the poem?

   ○ A. Each idea is spoken calmly, with hope, and with confidence.
   ○ B. The speaker sounds angry, rushing to express something upsetting.
   ○ C. The short lines and line breaks suggest the speaker is tired and depressed.
   ○ D. Each line seems to express a threatening demand.

SkillsTV

Project the SkillsTV episode ▶ and pause at the following times to prompt discussion:

0:43 How can a poem with a simple structure also be complex?

1:54 How do the students figure out that the poem is more complex than they thought? What do they discover?

2:47 How does looking for a rhythm and paying attention to the length of lines and line breaks affect how the students read the poem?

Your Turn

Ask students to complete the Your Turn Activity.

QUESTION 1

A. Incorrect. The words "tomorrow" and "then" suggest that something will happen.

B. **Correct.** The word "tomorrow" indicates that the speaker has hope that inequality will change soon, and "then" tells when things will be different in America.

C. Incorrect. The speaker does not suggest waiting; rather, he shows hope and confidence that something is about to happen.

D. Incorrect. The speaker does not suggest giving up.

QUESTION 2

A. Incorrect. The poem does not have a predictable rhythm scheme.

B. Incorrect. There are no rhyming words.

C. **Correct.** There is no regular meter, rhythm, or stanza length in this poem.

D. Incorrect. There is no pattern of stressed and unstressed syllables.

QUESTION 3

A. **Correct.** When read aloud, the lines show a calm speaker who is confident that one day, things will be better.

B. Incorrect. The line breaks do not create a sense of anger.

C. Incorrect. The short lines and line breaks suggest a speaker who is thoughtful rather than tired and depressed.

D. Incorrect. The structure does not suggest a threatening way of speaking.

Skill: Media

Introduce the Skill

Watch the Concept Definition video and read the following definitions with your students.

Media is the plural form of the word *medium*. A **medium** is a means of sending a communication to an intended audience. Throughout most of human history, people communicated through three main media: speech, writing, and visual arts such as drawing, painting, and sculpture. But in the 19th century media options suddenly exploded. The invention of photography, and then the telegraph and the telephone, changed the world. Within a century radio, motion pictures, and television followed.

Stories and ideas change as they are translated from one medium to another. A dialogue between two characters in a novel, for example, becomes very different when it is delivered by actors in a film—with close-ups, sound effects such as music, and other elements unique to the medium of film itself.

Today new media are being invented at a much faster pace than ever before, and each of these forms of online communication has its own "language" and creates its own experience.

TURN AND TALK

1. How does your favorite book differ from the movie version?

2. How does this difference impact the theme or how you visualized the book?

ELL SPEAKING FRAMES

- One difference between [book/movie title] is ____.
- This difference impacts the theme because ____.
- This difference impacts the way I visualized the book by ____.

I, Too

Skill:
Media

Use the Checklist to analyze Media in "I, Too, Sing America." Refer to the sample student annotations about Media in the text.

••• CHECKLIST FOR MEDIA

In order to determine how to compare and contrast reading a story, drama, or poem to listening to or viewing an audio, video, or live version of a text, do the following:

- ✓ choose a story that has been presented in multiple forms of media, such as a written story and a film adaptation

- ✓ think about the key features of the different media presentations

- ✓ consider how different kinds of media treat story elements in different ways

- ✓ think about what you "see"—or visualize—as well as "hear" when you read a story, drama, or poem and how it compares to seeing it as a film, or hearing it read aloud

To compare and contrast the experience of reading a story, drama, or poem to listening to or viewing an audio, video, or live version of the text, including contrasting what they "see" and "hear" when reading the text to what they perceive when they listen or watch, consider the following questions:

- ✓ What features of each medium are the most important?

- ✓ Do you listen to it or view it? Do you hear one voice or many? How do these affect the written work?

- ✓ How is the way you picture a character in your mind as you read similar to the way that same character is portrayed in a filmed version of the same story? How is it different?

V   SKILL VOCABULARY

medium / el medio *noun* a form of communication, such as television, the Internet, and radio   COGNATE

media / los medios *noun* the plural form of the word medium; a means of sending a communication to an intended audience

Skill:
Media

Reread lines 4–10 of "I, Too, Sing America." Then, using the Checklist on the previous page, answer the multiple-choice questions below.

⟳ YOUR TURN

1. How can comparing and contrasting different forms of media be useful for analyzing the theme of "I, Too?

   ○ A. Varying themes help the reader understand how the piece connects to the world today.
   ○ B. A shift in mood helps the reader draw further conclusions about the speaker.
   ○ C. Analyzing tone and use of pronouns helps the reader to better understand theme.
   ○ D. A shift in tone can help the reader visualize the events in the piece.

2. How are the audio and printed versions of the poem "I, Too" different?

   ○ A. The textual difference between the spoken and written version influences the audience's understanding of the poem's theme
   ○ B. The difference in the rhyming lines between the spoken and written version impacts how the reader imagines the speaker.
   ○ C. The difference in the theme between the spoken and written version allows the reader to relate to the speaker.
   ○ D. The student is better able to analyze the narrator's tone in the printed version.

⚙ Your Turn

Ask students to complete the Your Turn Activity.

QUESTION 1

A. Incorrect. The audio version does not offer a different theme for the poem.

B. Incorrect. There is not an overall shift in mood from the printed poem to the audio version, nor does the reader make specific conclusions about the speaker; rather, the reader analyzes the tone of the speaker and how it relates to theme.

C. **Correct.** The inflection in the speaker's voice in the audio version of the poem and the change from "I" to "we" allows the student to better understand the theme.

D. Incorrect. The shift in tone that is experienced in the audio version may help the reader visualize, but this is not the best answer because it does not pertain to theme.

QUESTION 2

A. **Correct.** The change from "I" to "we" helps the reader to more easily understand the theme.

B. Incorrect. Neither the audio or printed version of the poem contains rhyming lines.

C. Incorrect. There is no difference in theme between the audio version and the printed version of the poem.

D. Incorrect. The reader is better able to analyze the narrator's tone in the audio version since he is able to hear the tone and inflection of the narrator's voice.

Close Read

Skills Focus

QUESTION 1: Poetic Elements and Structure

See lines 3–14: The speaker uses these lines to contrast his negative treatment with his positive attitude. This hints at change.

QUESTION 2: Figurative Language

See lines 3 and 4: Hughes uses a dinner table as a metaphor to discuss racism. Hughes is not welcome now because of segregation, but he will be soon.

QUESTION 3: Media

See lines 3–7: By reading the poem, I can infer that the central theme of the poem is pride. The speaker shows pride in his ability to laugh during hard times, knowing that he will soon take his rightful place at the table.

QUESTION 4: Connect to Essential Question

See lines 2–7: By reading the poem, I can infer that the central theme of the poem is pride. The speaker shows pride in his ability to laugh during hard times, knowing that he will soon take his rightful place at the table.

I, Too

 Close Read

Reread "I, Too, Sing America." As you reread, complete the Skills Focus questions below. Then use your answers and annotations from the questions to help you complete the Write activity.

◎ SKILLS FOCUS

1. Explain the effect of two or three lines, or a stanza, on the poem's theme.

2. Hughes uses a dining table as a metaphor to explain American racism. Explain how this metaphor causes readers to think about the topic in a new way.

3. Compare and contrast the experience of determining the central theme of the poem by reading the poem and listening to the audio version. Explain your thinking using textual evidence.

4. Explain why it's important for the speaker to sit at the table, even though he was instructed to sit in the kitchen. Cite traits of the speaker that will help him achieve this goal.

✎ WRITE

LITERARY ANALYSIS: How does Langston Hughes use poetic elements and structure to explore the theme of change in his poem "I, Too"? Write a response in which you analyze the effect of the poem's poetic structure. Did the effect change when you listened to the poem? Be sure to use evidence from the text.

Please note that excerpts and passages in the StudySync® library and this workbook are intended as touchstones to generate interest in an author's work. The excerpts and passages do not substitute for the reading of entire texts, and StudySync® strongly recommends that students seek out and purchase the whole literary or informational work in order to experience it as the author intended. Links to online resellers are available in our digital library. In addition, complete works may be ordered through an authorized reseller by filling out and returning to StudySync® the order form enclosed in this workbook.

 ## Writer's Notebook

Connect to Essential Question: Give students time to reflect on how "I, Too" connects to the unit's essential question "How do we know what to do when there are no instructions?" by freewriting in their Writer's Notebooks.

 Beginning & Intermediate

Read aloud the unit's essential question: "How do we know what to do when there are no instructions?" Encourage students to draw their connections or allow students to write in their native language. Circulate around the room, prompting students for their thoughts as they respond orally or through pantomime.

Advanced & Advanced High

Allow students to share their connections orally in pairs or small groups before freewriting.

Collaborative Conversation

Break students into collaborative conversation groups to discuss the Close Read prompt. Remind them to reference their Skills Focus annotations in their discussion.

How does Langston Hughes use poetic elements and structure to explore the theme of change in his poem "I, Too"? Write a response in which you analyze the effect of the poem's poetic structure. Did the effect change when you listened to the poem? Be sure to use evidence from the text.

Use the scaffolds below to differentiate instruction for your **ELL** English Language Learners and **A** Approaching grade-level learners.

ELL **BEGINNING, INTERMEDIATE** Use the discussion guide and speaking frames to facilitate the discussion with support from the teacher.

ADVANCED, ADVANCED HIGH Use the discussion guide and speaking frames to facilitate the discussion in mixed-level groups.

A **APPROACHING** Use the discussion guide to facilitate the discussion in mixed-level groups.

APPROACHING
ADVANCED, ADVANCED HIGH
BEGINNING, INTERMEDIATE

Discussion Guide	Speaking Frames
1. In the poem, how does the speaker change between the present and the future?	• In the present, the hosts view the speaker ___. • In the future, the hosts will view the speaker ___.
2. In the poem, how does America change between the present and the future?	• In the present, America is a place where ___. • In the future, America will be a place where ___.
3. Did listening to the poem change the effect of the poetic structure?	• The audio clip did/did not influence the poetic structure because ___. • This impacts my analysis of the poem because ___.

Review Prompt and Rubric

Before students begin writing, review the writing prompt and rubric with the class.

LITERARY ANALYSIS: How does Langston Hughes use poetic elements and structure to explore the theme of change in his poem "I, Too"? Write a response in which you analyze the effect of the poem's poetic structure. Did the effect change when you listened to the poem? Be sure to use evidence from the text.

ELL **PROMPT GUIDE**

A
- What is poetic structure?
- What are some poetic elements and structure in the poem?
- How do the speaker and America change between the present and the future?

- In what ways does the poem's structure affect the theme of change?
- Did listening to the poem change the effect of the poetic structure?

Score	Poetic Elements and Structure	Media	Language and Conventions
4	The writer clearly analyzes and explains the author's use of poetic structure. The writer provides exemplary analysis, using relevant evidence from the text.	The writer clearly analyzes and explains how listening to the poem affects their understanding. The writer provides exemplary analysis, using relevant evidence from the text.	The writer demonstrates a consistent command of grammar, punctuation, and usage conventions. Although minor errors may be evident, they do not detract from the fluency or the clarity of the essay.
3	The writer analyzes and explains the author's use of poetic structure. The writer provides sufficient analysis, using relevant evidence from the text most of the time.	The writer analyzes and explains how listening to the poem effects their understanding. The writer provides sufficient analysis, using relevant evidence from the text most of the time.	The writer demonstrates an adequate command of grammar, punctuation, and usage conventions. Although some errors may be evident, they create few (if any) disruptions in the fluency of the writing or the clarity of the essay.
2	The writer begins to analyze or explain the author's use of poetic structure, but the analysis is incomplete. The writer uses relevant evidence from the text only some of the time.	The writer begins to analyze or explains how listening to the poem effects their understanding, but the analysis is incomplete. The writer uses relevant evidence from the text only some of the time.	The writer demonstrates a partial command of grammar, punctuation, and usage conventions. Some distracting errors may be evident, at times creating minor disruptions in the fluency or clarity of the writing.
1	The writer attempts to analyze or explain the author's use of poetic structure, but the analysis is not successful. The writer uses little or no relevant evidence from the text.	The writer attempts to analyze or explain how listening to the poem affects their understanding, but the analysis is not successful. The writer uses little or no relevant evidence from the text.	The writer demonstrates little or no command of grammar, punctuation, and usage conventions. Serious and persistent errors create disruptions in the fluency of the writing and sometimes interfere with meaning.
0	The writer does not provide a relevant response to the prompt or does not provide a response at all.	The writer does not provide a relevant response to the prompt or does not provide a response at all.	Serious and persistent errors overwhelm the writing and interfere with the meaning of the response as a whole, making the writer's meaning impossible to understand.

Write

Ask students to complete the writing assignment using textual evidence to support their answers.

Use the scaffolds below to differentiate instruction for your **ELL** English Language Learners and **A** Approaching grade-level learners.

ELL **BEGINNING** With the help of the <u>word bank</u>, write a response using <u>paragraph frame 1</u>.

INTERMEDIATE With the help of the <u>word bank</u>, write a response using <u>paragraph frames 1 and 2</u>.

ADVANCED, ADVANCED HIGH Write a response of differentiated length using the <u>sentence starters</u>.

A **APPROACHING** Write a response of differentiated length using the <u>sentence starters</u>.

| BEGINNING | | ADVANCED, ADVANCED HIGH |
| INTERMEDIATE | | APPROACHING |

Word Bank	Paragraph Frame 1	Paragraph Frame 2	Sentence Starters
America future equality stanza we	In the poem, the speaker changes from someone who eats in the kitchen to someone who eats at the table. This change will occur because the speaker feels that ____ will change. America will acknowledge and embrace all its citizens, black and white, like a family. The poem's structure supports this idea because the second ____ describes the present, and the third stanza describes the ____. Listening to the poem adds to the effect of the poetic structure by showing that African Americans are united and will receive equal rights. Hughes shows this when he substitutes "____" for "I" in the audio version of the poem. This emphasizes the theme of change and need for ____.	In the first line of the poem, the speaker sings ____. He sings as if he is not ____. In the last line of the poem, the speaker says that he ____. He speaks as if he is ____. The change in the speaker is ____ in the structure of the poem.	• In the present, the speaker is . . . • In the future, the speaker is . . . • This change in the speaker occurs because there is a change in . . . • The poem's line breaks support the theme of change in that . . . • The poem's stanzas (punctuation) support(s) the theme of change in that . . . • Listening to the poem adds to the effect of the poetic structure because . . .

Peer Review

Students should submit substantive feedback to two peers using the review instructions below.

- How well does this response answer the prompt?
- How well does the writer support his or her ideas with details and examples from the poem?
- Which sentence in the writer's response makes you think differently about the poem?
- What does the writer do well in this response? What does the writer need to work on?

Rate

Respond to the following with a point rating that reflects your opinion.

	1 2 3 4
Ideas	■ ■ ■ □
Evidence	■ ■ ■ ■
Language and Conventions	■ ■ □ □

Submit

ELL **SENTENCE FRAMES**

A
- You were able to (completely / partly / almost) ____ answer the prompt because ____.
- You could answer the prompt more completely by ____.
- You supported the idea of ____ with the detail of ____.

- One idea that needs more support is ____.
- I thought differently about the poem after reading ____.
- My favorite part of your response is ____.

Everybody Jump
(from 'What If?')

INFORMATIONAL TEXT
Randall Munroe
2014

Introduction

Randall Munroe (b. 1984) is a physicist and former NASA computer programmer and roboticist. After leaving NASA, he became a popular webcomic artist and blogger, and in 2014, Munroe published a collection of writings and blog posts titled *What If? Serious Scientific Answers to Absurd Hypothetical Questions*. True to the collection's title, the excerpted essay explores what might happen if everyone on Earth jumped at the exact same moment. In answering this, Munroe contrasts human beings' relative unimportance in the physical universe to our profound effects on one another.

Answering a hypothetical question, Randall Munro explores what would happen if everyone on Earth stood close to each other and jumped at the same time. Munro asks readers to imagine that everyone on the planet is in Rhode Island. After everyone jumps, a lot of energy would be created, but nothing much would happen beyond generating a loud roar and a lot of footprints. Next, Munro posits that chaos would ensue due to the fact that everyone would try to leave at the same time, which would overload local airports and train stations. Likewise, the roads would be clogged with traffic. In short, Munro proposes that within weeks of this jumping experiment, the majority of humanity would die and the survivors would struggle to build a new civilization.

ELL Proficiency-leveled summaries and summaries in multiple languages are available digitally.

🔊 Audio and audio text highlighting are available with this text.

CONNECT TO ESSENTIAL QUESTION

How do we know what to do when there are no instructions?

Imagine if everyone in the world gathered in the same place and jumped at exactly the same time! What would the aftermath be? Would planet Earth be affected?

Access Complex Text

LEXILE: 860L   WORD COUNT: 626

The following areas may be challenging for students, particularly **ELL** English Language Learners and **A** Approaching grade-level learners.

Genre	Connection of Ideas	Specific Vocabulary
• The selection contains text features, such as stick figure drawings, that are not common in informational texts. Some students may struggle to connect these graphic features, particularly the area on the map and what they represent, to the text.	• The blend of humor—in particular humorous asides—with facts may make it difficult for students to synthesize information from the text. They may require assistance to determine the author's purpose and message.	• Words such as *kinematics* may need clarification. • Context clues or a dictionary can help students define unfamiliar words.

📶 **SCAFFOLDS**   **ENGLISH LANGUAGE LEARNERS**   **APPROACHING GRADE LEVEL**   **BEYOND GRADE LEVEL**

These icons identify differentiation strategies and scaffolded support for a variety of students. See the digital lesson plan for additional differentiation strategies and scaffolds.

Instructional Path

The print teacher's edition includes essential point-of-use instruction and planning tools. Complete lesson plans and program documents appear in your digital teacher account.

First Read: Everybody Jump (from 'What If?')

Objectives: After an initial reading and discussion of the informational essay, students will be able to identify and restate the text's key ideas and details.

Skill: Informational Text Structure

Objectives: After rereading and discussing a model of close reading, students will be able to analyze how particular sections fit into the overall structure of an informational text and contribute to the development of ideas.

Skill: Technical Language

Objectives: After rereading and discussing a model of close reading, students will be able to identify and define technical language in an informational text using context.

Close Read: Everybody Jump (from 'What If?')

Objectives: After engaging in a close reading and discussion of the text, students will be able to analyze informational text structures and technical language in order to participate in a collaborative conversation and use key ideas and details to write a short, written response.

Blast: Emojis Speak Louder Than Words

Objectives: After exploring background information and research links about a topic, students will respond to a question with a 140-character response.

DIGITAL ONLY

Progress Monitoring

Opportunities to Learn	Opportunities to Demonstrate Learning	Opportunities to Reteach

Informational Text Structure

⚙ Skill: Informational Text Structure	⚙ Skill: Informational Text Structure • Your Turn ▣ Close Read • Skills Focus • Write	⚙ Unit 4 Skill: Informational Text Structure - Malala Yousafzai-Nobel Lecture ⚙ Unit 5 Skill: Informational Text Structure - Warriors Don't Cry ⚙ Spotlight Skill: Informational Text Structure

Technical Language

⚙ Skill: Technical Language	⚙ Skill: Technical Language • Your Turn ▣ Close Read • Complete Vocabulary Chart • Skills Focus	⚙ Unit 3 Skill: Technical Language - Margaret Bourke-White: Fearless Photographer ⚙ Spotlight Skill: Technical Language

First Read

Randall Munroe

Everybody Jump!

 ## Introduce the Text

As a class, watch the video preview and have students read the introduction in pairs to make connections to the video preview.

To activate prior knowledge and experiences, ask students:

- What key words or images from the video do you think will be most important to the essay you are about to read?

- What do you think the phrase "unimportance in the physical universe" means?

ELL SPEAKING FRAMES

- The ____ in the video makes me think ____.
- The video shows ____. This makes me wonder ____.
- I think the text will ____. I think this because ____.
- I predict that there will be ____. I believe this because ____.

Entry Point

As students prepare to read "Everybody Jump," share the following information with them to provide context.

✓ There are around 7,600,000,000 (that's 7.6 billion) people alive on Earth.

✓ The world's population has grown exponentially, meaning the rate of growth increases as the population increases. So the doubling of the world's population from one billion people to two billion people took 127 years, but only 47 years for it to double again.

✓ In an interview with *The Atlantic*, Randall Monroe talks about how he gets ideas for his *What If?* blog. He says, "What I like doing is finding the places in those questions where normal people -- or, people who have less spare time than I do -- think, 'This is stupid,' and stop." He goes on to say that math and physics are really cool because they give him the tools to answer the questions.

"At the stroke of noon, everyone jumps."

Skill: Technical Language

I think the subject of the text is "science" because the author mentions ScienceBlogs. I can guess that "kinematics" has to do with motion because everyone will jump. If the text is about motion, the type of science is probably physics.

1   *What would happen if everyone on earth stood as close to each other as they could and jumped, everyone landing on the ground at the same instant? —Thomas Bennett (and many others)*

2   This is one of the most popular questions submitted to this blog. It's been examined before, including by a ScienceBlogs post and a Straight Dope article. They cover the kinematics pretty well. However, they don't tell the whole story.

3   Let's take a closer look.

4   At the start of the **scenario,** the entire Earth's population has been magically transported together into one place.

5   This crowd takes up an area the size of Rhode Island. But there's no reason to use the vague phrase "an area the size of Rhode Island". This is our scenario; we can be specific. They're *actually* in Rhode Island.

Copyright © BookheadEd Learning, LLC

SELECTION VOCABULARY

scenario / el escenario *noun* a description of something that could happen **COGNATE**

Analyze Vocabulary Using Context Clues

In paragraph 4, focus on the sentence that uses the word scenario. Point out these context clues:

1.   First I notice that the word *scenario* contains the word *scene,* like a scene or a plot or setting in a movie.

2.   I also notice that the described setting—Earth's population transported to one place—isn't real. I'm supposed to engage in magical thinking to envision it.

3.   I think a *scenario* is an "imagined setting or sequence of events."

Technical Language

What words helped the reader figure out the subject of the text?

The reader highlighted "ScienceBlogs", "jumped" and "kinematics" to figure out that this is a science text, and more specifically, about physics.

TEXT TALK

What does the term *kinematics* mean?

See paragraph 2: The term *kinematics* refers to "a branch of science that deals with aspects of motion."

Informational Text Structure

What was the first clue about text structure that the reader identified? How did he use this clue to help him understand the text?

The reader first noticed the word "next." He then looked for other words and phrases that would signal an order of events, which helped him understand the scenario being described.

6   At the stroke of noon, everyone jumps.

7   As discussed elsewhere, it doesn't really affect the planet. Earth outweighs us by a factor of over ten trillion. On average, we humans can vertically jump maybe half a meter on a good day. Even if the Earth were **rigid** and responded instantly, it would be pushed down by less than an atom's width.[1]

8   Next, everyone falls back to the ground.

9   Technically, this delivers a lot of energy into the Earth, but it's spread out over a large enough area that it doesn't do much more than leave footprints in a lot of gardens. A slight pulse of pressure spreads through the North American continental crust and dissipates with little effect. The sound of all those feet hitting the ground creates a loud, drawn-out roar which lasts many seconds.

10   Eventually, the air grows quiet.

11   Seconds pass. Everyone looks around.

Skill: Informational Text Structure

Next is one of the key signal words for sequential order, so I know to look out for other words or phrases that signal events are happening in a specific order, like "eventually" and "seconds pass" below. The sequential order helps me understand what's going to happen next in the scenario.

1.   **atom's width:** the atom is the basic unit of matter

Reading & Writing Companion   **43**

V   **SELECTION VOCABULARY**

rigid / rígido/a *adjective* not flexible or able to change shape   COGNATE

ELL
- Does Earth bend easily when force is applied?
- Does Earth stay stiff when force is applied?

NOTES

12 There are a lot of uncomfortable glances. Someone coughs.

Skill: Informational Text Structure

The author is using cause-and-effect structure here to develop the story. The cause is that everybody tries to use their cell phones at the same time. The effect is that the cell networks stop working. This helps me understand the consequences of the jump.

13 A cell phone comes out of a pocket. Within seconds, the rest of the world's five billion phones follow. All of them—even those **compatible** with the region's towers—are displaying some version of "NO SIGNAL." The cell networks have all collapsed under the unprecedented load.

14 The T. F. Green airport in Warwick, Rhode Island handles a few thousand passengers a day. Assuming they got things organized (including sending out scouting missions to retrieve fuel), they could run at 500% **capacity** for years without making a dent in the crowd.

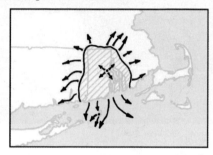

15 The addition of all the nearby airports doesn't change the equation much. Nor does the region's light rail system. Crowds climb on board container ships in the deepwater port of Providence, but stocking sufficient food and water for a long sea voyage proves a challenge.

16 Rhode Island's half-million cars are commandeered. Moments later, I-95, I-195, and I-295 become the sites of the largest traffic jam in the history of the planet. Most of the cars are engulfed by the crowds, but a lucky few get out and begin wandering the abandoned road network.

Copyright © BookheadEd Learning, LLC

44 Reading & Writing Companion

SELECTION VOCABULARY

compatible / compatible *adjective* agreeable or in harmony COGNATE

ELL
- Are the cell phones designed to work with the towers?
- Do the towers usually support these cell phones?

capacity / la capacidad *noun* the maximum amount that can be used or contained within something COGNATE

ELL
- Is the airport transporting the most or least amount of people that it can?
- Is a few thousand passengers per day the most or the least the airport can handle?

Informational Text Structure

What event does the reader focus on to identify a text structure?

The reader focuses on the major event of cell phone networks collapsing. He identifies a cause, which reveals the cause-and-effect structure of that paragraph.

Skills Focus

QUESTION 2: Informational Text Structure

The author uses cause and effect and sequential order to describe what happens when people commandeer Rhode Island's cars. This helps develop the central idea that the jump would create total chaos for humankind. The details about commandeering cars and the resulting traffic jam reveal the cause-and-effect text structure. The phrase "moments later" signals sequential order.

Skills Focus

QUESTION 3: Technical Language

The author uses the word "load" at the end of this paragraph in a specific way. "Load" can mean many things, like doing a load of laundry or carrying a load of books. In this context, however, it has a technical meaning of the amount of data being sent to the cell phone towers.

TEXT TALK

How will Munroe's essay differ from other articles that address this same question?

See paragraphs 2, 13, and 14: While other essays have addressed the physics of the question, Munroe's essay will address the effects on humanity.

After the imagined scenario ends, how many people will need to travel out of Rhode Island to get home?

See paragraph 13: About five billion people will need to travel.

What problems will these people face in trying to travel out of Rhode Island?

See paragraphs 15 and 16: The people will face problems with transportation, food, and water.

Skills Focus

QUESTION 1: Informational Text Structure

This paragraph contains a series of causes and effects. The author first lists factors that lead to the collapse of social hierarchies. The collapse then produces its own effects of violence, hunger, and thirst, as food and water become scarce.

Skills Focus

QUESTION 4: Connect to Essential Question

Laws are instructions for good behavior. Without police to enforce the laws, the author thinks people would steal cars to escape Rhode Island.

TEXT TALK

What will be the primary effect as people face these travel problems?

See paragraphs 19 and 20: Many people will die, greatly reducing the population of Earth.

What other information have you read that will help you understand this essay through synthesis?

Answers will vary.

How do the people in the scenario react to emergencies? What should they do to combat panic?

Answers will vary.

> **B** Ask each Beyond grade-level student to write one additional discussion question. Then, have one or two students facilitate a discussion, using their questions to guide the conversation.

NOTES

17 Some make it past New York or Boston before running out of fuel. Since the electricity is probably not on at this point, rather than find a working gas pump, it's easier to just abandon the car and steal the new one. Who can stop you? All the cops are in Rhode Island.

18 The edge of the crowd spreads outward into southern Massachusetts and Connecticut. Any two people who meet are unlikely to have a language in common, and almost nobody knows the area. The state becomes a patchwork chaos of **coalescing** and collapsing social hierarchies.[2] Violence is common. Everybody is hungry and thirsty. Grocery stores are emptied. Fresh water is hard to come by and there's no efficient system for distributing it.

19 Within weeks, Rhode Island is a graveyard of billions.

20 The survivors spread out across the face of the world and struggle to build a new civilization atop the pristine ruins of the old. Our species staggers on, but our population has been greatly reduced. Earth's orbit is completely unaffected—it spins along exactly as it did before our species-wide jump.

21 But at least now we know.

Everybody Jump" from WHAT IF?: Serious Scientific Answers to Absurd Hypothetical Questions by Randall Munroe. Copyright © 2014 by xked Inc. Reprinted by permission of Houghton Mifflin Harcourt Publishing Company. All rights reserved.

2. **hierarchies:** structures of status or value, from the powerful to the subjugated

Reading & Writing Companion   45

SELECTION VOCABULARY

coalescing / fusionarse *verb* to come together to form one group or mass

> **ELL** • Is patchwork something that comes together or is torn apart?
> • If *collapsing* is an antonym, what might *coalescing* mean?

Reading Comprehension OPTIONAL

Have students complete the digital reading comprehension questions ✓ when they finish reading.

ANSWER KEY

QUESTION 1: B	**QUESTION 5:** B	**QUESTION 9:** D
QUESTION 2: D	**QUESTION 6:** B	**QUESTION 10:**
QUESTION 3: A	**QUESTION 7:** C	*See chart below.*
QUESTION 4: B	**QUESTION 8:** C	

First	Second	Third	Fourth
Everybody appears in Rhode Island at the same time.	Everybody jumps at the same time.	Everybody checks their phone, but there is no reception.	The scene descends into violence and chaos.

Connect and Extend OPTIONAL

CONNECT TO EXTENDED WRITING PROJECT

Students can use "Everybody Jump" as a mentor text for their Extended Writing Project. They may adopt the author's use of short sentences for emphasis in their informational essay.

BEYOND THE BOOK

Game: What If?

Break students into teams to play "What if?" The object of the game is to use research skills and teamwork to correctly answer "what if" questions.

Rules:

- Once students are in teams, ask each team to write 4 "what if" questions on four separate index cards. These will be your playing cards for the game.

- Each team will take a turn drawing a "what if" question from the pile. Then the rest of the teams will have 3 minutes to research the answer to the question and agree on an answer.

- Each team will share their answer to the question and the team that drew the card will select the answer they think is strongest.

- The team selecting the strongest answer can ask follow up questions about the credibility or accuracy of the information before selecting the winner for that round.

- The team to get to 5 first wins!

Think Questions

Circulate as students answer Think Questions independently. Scaffolds for these questions are shown on the opposite page.

QUESTION 1: Textual Evidence

The author of the essay chooses to answer this seemingly absurd question because it is "one of the most popular questions submitted to [his] blog." His purpose in doing so is to suggest that humans are more connected to each other than they are to the physical attributes of Earth.

QUESTION 2: Textual Evidence

A coordinated jump would greatly reduce Earth's population as transportation, food, and water systems would not support travel out of Rhode Island. However, the jump would leave Earth's orbit "completely unaffected."

QUESTION 3: Textual Evidence

Instead of affecting the motion of the planet as might be anticipated, the jump would affect the ability of the people to travel and survive after they have gathered in Rhode Island: "Everybody is hungry and thirsty . . . [the] population has been greatly reduced."

QUESTION 4: Greek and Latin Affixes and Roots

The word *compatible* comes from the Latin root *compati,* meaning "to sympathize with," or "to relate to," and the prefix *com-*, meaning "together or in association with." I think *compatible* must mean "designed to work together within a system." The word is used to describe cell phones that work with the region's cell towers.

QUESTION 5: Context Clues

I think *capacity* must mean "maximum operation." The context clues in the sentence support this meaning, because even at 500% capacity, or more than maximum operation, the author says the airport would barely make a dent in the crowd size.

Everybody Jump (from 'What If?')

First Read

Read the essay "Everybody Jump." After you read, complete the Think Questions below.

 THINK QUESTIONS

1. Why does the author of this essay choose to answer this seemingly absurd question? What is his purpose in doing so? Explain by citing textual evidence from the selection to support your answer.

2. According to the author, how would a coordinated jump affect the Earth's orbit? Describe in your own words what would happen, referring to specific details from the text.

3. Why is the outcome of this imaginary scenario surprising? Discuss how things turn out a little differently than expected. Be sure to cite examples.

4. The prefix *com-* means "together" or "in association with" something. Based on this clue and any other common affixes, what is the meaning of **compatible** as it is used in paragraph 13 of the excerpt? Write your definition here, explaining its roots and/or affixes.

5. According to paragraph 14, the T.F. Green airport "could run at 500% **capacity** for years." Based on context, what does the word *capacity* mean? Write your best definition here and explain how you figured out its meaning.

Think Questions

Use the scaffolds below to differentiate instruction for your **ELL** English Language Learners and **A** Approaching grade-level learners.

ELL **BEGINNING** Write a response using the word bank and sentence frames.

INTERMEDIATE Write a response using the sentence frames.

ADVANCED, ADVANCED HIGH Write a response using the Text-Dependent Question Guide.

A **APPROACHING** Write a response using the Text-Dependent Question Guide.

| | INTERMEDIATE | APPROACHING |
| BEGINNING | | ADVANCED, ADVANCED HIGH |

Word Bank	Sentence Frames	Text-Dependent Question Guide
connected Latin make a dent	The author chooses to answer this absurd question because it is "one of the most ___ submitted to [his] blog." His purpose is to suggest that humans are more ___ to each other than they are to the ___.	1. • How many people are interested in this question? • Has the question been addressed previously? • How will this author's answer differ?
maximum operation motion physical Earth	The jump would leave Earth's orbit "completely ___." However, it would greatly reduce Earth's ___ as ___, food, and water systems would not support travel out of Rhode Island.	2. • How will Earth be affected by the imagined scenario? • What will happen to the people as a result of the imagined scenario? • What will cause this result?
popular questions population reduced survive	The outcome is surprising because instead of affecting the ___ of the planet as might be expected, the experiment affects the ability of the people to ___ afterward: "Everybody is hungry and thirsty . . . [the] population has been greatly ___."	3. • Why are people interested in this question? • What do you expect the outcome of the imaginary scenario to be? • How is the result the same as or different from your expectation?
together towers transportation unaffected	The word *compatible* comes from ___. I think *compatible* means "designed to work ___ within a system." The word is used to describe cell phones that work together with the region's cell ___.	4. • Read: "All of them—even those **compatible** with the region's towers—are displaying some version of "NO SIGNAL."" • Are the cell phone meant to work with the towers? • What does that tell me about the meaning of the word *compatible*?
	I think *capacity* must mean " ___." The context clues in the sentence support this meaning, because even at 500%, the author says the airport would barely ___ in the crowd size.	5. • Read: "Assuming they got things organized (including sending out scouting missions to retrieve fuel), they could run at 500% **capacity** for years without making a dent in the crowd." • Is the airport transporting the most or least number of people? • Is 500% above or below the number of passengers the airport can handle?

Skill: Informational Text Structure

Introduce the Skill

Watch the Concept Definition video and read the following definitions with your students.

Text structure refers to the organizational pattern authors of nonfiction use to present information. Some of the most common informational text structures include **sequential, problem and solution, cause and effect, and comparison and contrast.** In a sequential text structure, authors present information about events or steps in a process, in the order in which they take or have taken place. Writers who specialize in history or science topics often use a cause and effect text structure to explain how or why something happened. Many authors use a compare and contrast text structure to present information about things that are different but have something in common, such as two points of view on a subject. Or a writer may present a problem or a series of problems, and offers solutions on how to solve them.

Authors may also use text structure to organize information about multiple topics, or use more than one organizational pattern within the same text.

Skill: Informational Text Structure

Use the Checklist to analyze Informational Text Structure in "Everybody Jump." Refer to the sample student annotations about Informational Text Structure in the text.

••• CHECKLIST FOR INFORMATIONAL TEXT STRUCTURE

In order to determine the overall structure of a text, note the following:

✓ the topic(s) and how the author organizes information about the topic(s)

✓ patterns in a paragraph or section of text that reveal the text structure, such as:

- sequences, including the order of events or steps in a process
- problems and their solutions
- cause-and-effect relationships
- comparisons

✓ the overall structure of the text and how each section contributes to the development of ideas

To analyze how a particular sentence, paragraph, chapter, or section fits into the overall structure of a text and contributes to the development of the ideas, use the following questions as a guide:

✓ What organizational patterns reveal the text structure the author uses to present information?

✓ How does a particular sentence, paragraph, chapter, or section fit into the overall structure of the text? How does it affect the development of the author's ideas?

✓ In what ways does the text structure contribute to the development of ideas in the text?

TURN AND TALK

1. What are some of your favorite informational texts or television programs?

2. How was information presented and organized?

ELL SPEAKING FRAMES

- One of my favorite informational texts/television programs is ____. I like this text/program because ____.
- The information is about ____. The information is presented as ____.
- The information is organized by ____.

V SKILL VOCABULARY

problem and solution / el problema y la solución *noun* a text structure that identifies a problem and offers a solution COGNATE

cause and effect / causa y efecto *noun* a text structure that explains how or why something happened

comparison and contrast / comparar y contrastar *noun* a text structure that compares and contrasts two or more things COGNATE

Everybody Jump (from 'What If?')

Skill:
Informational Text Structure

Reread paragraphs 14–18 of "Everybody Jump." Then, using the Checklist on the previous page, answer the multiple-choice questions below.

🔁 YOUR TURN

1. In paragraphs 14 and 15, the author uses a problem-and-solution structure. What problem are the suggested solutions trying to solve?

   ○ A. how to get people home from Rhode Island after the jump
   ○ B. how to find fuel for airplanes
   ○ C. how to direct people to the nearest train station
   ○ D. how to prepare ships for a long sea voyage

2. In paragraph 16, what text structure do the phrases "moments later" and "begin wandering" suggest?

   ○ A. classify information
   ○ B. compare and contrast
   ○ C. chronological order
   ○ D. order of important ideas

3. Which of the following descriptions in paragraph 18 is most relevant to the central idea of the text?

   ○ A. the disadvantages of knowing multiple languages
   ○ B. the effects of collapsing social hierarchies
   ○ C. the common problems when people don't know an area
   ○ D. the crowds in Massachusetts and Connecticut

SkillsTV

Project the SkillsTV episode and pause at the following times to prompt discussion:

1:42 How do the students determine the main text structure of the paragraph? What reading strategy do they use?

2:44 How do the students know that the author is using a text structure that is different from the first example they analyzed?

3:17 What conclusions do the students make? Do you agree or disagree? Why or why not?

⚙ Your Turn

Ask students to complete the Your Turn Activity.

QUESTION 1

A. **Correct.** The text does not directly state the problem, but the text is about the solutions to getting the crowd out of Rhode Island.

B. Incorrect. This detail is a part of the problem.

C. Incorrect. The rail system is described as a failed solution to the problem.

D. Incorrect. The difficulty of stocking ships for a long sea voyage is why this solution fails.

QUESTION 2

A. Incorrect. The phrases do not suggest classification.

B. Incorrect. The phrases do not set up a compare and contrast.

C. **Correct.** The phrases signal when events happen.

D. Incorrect. The phrases do not suggest an order of importance.

QUESTION 3

A. Incorrect. There is no evidence to support this answer, and it does not reflect the central idea of the text (the serious effects of the jump).

B. **Correct.** The many problems resulting from collapsing social hierarchies best relate to the central idea of the text, which is the serious effects of the jump.

C. Incorrect. This problem is not the focus of the paragraph, and is not relevant to the central idea of the text (the serious effects of the jump).

D. Incorrect. The crowds in the two states are not key to the central idea of the text (the serious effects of the jump).

Skill: Technical Language

Introduce the Skill

Watch the Concept Definition video and read the following definitions with your students.

Technical language refers to words that are used in certain fields of knowledge. The **subject** is the field of knowledge the author writes about, such as astronomy or computer science, and it is an important part of determining the meaning of technical language. For example, if you know that archaeologists study human history based on things found in ancient ruins, and you read that an archaeologist has discovered an important artifact, you can guess that in this context the word artifact refers to an object made by a human being, usually an item of cultural or historical interest. Writers include technical language to educate readers, to make their explanation more **precise** and accurate, or to establish their **authority** on a subject. When a writer is being precise, they must be detailed but straightforward in their explanations of complex ideas and concepts. Being an authority, or expert, on a subject gives the writer credibility with readers.

TURN AND TALK

1. Can you think of any words that are specific to your favorite subject but have multiple meanings?

2. How do you figure out which meaning is correct?

ELL SPEAKING FRAMES

- One word related to my favorite subject is ____.
- It can also mean ____.
- To figure out which meaning is being used, I ____.

Skill: Technical Language

Use the Checklist to analyze Technical Language in "Everybody Jump." Refer to the sample student annotations about Technical Language in the text.

••• CHECKLIST FOR TECHNICAL LANGUAGE

In order to determine the meaning of words and phrases as they are used in a text, note the following:

✓ the subject of the book or article

✓ any unfamiliar words that you think might be technical terms

✓ words have multiple meanings that change when used with a specific subject

✓ the possible contextual meaning of a word, or the definition from a dictionary

To determine the meaning of words and phrases as they are used in a text, including technical meanings, consider the following questions:

✓ What is the subject of the informational text?

✓ Are there any unfamiliar words that look as if they might be technical language?

✓ Do any of the words in the text have more than one meaning?

✓ Can you identify the contextual meaning of any of the words?

Reading & Writing Companion **49**

V SKILL VOCABULARY

technical language / el lenguaje técnico *noun* words that are used in certain fields of knowledge, such as astronomy or computer science COGNATE

subject / la materia *noun* an area of knowledge to study

authority / la autoridad *noun* the power or right to give orders or make decisions; the power to be in charge COGNATE

Everybody Jump (from 'What If?')

Skill:
Technical Language

Reread paragraphs 19–21 of "Everybody Jump." Then, using the Checklist on the previous page, answer the multiple-choice questions below.

⟳ YOUR TURN

1. Which of the following best defines "species" as it is used in the passage?

   ○ A. coined money
   ○ B. humans inhabiting the earth
   ○ C. animals of the same biological classification
   ○ D. plants of the same group

2. Which line helps you best determine the meaning of "orbit" in paragraph 20?

   ○ A. "The survivors spread out across the face of the world. . ."
   ○ B. "Our species staggers on. . ."
   ○ C. ". . . it spins along exactly as it did before our species-wide jump."
   ○ D. ". . . but our population has been greatly reduced."

Your Turn

Ask students to complete the Your Turn Activity.

QUESTION 1

A. Incorrect. The context does not suggest money.

B. **Correct.** The context suggests that the author is referring to people.

C. Incorrect. The context does not suggest animals.

D. Incorrect. The context does not suggest plants.

QUESTION 2

A. Incorrect. This statement does not provide any clues for the meaning of the word "orbit."

B. Incorrect. This statement does not provide any clues for the meaning of the word "orbit."

C. **Correct.** This statement includes the word "spin," which provides a context clue to understand the meaning of "orbit."

D. Incorrect. This statement does not provide any clues for the meaning of the word "orbit."

Close Read

Skills Focus

QUESTION 1: Informational Text Structure

See paragraph 18.

QUESTION 2: Informational Text Structure

See paragraph 16.

QUESTION 3: Technical Language

See paragraph 13.

QUESTION 4: Connect to Essential Question

See paragraph 17.

✓ CHECK FOR SUCCESS

If students struggle to respond to Skills Focus Question #1, ask students the following questions:

- What are the first two sentences in paragraph 18 about?

- What happens in the third sentence of paragraph 18? How is this sentence related to the first two sentences?

- What are the last four sentences of paragraph 18 about? How are these sentences related to the third sentence?

- What do these details reveal about the text structure?

Close Read

Reread "Everybody Jump." As you reread, complete the Skills Focus questions below. Then use your answers and annotations from the questions to help you complete the Write activity.

◎ SKILLS FOCUS

1. Identify examples of the author's use of a cause-and-effect text structure. Explain what details or signal words reveal the text structure.

2. Identify a place in the text where the author uses another text structure that helps develop the central idea of the text. Explain what details or signal words reveal the text structure.

3. Identify a technical meaning of a word in the text and the context clues you used to help you define it.

4. Think about the unit's essential question: How do you know what to do when there are no instructions? Identify textual evidence in Munroe's scenario that answers this question, and explain your reasoning.

✎ WRITE

NARRATIVE: Randall Munroe describes the effect of everyone on Earth jumping at the same time as they stand close together. Imagine that you are one of these jumping individuals. Write a scene describing the incident from your point of view. What do you see? How do you **maneuver** yourself and others through the chaos? Draw inspiration for your narrative using evidence from the various informational text structures in Munroe's essay as you write your narrative.

Copyright © BookheadEd Learning, LLC

▦ Writer's Notebook

Connect to Essential Question: Give students time to reflect on how "Everybody Jump" connects to the unit's essential question "How do you know what to do when there are no instructions?" by freewriting in their Writer's Notebooks.

ELL **Beginning & Intermediate**

Read aloud the unit's essential question: "How do you know what to do when there are no instructions?" Encourage students to draw their connections or allow students to write in their native language. Circulate around the room, prompting students for their thoughts as they respond orally or through pantomime.

Advanced & Advanced High

Allow students to share their connections orally in pairs or small groups before freewriting.

Collaborative Conversation

Break students into collaborative conversation groups to discuss the Close Read prompt. Remind them to reference their Skills Focus annotations in their discussion.

Randall Munroe describes the effect of everyone on Earth jumping at the same time as they stand close together. Imagine that you are one of these jumping individuals. Write a scene describing the incident from your point of view. What do you see? How do you **maneuver** yourself and others through the chaos?

Use the scaffolds below to differentiate instruction for your **ELL** English Language Learners and **A** Approaching grade-level learners.

ELL **BEGINNING, INTERMEDIATE** Use the discussion guide and speaking frames to facilitate the discussion with support from the teacher.

ADVANCED, ADVANCED HIGH Use the discussion guide and speaking frames to facilitate the discussion in mixed-level groups.

A **APPROACHING** Use the discussion guide to facilitate the discussion in mixed-level groups.

APPROACHING
ADVANCED, ADVANCED HIGH
BEGINNING, INTERMEDIATE

Discussion Guide	Speaking Frames
1. What do you see around you after the jump?	• One thing I see is ____. • This is a problem because ____.
2. What can you do to maneuver through the chaos?	• One thing I can do is ____. • This might help because ____.

Review Prompt and Rubric

Before students begin writing, review the writing prompt and rubric with the class.

NARRATIVE: Randall Munroe describes the effect of everyone on Earth jumping at the same time as they stand close together. Imagine that you are one of these jumping individuals. Write a scene describing the incident from your point of view. What do you see? How do you **maneuver** yourself and others through the chaos? Draw inspiration for your narrative using evidence from the various informational text structures in Munroe's essay as you write your narrative.

 PROMPT GUIDE

 • What does it mean to **maneuver?**
  • Based on the text, what do you see around you after the jump?

  • What can you do to maneuver yourself and others through the chaos?

Score	Informational Text Structure	Language and Conventions
4	The writer is able to skillfully imagine and describe the scene from his or her point of view by using descriptive details from various structures within the text.	The writer demonstrates a consistent command of grammar, punctuation, and usage conventions. Although minor errors may be evident, they do not detract from the fluency or the clarity of the essay.
3	The writer is able to clearly imagine and describe the scene from his or her point of view using details from various structures, though there may be minor lapses in focus.	The writer demonstrates an adequate command of grammar, punctuation, and usage conventions. Although some errors may be evident, they create few (if any) disruptions in the fluency of the writing or the clarity of the essay.
2	The writer is able to imagine and describe the scene from his or her point of view using some details from structures within the text, but they do not successfully contribute to the narrative.	The writer demonstrates a partial command of grammar, punctuation, and usage conventions. Some distracting errors may be evident, at times creating minor disruptions in the fluency or clarity of the writing.
1	Because the narrative is presented in a random or illogical way, the writer is not able to imagine and describe the scene from his or her point of view and fails to use details from structures within the text that contribute to the narrative.	The writer demonstrates little or no command of grammar, punctuation, and usage conventions. Serious and persistent errors create disruptions in the fluency of the writing and sometimes interfere with meaning.
0	The writer does not provide a relevant response to the prompt or does not provide a response at all.	Serious and persistent errors overwhelm the writing and interfere with the meaning of the response as a whole, making the writer's meaning impossible to understand.

Write

Ask students to complete the writing assignment using textual evidence to support their answers.

Use the scaffolds below to differentiate instruction for your **ELL** English Language Learners and **A** Approaching grade-level learners.

ELL **BEGINNING** With the help of the <u>word bank</u>, write a response using <u>paragraph frame 1</u>.

INTERMEDIATE With the help of the <u>word bank</u>, write a response using <u>paragraph frames 1 and 2</u>.

ADVANCED, ADVANCED HIGH Write a response of differentiated length using the <u>sentence starters</u>.

A **APPROACHING** Write a response of differentiated length using the <u>sentence starters</u>.

BEGINNING / INTERMEDIATE		ADVANCED, ADVANCED HIGH / APPROACHING
Word Bank	**Paragraph Frame 1**	**Paragraph Frame 2**	**Sentence Starters**

Word Bank	Paragraph Frame 1	Paragraph Frame 2	Sentence Starters
fuel cell phones maneuver signal airport	After the jump, I see everybody trying to use their ____. No one can get a ____. Luckily, I know the ____ isn't far. I yell to the crowd to ____ toward T.F Green. Once there, I organize a hunt for ____ to fill the planes.	Unfortunately, the fuel runs out before I can ____. So I tell the crowd to maneuver to ____. I lead the crowd to ____. However, my plan is far from perfect because we can't ____. In frustration, I ____.	• After the jump, I see everybody . . . • Luckily, I know . . . • Once there, I organize . . . • Unfortunately, I can't . . . • So I tell the crowd to . . . • Next I decide to . . . • Eventually, we . . .

Peer Review

Students should submit substantive feedback to two peers using the review instructions below.

- How well does this response answer the prompt?
- How well does the writer support his or her ideas with details from the text?
- Which sentence in the writer's response made you picture the scene vividly?
- What did the writer do well in this response? What does the writer need to work on?

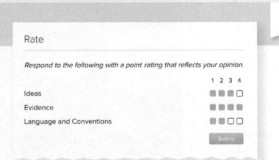

Rate

Respond to the following with a point rating that reflects your opinion.

	1 2 3 4
Ideas	▪▪▪□
Evidence	▪▪▪▪
Language and Conventions	▪▪□□

Submit

ELL **SENTENCE FRAMES**

A
- You were able to (completely / partly / almost) ____ answer the prompt because ____ .
- You could answer the prompt more completely by ____
- You supported the idea of ____ with the detail of ____ .

- One idea that needs more support is ____
- I thought differently about the text after reading ____ .
- My favorite part of your response is ____ .

Hoot

FICTION
Carl Hiaasen
2002

Introduction

studysync tv

After a move from Montana to Florida, Roy is the new kid in town, with no friends and no allies—not yet, anyway. One day, with his face smashed against the school bus window courtesy of the school bully, Roy sees something that attracts his curiosity. This coming-of-age novel, written by Carl Hiaasen (b. 1953), was awarded a Newbery Honor in 2003.

On the bus to school on a Monday morning, Roy is ambushed by the school bully, Dana Matherson, who pushes Roy's face against the window. Through the window, Roy sees a boy, whom he thinks is running to catch the school bus. He is wearing a basketball jersey and shorts, but he isn't wearing shoes or carrying a backpack. Roy imagines how Dana will pick on this kid. Instead of boarding the bus, the boy keeps running, cutting through people's front yards and jumping over a German Shepherd that leaps out at him. At this point, Dana, who is still pushing Roy against the window, begins to taunt him. Roy knows that getting angry is pointless, as Dana is much bigger than Roy. When Roy says that he has had enough, Dana releases him. Roy opens the window to look for the strange boy, but he does not see him anywhere. He wonders if anyone else on the bus noticed him.

ELL Proficiency-leveled summaries and summaries in multiple languages are available digitally.

◀)) Audio and audio text highlighting are available with this text.

CONNECT TO ESSENTIAL QUESTION

How do we know what to do when there are no instructions?

Roy becomes the new kid in town when his family moves to Florida from Montana. Before he has a chance to make friends, Roy has a run-in with the school bully, Dana Matherson. How can the new kid cope with a bully?

Access Complex Text

LEXILE: 990L   WORD COUNT: 672

The following areas may be challenging for students, particularly **ELL** English Language Learners and **A** Approaching grade-level learners.

Genre	Sentence Structure	Prior Knowledge
• Although it is an example of realistic fiction, the story contains some elements readers may perceive as fantasy. Students may need to attend to these elements to comprehend the text. • Discuss with students why Roy questions whether he really sees the mysterious boy.	• The author's use of dashes and ellipses to denote pauses and continuing action may need explanation. • Remind readers to pause for two beats when they reach such punctuation.	• Students may not be familiar with the state of Montana in the northwestern part of the U.S.. Cowboys play an important role in the state, where ranching and farming are key to the economy.

 SCAFFOLDS   **ENGLISH LANGUAGE LEARNERS**   **A** **APPROACHING GRADE LEVEL**   **B** **BEYOND GRADE LEVEL**

These icons identify differentiation strategies and scaffolded support for a variety of students. See the digital lesson plan for additional differentiation strategies and scaffolds.

Instructional Path

The print teacher's edition includes essential point-of-use instruction and planning tools. Complete lesson plans and program documents appear in your digital teacher account.

First Read: Hoot

Objectives: After an initial reading and discussion of the excerpt, students will be able to identify and describe character traits and setting details as well as articulate the conflict that is central to the story's plot.

Skill: Theme

Objectives: After rereading and discussing a model of close reading, students will be able to determine a theme of a text and explain how it is conveyed through particular details.

Close Read: Hoot

Objectives: After engaging in a close reading and discussion of the text, students will be able to determine a theme of the story, explain how it is conveyed through the character's responses and other textual details, and give an opinion about the author's message in a short, written response.

Progress Monitoring

Opportunities to Learn	Opportunities to Demonstrate Learning	Opportunities to Reteach

Theme

⚙ Skill: Theme	⚙ Skill: Theme • Your Turn ▣ Close Read • Skills Focus • Write	⚙ Unit 4 Skill: Theme — All Summer in a Day ⚙ Spotlight Skill: Theme

First Read

Carl Hiaasen

Hoot

Introduce the Text

As a class, watch the video preview and have students read the introduction in pairs to make connections to the video preview.

To activate prior knowledge and experiences, ask students:

- How do the images, words, and music in this video make you feel?

- How do the images, words, and music in the video connect to the information in the introduction?

ELL SPEAKING FRAMES

- The ____ in the video makes me think ____.
- The video shows ____. This makes me wonder ____.
- I think the text will ____. I think this because ____.
- I predict that there will be ____. I believe this because ____.

Entry Point

As students prepare to read *Hoot,* share the following information with them to provide context.

✓ Carl Hiaasen lives in Florida where he was born and raised. He graduated from the University of Florida and then worked as a reporter for the *Miami Herald*. He has been writing a regular column for the *Herald* since 1983, which according to his own website "at one time or another has pissed off just about everybody in South Florida, including his own bosses."

✓ Hiaasen began writing novels in the early 1980s in collaboration with his good friend and fellow journalist, William D. Montalbano. Since then he has been the solo author on most of his books, many of which are set in Florida. He has written novels for both adults and young people, as well as nonfiction.

✓ *Hoot* was turned into a movie in 2006. Jimmy Buffett plays a teacher.

"... Roy lowered the window and stuck out his head. The strange boy was gone."

1 Excerpted from Chapter 1

2 Roy would not have noticed the strange boy if it weren't for Dana Matherson, because Roy ordinarily didn't look out the window of the school bus. He preferred to read comics and mystery books on the morning ride to Trace Middle.

3 But on this day, a Monday (Roy would never forget), Dana Matherson grabbed Roy's head from behind and pressed his thumbs into Roy's temple, as if he were squeezing a soccer ball. The older kids were supposed to stay in the back of the bus, but Dana had snuck up behind Roy's seat and **ambushed** him. When Roy tried to wriggle free, Dana mushed his face against the window.

4 It was then, squinting through the smudged glass, that Roy spotted the strange boy running along the sidewalk. It appeared as if he was hurrying to catch the school bus, which had stopped at a corner to pick up more kids.

5 The boy was straw-blond and wiry, and his skin was nutbrown from the sun. The **expression** on his face was **intent** and serious. He wore a faded Miami Heat basketball jersey and dirty khaki shorts, and here was the odd part: no shoes. The soles of his bare feet looked as black as barbecue coals.

6 Trace Middle School didn't have the world's strictest dress code, but Roy was pretty sure that some sort of footwear was **required**. The boy might have been carrying sneakers in his backpack, if only he'd been wearing a backpack. No shoes, no backpack, no books—strange, indeed, on a school day.

7 Roy was sure that the barefoot boy would catch all kinds of grief from Dana and the other big kids once he boarded the bus, but that didn't happen. . . .

8 Because the boy kept running—past the corner, past the line of students waiting to get on the bus; past the bus itself. Roy wanted to shout, "Hey, look at that guy!" but his mouth wasn't working so well. Dana Matherson still had him from behind, pushing his face against the window.

Copyright © BookheadEd Learning, LLC

Reading & Writing Companion **53**

Analyze Vocabulary Using Context Clues

In paragraph 2, focus on the sentence that uses the word *ambushed*. Point out these context clues:

1. First I notice that the word *ambushed* describes what Dana does to Roy.

2. When I read earlier in the paragraph, I notice that Dana sneaks up behind Roy and grabs his head.

3. I think *ambushed* must mean "attacked suddenly."

TEXT TALK

What does Roy usually do on the school bus?

See paragraph 1: Roy usually reads comics and mystery books on the bus.

In what two ways is Roy's bus ride different today?

See paragraphs 1 and 2: Today, Roy is bullied by Dana Matherson, and Roy sees a mysterious boy running outside the bus.

In what two ways is the mysterious boy particularly strange?

See paragraphs 4, 5, and 7: The boy is shoeless and without school supplies, and he doesn't board the bus.

SELECTION VOCABULARY

ambush / emboscar *verb* to make a sudden, surprise attack against another person or group

expression / la expresión *noun* a particular look, action, or vocal intonation indicating something such as a thought or feeling **COGNATE**

 ELL
• What does the word *expression* have to do with the look on the boy's face?
• Is the boy is serious as he runs, how does this affect his *expression*?

intent / decidido / a *adjective* showing determination or focused attention

 ELL
• What does the word *serious* suggest about the meaning of the word *intent*?

required / necesario / a *adjective* essential, or necessary; something that must be had or done

 ELL
• What items are commonly mentioned in a dress code?

Theme

How does the reader use a character's response to infer theme?

The reader notices how Roy first reacts to Dana's bullying. Roy doesn't feel any pain because he is paying attention to something going on outside the bus.

Prepare for Advanced Courses

Use the activity below to differentiate instruction for your **B** Beyond grade-level learners.

Reread paragraph 2.

Ask students: How does the author's choice of verbs in this paragraph help the reader understand the action and the personalities of the characters in this scene?

Sample answer; answers will vary: The author uses verbs like "squeezing," "ambushed," and "mushed" to describe Dana's actions, which shows how physically violent he is. The author uses the verb "wriggle" to describe Roy's reaction to Dana's attack, which shows how weak Roy is.

 TEXT TALK

Why does Dana refer to Roy as "cowgirl" and "Tex"?

See paragraphs 12, 13, and 14: Roy has recently relocated from Montana to Florida, and Dana judges Roy to be a country boy.

Why does Roy wonder whether he's really seen the mysterious boy?

See paragraphs 10, 16, and 18: The boy does some incredible things such as jumping over a German shepherd and then disappearing.

 Ask each Beyond grade-level student to write one additional discussion question. Then, have one or two students facilitate a discussion, using their questions to guide the conversation.

Hoot

 NOTES

 Skill: Theme

One detail I notice is that Roy is getting bullied. When I read how Roy reacts to Dana's bullying, I can infer a theme. Roy's curiosity about the running boy makes him immune to his pain. Maybe one way to escape bullying is to check out mentally.

9   As the bus pulled away from the intersection, Roy hoped to catch another glimpse of the boy farther up the street. However, he had turned off the sidewalk and was now cutting across a private yard—running very fast, much faster than Roy could run and maybe even faster than Richard, Roy's best friend back in Montana. Richard was so fast that he got to work out with the high school track squad when he was only in seventh grade.

10   Dana Matherson was digging his fingernails into Roy's scalp, trying to make him squeal, but Roy barely felt a thing. He was gripped with curiosity as the running boy dashed through one neat green yard after another, getting smaller in Roy's vision as he put a wider distance between himself and the school bus.

11   Roy saw a big pointy-eared dog, probably a German shepherd, **bound** off somebody's porch and go for the boy. Incredibly, the boy didn't change his course. He vaulted over the dog, crashed through a cherry hedge, and then disappeared from view.

12   Roy gasped.

13   "Whassamatter, cowgirl? Had enough?"

14   This was Dana, hissing in Roy's right ear. Being the new kid on the bus, Roy didn't expect any help from the others. The "cowgirl" remark was so lame, it wasn't worth getting mad about. Dana was a well-known idiot, on top of which he outweighed Roy by at least fifty pounds. Fighting back would have been a complete waste of energy.

15   "Had enough yet? We can't hear you, Tex." Dana's breath smelled like stale cigarettes. Smoking and beating up smaller kids were his two main hobbies.

16   "Yeah, okay," Roy said impatiently. "I've had enough."

17   As soon as he was freed, Roy lowered the window and stuck out his head. The strange boy was gone.

18   Who was he? What was he running from?

19   Roy wondered if any of the other kids on the bus had seen what he'd seen. For a moment he wondered if he'd really seen it himself.

Excerpted from *Hoot* by Carl Hiaasen, published by Alfred A. Knopf.

 SELECTION VOCABULARY

bound / saltar *verb* to move by jumping or leaping

- Does the dog more likely jump or walk off the porch to chase the boy?
- In chasing the boy, does the dog more likely move quickly or slowly?

Reading Comprehension OPTIONAL

Have students complete the digital reading comprehension questions ✓ when they finish reading.

ANSWER KEY

QUESTION 1: A	**QUESTION 5:** B	**QUESTION 9:**
QUESTION 2: D	**QUESTION 6:** D	*See first chart*
QUESTION 3: B	**QUESTION 7:** B	**QUESTION 10:**
QUESTION 4: A	**QUESTION 8:** A	*See second chart*

Synonym	Word
lean	wiry
purpose	intent
tan	khaki
leap	bound
brow	temples

First	Second	Third	Fourth
The running boy is sprinting toward the corner where kids are waiting to get on the bus.	The running boy runs past the bus.	The running boy crosses through someone's yard.	The running boy leaps over a dog.

Connect and Extend OPTIONAL

CONNECT TO EXTENDED WRITING PROJECT

Students can use *Hoot* as a mentor text for their Extended Writing Project. They may adopt the author's use of sensory language and descriptive words within the format of their informational essay.

BEYOND THE BOOK

Writing: An Onlooker Story

Tell students:

- At the end of the excerpt from *Hoot*, the narrator says, "Roy wondered if any of the other kids on the bus had seen what he'd seen. For a moment he wondered if he'd really seen it himself."

- Imagine you are one of the other kids on the bus. Describe the events that took place from that kid's perspective.

- Write what you saw in the form of a journal entry, using first-person point of view.

Have students consider the following questions as they write their entries:

- Did you see Dana bully Roy, or were you too distracted by the mysterious boy?

- Did you see something Roy didn't?

- Have you seen Dana bully other people?

- Did something else take place on the bus that day that only you noticed?

Think Questions

Circulate as students answer Think Questions independently. Scaffolds for these questions are shown on the opposite page.

QUESTION 1: Textual Evidence

Roy is looking out the bus window because the bully Dana Matherson is smashing Roy's face against the glass: "Dana mushed [Roy's] face against the window."

QUESTION 2: Textual Evidence

Based on text clues such as the fact that the boy is "wiry," his clothes are "faded" and "dirty," and his feet are shoeless and "black," the reader might infer that the mysterious boy is poor. The boy may even be homeless, as "his skin was nutbrown from the sun."

QUESTION 3: Textual Evidence

The relationship is antagonistic. Dana is older, and bullies younger boys. On the bus, Dana "[grabs] Roy's head from behind and [presses] his thumbs into Roy's temple . . . [mushing] his face against the window." This develops the action because that's how Roy catches his first sight of the mysterious boy.

QUESTION 4: Context Clues

I think *required* must mean "necessary." The word is used to describe footwear according to the school's dress code, and it makes sense for a school to have a rule that students need to wear some sort of footwear.

QUESTION 5: Context Clues

I think *bound* must mean "to move by jumping or leaping." The context clues in the sentence support this meaning, because the German shepherd leaves the porch quickly, likely by jumping or leaping, and chases the boy.

First Read

Read *Hoot*. After you read, complete the Think Questions below.

☁ THINK QUESTIONS

1. Why is Roy looking out the window? Cite textual evidence from the selection to support your answer.

2. Based on paragraph 4, what inferences can you make about the mysterious boy? What clues does the text give?

3. Describe the relationship between Dana and Roy, using specific examples from the text.

4. Find the word **required** in paragraph 5 of *Hoot*. Use context clues in the surrounding sentences, as well as the sentence in which the word appears, to determine the word's meaning.

5. Use context clues to determine the meaning of **bound** as it is used in paragraph 10 of *Hoot*. Write your definition here and identify clues that helped you figure out its meaning. Then check the meaning in the dictionary.

Reading & Writing Companion **55**

Think Questions

Use the scaffolds below to differentiate instruction for your **ELL** English Language Learners and **A** Approaching grade-level learners.

ELL **BEGINNING** Write a response using the <u>word bank</u> and <u>sentence frames.</u>

INTERMEDIATE Write a response using the <u>sentence frames.</u>

ADVANCED, ADVANCED HIGH Write a response using the <u>Text-Dependent Question Guide.</u>

A **APPROACHING** Write a response using the <u>Text-Dependent Question Guide.</u>

| | INTERMEDIATE | APPROACHING |
BEGINNING		ADVANCED, ADVANCED HIGH
Word Bank	**Sentence Frames**	**Text-Dependent Question Guide**
bully dress code chases dirty enemies face faded jumping necessary mushing older poor sneaks up younger	Roy looks out the bus window because the ___ Dana Matherson is ___ [Roy's] ___ against the window."	1. • Who attacks Roy? • How does this person attack Roy? • In what ways does this person abuse Roy?
	Because the boy is "wiry" and dressed in "___" and "___" clothes, the reader might infer that the mysterious boy is ___.	2. • Is the mysterious boy thin or fat? • Is the mysterious boy clean or dirty? • Is the mysterious boy well dressed or poorly dressed?
	Dana and Roy are ___. Dana is an ___ boy who bullies ___ boys such as Roy. On the bus, Dana ___ behind Roy and "[grabs] Roy's head."	3. • Are Dana and Roy friends or enemies? • How does Dana treat Roy? • Is Dana kind or abusive toward Roy?
	I think *required* means " ___." The word is used to describe wearing footwear according to the school's ___.	4. • Read: "Trace Middle School didn't have the world's strictest dress code, but Roy was pretty sure that some kind of footwear was **required.**" • Why does Roy think about the school's dress code when he sees the barefoot boy? • What does Roy think might have been in the boy's backpack if he had one?
	I think *bound* means "to move by ___ or leaping." The context clues in the sentence support this meaning, because the German shepherd leaves the porch quickly and ___ the boy.	5. • Read: "Roy saw a big pointy-eared dog, probably a German shepherd, **bound** off somebody's porch and go for the boy." • How does the dog move off the porch? • How do dogs usually act when they're chasing something?

Skill: Theme

Introduce the Skill

Watch the Concept Definition video  and read the following definitions with your students.

The **topic** of a literary work is the subject of the work. It is usually expressed as a noun. The **theme** is the central idea or message of a work of literature. It is often expressed as a general statement about life. For example, the topic of a literary work might be love. The theme would be what the writer suggests about love: that it is wonderful or painful or maybe both at once. A literary work may have more than one theme.

Sometimes a writer states a theme directly. More often, though, theme is revealed gradually. In short stories, novels, and dramas, theme is revealed through elements such as character, setting, and plot, what the characters do and say, and how these elements affect the events that take place. When a theme is not stated directly, a reader will have to infer the theme. To **infer** means to determine something by using reasoning and textual evidence.

 TURN AND TALK

1. What is one of your favorite books, TV shows, or movies?
2. How do the main characters grow or change as a result of the plot events or particular details in the story? What do the main characters learn?
3. Have you ever read a story or novel that had more than one theme? If so what were the multiple themes?

ELL SPEAKING FRAMES

- One of my favorite books (TV shows/movies) is ____. I like this book (TV show/movie) because ____.
- As a result of the plot events and particular details, the character ____.
- One theme that is revealed is ____.

Hoot

 Skill: Theme

Use the Checklist to analyze Theme in *Hoot*. Refer to the sample student annotations about Theme in the text.

••• CHECKLIST FOR THEME

In order to identify a theme or central idea in a text, note the following:

✓ the topic of the text

✓ whether or not the theme is stated directly in the text

✓ details in the text that may reveal the theme

- the title and chapter headings
- details about the setting
- a narrator's or speaker's tone
- characters' thoughts, actions, and dialogue
- the central conflict in the story's plot
- the resolution of the conflict

✓ analyze how characters and the problems they face are affected by the setting, and what impact this may have on how the theme is developed

To determine a theme or central idea of a text and how it is conveyed through particular details, consider the following questions:

✓ What is a theme or central idea of the text?

✓ What details helped to reveal that theme or central idea?

✓ When did you become aware of that theme? For instance, did the story's conclusion reveal the theme?

V SKILL VOCABULARY

topic / el tema *noun* the subject of a literary work, usually expressed as a single word or phrase in the form of a noun

theme / el tema *noun* the central idea or message of a work of literature, often expressed as a general statement about life

infer / inferir *verb* to determine something by using reasoning and evidence from the text COGNATE

Skill:
Theme

Reread paragraphs 14–18 from *Hoot*. Then, using the Checklist on the previous page, answer the multiple-choice questions below.

⟳ YOUR TURN

1. This question has two parts. First, answer Part A. Then, answer Part B.

   Part A: In paragraph 15, how does Roy end the conflict with Dana?

   ○ A. Roy insults Dana's smoking habit, escalating the situation.
   ○ B. Roy gives in, allowing Dana to maintain the upper hand.
   ○ C. Roy begs the smaller kids on the bus for help, causing Dana to laugh.
   ○ D. Roy tells Dana not to call him "Tex," causing Dana to grab Roy's head.

   Part B: What theme can be inferred from the way Roy ends the conflict with Dana in paragraph 15?

   ○ A. During a conflict, it's best to stand up for yourself and fight back.
   ○ B. During a conflict, it's best to call someone names and invade his personal space.
   ○ C. During a conflict, it's best to stay calm and rational.
   ○ D. During a conflict, it's best to taunt and make physical attacks.

2. Throughout the story, Roy's reaction to Dana Matherson supports a theme that illustrates the value of –

   ○ A. bullying
   ○ B. curiosity
   ○ C. cleverness
   ○ D. running

Reading & Writing Companion **57**

Your Turn

Ask students to complete the Your Turn Activity.

QUESTION 1

PART A

A. Incorrect. Roy does not insult Dana.

B. Correct. Roy answers that he's had enough, and Dana releases Roy.

C. Incorrect. Roy does not ask for help.

D. Incorrect. Roy does not respond to the nickname "Tex."

PART B

A. Incorrect. Roy ends the conflict by staying calm, not by standing up for himself.

B. Incorrect. These are Dana's strategies, and they escalate the conflict.

C. Correct. Roy ends the conflict by staying calm and telling Dana what he wants to hear.

D. Incorrect. These are Dana's strategies, and they escalate the conflict.

QUESTION 2

A. Incorrect. Nothing in the story suggests that bullying has value.

B. Incorrect. While Roy is curious about the running boy, this is not the best description of his strategy for dealing with Dana.

C. Correct. Roy repeatedly uses aspects of his mind to deal with Dana.

D. Incorrect. The mysterious boy is running, not Roy.

Close Read

Skills Focus

QUESTION 1: Theme

See paragraphs 13–15: Roy thinks about bullying. He knows he shouldn't be upset when he's called "a cowgirl." When Roy gives up he isn't giving in, he wants a nonviolent end. I can infer that one theme of the story is how best to handle bullies.

QUESTION 2: Theme

See paragraphs 1–3: During the bullying, the author describes Roy's first sighting of the boy. These events are related because Roy wouldn't have noticed the boy if Dana hadn't smashed Roy's face into the window. Roy's curiosity distracts him. Roy focuses on the mysterious boy. This is a second theme: You can respond constructively, even in negative circumstances.

QUESTION 3: Character

See paragraph 15: Roy gives in and tells Dana what he wants to hear in order to avoid more trouble. This response shows that Roy is level-headed and able to keep his cool in a difficult situation.

QUESTION 4: Connect to Essential Question

See paragraph 13: Roy is used to newness—he doesn't expect help; he also doesn't seem upset. He ignores Dana's words and doesn't fight back. I think this is part of the author's message—it is better to think than just react.

Hoot

Close Read

Reread *Hoot*. As you reread, complete the Skills Focus questions below. Then use your answers and annotations from the questions to help you complete the Write activity.

◎ SKILLS FOCUS

1. Dealing with Dana's bullying is one of the challenges Roy faces in the story. Identify evidence of how Roy responds to this challenge. Explain what the response helps you infer about a theme in the story.

2. Dana's bullying is not the only plot event in the chapter. Identify evidence about the other event the author **describes** and about Roy's reaction to it. Explain how the two plot events are related and how this helps you infer a second theme.

3. The author uses Roy's thoughts and actions to develop the plot. Identify examples of Roy's responses that help you understand his character. Explain how these responses help develop the plot.

4. Roy is new to Trace Middle School, so he is on his own in figuring out how to handle Dana's bullying. Identify textual evidence that highlights Roy's methods. Explain what the evidence tells you about Roy's character and the author's message.

✎ WRITE

LITERARY ANALYSIS: In *Hoot*, Roy responds to bullying in a surprising way. How does the author use details and Roy's response to Dana's bullying to communicate a theme? Do you agree or disagree with the author's message in this story? Use evidence from the text as well as from your own experiences to support your response.

Writer's Notebook

Connect to Essential Question: Give students time to reflect on how Hoot connects to the unit's essential question "How do we know what to do when there are no instructions?" by freewriting in their Writer's Notebooks.

ELL Beginning & Intermediate

Read aloud the unit's essential question: "How do we know what to do when there are no instructions?" Encourage students to draw their connections or allow students to write in their native language. Circulate around the room, prompting students for their thoughts as they respond orally or through pantomime.

Advanced & Advanced High

Allow students to share their connections orally in pairs or small groups before freewriting.

StudySyncTV

Project the StudySyncTV episode  and pause at the following times to prompt discussion:

1:38 How do the students use textual evidence to determine how Roy deals with Dana's bullying?

2:32 How do the students use their own experiences to analyze how Roy deals with bullies?

4:48 How do the students sum up Roy's characteristics in support of Lorenzo's observation that Roy is a role model on how to survive a bully?

Collaborative Conversation

SCAFFOLDS

Break students into collaborative conversation groups to discuss the Close Read prompt. Ask students to use the StudySyncTV episode as a model for their discussion. Remind them to reference their Skills Focus annotations in their discussion.

In *Hoot*, Roy responds to bullying in a surprising way. How does the author use details and Roy's response to Dana's bullying to communicate a theme? Do you agree or disagree with the author's message in this story? Use evidence from the text as well as your own experiences to support your response.

Use the scaffolds below to differentiate instruction for your **ELL** English Language Learners and **A** Approaching grade-level learners.

ELL **BEGINNING, INTERMEDIATE** Use the <u>discussion guide</u> and <u>speaking frames</u> to facilitate the discussion with support from the teacher.

ADVANCED, ADVANCED HIGH Use the <u>discussion guide</u> and <u>speaking frames</u> to facilitate the discussion in mixed-level groups.

A **APPROACHING** Use the <u>discussion guide</u> to facilitate the discussion in mixed-level groups.

APPROACHING
ADVANCED, ADVANCED HIGH
BEGINNING, INTERMEDIATE

Discussion Guide	Speaking Frames
1. How does Roy respond to Dana's bullying?	• One way Roy responds to Dana's bullying is by ____.
2. What does Roy's response tell you about the theme?	• Roy's response tells me ____ about the theme. • I think this because ____.
3. What other details help you identify this theme?	• One detail in the text that helps me identify this theme is ____. • When the author writes ____, I think it means ____.
4. Do you agree with the author's message? Why or why not?	• I (agree/disagree) with the author's message that ____. • I think this because ____.

Review Prompt and Rubric

Before students begin writing, review the writing prompt and rubric with the class.

LITERARY ANALYSIS: In *Hoot*, Roy responds to bullying in a surprising way. How does the author use details and Roy's response to Dana's bullying to communicate a theme? Do you agree or disagree with the author's message in this story? Use evidence from the text as well as your own experiences to support your response.

ELL PROMPT GUIDE

A
- How does Roy respond to Dana's bullying?
- What does Roy's response tell you about the theme?
- What other details help you identify this theme?

- What is the author's message?
- Do you agree with the author's message? Why or why not?

Score	Theme	Language and Conventions
4	The writer clearly analyzes and explains how the author uses details and Roy's response to Dana's bullying to communicate a theme. The writer provides exemplary analysis, using relevant evidence from the text.	The writer demonstrates a consistent command of grammar, punctuation, and usage conventions. Although minor errors may be evident, they do not detract from the fluency or the clarity of the essay.
3	The writer analyzes and explains how the author uses details and Roy's response to Dana's bullying to communicate a theme. The writer provides sufficient analysis, using relevant evidence from the text most of the time.	The writer demonstrates an adequate command of grammar, punctuation, and usage conventions. Although some errors may be evident, they create few (if any) disruptions in the fluency of the writing or the clarity of the essay.
2	The writer begins to analyze or explain how the author uses details and Roy's response to Dana's bullying to communicate a theme, but the analysis is incomplete. The writer uses relevant evidence from the text only some of the time.	The writer demonstrates a partial command of grammar, punctuation, and usage conventions. Some distracting errors may be evident, at times creating minor disruptions in the fluency or clarity of the writing.
1	The writer attempts to analyze or explain how the author uses details and Roy's response to Dana's bullying to communicate a theme, but the analysis is not successful. The writer uses little or no relevant evidence from the text.	The writer demonstrates little or no command of grammar, punctuation, and usage conventions. Serious and persistent errors create disruptions in the fluency of the writing and sometimes interfere with meaning.
0	The writer does not provide a relevant response to the prompt or does not provide a response at all.	Serious and persistent errors overwhelm the writing and interfere with the meaning of the response as a whole, making the writer's meaning impossible to understand.

Write

Ask students to complete the writing assignment using textual evidence to support their answers.

Use the scaffolds below to differentiate instruction for your **ELL** English Language Learners and **A** Approaching grade-level learners.

ELL **BEGINNING** With the help of the <u>word bank</u>, write a response using <u>paragraph frame 1</u>.

INTERMEDIATE With the help of the <u>word bank</u>, write a response using <u>paragraph frames 1 and 2</u>.

ADVANCED, ADVANCED HIGH Write a response of differentiated length using the <u>sentence starters</u>.

A **APPROACHING** Write a response of differentiated length using the <u>sentence starters</u>.

| BEGINNING | | ADVANCED, ADVANCED HIGH |
| INTERMEDIATE | | APPROACHING |

Word Bank	Paragraph Frame 1	Paragraph Frame 2	Sentence Starters
head curiosity fighting lame remarks humor	Roy responds to Dana's bullying by focusing his ____ on the running boy. Roy also uses ____ to deal with the bullying. In addition, he ignores Dana's ____. By analyzing these details from the story, I think the author's message is that ____ is not the best way to handle a bully. I agree because I have used my ____ to stay calm rather than fight a bully.	I know from experience that you can distract yourself by ____. Using humor can keep you from ____. Ignoring lame remarks can also help you ____. The author's message is ____. Rather than fighting, you should ____.	• One way Roy responds to Dana's bullying is by . . . • Another way Roy responds to Dana's bullying is by . . . • I have found that one way to deal with a bully is . . . • I have also dealt with bullies by . . . • I think the author's message is . . . • I (agree/disagree) with this message because . . .

Peer Review

Students should submit substantive feedback to two peers using the review instructions below.

- How well does this response answer the prompt?
- How well does the writer support his or her ideas with details and examples from the text and from personal experiences?
- Which sentence in the writer's response made you think differently about the author's message or the writer's argument?
- What did the writer do well in this response? What does the writer need to work on?

Rate

Respond to the following with a point rating that reflects your opinion.

	1 2 3 4
Ideas	▪▪▪☐
Evidence	▪▪▪▪
Language and Conventions	▪▪☐☐

Submit

ELL **A** **SENTENCE FRAMES**

- You were able to (completely / partly / almost) ____ answer the prompt because ____.
- You could answer the prompt more completely by ____.
- You supported the idea of ____ with the detail of ____.

- One idea that needs more support is ____.
- I thought differently about the texts after reading ____.
- My favorite part of your response is ____.

Donna O'Meara: The Volcano Lady

INFORMATIONAL TEXT
McGraw Hill Education
2017

Introduction

Donna O'Meara is an explorer and adventurer like few others. As a photographer of some of the world's biggest volcanoes, her job is often quite perilous. In the face of danger, however, O'Meara often risks her life to obtain some of the most amazing up-close footage of volcanoes the world has ever witnessed. This short biography profiles O'Meara's life, from her time growing up in New England to how she came to be known as the "volcano lady."

Donna O'Meara is a photographer and biologist, who studies active volcanoes alongside her husband Steve. As a child, she was fascinated by thunder and lightning and enjoyed science, but O'Meara went on to pursue photography and the arts in college. It was only at the age of thirty-two that she went back to school to study science and discovered her passion for volcanoes. As her husband's research assistant, she visited her first volcano; while dodging lava bombs, she fell in love with the work. According to O'Meara, the scariest moment of her life was when her and her husband were stranded overnight on Mount Stromboli in freezing cold temperatures, two hundred feet above a fiery pit. Nonetheless, she loves her job and continues documenting active volcanoes so that scientists can better predict when an eruption is imminent.

 Proficiency-leveled summaries and summaries in multiple languages are available digitally.

 Audio and audio text highlighting are available with this text.

 COMPARING WITHIN AND ACROSS GENRES

"Donna O'Meara: The Volcano Lady," the story of a woman who frequently puts herself in many precarious situations at the tops of volcanoes around the world, is paired with "Dare to be Creative!" and "Margaret Bourke-White: Fearless Photographer" so that students may compare and contrast motivated individuals within the informational genre.

Access Complex Text

LEXILE: 940L   **WORD COUNT:** 673

The following areas may be challenging for students, particularly **ELL** English Language Learners and **A** Approaching grade-level learners.

Genre	Purpose	Organization
• The text contains features of a biography by relating the sequential story of a person's life. • Through vivid descriptions of dangerous encounters with volcanoes, the text has the qualities of an adventure story.	• The primary purpose of the text is to inform, but it also includes a focus on how one woman's dream was realized. There are entertaining elements in the opening narrative as well.	• After beginning with an exciting narrative, the text backtracks in time to relate biographical information interspersed with scientific facts about volcanoes, which may be confusing for some students.

SCAFFOLDS   **ELL** ENGLISH LANGUAGE LEARNERS   **A** APPROACHING GRADE LEVEL   **B** BEYOND GRADE LEVEL

These icons identify differentiation strategies and scaffolded support for a variety of students. See the digital lesson plan for additional differentiation strategies and scaffolds.

Instructional Path

The print teacher's edition includes essential point-of-use instruction and planning tools. Complete lesson plans and program documents appear in your digital teacher account.

Independent Read: Donna O'Meara: The Volcano Lady

Objectives: After reading the text, students will write a short response that demonstrates their understanding of and connection to the text.

Independent Read

Donna O'Meara: The Volcano Lady

Introduce the Text

As a class, watch the video preview ▶ and have students read the introduction in pairs to make connections to the video preview.

- What key words or images from the video do you think will be important in the text you are about to read?

- How does the information in the video connect to what you already know?

- Why do you think it's important to learn about this person?

ELL SPEAKING FRAMES

- The ___ in the video makes me think ___.
- The video shows ___. This makes me wonder ___.
- I think the text will ___. I think this because ___.
- I predict that there will be ___. I believe this because ___.

Entry Point

As students prepare to read "Donna O'Meara: The Volcano Lady," share the following information with them to provide context.

✓ Volcanoes happen where thick magma and large amounts of gas build up and break through the Earth's crust. They usually exist between the tectonic plates, the large rock slabs that make up the Earth's surface. The Ring of Fire along the edges of the Pacific Ocean accounts for about 90% of the volcanoes on Earth.

✓ There are about 1,900 active volcanoes on Earth. A volcano is active if it has produced some lava and is likely to explode again. Scientists estimate that in the past 300 years more than 260,000 people have died from volcanic eruptions and their aftermath. Volcanoes are dangerous not only because of lava flows, but also mud slides from melting snow, ash and toxic gases, and hardening lava that can rain down on people.

"They were stuck on a narrow ledge just 200 feet above a fiery, smoking pit."

NOTES

1   After a blistering hot day, a cold storm suddenly whipped the top of Mt. Stromboli, a volcano on an island off the coast of Sicily. The temperature quickly dropped more than 60 degrees. Donna O'Meara and her husband, Steve, didn't dare try to climb down the steep slopes in the dark. They were stuck on a narrow ledge just 200 feet above a fiery, smoking pit.

2   They huddled together, shivering nonstop in the cold air. Thundering blasts from the volcano and falling rocks the size of basketballs kept them awake and fearful. When the sun came up, Donna felt cinder burns on her face. There were sharp pieces of rock tangled in her hair.

3   Frightening experiences on top of a volcano are not unusual for Donna O'Meara. For over 25 years, she has worked with Steve to photograph and study volcanoes all over the world. They hope their documentation will someday be a written and visual record of information that helps scientists to better **predict** volcanic **eruptions.**

4   O'Meara grew up in the New England countryside. There are no volcanoes in Connecticut, but in the spring and summer there were fierce thunder and lightning storms that thrilled Donna. In school, her favorite classes were earth science and biology. However, instead of turning her love for science into a career after graduation, she became an artist, photographer, and writer. As she worked on different magazines and books, she gradually began to realize that something was missing in her life.

5   When Donna went back to school at the age of 32 to study science, her passion for volcanoes began. She took geology classes to learn more about what rocks and soil tell us about the earth. She found out that volcanism is one of the most **dynamic** forces in nature. Volcanoes constantly shape and change the earth. Many islands, such as the islands that make up Hawaii, were formed by volcanic activity.

6   In 1986, Donna visited her first volcano as Steve's research assistant. After dodging lava bombs and feeling the heat from underground lava melting her shoes, Donna was hooked. The following year, she and Steve were married

60 ☐ Reading & Writing Companion

 ## Analyze Vocabulary Using Context Clues

As students read the text, ask them to make predictions about each bold vocabulary word based on the context clues in the sentence. Have students use the annotation tool to make their predictions.

 TURN AND TALK

Have students discuss their original vocabulary predictions with a neighbor. Come to a consensus as a class before confirming their definitions.

 TEXT TALK

What happened to Donna O'Meara on Mt. Stromboli?

See paragraphs 1 and 2: She endured a temperature drop of 60 degrees, was stranded all night, was frightened by thundering blasts and falling rocks, felt cinder burns on her face and caught pieces of rock in her hair.

What do Donna and her husband do for a living, and for what purpose?

See paragraph 3: They photograph and study volcanoes with the intention of helping scientists to better predict eruptions.

What did Donna learn about volcanism when she went back to school to study science?

See paragraph 5: She learned that volcanoes shape and change the earth, even forming islands.

V **SELECTION VOCABULARY**

predict / predecir *verb* to guess or estimate what might happen COGNATE

 ELL • What do scientists want to do in the future?
• How would the ability to predict volcanic eruptions be helpful to communities living close to volcanoes?

eruption / la erupción *noun* bursting out after building pressure for a long time COGNATE

ELL • What happens when volcanoes are no longer quiet?
• What does O'Meara take pictures of?

dynamic / dinámico/a *adjective* constantly changing, improving or progressing COGNATE

 ELL • What did O'Meara learn about nature when she went back to school?
• What does volcanism aim to do?

on lava that had oozed from Kilauea on Hawaii and hardened. Lava that hardens creates new landforms, and some volcanoes, such as Surtsey off the coast of Iceland, actually create new islands!

7   Today, Donna can't imagine what her life would be like without volcanoes. She loves them so much she lives on one. Her home is on top of Kilauea, where she was married. This is one of the most **active** volcanoes in the world.

Kilauea, in Hawaii

8   From their home, Donna and Steve run Volcano Watch International (VWI). The O'Mearas' organization is dedicated to understanding how Earth's active volcanoes work. VWI uses photos and video to educate people about the dangers of volcanoes. Their mission is to travel to active volcanoes and **document** the eruptions. The first volcano Donna studied was Kilauea, which is a shield volcano.

9   Mt. Stromboli is a stratovolcano. A stratovolcano has the common cone shape people usually picture when they think of a volcano. It is formed from explosive eruptions that build layers of ash, lava, and cinders at the top of the mountain.

10 Donna says the experience of being stranded on Mt. Stromboli for one freezing night was the scariest experience of her life. Since the sides of this volcano are steep, it was impossible for the O'Mearas to travel down the slopes until the sun rose in the morning. So they were trapped on a ledge in the freezing cold with scalding rocks flying around them.

11 Donna O'Meara escaped from her scary night of Mt. Stromboli safe and sound. Now she and Steve hope that the knowledge they gather photographing and studying volcanoes will help save the lives of people who live near them. The O'Mearas' volcano photographs, videos, and samples of volcanic rock are part of the permanent collection of the Smithsonian Institution located in Washington, D.C.

12 Donna believes they have the best jobs on Earth, even though their work may be the most dangerous as well.

Used with permission of McGraw-Hill Education

Reading & Writing Companion   **61**

TEXT TALK

What is a stratovolcano?

See paragraph 9: It is the familiar cone-shaped volcano, like Stromboli, formed from layers of ash, lava, and cinders.

Where is Donna and her husband's collection of photos and videos kept?

See paragraph 11: At the Smithsonian Institution in Washington, DC.

> **B** Ask each Beyond grade-level student to write one additional discussion question. Then, have one or two students facilitate a discussion, using their questions to guide the conversation.

V SELECTION VOCABULARY

active / activo/a *adjective* (of a volcano) historically or currently erupting, and so likely to erupt again   COGNATE

> **ELL**
> • What is the opposite of a quiet volcano?
> • Why is O'Meara's home in such an unusual place?

document / documentar *verb* to make a record of something in writing, video, or photos   COGNATE

> **ELL**
> • How do Donna and Steve O'Meara show other people what a volcano is doing?
> • What can people learn from viewing a volcano over time?

✏ WRITE

PERSONAL RESPONSE: Donna O'Meara and her husband Steve risk their lives to collect close-up photos of volcanoes from around the world. If you were a scientist or researcher, what kind of natural phenomenon would you want to explore? Why? Support your response with evidence from the text and from your personal experience. As you make connections between Donna O'Meara's dream and your own, include any information that may have changed your understanding or opinion of what it means to be a scientist or researcher.

  Reading & Writing Companion

Reading Comprehension

Have students complete the digital reading comprehension questions ✓ when they finish reading.

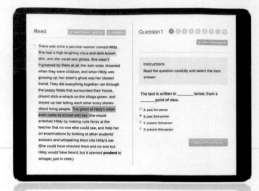

ANSWER KEY

QUESTION 1:	B	QUESTION 5:	D	QUESTION 9:
QUESTION 2:	C	QUESTION 6:	D	*See first chart.*
QUESTION 3:	C	QUESTION 7:	C	QUESTION 10:
QUESTION 4:	B	QUESTION 8:	A	*See second chart.*

Definition	Word
ongoing	active
forecast	predict
record	document
explosions	eruptions
changing	dynamic

First	Second	Third	Fourth
Donna works as an artist, photographer, and writer.	Donna goes back to school at age 32 to study science.	Donna visits her first volcano.	Donna and Steve are married on hardened lava rock.

Connect and Extend OPTIONAL

CONNECT TO EXTENDED WRITING PROJECT

Students can incorporate a similar structure to the article, "Donna O'Meara: The Volcano Lady" for their informational essays. Have students note how the author uses chronological text structure interspersed with scientific facts to organize her writing.

BEYOND THE BOOK

Research Project: Active Volcanoes Around the World

Donna O'Meara spent the night on the edge of an active volcano. To better understand active volcanoes, students will research active volcanoes in different parts of the world and present their findings to the class.

Break students into groups and ask each group to:

- Select an active volcano to research
  - > Where is this volcano?
  - > When was the last time it erupted?
  - > Do people live near this volcano who could be in danger if it erupted?
  - > When do scientists predict this volcano might erupt? How do they know?
  - > What is happening inside this active volcano?
- Present a photo collage combining photography and information to the class.

To reflect, ask students:

- What is the most surprising fact you learned about volcanoes from this project?
- After researching active volcanoes, can you imagine spending the night sleeping on the edge of one or living near a volcano?

Collaborative Conversation

■ SCAFFOLDS

Break students into collaborative conversation groups to discuss the writing prompt. Remind them to reference their Skills Focus annotations in their discussion.

Donna O'Meara and her husband risk their lives to get close-up photos of volcanoes all over the world. If you were a scientist or researcher, what kind of natural phenomena would you want to explore? Why? Support your response with evidence from the text as well as personal experience. As you make connections between Donna O'Meara's dream and your own, include any information that may have changed your understanding or opinion of what it means to be a scientist or researcher.

Use the scaffolds below to differentiate instruction for your **ELL** English Language Learners and **A** Approaching grade-level learners.

ELL **BEGINNING, INTERMEDIATE** Use the discussion guide and speaking frames to facilitate the discussion with support from the teacher.

ADVANCED, ADVANCED HIGH Use the discussion guide and speaking frames to facilitate the discussion in mixed-level groups.

A **APPROACHING** Use the discussion guide to facilitate the discussion in mixed-level groups.

APPROACHING
ADVANCED, ADVANCED HIGH
BEGINNING, INTERMEDIATE

Discussion Guide	Speaking Frames
1. What kind of natural phenomenon would you want to explore?	• I would want to explore ____ because ____.
2. What connections can you make from the text to your own knowledge and experiences?	• This story reminds me of ____. • This story connects to ____.
3. How has the text changed the way you think about what it means to be a scientist or researcher?	• The text has made me realize that ____. • I used to think ____. Now I think ____.

Review Prompt and Rubric

Before students begin writing, review the writing prompt and rubric with the class.

PERSONAL RESPONSE: Donna O'Meara and her husband risk their lives to get close-up photos of volcanoes all over the world. If you were a scientist or researcher, what kind of natural phenomenon would you want to explore? Why? Support your response with evidence from the text as well as personal experience. As you make connections between Donna O'Meara's dream and your own, include any information that may have changed your understanding or opinion of what it means to be a scientist or researcher.

ELL **A** **PROMPT GUIDE**

- What kind of natural phenomenon would you want to explore?
- What connections can you make from the text to your own knowledge and experiences?

- How has the text changed the way you think about what it means to be a scientist or researcher?

Score	Personal Response	Language and Conventions
4	The writer clearly explains his or her personal connection to the text, using relevant evidence from the text as needed.	The writer demonstrates a consistent command of grammar, punctuation, and usage conventions. Although minor errors may be evident, they do not detract from the fluency or the clarity of the essay.
3	The writer sufficiently explains his or her personal connection to the text, using relevant evidence from the text most of the time.	The writer demonstrates an adequate command of grammar, punctuation, and usage conventions. Although some errors may be evident, they create few (if any) disruptions in the fluency of the writing or the clarity of the essay.
2	The writer begins to explain his or her personal connection to the text, but the explanation is incomplete. The writer uses relevant evidence from the text only some of the time.	The writer demonstrates a partial command of grammar, punctuation, and usage conventions. Some distracting errors may be evident, at times creating minor disruptions in the fluency or clarity of the writing.
1	The writer attempts to explain his or her personal connection to the text, but the explanation is not successful. The writer uses little or no relevant evidence from the text.	The writer demonstrates little or no command of grammar, punctuation, and usage conventions. Serious and persistent errors create disruptions in the fluency of the writing and sometimes interfere with meaning.
0	The writer does not provide a relevant response to the prompt or does not provide a response at all.	Serious and persistent errors overwhelm the writing and interfere with the meaning of the response as a whole, making the writer's meaning impossible to understand.

Write

Ask students to complete the writing assignment using textual evidence to support their answers.

Use the scaffolds below to differentiate instruction for your **ELL** English Language Learners and **A** Approaching grade-level learners.

ELL **BEGINNING** With the help of the <u>word bank</u>, write a response using <u>paragraph frame 1</u>.

INTERMEDIATE With the help of the <u>word bank</u>, write a response using <u>paragraph frames 1 and 2</u>.

ADVANCED, ADVANCED HIGH Write a response of differentiated length using the <u>sentence starters</u>.

A **APPROACHING** Write a response of differentiated length using the <u>sentence starters</u>.

| BEGINNING | | ADVANCED, ADVANCED HIGH |
| INTERMEDIATE | | APPROACHING |

Word Bank	Paragraph Frame 1	Paragraph Frame 2	Sentence Starters
fossils studied dangerous scientists rocks space brave adventurous	Donna and Steve O'Meara have ____ volcanoes for over 25 years. The O'Meras want to help ____ learn more about volcanoes. If I were a researcher or scientist, I would explore ____. To have this job, I would have to be ____ like Donna O'Meara. Donna O'Meara may have the most ____ job in the world.	This text helps me understand that scientists and researchers can ____. For example, when I read ____, I thought ____. This text teaches me that when you have a dream, you sometimes have to ____ to make it come true.	• I want to explore . . . • The text reminds me of . . . • This text relates to . . . • This text helped me understand . . . • When I read . . . , I thought . . . • I used to think . . . , but now I think . . .

Peer Review

Students should submit substantive feedback to two peers using the instructions below.

• How well does this response answer the prompt?
• Which of the writer's comments inspired you to think differently about the text?
• What does the writer do well in this response? What does the writer need to work on?

Rate

Respond to the following with a point rating that reflects your opinion.

	1 2 3 4
Ideas	▪▪▪▫
Evidence	▪▪▪▪
Language and Conventions	▪▪▫▫

Submit

ELL **A** **SENTENCE FRAMES**

• You were able to (completely / partly / almost) ____ answer the prompt.
• You could answer the prompt more completely by ____.

• I thought differently about the text after reading ____.
• My favorite part of your responses is ____.

Dare To Be Creative!

INFORMATIONAL TEXT
Madeleine L'Engle
1983

Introduction

n 1983, renowned young adult author Madeleine L'Engle (1918–2007) delivered this lecture before the Library of Congress. "Dare to be creative!" is heralded as an inspirational manifesto on the beauty and power of words, the magic of reading, as well as a stunning rebuke of literary censorship. L'Engle is the author of such young adult classics as *A Wrinkle in Time* and *A Wind in the Door*.

Madeleine L'Engle states that we do not need to be afraid of disagreeing with people, even if they insist we're wrong. L'Engle also mentions that those who are zealous are not fully certain that they're right. When Dr. Semmelweis suggested surgeons wash their hands before delivering a baby, zealots within the medical establishment persecuted him. Luckily for us, their logic did not win out. Likewise, L'Engle herself sometimes finds herself zealously defending something. When she notices this, she takes it as a sign that she needs to take a step back and ask what's bothering her so much. Oftentimes, it turns out she's afraid of something that will make her change and grow. Fiction helps her in this regard, because L'Engle's writing forces her to ask questions she might otherwise avoid. Often, once the writing gets going, she's forced to confront those questions and the answers shake her world.

 Proficiency-leveled summaries and summaries in multiple languages are available digitally.

 Audio and audio text highlighting are available with this text.

COMPARING WITHIN AND ACROSS GENRES

 Like "Donna O'Meara: The Volcano Lady" and "Margaret Bourke-White: Fearless Photographer," this text focuses on the idea of what motivates individuals. Madeleine L'Engle's speech "Dare to be creative!" urges readers to make their own opinions and to ask questions that will help them "shake their universe."

Access Complex Text

LEXILE: N/A   WORD COUNT: 533

The following areas may be challenging for students, particularly English Language Learners and Approaching grade-level learners.

Genre	Purpose	Organization
• The text is a speech that contains features of a personal essay, including references to real people and real events, real memories, experiences, and influences, all from a first-person point of view.	• The primary purpose of the text is to inform. The author shares how she came to develop her belief in the power of independent thought, free of the need to conform and unafraid of other people's judgment.	• The speech uses a combination of text structures. The author uses a cause-and-effect text structure to relate how her experiences influenced her belief. She also uses specific examples from history in order to further convey her belief.

| SCAFFOLDS | ENGLISH LANGUAGE LEARNERS | APPROACHING GRADE LEVEL | BEYOND GRADE LEVEL |

These icons identify differentiation strategies and scaffolded support for a variety of students. See the digital lesson plan for additional differentiation strategies and scaffolds.

Instructional Path

The print teacher's edition includes essential point-of-use instruction and planning tools. Complete lesson plans and program documents appear in your digital teacher account.

Independent Read: Dare to be creative!

Objectives: After reading the text, students will write a short response that demonstrates their understanding of the speech through a personal connection.

Independent Read

Madeleine L'Engle

Dare to be Creative!

Entry Point

Introduce the Text

As a class, watch the video preview ▶ and have students read the introduction in pairs to make connections to the video preview.

• What part of the video stood out to you the most?

• What kind of text are you about to read? How can you tell?

• What information does the video provide that the introduction does not?

ELL SPEAKING FRAMES

• The ____ in the video makes me think ____.
• The introduction mentions ____. This connects to ____ in the video.
• The video shows ____. This makes me wonder ____.
• I think the text will ____. I think this because ____.
• I predict that there will be ____. I believe this because ____.

As students prepare to read "Dare to be creative!," share the following information with them to provide context.

✓ In her speech "Dare to be creative!," delivered to the Library of Congress, Madeleine L'Engle argues that, contrary to popular opinion, children have the ability to tackle difficult concepts and emotions. She calls for less censorship and a push for questioning the world around you. Her inspiring and thought-provoking speech is still celebrated today during National Children's Book week.

✓ The Library of Congress contains a singular of works, "which document the history and further the creativity of the American people and which record and contribute to the advancement of civilization and knowledge throughout the world…" The Library of Congress is preserving such works with the intent of promoting creativity and critical thinking. Aligned with the ideals of L'Engle, the Library of Congress invited her to speak about such concepts in 1985.

"My books push me and prod me and make me ask questions I might otherwise avoid."

NOTES

1 We need to dare disturb the universe by not being **manipulated** or frightened by judgmental groups who assume the right to insist that if we do not agree with them, not only do we not understand but we are wrong. How dull the world would be if we all had to feel the same way about everything, if we all had to like the same books, dislike the same books. For my relaxing reading I enjoy English murder mysteries, but my husband prefers spy thrillers. I like beet greens and he likes beet root. We would be a society of ants if we couldn't have personal tastes and honest differences. And how sad it would be if we had to give up all sense of mystery for the limited world of provable fact. I still can't read *The Happy Prince* or *The Selfish Giant* aloud without a lump coming into my throat, but I suppose that talking statues and giants are on someone's hit list.

2 Perhaps some of this zeal is caused by fear. But, as Bertrand Russell warns, "Zeal is a bad mark for a cause. Nobody had any zeal about arithmetic. It was the anti-vaccinationists,[1] not the vaccinationists, who were **zealous."** Yet because those who were not threatened by the idea of vaccination ultimately won out, we have **eradicated** the horror of smallpox[2] from the planet.

3 It is hard for us to understand the zeal of the medical **establishment** when Dr. Semmelweis sensibly suggested that it might be a good idea if surgeons washed their hands after dissecting a cadaver, before going to deliver a woman in labor. This, to us, obvious suggestions of cleanliness was so threatening to the medical establishment of the day that they zealously set about persecuting

Despite overzealous critics, Dr. Semmelweis convinced doctors to wash their hands when dealing with patients, which saved many lives.

1. **anti-vaccinationists:** activists or individuals who oppose the practice of giving vaccinations or shots
2. **smallpox:** a lethal and disfiguring infectious virus eradicated in 1980

 64 Reading & Writing Companion

 ## Analyze Vocabulary Using Context Clues

As students read the text, ask them to make predictions about each bold vocabulary word based on the context clues in the sentence. Have students use the annotation tool to make their predictions.

 ### TURN AND TALK

Have students discuss their original vocabulary predictions with a neighbor. Come to a consensus as a class before confirming their definitions.

 ### TEXT TALK

Why does Madeleine L'Engle contrast her preferences with her husband's?

See paragraph 1: She contrasts their tastes in books and in food. This helps to prove her point that it's important to think independently.

How does Madeleine L'Engle use medical events from history to help prove her point?

See paragraphs 2–3: She provides examples of zeal as the defining characteristic of those, like the anti-vaccinationists, who are opposed to progress in medical science.

 ### SELECTION VOCABULARY

manipulate / manipular *verb* to change something for a specific purpose or advantage COGNATE

zealous / ferviente *adjective* actively engaged and energetic

 ELL
- What do you know about anti-vaccinationists?
- How did anti-vaccinationists feel about their cause?

eradicate / erradicar *verb* to eliminate or destroy completely COGNATE

ELL
- What happened to the disease called smallpox?
- What does the word describe about the disease?

establishment / el establecimiento *noun* a place or business COGNATE

 ELL
- What did Dr. Semmelweis do?
- How does Dr. Semmelweis's suggestion affect the medical practice?

Semmelweis. But, thanks to him, many of us are alive because doctors now wash their hands. If the zealots had won, women would still be dying of septicemia[3] after childbirth.

4 Russell suggests that people are zealous when they are not completely certain they are right. I agree with him. When I find myself hotly defending something, when I am, in fact, zealous, it is time for me to step back and examine whatever it is that has me so hot under the collar. Do I think it's going to threaten my comfortable **rut?** Make me change and grow?—and growing always causes growing pains. Am I afraid to ask questions?

5 Sometimes. But I believe that good questions are more important than answers, and the best children's books ask questions, and make the reader ask questions. And every new question is going to disturb someone's universe.

6 Writing fiction is definitely a universe disturber, and for the writer, first of all. My books push me and prod me and make me ask questions I might otherwise avoid. I start a book, having lived with the characters for several years, during the writing of other books, and I have a pretty good idea of where the story is going and what I hope it's going to say. And then, once I get deep into the writing, unexpected things begin to happen, things which make me question, and which sometimes really shake my universe.

By Madeleine L'Engle, 1983. Used by permission of Crosswicks Ltd., c/o Aaron M. Priest Literary Agency

---

3. **septicemia:** a bacterial infection of the blood, skin or lungs

✏ WRITE

PERSONAL RESPONSE: In the speech "Dare to be Creative!," Madeleine L'Engle urges listeners to not be scared of thinking independently. Write about a time when you took a risk to do something creative or unexpected and it turned out well. Then, explain how this connects to the speech. Support your response with evidence from the text as well as personal experience.

Reading & Writing Companion **65**

👤 TEXT TALK

How does Madeleine L'Engle's reference to writing fiction contribute to her argument?

See paragraphs 5–6: She explains that writing fiction can shake the universe and make you question reality, thus allowing new, independent thoughts to form.

B Ask each Beyond grade-level student to write one additional discussion question. Then, have one or two students facilitate a discussion, using their questions to guide the conversation.

🗄 SELECTION VOCABULARY

rut / la rutina *noun* a habit or pattern of behavior that has become dull and unproductive but is hard to change

ELL
• What is L'Engle describing?
• How is L'Engle explaining zealous people?

Reading Comprehension

Have students complete the digital reading comprehension questions ✔ when they finish reading.

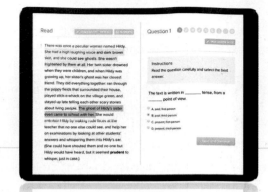

ANSWER KEY

QUESTION 1: C	**QUESTION 3:** D	**QUESTION 5:**
QUESTION 2: C	**QUESTION 4:** A	*See chart below.*

Definition	Word
To pursue with harassing or oppressive treatment, especially because of religious or political beliefs, ethnic or racial origin, gender identity, or sexual orientation	persecute
Utterly removed or destroyed	eradicated
A habit or pattern of behavior that has become dull and unproductive but is hard to change	rut
The dominant group or organization in a particular field	establishment

Connect and Extend OPTIONAL

CONNECT TO EXTENDED WRITING PROJECT

Students can find inspiration from Madeleine L'Engle's historical references within her speech. Have them work to research historical references that could be used in an informational writing assignment.

BEYOND THE BOOK

Writing: Motivational Speech

Madeleine L'Engle's speech intends to motivate us to be more independent-minded. Write your own speech that encourages others to do something that you find to be important.

To reflect, ask students:

- How did your own writing allow you to better understand the elements of influential speeches?

- What insights have you gained about genre and reader expectations based on writing your own speech?

Collaborative Conversation

SCAFFOLDS

Break students into collaborative conversation groups to discuss the writing prompt. Remind them to reference their Skills Focus annotations in their discussion.

In the speech "Dare to be creative!," Madeleine L'Engle urges listeners to not be scared of thinking independently. Write about a time when you took a risk to do something creative or unexpected and it turned out well. Then, explain how this connects to the speech. Support your response with evidence from the text as well as personal experience.

Use the scaffolds below to differentiate instruction for your **ELL** English Language Learners and **A** Approaching grade-level learners.

ELL **BEGINNING, INTERMEDIATE** Use the <u>discussion guide</u> and <u>speaking frames</u> to facilitate the discussion with support from the teacher.

ADVANCED, ADVANCED HIGH Use the <u>discussion guide</u> and <u>speaking frames</u> to facilitate the discussion in mixed-level groups.

A **APPROACHING** Use the <u>discussion guide</u> to facilitate the discussion in mixed-level groups.

APPROACHING
ADVANCED, ADVANCED HIGH
BEGINNING, INTERMEDIATE

Discussion Guide	Speaking Frames
1. What kind of risk did you take that turned out well?	• I decided to ____ because ____. • This turned out to be positive because ____.
2. How does the risk you took connect to Madeleine L'Engle's speech?	• My risk connects to the speech because ____. • After reading the speech, I learned that ____.

Review Prompt and Rubric

Before students begin writing, review the writing prompt and rubric with the class.

PERSONAL RESPONSE: In the speech "Dare to be creative!," Madeleine L'Engle urges listeners to not be scared of thinking independently. Write about a time when you took a risk to do something creative or unexpected and it turned out well. Then, explain how this connects to the speech. Support your response with evidence from the text as well as personal experience.

 PROMPT GUIDE

- What kind of risk did you take that turned out well?
- Why was this risk something creative or unexpected?

- How does the risk you took connect to Madeleine L'Engle's speech?

Score	Personal Response	Language and Conventions
4	The writer clearly explains the risk he or she took and the personal connection to the speech, using relevant evidence from the text as needed.	The writer demonstrates a consistent command of grammar, punctuation, and usage conventions. Although minor errors may be evident, they do not detract from the fluency or the clarity of the essay.
3	The writer sufficiently explains the risk he or she took and the personal connection to the speech, using relevant evidence from the text most of the time.	The writer demonstrates an adequate command of grammar, punctuation, and usage conventions. Although some errors may be evident, they create few (if any) disruptions in the fluency of the writing or the clarity of the essay.
2	The writer begins to explain the risk he or she took and the personal connection to the speech, but the explanation is incomplete. The writer uses relevant evidence from the text only some of the time.	The writer demonstrates a partial command of grammar, punctuation, and usage conventions. Some distracting errors may be evident, at times creating minor disruptions in the fluency or clarity of the writing.
1	The writer attempts to explain the risk he or she took and the personal connection to the speech, but the explanation is not successful. The writer uses little or no relevant evidence from the text.	The writer demonstrates little or no command of grammar, punctuation, and usage conventions. Serious and persistent errors create disruptions in the fluency of the writing and sometimes interfere with meaning.
0	The writer does not provide a relevant response to the prompt or does not provide a response at all.	Serious and persistent errors overwhelm the writing and interfere with the meaning of the response as a whole, making the writer's meaning impossible to understand.

Write

Ask students to complete the writing assignment using textual evidence to support their answers.

Use the scaffolds below to differentiate instruction for your **ELL** English Language Learners and **A** Approaching grade-level learners.

ELL **BEGINNING** With the help of the <u>word bank</u>, write a response using <u>paragraph frame 1</u>.

INTERMEDIATE With the help of the <u>word bank</u>, write a response using <u>paragraph frames 1 and 2</u>.

ADVANCED, ADVANCED HIGH Write a response of differentiated length using the <u>sentence starters</u>.

A **APPROACHING** Write a response of differentiated length using the <u>sentence starters</u>.

| BEGINNING | | ADVANCED, ADVANCED HIGH |
| INTERMEDIATE | | APPROACHING |

Word Bank	Paragraph Frame 1	Paragraph Frame 2	Sentence Starters
question opinion independently stood up for a boy positive	In her speech, Madeleine L'Engle reminds me that is it okay to have my own ____. This makes me realize that some people might be afraid to think ____. It is important to ____ the things around us. One time, I took a risk and ____ who was being bullied. Lots of kids thought it was okay to make fun of the boy, but not me. I went right up to the bully and asked him, "Do you think you're tough when you hurt others?" The bully unexpectedly answered, "No." I followed L'Engle's advice and asked the bully an important question to get him to think deeply about what he was doing. I think I made a ____ impact because the bully stopped.	This speech makes me feel motivated to ask more ____. For example, when I read ____, I thought about how ____. This speech reminds me that ____.	• Madeleine L'Engle's speech is about . . . • The speech reminds me of when I . . . • This speech relates to me because . . . • My family is . . . • I took a risk that was unexpected when . . . • When I read . . . , I thought . . . • L'Engle's speech connects with my risk because . . .

Peer Review

Students should submit substantive feedback to two peers using the review instructions below.

- How well does this response answer the prompt?
- Which of the author's comments inspired you to think differently about the speech?
- What did the writer do well in this response? What does the writer need to work on?

Rate

Respond to the following with a point rating that reflects your opinion.

	1 2 3 4
Ideas	
Evidence	
Language and Conventions	

Submit

ELL **SENTENCE FRAMES**

A
- You were able to (completely / partly / almost) ____ answer the prompt.
- You could answer the prompt more completely by ____.
- I thought differently about the speech after reading ____.
- My favorite part of your responses is ____.

Margaret Bourke-White:
Fearless Photographer

INFORMATIONAL TEXT
McGraw Hill Education
2017

Introduction

Margaret Bourke-White (1904–1971) was an American photographer who gained fame for traveling around the world and snapping photographs for high-profile magazines. As the first American female war photojournalist, her photographs earned her a spot on the cover of *Life* magazine and can be viewed to this day in museums nationwide, including the Library of Congress. This short biography of her life describes some of the challenges she faced and feats she accomplished throughout her career.

Born in 1904, Margaret Bourke-White grew up during a time when women were discouraged from seeking jobs in male-dominated fields. Interested in photography from an early age and encouraged by her parents, she had some of her photos published when she was in college. After graduation, she was hired to take photos of steel mills in Cleveland. To do so, she had to determine how to light the molten steel so that it would show up clearly in black and white. These photos caught the attention of Henry Luce, who hired Bourke-White to work as a photojournalist at *Fortune Magazine*. When World War II started, she traveled to Moscow, where she created a visual record of the firefight of the German invasion. Later, she went on to document labor injustice in South Africa as well as Gandhi's nonviolent resistance in India, showing women that they should pursue the careers of their dreams.

 Proficiency-leveled summaries and summaries in multiple languages are available digitally.

 Audio and audio text highlighting are available with this text.

COMPARING WITHIN AND ACROSS GENRES

 From the time she started making photographs and recognized that they could stir people's feelings to the culmination of her long record-breaking career as a photojournalist, Margaret Bourke-White's perseverance and adventurous attitude paved the way for women to take on roles beyond what society expected of them. Students should compare the motivations and achievements in the selections about Donna O'Meara and Margaret Bourke-White with the ideas from Madeleine L'Engle's speech, "Dare to be creative!"

Access Complex Text

LEXILE: 1040L　**WORD COUNT: 965**

The following areas may be challenging for students, particularly English Language Learners and Approaching grade-level learners.

Purpose	Sentence Structure	Specific Vocabulary
• An author may write for one or several purposes: to persuade, to inform, to describe, to explain, or to entertain, for example.	• Some sentences are lengthy and utilize time transition words and phrases to indicate the span of Margaret Bourke-White's career.	• Some terms such as *photojournalism* may need clarification.
• While the purpose of informing is generally clear in a biography, other purposes may not be as clear for some readers. Lead students to discuss and support other possible purposes.	• Point out such transitions, including dates, historical events, and words such as *after*, *during*, and *through*.	• Students may define such terms using print or digital resources, context, and word origin.

 SCAFFOLDS　 **ENGLISH LANGUAGE LEARNERS**　 **APPROACHING GRADE LEVEL**　Ⓑ **BEYOND GRADE LEVEL**

These icons identify differentiation strategies and scaffolded support for a variety of students. See the digital lesson plan for additional differentiation strategies and scaffolds.

Instructional Path

The print teacher's edition includes essential point-of-use instruction and planning tools. Complete lesson plans and program documents appear in your digital teacher account.

Skill: Synthesizing

Objectives: After reading and discussing a model, students will be able to synthesize information from multiple texts to create a new and fuller understanding.

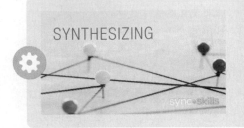

First Read: Margaret Bourke-White: Fearless Photographer

Objectives: After an initial reading and discussion of an informational text, students will be able to identify and restate the text's key ideas and details.

Skill: Textual Evidence

Objectives: After rereading and discussing a model of close reading, students will be able to cite textual evidence to support an analysis of what the text says explicitly, as well as draw inferences from the text.

Skill: Technical Language

Objectives: After rereading and discussing a model of close reading, students will be able to determine the meaning of words and phrases as they are used in a text, including technical meanings.

Close Read: Margaret Bourke-White: Fearless Photographer

Objectives: After engaging in a close reading and discussion of the texts, students will be able to compare and contrast authors' motivations in a short, written response.

Progress Monitoring

Opportunities to Learn	Opportunities to Demonstrate Learning	Opportunities to Reteach
Synthesizing		
⚙ Skill: Synthesizing	🖥 **First Read** • Practice Oral Reading Fluency • Read And Annotate	🖥 **Unit 6** **First Read: Shree Bose: Never Too Young to Change the World** ⚙ Spotlight Skill: Synthesizing
Textual Evidence		
⚙ Skill: Textual Evidence	⚙ **Skill: Textual Evidence** • Your Turn 🖥 **Close Read** • Writer's Notebook • Skills Focus • Collaborative Conversation • Write	⚙ Spotlight Skill: Textual Evidence
Technical Language		
⚙ Skill: Technical Language	⚙ **Skill: Technical Language** • Your Turn 🖥 **Close Read** • Complete Vocabulary Chart • Skills Focus • Write	⚙ Spotlight Skill: Technical Language

First Read

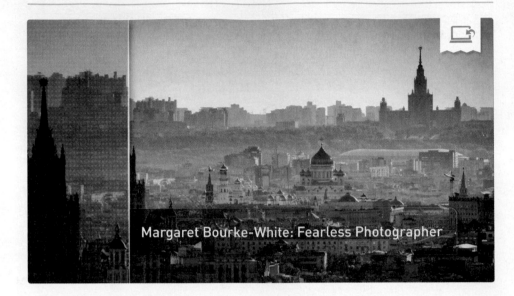

Margaret Bourke-White: Fearless Photographer

 ## Introduce the Text

As a class, watch the video preview and have students read the introduction in pairs to make connections to the video preview.

To activate prior knowledge and experiences, ask students:

- What other images could you imagine using in this video?
- How do the images, words, and music in the video connect to the information in the introduction?

ELL SPEAKING FRAMES
- The ____ in the video makes me think ____.
- The video shows ____. This makes me wonder ____.
- I think the text will ____. I think this because ____.
- I predict that there will be ____. I believe this because ____.

Entry Point

As students prepare to read "Margaret Bourke-White: Fearless Photographer," share the following information with them to provide context.

✓ Born in New York City, Margaret Bourke-White attended Clarence H. White School of Photography in pursuit of a photography career. After moving to Cleveland, Ohio, she opened her own studio and concentrated mainly on industrial photography. Henry Luce, publisher of Fortune magazine, admired her work and hired her. Bourke-White became the first foreign photographer to travel to the Soviet Union and capture images of industry. Thus began her career as a photojournalist. A photojournalist is a photographer who communicates the news through images they capture.

✓ While working for various famous magazines, Bourke-White photographed the Dust Bowl, the German Invasion of Moscow, allied bombing missions, and other major historical events. She is regarded as one of the most respected photojournalists of her time because of her respect for her subjects, her attention to detail, and the messages presented in her photos.

"... Margaret made the production of steel look magnificent, mysterious, and awe-inspiring."

1 In 1904, girls weren't supposed to dream of careers that took them flying into the sky on airplanes or climbing out onto ledges at the top of skyscrapers. And they certainly weren't encouraged to think about competing with men for the opportunity to photograph important people and events.

NOTES

2 Joseph White and Minnie Bourke, however, never told their daughter what to think and dream about. Instead, young Margaret, or "Peg" as her friends called her, got plenty of attention and encouragement from her parents to explore her world. Early on, they taught her to work hard and to go after what she wanted. They even gave her a motto: "You can." It's no wonder Margaret Bourke-White grew up to be one of the most accomplished women and talked-about photographers of the twentieth century.

Margaret Bourke-White paved the way for female photographers.

Skill: Textual Evidence

I can find evidence explicitly in the text that supports the idea that Margaret was a trailblazer. I highlighted the "firsts" in her career.

Skill: Technical Language

I'm not sure what a "commercial photography studio" is, but the text says that Margaret opened one, so it's probably a business.

3 Many photographers today owe thanks to Margaret. From the time she started taking photographs and recognized that they could stir up feelings to the **culmination** of her long career as a photojournalist, Margaret was a trailblazer.[1] She shaped the art of photography and the profession of photojournalism and showed that women photographers could travel all over the world and work alongside men in dangerous situations.

4 **A Star Photographer**

5 Her mother gave Margaret her first camera in 1921, when she was 17 years old. Her interest in photography grew as a result of her father's enthusiasm for cameras. A few years later, Margaret's classmates at Cornell University became her first admirers when photos she took of the campus appeared in

---

1. **trailblazer:** someone who does things for the first time, metaphorically burning a trail for others

Reading & Writing Companion **67**

Analyze Vocabulary Using Context Clues

In paragraph 3 focus on the sentence that uses the word *culmination*. Point out these context clues:

1. First I notice that the writer refers to Margaret as a trailblazer, which means someone who leads the way for others.

2. The writer explains that Margaret wasn't just a trailblazer for a short amount of time, but instead that she was a trailblazer from the beginning of her career to the *culmination* of her career.

3. I think *culmination* must mean "end."

Textual Evidence

How does the reader use textual evidence to support the author's central idea?

The reader defines a key word in the author's claim ("trailblazer") and then highlights textual evidence to support the central idea.

Technical Language

What was the technical language that the reader noticed?

The reader highlighted the language associated with Margaret's photography studio.

TEXT TALK

What was Margaret Bourke-White's motto, and why was it important?

See paragraphs 1 and 2: Her motto was, "You can." The motto was important because Margaret grew up during a time when women were not encouraged to compete in the workforce or engage in adventurous lives.

How did Margaret Bourke-White develop an interest in photography?

See paragraph 4: Margaret's mother gave her a camera, and her father had an enthusiasm for cameras.

[V] SELECTION VOCABULARY

culmination / la culminación *noun* end or final result COGNATE

interpret / interpretar *verb* to explain the meaning of (information, words, or actions) COGNATE

ELL
• What does it mean to summarize the news?
• What more might journalists do with the news?

Textual Evidence

How does the reader use textual evidence to make an inference?

The reader notes an interesting text detail about Margaret "bringing along a new style of flare" and uses it to make an inference regarding her as an innovator.

Skills Focus

QUESTION 2: Technical Language

I see a new technical term introduced in paragraph 8: photojournalism. The author describes Margaret's work in this section as "report [ing] the news through images." This must mean that Margaret was taking pictures that delivered important information to the public.

TEXT TALK

In what ways was Henry Luce important for Margaret Bourke-White's career?

See paragraphs 7 and 8: He gave her a job at a magazine that both summarized and interpreted the news. She was charged with telling stories through images

What world events did Margaret Bourke-White photograph?

See paragraphs 10, 11, and 12: She photographed World War II and Gandhi's protest in India.

Margaret Bourke-White: Fearless Photographer

NOTES

Skill:
Textual Evidence

Margaret Bourke-White was a great photographer, but she did more than just take photographs. The text doesn't explicitly say that she was an inventor because this sentence has an implicit meaning. I made an inference to figure it out.

the school newspapers. A year after graduating, Margaret moved to Cleveland, Ohio and opened a commercial photography studio.

6   One of Margaret's first clients was the Otis Steel Company. Her success was due both to her technique and her skills in dealing with people. At first, several people at the company wondered if a woman could stand up to the intense heat and generally dirty and gritty conditions inside a steel mill.[2] When Margaret finally got permission, the technical problems began. Black-and-white film at that time was sensitive to blue light, not the reds and oranges of hot steel. The pictures came out all black. Margaret solved this problem by bringing along a new style of flare (which produces white light) and having assistants hold them to light her scenes. Her abilities resulted in some of the best steel factory pictures of that era, and these earned her national attention.

7   The city's powerful businessmen soon began calling on her to take pictures of their mills, factories, and buildings. In the steel mills, she wanted to be right next to the melted metal. The extreme heat sometimes burned her face and damaged the paint on her camera. In her first well-known photographs, Margaret made the production of steel look magnificent, mysterious, and awe-inspiring. Her photos, filled with streams of melted steel and flying sparks, caught the eye of someone who would change her life.

8   **A New Sort of Storytelling**

9   Henry Luce was a powerful and important American publisher. In the 1920s and 1930s he started a series of magazines that would change journalism and the reading habits of Americans. Luce's magazine called *Time* summarized and **interpreted** the week's news. *Life* was a picture magazine of politics, culture and society that became very popular in the years before television, and *Fortune* explored the economy and the world of business. *Sports Illustrated* investigated the teams and important players of popular sports such as baseball and football.

10 In 1929, Henry Luce invited Margaret to work at *Fortune* Magazine. She jumped at the chance and became the first woman in a new field called photojournalism, in which photographers reported the news through images.

11 As Margaret snapped artistic shots of workplaces, she was able to find beauty in simple objects. Over time she **adapted** her techniques to photograph people and was **adept** at catching expressions and showing hardship. In 1930, she was the first photographer from a Western country to be allowed

---

2. **steel mill:** a plant where part or all of the steelmaking process is done

---

SELECTION VOCABULARY

adapt / adaptar *verb* to change something for a new use or purpose COGNATE

ELL
• What does Margaret do to her techniques over time?
• What is the purpose of these changes?

adept / experto/a *adjective* very skilled at something

ELL
• Is Margaret good or bad at catching expressions?
• Is Margaret good or bad at showing hardship?

into the Soviet Union (now Russia), where she took pictures of the workers in what was then a communist[3] country.

12 **World War II and After**

13 When World War II broke out in 1939, Margaret became the first female war correspondent. This is a journalist who covers stories first hand from a war zone. In 1941, she traveled to the Soviet Union again and was the only foreign photographer in Moscow when German forces invaded. Taking shelter in the U.S. Embassy,[4] she then captured much of the fierce battle on camera.

14 As the war continued, Margaret joined the U.S. Army Air Force in North Africa and then traveled with the U.S. Army in Italy and later Germany. She repeatedly came under fire in Italy as she traveled through areas of intense fighting.

15 After the war, Margaret continued to make the world's most complex events understandable. Her photos reflected stirring social issues of the time. She photographed South Africans laboring in gold mines and civil rights leader Mahatma Gandhi's nonviolent work in India.

16 **A Lasting Influence**

17 During the 1930s and 1940s, Margaret's adventurous attitude and perseverance paved the way for women to take on roles beyond the **norm**. Rather than snapping photos of high-society parties as other female photographers had done before her, she marched into steel plants and combat zones. She proved to women that they had every right to pursue the careers they wanted.

18 Through her work, Margaret became a role model for working women as well as a strong voice for the poor and powerless. She earned the respect of powerful businessmen when women were discouraged from working. When she died in 1971, she left behind not only an amazing photographic record of the human experience. She also left a message for women all over the world who wanted to make an impact: "You can."

Used with permission by McGraw Hill Education.

NOTES

 Skill:
Theme

I know the word "technique" can have many different meanings, like having a certain technique for cooking or skateboarding! I can use the subject of the text to understand that the word "technique" here means Margaret's skills in photography.

3. **communist:** a system of government which aims to eliminate class hierarchies by placing the means of production in common ownership
4. **U.S. Embassy:** the office of the United States in any other country

Please note that excerpts and passages in the StudySync® library and this workbook are intended as touchstones to generate interest in an author's work. The excerpts and passages do not substitute for the reading of entire texts, and StudySync® strongly recommends that students seek out and purchase the whole literary or informational work in order to experience it as the author intended. Links to online resellers are available in our digital library. In addition, complete works may be ordered through an authorized reseller by filling out and returning to StudySync® the order form enclosed in this workbook.

Reading & Writing Companion **69**

Skills Focus

QUESTION 1: Textual Evidence

Bourke-White was also a role model because she changed what was considered normal when it came to careers for women.

Skills Focus

QUESTION 3: Compare and Contrast

Donna O'Meara's: experiences on top of volcanoes qualify as adventurous. I think being holed up in the U.S. Embassy during a fierce battle is equally adventurous—especially when you're the only foreign correspondent there.

 TEXT TALK

What other information are you able to synthesize from the three articles?

Answers will vary.

Why were Margaret Bourke-White's photographs of Europe during World War II valuable to Americans?

Answers will vary.

 B Ask each Beyond grade-level student to write one additional discussion question. Then, have one or two students facilitate a discussion, using their questions to guide the conversation.

 SELECTION VOCABULARY

norm / la norma *noun* what is usual or standard; model or pattern regarded as typical COGNATE

ELL
• What roles were women expected to do during the time Margaret lived?
• Did Margaret follow or not follow these roles?

Think Questions

Circulate as students answer Think Questions independently. Scaffolds for these questions are shown on the opposite page.

QUESTION 1: Textual Evidence

Margaret Bourke-White used her hardworking attitude to advance her career when she "opened a commercial photography studio" in Cleveland, Ohio, after graduating from college.

QUESTION 2: Textual Evidence

Margaret Bourke-White photographed steel mills by using white light to illuminate the dark scenes and by taking close-up shots of molten metal. The results made the production of steel look "magnificent, mysterious, and awe-inspiring."

QUESTION 3: Textual Evidence

Margaret Bourke-White stood out from the crowd of traditional photojournalists in that her photographs were artistic, made complex events understandable, and "reflected stirring social issues." She also had opportunities to photograph events, such as the German forces invading Moscow, that other photographers did not.

QUESTION 4: Context Clues

The word is used to describe how Margaret Bourke-White's photography changed from focusing on "simple objects" to focusing on people. So, *adapted* must mean "changed."

QUESTION 5: Greek and Latin Affixes and Roots

I think *norm* must mean "the accepted standard or rule." The context clues in the sentence support this meaning because Margaret Bourke-White encouraged women to "take on roles beyond" what was normally expected for them or beyond the social rules.

MARGARET BOURKE-WHITE FEARLESS PHOTOGRAPHER

First Read

Read "Margaret Bourke-White: Fearless Photographer." After you read, complete the Think Questions below.

THINK QUESTIONS

1. Describe one example of when Margaret Bourke-White's hardworking attitude helped advance her career. Refer to specific passages or quotations from the text in your answer.

2. What was special about how Margaret Bourke-White photographed steel mills? Use evidence from the text in your response.

3. What made Margaret Bourke-White different from other photojournalists of her time? Identify several ways in which Margaret stood out from the crowd, citing textual evidence.

4. Which context clues helped you determine the meaning of the word **adapted** in paragraph 9? Write your definition of *adapted* and describe which words in the paragraph led you to your understanding of the word. Then look up the word in a print or online dictionary to confirm your definition.

5. The word **norm** is derived from the Latin *norma*, meaning "precept" or "rule." Knowing this, try to infer the meaning of *norm* as it is used in paragraph 13. Write your best definition here, along with any other words you know that could be derived from the same Latin root.

Think Questions

Use the scaffolds below to differentiate instruction for your **ELL** English Language Learners and **A** Approaching grade-level learners.

ELL **BEGINNING** Write a response using the <u>word bank</u> and <u>sentence frames</u>.

INTERMEDIATE Write a response using the <u>sentence frames</u>.

ADVANCED, ADVANCED HIGH Write a response using the <u>Text-Dependent Question Guide</u>.

A **APPROACHING** Write a response using the <u>Text-Dependent Question Guide</u>.

BEGINNING	INTERMEDIATE	APPROACHING
		ADVANCED, ADVANCED HIGH
Word Bank	**Sentence Frames**	**Text-Dependent Question Guide**
beyond objects close-up shots graduating changed magnificent photography opened rule social issues studio understandable white light	Margaret Bourke-White used her hardworking attitude to advance her career when she "____ a commercial photography ____" in Cleveland, Ohio, after ____ from college.	1. • What does it mean to be a hard worker? • What work did Margaret Bourke-White do while in college? • What work did Margaret Bourke-White do after college?
	Margaret Bourke-White photographed steel mills by using ____ to show dark scenes and by taking ____ of melted metal. The results made the production of steel look "____."	2. • How did Margaret Bourke-White solve the problem of dark shots? • From what point of view did Margaret Bourke-White photograph her subjects? • What were the results of these techniques?
	Margaret Bourke-White was different from other photojournalists in that her photographs were artistic, made complex events ____, and "reflected stirring ____."	3. • What word describes Margaret Bourke-White's photos? • How did Margaret Bourke-White help people understand world events? • What subjects did Margaret Bourke-White photograph?
	The word is used to describe a shift in Margaret Bourke-White's ____ techniques over time. She used to photograph ____ before she photographed people. So, *adapted* must mean "____."	4. • Read: "Over time she **adapted** her techniques to photograph people and was adept at catching expressions and showing hardship." • What did Margaret Bourke-White photograph before people? • Did her photography techniques stay the same over time?
	I think *norm* must mean "the accepted standard or ____." The context clues in the sentence support this meaning because Margaret Bourke-White encouraged women to "take on roles ____" the social rules or expectations.	5. • Read: "During the 1930s and 1940s, Margaret's adventurous attitude and perseverance paved the way for women to take on roles beyond the **norm**." • Did Margaret Bourke-White live the life expected of women? • What is normal for many women at the time?

Reading Comprehension OPTIONAL

Have students complete the digital reading comprehension questions ✓ when they finish reading.

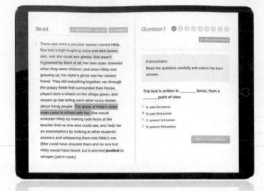

ANSWER KEY

QUESTION 1: B	QUESTION 5: D	QUESTION 9:
QUESTION 2: B	QUESTION 6: D	*See first chart.*
QUESTION 3: C	QUESTION 7: D	QUESTION 10:
QUESTION 4: D	QUESTION 8: A	*See second chart.*

Definition	Word
Skilled at something	adept
To make something useful in a new situation	adapted
Point of highest development	culmination
Something that is usual	norm
To explain the meaning of something	interpreted

First	Second	Third	Fourth
Margaret took photographs at the Otis Steel Mill.	Henry Luce contacted Margaret to work for *Fortune* magazine.	Margaret traveled to the Soviet Union as the first Western photographer allowed to enter.	Margaret travelled to World War II battlefronts as the first female war photojournalist.

Connect and Extend OPTIONAL

CONNECT TO EXTENDED WRITING PROJECT

Students can use "Margaret Bourke-White: Fearless Photographer" as a mentor text for their Extended Writing Project. They may adopt the author's use of chronological text structure in their informational essay.

BEYOND THE BOOK

Photojournalism: Current Event

Margaret Bourke-White was the first woman to enter the field of photojournalism. To better understand this field, students will need to become photojournalists to tell the story of a current event or issue on campus.

Ask students to:

- Select a current issue or event they are interested in and want to report on.
- Use their devices to take photos of images that tell the story of this event.
- Post their images online with short captions.

Once everyone has posted their photos and simple captions online, allow the class to do an online gallery walk to view each other's images.

To reflect, ask students:

- Which events or issues were covered by multiple students? Why do you think so many students selected these events or issues?
- Which images were most effective at telling a story? What do you think made these images so effective?

Margaret Bourke-White: Fearless Photographer

Skill:
Textual Evidence

Use the Checklist to analyze Textual Evidence in "Margaret Bourke-White: Fearless Photographer." Refer to the sample student annotations about Textual Evidence in the text.

↻ CHECKLIST FOR TEXTUAL EVIDENCE

In order to support an analysis by citing textual evidence that is explicitly stated in the text, do the following:

- ✓ read the text closely and critically
- ✓ identify what the text says explicitly
- ✓ find the most relevant textual evidence that supports your analysis
- ✓ consider why the author explicitly states specific details and information
- ✓ cite the specific words, phrases, sentences, or paragraphs from the text that support your analysis

In order to interpret implicit meanings in a text by making inferences, do the following:

- ✓ combine information directly stated in the text with your own knowledge, experiences, and observations
- ✓ cite the specific words, phrases, sentences, or paragraphs from the text that support this inference

In order to cite textual evidence to support an analysis of what the text says explicitly as well as inferences drawn from the text, consider the following questions:

- ✓ Have I read the text closely and critically?
- ✓ What inferences am I making about the text? What textual evidence am I using to support these inferences?
- ✓ Am I quoting the evidence from the text correctly?
- ✓ Does my textual evidence logically relate to my analysis?

Reading & Writing Companion 71

Ⅴ SKILL VOCABULARY

cite / citar *verb* to quote as evidence to support a response

textual evidence / la evidencia del texto *noun* details from the text that a reader can use to support his or her ideas and opinions about the text

explicit / explícito/a *adjective* precisely and clearly expressed COGNATE

implicit / implícito/a *adjective* implied but not stated directly COGNATE

make inferences / hacer inferencias *verb* to use your understanding of a text and your own experiences, to draw conclusions

Skill: Textual Evidence

Introduce the Skill

Watch the Concept Definition video ▶ and read the following definition with your students.

Any time you're discussing a text, you need to **cite**, or point out, **textual evidence**, the details that readers use to support their ideas and opinions. Readers may cite evidence that is directly stated, or **explicit**, in the text. Other times, textual evidence may be implicit, which means it is suggested but not directly stated. One way to interpret implicit meanings is to **make inferences**, using clues from the text and your own experiences to make logical decisions about characters and events that are not stated directly.

Readers must also refer to textual evidence when they **analyze** and examine the different parts of a text. Analyzing specific parts of the text, such as the actions of a character or the cause-and-effect relationships between events in nonfiction, helps a reader **interpret** and explain the meaning, theme, or central idea of the text as a whole. When you cite textual evidence, someone else can look back at a particular part of a text you read and understand your analysis.

⚙ TURN AND TALK

1. What inference can you make about this class? Is it interesting? Challenging? Unusual? Something else?

2. Now, look around the classroom. Which pieces of textual evidence—posters, writing on the board, books, student assignments—support your inference?

⒠ SPEAKING FRAMES

- This class is ____.
- Posters (books) such as ____. support this inference because ____.
- Student (board) work such as ____ supports this inference because ____.

⚙ Your Turn

Ask students to complete the Your Turn Activity.

QUESTION 1

A. Incorrect. Margaret Bourke-White was an advocate for women.

B. Incorrect. There is no evidence in this paragraph to support this statement.

C. Incorrect. There is no evidence in this paragraph to support this statement.

D. **Correct.** Margaret Bourke-White created her own path and encouraged women to pursue the careers they wanted.

QUESTION 2

A. Incorrect. There is no mention of poverty on Margaret Bourke-White's college campus.

B. Incorrect. Powerful businessmen are more likely rich than poor.

C. Incorrect. This textual evidence mentions art and beauty, not poverty.

D. **Correct.** South Africans laboring in gold mines were likely poor, and Gandhi worked on behalf of the poor and powerless in India.

Margaret Bourke-White: Fearless Photographer

Skill:
Textual Evidence

Reread paragraphs 13–14 of "Margaret Bourke-White: Fearless Photographer." Then, using the Checklist on the previous page, answer the multiple-choice questions below.

↻ YOUR TURN

1. Using the textual evidence in paragraph 13, what is most likely an inference you can make about Margaret Bourke-White?

    ○ A. She was unable to become an advocate for women because of her profession.
    ○ B. She was able to become successful because her father was a powerful businessman.
    ○ C. She encouraged other women to pursue photography as a way to support equal rights.
    ○ D. She was an innovator and a symbol for women's rights and equality.

2. Which textual evidence best supports the author's claim in paragraph 14 that Margaret Bourke-White was "a strong voice for the poor and powerless"?

    ○ A. "Margaret's classmates at Cornell University became her first admirers when photographs she took of the campus appeared in the school newspapers."
    ○ B. "The city's powerful businessmen soon began calling on her to take pictures of their mills, factories, and buildings."
    ○ C. "As Margaret snapped artistic shots of workplaces, she was able to find beauty in simple objects."
    ○ D. "She photographed South Africans laboring in gold mines and civil rights leader Mahatma Gandhi's nonviolent work in India."

---

72   Reading & Writing Companion

ⓥ SKILL VOCABULARY

analyze / analizar *verb* to consider in detail and discover essential features or meaning COGNATE

interpret / interpretar *verb* to explain the meaning of (information, words, or actions) COGNATE

Skill: Technical Language

Skill: Technical Language

Use the Checklist to analyze Technical Language in "Margaret Bourke-White: Fearless Photographer." Refer to the sample student annotations about Technical Language in the text.

🔄 CHECKLIST FOR TECHNICAL LANGUAGE

In order to determine the meaning of words and phrases as they are used in a text, note the following:

- ✓ the subject of the book or article
- ✓ any unfamiliar words that you think might be technical terms
- ✓ words have multiple meanings that change when used with a specific subject
- ✓ the possible contextual meaning of a word, or the definition from a dictionary

To determine the meaning of words and phrases as they are used in a text, including technical meanings, consider the following questions:

- ✓ What is the subject of the informational text?
- ✓ Are there any unfamiliar words that look as if they might be technical language?
- ✓ Do any of the words in the text have more than one meaning?
- ✓ Can you identify the contextual meaning of any of the words?

Introduce the Skill

Watch the Concept Definition video and read the following definition with your students.

Technical language refers to words that are used in certain fields of knowledge. The **subject** is the field of knowledge the author writes about, such as astronomy or computer science, and it is an important part of determining the meaning of technical language. For example, if you know that archaeologists study human history based on things found in ancient ruins, and you read that an archaeologist has discovered an important artifact, you can guess that in this context the word *artifact* refers to an object made by a human being, usually an item of cultural or historical interest. Writers include technical language to educate readers, to make their explanation more **precise** and accurate, or to establish their **authority** on a subject. When a writer is being precise, they must be detailed but straightforward in their explanations of complex ideas and concepts. Being an authority, or expert, on a subject gives the writer credibility with readers.

TURN AND TALK

1. What are some examples of technical language associated with your favorite sport?

2. What do you do to explain the meaning of this technical language to a friend?

ELL SPEAKING FRAMES
- My favorite sport is ____.
- One example of technical language associated with my favorite sport is ____.
- I can explain [technical language] as ____.

V SKILL VOCABULARY

technical language / el lenguaje técnico *noun* words that are used in certain fields of knowledge, such as astronomy or computer science COGNATE

subject / la materia *noun* an area of knowledge to study

precise / preciso / a *adjective* clearly defined and accurate COGNATE

authority / la autoridad *noun* the power or right to give orders or make decisions; the power to be in charge COGNATE

Your Turn

Ask students to complete the Your Turn Activity.

QUESTION 1

A. **Correct.** This context clue allows the reader to understand that a flare is a type of illumination that produces white light.

B. **Incorrect.** This context clue provides information about the problem and why she introduced the flare, but not the meaning of the word "flare."

C. **Incorrect.** This context clue describes what the flare does, but not what the term itself means.

D. **Incorrect.** The flare cause national attention, but this context clue does not describe the meaning of the technical term.

QUESTION 2

A. **Incorrect.** She is not wanting to illuminate her camera. She needs to illuminate what she is photographing.

B. **Correct.** Margaret wants to illuminate what she is photographing.

C. **Incorrect.** A scene can refer to a part of a theater production, but this answer does not fit within the context of this text.

D. **Incorrect.** She is not trying to light the film; the film goes inside the camera. She needs to illuminate what she is photographing.

Margaret Bourke-White: Fearless Photographer

Skill:
Technical Language

Reread paragraph 5 of "Margaret Bourke-White: Fearless Photographer." Then, using the Checklist on the previous page, answer the multiple-choice questions below.

⟳ YOUR TURN

1. Which of the following context clues in the text help you to define the technical term "flare"?

   ○ A. "produces white light"
   ○ B. "came out all black"
   ○ C. "light her scenes"
   ○ D. "national attention"

2. Which of the following best defines "scenes" as it's used in the passage?

   ○ A. a type of camera
   ○ B. the subjects/locations of her photographs
   ○ C. a theater production
   ○ D. the film used

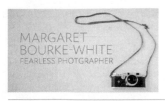

Close Read

Reread "Margaret Bourke-White: Fearless Photographer." As you reread, complete the Skills Focus questions below. Then use your answers and annotations from the questions to help you complete the Write activity.

◎ SKILLS FOCUS

1. "Margaret Bourke-White: Fearless Photographer" claims that Bourke-White "became a role model for working women." Identify textual evidence that supports this claim. Explain your reasoning.

2. Identify technical terms in "Margaret Bourke-White: Fearless Photographer" that relate to the subject of photography. Cite the evidence that helped you identify the terms' meanings.

3. In "Donna O'Meara: The Volcano Lady," the author presents textual evidence that suggests that O'Meara is attracted to the adventure of

photographing volcanoes. Identify evidence in "Margaret Bourke-White: Fearless Photographer" that suggests that Bourke-White was also motivated by a sense of adventure. Use the evidence to compare and contrast the career motivations of the two women.

4. "Margaret Bourke-White: Fearless Photographer" calls Bourke-White a trailblazer. Identify textual evidence that supports this claim. Explain how the evidence relates to the unit's essential question: How do you know what to do when there are no instructions?

✏ WRITE

COMPARATIVE: "Donna O'Meara: The Volcano Lady," "'Dare to Be Creative!,'" and "Margaret Bourke-White: Fearless Photographer" each describe a person motivated to do something other people see as impossible. They refuse to be manipulated into one way of thinking or living. Some people are motivated by role models or successes, while other people derive motivation from their experiences. Compare and contrast the main motivation of each individual in these three texts, using technical language when possible. Remember to use evidence from all three texts to support your ideas.

Reading & Writing Companion **75**

Close Read

Skills Focus

QUESTION 1: Textual Evidence

See paragraph 13.

QUESTION 2: Technical Language

See paragraphs 8 and 9.

QUESTION 3: Compare and Contrast

See paragraph 10.

QUESTION 4: Connect to Essential Question

See paragraphs 8 and 9. Being the first to do something makes you a trailblazer. Bourke-White was the first woman in photojournalism. The textual evidence indicates that she was willing to adapt her techniques to new situations. That is one way to handle situations when you don't have instructions.

✓ CHECK FOR SUCCESS

If students struggle to respond to Skills Focus Question #1, ask students the following questions:

- According to paragraph 3, what did Bourke-White do?

- What do you learn about Bourke-White's achievements in paragraph 13?

- How do these details support the claim that Bourke-White was a role model for working women?

📖 Writer's Notebook

Connect to Essential Question: Give students time to reflect on how "Margaret Bourke-White: Fearless Photographer" connects to the unit's essential question "How do we know what to do when there are no instructions?" by freewriting in their Writer's Notebooks.

ELL Beginning & Intermediate

Read aloud the unit's essential question: "How do we know what to do when there are no instructions?" Encourage students to draw their connections or allow students to write in their native language. Circulate around the room, prompting students for their thoughts as they respond orally or through pantomime.

Advanced & Advanced High

Allow students to share their connections orally in pairs or small groups before freewriting.

Collaborative Conversation

Break students into collaborative conversation groups to discuss the Close Read prompt. Remind them to reference their Skills Focus annotations in their discussion.

"Donna O'Meara: The Volcano Lady," "'Dare to Be Creative!," and "Margaret Bourke-White: Fearless Photographer" each describe a person motivated to do something other people see as impossible. They refuse to be manipulated into one way of thinking or living. Some people are motivated by role models or successes, while other people derive motivation from their experiences. Compare and contrast the main motivation of each individual in these three texts, using technical language when possible. Remember to use evidence from all three texts to support your ideas.

Use the scaffolds below to differentiate instruction for your **ELL** English Language Learners and **A** Approaching grade-level learners.

ELL **BEGINNING, INTERMEDIATE** Use the <u>discussion guide</u> and <u>speaking frames</u> to facilitate the discussion with support from the teacher.

ADVANCED, ADVANCED HIGH Use the <u>discussion guide</u> and <u>speaking frames</u> to facilitate the discussion in mixed-level groups.

A **APPROACHING** Use the <u>discussion guide</u> to facilitate the discussion in mixed-level groups.

APPROACHING

ADVANCED, ADVANCED HIGH

BEGINNING, INTERMEDIATE

Discussion Guide	Speaking Frames
1. What motivates Margaret Bourke-White?	• One thing that motivates Margaret Bourke-White is ____. • I know this because ____.
2. What motivates Donna O'Meara?	• One thing that motivates Donna O'Meara is ____. • I know this because ____.
3. How are the individuals' motivations similar or different?	• One way the motivations are similar is ____. • One way the motivations are different is ____.

Review Prompt and Rubric

Before students begin writing, review the writing prompt and rubric with the class.

COMPARATIVE: "Donna O'Meara: The Volcano Lady," "'Dare to be creative!," and "Margaret Bourke-White: Fearless Photographer" each describe a person motivated to do something other people see as impossible. They refuse to be manipulated into one way of thinking or living. Some people are motivated by role models or successes, while other people derive motivation from their experiences. Compare and contrast the main motivation of each individual in these three texts, using technical language when possible. Remember to use evidence from all three texts to support your ideas.

  PROMPT GUIDE

• What motivates Margaret Bourke-White?	• What motivates Madeleine L'Engle?
• What motivates Donna O'Meara?	• How are the individuals' motivations similar or different?

Score	Compare and Contrast	Technical Language	Language and Conventions
4	The writer clearly compares and contrasts the main motivation of each individual in the three texts. The writer provides exemplary analysis, using relevant evidence from the text.	The writer uses exemplary technical language to support his or her writing.	The writer demonstrates a consistent command of grammar, punctuation, and usage conventions. Although minor errors may be evident, they do not detract from the fluency or the clarity of the essay.
3	The writer compares and contrasts the main motivation of each individual in the three texts. The writer provides sufficient analysis, using relevant evidence from the text most of the time.	The writer uses sufficient technical language to support his or her writing.	The writer demonstrates an adequate command of grammar, punctuation, and usage conventions. Although some errors may be evident, they create few (if any) disruptions in the fluency of the writing or the clarity of the essay.
2	The writer begins to compare and contrast the main motivation of each individual in the three texts, but the analysis is incomplete. The writer uses relevant evidence from the text only some of the time.	The writer uses some technical language to support his or her writing, but the language does not provide much context for the response.	The writer demonstrates a partial command of grammar, punctuation, and usage conventions. Some distracting errors may be evident, at times creating minor disruptions in the fluency or clarity of the writing.
1	The writer attempts to compare and contrast the main motivation of each individual in the three texts, but the analysis is not successful. The writer uses little or no relevant evidence from the text.	The writer attempts to use technical language to support his or her writing, but makes errors that leave the reader with little or no context for the response.	The writer demonstrates little or no command of grammar, punctuation, and usage conventions. Serious and persistent errors create disruptions in the fluency of the writing and sometimes interfere with meaning.
0	The writer does not provide a relevant response to the prompt or does not provide a response at all.	The writer does not use technical language to support his or her writing.	Serious and persistent errors overwhelm the writing and interfere with the meaning of the response as a whole, making the writer's meaning impossible to understand.

Write

Ask students to complete the writing assignment using textual evidence to support their answers.

Use the scaffolds below to differentiate instruction for your **ELL** English Language Learners and **A** Approaching grade-level learners.

ELL **BEGINNING** With the help of the <u>word bank</u>, write a response using <u>paragraph frame 1</u>.

INTERMEDIATE With the help of the <u>word bank</u>, write a response using <u>paragraph frames 1 and 2</u>.

ADVANCED, ADVANCED HIGH Write a response of differentiated length using the <u>sentence starters</u>.

A **APPROACHING** Write a response of differentiated length using the <u>sentence starters</u>.

| BEGINNING | | ADVANCED, ADVANCED HIGH |
| INTERMEDIATE | | APPROACHING |

Word Bank	Paragraph Frame 1	Paragraph Frame 2	Sentence Starters
adventure skills and abilities daring fitting in critics	Margaret Bourke-White, Donna O'Meara, and Madeleine L'Engle derive motivation from a sense of ____. L'Engle wrote a passionate speech about "shaking up the universe" by daring to be different, and Bourke-White and O'Meara are also considered to be ____ in their fields of work. Bourke-White and L'Engle are motivated by something else, too. They are motivated by the challenge of ____. Bourke-White even convinced ____ that she belonged by using her ____.	O'Meara and Bourke-White were also motivated by the ____. O'Meara was able to succeed in part because ____. Bourke-White was able to succeed in part because ____. Bourke-White appears to have dreamed of ____. O'Meara, on the other hand, developed her passion for ____. L'Engle had a passion for ____.	• Margaret Bourke-White, Donna O'Meara, and Madeleine L'Engle derived motivation from . . . • Bourke-White/O'Meara/L'Engle was . . . • Like O'Meara, Bourke-White . . . • Like L'Engle, Bourke-White . . . • Unlike O'Meara, Bourke-White . . . • Unlike O'Meara, L'Engle . . . • I know this because . . .

Peer Review

Students should submit substantive feedback to two peers using the review instructions below.

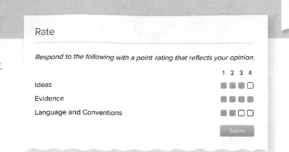

- How well does this response answer the prompt?
- How well does the writer support his or her ideas with details and examples from each text?
- Which sentence in the writer's response made you think differently about each text?
- What does the writer do well in this response? What does the writer need to work on?

 SENTENCE FRAMES

- You were able to (completely / partly / almost) ____ answer the prompt because ____.
- You could answer the prompt more completely by ____.
- You supported the idea of . . . with the detail of ____.

- One idea that needs more support is ____.
- I thought differently about the texts after reading ____.
- My favorite part of your responses is ____.

Blast: A Single Line

TEXT TALK

What are you thinking after finishing the *In the Dark* unit? What is your opinion of this theme based on the unit's selections? Answers may vary.

What is one strategy you can use for self-selecting a new text? How does it work? I can look at visual information to help me decide what I want to read.

What should you do once you choose a text that interests you? Start reading the text to confirm my interest. If I like it, I should keep reading.

Create Your Own Blast

SCAFFOLDS

Ask students to write a 140-character Blast after they complete the QuikPoll.

Use the scaffolds below to differentiate instruction for your **ELL** English Language Learners.

ELL **BEGINNING** Write a response using the <u>word bank</u> to complete the <u>sentence frames</u>.

INTERMEDIATE Write a response using the <u>sentence frames</u>.

ADVANCED, ADVANCED HIGH Write a response using the <u>sentence starter</u>.

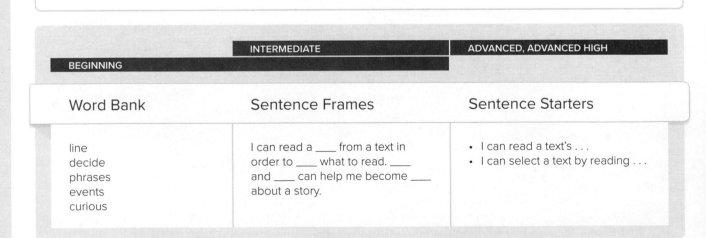

BEGINNING	INTERMEDIATE	ADVANCED, ADVANCED HIGH
Word Bank	Sentence Frames	Sentence Starters
line decide phrases events curious	I can read a ___ from a text in order to ___ what to read. ___ and ___ can help me become ___ about a story.	• I can read a text's . . . • I can select a text by reading . . .

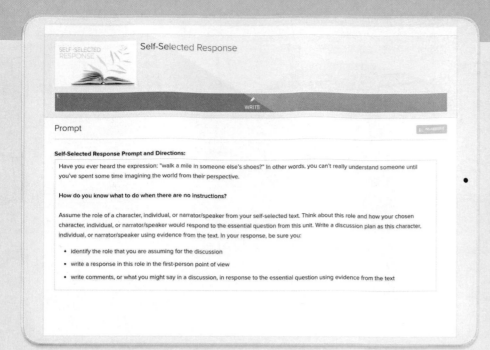

 Self-Selected Response

Introduce the Prompt

Read aloud the prompt. Ask students to discuss:

- What is the prompt asking you to do?

- Why might it be helpful to think about the world from another person's point of view?

Write

SCAFFOLDS

Ask students to complete the writing assignment using text evidence to support their answers.

Use the scaffolds below to differentiate instruction for your **ELL** English Language Learners and **A** Approaching grade level learners.

ELL **BEGINNING** With the help of the <u>word bank</u>, write a response using <u>paragraph frame 1</u>.

INTERMEDIATE With the help of the <u>word bank</u>, write a response using <u>paragraph frames 1 and 2</u>.

ADVANCED, ADVANCED HIGH Write a response of differentiated length using the <u>sentence starters</u>.

A **APPROACHING** Write a response of differentiated length using the <u>sentence starters</u>.

BEGINNING / INTERMEDIATE		INTERMEDIATE	ADVANCED, ADVANCED HIGH / APPROACHING
Word Bank	Paragraph Frame 1	Paragraph Frame 2	Sentence Starters
happy nervous difficult sad tense mysterious angry anxious upsetting surprised frustrated scary excited relieved thrilling	I am (character/individual/speaker/narrator) ____ from the text (title) ____ by (author) ____. One event where I needed to know what to do without any instruction was ____. I ____ when this event happened because ____. Some comments I might make in the discussion include: 1. I felt ____ when ____. 2. When there are no directions, I can ____. 3. I would describe this event as ____.	I am (character/individual/speaker/narrator) ____ from the text (title) ____ by (author) ____. One event where I needed to know what to do without any instruction was ____. I ____ when this event happened because ____. Some comments I might make in the discussion include: 1. I felt ____ when ____. 2. When there are no directions, I can ____. 3. I would describe this event as ____. I think it will be especially hard to know ____. I am also unsure of ____.	• I am . . . from the text . . . • One important event from the story is . . . • I felt . . . when this event happened to me . . . • I would . . . when there are no instructions • I would do this because . . . • Another thing I would do is . . .

Extended Writing Project

EXTENDED WRITING PROJECT INFORMATIVE WRITING

The Extended Writing Project (EWP) in Grade 6, Unit 3 focuses on informative writing. Students consider the following question—What motivates us to conquer feelings of uncertainty?—as they write a proposal identifying three people from the selection and explaining what drives them to respond, take action, or make a decision. The unit's selections about individual bravery provide many examples to analyze. Specific skill lessons teach developing ideas, organization, and conventions, while other skill lessons focus on thesis statement, supporting details, and introductions and conclusions, and help students convey information clearly. Directed revision leads students through the process of revising for clarity, development, organization, word choice, and sentence variety. Throughout the EWP, students have the opportunity to practice using created student writing, authentic texts, and their own work.

 Audio and audio text highlighting are available in select lessons in the Extended Writing Project.

CONNECT TO ESSENTIAL QUESTION

How do you know what to do when there are no instructions?

In this unit students read about motivation in the face of uncertainty. Now students will synthesize the experiences of the characters, subjects, and authors of this unit's texts into an informative essay about conquering uncertainty.

Extended Writing Project Prompt

What motivates us to conquer feelings of uncertainty?

Think about the individuals from this unit who take action even when they are unsure of what lies ahead. Identify three of these individuals and write an informative essay explaining what drives them to respond, take action, or make a decision when there are no guidelines to help them.

 **SCAFFOLDS**    **ELL ENGLISH LANGUAGE LEARNERS**    **A APPROACHING GRADE LEVEL**    **B BEYOND GRADE LEVEL**

These icons identify differentiation strategies and scaffolded support for a variety of students. See the digital lesson plan for additional differentiation strategies and scaffolds.

Instructional Path

Informative Writing Process: Plan

Objectives: After learning about genre characteristics and craft, students will analyze a sample Student Model and plan a meaningful informative essay in response to a prompt.

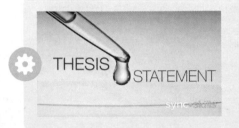

Skill: Thesis Statement

Objectives: After reading and discussing a model of student writing, students will write a clear thesis statement that explains the main or controlling idea of an essay.

Skill: Organizing Informative Writing

Objectives: After reading and discussing a model of student writing, students will identify a purpose for writing an informative essay and choose a text structure that supports the purpose.

Skill: Supporting Details

Objectives: After reading and discussing a model of student writing, students will use details to support the writer's main idea in an informative essay.

Informative Writing Process: Draft

Objectives: After reading a Student Model draft and reviewing a writing checklist, students will draft a focused, organized, and coherent informative essay in response to a prompt.

Skill: Introductions

Objectives: After reading and discussing a model of student writing, students will improve an informative essay by revising the introduction to grab a reader's attention.

The print teacher's edition includes essential point-of-use instruction and planning tools. Complete lesson plans and program documents appear in your digital teacher account.

Skill: Transitions

Objectives: After reading and discussing a model of student writing, students will develop their drafts by using appropriate transitions to clarify the relationships among ideas and concepts.

Skill: Precise Language

Objectives: After reading and discussing a model of student writing, students will develop their drafts by using precise language and domain-specific vocabulary to inform the reader or explain the topic.

Skill: Style

Objectives: After reading and discussing a model of student writing, students will develop their drafts by establishing and maintaining a formal style.

Skill: Conclusions

Objectives: After reading and discussing a model of student writing, students will improve an informative essay by revising the conclusion to rephrase the main idea so that readers remember it.

Informative Writing Process: Revise

Objectives: Revise an informative essay draft for clarity, development, organization, style, word choice, and sentence variety.

Grammar: Parentheses, Brackets, and Ellipses

Objectives: After learning about parentheses, brackets, and ellipses and seeing how they are used in text examples, students will practice using parentheses, brackets, and ellipses correctly.

Instructional Path

The print teacher's edition includes essential point-of-use instruction and planning tools. Complete lesson plans and program documents appear in your digital teacher account.

Grammar: Prefixes

Objectives: After learning about prefixes and seeing how they are used in text examples, students will practice using prefixes correctly.

Grammar: Spelling Rules II

Objectives: After learning about spelling rules and seeing how they are used in text examples, students will practice using spelling rules correctly.

Informative Writing Process: Edit and Publish

Objectives: After seeing an example of editing in the Student Model and reviewing an editing checklist, students will edit and publish the final draft of their informative essay.

Progress Monitoring

Opportunities to Learn	Opportunities to Demonstrate Learning	Opportunities to Reteach
Informative Writing Process: Plan		
Informative Writing Process: Plan	Informative Writing Process: Plan • Write	Units 4–6 Process: Plan
Informative Writing Process: Draft		
Informative Writing Process: Draft	Informative Writing Process: Draft • Write	Units 4–6 Process: Draft

Opportunities to Learn	Opportunities to Demonstrate Learning	Opportunities to Reteach

Informative Writing Process: Revise

Informative Writing Process: Revise	Informative Writing Process: Revise • Write	Units 4–6 Process: Revise

Informative Writing Process: Edit and Publish

Informative Writing Process: Edit and Publish	Informative Writing Process: Edit and Publish • Write	Units 4, 6 Process: Edit and Publish Unit 5 Process: Edit and Present

Thesis Statement

Skill: Thesis Statement	Skill: Thesis Statement • Your Turn Informative Writing Process: Draft	Unit 4 Skill: Thesis Statement Spotlight Skill: Thesis Statement

	Opportunities to Learn	Opportunities to Demonstrate Learning	Opportunities to Reteach

Organizing Informative Writing

| Skill: Organizing Informative Writing | Skill: Organizing Informative Writing
 • Your Turn

 Informative Writing Process: Draft | Spotlight Skill: Organizing Informative Writing |

Supporting Details

| Skill: Supporting Details | Skill: Supporting Details
 • Your Turn

 Informative Writing Process: Draft | Spotlight Skill: Supporting Details |

Introductions

| Skill: Introductions | Skill: Introductions
 • Your Turn

 Informative Writing Process: Revise | Unit 4
 Skill: Introductions

 Spotlight Skill: Introductions |

Transitions

| Skill: Transitions | Skill: Transitions
 • Your Turn

 Informative Writing Process: Revise | Unit 4
 Skill: Transitions

 Spotlight Skill: Transitions |

Opportunities to Learn	Opportunities to Demonstrate Learning	Opportunities to Reteach

Precise Language

⚙ Skill: Precise Language	⚙ Skill: Precise Language • Your Turn ✏ Informative Writing Process: Revise	⚙ Spotlight Skill: Precise Language

Style

⚙ Skill: Style	⚙ Skill: Style • Your Turn ✏ Informative Writing Process: Revise	⚙ Unit 4 Skill: Style ⚙ Spotlight Skill: Style

Conclusions

⚙ Skill: Conclusions	⚙ Skill: Conclusions • Your Turn ✏ Informative Writing Process: Revise	⚙ Unit 4 Skill: Conclusions ⚙ Spotlight Skill: Conclusions

Opportunities to Learn	Opportunities to Demonstrate Learning	Opportunities to Reteach

Parentheses, Brackets, and Ellipses

⚙ Grammar: Parentheses, Brackets, and Ellipses	⚙ Grammar: Parentheses, Brackets, and Ellipses • Your Turn ✎ Informative Writing Process: Edit and Publish	⚙ Grammar: Colons and Semicolons — Semicolons

Prefixes

⚙ Grammar: Prefixes	⚙ Grammar: Prefixes • Your Turn ✎ Informative Writing Process: Edit and Publish	⚙ Grammar: Spelling — Suffixes

Basic Spelling Rules II

⚙ Grammar: Basic Spelling Rules II	⚙ Grammar: Basic Spelling Rules II • Your Turn ✎ Informative Writing Process: Edit and Publish	⚙ Grammar: Spelling — Homophones

Informative Writing Process: Plan

Introduce the Extended Writing Project

- What is the prompt asking you to do?

- What are the five characteristics of informative writing?

- Which characteristics of informative writing will you need to learn more about in order to respond to the prompt?

DIFFERENTIATED QUESTIONS

A
- What do *motivate* and *uncertainty* mean?

- What are some situations that might lead to feelings of uncertainty?

- How can we become more sure of what lies ahead?

Informative Writing Process: Plan

PLAN	DRAFT	REVISE	EDIT AND PUBLISH

The texts in this unit feature individuals who are driven to act without instructions, a clear plan, or a certain outcome. Margaret Bourke-White became the first female war photojournalist, sacrificing her safety in order to capture important moments in history. In one of the most popular Greek myths, Perseus sets out on a quest to defeat the snake-haired Gorgon, Medusa. He does not know if he'll survive the battle. Hatshepsut became the first female leader in ancient Egypt to call herself "pharaoh," breaking tradition and gender barriers throughout her reign. What motivates, or moves, these individuals to attempt something no one has done before?

WRITING PROMPT

What motivates us to conquer feelings of uncertainty?

Think about the individuals from this unit who take action even when they are unsure of what lies ahead. Identify three of these individuals and write an informative essay explaining what drives them to respond, take action, or make a decision when there are no guidelines to help them. Be sure your informative essay includes the following:

- an introduction
- a thesis or controlling idea
- coherent body paragraphs
- supporting details
- a conclusion

Writing to Sources

As you gather ideas and information from the texts in the unit, be sure to:

- use evidence from multiple sources; and
- avoid overly relying on one source.

Reading & Writing Companion

Introduction to Informative Writing

Writers of informative texts provide facts and details related to historical, scientific, and cultural topics. An informative text presents readers with information, facts, and ideas about real people, places, things, and events. The text should include an introduction with a thesis statement, or the main idea about the topic, body paragraphs that include details that support the main idea, and a conclusion.

Text structure refers to the way a writer organizes the information in a nonfiction text. It is an organizational pattern that is used to present facts and other information clearly. There are several different types of informative text structures. For instance, a writer may:

- describe a process or a series of steps to follow in sequential order
- tell about events in chronological order
- discuss ideas in order of importance
- compare and contrast information
- present cause and effect relationships
- list advantages and disadvantages
- describe a problem and offer a solution
- define the essential, or most important, qualities of a subject
- classify, or organize, information into categories and subcategories

A writer may use more than one organizational pattern within the same text. In addition, a text structure can be used to organize information about more than one topic.

Analyzing the structure of an informative text helps a reader to follow what a writer is trying to say and understand how different facts and details are related. It can also help a reader identify the main, or controlling, idea.

As you continue with this Extended Writing Project, you'll receive more instruction and practice at crafting each of the characteristics of informative writing. This will help you to create your own informative text.

Review the Rubric

Have students examine the Informative Writing Rubric—Grade 6 grading rubric this Student Model was written to satisfy. Inform students that this is the same rubric that will be used to evaluate their completed Informative Extended Writing Project.

Read and Annotate

As students read, have them use the Annotation Tool to identify and label the five characteristics of informative writing:

- an introduction
- a thesis or controlling idea
- coherent body paragraphs
- supporting details
- a conclusion

When students finish reading, ask them to share their annotations in small groups.

ELL ANNOTATION GUIDE

Find the following quotes in the Student Model. Then, use the Annotation Tool to label each quote as an example of comparing and contrasting information, a cause-and-effect relationship, or defining the essential qualities of a subject.

- Like Donna O'Meara, the character Roy in *Hoot* is motivated by a desire for knowledge.
- When Roy tells Dana "I've had enough," Dana lets him go.
- Each person or character is motivated by a desire to know something for certain.
- When these billions of people tried to go back to their homes, they would run out of food, water, and fuel.

A READ AND ANNOTATE

Pair students with on-grade-level peers to complete the annotation activity.

Before you get started on your own informative text, read this informative essay that one student, Colin, wrote in response to the writing prompt. As you read the Model, highlight and annotate the features of informative writing that Colin included in his text.

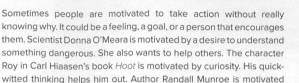

1 Sometimes people are motivated to take action without really knowing why. It could be a feeling, a goal, or a person that encourages them. Scientist Donna O'Meara is motivated by a desire to understand something dangerous. She also wants to help others. The character Roy in Carl Hiaasen's book *Hoot* is motivated by curiosity. His quick-witted thinking helps him out. Author Randall Munroe is motivated by mathematical reasoning. He wants to answer what seems to be an impossible question. Each of these people or characters has a different motivation and faces different obstacles and problems, but they all learn something important.

2 Donna O'Meara's desire to understand how volcanoes work has sometimes put her in danger. Most people would probably be afraid to get close to a volcano. There's a lot we don't know about them. But O'Meara has risked her life to study them. During her first visit to a volcano, she dodged "lava bombs," and hot lava melted her shoes. Another time, she and her husband Steve "were trapped on a ledge in the freezing cold with scalding rocks flying around them." The desire for knowledge has pushed O'Meara to conquer the unknown and hazardous world of volcanoes. Now she's an expert on volcanoes. She shares her knowledge to help keep others safe when volcanoes erupt. She hopes her work will "help save the lives of people who live near" volcanoes.

3 Like Donna O'Meara, the character Roy in *Hoot* is motivated by a desire for knowledge. He's also clever when it comes to dealing with problems. These qualities help Roy, who's the new kid at school, deal with Dana the bully. Dana is attacking Roy on his way to school when Roy sees a boy running past the school bus. Even though Dana is hurting him, Roy is "gripped with curiosity" about the boy: "Who was he? What was he running from?" Roy doesn't care about the pain. He just wants Dana to stop bothering him, and he is smarter than Dana. Although Roy might not know the boy running past the

Reading & Writing Companion **79**

TEXT TALK

Purpose

Where does Colin introduce the thesis, or purpose, in his essay?

See paragraph 1: Colin's thesis comes at the end of his first paragraph, or introduction: "Each of these people or characters has a different motivation and faces different obstacles and problems, but they all learn something important."

Focus

How does Colin begin each body paragraph to maintain a coherent structure in his essay?

Each body paragraph begins with a sentence explaining the character's motivation.

NOTES

bus, he does know that Dana is "a well-known idiot." Roy also knows that fighting back would be "a complete waste of energy." When Roy tells Dana "I've had enough," Dana lets him go. Now Roy, released from the grip of Dana's hands, is free to wonder about the strange boy. Roy's curiosity and his intelligence help him get out of a bad situation.

4 In "Everybody Jump," scientist Randall Munroe is motivated to use mathematical reasoning to answer a difficult question: "What would happen if everyone on earth stood as close to each other as they could and jumped . . . at the same instant?" This could never happen in real life, but Munroe takes the question seriously. He knows that "many others" are curious about this topic and uncertain about the answer. Munroe uses mathematical reasoning, or logic, to explain the unknown. In his conclusion, he says that everyone jumping at once in the same place would have "little effect" on the planet. But then some terrible things would happen. When these billions of people tried to go back to their homes, they would run out of food, water, and fuel. They would probably become violent and die "within weeks." Munroe paints an ugly picture, but it's where his reasoning takes him. He ends by stating certainly, "at least now we know."

5 Donna O'Meara could have been hurt as she tried to find answers to her questions about volcanoes, but her wish to learn more and help others kept her pushing forward. Curiosity and intelligence help Roy get through the experience of being bullied. Randall Munroe's logic leads him to conquer feelings of uncertainty about a frightening event. Each person or character is motivated by a desire to know something for certain. Even though none of them is sure what will happen next, they are all motivated into action. As a result, they learn something about themselves and the world.

TEXT TALK

Organization

How does Colin organize his main ideas in support of his thesis? See paragraphs 2–4: Colin organizes each main body paragraph around one of the characters he introduced in the first paragraph. He explains each person's motivation and the obstacles she or he overcame.

Evidence

How does Colin use specific examples from each text to support his ideas? Answers will vary. Sample answer: In paragraph 3, Colin includes specific quotations from the text, *Hoot,* to support the idea that Roy is motivated by curiosity: "Even though Dana is hurting him, Roy is 'gripped with curiosity' about the boy: 'Who was he? What was he running from?'"

Elaboration

Are Colin's supporting details effective? Why or why not? Answers will vary. Sample answer: Yes, I think Colin chooses effective examples from the texts to explain the people's and characters' motivations.

Word Choice

Are there any places where Colin's word choice could be stronger or more effective? Answers will vary. Sample answer: Yes. In paragraph 4, Colin writes, "Munroe paints an *ugly picture*, but it's where his reasoning takes him." He could have used a more specific phrase, such as "a frightening picture of the outcome."

Sentence Fluency

Do the last three sentences of the conclusion provide an effective closing statement? Why or why not? Answers will vary. Sample answer: Yes, the last three sentences restate the essay's thesis effectively and leave the reader with a strong final impression.

Conventions

Does Colin correctly use prefixes throughout his essay? Answers will vary. Sample answer: Yes, he correctly uses prefixes, such as in the words *impossible, unknown,* and *uncertain.*

Write

Circulate as students use the questions in the bulleted list to plan their writing. See the instructions for scaffolding and differentiation that follow.

✔ CHECK FOR SUCCESS

If students struggle to come up with answers for the questions in the lesson, work with students to provide an answer to one question and then help them build from there.

For example, start by asking students, "Which individual from the unit interested you the most?" Once students have answered one question, help them to work through a second question until they've begun to build some momentum. It may be helpful to start with a different question than the one that's listed first in the lesson.

✏ WRITE

Writers often take notes about their ideas before they sit down to write. Think about what you've learned so far about informative writing to help you begin prewriting.

- Which three individuals from this unit will you focus on in your informative text?

- What steps did they take in order to move forward even when they felt uncertain?

- Were there any cause and effect relationships that set each individual's story in motion?

- How will you compare and contrast each individual's situation?

- Which texts will you use to support your ideas? Will you need to do more research?

Response Instructions

Use the questions in the bulleted list to write a one-paragraph summary. Your summary should describe what your informative essay will be about.

Don't worry about including all of the details now; focus only on the most essential and important elements. You will refer back to this short summary as you continue through the steps of the writing process.

Review Prompt and Rubric

Before students begin writing, review the writing prompt and rubric with the class.

Response Instructions

Use the questions in the bulleted list on the previous page to write a one-paragraph summary. Your summary should describe what your informative essay will be about.

Don't worry about including all of the details now; focus only on the most essential and important elements. You will refer back to this short summary as you continue through the steps of the writing process.

Score	Informative Plan	Language and Conventions
4	The writer responds to the questions, and the writing is clear and focused.	The writer demonstrates a consistent command of grammar, punctuation, and usage conventions. Although minor errors may be evident, they do not detract from the fluency or clarity of the writing.
3	The writer responds to the questions, but the writing is not always clear or focused.	The writer demonstrates an adequate command of grammar, punctuation, and usage conventions. Although some errors may be evident, they create few (if any) disruptions in the fluency or clarity of the writing.
2	The writer responds to the questions, but the writing is somewhat unclear and unfocused.	The writer demonstrates a partial command of grammar, punctuation, and usage conventions. Some distracting errors may be evident, at times creating minor disruptions in the fluency or clarity of the writing.
1	The writer responds to the questions, but the writing is very unclear and unfocused.	The writer demonstrates little or no command of grammar, punctuation, and usage conventions. Serious and persistent errors create disruptions in the fluency of the writing and sometimes interfere with meaning.
0	The writer does not provide a relevant response to the prompt or does not provide a response at all.	Serious and persistent errors overwhelm the writing and interfere with the meaning of the response as a whole, making the writer's meaning impossible to understand.

Write

SCAFFOLDS

Use the scaffolds below to differentiate instruction for your **ELL** English Language Learners and **A** Approaching grade-level learners.

ELL **BEGINNING, INTERMEDIATE** With the help of the <u>word bank</u>, write a response using the <u>paragraph frame</u>.

ADVANCED, ADVANCED HIGH Write a response using the <u>sentence starters</u>.

A **APPROACHING** Write a response using the <u>sentence starters</u>.

BEGINNING	ADVANCED, ADVANCED HIGH
INTERMEDIATE	APPROACHING

Word Bank	Paragraph Frame	Sentence Starters
Percy Jackson learning about his father themselves "shaking the universe" volcanoes Madeleine L'Engle Donna O'Meara	My essay will be about ____, ____, and ____. Donna O'Meara wants to learn about ____, so she risks her life to study them. ____ is motivated by ____, which helps him discover that he's not an ordinary boy, but rather, the son of a god. I will include supporting details about ____ and how she gave a speech about ____. These three people's experiences teach them something about ____ and the world.	• My essay will be about . . . • [Individual] wanted to . . . • He/she was motivated by . . . • I will include supporting details from . . . • I will conclude by . . .

Peer Review

Students should submit substantive feedback to two peers using the review instructions below.

• How well does this response answer the prompt?
• What part of the informative essay are you most excited to read about?
• Are there any ideas that could be improved on? How so?

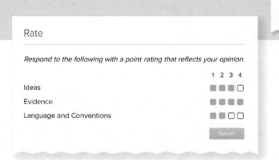

Rate

Respond to the following with a point rating that reflects your opinion.

	1 2 3 4
Ideas	■ ■ ■ □
Evidence	■ ■ ■ ■
Language and Conventions	■ ■ □ □

Submit

ELL
A **SENTENCE FRAMES**

• The response does a good job of addressing ____ from the prompt.
• The response would improve by addressing ____ from the prompt.

• I am most excited to read about ____.
• I think you could improve ____ by (adding / clarifying / describing) ____.

Extended Writing Project

Skill:
Thesis Statement

••• CHECKLIST FOR THESIS STATEMENT

Before you begin writing your thesis statement, ask yourself the following questions:

- What is the prompt asking me to write about?
- What is the topic of my essay?
- What claim do I want to make about the topic of this essay? Is my opinion clear to my reader?
- Does my thesis statement introduce the body of my essay?
- Where should I place my thesis statement?

Here are some methods to introduce and develop your claim and topic:

- think about the topic and central idea of your essay
  - > the central idea of an argument is stated as a claim, or what will be proven or shown to be true
  - > identify as many claims as you intend to prove
- write a clear statement about the central idea or claim. Your thesis statement should:
  - > let the reader anticipate the body of your essay
  - > respond completely to the writing prompt
- consider the best placement for your thesis statement
  - > if your response is short, you may want to get right to the point. Your thesis statement may be presented in the first sentence of the essay.
  - > if your response is longer (as in a formal essay), you can build up your thesis statement. In this case, you can place your thesis statement at the end of your introductory paragraph.

Introduce the Skill

Watch the Concept Definition video ▶ and read the following definition with your students.

In an essay, a **thesis statement** expresses the writer's main idea about a topic. The thesis statement usually appears in the **introduction,** or opening paragraph of your essay, and is often the last sentence of the introduction. The **body paragraphs** of the essay should offer a thorough explanation of the thesis statement as well as supporting details, reasons, and relevant evidence. The thesis is often restated in the **conclusion** of an essay.

ⓥ SKILL VOCABULARY

thesis statement / la presentación de la tesis *noun* a statement that shares the main idea of an argumentative or informative essay

introduction / la introducción *noun* the opening paragraph or section of an essay COGNATE

body paragraph / el párrafo del cuerpo *noun* a paragraph that appears between the introduction and the conclusion of an essay

conclusion / la conclusión *noun* the closing paragraph or section of an essay; a closing argument in an argumentative text COGNATE

⚙ TURN AND TALK

Turn to your partner and brainstorm a list of nonfiction books, articles, and documentaries and each of their corresponding main ideas.

ELL SPEAKING FRAMES

- The main idea of ___ is ___.
- Another example of a main idea of a book or article is ___.

Your Turn

Ask students to complete the Your Turn activity.

When Donna went back to school . . .	not thesis
For over 25 years . . .	thesis
Donna says the experience . . .	not thesis
The following year . . .	not thesis

Write

Ask students to complete the writing assignment.

ELL **REWRITE CHECKLIST**

A
☐ What ideas would you like to discuss in your essay?

☐ How do these ideas relate to one larger idea? This larger idea is your thesis statement.

☐ How can you clearly express your thesis in one or two short sentences? Remember that your thesis statement should:

  ☐ let the reader know what the rest of your essay will be about.

  ☐ respond to the writing prompt.

↻ YOUR TURN

Read the excerpts from *Donna O'Meara: Volcano Lady* below. Then, complete the chart by sorting them into those that are thesis statements and those that are not. Write your answer in the second column.

Excerpts	Thesis Statement or Not Thesis Statement?
When Donna went back to school at the age of 32 to study science, her passion for volcanoes began.	
For over 25 years, she has worked with Steve to photograph and study volcanoes all over the world. They hope their documentation will someday be a written and visual record of information that helps scientists to better predict volcanic eruptions.	
Donna says the experience of being stranded on Mt. Stromboli for one freezing night was the scariest experience of her life.	
The following year, she and Steve were married on lava that had oozed from Kilauea on Hawaii and hardened. Lava that hardens creates new landforms, and some volcanoes, such as Surtsey off the coast of Iceland, actually create new islands!	

Copyright © BookheadEd Learning, LLC

✏ WRITE

Use the list and questions from the checklist to write a thesis statement for your essay.

Reading & Writing Companion **83**

Writer's Notebook

Project the following list of questions on the board. Ask students to choose one question and imagine that it is a writing prompt for an essay. Instruct them to write a sample thesis statement for the essay.

1. How much television should kids be allowed to watch each day?
2. At what age should kids be allowed to have cell phones?
3. Who is a better entertainer: Taylor Swift or Beyoncé?

ELL **TURN AND TALK**

Allow students to share their thesis statements orally in pairs or small groups before writing.

Extended Writing Project

Skill:
Organizing Informative Writing

••• CHECKLIST FOR ORGANIZING INFORMATIVE WRITING

As you consider how to organize your writing for your informative essay, use the following questions as a guide:

- What is my topic? How can I summarize the main idea?
- What is the logical order of my ideas, concepts, and information? Do I see a pattern that is similar to a specific text structure?
- Which organizing structure should I use to present my information?
- How might using graphics, headings, or some form of multimedia help to present my information?

Here are some strategies to help you organize ideas, concepts, and information and aid comprehension:

- definition is useful for:
  - > defining a difficult idea or concept
  - > defining the essential qualities of a subject
  - > teaching readers about a topic or how to do something
  - > providing examples
  - > restating a definition in different ways to help readers understand the subject
- classification is useful for:
  - > dividing larger ideas and concepts into subcategories that are easier to understand
  - > sorting information into subcategories
  - > using subcategories to clarify ideas and provide detailed descriptions
- compare and contrast is useful for:
  - > comparing the similarities and differences between two texts, ideas, or concepts
- cause and effect is useful for:
  - > explaining what and why something happened
  - > understanding how things change over time

Copyright © BookheadEd Learning, LLC

84 Reading & Writing Companion

V SKILL VOCABULARY

informative writing / la escritura informativa *noun* nonfiction writing that presents information about real people, places, things, and events

organizational structure / la estructura organizativa *noun* the order or pattern that a writer uses to organize information, such as cause-and-effect or compare-and-contrast COGNATE

heading / el título *noun* the title given to a particular section of text

graphics / las gráficas *noun* charts or tables that can make complex information easier to understand COGNATE

multimedia / multimedia *adjective* using several communications media at the same time COGNATE

Skill: Organizing Informative Writing

Introduce the Skill

Watch the Concept Definition video and read the following definition with your students.

The purpose of **informative writing** is to inform readers about real people, places, things, and events, so authors need to organize their ideas, concepts, and information in a logical way. Experienced authors carefully choose an **organizational structure,** such as definition, classification, compare/contrast, and cause/effect, that best suits their material. Writers often use an outline to decide which organizational structure will help them express their ideas. For example, texts about historical topics might need a cause/effect structure to explain why something happened. **Headings** that divide a series of paragraphs can make organization obvious. They tell readers how information is arranged and presented. A reader can scan a document and find specific information. Some writers also use **graphics,** such as charts and tables, or **multimedia,** such as video, sound, and hypertext links, to make complex information easier to understand. The organizational structure should always be appropriate for the writing purpose.

TURN AND TALK

Turn to your partner and brainstorm a list of informative texts you've read recently.

ELL SPEAKING FRAMES
- One example of an informative text is ___.
- It is organized using a ___ text structure.

- visual elements
  > use headings to organize your essay into groups of information
  > use graphics, such as charts or tables, to visually represent large amounts of information
  > use multimedia, such as video, sound, and hypertext links, to help readers understand complex ideas and concepts

Extended Writing Project

 YOUR TURN

Read the thesis statements and descriptions of each writer's overall purpose for writing below. Then, complete the chart by writing the organizational structure that would best develop the thesis and achieve the writer's overall purpose.

Organizational Structure Options
Cause and Effect   Steps in a Process in Sequential Order   Compare and Contrast   Problem and Solution

Thesis	Purpose	Organizational Structure
The Civil War reshaped American ideas about freedom by resolving the question of slavery.	to show how the Civil War caused Americans to change the way they think about freedom	
Although many people prefer cats, some people find dogs to be the best companions.	to show the differences and similarities between cat ownership and dog ownership	
Bullying is a serious issue for some students, but with support from teachers, parents, and administrators, we can eliminate the problem.	to present a possible solution for the problem of bullying in schools	
The Hudson River is the longest glacial river in America, and the way it was formed is quite fascinating.	to explain how the Hudson River was formed	

✏️ **WRITE**

Use the steps in the checklist to plan out the organization of your informative essay.

 Your Turn

Ask students to complete the Your Turn activity.

The Civil War reshaped American ideas about freedom by resolving the question of slavery.	to show how the Civil War caused Americans to change the way they think about freedom	Cause and Effect
Although many people prefer cats, some people find dogs to be the best companions.	to show the differences and similarities between cat ownership and dog ownership	Compare and Contrast
Bullying is a serious issue for some students, but with support from teachers, parents, and administrators, we can eliminate the problem.	to present a possible solution for the problem of bullying in schools	Problem and Solution
The Hudson River is the longest glacial river in America, and the way it was formed is quite fascinating.	to explain how the Hudson River was formed	Steps in a Process in Sequential Order

 Write

Ask students to complete the writing assignment.

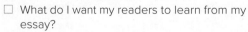

ELL REWRITE CHECKLIST

A ☐ What am I being asked to write about?

☐ What do I want my readers to learn from my essay?

Skill: Supporting Details

Introduce the Skill

Watch the Concept Definition video and read the following definition with your students.

In informative and argumentative writing, writers develop their thesis statements or claims with information called **supporting details.** These details can include any kind of textual evidence, such as descriptions, examples, reasons, quotations that reveal expert opinions, facts, and statistics. Supporting details help explain key ideas and are closely related to the topic.

Supporting details that develop a thesis statement or claim must be **relevant,** necessary, or concrete. Relevant supporting details are appropriate and logically related to the topic. **Necessary** details are essential and required for developing a writer's thesis statement or proving a writer's claim. A **concrete detail** is very specific. It helps readers visualize and understand the topic or the idea in the writer's mind.

Though information is plentiful, the writer must be careful to **evaluate,** or judge, the quality of information to determine what is most important and most closely related to the thesis statement or claim.

SUPPORTING DETAILS

sync•skills

Skill: Supporting Details

••• CHECKLIST FOR SUPPORTING DETAILS

As you look for supporting details to develop your topic, claim, or thesis statement, ask yourself the following questions:

- What is my main idea about this topic?
- What does a reader need to know about the topic in order to understand the main idea?
- What details will support my thesis?
- Is this information necessary to the reader's understanding of the topic?
- Does this information help to develop and refine my key concept or idea?
- Does this information relate closely to my thesis or claim?
- Where can I find better evidence that will provide stronger support for my point?

Here are some suggestions for how you can develop your topic:

- review your thesis or claim
- consider your main idea
- note what the reader will need to know in order to understand the topic
- be sure to consult credible sources
- use different types of supporting details, such as:
  - > facts that are specific to your topic and enhance your discussion to establish credibility with your reader and build information
  - > definitions to explain difficult concepts, terms, or ideas in your topic, claim, or thesis statement
  - > concrete details that will add descriptive and detailed material to your topic
  - > quotations to directly connect your thesis statement or claim to the text
  - > examples and other information to deepen your claim, topic, or thesis statement

Copyright © BookheadEd Learning, LLC

Reading & Writing Companion **87**

 TURN AND TALK

Turn to your partner and brainstorm a list of details you might use to support the following idea: Curiosity is an important quality for personal success.

 SPEAKING FRAMES
- One reason curiosity is important to success is ____.
- Another reason is ____.

 SKILL VOCABULARY

supporting detail / el detalle de apoyo *noun* a piece of text evidence, a description, an example, a reason, an expert opinion, a fact, or a statistic that further explains a key idea and closely relates to the thesis or claim

relevant / relevante *adjective* appropriate and logically related to the topic
COGNATE

necessary / necesario/a *adjective* essential, and required COGNATE

Extended Writing Project

⟳ YOUR TURN

Choose the best answer to each question.

1. The following is a section from a previous draft of Colin's essay. Colin would like to add a sentence to support the idea that he has presented in the underlined sentence. Which of these would BEST follow and support the underlined sentence?

> In "Everybody Jump," scientist Randall Munroe is motivated to use logic to answer a difficult question: "What would happen if everyone on earth stood as close to each other as they could and jumped . . . at the same instant?" <u>He knows that this could never really happen, but Munroe takes the question seriously.</u>

- ○ A. He knows that other people are curious about this topic and uncertain about the answer.
- ○ B. It's an interesting scenario, even if it can't happen in real life.
- ○ C. It's a chance for him to impress readers with his ability to use mathematical reasoning to solve real-life problems.
- ○ D. He hopes to advance the science of kinematics.

2. The following is a paragraph from a previous draft of Colin's informative essay. Colin has included an irrelevant sentence in the paragraph. Which sentence should be deleted from this paragraph?

> (1) Roy is motivated by a desire for knowledge. (2) He's also clever at dealing with problems. (3) These qualities help Roy—who's the new kid at school—deal with Dana the bully. (4) Roy's family has recently moved from Montana to Florida. (5) Dana is attacking Roy on the way to school when Roy sees a boy running past the school bus. (6) Even though Dana is hurting him, Roy is curious about the boy: "Who was he? What was he running from?" (7) Roy doesn't care about the pain. (8) He just wants Dana to stop bothering him. (9) When Roy tells Dana "I've had enough," Dana lets him go. (10) Now Roy is free to wonder about the strange boy.

- ○ A. Sentence 2
- ○ B. Sentence 4
- ○ C. Sentence 6
- ○ D. Sentence 9

✎ WRITE

Use the steps and questions in the checklist to revise the body of your informative essay.

🖥 Reading & Writing Companion

🗄 SKILL VOCABULARY

concrete detail / el detalle concreto *noun* a specific detail that helps readers visualize or understand the topic or the idea in the writer's mind COGNATE

evaluate / evaluar *verb* to judge or decide; to estimate the quality of COGNATE

Informative Writing

Your Turn

Ask students to complete the Your Turn activity.

QUESTION 1

A. Correct. This detail illustrates why Munroe is taking the question seriously.

B. Incorrect. This point isn't relevant to the main idea.

C. Incorrect. The question doesn't involve a real-life problem.

D. Incorrect. Munroe isn't interested in kinematics.

QUESTION 2

A. Incorrect. Sentence 2 supports how Roy conquers his challenges.

B. Correct. Sentence 4 goes into unnecessary detail.

C. Incorrect. Sentence 6 focuses on Roy's curiosity.

D. Incorrect. Sentence 9 illustrates how Roy deals with problems.

Write

Ask students to complete the writing assignment.

> **ELL REWRITE CHECKLIST**
>
> **A Step 1: Prepare your thesis statement**
> ☐ What is your main idea about this topic?
>
> **Step 2: Search for sources**
> ☐ Identify texts from your reading that support the idea reflected in your thesis statement.
>
> **Step 3: Identify relevant supporting details**
> ☐ Review your supporting details to make sure they are relevant and necessary.

Informative Writing Process: Draft

Write

Ask students to complete the writing assignment.

Extended Writing Project

Informative Writing Process: Draft

PLAN	DRAFT	REVISE	EDIT AND PUBLISH

You have already made progress toward writing your informative essay. Now it is time to draft your informative essay.

✎ WRITE

Use your Plan and other responses in your Binder to draft your informative essay. You may also have new ideas as you begin drafting. Feel free to explore those new ideas as they occur to you. You can also ask yourself these questions:

☐ Does my essay fully address the prompt?

☐ Have I included a clear thesis statement or controlling idea?

☐ Does my thesis statement let readers know what to expect in the body of my essay?

☐ Does the organizational text structure support my purpose for writing? Would another text structure be more effective?

Before you submit your draft, read it over carefully. You want to be sure you've responded to all aspects of the prompt.

✔ CHECK FOR SUCCESS

If students struggle to begin drafting their informative essay, ask them the following questions:

- Which three individuals have you identified?
- What is your thesis statement?
- What text structure are you thinking about using?
- What motivations and actions, responses, or decisions are most relevant to your thesis?

ELL DRAFT CHECKLIST

☐ Does my essay address the prompt?
☐ Have I clearly stated my thesis?
☐ Does my text structure support my purpose?
☐ Have I clearly stated each individual's motivations?
☐ Have I clearly stated relevant responses, actions, or decisions for each individual?

Peer Review

Students should submit substantive feedback to two peers using the review instructions below.

- Does the writer's essay fully address the prompt? Is there anything that needs to be added or improved?
- Does the writer include a clear thesis statement or controlling idea? If not, can you offer any suggestions?
- Does the writer's thesis statement let readers know what to expect in the body of the essay? If not, can you offer any suggestions?
- Does the organizational text structure support the writer's purpose? If not, what other text structure might be more effective?
- Has the writer included relevant information about the motivations and responses, actions, or decisions for each individual?

ELL SENTENCE FRAMES

- Your thesis statement is clear because ____.
- Your thesis statement would be clearer if ____.
- I like your choice of organizational structure because ____.
- I think your organizational structure could be improved by ____.
- I like your example of ____.
- Another example you might add is ____.

Extended Writing Project

Here is Colin's informative essay draft. As you read, identify how effectively he has presented his thesis statement or controlling idea and organized his information.

NOTES

Skill:
Introductions

By adding a "hook" to his introduction, Colin has made his essay more interesting to readers. He has also made his thesis more concise while keeping important details.

Skill:
Precise Language

Colin notices that he's using some inexact words. He replaces the phrase "triumph over" with the more precise word "conquer."

Skill:
Style

In order to make his writing have an academic tone, Colin decides to replace the words "scary job" with more sophisticated vocabulary, such as "the unknown and hazardous world of volcanoes."

≡ **STUDENT MODEL: FIRST DRAFT**

~~Scientist Donna O'Meara is motivated by a desire to understand something dangerous. She also wants to help others. The character Roy in Carl Hiaasen's book Hoot is motivated by curiosity. His quick-witted thinking helps him out. Author Randall Munroe is motivated by mathematical reasoning to answer what seems to be an impossible question. Each of these people or characters has a different motivation. Each of them faces different obstacles and problems. But each of them learns something important.~~

Sometimes people are motivated to take action without really knowing why. It could be a feeling, a goal, or a person that encourages them. Scientist Donna O'Meara is motivated by a desire to understand something dangerous. She also wants to help others. The character Roy in Carl Hiaasen's book *Hoot* is motivated by curiosity. His quick-witted thinking helps him out. Author Randall Munroe is motivated by mathematical reasoning. He wants to answer what seems to be an impossible question. Each of these people or characters has a different motivation and faces different obstacles and problems, but they all learn something important.

~~Donna O'Meara's desire to understand how volcanoes work has some-times put her in danger. Most people would probably be afraid to get close to a volcano. There's a lot we don't know about them. But O'meara has risked her life to study them. The desire for knowledge has pushed O'Meara to triumph over her scary job. Now she's an expert on volcanoes and shares her knowledge to help keep others safe. She hopes her work will "help (save the lives) of people who live near" volcanoes.~~

Donna O'Meara's desire to understand how volcanoes work has sometimes put her in danger. Most people would probably be afraid to get close to a volcano. There's a lot we don't know about them. But O'Meara has risked her life to study them. During her first visit to a volcano, she dodged "lava bombs," and hot lava melted her shoes. Another time, she and her husband Steve "were trapped on a ledge

Copyright © Bookhead Learning, LLC

---

90 Reading & Writing Companion

 PEER TO PEER NOTES

Have students review the checklist and Student Model. Ask students to create notes to teach other students. Encourage each student to re-write the checklist in a simpler way and create their own model or example. If time permits, pair the student with an English language learner to explain and share their notes and ideas.

 ## Analyze Student Model

Have students discuss the questions in the lesson as well as the Student Model draft. Ask:

- Which three individuals has Colin chosen?

- Has Colin included a clear thesis statement? What makes you say this?

Encourage students to share ideas for their own informative essays based on the questions in the lesson.

 SPEAKING FRAMES

- The three individuals Colin has chosen to write about are ___, ___, and ___.
- I think Colin (has / has not) included a clear thesis statement. The thesis statement (is / is not) clear because ___.
- One idea I have for my informative essay is ___.

 ## Introductions

Discuss the Model

How did Colin change his introduction? He added a "hook" to the beginning.

 SPEAKING FRAMES

- Colin changed his introduction by ___.
- This change improved his introduction because ___.

 ## Precise Language

Discuss the Model

What domain-specific vocabulary does Colin add to his essay? Colin adds the term "lava bombs."

 SPEAKING FRAMES

- Colin used ___, an example of domain-specific vocabulary, in his essay.
- This vocabulary changed his essay ___.
- Colin used ___, an example of precise language, in his essay.
- This language changed his essay ___.

Style

Discuss the Model

What type of style and language should Colin use in an informative essay? He should use formal style and academic and domain-specific language.

ELL SPEAKING FRAMES

- Colin should use ____ type of style and language in an informative essay.
- Colin should check for ____.
- These change improve his essay because ____.
- Colin could also change ____.

Transitions

Discuss the Model

Where have you seen the different types of transitions in movies, TV shows, or books? Answers will vary. Sample answers: music signaling the end/start of a scene, scenes fading in/out.

ELL SPEAKING FRAMES

- I have seen ____ transitions in ____.
- In Colin's draft, he writes ____, but in his final draft he adds ____.
- These transitions improve his essay because ____.

Copyright © BookheadEd Learning, LLC

NOTES

in the freezing cold with scalding rocks flying around them." The desire for knowledge has pushed O'Meara to conquer the unknown and hazardous world of volcanoes. Now she's an expert on volcanoes. She shares her knowledge to help keep others safe when volcanoes erupt. She hopes her work will "help save the lives of people who live near" volcanoes.

~~The character Roy is motivated by a desire for knowledge. He's also clever when it comes to dealing with problems. These qualities help Roy who's the new kid at school deal with Dana the bully. Dana is attacking Roy on his way to school, when Roy sees a boy running past the school bus. Roy is "griped with curiousity" about the boy: "... Who was he? What was he runing from?" Roy doesn't care about the pain. He just wants Dana to stop bothering him, and he is smarter than Dana. He does know that Dana is "a well-known [idiot]." Roy also knows that fighting back would be "a complete waste of (energy)." When Roy tells Dana "I've had enough," Dana lets him go. Now Roy, released from the grip of Dana's hands, are free to wonder about the strange boy. Roy's curiousity and his intelligence help him get out of a bad situation~~

Like Donna O'Meara, the character Roy in *Hoot* is motivated by a desire for knowledge. He's also clever when it comes to dealing with problems. These qualities help Roy, who's the new kid at school, deal with Dana the bully. Dana is attacking Roy on his way to school when Roy sees a boy running past the school bus. Even though Dana is hurting him, Roy is "gripped with curiosity" about the boy: "Who was he? What was he running from?" Roy doesn't care about the pain. He just wants Dana to stop bothering him, and he is smarter than Dana. Although Roy might not know the boy running past the bus, he does know that Dana is "a well-known idiot." Roy also knows that fighting back would be "a complete waste of energy." When Roy tells Dana "I've had enough," Dana lets him go. Now Roy, released from the grip of Dana's hands, is free to wonder about the strange boy. Roy's curiosity and his intelligence help him get out of a bad situation.

In "Everybody Jump," scientist Randall Munroe is motivated to use mathematical reasoning to answer a difficult question: "What would happen if everyone on earth stood as close to each other as they

Skill:
Transitions

Colin continues to add transitions to his draft in order to clarify ideas between paragraphs and make apparent his organizational structure. He realizes that there is no connection between the paragraph about Donna O'Meara and the one about Roy from Hoot. Therefore, he adds the transitional phrase "Like Donna O'Meara" before introducing the character Roy. Colin also adds cohesion and clarity to the ideas within this paragraph by adding other transitions, such as "Even though Dana is hurting him" and "Although Roy might not know the boy running past the bus."

NOTES

could and jumpped . . . at the same instant?" This could never sucsede in real life since it would totally be unpossible to get everyone in the same place at the same time, but Munroe takes the question seriously. He knows that "many others" are curious about this topic and discertain about the answer. Munroe uses mathematical reasoning, or logic, to explain the inknown. In his conclusion, he says that everyone jumping at once in the same place. Would have "little effect" on the planet. But then some terrible things would happen. When these billions of people tried to go back to their homes, they would be come violent and die "within weeks." Munroe paints an ugly picture, but it's where his reasoning takes him. He ends by stating certainly, "at least now we know."

Skill:
Conclusions

Colin decides that his conclusion does a good job of wrapping up his main points about each person. However, he realizes that he has not rephrased his main idea, or thesis. Thus, he adds several sentences that show his depth of knowledge about his main idea.

Donna O'Meara could have been hurt as she tried to find answers to her questions about volcanoes, but her wish to learn more and help others kept her pushing forward. Curiosity and intelligence help Roy get through the experience of being bullied. Randall Munroe's logic leads him to conquer feelings of uncertainty about a frightening event. Each person or character is motivated by a desire to know something for certain. Even though none of them is sure what will happen next, they are all motivated into action. As a result, they learn something about themselves and the world.

Conclusions

Discuss the Model

How did Colin improve his conclusion? He rephrased his thesis by adding sentences that show his depth of knowledge about his main idea.

>
> **ELL** **SPEAKING FRAMES**
>
> - Colin improved his conclusion by ___.
> - Colin needs to restate his thesis because ___.
> - This change improved his conclusion because ___.

Conclusions

Connect to Mentor Text

Project the following conclusion:

Through her work, Margaret became a role model for working women as well as a strong voice for the poor and powerless. She earned the respect of powerful businessmen when women were discouraged from working. When she died in 1971, she left behind not only an amazing photographic record of the human experience. She also left a message for women all over the world who wanted to make an impact: "You can." ("Margaret Bourke-White: Fearless Photographer")

Ask students:

- What do you notice about this conclusion?

- What about the conclusion appeals to you as a reader?

- Does information sum up the essay? Why or why not?

Skill: Introductions

Introduce the Skill

Watch the Concept Definition video ▶ and read the following definition with your students.

The **introduction** is the opening paragraph or section of an essay or other nonfiction text. To begin an argumentative essay, writers identify the **topic,** or what the essay will be about. The most important part of the introduction in an argumentative essay is the **thesis statement.** This statement contains the writer's **claim,** or main argument, and it states something that the writer believes to be true.

In an informative/explanatory text, the introduction should provide readers with necessary information in order to introduce a topic. It should state the thesis, which in an informative/explanatory essay is a short statement that summarizes the main point of the essay and previews the ideas that will follow in the text. In an informative/explanatory essay, many writers also include one or two sentences that are called a "hook." They are intended to engage readers' interest and grab their attention so they keep reading.

TURN AND TALK

Turn to your partner and brainstorm a list of ways to quickly hook a reader when writing an informative essay.

> **ELL SPEAKING FRAMES**
> - One way to hook a reader is to use a ____.
> - This method is effective because ____.

Extended Writing Project

Skill: Introductions

> **••• CHECKLIST FOR INTRODUCTIONS**

Before you write your introduction, ask yourself the following questions:

- What is my claim? How can I introduce my claim(s) so it is clear to my reader?
- What is the best way to organize my ideas, concepts, reasons, and evidence in a clear and logical order?
- How will you "hook" your reader's interest? You might:
  > start with an attention-grabbing statement
  > begin with an intriguing question
  > use descriptive words to set a scene

Below are two strategies to help you introduce your topic and claim, and organize reasons and evidence clearly in an introduction:

- Peer Discussion
  > talk about your topic with a partner, explaining what you already know and your ideas about your topic
  > write notes about the ideas you have discussed and any new questions you may have
  > review your notes and think about what will be your claim or controlling idea
  > briefly state your claim or thesis
  > organize your reasons and evidence in an order that is clear to readers, presenting your reasons first, followed by evidence
  > write a possible "hook"

- Freewriting
  > freewrite for 10 minutes about your topic. Don't worry about grammar, punctuation, or having fully formed ideas. The point of freewriting is to discover ideas.
  > review your notes and think about what will be your claim or controlling idea

Reading & Writing Companion **93**

SKILL VOCABULARY

introduction / la introducción *noun* the opening paragraph or section of an essay COGNATE

topic / el tema *noun* the subject of a literary work, usually expressed as a single word or phrase in the form of a noun

thesis statement / la presentación de la tesis *noun* a statement that shares the main idea of an argumentative or informative essay

claim / la afirmación *noun* the writer's or speaker's position on a debatable issue or problem

> briefly state your claim or thesis

> organize your reasons and evidence in an order that is clear to readers, presenting your reasons first, followed by evidence

> write a possible "hook"

Your Turn

Ask students to complete the Your Turn activity.

QUESTION 1

A. Incorrect. This sentence does not provide details that might grab a reader's attention.

B. **Correct.** This sentence provides some examples of what motivates people.

C. Incorrect. This sentence hints at something that might be interesting, but does not provide details.

D. Incorrect. This sentence defines a term but does not provide details.

QUESTION 2

A. Incorrect. This revision does not mention the obstacles or problems of the person or character.

B. Incorrect. This revision does not mention motivations, obstacles, or problems.

C. **Correct.** This sentence states the thesis in a memorable way.

D. Incorrect. This revision does not mention the different motivations or that the person or character learns something important.

Write

Ask students to complete the writing assignment.

 REWRITE CHECKLIST

 Introduction

☐ How can I "hook" my reader with an attention-grabbing statement or question?

🔄 YOUR TURN

Choose the best answer to each question.

1. Below is the introduction from a previous draft of Colin's essay. The first sentence is a weak "hook." How could Colin rewrite the sentence to better grab the reader's attention?

> <u>Lots of things motivate people.</u> Scientist Donna O'Meara is motivated to understand volcanoes, even if it means putting herself in danger. Roy in Carl Hiaasen's novel *Hoot* is motivated by curiosity. Author Randall Munroe is motivated by the challenge of using mathematical reasoning to answer a seemingly impossible question.

○ A. People are motivated by different things.

○ B. A quest for understanding, a keen sense of curiosity, a sharp mind—many different things motivate people to act.

○ C. Motivation comes from surprising places.

○ D. Motivation—the reason or reasons that drive people to take action—comes from many sources.

2. Colin wants to improve the introduction in an earlier draft of his informative essay. Which of these revisions to the following three sentences makes a more concise thesis?

> Each of these people or characters has a different motivation. Each of them faces different obstacles and problems. But each of them learns something important.

○ A. Each person learns something important through a different motivation.

○ B. In each case, they all learn something different.

○ C. Despite unique motivations and different obstacles, each of them learns something important.

○ D. In each case, they face different problems and overcome uncertainty.

✏️ WRITE

Use the questions in the checklist to revise the introduction of your informative essay.

Reading & Writing Companion 95

📓 Writer's Notebook

Provide a list of types of attention-grabbers on the board, such as quotations, descriptions, interesting or startling facts, riddles or mysteries, anecdotes, questions, or puns. Ask students to choose their two or three favorite types and mimic them as first lines for an informative essay topic of their choosing.

 TURN AND TALK

Allow students to share their first lines orally in pairs or small groups before writing.

Extended Writing Project

TRANSITIONS

sync•skills

Skill:
Transitions

••• CHECKLIST FOR TRANSITIONS

Before you revise your current draft to include transitions, think about:

- the key ideas you discuss in your body paragraphs
- the organizational structure of your essay
- the relationships among ideas and concepts

Next, reread your current draft and note areas in your essay where:

- the organizational structure is not yet apparent

  > For example, if you are comparing and contrasting two texts, your explanations about how two texts are similar and different should be clearly stated.

- the relationship between ideas from one paragraph to the next is unclear

  > For example, an essay that describes a process in sequential order should make clear the order of steps using transitional words like *first, then, next,* and *finally.*

- the relationship between ideas within a paragraph is unclear

  > For example, when providing evidence to support an idea in a topic sentence, you should introduce the evidence with a transition such as *for example* or *to illustrate.*

Revise your draft to use appropriate transitions to clarify the relationships among ideas and concepts, using the following questions as a guide:

- What kind of transitions should I use to make the organizational structure clear to readers?
- Which transition best connects the ideas within a paragraph?
- Which transition best connects ideas across paragraphs?

Skill: Transitions

Introduce the Skill

Watch the Concept Definition video and read the following definition with your students.

Transitions are connecting words, phrases, and clauses that writers use to **clarify** the relationships among ideas and details in a text. Transitions have different functions depending on whether the text is argumentative, informative, or narrative.

In an argumentative essay, writers state claims and provide reasons and evidence for their claims. To clarify a relationship between a claim and a reason or supporting evidence, transitions such as *although* and *on the other hand* help make connections clear.

For informative essays, transitions such as *however, in addition,* and *for example* may help create **cohesion** among ideas and concepts.

In narrative writing, authors use a variety of words, phrases, and clauses to signal shifts in time, setting, and action. Transitions such as *until now, meanwhile,* and *once it was over* may make narrative events more **coherent.**

Transitions also help to connect ideas both within and across paragraphs and between major sections of text.

TURN AND TALK

Turn to your partner and explain how your favorite movie transitions from one scene to another.

 SPEAKING FRAMES

- My favorite movie is ____.
- It transitions from one scene to another by ____.

SKILL VOCABULARY

transition / la transición *noun* a connecting word or phrase that a writer may use to clarify the relationship between ideas in a text; set off with a comma COGNATE

clarify / aclarar *verb* to make clear and more comprehensible

cohesion / la cohesión *noun* the quality of parts working together as a whole COGNATE

coherent / coherente *adjective* marked by being orderly and logical; easy to understand COGNATE

⚙ Your Turn

Ask students to complete the Your Turn activity.

A. **Correct.** This transition creates cohesion among ideas because sentence 3 contradicts sentence 2.

B. Incorrect. Sentences 2 and 3 are contradictions of each other.

C. Incorrect. This transition indicates a further detail rather than a contradiction.

D. Incorrect. This transition suggests the final step or sentence, not a contradiction.

⚙ Your Turn

Ask students to complete the Your Turn activity. Answers will vary.

However	Most kids are terrified of bullies. However, Roy doesn't let the bully bother him.
To illustrate	Many people would never get close to a volcano. But not Donna O'Meara. To illustrate, she and her husband live on an active volcano.
In addition	In addition to wearing men's clothing, Hatshepsut even wore a fake male beard.
For example	Margaret Bourke-White was not afraid to photograph intense situations. For example, she traveled to photograph many countries during World War II.

⟳ YOUR TURN

Choose the best answer to the question.

1. Below is a section from Colin's essay. Which transition would make the most sense to add to the beginning of sentence 3?

> 1. Munroe uses mathematical reasoning, or logic, to explain the unknown. 2. In his conclusion, he says that everyone jumping at once in the same place would have "little effect" on the planet. 3. Some terrible things would happen.

- ○ A. However,
- ○ B. To illustrate,
- ○ C. In addition,
- ○ D. Finally,

⟳ YOUR TURN

Complete the chart by adding the following transitions to sentences of your informative essay.

Transition	Rewritten Sentence
However	
To illustrate	
In addition	
For example	

📓 Writer's Notebook

Have students write out a typical day's schedule with descriptions of each activity, in paragraph form, using transition words.

 TURN AND TALK

Allow students to share their schedules orally in pairs or small groups before freewriting.

Extended Writing Project

Skill:
Precise Language

sync•skills

••• CHECKLIST FOR PRECISE LANGUAGE

As you consider precise language and domain-specific vocabulary related to a subject or topic, use the following questions as a guide:

- What information am I trying to convey or explain to my audience?
- Are there any key concepts that need to be explained or understood?
- What domain-specific vocabulary is relevant to my topic and explanation?
- Where can I use more precise vocabulary in my explanation?

Here are some suggestions that will help guide you in using precise language and domain-specific vocabulary to inform about or explain a topic:

- determine the topic or area of study you will be writing about
- identify key concepts that need explanation in order to inform readers
- research any domain-specific vocabulary that you may need to define
- substitute vague, general, or overused words and phrases for more precise, descriptive, and domain-specific language
- reread your writing to refine and revise if needed

▼ SKILL VOCABULARY

precise language / el lenguaje preciso *noun* exact language that includes specific nouns and action verbs COGNATE

domain-specific vocabulary / el vocabulario específico de un campo *noun* words and phrases that are limited to specific domains, or fields of study, such as law or medicine

---

 # Skill: Precise Language

Introduce the Skill

Watch the Concept Definition video and read the following definition with your students.

Precise language refers to clear and direct words or phrases that have very specific meanings. **Domain-specific vocabulary** are words and phrases that are used to explain concepts that are related to a particular subject or topic. A scientist writing about astronomy might use terms such as "airglow," for example, which is a glow in the night sky caused by radiation from the upper atmosphere.

When writers have to explain a complicated subject or topic, using precise language allows readers to develop a deeper understanding of the text and make connections between facts and other information. For example, the word *observe* is a synonym for the words *notice* or *see,* but it has a more precise meaning. To observe something means "to notice something and recognize it as significant." This difference, when used to describe a scientific experiment, can help readers develop their own ideas about the subject matter.

 ## TURN AND TALK

Turn to your partner and explain when you've used precise language (perhaps in English/language arts) or domain-specific language (perhaps in science/math).

ELL SPEAKING FRAMES
- I used precise language in ____.
- I used domain-specific language in ____.

⚙ Your Turn

Ask students to complete the Your Turn activity.

A. Incorrect. The addition of the word "fantasy" contradicts the meaning of the phrase "real life."

B. Correct. The addition of precise language, such as "reality" in place of "real life," and "query" in place of "question," makes the essay more vivid and attractive for the reader.

C. Incorrect. The word "debate" is not a good use of precise language because it doesn't fit into the context of the section.

D. Incorrect. The addition of the word "totally" is informal language, not precise language.

⚙ Your Turn

Ask students to complete the Your Turn activity. Answers will vary.

precise language	Margaret Bourke-White was a dynamic and unusual 20th-century woman.
domain-specific vocabulary	Hatshepsut was an extraordinary woman. It all began when she married the heir to the Egyptian throne. In this case, an heir is a person next in line for the throne.

⟳ YOUR TURN

Choose the best answer to the question.

1. Below is a section from a previous draft of Colin's essay. How could Colin change sentence 2 to add more precise language?

> 1. In "Everybody Jump," scientist Randall Munroe is motivated to use mathematical reasoning to answer a difficult question: "What would happen if everyone on earth stood as close to each other as they could and jumped . . . at the same instant?" 2. This could never happen in real life, but Munroe takes the question seriously.

○ A. This could never happen in fantasy, but Munroe takes the question seriously.
○ B. This could never happen in reality, but Munroe considers the query seriously.
○ C. This could never happen in real life, but Munroe takes the debate seriously.
○ D. This could never happen in real life, but Munroe takes the question totally seriously.

⟳ YOUR TURN

Complete the chart by adding an example of precise language and domain-specific language to your essay.

Type of Language	Rewritten Sentence
precise language	
domain-specific vocabulary	

Please note that excerpts and passages in the StudySync® library and this workbook are intended as touchstones to generate interest in an author's work. The excerpts and passages do not substitute for the reading of entire texts, and StudySync® strongly recommends that students seek out and purchase the whole literary or informational work. In order to experience it as the author intended. Links to online resellers are available in our digital library. In addition, complete works may be ordered through an authorized reseller by filling out and returning to StudySync® the order form enclosed in this workbook.

📖 Writer's Notebook

Have students write about a time in science or math class when they needed to know and understand domain-specific language, and how this helped them in the subject.

ELL TURN AND TALK

Allow students to share their experiences orally in pairs or small groups before freewriting.

Extended Writing Project

Skill:
Style

••• CHECKLIST FOR STYLE

First, reread the draft of your informative essay and identify the following:

- places where you use slang, contractions, abbreviations, and a conversational tone

- areas where you could use subject-specific or academic language in order to help persuade or inform your readers

- moments where you use first-person (*I*) or second person (*you*)

- areas where sentence structure lacks variety

- incorrect uses of the conventions of standard English for grammar, spelling, capitalization, and punctuation

Establish and maintain a formal style in your essay, using the following questions as a guide:

- Have I avoided slang in favor of academic language?

- Did I consistently use a third-person point of view, using third-person pronouns (*he, she, they*)?

- Have I varied my sentence structure and the length of my sentences? Apply these specific questions where appropriate:

  > Where should I make some sentences longer by using conjunctions to connect independent clauses, dependent clauses, and phrases?

  > Where should I make some sentences shorter by separating any independent clauses?

- Did I follow the conventions of standard English, including:

  > grammar?

  > spelling?

  > capitalization?

  > punctuation?

100 Reading & Writing Companion

Please note that excerpts and passages in the StudySync® library and this workbook are intended as touchstones to generate interest in an author's work. The excerpts and passages do not substitute for the reading of entire texts, and StudySync® strongly recommends that students seek out and purchase the whole literary or informational work in order to experience it as the author intended. Links to online resellers are available in our digital library. In addition, complete works may be ordered through an authorized reseller by filling out and returning to StudySync® the order form enclosed in this workbook.

Copyright © BookheadEd Learning, LLC

Skill: Style

Introduce the Skill

Watch the Concept Definition video ▶ and read the following definition with your students.

Style is the way a writer uses language to express ideas and convey information. It is revealed through the writer's choice of words and sentence construction. Style also involves being aware of the rules for writing standard English.

Choosing an appropriate style depends on the audience and the purpose for writing. Different subjects require different styles of writing. For both argumentative and informative writing, writers must use a formal style. With a **formal style,** a writer chooses **academic** language—the type of vocabulary used in school texts, for example—rather than informal or conversational language. The writer might also use special vocabulary unique to a particular topic, sometimes called **domain-specific** language.

Finally, to help maintain a formal style, writers must be sure to follow conventional rules for grammar, spelling, capitalization, and punctuation.

⚙ TURN AND TALK

Turn to your partner and discuss the style of your favorite movie. Is it formal or informal? What information (scenes, characters, elements) are unique to that movie/movie genre?

> **ELL** SPEAKING FRAMES
>
> - My favorite movie is ____.
> - The style of it is ____.
> - ____ is unique to this movie/genre because ____.

ⓥ SKILL VOCABULARY

style / el estilo *noun* a way of expressing something that is characteristic of the person or time period COGNATE

formal style / el estilo formal *noun* a writing style or way of writing for academic essays

academic / académico/a *adjective* having to do with school COGNATE

domain-specific / específico/a del campo *adjective* having to do with a particular topic

Your Turn

Ask students to complete the Your Turn activity.

A. **Incorrect.** The commas from the original draft are necessary.

B. **Incorrect.** The pronouns "him" and "he" are incorrect in the second sentence.

C. **Incorrect.** "And" makes the sentence a run-on.

D. **Correct.** The change from "are" to "is" and the correct spelling of "curiosity" follow conventions of standard English.

Your Turn

Ask students to complete the Your Turn activity. Answers will vary.

Eliminate slang, contractions, abbreviations, or a conversational tone.	Hatshepsut broke cultural norms in order to lead Egypt. She took control of her life, and she is an inspiration to this day.
Use domain-specific or academic language.	Randall Munroe uses mathematical reasoning to hypothesize an outcome to a common query: What would happen if everyone on earth jumped at exactly the same time?
Vary sentence structure and the length of sentences.	Margaret Bourke-White was fearless. She traveled to many dangerous places in times of war, including the Soviet Union, North Africa, Italy, and even Germany.

 YOUR TURN

Choose the best answer to the question.

1. Below is a section from a previous draft of Colin's essay. Which of the following revisions shows correct conventions of English?

> Now Roy, released from the grip of Dana's hands, are free to wonder about the strange boy. Roy's curiosity and his intelligence help him get out of a bad situation.

○ A. Now Roy released from the grip of Dana's hands is free to wonder about the strange boy. Roy's curiosity and his intelligence help him get out of a bad situation.

○ B. Now Roy, released from the grip of Dana's hands, is free to wonder about the strange boy. Roy's curiosity and him intelligence help he get out of a bad situation.

○ C. Now Roy, released from the grip of Dana's hands, is free to wonder about the strange boy and Roy's curiosity and his intelligence help him get out of a bad situation.

○ D. Now Roy, released from the grip of Dana's hands, is free to wonder about the strange boy. Roy's curiosity and his intelligence help him get out of a bad situation.

YOUR TURN

Complete the chart by making style changes within your informative essay.

Style Change	Rewritten Sentence
Eliminate slang, contractions, abbreviations, or a conversational tone.	
Use domain-specific or academic language.	
Vary sentence structure and the length of sentences.	

Reading & Writing Companion   **101**

Writer's Notebook

Have students think of a funny or memorable experience from their lives. Have students write out the story as if they were telling it to the principal or their grandparent (or someone they look up to and respect). Then, have students write the same story as if they were telling it to their best friend.

ELL **TURN AND TALK**

Allow students to share their stories orally in pairs or small groups before freewriting.

Extended Writing Project

Skill:
Conclusions

••• CHECKLIST FOR CONCLUSIONS

Before you write your conclusion, ask yourself the following questions:

- How can I restate the thesis or main idea in my concluding section or statement? What impression can I make on my reader?

- How can I write my conclusion so that it follows logically from the information I presented?

- Have I left out any important information in my concluding statement that I have presented in my essay?

Below are two strategies to help you provide a concluding statement or section that follows from the information or explanation presented:

- Peer Discussion

  > after you have written your introduction and body paragraphs, talk with a partner and tell them what you want readers to remember, writing notes about your discussion

  > review your notes and think about what you wish to express in your conclusion

  > do not simply restate your claim or thesis statement. Rephrase your main idea to show the depth of your knowledge.

  > write your conclusion

- Freewriting

  > freewrite for 10 minutes about what you might include in your conclusion. Don't worry about grammar, punctuation, or having fully formed ideas. The point of freewriting is to discover ideas.

  > review your notes and think about what you wish to express in your conclusion

  > do not simply restate your claim or thesis statement. Rephrase your main idea to show the depth of your knowledge.

  > write your conclusion

 102 Reading & Writing Companion

SKILL VOCABULARY

conclusion / la conclusión *noun* the closing paragraph or section of an essay; a closing argument in an argumentative text COGNATE

thesis statement / la presentación de la tesis *noun* a statement that shares the main idea of an argumentative or informative essay

claim / la afirmación *noun* the writer's or speaker's position on a debatable issue or problem

narrative / la narración *noun* a story, real or imagined, consisting of connected events

---

 ## Skill: Conclusions

Introduce the Skill

Watch the Concept Definition video ▶ and read the following definition with your students.

A **conclusion** is the closing paragraph or section of an essay, argument, or narrative. It is where the writer brings an essay to a close by restating the main idea or **thesis statement** or the claim in an argument. It also summarizes the evidence and research that support the **claim** or thesis. The conclusion should follow logically from the information, explanations, or claim that has been presented. A conclusion is a good way to suggest to your readers that you have accomplished what you set out to do. In addition, try to leave readers with an interesting final impression. This might be accomplished by closing with a quote, an anecdote, or a call to action.

In a **narrative,** a conclusion should follow logically from the events of the plot and what the characters have experienced. It might include characters reflecting on events, why they matter, and how they feel about them.

 ### TURN AND TALK

Turn to your partner and brainstorm a list of ways to conclude your ideas when writing an informative essay.

> **ELL** SPEAKING FRAMES
> - One way to conclude an essay is to ____.
> - This method is effective because ____.

Your Turn

Ask students to complete the Your Turn activity.

QUESTION 1

A. Incorrect. Colin has mentioned all three people or characters in the conclusion.

B. **Correct.** Colin has not restated his thesis.

C. Incorrect. The "hook" is present in the introduction, not the conclusion.

D. Incorrect. Colin has restated each person or character's motivation.

QUESTION 2

A. Incorrect. This is not memorable.

B. Incorrect. The focus of the thesis is not the desire to push past uncertainty.

C. **Correct.** This sentence rephrases the thesis in a memorable way.

D. Incorrect. The thesis focuses on the desire for knowledge as a motivation for action.

Write

Ask students to complete the writing assignment.

ELL REWRITE CHECKLIST

A Conclusion

☐ Have I rephrased my main idea, or thesis, in a way that shows the depth of my knowledge?

☐ Will my reader remember the most important idea I am expressing?

Extended Writing Project

↻ YOUR TURN

Choose the best answer to each question.

1. Below is the conclusion from a previous draft of Colin's essay. What key component is Colin missing from his conclusion?

> Donna O'Meara could have been hurt as she tried to find answers to her questions about volcanoes, but her wish to learn more and help others kept her pushing forward. Curiosity and intelligence help Roy get through the experience of being bullied. Randall Munroe's logic leads him to conquer feelings of uncertainty about a frightening event.

○ A. restating all three people or characters
○ B. restating the essay's thesis
○ C. a "hook"
○ D. descriptions of the motivation of each person or character

2. Colin wants to improve the conclusion to an earlier draft of his informative essay. What is the most effective revision to make to the underlined sentence in order to end with a memorable comment that expresses the essay's thesis?

> Donna O'Meara could be hurt trying to understand volcanoes, but her wish to learn more spurs her on. Curiosity helps Roy cope with being bullied. Randall Munroe's logic leads him to overcome uncertainty about a frightening event. In each case, the person or character learns something.

○ A. In each case, the person learns something important through motivation.
○ B. In each case, the desire to push past uncertainty leads to knowledge about themselves and the world.
○ C. In each case, the desire to know something pushes the person or character past uncertainty to learn something about themselves and the world.
○ D. In each case, knowledge of the world helps them overcome uncertainty.

✎ WRITE

Use the questions in the checklist to revise the conclusion of your informative essay.

Reading & Writing Companion **103**

📓 Writer's Notebook

Provide a list of types of endings on the board, such as quotations, descriptions, anecdotes, questions, or puns. Ask students to choose their two or three favorite types and mimic them as ending lines for an informative essay topic of their choice.

ELL TURN AND TALK

Allow students to share their ending lines orally in pairs or small groups before writing.

Informative Writing Process: Revise

PLAN	DRAFT	REVISE	EDIT AND PUBLISH

You have written a draft of your informative essay. You have also received input from your peers about how to improve it. Now you are going to revise your draft.

◀ REVISION GUIDE

Examine your draft to find areas for revision. Keep in mind your purpose and audience as you revise for clarity, development, organization, and style. Use the guide below to help you review:

Review	Revise	Example
Clarity		
Highlight any place in your essay where there are unnecessary details that lack a formal style and hinder clarity.	Remove irrelevant information and informal language from sentences.	This could never happen in real life ~~since it would totally be impossible to get everyone in the same place at the same time~~, but Munroe takes the question seriously.
Development		
Identify places where you give details in support of your thesis. Note reasons, descriptions, and examples you could incorporate to add support.	Focus on a single idea and add reasons, descriptions, or examples to support your idea.	In his conclusion, he says that everyone jumping at once in the same place would have "little effect" on the planet. But then some terrible things would happen. When these billions of people tried to go back to their homes, they would run out of food, water, and fuel. They ~~they~~ would become violent and die "within weeks."

Copyright © BookheadEd Learning, LLC

Informative Writing Process: Revise

Review Revision Guide

Break the class into five groups, and assign each group a category of the revision guide. Ask:

- What is the purpose of this section of the guide?
- How did it improve Colin's writing?
- How will it help to improve your writing?

Allow groups to share their ideas with the class.

> **ELL** SPEAKING FRAMES
>
> - I think ____ (clarity / development / organization / word choice / sentence variety) improved Colin's writing by ____.
> - I think ____ (clarity / development / organization / word choice / sentence variety) will improve my writing because ____.

Revise

Students should start this activity with a copy of their drafts either printed on paper or open in a word-processing program, such as Google Docs. Allow students time to revise their drafts using the instructions in the revision guide. Once students have finished revising their informative essay, have them submit their work.

✓ CHECK FOR SUCCESS

Circulate around the room to spend time with individual students. Ask:

- What category are you working on?
- Why are you revising this specific section?
- How are you revising it?
- How does this change support your purpose?
- Does this change make your writing appropriate for your audience?

If students struggle while revising their drafts, choose an exemplary revision to share with the class while the student talks through the process. You could also invite a student to share a dilemma in the revision process and allow the class to offer feedback or suggestions.

ORGANIZATION

Select sentences from your draft that could be replaced to create a stronger organization. Revise your draft, focusing on organization.

Ⓐ ORGANIZATION

Tell students to revise their drafts using the revision guide, focusing on organization. In addition, have students make revisions that focus on development, as practiced in the previous unit.

Write

Ask students to complete the writing assignment.

Review	Revise	Example
Organization		
Review whether your text structure supports your purpose. Annotate places where the organization can be improved.	Rewrite the transition between paragraphs to make the text structure clear to readers.	She shares her knowledge to help keep others safe when volcanoes erupt. She hopes her work will "help save the lives of people who live near" volcanoes. Like Donna O'Meara, the ~~The~~ character Roy is motivated by a desire for knowledge. He's also clever when it comes to dealing with problems.
Style: Word Choice		
Identify prefixes in your writing (such as *in-* and *un-*).	Select sentences to rewrite using correct prefixes.	Munroe uses mathematical reasoning, or logic, to explain the ~~inknown~~ unknown.
Style: Sentence Variety		
Review your essay for precise language. Create comprehensible sentences by using language that is specific to the text.	Rewrite sentences to include domain-specific vocabulary.	The desire for knowledge has pushed O'Meara to conquer ~~her scary job~~ the unknown and hazardous world of volcanoes.

WRITE

Use the guide above, as well as your peer reviews, to help you evaluate your informative essay to determine areas that should be revised.

REVISION CHECKLIST

- ☐ Find areas of weak organization.
- ☐ Consider how additional details can improve the organization of your essay.
- ☐ Replace the weak sentences with details or sentences that create a stronger organization.

Extended Writing Project

PARENTHESES, BRACKETS, AND ELLIPSES
PARENTHESES
sync•skills

Grammar: Parentheses,
Brackets, and Ellipses

Parentheses

Parentheses ( ) are punctuation marks used to set off supplemental or explanatory material that is not part of the main sentence. Supplemental material often includes words that define or explain another word.

Text	Explanation
The fine sarcophagus **(sar-KOFF-ah-guss)**, or stone coffin, which would hold his body was also ready. His Majesty, Herself	The pronunciation is explanatory material, so it is set off in parentheses.

Brackets

Brackets [ ] are punctuation marks used in quotations to set off information inserted by someone besides the original writer or speaker in order to clarify the quotation.

Text	Explanation
Hail, Ari-em-ab-f, who comest forth from Tebu, I have never stopped **[the flow of]** water. Book of the Dead	The words *the flow of* clarify the sentence and were inserted by someone besides the original writer. Therefore, they are set off in brackets.

Ellipses

When writers quote other texts, sometimes they need to leave out some of the material. They use ellipses [. . .], or three spaced points, to indicate that material from a quotation has been left out.

Text	Explanation
"Troy . . . was sacked twice," modern archaeologists remark, "once by the Greeks and once by Heinrich Schliemann." The Hero Schliemann: The Dreamer Who Dug for Troy	The ellipses indicate the omission of material from the middle or end of a quotation.

Reading & Writing
Companion

Grammar: Parentheses, Brackets, and Ellipses

Introduce the Skill

Review the terms and definitions for parentheses, brackets, and ellipses as a class.

- parentheses: punctuation that sets off supplemental material that is not meant to be part of the main statement

- brackets: punctuation that encloses information that you insert into a quotation from someone else's work in order to clarify the quotation

- ellipses: punctuation made up of equally spaced points generally used to indicate the omission of material from a quotation

Discuss the Model

1. What are parentheses meant to do? Parentheses are used to set off supplemental or explanatory material that is not meant to be part of the main sentence.

2. Why might someone choose to use brackets? Brackets are used in quotations to set off information inserted by someone besides the original writer or speaker, and they help clarify the quotation.

3. What's the purpose of ellipses? Ellipses are used to indicate that material from a quotation has been left out.

⚙ Your Turn

Ask students to complete the Your Turn activity.

QUESTION 1

A. Incorrect.

B. Incorrect.

C. **Correct.** Parentheses are needed to set off the supplemental material *21,780 square feet*.

D. Incorrect.

QUESTION 2

A. Incorrect.

B. Incorrect.

C. **Correct.** This sentence makes sense with the omission.

D. Incorrect.

QUESTION 3

A. Incorrect.

B. **Correct.** Brackets are needed to set off the name *Susan B. Anthony*, which was inserted by someone besides the original writer.

C. Incorrect.

D. Incorrect.

Extended Writing Project

↻ YOUR TURN

1. How should this sentence be changed?

   > Their property consists of one-half acre 21,780 square feet.

   ○ A. Insert brackets around the words *one-half acre*.
   ○ B. Insert brackets around the words *21,780 square feet*.
   ○ C. Insert parentheses around the words *21,780 square feet*.
   ○ D. No change needs to be made to this sentence.

2. Which revision of the quotation uses ellipses correctly?

   > The news anchor explained, "Although his lawyer presented an eloquent defense, he was found guilty and sentenced to life in prison."

   ○ A. The news anchor explained, "Although his lawyer presented an eloquent defense, he was found guilty . . ."
   ○ B. The news anchor explained, "Although his lawyer presented an eloquent defense, he was . . . life in prison."
   ○ C. The news anchor explained, "Although his lawyer presented an eloquent defense, he was . . . sentenced to life in prison."
   ○ D. None of the above

3. How should this sentence be changed?

   > According to Anika's history book, "she (Susan B. Anthony) played a major role in winning American women the right to vote."

   ○ A. Remove the parentheses around the words *Susan B. Anthony*.
   ○ B. Remove the parentheses and insert brackets around the words *Susan B. Anthony*.
   ○ C. Remove the parentheses and insert commas around the words *Susan B. Anthony*.
   ○ D. No change needs to be made to this sentence.

Reading & Writing Companion

Grammar: Prefixes

Grammar: Prefixes

A prefix is a word part that is added to the beginning of a base word and changes its meaning. Prefixes help develop meaning in words and sentences. An understanding of prefixes and their meanings will help you learn new words.

Prefix	Meaning	Examples	Meaning
in-	not	**in**direct **in**visible	not direct not visible
non-	without, not	**non**stop **non**fiction	without stop not fiction
un-	opposite of, not, reverse	**un**clean **un**tie	not clean to loosen
pre-	before	**pre**pay **pre**heat	to pay in advance to heat in advance
de-	remove from, reduce	**de**grade **de**throne	to make lower to remove from the throne
dis-	opposite of, not, remove from	**dis**agree **dis**appear	to not agree to vanish

Copyright © BookheadEd Learning, LLC

Introduce the Skill

Review the image and definition for prefixes as a class.

- base word: word before the attachment of any affixes

- prefix: an affix attached to the beginning of a word; spelling of the word remains the same with attached prefix

Discuss the Model

1. What is a prefix, and what are some examples? A prefix is a word part that is added to the beginning of a base word, such as *un-*, *non-*, *dis-*, and *pre-*.

2. How can understanding prefixes and their meanings help you learn new words? Answers will vary; sample answer: Understanding that *in-*, *non-*, and *un-* are all prefixes that mean "not" will help me determine the meanings of unknown words.

Your Turn

Ask students to complete the Your Turn activity.

QUESTION 1

A. Incorrect.

B. Incorrect.

C. **Correct.** *Unkind* means "not kind."

D. Incorrect.

QUESTION 2

A. **Correct.** *Discard* means "to get rid of or remove a card."

B. Incorrect.

C. Incorrect.

D. Incorrect.

QUESTION 3

A. Incorrect.

B. Incorrect.

C. **Correct.** *Deplane* means "to remove oneself from a plane."

D. Incorrect.

QUESTION 4

A. **Correct.** *Pregame* means "before the game."

B. Incorrect.

C. Incorrect.

D. Incorrect.

YOUR TURN

1. Which word with a prefix best replaces the bolded words in the following sentence?

> His actions were **not kind**.

- A. cruel
- B. insane
- C. unkind
- D. None of the above

2. Which word with a prefix best replaces the bolded words in the following sentence?

> When playing this card game, after each turn you must **remove a card** from your hand.

- A. discard
- B. disallow
- C. draw
- D. None of the above

3. Which word with a prefix best replaces the bolded words in the following sentence?

> Passengers may **remove themselves from the plane** upon landing.

- A. disrobe
- B. disagree
- C. deplane
- D. None of the above

4. Which word with a prefix best replaces the bolded words in the following sentence?

> The team got together to enjoy a **before the game** snack.

- A. pregame
- B. early
- C. preapproved
- D. None of the above

Reading & Writing Companion

Grammar:
Basic Spelling Rules II

Doubled Consonants

Spelling Conventions	Correct Spelling	Incorrect Spelling
Before adding -ed or a suffix: When a word ends in a single consonant following one vowel, double the final consonant if the word is one syllable.	slap + -ed = slapped sit + -ing = sitting	slaped siting
Before adding -ed or a suffix: Double the final consonant if the last syllable of the word is accented and the accent stays there after the suffix is added.	refer + -ed = referred occur + -ence = occurrence deter + -ing = deterring admit + -ed = admitted	refered occurence detering admited
Before adding -ly to a double l: When adding -ly to a word that ends in ll, drop one l.	full + -ly = fully dull + -ly = dully	fullly dullly

Compound Words

Spelling Conventions	Original Words	Compound Words
Compound words are made up of two or more words. When forming compound words, maintain all original spellings.	back + pack honey + bee fly + wheel	backpack honeybee flywheel

Spelling -cede, -ceed, and -sede

Spelling Conventions	Correct Spelling	Incorrect Spelling
The only English word ending in -sede is supersede.	supersede	superceed
Three words end in -ceed: proceed, exceed, and succeed.	proceed exceed succeed	procede exsede succede
All other words ending with the "seed" sound are spelled with -cede.	precede recede	preceed receed

 Reading & Writing Companion

Grammar: Basic Spelling Rules II

Introduce the Skill

Review the image and definition for basic spelling rules II as a class.

- **doubled consonants**: with the addition of some suffixes, the final consonant of a word is doubled.

- **compound word**: when forming compound words, keep the original spelling of both words.

- **spelling -cede, -ceed, and -sede**: because c and s are often pronounced the same way, confusion arises in spelling words ending in -cede, -ceed, and -sede.

Discuss the Model

1. When might someone need to double a final consonant before adding -ed or a suffix? Answers will vary; sample answer: Double the final consonant if the last syllable of the word is accented and the accent stays there after the suffix is added.

2. What are compound words? They are words that are made up of two or more words. When forming compound words, you maintain all original spellings.

3. What is important to remember about words that end in -sede, -ceed, and -cede? Answers will vary; sample answer: In English, only one word ends in -sede, three words end in -ceed, and all other words ending with the "seed" sound are spelled with -cede.

Your Turn

Ask students to complete the Your Turn activity.

QUESTION 1

A. **Correct.** The last syllable of *occur* is accented, and the accent stays there after *-ing* is added, so the *r* is doubled. *Earthquake* is a compound word.

B. Incorrect.

C. Incorrect.

D. Incorrect.

QUESTION 2

A. Incorrect.

B. Incorrect.

C. **Correct.** *Succeed* is one of the three "seed" words ending in *-ceed,* and *somewhere* is a compound word.

D. Incorrect:

QUESTION 3

A. **Correct.** *Supersede* is the only English word ending in *-sede.*

B. Incorrect.

C. Incorrect.

D. Incorrect.

QUESTION 4

A. Incorrect.

B. Incorrect.

C. Incorrect.

D. **Correct.** The sentence contains no spelling errors.

⟳ YOUR TURN

1. How should the spelling error in this sentence be corrected?

   > No one in our class has ever experienced a naturally occuring disaster such as an earth quake.

   ○ A. Change *occuring* to *occurring* and *earth quake* to *earthquake.*
   ○ B. Change *occuring* to *occurring.*
   ○ C. Change *earth quake* to *earthquake.*
   ○ D. No change needs to be made to this sentence.

2. How should the spelling error in this sentence be corrected?

   > If you look very carefully you will succede in finding the book some where in this room.

   ○ A. Change *succede* to *succeed.*
   ○ B. Change *some where* to *somewhere.*
   ○ C. Change *succede* to *succeed* **and** *some where* to *somewhere.*
   ○ D. No change needs to be made to this sentence.

3. How should the spelling error in this sentence be corrected?

   > The founders of the religion believed that the new faith would fully superceed all existing forms of belief.

   ○ A. Change *superceed* to *supersede.*
   ○ B. Change *fully* to *fullly.*
   ○ C. Change *fully* to *fuly.*
   ○ D. No change needs to be made to this sentence.

4. How should the spelling error in this sentence be corrected?

   > When the rock hit the windshield, the driver slammed on the brakes, and then she proceeded through the traffic light.

   ○ A. Change *windshield* to *wind shield.*
   ○ B. Change *slammed* to *slamed.*
   ○ C. Change *proceeded* to *proceded.*
   ○ D. No change needs to be made to this sentence.

Reading & Writing Companion

Informative Writing Process: Edit and Publish

Extended Writing Project

Informative Writing
Process: Edit And Publish

| PLAN | DRAFT | REVISE | EDIT AND PUBLISH |

You have revised your informative essay based on your peer feedback and your own examination.

Now, it is time to edit your informative essay. When you revised, you focused on the content of your essay. You probably looked at your essay's thesis statement, introduction, organizational text structure, supporting details, transitions, precise language, style, and conclusion. When you edit, you focus on the mechanics of your essay, and pay close attention to things like grammar and punctuation.

Use the checklist below to guide you as you edit:

☐ Have I correctly used parentheses, brackets, and ellipses?

☐ Have I correctly used prefixes?

☐ Did I follow spelling rules, especially regarding doubled consonants, compound words, and words ending with the "seed" sound?

☐ Do I have any sentence fragments or run-on sentences?

☐ Have I spelled everything correctly?

Notice some edits Colin has made:

• Corrected the incorrect use of parentheses.

• Corrected incorrect prefixes.

• Used basic spelling rules to correct spelling errors, especially in words with doubled consonants and compound words.

• Changed a verb so that it matches the subject.

• Corrected a sentence fragment.

Practice with Student Model (optional)

Provide groups with a different section of Colin's draft. Each group should practice editing Colin's model using the checklist in the lesson: Has he:

☐ correctly used parentheses, brackets, and ellipses?

☐ correctly used prefixes?

☐ followed spelling rules, especially regarding doubled consonants, compound words, and words ending with the "seed" sound?

☐ corrected any sentence fragments or run-on sentences?

☐ spelled everything correctly?

After the groups have finished, call on volunteers from each group to make edits until all the mistakes have been found and edited, pausing to discuss points of disagreement.

ELL SPEAKING FRAMES

A
• Colin (did / did not) correctly use parentheses, brackets, or ellipses when he wrote ____.
• Colin (did / did not) correctly use prefixes when he wrote ____.
• Colin (did / did not) make sure he followed the spelling rules for doubled consonants, compound words, and words ending in the "seed" sound when he wrote ____.
• ____ is an example of a (run-on sentence / sentence fragment) that Colin (has / has not) corrected.
• ____ is spelled incorrectly. The correct spelling is ____.

Write

After students finish editing, suggest, if there's time, that they set their essays aside for a few minutes, and that they then proofread them one more time. Once students have completed their writing, have them submit their work.

✓ CHECK FOR SUCCESS

If students struggle to edit successfully, help them determine where edits are needed, and what changes need to be made.

Direct students to the grammar lessons in this unit if they are uncertain about the rules for specific concepts.

ELL READ ALOUD

Encourage students to read their essays aloud to themselves or to a partner in order to catch any remaining mistakes.

A READ ALOUD

Encourage students to read their essays aloud to themselves or to an on-grade-level peer in order to catch any remaining mistakes.

B PULL QUOTE

Remind students that a pull quote is a short section of a piece of writing—usually no more than a sentence—that expresses an essential message about a work or conveys the overall tone of the writing. Have students identify a pull quote from their writing and explain why it is an effective choice for their work. Alternately, have students identify pull quotes from other students' essays and post them around the room.

Roy also knows that fighting back would be "a complete waste of (energy) energy." When Roy tells Dana "I've had enough," Dana lets him go. Now Roy, released from the grip of Dana's hands, ~~are~~ is free to wonder about the strange boy. Roy's ~~curiousity~~ curiosity and his intelligence help him get out of a bad situation.

In "Everybody Jump," scientist Randall Munroe is motivated to use mathematical reasoning to answer a difficult question: "What would happen if everyone on earth stood as close to each other as they could and ~~jumpped~~ jumped . . . at the same instant?" This could never happen in real life, but Munroe takes the question seriously. He knows that "many others" are curious about this topic and ~~discertain~~ uncertain about the answer. Munroe uses mathematical reasoning, or logic, to explain the ~~inknown~~ unknown. In his conclusion, he says that everyone jumping at once in the same place. ~~W~~ would have "little effect" on the planet. But then some terrible things would happen. When these billions of people tried to go back to their homes, they would run out of food, water, and fuel. They would probably ~~be come~~ become violent and die "within weeks."

✏ WRITE

Use the questions on the previous page, as well as your peer reviews, to help you evaluate your informative essay to determine areas that need editing. Then edit your essay to correct those errors.

Once you have made all your corrections, you are ready to publish your work. You can distribute your writing to family and friends, hang it on a bulletin board, or post it on your blog. If you publish online, share the link with your family, friends, and classmates.

English Language Learner Resources

studysync

GRADE 6 > UNIT

USERS   ASSIGNMENTS

6 7

Add to booksh

In the Dark
Core ELA
Grade 6
30 Days

Unit Overview

Integrated Reading and Writing

Extended Writing Project

ELL Resources

Novel Study

End-of-Unit Assessment

Instructional Path

Tracking Down Typhoid Mary

The Notice

Skill: Classroom Vocabulary

Students will learn and recognize routine classroom vocabulary and practice using them in a variety of contexts.

CLASSROOM VOCABULARY
THE NOTICE

sync•skills

+ Assign

Skill: Making Predictions

Students will learn and practice the skill of making predictions by using clues from the text, background knowledge, and previewing the text before reading.

Teacher Resources: Lesson Plan

MAKING PREDICTIONS
THE NOTICE

sync•skills

+ Assign

Lessons in the English Language Learner Resources section offer explicit ELL instruction. These lessons share a thematic and genre focus with all other lessons in the Core ELA unit.

The twenty ELL Resources are developed around two texts, "Tracking Down Typhoid Mary" and "The Notice," and an Extended Oral Project. Each text is written at four distinct levels. For ELLs, these texts serve as structural and thematic models of authentic texts in the Integrated Reading and Writing section of the unit. Thus, teachers may use the ELL texts in place of or as extensions for *Hatshepsut: His Majesty, Herself* and *Elena*.

ELL lessons modify the routines used with texts in the Integrated Reading and Writing section. Explicit vocabulary instruction is emphasized, and reading and writing Skills lessons focus strongly on language acquisition and reading comprehension.

After reading texts about dealing with the uncertain, students will complete an Extended Oral Project that can be used in place of or as an extension to the Extended Writing Project. In this unit, students will plan and present a short biography of someone who overcame an uncertain, challenging situation.

Focus on English Language Proficiency Levels

ELL Resources provide targeted support for four levels of proficiency: Beginning, Intermediate, Advanced, and Advanced High. Instruction and scaffolds, as well as the texts themselves, are differentiated based on these levels.

Additional differentiated scaffolds include visual glossaries, speaking and writing frames, and suggested grouping for peer and teacher support. Lessons also include suggested extension activities to challenge Advanced and Advanced High students as they progress through the year.

ELL Resources

ELL TEXTS

Tracking Down Typhoid Mary

- Skill: Sight Vocabulary and High-Frequency Words
- Skill: Using Prereading Supports
- First Read
- Skill: Language Structures
- Skill: Main Ideas and Details
- Skill: Spelling Patterns and Rules
- Close Read

The Notice

- Skill: Classroom Vocabulary
- Skill: Making Predictions
- First Read
- Skill: Analyzing Expressions
- Skill: Compare and Contrast
- Skill: Verb Tenses
- Close Read

EXTENDED ORAL PROJECT

- Introduction
- Skill: Acquiring Vocabulary
- Plan

- Skill: Connecting Words
- Practice
- Present

Tracking Down Typhoid Mary

INFORMATIONAL TEXT

Introduction

This true-life mystery tells about a serious illness and the man who tracked down its source. The story is set in the early 1900s, when people were just starting to understand the causes of disease.

In 1906, some people in Charles Warren's house got sick. They had typhoid fever. Warren wanted to know how the people got sick. He hired an investigator. The investigator discovered that the illness came from a woman named Mary Mallon. Mary worked as a cook in other houses. Wherever Mary worked, people got typhoid fever. But Mary was just a carrier of the disease. She did not get sick. Mary was angry that she was accused of causing the disease. Usually, cooking kills germs. But Mary made ice cream. That is how the disease spread. Mary went to prison for four years. When she got out, she cooked for people again. Again, people got sick. Mary went to jail again. This time, she went for twenty-three years.

ELL Summaries in multiple languages are available digitally.

🔊 Audio and audio text highlighting are available with this text.

CONNECT TO ESSENTIAL QUESTION

How do you know what to do when there are no instructions?

In this informational text, people in one community are dying of typhoid fever. The year is 1906, and George Soper is trying to solve the mystery of how these people are getting sick. Will he find out before another person gets sick and dies from this serious illness?

Core ELA Connections

Texts	Theme	Genre
Hatshepsut: His Majesty, Herself	At the turn of the twentieth century, Mary Mallon was a healthy carrier of typhoid fever. This text explores the topics of individual actions and their larger impacts.	"Tracking Down Typhoid Mary" is a narrative non-fiction article that describes the search for the infamous carrier of typhoid fever.

Differentiated Text Levels

ELL LEVEL	BEGINNING	INTERMEDIATE	ADVANCED	ADVANCED HIGH
WORD COUNT	312	463	543	533
LEXILE	360L	430L	620L	680L

Instructional Path

The print teacher's edition includes essential point-of-use instruction and planning tools. Complete lesson plans and program documents appear in your digital teacher account.

Skill: Sight Vocabulary and High-Frequency Words

Objectives: Students will be able to learn and recognize sight vocabulary and high-frequency words in English.

Objectives: Students will be able to recognize sight vocabulary and high-frequency words when listening and reading, and produce sight vocabulary and high-frequency words when speaking and writing.

Skill: Using Prereading Supports

Objectives: Students will be able to learn and practice the skill of using prereading supports when reading a new text.

Objectives: Students will be able to read a new or unfamiliar text using prereading supports such as graphic organizers, illustrations, and topic vocabulary.

First Read: Tracking Down Typhoid Mary

Objectives: Students will be able to perform an initial reading of a text using the strategy of using prereading supports.

Objectives: Students will be able to demonstrate comprehension of a text by responding to questions orally and in writing using textual evidence.

Skill: Language Structures

Objectives: Students will be able to understand and practice the rules of language structures, like verbs followed by prepositions.

Objectives: Students will be able to understand and apply the rules of language structures, like verbs followed by prepositions, while reading and speaking.

Skill: Main Ideas and Details

Objectives: Students will be able to distinguish between main ideas and details.

Objectives: Students will be able to distinguish between main ideas and details when reading and justify their decision when speaking.

Skill: Spelling Patterns and Rules

Objectives: Students will be able to recognize and apply spelling patterns and rules.

Objectives: Students will be able to recognize spelling patterns and rules when reading and apply spelling patterns and rules when writing.

Close Read: Tracking Down Typhoid Mary

Objectives: Students will be able to perform a close reading of a text in order to analyze main ideas and details.

Objectives: Students will be able to demonstrate analysis of main ideas and details by participating in a collaborative conversation and writing a short constructed response.

Progress Monitoring

Opportunities to Learn	Opportunities to Demonstrate Learning	Opportunities to Reteach

Sight Vocabulary and High-Frequency Words

⚙ Skill: Sight Vocabulary and High Frequency Words	⚙ Skill: Sight Vocabulary and High Frequency Words • Your Turn 💬 First Read • Sight Vocabulary and High Frequency Words Focus	⚙ Spotlight Skill: Sight Vocabulary and High Frequency Words

Using Prereading Supports

⚙ Skill: Using Prereading Supports	⚙ Skill: Using Prereading Supports • Your Turn 💬 First Read • Practice Prereading Skill	⚙ Spotlight Skill: Using Prereading Supports

Language Structures

⚙ Skill: Language Structures	⚙ Skill: Language Structures • Your Turn	⚙ Spotlight Skill: Language Structures

Main Ideas and Details

⚙ Skill: Main Ideas and Details	⚙ Skill: Main Ideas and Details • Your Turn 📄 Close Read • Skills Focus • Write	⚙ Spotlight Skill: Main Ideas and Details

Spelling Patterns and Rules

⚙ Skill: Spelling Patterns and Rules	⚙ Skill: Spelling Patterns and Rules • Your Turn 📄 Close Read • Write	⚙ Spotlight Skill: Spelling Patterns and Rules

First Read

StudySync

Tracking Down Typhoid Mary

Introduce the Text

As a class, watch the video preview ▶ and have students read the introduction in pairs to make connections to the video preview. Ask students various "wh" questions such as:

- What did you see in the video? How does it make you feel?
- What do you think the text will be about?
- Is there something in the video or introduction that surprised you?

ELL Beginning & Intermediate

SPEAKING FRAMES
- I see ___. I feel ___.
- I think the text will be about ___.
- I was surprised by ___.

Practice Prereading Skill

Remind students that **Using Prereading Supports:**

Helps you prepare to read a text. An example of this is learning topic vocabulary. When you scan a text and discover words that are important to the topic, you can look them up in a dictionary or ask your teacher or peers for support.

Have students work in small, mixed-level groups to skim the passage looking for topic vocabulary related to medicine. Prompt students to use a dictionary, context clues, and each other to define unknown words.

As students are working in small groups, circulate to listen for sample questions such as:

- *What does this word mean?*
- *What meaning does the dictionary give?*

Activate Prior Knowledge and Experiences OPTIONAL

Have students make connections while practicing their oral language by discussing what they know about how diseases are spread.

Generate a list (on the board or on paper) of any information or ideas your students have about how diseases are spread.

Ask students to share where their background knowledge came from. For example, did their ideas come from a movie, friend, television show, book, or family member?

V VOCABULARY

mansion
a large and impressive house

thoroughly
completely; in a detailed way

carrier
a person or animal that transmits a disease without suffering from or showing signs of the disease

isolation
the condition of being alone

inspector
someone whose job is to examine something closely

☰ READ

NOTES

1 It was a lovely day in Oyster Bay. The sun was shining. The sky was blue. At Charles Warren's **mansion** on the shore, though, all was not well. Six people in the house were fighting for their lives. All were very ill with symptoms that included a very high fever. One of them was Charles's little daughter.

2 As it turned out, the six people had typhoid fever. In 1906 it was a common illness, found in crowded parts of the city. However, no one had ever seen it in rich Oyster Bay homes. How did it get there? Where had it come from? Charles wanted to know.

3 Charles hired a man named George Soper. George had an unusual job. He was a sanitation engineer. He worked to make buildings cleaner because making them cleaner kept sickness from spreading. Dirty water and dirty hands made germs spread. One of those germs caused typhoid fever. George set to work in the Warrens' house, looking for the cause of disease.

Reading & Writing Companion **109**

 Preteach Vocabulary

Model the first word and example for the class.

1. The first word is *mansion* and its meaning is "a large and impressive house."

2. When I hear the word *mansion*, I think of places where very wealthy people might live.

3. For example, you might see a *mansion* in the fanciest parts of town.

4. A governor or a president might also live in a *mansion* because a *mansion* is big enough to hold many guests at once.

Continue this exercise with each word in the glossary, calling on individuals or groups of students to share out.

ELL Beginning

PRETEACH VOCABULARY

Use the gestures to clarify meanings.

- **mansion** (Pantomime looking up in awe at a grand house.)
- **carrier** (Pantomime coughing or sneezing at someone.)
- **inspector** (Look closely at an object, turning it over in your hands.)
- **thoroughly** (Pantomime washing hands thoroughly.)
- **isolation** (Remove yourself from the group and stand alone in the corner.)

🔊 AUDIO TEXT HIGHLIGHTING

Allow students to use the audio text highlight feature to follow along as they read. Alternately, you may wish to work directly with students or group them in twos or threes for partner reading or choral reading.

Sight Vocabulary and High-Frequency Words Focus

Remind students of the sight vocabulary and high-frequency words that they studied at the beginning of the unit. Point out that some of the words may be useful as they think about and discuss the text. For example:

- away (Mary runs **away** from the inspector . . .)
- make (Mary likes to **make** ice cream . . .)
- not (If you do **not** wash thoroughly . . .)
- see (If no one can **see** germs, they may not believe in them . . .)
- to (They send her **to** an island . . .)

TEXT TALK

Have students discuss the questions in small groups. Circulate and check for understanding.

1. What is the text about?
2. What is the author mainly discussing?
3. What are some details that the author gives?
4. Does the text change the way you feel about the topic?

 All Levels

SPEAKING FRAMES
Giving Information:

- This text is about ____.
- The main idea is ____.
- Some examples the author gives about ____ include ____.
- This text makes me think ____.

Asking for Information:

- Can you explain ____?
- What do you think about ____?
- Why do you think ____?

Tracking Down Typhoid Mary

 NOTES

4 George found nothing wrong with the water pipes. Nothing was wrong with the drains. Could bad seafood be making people sick? George checked the kitchen. Everything seemed fresh and clean. He talked to everyone in the household. By spring, he had the answer. He tracked the fever to one woman. She had worked in the house as a cook. She had worked in other homes before that, and people at those homes had become sick. The woman's name was Mary Mallon.

5 Mary had never been sick herself. Others became sick, but she did not. She was a **carrier** of the disease. She did not believe that she had made anyone sick. She was angry. In fact, she chased George away with a fork!

6 Mary was still a cook. Now she worked for a different family. George was worried. Would she make them sick, too? He called the Health Department. An **inspector** came to talk to Mary, but she ran away. Finally, the police picked her up. They took her to a hospital. There, doctors tested her blood. She was loaded with the germ that caused typhoid fever.

7 How did Mary make people sick? The doctors figured it out. Mary made great peach ice cream. She did not wash her hands **thoroughly**, so germs could spread. The peaches were raw, so cooking did not kill the germs.

8 The Health Department locked Mary away in **isolation**. She lived alone on an island for three years. She went to court. The judge agreed that she was dangerous. Finally, in 1910, she was freed.

9 Mary continued to work as a cook. Everywhere she worked, people got sick. Many people got typhoid fever from Mary Mallon. At least three people died from her cooking.

10 In 1915, the courts locked Mary up again. She died on the island 23 years later. She had never once had typhoid fever. Even so, people everywhere called her "Typhoid Mary."

First Read

Read the text. After you read, answer the Think Questions below.

☁ THINK QUESTIONS

1. Whom did Charles Warren hire? Why did he hire that person?

   Charles Warren hired _____.

   He hired him _____.

2. How did Mary get people sick?

   Mary got people sick because _____.

3. What happened to Mary after she was freed in 1910?

   After Mary was freed she _____.

4. Use context to confirm the meaning of the word *isolation* as it is used in "Tracking Down Typhoid Mary." Write your definition of *isolation* here.

   Isolation means _____.

   A context clue is _____.

5. What is another way to say that you cleaned your room *thoroughly*?

   I cleaned my room _____.

Reading & Writing Companion **111**

🖥 Think Questions

Circulate as students answer Think Questions independently. Answers will vary.

QUESTION 1: Comprehension

He hired George Soper to find out what made his daughter sick.

QUESTION 2: Comprehension

She did not wash her hands. Germs got into the ice cream she made. People ate the ice cream and got sick.

QUESTION 3: Comprehension

Answers will vary, but may include the following details:

- She kept cooking and made people sick.
- She was locked up again and died on the island.

Student responses should refer to specific details from the passage.

QUESTION 4: Language

Mary is locked away and lives alone on an island. A definition for *isolation* might be "alone in a separate place."

QUESTION 5: Language

I cleaned my room totally and completely.

Skill: Language Structures

Introduce the Skill

Watch the Concept Definition video and read the definition for Language Structures.

TURN AND TALK

1. What is one thing that language rules may tell us?

2. What is one example of a basic sentence structure?

3. If a sentence is not basic, what do we call it?

ELL Beginning & Intermediate

SPEAKING FRAMES

- Language rules may tell the correct order of ____.
- A basic sentence structure might be ____.
- Some sentences are basic, and some are more ____.

ELL Advanced & Advanced High

SPEAKING FRAMES

- Language rules may tell the correct order of ____.
- A basic sentence structure might be ____. One example is ____.
- Some sentences are basic, and some are more ____. For example, ____.

Skill:
Language Structures

★ DEFINE

In every language, there are rules that tell how to **structure** sentences. These rules define the correct order of words. In the English language, for example, a **basic** structure for sentences is subject, verb, and object. Some sentences have more **complicated** structures.

You will encounter both basic and complicated **language structures** in the classroom materials you read. Being familiar with language structures will help you better understand the text.

••• CHECKLIST FOR LANGUAGE STRUCTURES

To improve your comprehension of language structures, do the following:

✓ Monitor your understanding.

- Ask yourself: Why do I not understand this sentence? Is it because I do not understand some of the words? Or is it because I do not understand the way the words are ordered in the sentence?

✓ Pay attention to verbs followed by prepositions.

- A **verb** names an action.

  > Example: I **sit** on my chair.

  > This tells the reader what the subject of the sentence is doing (sitting).

- A **preposition** defines the relationship between two or more nouns or verbs in a sentence.

  > Example: I sit **on** my chair.

  > This tells the reader where the subject is doing the action (on a chair).

---

112 Reading & Writing Companion

V SKILL VOCABULARY

structure / la estructura *noun* the order of parts

basic / básico *adjective* the most important parts without anything extra

complicated / complicado *adjective* having many parts

language structure / la estructura de lenguaje *noun* the order of words in a sentence

- Sometimes the preposition comes directly after the verb, but it can also be separated by another word.

    Example: I **took** it **to** school with me.

- Sometimes the preposition changes the meaning of the verb. This is called a **phrasal verb**.

    > Example: The teacher liked to **call on** the students in the front of the class.

    > The phrasal verb *call on* means "to select someone to share information."

✓ Break down the sentence into its parts.

- Ask yourself: What words make up the verbs in this sentence? Is the verb followed by a preposition? How does this affect the meaning of the sentence?

✓ Confirm your understanding with a peer or teacher.

Reading & Writing Companion **113**

Discuss the Skill Model

1. What did the student highlight?

   The student highlighted some phrasal verbs.

2. How can prepositions change a sentence?

   Adding a preposition to a verb can change its meaning.

3. Where may prepositions appear?

   Prepositions may appear after verbs.

4. What can the student do if he is unsure of the meaning of a phrasal verb?

   Answers may vary, but should include: He can practice. He can ask a teacher or classmate for help.

ELL Beginning & Intermediate

Have students use the <u>speaking frames</u> and <u>helpful terms</u> to participate in the group discussion. If beginning students are hesitant to participate in a discussion, encourage them by prompting with *yes* or *no* questions.

Advanced & Advanced High

Have students use the <u>speaking frames</u> to participate in the group discussion.

SPEAKING FRAMES

- The student highlighted some ____.
- Adding a preposition may ____. For example, ____.
- Prepositions may appear ____.
- If he is unsure, he can ____. For example, ____.

HELPFUL TERMS FOR DISCUSSION

- structure
- verb
- separated
- preposition
- practice
- teacher
- verbal phrase
- after
- follows

↻ YOUR TURN

Read each sentence from the text. Find the verb and preposition that goes along with it. Then, write the verb in the center column and the preposition in the last column. Remember, the preposition may not always directly follow the verb.

Sentences	Verbs	Prepositions
At least three people died from her cooking.		
He tracked the fever to one woman.		
She lived alone on an island for three years.		
She went to court.		

Your Turn Ask students to complete the Your Turn activity.

Verbs	Prepositions
died	from
tracked	to
lived	on
went	to

Skill:
Main Ideas and Details

★ DEFINE

The **main ideas** are the most important ideas of a paragraph, a section, or an entire text. The **supporting details** are details that describe or explain the main ideas.

To **distinguish** between the main ideas and the supporting details, you will need to decide what information is the most important and supports or explains the main ideas.

••• CHECKLIST FOR MAIN IDEAS AND DETAILS

In order to distinguish between main ideas and supporting details, do the following:

✓ Preview the text. Look at headings, topic sentences, and boldface vocabulary.

• Ask yourself: What seems to be the main idea in this text?

✓ Read the text.

• Ask yourself: What are the most important ideas? What details support or explain the most important ideas?

✓ Take notes or use a graphic organizer to distinguish between main ideas and supporting details.

Reading & Writing Companion **115**

V SKILL VOCABULARY

main idea / la idea principal *noun* the most important idea of a paragraph, a section, or an entire text

supporting details / los detalles que desarrollan la idea central *noun* details that describe or explain the main idea

distinguish / distinguir *verb* to determine the difference between two things COGNATE

Skill: Main
Ideas and Details

Introduce the Skill

Watch the Concept Definition video and read the definition for Main Ideas and Details.

TURN AND TALK

1. What does it mean to distinguish between main ideas and details?

2. Why might it be difficult to distinguish between main ideas and details?

3. What can you do if you are struggling to keep track of a text's main ideas and supporting details?

ELL Beginning & Intermediate

SPEAKING FRAMES
• To distinguish between main ideas and details means to decide ____.
• You may not be able to ____.
• You could use a ____ to keep track of main ideas and supporting details.
• You could also ____.

ELL Advanced & Advanced High

SPEAKING FRAMES
• To distinguish between main ideas and details means ____.
• You may not be able to ____ because ____.
• You could use a ____.
• You could also try ____ or ____.

Discuss the Skill Model

1. What does the student do to find the main idea of the text?

    The student reads the text and thinks about the most important idea in the paragraph.

2. What is the main idea of the paragraph?

    The main idea is that Mary was a carrier for the disease.

3. What does the student look for next?

    She looks for details that support the main idea.

4. Why does the student take notes?

    Taking notes helps the student distinguish between and confirm the main ideas and details.

ELL   Beginning & Intermediate

Have students use the <u>speaking frames</u> and <u>helpful terms</u> to participate in the group discussion. If beginning students are hesitant to participate in a discussion, encourage them by prompting with *yes* or *no* questions.

Advanced & Advanced High

Have students use the <u>speaking frames</u> to participate in the group discussion.

SENTENCE FRAMES

*   To find the main idea of the paragraph, the student ____.
*   The main idea is that ____.
*   Next the student looks for ____.
*   Taking notes helps ____. For example, ____.

HELPFUL TERMS FOR DISCUSSION

• most important	• confirm
• carrier	• read
• better understand	• distinguish

↻ YOUR TURN

Read the following excerpt from the text. Then, complete the multiple-choice questions below.

> **from "Tracking Down Typhoid Mary"**
>
> How did Mary make people sick? The doctors figured it out. Mary made great peach ice cream. She did not wash her hands thoroughly, so germs could spread. The peaches were raw, so cooking did not kill the germs.

1. What is the main idea of the paragraph?

    ○ A. Mary never learned to clean her tools.
    ○ B. Mary wanted to make people sick.
    ○ C. Mary's peach ice cream made people sick.
    ○ D. Mary's ice cream needed further cooking.

2. Which detail supports the main idea?

    ○ A. Mary made great ice cream.
    ○ B. Cooking did not kill the germs.
    ○ C. Peaches may be used in ice cream.
    ○ D. Germs spread when Mary washed up.

3. Which other detail supports the main idea of the paragraph?

    ○ A. Mary did not wash her hands properly.
    ○ B. Peaches are often loaded with germs.
    ○ C. Mary forgot to cook the peaches.
    ○ D. Ice cream can cause stomach pains.

Your Turn   Ask students to complete the Your Turn activity.

QUESTION 1: C) The doctor claims the ice cream made people sick.

QUESTION 2: B) This detail best supports the claim that the ice cream made people sick.

QUESTION 3: A) This detail tells us how Mary spread the disease.

Close Read

✏ WRITE

PERSONAL RESPONSE: Imagine that you were Mary Mallon in this story. How would you feel about George? How would you react to being told you were spreading disease, and why? Write about your experience as Mary. Recount details from the original story in your response. Pay attention to spelling patterns and rules as you write.

Use the checklist below to guide you as you write.

☐ How do you think Mary Mallon feels?

☐ Why does George look for Mary?

☐ What information from the text supports your ideas?

Use the sentence frames to organize and write your personal response.

Mary is not sure why George _____.

I would feel _____ if _____.

I think I would _____.

Spreading germs is bad because _____.

I practice healthy habits to _____.

Please note that excerpts and passages in the StudySync® library and this workbook are intended as touchstones to generate interest in an author's work. The excerpts and passages do not substitute for the reading of entire texts, and StudySync® strongly recommends that students seek out and purchase the whole literary or informational work in order to experience it as the author intended. Links to online resellers are available in our digital library. In addition, complete works may be ordered through an authorized reseller by filling out and returning to StudySync® the order form enclosed in this workbook.

Reading & Writing Companion   **117**

Close Read

Model Skills Focus

Remind students of the Reading Skill Main Idea and Details. Tell students that one way you can identify main ideas and details is to determine what information is most important and how the text supports it. Direct students to the Skills Focus and remind them to track as you read aloud.

Find the main idea and details of the text.

Model Main Idea and Details for students:

- I am going to focus on paragraph 7.

- I reread the paragraph and ask myself what the most important idea is in this paragraph.

- The most important idea is that Mary's peach ice cream made people sick.

- I ask myself "What details support this main idea?"

- I notice the detail "She did not wash her hands thoroughly." This explains how the germs got into her food. I also notice the detail "cooking did not kill germs." This explains how people ended up getting sick from Mary's food. Both of these details support the main idea that it was Mary's cooking

Complete Skills Focus

Use a Jigsaw strategy to have students complete the Skills Focus. Divide students into three groups. Assign each group the beginning, middle, or end of the text (paragraphs 1–4, 5 and 6, and 7–10). Prompt groups to:

- Find the main ideas and details of each paragraph in their section.

- Decide on the main idea of the section as a whole.

Circulate and monitor groups as they work.

Collaborative Conversation

Rearrange students so they have a representative from each of the original groups. Prompt partners to combine the main ideas and details they found to better understand the whole text.

- How did you determine the main idea?
- How did you determine supporting details?

- How did distinguishing main ideas from details help you better understand the text?

Collaborative Conversation

▲ SCAFFOLDS

 ELL   **BEGINNING, INTERMEDIATE** Use the word bank to participate in the group discussion.

ADVANCED Use the speaking frames to participate in the group discussion.

BEGINNING, INTERMEDIATE	ADVANCED
Word Bank	**Speaking Frames**
• most important • information • idea • explain • section • now I understand	• I ____ to determine the main ideas. • I ____ to determine the supporting details. • Distinguishing main ideas from details helped me better understand ____ about the text.

Write

Ask students to complete the writing assignment. Remind students to pay attention to the spelling of words with suffixes.

ELL **BEGINNING** Write a response using the <u>paragraph frames</u> and <u>word banks</u>.

INTERMEDIATE Write a response using the <u>paragraph frames</u>.

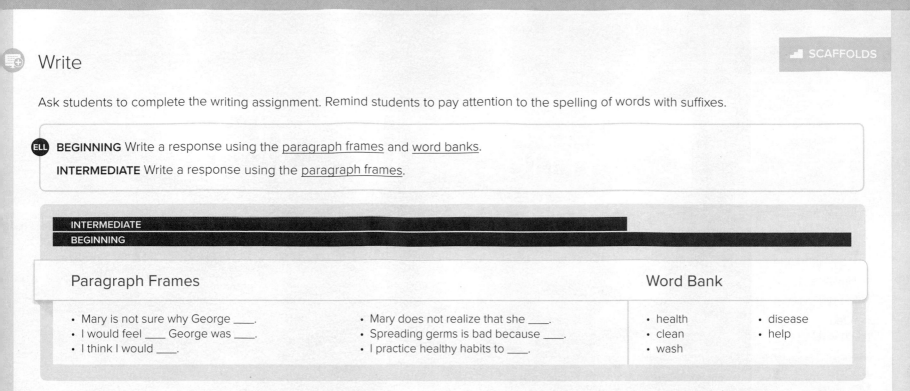

INTERMEDIATE

BEGINNING

Paragraph Frames

- Mary is not sure why George ____.
- I would feel ____ George was ____.
- I think I would ____.

- Mary does not realize that she ____.
- Spreading germs is bad because ____.
- I practice healthy habits to ____.

Word Bank

- health
- clean
- wash

- disease
- help

The Notice

FICTION

Introduction

New York City in the 1930s was home to immigrant families who traveled there from every corner of the world in search of a happy life. At times, they faced a less-than-warm welcome. In the story "The Notice," two Czech families experience a dilemma: can they keep their livelihood when their landlord prefers not to rent to immigrants?

A young child watches his father, Dominik. It is the end of the day. Dominik closes his shop. The shop sells glass articles made by the Vaceks. The Vaceks work in the back of the shop. Dominik usually smiles. Today, Dominik is not happy. The Vaceks, the child, and the child's mother watch Dominik. Dominik pulls a notice out of his pocket. Mr. Davis, the landlord, left the notice on the door. Mr. Davis says the shop's rent is now double. Mr. Davis says that it is a difficult financial time. Dominik recently came from Prague. He knows that Mr. Davis does not like immigrants. That is why Mr. Davis is raising the rent. Mr. Vacek asks Dominik what he will do. Mr. Vacek and his wife need the work. The two men have been friends since childhood. Dominik tells Mr. Vacek that he will find a solution.

ELL Summaries in multiple languages are available digitally.

🔊 Audio and audio text highlighting are available with this text.

CONNECT TO ESSENTIAL QUESTION

How do you know what to do when there are no instructions?

Two long-time friends own a business together in New York City in the 1930s. Their landlord is going to double their rent because they are immigrants. They need their business to survive, but they are tired of the discrimination. What will they do?

Core ELA Connections

Texts	Theme	Genre
Elena	A group of immigrants from Czechoslovakia are evicted from their store in New York City. This story builds on ideas of family, hardships, and adjusting to a new place.	Set in the 1930s in New York City, "The Notice" is a short story that depicts the hardships faced by immigrant families.

Differentiated Text Levels

ELL LEVEL	BEGINNING	INTERMEDIATE	ADVANCED	ADVANCED HIGH
WORD COUNT	275	377	429	477
LEXILE	480L	550L	630L	760L

Instructional Path

The print teacher's edition includes essential point-of-use instruction and planning tools. Complete lesson plans and program documents appear in your digital teacher account.

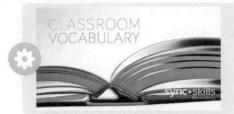

Skill: Classroom Vocabulary

Objectives: Students will be able to learn and recognize routine classroom vocabulary in English.

Objectives: Students will be able to recognize routine classroom vocabulary when listening and reading, and produce routine classroom vocabulary when speaking and writing.

DIGITAL ONLY

Skill: Making Predictions

Objectives: Students will be able to learn and practice the skill of making predictions about a text before reading.

Objectives: Students will be able to make predictions by using clues from the text, background knowledge, and previewing the text when reading a new or unfamiliar text.

DIGITAL ONLY

First Read: The Notice

Objectives: Students will be able to perform an initial reading of a text using the strategy of making predictions.

Objectives: Students will be able to demonstrate comprehension of a text by responding to questions orally and in writing using textual evidence.

Skill: Analyzing Expressions

Objectives: Students will be able to analyze expressions.

Objectives: Students will be able to analyze and understand expressions when reading and speaking.

Skill: Comparing and Contrasting

Objectives: Students will be able to compare and contrast characters in a text.

Objectives: Students will be able to compare and contrast when reading and justify their comparisons when speaking.

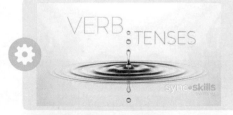

Skill: Verb Tenses

Objectives: Students will be able to recognize and apply correct verb tense rules.

Objectives: Students will be able to recognize correct verb tense when reading and apply correct verb tense rules when writing.

DIGITAL ONLY

Close Read: The Notice

Objectives: Students will be able to perform a close reading of a text in order compare and contrast.

Objectives: Students will be able to demonstrate their ability to compare and contrast by participating in a collaborative conversation and writing a short constructed response.

Progress Monitoring

Opportunities to Learn	Opportunities to Demonstrate Learning	Opportunities to Reteach
Classroom Vocabulary		
⚙ Skill: Classroom Vocabulary	⚙ Skill: Classroom Vocabulary • Your Turn 📖 First Read • Classroom Vocabulary Focus	⚙ Spotlight Skill: Classroom Vocabulary
Making Predictions		
⚙ Skill: Making Predictions	⚙ Skill: Making Predictions • Your Turn 📖 First Read • Practice Prereading Skill	⚙ Spotlight Skill: Making Predictions
Analyzing Expressions		
⚙ Skill: Analyzing Expressions	⚙ Skill: Analyzing Expressions • Your Turn	⚙ Spotlight Skill: Analyzing Expressions
Comparing and Contrasting		
⚙ Skill: Comparing and Contrasting	⚙ Skill: Comparing and Contrasting • Your Turn 📄 Close Read • Skills Focus • Write	⚙ Spotlight Skill: Comparing and Contrasting
Verb Tenses		
⚙ Skill: Verb Tenses	⚙ Skill: Verb Tenses • Your Turn 📄 Close Read • Write	⚙ Spotlight Skill: Verb Tenses

First Read

StudySync

The Notice

Introduce the Text

As a class, watch the video preview ▶ and have students read the introduction in pairs to make connections to the video preview. Ask students various "wh" questions such as:

1. What did you see in the video? How does it make you feel?

2. What do you think the text will be about?

3. Is there something in the video or introduction that surprised you?

ELL Beginning & Intermediate

SPEAKING FRAMES

- I see _____. I feel _____.
- I think the text will be about _____.
- I was surprised by _____.

Practice Prereading Skill

Remind students that Making Predictions:

Is making guesses about what will happen next in a story or what information a non-fiction text will provide. A reader can use clues from the text and their background knowledge to make predictions. Making predictions before and during reading can help a reader maintain focus and interest in a text.

Have students work in small, homogeneous groups to make predictions about the summary.

As students are working in small groups, circulate to listen for sample questions such as:

- *What will this story be about?*
- *What will happen next?*
- *Why do you think that?*

Activate Prior Knowledge and Experiences OPTIONAL

Have students make connections while practicing their oral language by discussing what they know about Ellis Island.

Generate a list (on the board or on paper) of any information or ideas your students have about Ellis Island.

Ask students to share where their background knowledge came from. For example, did their ideas come from a movie, friend, television show, book, or family member?

V VOCABULARY

 impatient
unwilling to wait for someone or something

 property
a piece of land or a building that is owned by a person or business

 counter
a flat surface over which goods are bought or food is served.

 admit
to tell the truth, but in an unwilling way

 glassware
objects made of glass

≡ READ

1 The last customer put on her coat and left. It was a cold January night. My *táta* locked the door and looked out. He stood there for a while. I began to grow **impatient**. I wanted to see his warm smile. I saw that smile every day, after he closed our shop for the day.

2 He turned at last, but he didn't look happy. He placed his hand on my shoulder and walked past me.

3 My *máma* and I watched him stand behind the **counter**. He took out a folded piece of paper from a small wooden box. He spread the paper out before him. Delicate glass vases, bowls, and plates sparkled in the display case below. Our family and the Vaceks made them in the back of the shop. We used to make the same **glassware** in Prague. The Vaceks were watching my *táta* too.

Reading & Writing
Companion **119**

 ## Preteach Vocabulary

Model the first word and example for the class.

1. The first word is *impatient* and its meaning is "unwilling to wait for someone or something."

2. When I hear the word *impatient*, I think of people who don't like to wait for something.

3. For example, if I am *impatient*, I will not wait for my family to begin eating dinner.

4. This is an example of *impatient* behavior.

Continue this exercise with each word in the glossary, calling on individuals or groups of students to share out.

ELL Beginning

PRETEACH VOCABULARY

Use the gestures to clarify meanings.

- **impatient** (Point to your watch or wrist with an anxious face.)

- **counter** (Pantomime the action of putting things on a counter.)

- **property** (Take something that is yours and make a gesture that you own it.)

- **glassware** (Draw things that are normally made of glass.)

- **admit** (Say: I didn't want to say this, but I'm bored.")

🔊 AUDIO TEXT HIGHLIGHTING

Allow students to use the audio text highlight feature to follow along as they read. Alternately, you may wish to work directly with students or group them in twos or threes for partner reading or choral reading.

Classroom Language Focus

Remind students of the sight vocabulary and high-frequency words that they studied at the beginning of the unit. Point out that some of the words may be useful as they think about and discuss the story. For example:

- disagree (Dominik and Mr. Vacek **disagree** with Mr. Davis because . . .)

- agree (I **agree** with Táta . . .)

- admit (Mr. Vacek doesn't want to **admit** that . . .)

- work on (I don't think Mr. Davis wants them to **work on** his . . .)

The Notice

NOTES

4 "What can we do, Dominik?" Josefa asked. Her husband, Miroslav, winced slightly.

5 Eventually my *táta* looked up. Josefa's question brought him back from some faraway place.

6 "Mr. Davis hasn't given us much of a choice." There was anger in his voice. "He has already made his choice. He will give our shop to anyone who didn't pass through Ellis Island. Or, he will *allow* us to pay extra for letting us work on his **property**."

7 *Máma* knew what my *táta* said was true.

8 *Táta* gripped the edges of the display case. Like the glassware the case contained, his expression was easy for everyone to see.

9 Mr. Vacek read the notice again. Mr. Davis left it on our shop door this morning. He didn't even hand it to my *táta* or Mr. Vacek.

10 I glanced at it. Mr. Davis blamed the doubling of our rent on hard times. It was difficult to imagine that he knew about hard times.

11 Mr. Vacek cleared his throat and said, "Josefa and I, we need this place." He didn't want to **admit** it, but it was true.

12 My *táta* looked at Mr. Vacek and nodded. They had known each other since they were children. My *táta* didn't want to hear his friend say that. But I knew my *táta* wasn't going to abandon him now.

13 "Whatever we decide, we will decide it together," my táta said.

Copyright © BookheadEd Learning, LLC

TEXT TALK

- What is the story about?
- What will the story's characters do?
- Where does the story take place?
- How does the story make you feel?

 All Levels

SPEAKING FRAMES

Giving Information:

- This story is about ____.
- The story's characters will ____.
- This story takes place in ____.
- This story makes me feel ____.

Asking Information:

- Can you explain ____?
- What do you think about ____?
- Why do you think ____?

Think Questions

First Read

Read the text. After you read, answer the Think Questions below.

☁ THINK QUESTIONS

1. Who are the main characters in the story? What is their relationship?

   The main characters are _____.

   They are _____.

2. Write two or three sentences describing the setting of the story.

   The setting _____
   _____.

3. At the end of the story, why does the narrator still have hope?

   The narrator still has hope because _____.

4. Use context to confirm the meaning of the word *admit* as it is used in "The Notice." Write your definition of *admit* here.

   Admit means _____.

   A context clue is _____.

5. What is another way to say the word *abandon*?

   Another way to say *abandon* is _____.

Circulate as students answer Think Questions independently. Answers will vary.

QUESTION 1: Comprehension

The kid, Táta, Máma, and the Vacek family. They are friends and work together.

QUESTION 2: Comprehension

They are in a glassware shop. It is a cold January night.

QUESTION 3: Comprehension

Answers will vary, but may include the following examples:

- "They had known each other since they were children"

- "But I knew my *táta* wasn't going to abandon him now."

Student responses should provide an example from the story and an explanation that describes how the example causes the narrator to still have hope.

QUESTION 4: Language

Mr. Vacek didn't want to admit that they needed to keep the store to be able to survive because it was hard for him. He didn't want to say that truth to everybody, but he had to say it anyway. A definition for *admit* is "to tell the truth unwillingly."

QUESTION 5: Language

Another way to say *abandon* is "to leave."

Reading & Writing
Companion **121**

Skill: Analyzing Expressions

Introduce the Skill

Watch the Concept Definition video and read the definition for Analyzing Expressions.

Skill: Analyzing Expressions

 ★ DEFINE

When you read, you may find English expressions that you do not know. An **expression** is a group of words that communicates an idea. Three types of expressions are idioms, sayings, and figurative language. They can be difficult to understand because the meanings of the words are different from their **literal**, or usual, meanings.

An **idiom** is an expression that is commonly known among a group of people. For example: "It's raining cats and dogs" means it is raining heavily. **Sayings** are short expressions that contain advice or wisdom. For instance: "Don't count your chickens before they hatch" means do not plan on something good happening before it happens. **Figurative** language is when you describe something by comparing it with something else, either directly (using the words *like* or *as*) or indirectly. For example, "I'm as hungry as a horse" means I'm very hungry. None of these expressions are actual animals.

••• CHECKLIST FOR ANALYZING EXPRESSIONS

To determine the meaning of an expression, remember the following:

✓ If you find a confusing group of words, it may be an expression. The meaning of words in expressions may not be their literal meaning.

- Ask yourself: Is this confusing because the words are new? Or because the words do not make sense together?

✓ Determining the overall meaning may require that you use one or more of the following:

- context clues
- a dictionary or other resource
- teacher or peer support

✓ Highlight important information before and after the expression to look for clues.

 TURN AND TALK

1. Why might it be difficult to understand expressions?

2. What can you do if you are struggling to understand expressions?

ELL **Beginning & Intermediate**

SPEAKING FRAMES

- It can be difficult to understand because ____.
- If I am struggling, I can ____.

ELL **Advanced & Advanced High**

SPEAKING FRAMES

- Expressions can be difficult to understand because ____. For example, ____.
- To determine the meaning of an expression, I can ____. For example, ____.

 SKILL VOCABULARY

expression / la expresión *noun* a phrase used to express an idea

literal / literal *adjective* describing the usual meaning of a word

idiom / el modismo *noun* a common expression that cannot be taken literally

saying / el dicho *noun* an expression that contains advice or wisdom

YOUR TURN

Read paragraphs 5–6 and 10–11 from the text. Then complete the multiple-choice questions below.

---

from **"The Notice"**

Eventually my *táta* looked up. Josefa's question brought him back from some faraway place.

"Mr. Davis hasn't given us much of a choice." There was anger in his voice. "He has already made his choice. He will give our shop to anyone who didn't pass through Ellis Island. Or, he will allow us to pay extra for letting us work on his property."

. . .

I glanced at it. Mr. Davis blamed the doubling of our rent on hard times. It was difficult to imagine that he knew about hard times.

Mr. Vacek cleared his throat and said, "Josefa and I, we need this place." He didn't want to admit it, but it was true.

---

1. What does the narrator mean by "brought him back from a faraway place" in paragraph 5?

○ A. He came back from a distant country.
○ B. Josefa brought *táta* from a distant place.
○ C. Josefa's question rescued *táta*.
○ D. The question brought *táta's* attention back.

2. Which context clue helped you determine the meaning of the expression?

○ A. "Mr. Davis hasn't given us much of a choice."
○ B. "He has already made his choice."
○ C. "There was anger in his voice."
○ D. "...Eventually my *táta* looked up..."

Please note that excerpts and passages in the StudySync® library and this workbook are intended as touchstones to generate interest in an author's work. The excerpts and passages do not substitute for the reading of entire texts, and StudySync® strongly recommends that students seek out and purchase the whole literary or informational work in order to experience it as the author intended. Links to online resellers are available in our digital library. In addition, complete works may be ordered through an authorized reseller by filling out and returning to StudySync® the order form enclosed in this workbook.

Reading & Writing Companion   123

 Your Turn   Ask students to complete the Your Turn activity.

QUESTION 1:   D) Táta was distracted and the questions made him pay attention.

QUESTION 2:   D) This clue tells us that Táta is not longer distracted.

QUESTION 3:   A) Here, "hard times" refers to times of financial struggle.

QUESTION 4:   D) Doubling rent shows that Mr. Davis is trying to make more money and is using "hard times" as his excuse.

 ## Discuss the Skill Model

1. What does the student not understand?

   He doesn't understand the meaning of the expression "warm smile."

2. How does the student analyze the expression?

   He searches for context clues.

3. What context clue does the student highlight? What does he conclude in his annotation?

   "I saw that smile every day" and "he didn't look happy. He placed his hand on my shoulder." He concludes that táta is a caring person, and maybe *warm* means "caring."

4. What does the student do to confirm his analysis of the expression?

   The student asks the teacher or peers what the expression means.

 Beginning & Intermediate

Have students use the speaking frames and helpful terms to participate in the group discussion. If beginning students are hesitant to participate in a discussion, encourage them by prompting with *yes* or *no* questions.

Advanced & Advanced High

Have students use the speaking frames to participate in the group discussion.

SPEAKING FRAMES

- The student does not understand the expression ____.
- The student analyzes the expression by searching for ____ in the text.
- The student highlights ____.
- The student concludes that ____ because ____.
- The student can ____ to confirm his understanding. For example, ____.

HELPFUL TERMS FOR DISCUSSION

- context
- teacher
- highlight
- conclude
- confirm
- improve
- expression
- understanding
- clues

3. What does the narrator mean when she says "hard times" in paragraph 10?

○ A. a time where people need money

○ B. a strong, solid period of time

○ C. events that happened long ago

○ D. the due date for paying your bills

4. Which context clue helped you determine the meaning of the expression?

○ A. "Josefa and I, we need this place"

○ B. "I glanced at it."

○ C. "He has already made his choice."

○ D. "Mr. Davis blamed the doubling of our rent …"

The Notice

Skill:
Comparing and Contrasting

★ DEFINE

To **compare** is to show how two or more pieces of information or literary elements in a text are similar. To **contrast** is to show how two or more pieces of information or literary elements in a text are different. By comparing and contrasting, you can better understand the **meaning** and the **purpose** of the text you are reading.

••• CHECKLIST FOR COMPARING AND CONTRASTING

In order to compare and contrast, do the following:

✓ Look for information or elements that you can compare and contrast.

  • Ask yourself: How are these two things similar? How are they different?

✓ Look for signal words that indicate a compare-and-contrast relationship.

  • Ask yourself: Are there any words that indicate the writer is trying to compare and contrast two or more things?

✓ Use a graphic organizer, such as a Venn diagram or chart, to compare and contrast information.

Reading & Writing Companion **125**

SKILL VOCABULARY

compare / comparar *verb* to explain how two or more things are similar COGNATE

contrast / contrastar *verb* to explain how two or more things are different COGNATE

meaning / el significado *noun* the general message of a text

purpose / el propósito *noun* the reason the writer wrote a text COGNATE

Skill: Comparing and Contrasting

Introduce the Skill

Watch the Concept Definition video and read the definition for Comparing and Contrasting.

TURN AND TALK

1. What does it mean to compare and contrast?

2. What type of information can be compared and contrasted in a text?

3. What can you do if you are struggling to determine what to compare and contrast in a text?

ELL Beginning & Intermediate
SPEAKING FRAMES
  • To compare and contrast means to show how ____.
  • You can compare and contrast information that is ____ or ____.
  • You could look for ____.
  • You could also use a ____.

ELL Advanced & Advanced High
SPEAKING FRAMES
  • To compare and contrast means ____.
  • You can compare and contrast ____, such as ____.
  • You could look for ____. For example, ____.
  • You could also use a ____, like a ____.

Discuss the Skill Model

- What does the student notice when she starts reading the text?

  She notices the two characters, Táta and Mr. Davis.

- What does the student do first?

  She wonders how the characters are similar and different.

- What does the student do next?

  She highlights clues that give more information about the characters.

- What does the student do with this information?

  Answers will vary, but should include: She makes a note that shows the similarities and differences. She makes a chart to compare and contrast the characters. She shares her conclusions with a peer.

ELL **Beginning & Intermediate**

Have students use the speaking frames and helpful terms to participate in the group discussion. If beginning students are hesitant to participate in a discussion, encourage them by prompting with *yes* or *no* questions.

Advanced & Advanced High

Have students use the speaking frames to participate in the group discussion.

SENTENCE FRAMES

- The student notices ____.
- The student wonders about ____.
- The student highlights ____. For example, ____.
- The student uses this information to ____. She also ____.

HELPFUL TERMS FOR DISCUSSION

- compare
- contrast
- similar
- common
- share
- chart

The Notice

⟳ YOUR TURN

Read the following excerpt from the text. Then complete the Compare-and-Contrast chart by writing the letter of the correct example in chart below.

---

from **"The Notice"**

Mr. Vacek read the notice again. Mr. Davis left it on our shop door this morning. He didn't even hand it to my *táta* or Mr. Vacek.

I glanced at it. Mr. Davis blamed the doubling of our rent on hard times. It was difficult to imagine that he knew about hard times.

Mr. Vacek cleared his throat and said, "Josefa and I, we need this place." He didn't want to admit it, but it was true.

My *táta* looked at Mr. Vacek and nodded. They had known each other since they were children. My *táta* didn't want to hear his friend say that. But I knew my *táta* wasn't going to abandon him now.

Examples
A	know Mr. Vacek
B	would never abandon his friend
C	left a notice without talking in person

Mr. Davis	Both	Táta

 ## Your Turn   Ask students to complete the Your Turn activity.

Mr. Davis	Both	Táta
left a notice without talking in person	know Mr. Vacek	would never abandon his friend

Close Read

Close Read

✏ **WRITE**

PERSONAL RESPONSE: Beginning a new life in a new country can be difficult. Imagine that like the families in "The Notice," you are starting over in a new country and trying to find a job. However, even though you are qualified, no one wants to hire you because you weren't born in their country. Think about the types of information you would need to provide in order to prove that you are able to do the work. Explain why that information is important. Pay attention to verb tenses as you write.

Use the checklist below to guide you as you write.

☐ What is a time when you were treated unfairly?

☐ How did you feel?

☐ What did you do?

☐ How does your experience compare to the families in "The Notice"?

☐ How does your experience contrast to the families in "The Notice"?

Use the sentence frames to organize and write your personal response.

I was once treated unfairly when _____.

It made me feel _____ because _____ .

My experience is like the story "The Notice" because _____.

Unlike in the story, I _____.

Reading & Writing Companion **127**

Model Skills Focus

Remind students of the Reading Skill Comparing and Contrasting. Tell students they can compare and contrast information within the text, across different texts, or even with their personal experiences. Direct students to the Skills Focus and remind them to track as you read aloud.

Think of a time that you have been treated unfairly. Compare and contrast your experience with the experience of the families in "The Notice."

Model Comparing and Contrasting for students:

- I am going to focus on *Táta's* behavior in the beginning of the story.

- When I was younger, I had a neighbor that was very mean to me. He used to pick on me because I was the youngest kid on the block.

- One day, he went to the park with a group of kids but said I wasn't allowed to go with them. Even my older sister went, and I had to spend the afternoon by myself.

- Just like *Táta*, I was being treated unfairly because I wasn't like the other kids on the street. Just because I was the youngest.

- However, unlike *Táta*, I didn't hide my frustration very well. I yelled and my sister and ended up getting grounded!

Complete Skills Focus

Use a Jigsaw strategy to have students complete the Skills Focus. Divide students into pairs. Have each pair focus on one of the following points of comparison:

- *Táta's* behavior in the beginning of the story.

- *Táta's* dialogue in the middle of the story.

- The Vaceks' reaction to the news.

- *Táta's* response at the end of the story.

Circulate and monitor groups as they work.

Collaborative Conversation

Rearrange partners so that they are talking with someone who worked on a different point of comparison. Prompt partners to take turns sharing their personal comparisons with the events in text.

- How did your experience compare with what happened in the story?
- How did your experience contrast with what happened in the story?

- How did comparing and contrasting help your understanding of the story?

Collaborative Conversation

SCAFFOLDS

 ELL **BEGINNING, INTERMEDIATE** Use the <u>word bank</u> to participate in the group discussion.

ADVANCED Use the <u>speaking frames</u> to participate in the group discussion.

BEGINNING, INTERMEDIATE	ADVANCED
Word Bank	**Speaking Frames**
• experience • different • like • understand • the same as • I felt • unlike • I responded by	• I focused on ____. • It is similar because ____. • It is different because ____. • This helps me understand the text because ____.

Write

Ask students to complete the writing assignment. Remind students to pay attention while using verb tenses.

ELL **BEGINNING** Write a response using the <u>paragraph frames</u> and <u>word banks</u>.

INTERMEDIATE Write a response using the <u>paragraph frames</u>.

INTERMEDIATE

BEGINNING

Paragraph Frames

1. I was once treated unfairly when ____. It made me feel ____ because ____.
2. My experience is like the story "The Notice" because ____. Unlike in the story, I ____.

Word Bank

- upset
- punish
- angry
- treat
- mean

In the Extended Oral Project, students plan, draft, practice, and deliver an oral presentation that ties into the theme of the unit and spans informative, argumentative, and narrative genres. Lessons provide explicit instruction to prepare students for the unique challenges of an oral presentation, and to help break down the genre characteristics of each prompt. At each step in the process, students focus in-depth on specific writing and speaking skills as they brainstorm, organize, and refine their presentation. Students also receive discussion prompts and frames to guide them in providing effective peer feedback as they practice and discuss in small group before presenting to the class on the final day.

CONNECT TO ESSENTIAL QUESTION

How do you know what to do when there are no instructions?

In this unit, students practiced effective collaborative communication skills, such as making predictions and comparing and contrasting, while reading and analyzing two texts about uncertainty. Now students will apply those skills to work together in writing and presenting a biography.

Developing Effective Presentations

Form	Language and Conventions	Oral Language Production
Students may struggle with the academic demands of developing the biography, such as chronological order and references.	Students should be encouraged to experiment with new sentence patterns and lengths to make their biography sound natural and interesting.	Students may make mistakes when they transfer grammatical forms from their native languages into English. Remind students to monitor their use of pronouns.

SCAFFOLDS   **ELL** **ENGLISH LANGUAGE LEARNERS**

Vocabulary, discussion, and peer and teacher support in the Extended Oral Project is differentiated for Beginning, Intermediate, Advanced, and Advanced High English Language Learners. See individual lesson plans for additional scaffolding and support.

Instructional Path

 All Extended Oral Project lessons lesson plans appear in your digital teacher account.

Introduction

Objectives: Students will be able to identify the components of a biography in order to brainstorm and plan their own.

Objectives: Students will be able to record ideas for a biography in writing.

DIGITAL ONLY

Skill: Acquiring Vocabulary

Objectives: Students will be able to use a graphic organizer to make connections between words and acquire new vocabulary for their biography.

Objectives: Students will be able to brainstorm new words to use in writing their biography.

DIGITAL ONLY

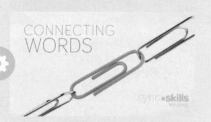

Plan

Objectives: Students will be able to plan and write a first draft of their biography.

Objectives: Students will be able to organize their first draft using an outline.

DIGITAL ONLY

Skill: Connecting Words

Objectives: Students will be able to apply knowledge of connecting words to revise their biographies.

Objectives: Students will be able to use connecting words to show how ideas are related orally and in writing.

DIGITAL ONLY

Practice

Objectives: Students will be able to practice and revise their biography based on peer feedback.

Objectives: Students will be able to practice reading a biography orally and make revisions in writing.

DIGITAL ONLY

Present

Objectives: Students will be able to listen to and read aloud a biography in order to give and receive peer feedback.

Objectives: Students will be able to use connecting words in an oral presentation and give peer feedback orally and in writing.

DIGITAL ONLY

Unit Overview

Integrated Reading and Writing

Extended Writing Project

English Language Learner Resources

Novel Study

End-of-Unit Assessment

Novel Study

Each Core ELAR Unit contains two texts designated for Novel Study. The Novel Study supports the close reading of the complete text through its associated Reading Guide and a series of comparative reading and writing lessons. Novel Studies are not a part of each grade-level's 180 days of instruction; however, teachers may choose to draw from them if they wish to incorporate materials from other disciplines or develop an alternative, novel-based approach to instruction.

Each novel comes with a **Reading Guide** that provides both teacher and student support. Each lesson provides key vocabulary words and close reading questions, as well as a key passage that will help teachers guide students through an exploration of the essential ideas, events, and character development in the novel. This passage will also serve as the point from which students will engage in their own StudySyncTV-style group discussion. Each novel study's **Comparative Reading and Writing** lessons contain resources to support comparative analyses. Students read passages of other texts drawn from across the disciplines and compare those passages to specific sections of the novel in written responses.

Suggested Novel Studies

Title	Genre	Summary	Themes and Topics
The Lightning Thief (2005)	Fiction	Twelve-year-old Percy Jackson finds out he's the son of the Greek god Poseidon—and must find a way to prevent a war between the gods that will destroy the world.	• Greek Mythology • Coming of Age • Fantasy
Hoot (2002)	Fiction	New kid in town Roy makes himself even less popular by joining the fight against the construction of a Mrs. Paula's Pancake House, which threatens a colony of burrowing owls.	• Alienation • Adolescence • Coming of Age

The Lightning Thief

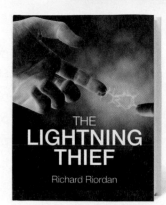

When 12-year-old Percy is kicked out of his sixth boarding school, his mother lets him in on the family secret—his absent father is a Greek god, making young Percy a demigod. When Percy arrives at Camp Half-Blood, a demigod refuge, Zeus's lightning bolt goes missing and Percy is the prime suspect. He has ten days to find the thief and return the lightning to Zeus or the gods will declare war, ending life on Earth.

The Lightning Thief is the first in a series by Rick Riordan (b. 1964), preceding *The Sea of Monsters, The Titan's Curse, The Battle of the Labyrinth*, and *The Last Olympian*. A feature film, *Percy Jackson and the Olympians: The Lightning Thief*, was released in 2010, and a sequel, *Percy Jackson: Sea of Monsters* followed in 2013.

Hoot

Roy Eberhardt is sad to leave his beloved Montana and become the new kid in town in humid Florida—as the bullies of Coconut Cove keep reminding him. One day, Roy sees a strange, shoeless wild boy and works to unravel his mysterious identity. When the site of the future Mrs. Paula's Pancake House is repeatedly vandalized because construction endangers a colony of burrowing owls, Roy is faced with a greater mystery: should he follow his heart or his head?

Hoot is the story of Roy's journey to self-acceptance and the challenges of burgeoning adolescence. Written by Carl Hiaasen (b. 1953), it was awarded the Newbery Honor in 2003. An author of colorful Floridian mysteries, Hiaasen has received the Damon Runyon Award for journalism and the Florida Lifetime Achievement Award for Writing.

Spotlight Skills Review

A review day before the end-of-unit assessment gives you an opportunity to review difficult concepts with students using Spotlight Skills lessons. Spotlight Skills are targeted lessons that provide you resources to reteach or remediate without assigning additional readings. Every Core ELA Skill lesson has a corresponding Spotlight Skill lesson. Spotlight Skills can be assigned at any point in the year, but the end of each unit provides a natural moment to pause, review data collected throughout the unit, and reteach skills students have not yet mastered.

Progress Monitoring

The Progress Monitoring charts that appear before every text in this unit identify standards and associated Spotlight Skills. On review day, you may want to give preference to reteaching skills that are not revisited in later units. You can see where Skills are covered again in the Opportunities to Reteach column.

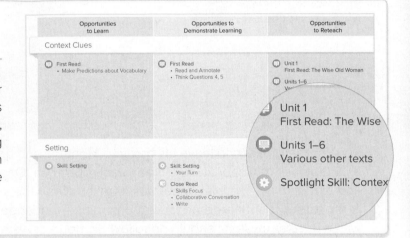

StudySync Gradebook

As students submit assignments on StudySync, their mastery of skills and standards is tracked via the gradebook. The gradebook can be sorted and viewed in a variety of ways. Sorting by assignment shows overall student performance, while sorting by standards or by Skill lessons displays student progress toward mastery goals.

Skills Library

Spotlight Skills are located in the Skills section of the StudySync Library. You can assign Spotlight Skills to individual students or groups of students. Search tools allow you to search by Skill type or name.

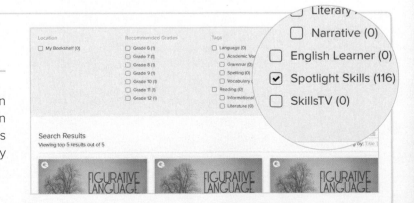

End-of-Unit Assessment

The end-of-unit assessment can be found in two places. The digital version of the assessment can be assigned from the Online Assessment tab inside your ConnectED account. The paper-based version of the assessment can be printed from the End-of-Unit Assessment tab inside this unit in your StudySync account.

Assessment Section	Content	Assessed Skills	
READING	Education Reformers Genre: Non-fiction Word Count: 602 Lexile: 1010	• Technical Language • Textual Evidence • Informational Text Structure	• Informational Text Elements • Central or Main Idea • Word Meaning
	Helping to Build the Pyramid of Giza Genre: Fiction Word Count: 690 Lexile: 1010	• Character • Word Meaning • Textual Evidence	• Theme • Greek and Latin Affixes and Roots • Story Structure
	Searching for a Future Home Genre: Non-fiction Word Count: 693 Lexile:1000	• Informational Text Elements • Informational Text Structure • Textual Evidence	• Greek and Latin Affixes and Roots • Technical Language • Central or Main Idea
	Where Am I? Genre: Non-fiction Word Count: 891 Lexile: 1000	• Central or Main Idea • Technical Language • Textual Evidence	• Informational Text Structure • Informational Text Elements
REVISING and **EDITING**	Student Passage #1	• Spelling • Prefixes	• Parentheses, Brackets, Ellipses
	Student Passage #2	• Organizing Informational Writing • Introductions • Thesis	• Supporting Details • Precise Language • Conclusions
WRITING	Prompt: Informative Writing	• Informative Writing	

What's Next?

Assessment results can be viewed by item, standard, and skill to monitor mastery and make decisions for upcoming instruction.

RETEACH skills that students have not yet mastered, using Spotlight Skills or the Test Preparation and Practice book.

REVISE your teaching plan to provide more or less explicit instruction into a skill or text, using Beyond the Book activities for enrichment.

REGROUP students and levels of scaffolding based on standards progress.

Teacher's Edition Credits

PHOTO/IMAGE CREDITS:

Cover, iStockphoto.com
p. 4, iStock.com/Delpixart
p. 5, iStock.com/Delpixart
p. 6, iStockphoto.com
p. 7, iStock.com/urbancow
p. 8, iStock.com/urbancow
p. 9, iStock/2jenn
p. 10, iStock/2jenn
p. 11, iStockphoto.com
p. 12, iStock.com/karandaev
p. 18, iStock.com/karandaev
p. 19, iStock.com/deimagine
p. 20, iStock.com/deimagine
p. 21, iStock.com/karandaev
p. 22, iStock.com/hdtravelpix
p. 26, iStock.com/technotr
p. 30, iStock.com/technotr
p. 31, iStock.com/Max_Xie
p. 32, iStock.com/Max_Xie
p. 33, iStock.com/Martin Barraud
p. 34, iStock.com/Martin Barraud
p. 35, iStock.com/technotr
p. 36, iStock.com/isaro
p. 38, iStock.com/CasarsaGuru
p. 45, iStock.com/isaro
p. 46, iStock.com/Spanishalex
p. 47, iStock.com/Spanishalex
p. 48, iStock.com/isaro
p. 49, iStock.com/eclipse_images
p. 60, iStock.com/eclipse_images
p. 61, iStock.com/ValentinaPhotos
p. 62, iStock.com/ValentinaPhotos
p. 63, iStock.com/Gemini-Create
p. 64, iStock.com/Gemini-Create
p. 65, iStock.com/eclipse_images
p. 66, iStock.com/gaiamoments
p. 73, iStock.com/gaiamoments
p. 74, ©iStockphoto.com
p. 75, ©iStockphoto.com
p. 76, iStock.com/gaiamoments
p. 77, iStock.com/cyberhawk
p. 78, iStock.com/THEPALMER
p. 80, iStock.com/Melnikof
p. 85, iStock.com/Mordolff
p. 89, iStock.com/Mordolff
p. 90, iStock.com/donatas1205
p. 91, iStock.com/donatas1206
p. 92, iStock.com/Mordolff
p. 93, iStock.com/Martin Barraud
p. 94, iStock.com/Martin Barraud
p. 99, Stock.com/oonal

p. 102, iStock.com/Martin Barraud
p. 108, iStock.com/truelight
p. 110, iStock.com/Jasmina007
p. 113, iStock.com/Jinnawat
p. 116, iStock.com/Jeff_Hu
p. 118, iStock.com/stevedangers
p. 120, iStock.com/Martin Barraud
p. 122, iStock.com/Martin Barraud
p. 124, iStock.com/anyaberkut
p. 125, iStock.com/woraput
p. 125, iStock.com/irabell
p. 125, iStock.com/montreehanlue
p. 125, iStock.com/diverroy
p. 125, iStock.com/narvikk
p. 125, iStock.com/FangXiaNuo
p. 127, iStock.com/anyaberkut
p. 128, iStock.com/Ales_Utovko
p. 130, iStock.com/BlackJack3D
p. 132, iStock.com/anyaberkut
p. 133, iStock.com/jrwasserman
p. 134, iStock.com/gzorgz
p. 134, iStock.com/PeskyMonkey
p. 134, iStock.com/Rawpixel Ltd
p. 134, iStock.com/3dts
p. 134, iStock.com/mevans
p. 137, iStock.com/jrwasserman
p. 138, iStock.com/BlackJack3D
p. 140, iStock.com/eugenesergeev
p. 142, iStock.com/jrwasserman

Reading & Writing Companion **143**

Teacher's Edition Credits

p. 294, iStock.com/criene
p. 295, iStock.com/criene
p. 296, iStock.com/criene
p. 297, bestdesigns/iStock.com
p. 297, mphillips007/iStock.com
p. 297, JoeRosh/iStock.com
p. 297, bpalmer/iStock.com
p. 303, bestdesigns/iStock.com
p. 303, mphillips007/iStock.com
p. 303, iStock.com/
p. 306, iStock/piola666
p. 306, iStock.com/GeorgeRudy
p. 306, iStock.com/hkeita
p. 306, iStock.com/5second
p. 307, iStock.com/borchee
p. 307, iStock.com/GeorgeRudy
p. 308, iStock.com/borchee
p. 308, iStock.com/jakkapan21
p. 309, iStock.com/borchee
p. 309, iStock.com/5second
p. 310, bpalmer/iStock.com
p. 312, iStock.com/from2015
p. 312, bpalmer/iStock.com
p. 312, iStock.com/antoni_halim
p. 312, iStock.com/urbancow
p. 314, HadelProductions/iStock.com
p. 320, ©iStock.com/cougarsan
p. 330, JoeRosh/iStock.com
p. 332, JoeRosh/iStock.com
p. 320, iStock.com/Orla
p. 320, iStock.com/Dominique_Lavoie
p. 320, iStock.com/ValentinaPhotos
p. 334, iStock.com/JoeRosh
p. 339, ©iStock.com/cougarsan
p. 352, ©iStock.com/chaiwarin
p. 354, iStock.com/mycola
p. 354, ©iStock.com/chaiwarin
p. 354, iStock.com/fotogaby
p. 354, iStock.com/SrdjanPav
p. 356, iStock.com/SteveRosset
p. 359, ©iStock.com/cougarsan
p. 368, ©iStock.com/didecs
p. 370, ©iStock.com/didecs
p. 370, iStock.com/KM6064
p. 370, iStock.com/Andrey_A
p. 372, Bill Chizek/iStock.com
p. 375, ©iStock.com/cougarsan
p. 384, @iStock.com/FS-Stock
p. 386, @iStock.com/FS-Stock
p. 386, iStock.com/Montes-Bradley
p. 393, ©iStock.com/cougarsan
p. 398, ©iStock.com/timeless
p. 400, ©iStock.com/timeless

p. 387, iStock.com/Smithore
p. 387, iStock.com/Eric_Schroeder
p. 402, skynesher/iStock.com
p. 405, ©iStock.com/cougarsan
p. 414, ©iStock.com/MilosJokic
p. 416, ©iStock.com/MilosJokic
p. 416, iStock.com/yipengge
p. 418, MATJAZ SLANIC/iStock.com
p. 429, ©iStock.com/cougarsan
p. 438, Universal History Archive/Universal Images Group/Getty Images
p. 440, Universal History Archive/Universal Images Group/Getty Images
p. 440, ImagineGolf/iStock.com
p. 447, ©iStock.com/cougarsan
p. 452, ©iStock.com/Popartic
p. 454, ©iStock.com/Popartic
p. 454, bauhaus1000/iStock.com
p. 456, ©iStock.com/cougarsan
p. 460, Candice Cusack/iStock.com
p. 462, Candice Cusack/iStock.com
p. 462, iStock.com/Martin Barraud
p. 464, iStock.com/vondoome
p. 467, ©iStock.com/cougarsan
p. 476, iStock.com/borchee
p. 476, iStock/shironosov
p. 477, iStock.com/EasternLightcraft
p. 477, iStock.com/borchee
p. 478, iStock.com/hanibaram, iStock.com/seb_ra, iStock.com/Martin Barraud
p. 480, iStock.com/SerrNovik
p. 480, iStock.com/fstop123
p. 480, iStock.com/gopixa
p. 480, iStock.com/Domin_domin
p. 481, iStock.com/bo1982
p. 481, iStock.com/Jeff_Hu
p. 481, iStock/Fodor90
p. 481, iStock.com/stevedangers
p. 481, iStock.com/SerrNovik
p. 482, iStock.com/efks
p. 482, iStock.com/Andrey-Kobylko
p. 482, ©iStock.com/Elnur
p. 482, iStock.com/SerrNovik
p. 482, iStock.com/efks
p. 526, iStock.com/borchee
p. 526, iStock.com/criene
p. 526, iStock.com/eskymaks
p. 526, iStock.com/NUMAX3D
p. 528, iStock.com/bestdesigns
p. 530, iStock.com/blackred
p. 530, iStock.com/artisteer
p. 530, iStock.com/bestdesigns
p. 530, iStock.com/Ales_Utovko

p. 530, iStock.com/Zoran Kolundzija
p. 530, iStock.com/eugenesergeev
p. 532, iStock.com
p. 542, iStock.com/mphillips007
p. 544, iStock.com/eskymaks
p. 544, iStock.com/NUMAX3D
p. 544, iStock.com/mphillips007
p. 544, iStock.com/BlackJack3D
p. 544, iStock.com/serggn
p. 544, iStock.com/borzaya
p. 546, recep-bg/iStock.com
p. 557, iStock.com/nikkytok
p. 557, iStock.com/juhide
p. 557, iStock.com/Ivan Bajic
p. 559, iStock.com/bpalmer
p. 559, iStock.com/JoeRosh

PHOTO/IMAGE CREDITS:

Cover, iStock.com/bpalmer
p. 4, iStock.com/bpalmer
p. 5, iStock.com/antoni_halim
p. 6, iStock.com/antoni_halim
p. 7, istock.com/urbancow
p. 8, istock.com/urbancow
p. 9, iStock.com/bpalmer
p. 10, iStock.com/JoeRosh
p. 15, iStock.com/JoeRosh
p. 16, iStock.com/Orla
p. 17, iStock.com/Orla
p. 18, iStock.com/Dominique_Lavoie
p. 19, iStock.com/Dominique_Lavoie
p. 20, iStock.com/ValentinaPhotos
p. 21, iStock.com/ValentinaPhotos
p. 22, iStock.com/JoeRosh
p. 23, iStock.com/chaiwarin
p. 25, iStock.com/chaiwarin
p. 26, iStock.com/fotogaby
p. 27, iStock.com/fotogaby
p. 28, iStock.com/JoeRosh
p. 29, iStock.com/didecs
p. 31, iStock.com/didecs
p. 31, iStock.com/
p. 33, iStock.com/
p. 34, iStock.com/didecs
p. 35, iStock.com/FS-Stock
p. 42, iStock.com/timeless
p. 44, iStock.com/topten22photo
p. 45, iStock.com/timeless
p. 46, iStock.com/
p. 47, iStock.com/
p. 48, iStock.com/timeless
p. 49, iStock.com/NoSystem images
p. 60, iStock.com/NoSystem images
p. 61, iStock.com/yipengge
p. 62, iStock.com/yipengge
p. 63, iStock.com/NoSystem images
p. 64, Universal History Archive/Universal Images
Group/Getty Images
p. 71, iStock.com/Popartic
p. 73, iStock.com/Candice Cusack
p. 76, iStock.com/Candice Cusack
p. 77, iStock.com/Martin Barraud
p. 78, iStock.com/Martin Barraud
p. 79, iStock.com/Candice Cusack
p. 80, iStock.com/Martin Barraud
p. 81, iStock.com/Martin Barraud
p. 86, iStock.com/fstop123
p. 88, iStock.com/gopixa
p. 91, iStock.com/Dominik Pabis

p. 93, iStock.com/Martin Barraud
p. 97, iStock.com/bo1982
p. 100, iStock/Jeff_Hu
p. 103, iStock/Fodor90
p. 106, iStock.com/stevedangers
p. 108, iStock.com/Martin Barraud
p. 110, iStock.com/Martin Barraud
p. 112, iStock.com/bestdesigns
p. 113, iStock.com/michaeljung
p. 113, iStock.com/CREATISTA
p. 113, iStock.com/SKAI
p. 113, iStock.com/
p. 113, iStock.com/RBFried
p. 113, iStock.com/lmgorthand
p. 113, iStock.com/GlobalStock
p. 115, iStock.com/bestdesigns
p. 116, iStock.com/Ales_Utovko
p. 118, iStock.com/Zoran Kolundzija
p. 120, iStock.com/bestdesigns
p. 121, iStock.com/mphillips007
p. 122, inhauscreative/iStock
p. 122, gcoles/iStock
p. 122, CREATISTA/iStock
p. 122, Antonio_Diaz/iStock
p. 122, Yuri_Arcurs/iStock
p. 124, iStock.com/mphillips007
p. 125, iStock.com/BlackJack3D
p. 127, Stock.com/serggn
p. 129, iStock.com/mphillips007

Reading & Writing Companion

Teacher's Edition Credits

p. 562, iStock.com/Boyloso
p. 563, iStock.com/Boyloso
p. 564, iStock.com/Boyloso
p. 565, iStock.com/cycaroon
p. 565, iStock.com/Lisa-Blue
p. 565, iStock.com/Michael Sick
p. 565, iStock.com/ABDESIGN
p. 569, iStock.com/
p. 571, iStock.com/cycaroon
p. 571, iStock.com/Lisa-Blue
p. 571, iStock.com/
p. 574, borchee/iStock.com
p. 574, gawrav/iStock.com
p. 574, iStock.com/hkeita
p. 574, iStock.com/5second
p. 575, gawrav/iStock.com
p. 575, iStock.com/borchee
p. 576, iStock.com/borchee
p. 576, iStock.com/SergeyTinyakov
p. 577, iStock.com/borchee
p. 577, iStock.com/5second
p. 578, ©iStock.com/timurka
p. 580, iStock.com/LoveTheWind
p. 580, ©iStock.com/timurka
p. 580, iStock.com/deimagine
p. 582, cineuno/iStock.com
p. 589, ©iStock.com/cougarsan
p. 598, iStock.com/ABDESIGN
p. 600, iStock.com/ABDESIGN
p. 600, iStock.com/ValentinaPhotos
p. 600, iStock.com/PhotoTalk
p. 602, pb505/iStock.com
p. 608, ©iStock.com/cougarsan
p. 616, iStock.com/RapidEye
p. 618, iStock.com/RapidEye
p. 618, dhughes9/iStock.com
p. 620, ©iStock.com/cougarsan
p. 624, ©iStock.com/gautier075
p. 626, ©iStock.com/gautier075
p. 626, iStock.com/eskaylim
p. 626, iStock.com/ThomasVogel
p. 628, iStock.com/MCCAIG
p. 633, ©iStock.com/cougarsan
p. 646, ©iStock.com/yuriz
p. 648, ©iStock.com/yuriz
p. 648, iStock.com/Andrey_A
p. 648, iStock.com/Hohenhaus
p. 650, Library of Congress/Corbis/VCG via Getty Images
p. 653, ©iStock.com/cougarsan
p. 664, ©iStock.com/Vladimir Vladimirov
p. 666, ©iStock.com/Vladimir Vladimirov
p. 666, iStock.com/Caval

p. 666, iStock.com/Orla
p. 666, iStock.com/martin-dm
p. 668, Nikolas_jkd/iStock.com
p. 673, ©iStock.com/cougarsan
p. 684, iStock.com/Michael Sick
p. 686, iStock.com/Michael Sick
p. 686, iStock.com/Dominique_Lavoie
p. 688, Gannet77/iStock.com
p. 691, ©iStock.com/cougarsan
p. 700, ©iStock.com/geyzer
p. 702, ©iStock.com/geyzer
p. 702, PatricioHidalgoP/iStock.com
p. 706, ©iStock.com/cougarsan
p. 710, ©iStock.com/carton_king
p. 712, ©iStock.com/carton_king
p. 712, Neustockimages/iStock.com
p. 715, ©iStock.com/cougarsan
p. 720, ©iStock.com/AntoniaLorenzo
p. 722, ©iStock.com/coscaron
p. 722, ©iStock.com/AntoniaLorenzo
p. 722, iStock.com/urbancow
p. 722, iStock.com/Orla
p. 724, iStock.com/
p. 730, ©iStock.com/cougarsan
p. 740, iStock.com/borchee
p. 740, iStock.com/shironosov
p. 741, iStock.com/borchee
p. 741, iStock.com/EasternLightcraft
p. 744, iStock.com/hanibaram, iStock.com/seb_ra, iStock.com/Martin Barraud
p. 744, iStock.com/Martin Barraud
p. 744, iStock.com/gopixa
p. 744, iStock.com/ThomasVogel
p. 744, iStock.com/Tevarak
p. 744, iStock.com/Martin Barraud
p. 744, iStock.com/bo1982
p. 744, iStock.com/Jeff_Hu
p. 745, iStock.com/peepo
p. 745, iStock/Fodor90
p. 745, iStock.com/stevedangers
p. 745, iStock.com/Martin Barraud
p. 745, iStock.com/peshkov
p. 746, iStock.com/efks
p. 746, iStock.com/efks
p. 746, iStock.com/peshkov
p. 792, iStock.com/Boyloso
p. 792, iStock.com/eskymaks
p. 792, iStock.com/enot-poloskun
p. 792, iStock.com/borchee
p. 794, iStock.com/cycaroon
p. 796, iStock.com/blackred
p. 796, iStock.com/mukem
p. 796, iStock.com/cycaroon

p. 796, iStock.com/BlackJack3D
p. 796, iStock.com/14951893
p. 796, iStock.com/eugenesergeev
p. 798, Luke Abrahams/iStock.com
p. 786, iStock.com/Lisa-Blue
p. 810, iStock.com/Lisa-Blue
p. 812, iStock.com/eskymaks
p. 812, iStock.com/enot-poloskun
p. 812, iStock.com/Ales_Utovko
p. 812, iStock.com/RazvanDP
p. 812, iStock.com/peeterv
p. 814, iStock.com/Lisa-Blue
p. 827, iStock.com/nikkytok
p. 827, iStock.com/juhide
p. 827, iStock.com/Aslan Alphan
p. 829, iStock.com/ABDESIGN
p. 829, iStock.com/Michael Sick

PHOTO/IMAGE CREDITS:

cover, iStock.com/timurka
p. 5, Public Domain Image
p. 7, iStock.com/timurka
p. 8, ©iStock.com/deimagine
p. 9, ©iStock.com/deimagine
p. 10, iStock.com/timurka
p. 11, iStock.com/ABDESIGN
p. 15, iStock.com/ABDESIGN
p. 16, ©iStock.com/ValentinaPhotos
p. 17, ©iStock.com/ValentinaPhotos
p. 18, ©iStock.com/ABDESIGN
p. 19, ©iStock.com/RapidEye
p. 21, iStock.com/gautier075
p. 24, ©iStock.com/ewg3D
p. 26, iStock.com/gautier075
p. 27, ©iStock.com/eskaylim
p. 28, ©iStock.com/eskaylim
p. 30, ©iStock.com/ThomasVogel
p. 31, ©iStock.com/ThomasVogel
p. 32, iStock.com/gautier075
p. 33, iStock.com/yuriz
p. 35, iStock.com/yuriz
p. 36, ©iStock.com/Andrey_A
p. 37, ©iStock.com/Andrey_A
p. 38, ©iStock.com/Hohenhaus
p. 39, ©iStock.com/Hohenhaus
p. 40, iStock.com/yuriz
p. 41, ©iStock.com/Vladimir Vladimirov
p. 42, Serious Scientific Answers to Absurd Hypothetical Questions by Randall Munroe. Copyright © 2014 by xkcd Inc. Reprinted by permission of Houghton Mifflin Harcourt Publishing Company. All rights reserved.
p. 43, Serious Scientific Answers to Absurd Hypothetical Questions by Randall Munroe. Copyright © 2014 by xkcd Inc. Reprinted by permission of Houghton Mifflin Harcourt Publishing Company. All rights reserved.
p. 44, Serious Scientific Answers to Absurd Hypothetical Questions by Randall Munroe. Copyright © 2014 by xkcd Inc. Reprinted by permission of Houghton Mifflin Harcourt Publishing Company. All rights reserved.
p. 45, Serious Scientific Answers to Absurd Hypothetical Questions by Randall Munroe. Copyright © 2014 by xkcd Inc. Reprinted by permission of Houghton Mifflin Harcourt Publishing Company. All rights reserved.
p. 46, ©iStock.com/Vladimir Vladimirov
p. 47, ©iStock.com/Caval
p. 48, ©iStock.com/Caval
p. 49, ©iStock.com/Orla

p. 50, ©iStock.com/Orla
p. 51, ©iStock.com/Vladimir Vladimirov
p. 52, iStock.com/Michael Sick
p. 55, iStock.com/Michael Sick
p. 56, ©iStock/Dominique_Lavoie
p. 57, ©iStock/Dominique_Lavoie
p. 58, iStock.com/Michael Sick
p. 59, ©iStock.com/geyzer
p. 61, ©iStock.com/AZ68
p. 63, ©iStock.com/carton_king
p. 64, ©iStock.com/robertprzybysz
p. 66, ©iStock.com/AntoniaLorenzo
p. 67, Alfred Eisenstaedt / Contributor/The LIFE Picture Collection
p. 70, ©iStock.com/AntoniaLorenzo
p. 71, @istock.com/urbancow
p. 72, @istock.com/urbancow
p. 73, ©iStock.com/Orla
p. 74, ©iStock.com/Orla
p. 75, ©iStock.com/AntoniaLorenzo
p. 76, iStock.com/hanibaram, iStock.com/seb_ra, iStock.com/Martin Barraud
p. 77, ©iStock.com/Martin Barraud
p. 82, ©iStock.com/gopixa
p. 84, ©iStock.com/ThomasVogel
p. 87, ©iStock.com/Tevarak
p. 89, ©iStock.com/Martin Barraud
p. 93, ©iStock.com/bo1982
p. 96, ©iStock/Jeff_Hu
p. 98, ©iStock.com/peepo
p. 100, ©iStock/Fodor90
p. 102, ©iStock.com/stevedangers
p. 104, iStock.com/Martin Barraud
p. 106, iStock.com/Martin Barraud
p. 108, @iStock.com/cycaroon
p. 109, ©iStock.com/auimeesri
p. 109, ©iStock.com/milanvirijevic
p. 109, ©iStock.com/Jewelsy
p. 109, ©iStock.com/TerryJ
p. 109, ©iStock.com/PavelRodimov
p. 111, ©iStock.com/cycaroon
p. 112, ©iStock.com/BlackJack3D
p. 115, ©iStock.com/14951893
p. 117, ©iStock.com/cycaroon
p. 118, iStock.com/Lisa-Blue
p. 119, iStock.com/
p. 119, iStock.com/
p. 119, iStock.com/
p. 119, iStock.com/
p. 119, iStock/Feverpitched
p. 121, iStock.com/Lisa-Blue
p. 122, ©iStock.com/Ales_Utovko
p. 125, ©iStock.com/RazvanDP
p. 127, iStock.com/Lisa-Blue

Reading & Writing Companion

Text Fulfillment Through StudySync

If you are interested in specific titles, please fill out the form below and we will check availability through our partners.

ORDER DETAILS

Date:

TITLE	AUTHOR	Paperback/ Hardcover	Specific Edition *If Applicable*	Quantity

SHIPPING INFORMATION

Contact:

Title:

School/District:

Address Line 1:

Address Line 2:

Zip or Postal Code:

Phone:

Mobile:

Email:

BILLING INFORMATION ☐ *SAME AS SHIPPING*

Contact:

Title:

School/District:

Address Line 1:

Address Line 2:

Zip or Postal Code:

Phone:

Mobile:

Email:

PAYMENT INFORMATION

☐ CREDIT CARD

Name on Card:

Card Number:

Expiration Date:

Security Code:

☐ PO

Purchase Order Number:

StudySync Text Fulfillment, BookheadEd Learning, LLC
610 Daniel Young Drive | Sonoma, CA 95476